CONTEMPORARY
GAY
AMERICAN NOVELISTS

CONTEMPORARY GAY AMERICAN NOVELISTS

A Bio-Bibliographical Critical Sourcebook

EDITED BY

Emmanuel S. Nelson

GREENWOOD PRESS
Westport, Connecticut • London

Library of Congress Cataloging-in-Publication Data

Contemporary gay American novelists : a bio-bibliographical critical
  sourcebook / edited by Emmanuel S. Nelson.
     p.   cm.
  Includes bibliographical references and index.
  ISBN 0–313–28019–3
  1. Novelists, American—20th century—Biography—Dictionaries.
2. Homosexuality and literature—United States—History—20th
century. 3. American fiction—20th century—Bio-bibliography.
4. American fiction—Men authors—Bio-bibliography. 5. Gay men—
United States—Biography—Dictionaries. 6. American fiction—20th
century—Dictionaries. 7. American fiction—Men authors—
Dictionaries. 8. Gays' writings, American—Bio-bibliography.
9. Gays' writings, American—Dictionaries. 10. Gay men in
literature. I. Nelson, Emmanuel S. (Emmanuel Sampath).
PS374.N63C66 1993
813'.54099206642—dc20   92–25762

British Library Cataloguing in Publication Data is available.

Library of Congress Catalog Card Number: 92–25762
ISBN: 0–313–28019–3

First published in 1993

Greenwood Press, 88 Post Road West, Westport, CT 06881
An imprint of Greenwood Publishing Group, Inc.

Printed in the United States of America

∞

The paper used in this book complies with the
Permanent Paper Standard issued by the National
Information Standards Organization (Z39.48–1984).

10 9 8 7 6 5 4 3 2 1

In gratitude to James Baldwin (1924–1987),
who shared with us his pain, his courage,
his vision of another country

CONTENTS

PREFACE

In the fall of 1975 I entered the graduate program in English at the University of Tennessee at Knoxville. Barely twenty years old, I had just arrived in the United States from India to work toward a doctorate in twentieth-century American literature. Before long I grew uncomfortable and impatient with a good deal of American literature that was the staple of my graduate courses: the works of white, straight authors. Though I did find some of their writing intellectually engaging, virtually none of it was emotionally compelling. I had, quite naively, expected a multicultural fare—in Tennessee, of all places, in the mid–1970s! The exclusive focus on white writers, therefore, was tiresome and frustrating. The equally relentless focus on heterosexual works—and the determined silence on gay texts and traditions in American literature—was just as uninspiring and disappointing. And, of course, the unspoken political assumptions that so unapologetically privileged white authors and straight narratives were profoundly alienating. Though my interest in and curiosity about American culture remained strong, my initial fascination with American literature began to fade.

It was then I started to discover, on my own, those literary territories whose existence was either unacknowledged or derisively dismissed in the classrooms. Prompted at least in part by my own increasing sense of isolation in a vulgarly racist and homophobic environment, I began to seek reflections of my own realities within the ethnic and gay spaces of American literature. In particular, I was drawn to the works of James Baldwin and John Rechy. I was drawn to Baldwin because of his elegant prose, his expansive humanity, his sharp challenges to the logic of racism, and his uncompromising deconstructions of conventional sexual assumptions. I was drawn to Rechy because of his authentic style and his rebellious stance; moreover, I imagined an affinity with his dark, Latino protagonists and their familiar and frantic journeys through the anarchic sexual underworlds. That Baldwin and Rechy were, like me, ethnic as well as sexual outsiders in American culture made their perspectives recognizable; their voices and visions became reassuring, even liberating. Their widely different styles of managing their competing ethnocultural and homosexual subjectivities offered me potential models to reconcile the conflicting claims of my own multiple identities. Above all, Baldwin and Rechy enabled me to rediscover American literature.

Understandably, therefore, I decided in 1981 to write my dissertation on the novels of James Baldwin and John Rechy, focusing specifically on the impact of their ethnic gay consciousness on their fictional constructions. Quite predictably, a majority of the faculty members in the English department responded to the announcement of my dissertation topic as if I had told a prurient joke in a totally inappropriate social context. They saw no academic merit or intellectual validity in my declared pursuit. A response I remember in particular came from one of the elderly professors, a southern "gentleman," who had been until then a concerned and genial mentor. He invited me into his office and confessed his consternation over what he considered to be my most bizarre choice of topic for the dissertation. He assured me that any interest in such a topic was exceedingly unbecoming of a well-bred postcolonial like me and solemnly predicted—in a tone that was more paternal than professorial—that no college in the United States would hire me if I persisted in my scholarly perversion. Persist I did. Happily, however, the kind professor's hasty prediction of my professional doom did not actualize.

I recall this encounter now, not in malice or in self-congratulatory amusement, but in order to register a larger statement: though this incident occurred only about a decade ago, the dramatic rise of gay/lesbian studies during the 1980s—the devastation of AIDS notwithstanding—makes the episode seem almost remotely medieval. While I do not wish to romanticize the present status of gay/lesbian studies or to downplay the very real personal and professional dilemmas that many gay/lesbian scholars face in their daily lives, I do wish to acknowledge the fact that gay/lesbian literature now enjoys a degree of academic respectability unimaginable even a decade ago. Courses in gay/lesbian literature, for example, have become institutionalized on many campuses. Many of the most innovative texts in cultural studies are being produced by gay/lesbian scholars. Even major academic conferences devoted exclusively to gay/lesbian studies are no longer uncommon.

The publication of this sourcebook on contemporary gay American novelists, then, is part of the current wave of significant academic interest in gay/lesbian studies. While this is the first volume of its kind, two companion volumes are already in progress: Sandra Pollack and Denise Knight's *Contemporary Lesbian Writers of the United States: A Bio-Bibliographical Critical Sourcebook* and David William Foster's *Latin American Gay and Lesbian Narrative: A Bio-Bibliographical Critical Sourcebook* are forthcoming from Greenwood Press, and others are planned. I hope these volumes, collectively, will give sharper definition and further legitimacy to American as well as international gay/lesbian literatures.

The central objective of this sourcebook is to offer reliable, thorough, and up-to-date biographical, bibliographical, and critical information on over fifty representative contemporary gay American novelists. Advanced scholars will find this volume a useful research tool; however, its user-friendly style, format, and level of complexity should make it accessible to a much wider audience. Each of the entries begins with relevant biographical information on the novelist, offers an interpretive summary of his major texts, provides an overview of the critical reception accorded his work, and concludes with a selected bibliography that lists, separately, the primary works and the secondary sources. To facilitate cross-referencing, whenever a writer who is also the subject of a chapter in this volume is first mentioned, an asterisk (*) appears next to his name. The critical essay by Gregory W. Bredbeck that follows these remarks offers a concise and lively introduction to contemporary gay American fiction.

My purpose in editing this volume is not to help define a gay literary canon. I am, however, uncomfortably conscious of the fact that a text such as this inevitably, even if unintentionally, will play a role in canon formation. While I do not lay claim to any firmly objective criteria, I have indeed attempted to operate within a set of reasonable guidelines in determining the scope and inclusiveness of this volume. However, I will concede readily that my personal and critical idiosyncrasies have probably played a role in shaping the text.

This sourcebook does not claim to be comprehensive in its coverage: by no means can all contemporary gay American novelists be considered in detailed, individual essays in a single volume. I have not, for example, included authors who write only erotic fiction or pulp novels. Though there are many gay science fiction writers, I have included only the most eminent one among them: Samuel Delany. From among the many who publish gay detective fiction, I have chosen to include only two representative novelists: Joseph Hansen, because he is a prolific writer who commands a large and loyal gay audience; Michael Nava, because his award-winning novels have placed him at the forefront of gay American detective fiction.

Unfortunately, while I was in the process of editing this volume, three rather well-known gay novelists contacted me and specifically requested me not to include them in the volume; two of them cited personal reasons, and the third cited professional considerations. I have respected their wishes and removed them from the volume. Two other novelists eliminated themselves less gracefully: they refused to cooperate with the scholars assigned to write the entries on them.

I have included a few lesser-known novelists because I feel that their works deserve wider attention. But in reaching such decisions I have often relied on the few available reviews of their works in the gay press for guidance. Some of the entries in the sourcebook are substantially longer than the others; in most cases, the length is determined by the amount of biographical information available, the number of gay-themed works the author has published, and the volume of critical attention his work has elicited. Often, though not always, the length of the essay does reflect the novelist's prominence in the gay American literary context.

I would like to take this opportunity to thank all of the contributors to this volume. Their prompt, enthusiastic, and professional handling of the assignments has made my editorial role a genuinely enjoyable one. Many thanks to Marilyn Brownstein, senior editor at Greenwood Press, for her unfailing support and to Susan Stout and Pat Hazard for their meticulous secretarial assistance. And thanks also to Jane Carducci, Ann Gebhard, and Denise Knight: one could not ask for finer colleagues or nicer friends.

Emmanuel S. Nelson

INTRODUCTION: GAY/LITERATURE—CROSSING THE DIVIDE

Gregory W. Bredbeck

The chapters in this volume share three common assumptions: that there is, first, "gay literature"; that, second, "we" can identify it and talk about it; and that, third, there is some degree of importance in doing so. The final assumption is indisputable. If, as ACT UP has so poignantly taught us, silence = death, then speaking becomes an act of affirmation and survival. About what we speak is not so much the issue, but that we speak about something *as* gay men and lesbians is precisely the issue. For the act of speech, whether it be in criticism, in politics, or in the bar, disco, or drawing room, asserts ourselves as speaking, thinking, and viable people. In this context, this volume is, in its very conception, a political-speech act and a material embodiment of gay power. While I acknowledge this political act to be of paramount importance, I would also like to suggest that its centrality frequently forces gay men and lesbians to elide some very real and very important issues of identity politics, issues signaled by the more disputable concepts of "gay literature" and "we." I would like to explore these two concepts in some detail as a prelude to reading, as a way of determining what it might mean when "we" read "gay literature."

The very idea of "gay literature" links two terms that are possibly antithetical and, certainly, in their own rights difficult to determine. What is gay? The French equivalent, *gaie*, may have referred to homosexual men as early as the sixteenth century, but until recently in Britain the word most typically was used to explain female heterosexual transgression (a "gay girl" was a whore). In America the term probably did not become commonly associated with male homosexuality until the 1950s or 1960s, and even today there is considerable debate as to what it means and why. Hence I write today from a culture in which I am a "homosexual queer gay white male," the exact emphasis of each word being determined by the exact crowd I happen to be in, the exact statement I am trying to make, or the exact statement being made about me. And while I believe it to be the case that there are both gay men and gay women, the standard phrase "gay men and lesbians" seems to associate "gay" with male sexual identity. Already "we" can see some of the tensions involved in speaking of "us."

It is, of course, easy to see how this troubled history of "gay" finds an analogue in the history of "literature." On the one hand, there is the notion that literature refers somehow to a rarefied or imaginative production, yet we also use the term to refer to any publication, as when we see religious or political advocates distributing "literature" on street corners. Indeed, for most of the history of writing, "poetry" (or, in a variant form, "poesy") was used to describe an imaginative written text. Even the criterion of imagination fails to determine literature, for most would agree that the new journalism of Tom Wolfe or the essays of Joan Didion, both of which derive from "fact," are "literature," while some would say that the romances of Barbara Cartland or Gordon Merrick, all of which are wholly imaginative, are not. When Larry Kramer's *Faggots* was first published, it was routinely derided in the gay media as being both fabricated and nonliterary—a double shot that clearly problematizes the relationship between imaginative production and literary importance.

The problems of using these two terms to specify an identifiable mode of writing should be entirely obvious at this point. Yet the situation becomes even more troublesome when we link the two terms, for the phrase seems to demand some prioritization. When we say "gay literature," are we talking about "gay" in the form of "literature," or "literature" that happens to be "gay"? The first formulation assumes that identity precedes the text and that a gay novel is a literary expression of an already existing identity concept. The second formulation assumes that the form precedes identity and that a gay novel is a literary form that incorporates "gayness" as a theme or motif. In the first, who "I" am determines how "it" appears; in the second, how "it" appears determines who "I" am. These issues become even more problematic when we consider the role of the reader. When "I," as a "homosexual, queer, gay, white male," read *Hamlet*, does it become "gay literature"? When Jesse Helms reads Andrew Holleran's *Dancer from the Dance*, is he reading "gay literature" or reading a heterosexual and, possibly, homophobic fantasization of what "gay" means? It is a question of which comes first, the chicken or the egg, the text or the reader, the text or the identity—and how we choose to answer these questions is entirely contingent on how and why we choose to engage a system of identity politics.

Two texts in particular provide a compelling demonstration of the tensions inherent in "gay literature." In 1987 Grove Press published Stephen Spender's *The Temple*, a novel revised from a manuscript originally written in 1929; in 1971 W. W. Norton published E. M. Forster's *Maurice*, which was originally written in 1913–1914. Publication of both novels was delayed because of strict censorship laws and fear of legal reprisals; both novels also incorporate strongly autobiographical plots, and each relates to the development of British high modernism: Forster, of course, is associated with the Bloomsbury tradition of the novel. Spender's novel originates from his friendship with Christopher Isherwood and W. H. Auden and is set in the same Germany that frames Isherwood's early writings. While these similarities seem to beg a comparison, the exact circumstances of each novel also mark a difference. In the afterword to *Maurice*, Forster pinpoints the motive of the novel as a primarily literary one: "The working out of such a character [as Maurice], the setting of traps for him which he sometimes eluded, sometimes fell into, and finally did smash, proved a welcome task" (251). Spender, contrastingly, begins with an idea of individual identity: the original manuscript "was written in the form of a journal in the first person and was autobiographical" (ix). It seems as if for Forster the idea of the novel precedes the idea of gayness, while the opposite is true for Spender. Not to put too fine a point on it, it seems as if *Maurice* was conceived of as a gay *modern* novel, while *The Temple* was conceived of a modern *gay* novel.

If this analysis seems to belabor what appears to be simply a matter of accent and emphasis, it is because this issue is by and large one that underpins each and every author and novel discussed in this anthology. Discussing the extraordinarily undervalued works of Arturo Islas, David Román suggests to us that Islas's "gay literature" is, in reality, generated more by an iden- tification with Chicano culture and with the Chicano political movements of the early 1960s than by a gay identification. The baroque fictions of Violet Quill author Robert Ferro, Joseph Dewey reminds us, are not pro- duced so much by a gay identity as they are by an irreconcilable tension between this gay identity and another identity as a Catholic American. My own essay on John Rechy attempts to point out that when we approach the topic of "gay identity" in a text, the topic may be *either* "gay" or "identity," but not *necessarily* both. When we read the works of Edmund White, Andrew Holleran, and William S. Burroughs, are we reading "gay literature" and encountering "gay identity"? The essays in this anthology would seem to suggest three different answers in this order: certainly so, closeted-ly so, repressed-ly so. Contributor Thomas Dukes supplies us with the idea from novelist David Plante that summarizes the uncertainty at work here: Plante argues that all of us who live in multicultural contemporary societies must be conscious of the influences that other groups exert on us. Following this line of reason, I would add that a "gay text" must necessarily always be aware of other influences and that gay readers, by extension, must also be able to read these other influences. When we posit an identi- fiable and solidified "gay identity" as the origin for "gay literature," it is frequently at the expense of an immense complexity and an irreducibility that may, in fact, be the very conditions of any identity politics. The prob- lems of "gay/literature," then, and the divide between the two terms, intersect that most problematic and pressing question at the basis of every gay man and lesbian's identity: am I a *gay* person, or am I a *person* who is gay?

I have suggested that, in the very basis of its terms, it may be an impossibility to speak of "gay literature." However, it seems to me to be equally important to stress the importance of undertaking this task and all its impossibilities. One immediate and pressing reason seems to me to be the extent to which the representation of homosexuality in the American novel has been achieved primarily from a heterosexual perspective. In the early 1900s, for example, the American penchant for "naturalism" (a literary movement popularized in Europe by, among others, Émile Zola) produced a number of texts that might be considered the genesis of the contemporary gay American novel, but that also heterosexualize the display of the homosexual. Alfred J. Cohen's 1899 novel, *A Marriage Below Zero*, tells the tale of a young woman who marries a man who, unknown to her, is a homosexual. The story, as is typical, ends with the homosexual dead from an opium overdose. Moreover, the preface to the novel suggests that it has been written to offer advice to young women about how to avoid such terrible pitfalls as marrying a sexual deviant. Contrastingly, Xavier Mayne's 1908 novel, *Imre: A Memorandum*, attempts to justify the conduct of a homosexual to the heterosexual reading community. Although this liberalism seems a far cry from Cohen's homophobia, both stances begin with the assumption that it is the task of literature about homosexuality to speak to the heterosexual community. Homosexuality becomes simply a figure or plot line in what is by and large a heterosexual identity politics.

The early American naturalist novel of homosexuality seems to pick up the course of the great English Victorian sexologists such as Havelock Ellis and John Addington Symonds, who attempted to justify homosexuality "scientifically" by explaining to the public that it is as "natural" and "necessary" as heterosexuality. Such strategies achieve a degree of tolerance, perhaps, but they also backhandedly reaffirm heterosexuality as the central standard of meaning. Gay identity—who "we" are—becomes simply a deviation from an assumed heterocentric norm; and hence "we" are not "us," but simply *"not* them." One of the primary purposes behind speaking of "gay/literature" is to posit the possibility of an "us" that is not simply a heterosexual fantasy of who "we" *should* be. Modern American gay novels that begin with the assumption of gay identity, either in the reader or in the text, may obscure the complexity of material sexuality—but they also imaginatively produce the possibility that "we" are "we" and, in the process, begin to question the tacit and repressive heterosexual assumptions that have underpinned the construction of the homosexual in modern cultures.

Another primary example of the importance of "gay/literature" in the development of a gay-identified definition of homosexuality can be found in David R. Feinberg's 1989 best-seller, *Eighty-Sixed*. In one of the brief satirical essays that separate the chapters of the novel, Feinberg explains "Why I Always Wanted to Be a Clone":

Nothing fazes the clone. With expert detachment and practiced nonchalance, he holds the menu disdainfully, as if it were unclean. He flicks his ashes without reflection on the ground. The world is his ashtray. Behind his mirrored policeman sunglasses, the color of his eyes is anyone's guess.... The clone speaks in monosyllables. He dances alone in the discotheque, pinching his own nipples. The clone is self-sufficient. (17)

Feinberg ends his tribute to the clone with an analysis of his own attraction to this recognizable and stereotyped gay male identity: "Invisibility is what I sought. I've always wanted to be exactly like everyone else. I wanted to blend into a crowd of clones and disappear" (17). What is most striking about this essay, as well as the novel as a whole, is the freedom that it manifests to critique the very gay male identity that generates the text in the first place. In the day-to-day political struggles of fighting for rights, opposing violence and discrimination, and asserting the basic human dignity of gay and lesbian lives, "we" cannot afford the luxury of self-doubt. To admit doubt in the face of the compulsory heterosexuality that dominates contemporary society is to admit defeat. "Gay/literature," however, provides a space where we can both find the "we" that is "us" and at the same time ask the equally important question, *should* this "we" be "us"? Increasingly, contemporary and postmodern "gay/literature" has seen this imaginative freedom as the very point of importance in the act of writing. Indeed, this element has been present in almost all post-Stonewall gay male writing and probably accounts for the hostility within the gay and lesbian communities to breakthrough novels such as *Faggots* and *Dancer from the Dance*.

The essays that comprise this anthology do not begin to answer the question, What is Gay American Literature? Nor do they adequately address the issues of racism, misogyny, and class oppression that frequently operate within the gay male community and, by extension, within much white gay male writing. What they achieve, however, is the opening of a space of speech, the possibility that there *may* be a voice that is not heterosexual, an imagination that is not homophobic, and a life that is nondiscriminatory and, indeed, liberational. This seems to me to be an important achievement. In recent years an extraordinary amount of critical work has been done on gay and lesbian identity and gay and lesbian textuality. Readers who find an interest in the male-oriented essays in this volume will have no problem proceeding further in their research. Limiting my suggestions here to book-length studies focusing on the development of the gay male novel in America, I have attempted to sketch a brief chronology of criticism through the texts I mention. Three initial sources, though each problematic in its own right, deserve recognition. James Levin's *The Gay Novel: The Male Homosexual Image in America* (1983) provides a wide-ranging chronological description of the development of gay writing in America from the late 1800s through the 1980s. The argument relies primarily on plot summaries of individual texts, and at times these summaries are summarily dismissive of novels that do not seem to present a "correct" view of homosexuality. A similar statement could be made about Roger Austen's *Playing the Game* (1977), which is perhaps more noteworthy if only because its relatively early date in the history of gay criticism marks it as courageous. An extraordinarily thorough bibliography of gay male writing is Ian Young's *The Male Homosexual in Literature: A Bibliography* (1982), which can be supplemented with the section on the humanities in Wayne R. Dynes's *Homosexuality: A Research Guide* (1987).

The issue of gay criticism—that is, the interpretation of gay-written or gay-themed works—is much more difficult to outline succinctly. One of the first and most important book-length studies of American gay writing relates not to the novel, but to poetry. Nonetheless, Robert K. Martin's *The Homosexual Tradition in American Poetry* (1979) will provide many helpful insights to readers of gay American novels. A roughly contemporaneous though less sophisticated study, Stephen Adams's *The Homosexual as Hero in Contemporary Fiction* (1980), provides some basic terms for examining the gay novel. Two collections of essays have been especially responsible for opening the possibility of gay male criticism: *Essays on Gay Literature* (1985), edited by Stuart Kellogg, ranges from classical pastoral poetry to the fiction of William Faulkner for its topics of discussion; and the section on literature in *The Gay Academic* (1978), edited by Louie Crew, contains essays on Mailer, Merrick, Vidal, Howard, and Crane. In the past few years the practice of gay criticism has been by and large replaced by gay male, lesbian, and "queer" theory. Heavily influenced by postmodern literary theory, this branch of the academic project typically examines the construction and deployment of sexual identity in a number of cultural arenas, one of which is frequently literature and textuality. While the practices of gay male, lesbian, and queer theory frequently presuppose specialized training in philosophy, it is also true that some of the most exciting work in the area of identity politics happens within these rubrics. Readers interested in familiarizing themselves with this field should consult either *Inside/Out: Lesbian Theories, Gay Theories* (1991), edited by Diana Fuss, or the "Queer Theory" issue of the journal *Differences*, edited by Teresa de Laurentis.

SELECTED CRITICAL WORKS

Adams, Stephen. *The Homosexual as Hero in Contemporary Fiction*. New York: Barnes and Noble, 1980.

Austen, Roger. *Playing the Game: The Homosexual Novel in America*. Indianapolis: Bobbs-Merrill, 1977.

Bergman, David. *Gaiety Transfigured: Gay Self-Representation in American Literature*. Madison: University of Wisconsin Press, 1991.

Bruce-Novoa, Juan. "Homosexuality and the Chicano Novel." *Confluencia* 2, no. 1 (Fall 1986): 69–71.

Butters, Ronald, John M. Clum, and Michael Moon. *Displacing Homophobia: Gay Male Perspectives in Literature and Culture*. Durham, N.C.: Duke University Press, 1990.

Clark, Mitchell J. *Liberation & Disillusionment: The Development of Gay Male Criticism & Popular Fiction a Decade after Stonewall*. Las Colinas, Tex.: Liberal Press, 1987.

Crew, Louie, ed. *The Gay Academic*. Palm Springs, Calif.: ETC Publishers, 1978.

de Laurentis, Teresa, ed. "Queer Theory." *Differences* 3, no. 2 (Summer 1991).

Dynes, Wayne R. *Homosexuality: A Research Guide*. New York: Garland Publishing, Inc., 1987.

Fuss, Diana, ed. *Inside/Out: Lesbian Theories, Gay Theories*. New York: Routledge, 1991.

Hall, Richard. "Gay Fiction Comes Home." *New York Times Book Review* 19 (June 1988): 1, 25–27.

Kellogg, Stuart, ed. *Essays on Gay Literature*. New York: Harrington Park Press, 1985.

Levin, James. *The Gay Novel: The Male Homosexual Image in America*. New York: Irvington Publishers, Inc., 1983.

———. *The Gay Novel in America*. New York: Garland, 1991.

Lilly, Mark. *Lesbian and Gay Writing: An Anthology of Critical Essays*. Philadelphia: Temple University Press, 1990.

Nero, Charles. "Towards a Black Gay Aesthetic: Signifying in Contemporary Black Gay Literature." *Brother to Brother: New Writings by Black Gay Men*. Ed. Essex Hemphill. Boston: Alyson Publication, Inc., 1991.

Norton, Rictor. *The Homosexual Literary Tradition: An Interpretation*. New York: The Revisionist Press, 1974.

Sarotte, Georges-Michel. *Like a Brother, Like a Lover: Male Homosexuality in the American Novel and Theatre from Herman Melville to James Baldwin*. Garden City, N.Y.: Anchor Press/Doubleday, 1978.

Summers, Claude. *Gay Fictions: Wilde to Stonewall*. New York: Continuum, 1990.

Young, Ian. *The Male Homosexual in Literature: A Bibliography*. Metuchen, N.J.: The Scarecrow Press, Inc., 1982.

CONTEMPORARY
GAY
AMERICAN NOVELISTS

STEVE ABBOTT (1943–   )
Seth Silberman

BIOGRAPHY

Steve Abbott was raised in Lincoln, Nebraska, where he later studied literature at the University of Nebraska. Abbott dabbled in poetry, but eventually he stopped because his university studies did not encourage this. After graduating in 1967, he went to a Benedictine monastery for two years. Abbott then left the monastery, which he found corrupt, and drifted around France with a wealthy English friend.

By 1971, he had married and moved to Atlanta, where he began graduate studies at Emory University. In Atlanta he lived in a commune, had a daughter, and became involved in the civil rights and antiwar movements. With his wife's encouragement, Abbott "came out" and became involved in the gay liberation movement. In 1972, his wife was killed in a car accident. The same year Abbott also lost his first gay lover, who was killed by an AWOL marine.

Abbott started to write again after he and his daughter moved to San Francisco in 1973, where he was introduced to the poetry of Jack Spicer. Spicer's work showed Abbott that poetry was a way to get in touch with his gay identity. Abbott says that it was like being reborn. Poetry was his raison d'être.

The first poet he admired was Aaron Shurin. Shurin introduced Abbott to Robert Duncan's poem "Torso," which is about the poet's feelings for his lovers. Abbott was deeply moved and responded by writing a poem called "Wrecked Hearts." The poem was later to become the title poem to his first book of poetry, which he self-published in 1978. His second collection of poetry, *Transmuting Gold*, was published in the same year.

In 1979 Steve Abbott began to establish a reputation for himself both as a poet and as a critic. He founded *Poetry Flash*, a monthly poetry magazine that showcased the San Francisco Beat poetry scene. Shortly thereafter, however, Abbott began reading the work of Dennis Cooper,* Kathy Acker, and other writers who excited him more than the Beat poets. Their writing, which grew from the avant-garde poetry and art scenes of San Francisco and New York, prompted Abbott to start *Soup* magazine in 1980 to showcase their work. Abbott later wrote about this growing group of writers called the "New Narrative Movement" in an article in *Soup*, an article that was subsequently published in his collection of essays, *View Askew*.

This new narrative writing, which Abbott has characterized as "speaking to and creating community" (42) while agonizing over those responsibilities and as employing "deconstructive writing techniques and popular culture to show how personality is constructed" (a letter to the author dated 10 February 1991), became influential in Abbott's subsequent works. After publishing his last collection of poetry, *Stretching the Agapé Bra*, he started to write a pastiche-style prose, first introduced to him by the work of Kathy Acker. Like other new narrative writing, Abbott's fiction arises from a grid of autobiographical snippets.

During the 1980s he also wrote essays and book reviews, as well as conducted interviews for *The Advocate* and *The James White Review*. Abbott's work has also been published in numerous gay 'zines like *Homocore* and the *Dear World*. Abbott has published two chapbooks, *Lives of the Poets* and *Skinny Trip to a Far Place*, and a novel, *Holy Terror*. An excerpt from his unpublished novel, *The Lizard Club*, appears in Dennis Cooper's anthology, *Discontents*. His work also appears in several anthologies including *Homeless, not Helpless*, *An Ear of the Ground*, and *Men Confront Pornography*.

Steve Abbott's collection of essays, *View Askew*, could be seen as his best work to date. The book's informal essays are often as much about him and his life in San Francisco as they are about their subjects. In approach *View Askew* is similar to his novels. However, Abbott here explicitly addresses his questions and concerns about art, life, and community.

In that book, Abbott also reveals his HIV-positive status in the last section of the epilogue, where he recounts caring for a friend with AIDS:

Because I'm antibody positive, I know I'll be in J. D.'s position myself someday—still alive but fading with little control of body or mind. We all die differently, just as we all live differently. I don't know what it will be like for me but I'm no longer afraid. I still feel angry, frustrated or self-pitying sometimes—often over the most trivial incidents—but when I'm with J. D. these feelings drop away. And I'm filled with such a profound gratitude to be alive, to be Gay and to have the friends I have and have had that I cannot explain it. (176)

MAJOR WORKS AND THEMES

For Steve Abbott what he writes is a function of what he reads. This belief has attracted him to a pastiche-style of writing. With pastiche, what he reads literally becomes what he writes. Abbott takes passages from other works and uses them in different contexts in order to deconstruct genres, stereotypes, and clichés. Far from engaging in a detached intellectual exercise, however, Abbott uses pastiche in order to tell the stories of his life.

His first and still unpublished novel, *Lost Causes*, is based upon his experiences living in a group house in Atlanta in the early 1970s. It is a shifting amalgamation of interviews, narratives, and journal entries that documents the lives of a group living in a commune. This heterogeneous narrative represents the attempts of the members of the commune to form a community. As the narrative moves toward and away from cohesion, so do the characters in the commune.

Consisting of people involved with *The Phoenix*, a leftist political paper, the commune rebuilds a deteriorating yellow mansion, which is haunted by the ghost of one of its first owners. *Lost Causes* documents the slow disintegration of this commune, which ultimately causes the destruction of the mansion itself. Despite the members' shared political activism against President Nixon or in support of the gay liberation movement, the commune is torn apart by blackmail and jealousy.

Pastiche is also central to Abbott's first published chapbook, *Lives of the Poets*, a takeoff on Samuel Johnson's eighteenth-century study of the great English poets of the day. *Lives* challenges not only Johnson's work but the very structure of biography by subverting the expected incremental chronology of one individual's life with parallel and contradicting snippets from several poets' lives. Even the idea of "poet" is challenged. Abbott's poets can be anyone: Elvis, Arthur Rimbaud, Jane Goodall, Bruce Boone,* John Lennon, or Mao Tse Tung.

The collision of their lives, however, is inextricably about Abbott himself. Through its lushly minimalistic prose, Abbott looks to the lives of gay poets and writers, as well as other stars, to find himself. In one section, Abbott writes of their relationships with their mothers:

His mother made him memorize 200 verses of Latin each night before he could eat dinner. She slapped him often and forced him to run to lose weight. His mother's ridicule made him violently ill and he cried for two days when she refused to let him wear dresses. Yet she combed his fair curls and nursed his frequent colds. His mother committed suicide when he was 18 months old. When she died he threw himself on the floor and tore his hair. "Mamma, your son is ill," he wrote in a poem.... When he was bad, mother locked him in a closet in "the tower." When he was good, she took him with her to the shrine on top of Mt. Shaoshan, legendary birthplace of the phoenix. He argued all night with her as to whether Valenciennes lace was made in colors or not. His mother laughed when she heard he walked down the street with her panties on his head. When he was fired from his teaching job for molesting boys, he eloped with his mother to Rome. She cautioned him about his outrageous behavior. He was embarrassed to have to take his mother to a mental institution on the bus. When his third wife refused to make him a spice cake at 5 a.m., his mother made one for him. His mother drank, gambled, was a whore, was a virtuous but cold woman who belonged to a separatist religious sect. He never knew his mother. He first met his mother when he was thirty-six. We know nothing at all about his mother. (10)

Abbott continues his search for identity in another deceptively minimalist chapbook, *Skinny Trip to a Far Place*, a collection of twenty-one presumably autobiographical prose poems about a trip to Japan his daughter arranges for them both. In Japan, Abbott attempts to link himself with the Japanese poetic tradition of haiku, but his attempts at "American haiku" only emphasize his creative and spiritual dislocation. On day ten of his trip he concedes, "Impossible to write haiku in English" (12).

The tension in the narration of *Skinny Trip* between prose and haiku is finally alleviated on day seventeen when Abbott lets himself write a poem about leaving Japan. Although it is through the writing of this poem and his return to San Francisco that Abbott "regains" himself, this journey actually shows how much his "poetic" life depends upon his environment and therefore how tenuous this "poetic" life is.

Abbott's first published novel, *Holy Terror*, also has autobiographical roots. The novel, which Abbott claims in its prologue is "fiction based on dream journals," follows the life of Armand Dupre. *Holy Terror* starts with the protagonist's experiences in an Iowan monastery with his first true love, a saintly seminarian student who dies when a monk discovers the two together. Armand then flees to France where he and a handsome young Italian movie star go on a nightmarish pilgrimage with drugs, orgies, parties, and finally a Satanic ritual with captive boys and decapitated chickens.

In form, *Holy Terror* is a *bildungsroman*; it shows Armand's growth through his journey. Accompanying this character growth is a shift in the narrative style as well. Starting with a somewhat awkward style of gothic romance in the tradition of Vincent Virgo's *Gaywyck*, the narration shifts to the more daring construction of the styles of Genet, Baudelaire, Robbe-Grillet, and Bataille.

Abbott's most recent (and as yet unpublished) novel, *The Lizard Club*, is a playful collage of interviews, history, poetry, narrative, and a play, which tells the story of a gay lizard that has a nasty habit of swallowing people whole. Through its shifting narrative styles, *The Lizard Club* is the story of this lizard's coming to terms with his "lizardness," with lizard history and the importance of lizard unification.

The aim of Abbott's pastiche in *The Lizard Club* is not only to merge different genres but also to merge his novel with "the real world," with the lives of everyone: "Everyone's autobiography is fantastic, the more so the more detail that's provided" (10). The appendix to *The Lizard Club*, a collection of responses to a questionnaire Abbott sent to artists, writers, and correspondents around the world entitled "A Final Desperate Stab at Enlarging This Novel's Universe," clearly demonstrates Abbott's agenda.

CRITICAL RECEPTION

So far Steve Abbott has received more attention for his poetry than for his prose. His only published novel, *Holy Terror* was reviewed favorably in some major gay publications. Typical is Clifton Snider's comment in *The Advocate* that "despite some discrepancies in song titles, dates, and geography, I found myself willingly suspending my disbelief, absorbed in Abbott's phantasmagoric world of hot sex and excitement" (70). More comprehensive studies of his works will appear as more of it is published.

WORKS BY STEVE ABBOTT

Transmuting Gold. San Francisco, Calif.: Androgyne Press, 1978.
Wrecked Hearts. San Francisco, Calif.: Dancing Rock Press, 1978.
Stretching the Agapé Bra. San Francisco, Calif.: Androgyne Press, 1981.
Lost Causes (unpublished).
The Lives of the Poets. San Francisco, Calif.: Black Star Series, 1987.
Skinny Trip to a Far Place. San Francisco, Calif.: e.g. Press, 1988.
Holy Terror. San Francisco, Calif.: The Crossing Press, 1989.
View Askew: Postmodern Investigation. San Francisco, Calif.: Androgyne Press, 1989.
"From Jennifer Blowdryer to Nightmare on Elm Street III" (excerpted from *The Lizard Club*). *Discontents.* Ed. Dennis Cooper, New York: Amethyst Press, 1992.

SELECTED STUDIES OF STEVE ABBOTT

Huerta, Alberto. "The Lessons of 'Failure.' " *San Francisco Sentinel* 10 April 1987: 28.
Koch, Michael. "Biography, Diary and Investigation." *Poetry Flash* (Spring 1990): 3.
Snider, Clifton. "Simple Truths: *Holy Terror* and *View Askew.*" *The Advocate* 16 January 1990: 70–71.
Willkie, Phil. "Interview with Steve Abbott." *James White Review* (Summer 1984): 11.

JAMES BALDWIN (1924–1987)
Emmanuel S. Nelson

BIOGRAPHY

Grandson of a slave, James Baldwin was born at Harlem Hospital on August 2, 1924, to Emma Berdis Jones—an unwed mother of twenty. He died of cancer at age sixty-three at his home in St. Paul de Vence, France, on December 1, 1987. During those sixty-three years he lived one of the most remarkable American lives of the twentieth century. He was born poor, and he died a reasonably wealthy man; he was born into obscurity, and he died an international celebrity. He was one of the most formidable intellectuals of his generation, though his formal schooling ended when he graduated from De Witt Clinton High School in Brooklyn in 1942. A brilliant essayist, an accomplished short-story writer, a talented novelist, a perceptive literary critic, a good playwright, and a promising poet, Baldwin was also a tireless public speaker and a passionately committed civil rights activist. Relegated to the shabby margins of American society—because he was poor, black, gay, and gifted—he literally wrote his way into the very center of his nation's cultural life and into the heart of his country's conscience. James Baldwin was much more than a celebrated American writer: he was a cultural phenomenon.

Three years after the birth of her son James, Emma Jones married David Baldwin, many years her senior, who was a laborer and a fundamentalist Baptist minister. With him she had eight children. Her husband, meanwhile, grew increasingly angry, abusive, and violent; soon he began to terrorize his wife and children. James, presumably because he was a stepchild, became a favorite target for the elder Baldwin's violent outbursts. This deeply troubled relationship with his stepfather would haunt Baldwin for many years to come.

At age fourteen, Baldwin underwent an experience of spiritual conver-

sion—an experience vividly re-created in his first and explicitly autobiographical novel, *Go Tell It on the Mountain*—and for the next three years
he was a teenage minister who preached regularly in evangelical churches
in and around Harlem. He left the church at age seventeen, but the three
years in the ministry were crucial to his personal and artistic development.
Though he formally abandoned the pulpit when he was seventeen, Baldwin
remained very much a preacher for the rest of his life. The language of the
church—the biblical imagery and cadences, the grand rhetorical strategies
of black pulpit oratory—left its unmistakable imprint on his distinct prose
style. And the social and theological imperatives of African-American Prot-
estantism fundamentally shaped his vision and granted authority and urgency to his message.

Soon after graduating from high school, Baldwin, at the recommendation
of a friend, became a laborer at a railroad construction site across the
Hudson in New Jersey. Although Baldwin had been subjected to racial taunts
and occasionally to racial violence in New York City, he was totally unprepared for the brutally racist hostility that greeted him in New Jersey. A
long series of encounters with petty apartheid culminated in a spectacular
incident at a diner that Baldwin later recounted in his classic essay, "Notes
of a Native Son." Soon he relocated to Greenwich Village, supported himself
by doing a variety of odd jobs—he was at times a busboy, a waiter, and
an elevator operator—and started to write. His book reviews and essays
began to appear in some of the most prestigious journals of the Eastern
intellectual establishment. He was gaining attention. But everyday encounters with racism, coupled with his growing awareness of the personal and
political implications of his homosexuality, left him deeply troubled. In a
frantic attempt to escape what he felt was impending madness, Baldwin,
with the money he had received as part of a Rosenwald Fellowship, purchased a one-way ticket to Paris. He was twenty-four, spoke no French,
and had forty dollars in his pocket when he landed in Paris on November
11, 1948. Thus began his trans-Atlantic exile, which would continue, on
and off, for the rest of his life.

Given the many dilemmas generated by Baldwin's profound sense of
racial, sexual, and artistic exclusion from his homeland, expatriation for
him was not merely a desirable option but a compelling necessity. But
Baldwin, though he commented extensively in his essays and interviews on
the reasons for and the consequences of his exilic wandering in France and
elsewhere, generally shied away from explicitly linking his expatriation to
his problematic sexuality. In fact, he chose to speak of his exile largely in
racial and artistic terms: he asserted that he left the United States to escape
the unceasing racial nightmare and to become a writer. While I do not want
to diminish the significance of those assertions—there is no doubt that
Baldwin left his country "to survive the fury of the color problem" there
(*Nobody Knows My Name* 17)—I wish to insist on the sexual dimension

of his exile as well. The question of sexual identity, after all, is as central to Baldwin's personal theology as the issue of race, and I do not believe that any meaningful assessment of the significance of Baldwin's life and work is possible if we persist in peripheralizing his sexual concerns. In other words, rather than privilege his ethnicity over his sexuality or vice versa, we need to seek an understanding of the enormous cultural significance of Baldwin's life and work in the context of his peculiar predicament as a twentieth-century American writer who was black as well as gay. His multiple subjectivities—that is, his national, racial, sexual, and class identities—do compete and clash, but a central achievement of Baldwin lies precisely in his confrontations with and management of his complex and conflicting inheritances.

Therefore, despite Baldwin's foregrounding of the racial and artistic dimensions of his exile, it is important to acknowledge its sexual component as well. When he left for France in 1948, he was fleeing not only the racial lunacy of his country but also the personal troubles of his sexuality. Indeed his flight to France was a flight away from American as well as African-American sexual codes. His physical departure from Harlem entailed a radical break from community and its constraints; his arrival in Paris and his entry into a new cultural formation where he, as an outsider, was exempt from the local definitions and expectations signaled his most crucial attempt at sexual self-determination. It was there he would meet and fall in love with Lucien Happersberger, with whom he would forge one of the most enduring relationships of his life. France, then, became a place of imaginative liberation—a space where American scripts of masculinity could be jettisoned, a place where sexuality could be explored in greater freedom and anonymity. It is there he began to chart the troublesome geography of his homosexual longing.

Race and sexuality—two of Baldwin's primary preoccupations—became the subjects of his first three major works, *Go Tell It on the Mountain* (1953), *Notes of a Native Son* (1955), and *Giovanni's Room* (1956), all of which he wrote during his early years of exile. All three books were successful, critically if not commercially, and helped establish him as a powerful new voice in American literature.

Seeking personal involvement in the burgeoning civil rights movement, Baldwin returned to the United States in 1957. During the 1960s—perhaps the finest decade in Baldwin's career—he emerged as a most eloquent spokesperson for the movement. Though an angry prophet, Baldwin advocated not a program of violence but a path of reconciliation, forgiveness, and love. With such a message, often articulated in precise and elegant prose, he soon drew a very large American as well as international audience. Works such as *Nobody Knows My Name, Another Country, Blues for Mister Charlie, Going to Meet the Man,* and *Tell Me How Long the Train's Been*

Gone, all published during the 1960s, made him one of the preeminent artists of his generation.

During the 1970s, though still quite prolific, Baldwin began to show signs of exhaustion. With the civil rights movement largely over, the reception of Baldwin's message began to grow less enthusiastic. The emergence of black women writers, such as Alice Walker and Toni Morrison, during the late 1970s and 1980s meant that Baldwin no longer held the center stage of the African-American literary scene. His failing health, which was complicated by heavy drinking, began to compromise the quality of his writing. He became clearly disillusioned by the emergence of the New Right in American politics, the election and landslide reelection of Ronald Reagan to the White House, and the escalation of racial animosities—though he continued to insist, even during the reactionary 1980s, on his vision of an America free of its racial pathologies and sexual repression.

Baldwin chose to die in France. On December 8, 1987, after an emotional funeral service at St. John the Divine Cathedral in New York City attended by thousands of friends and fans, the casket carrying his frail body was driven through the streets of Harlem—the streets of his childhood. Baldwin's journey ended at Ferncliff Cemetery, a few miles outside the city.

MAJOR WORKS AND THEMES

The international reputation of James Baldwin has rested largely on his insightful analysis of racism and on his interpretations of the African-American experience. Such a reputation, however, has served to de-emphasize the fact that he is one of the most important and influential gay writers of the twentieth century. Simultaneously a racial and a sexual outsider, he articulated a sustained intellectual challenge not only to the discourses of American racism but also to the dominant narratives of mandatory heterosexuality. By insisting on honest explorations of gay and bisexual themes in his novels, Baldwin made a sharp break from the African-American literary conventions; through such a radical departure from tradition, he helped create the space for a generation of young African-American gay writers who succeeded him. Long before the Stonewall Riots of 1969 helped liberate the gay literary imagination in the United States, Baldwin boldly made his sexuality a vital part of the vision he projected in his art. He was, in the finest sense of the word, a revolutionary.

Go Tell It on the Mountain, a modern classic and perhaps Baldwin's magnum opus, was published in 1953. Given the abundant evidence of autobiographical material present in the narrative, *Go Tell* is arguably a record of its author's attempt to come to terms with the given of his complex inheritance. But *Go Tell* is much more than an autobiographical tale. Imbued with an epic sense of history and resonant with elaborate biblical imagery, it is a universal story of initiation, of coming of age, of a young man's struggle to forge an autonomous identity in opposition to surrounding authority figures.

Go Tell is divided into three parts. Book I focuses on the consciousness of the adolescent protagonist, John Grimes. Book II, the longest of the three, follows a historical-generational pattern: subdivided into "Florence's Prayer," "Gabriel's Prayer," and "Elizabeth's Prayer," it familiarizes the reader with the personal histories of the three characters through flashbacks. Although John is unaware of the struggles of Florence, his aunt, Gabriel, his raging father, and Elizabeth, his mother, the reader is given a telescopically expanding vision of the protagonist's familial and racial histories, which have shaped aspects of his identity. The three "Prayers" provide a broad framework for the novel's central situation, John's search for self; they also, collectively, reveal the historical essence of African-American experience. As we understand the protagonist's history, we begin to grasp the various forces that inform his inheritance, the interconnectedness of the past and the present, the link between self and history. Book III culminates in John's spiritual conversion, his acceptance of the Holy Spirit, before the altar of the Temple of the Fire Baptized.

Because critics in general have privileged the novel's racial content, many have failed to acknowledge fully the sexual dimension of John's struggle for identity. *Go Tell*, in fact, offers one of the most sensitive portrayals of the developing adolescent gay consciousness in American fiction. The first suggestion of John's homosexual leanings becomes evident when he keeps staring at Elisha, as the seventeen-year-old Sunday school teacher explains a biblical lesson. John finds himself "admiring the timbre of Elisha's voice, much deeper and manlier than his own, admiring the leanness and grace, the strength, the darkness of Elisha in his Sunday suit" (13). When Elisha dances in a state of religious frenzy, the adolescent protagonist is fascinated by the "muscles leaping and swelling in his long, dark neck" and his thighs that move "terribly against the cloth of his suit" (16). Also, John feels guilty about his recently learned practice of masturbation, but what terrifies him most is that his masturbatory fantasies center around the boys he sees in the school restroom, boys who are "older, bigger, braver, who made bets with each other as to whose urine could arch higher" (19). Such fantasies produce in him "a transformation of which he would never dare speak" (19).

John and Elisha's playful wrestling on the church floor has obvious sexual overtones. After the wrestling, the protagonist stares "in a dull paralysis of terror at the body of Elisha" and looks at the older boy's face with "questions he would never ask" (54). Towards the end of the novel, after John's spiritual conversion, he touches Elisha's arm and finds himself "trembling" (220). He looks at his Sunday school teacher and struggles "to tell him something

...all that never could never be said" (220). When Elisha places a "holy kiss" on John's forehead, the new convert views it as "a seal ineffaceable forever" (221), thereby suggesting a new awareness on his part. Thus Baldwin reveals the doubts, anxieties, fears, and moments of dim excitement that accompany John's sexual awakening.

It is this theme of sexual identity that dominates Baldwin's second novel, *Giovanni's Room* (1956). Prior to the publication of *Giovanni's Room*, Baldwin had already established himself as an eloquent essayist and gifted novelist. Readers and critics had come to recognize him as an insightful interpreter of the African-American experience. Therefore, *Giovanni's Room*, with its all-white cast and its focus on the issue of sexual identity, disappointed and disturbed many. But publishing such a novel in the mid– 1950s was a singular act of courage and defiance on the part of Baldwin, because by doing so he risked his career and the very real possibilities of alienating a substantial segment of his white audience and antagonizing a good many black readers. Yet now nearly four decades after its publication, *Giovanni's Room* remains a classic piece of American gay fiction.

As much a Jamesian tale of expatriation and its discontents as it is a lyrical novel of remembrance and atonement, *Giovanni's Room* begins with David, the narrator, standing "at the window of this great house in the south of France as the night falls" and "dreading the most terrible morning" (7) of his life. An American in his late twenties, he has fled to France to escape the haunting memories of a dead mother, a domineering aunt, an irresponsible father, and an adolescent homosexual affair with Joey, a schoolmate. In Paris, after a brief affair with Hella, an American drifter who soon leaves for Spain, he reluctantly falls in love with Giovanni, a handsome Italian. But David remains sexually confused: he is simultaneously attracted to and repelled by his lover; sometimes he goes out alone in order "to find a girl, any girl at all" (126) to reassure himself that he is indeed capable of functioning heterosexually. When Hella returns to Paris from Spain, David leaves Giovanni to resume his difficult relationship with her. Abandoned by his only close friend, Giovanni resorts to prostitution to pay for his room and food. In a rather sensational turn of events, Giovanni murders Guillaume, an employer who humiliates and exploits him. Soon Giovanni is caught, tried, found guilty, and sentenced to death. It is on the eve of his execution that the narrative begins; in an extended flashback David reconstructs his relationship with Giovanni and his own role in pushing Giovanni to his present plight.

Its despair and violent conclusion notwithstanding, *Giovanni's Room* is a bittersweet remembrance of a gay romance. In it Baldwin forcefully reveals one of the primary dilemmas of the American gay male: on the one hand, he is faced with rigid social definitions of masculinity and cultural expectations of heterosexual conduct; on the other hand, he has to deal with his sexual feelings for other men, feelings that militate against all the beliefs systems that he has, for the most part, internalized. The crisis resulting from such a conflict provides the central drama of Baldwin's second novel.

This inability to love authentically resurfaces as a dominant theme in *Another Country* (1962), Baldwin's best-selling third major work of fiction. Here Baldwin, for the first time, explicitly combines racial and sexual protest. Though an angry work, it nevertheless embodies Baldwin's vision of "another country"—a new Jerusalem, an imaginary America—free of repressive racial boundaries and sexual categories.

Another Country is a complex narrative, structured to reveal Baldwin's outrage with maximum force. It has a multiethnic cast of eight major characters: Rufus is a black jazz musician; Leona is a poor white from the South; Ida, Rufus's sister, is an angry and ambitious blues singer; Vivaldo, an aspiring writer of Irish and Italian stock, is a friend of Rufus and lover of Ida; Richard, a Polish-American of working-class background, is a friend of Vivaldo, an ex-English teacher and a fairly successful novelist; his wife, Cass, is a WASP from a wealthy New England family; Eric, a Southern white male, is an actor; and Yves, a former Parisian male prostitute, is Eric's lover. All the women are exclusively heterosexual. Among the male characters, Rufus and Vivaldo are bisexual, although they generally prefer women; Eric and Yves are also bisexual, but their primary preference is for men; and Richard, the least likeable character, is the novel's only exclusively heterosexual male. This regionally, economically, ethnically, and sexually diverse group of characters constitutes a microcosmic America; Baldwin's exploration of the conflicts among them, then, is a commentary on the larger tensions in American society.

In *Another Country* Baldwin argues, on the one hand, that labels and categories warp human relationships, that racial histories inform individual encounters, that the politics of color shapes even the most casual of cross-racial connections. Yet, on the other hand, Baldwin insists that labels and categories are merely artificial constructions, that history can indeed be transcended, that color has no intrinsic validity in any genuinely human terms. "Another country," then, is a territory without barriers, a place where individuals can connect with one another unhindered by any imposed labels. But that country is not merely a geographical place but also a symbolic space within ourselves—a space where we may imaginatively transcend national, racial, and sexual categories.

For a pre-Stonewall novel, the treatment of homosexuality in *Another Country* is remarkably sophisticated. Refreshingly absent here is the ubiquitous Freudian pattern of ineffectual fathers, overprotective mothers, and homosexually inclined sons that recurs insistently in many a "gay" American novel published prior to the 1970s. Here homosexuality is hardly an occasion for panic or reason for guilt. True, it causes suffering, as it does in the case of Eric, but in Baldwin's theology suffering can lead to redemptive self-knowledge, to a more humane understanding of the self and the Other. Gayness, therefore, has redemptive potential. And, significantly, *Another Country* is one of very few pre-Stonewall novels in which gay romance does not terminate in murder or suicide; on the contrary, the relationship between Eric and Yves at the end of the narrative reveals at least tentative signs of wholeness and durability.

That homosexuality may contain redemptive possibilities is developed even more vigorously in Baldwin's fourth novel, *Tell Me How Long the Train's Been Gone* (1968). It is the story of Leo Proudhammer, a bisexual, thirty-nine-year-old, highly successful black actor. While recuperating in a San Francisco hospital from a massive heart attack, which he suffered on stage during a performance, Leo looks back at his life, a journey from a bleak childhood in a rat-infested tenement house in Harlem to his present status as a phenomenally successful actor. The story is narrated entirely through Leo's flashbacks, with shorter flashbacks embedded in larger ones. Leo examines his life, his memories, seeking a pattern that would grant at least a semblance of order to the accumulated anarchy of his experience. He wants to invest his suffering "with a coherence and authority" (99). It is his larger quest that unifies his elaborate and sometimes disjointed recollections.

In Book I of *Tell Me*, Leo recalls memories of his life in Harlem and his relationships with his father, mother, and Caleb, his older brother. Leo's childhood, like Baldwin's own, is strikingly similar to John's in *Go Tell It on the Mountain*. Book II relates Leo's early days in professional acting; his romantic involvement with Barbara, a white actress; and the racist disapproval of society, which eventually destroys that relationship. Book III recapitulates Leo's gay relationship with black Christopher, a young militant committed to revolutionary change. Drifting away from Barbara, Leo grows closer to Christopher, begins to identify with his revolutionary zeal, and feels almost a paternal bond to him. It is in his relationship with Christopher that Leo is able to find some justification for his own life. The last paragraph of the novel briefly summarizes some highlights of Leo's life after the heart attack. He returns to Harlem with Christopher for a few days but soon decides to leave for Europe—alone. He comes back to New York a few years later, acts in a movie and in a play, and finds himself "presently standing in the wings again, waiting for my cue" (484).

Many of Baldwin's thematic concerns—such as the failure of love, the loneliness of the artist, the maiming impact of racism on individuals and on human relationships—resurface in *Tell Me*. Once again, Baldwin casts the homosexual in a redemptive role. Black Christopher's name itself, for example, suggests his role as a racial savior; his absolute commitment to revolutionary politics shows that he is part of the transforming process that is challenging and changing America. But Christopher is also comfortably and confidently gay. By combining black militancy and gay sexuality in

Christopher's character, Baldwin suggests that there is no fundamental conflict between the two traits. One is tempted, of course, to speculate whether Baldwin, in creating black Christopher's character, is responding to the irresponsible criticism that the gay content of *Giovanni's Room* and *Another Country* elicited from homophobic black militants such as Eldridge Cleaver and Amiri Baraka. It is not unreasonable to assume that Baldwin, by making militant Christopher go to bed with Leo (a largely autobiographical persona), is perhaps determined to have the last laugh.

There is in Baldwin's next novel, *If Beale Street Could Talk* (1974), a conspicuous absence of gay themes. But in his sixth and last novel, *Just above My Head* (1979), the focus is on the life of Arthur Montana, a black gay gospel singer, as seen through the eyes of his surviving brother, Hall Montana, a forty-eight-year-old advertising executive. Arthur, at age thirty-nine, was found dead in the men's room of a London pub. Hall's thoughts about Arthur's life and death are triggered by his fifteen-year-old son's asking why his friends at school call his musically renowned, now deceased, Uncle Arthur a "faggot." Troubled by his son's query, Hall begins to reconstruct the past, his brother's and his own, in an attempt to understand their particular fates so that he may face "both love and death" (497).

Interwoven into many of Hall's recollections are lengthy bits of Arthur's life. Early in childhood Arthur shows signs of musical genius and joins Harlem's Trumpets of Zion, a church-related quartet. His sexual initiation occurs at age thirteen, when a desperate middle-aged man who takes him into an abandoned building and hurriedly fellates him puts two dimes and a quarter in his hand and then runs away. This incident frightens Arthur, yet it also makes him sexually curious. A few years later he falls in love with Crunch, another member of the quartet. Later, while living in Paris, he has a short-lived affair with Guy Lazer, a Frenchman. Eventually, however, Arthur establishes a steady relationship with Jimmy, someone he was close to in Harlem; their love lasts almost until Arthur's untimely death. A minor misunderstanding comes between them just prior to Arthur's departure for London. He dies there—alone—in the basement of a pub, without realizing that Jimmy is contrite and that their love is very much alive.

But the plot of *Just above My Head* is much more complex than the preceding summary might suggest. Arthur's story, for example, intersects with the stories of Hall, Crunch, Jimmy, and Jimmy's sister, Julia. Gay sexuality, as in *Another Country* and *Tell Me*, is only one of the major issues the novel addresses; however, compared to those two earlier works, here Baldwin treats it less self-consciously, less polemically, and less stridently. The gay theme, in fact, is more smoothly woven into the narrative; and it is presented as an essentially unsensational, though problematic, element in Arthur's search for identity and meaning.

CRITICAL RECEPTION

Baldwin's work has attracted a good deal of critical attention: there are at least a dozen book-length studies, about 200 scholarly articles, and over 1,000 reviews of his individual books. Generally speaking, critics and reviewers seem most comfortable with and enthusiastic about his nonfiction; his fiction, on the other hand, has received a decidedly mixed reception. Though a number of legitimate, critically sound reasons might explain this discrepancy, an obvious fact remains: Baldwin almost entirely avoids the subject of homosexuality in his nonfiction, whereas he insists on speaking about it in many of his novels. It would be naive, then, to assume that the gay content of his fiction is not at least partly responsible for the mixed criticism his novels have provoked.

Critically engaging Baldwin's fiction proves to be too much of a challenge for many white heterosexual critics, although there are a few exceptions. To many the task of examining the perspective of a racially as well as a sexually othered artist proves too taxing on their imaginary resources. Homophobia, sometimes mixed with racism, mars their responses to a considerable degree. African-American critics, again with some notable exceptions, are enthusiastic about Baldwin's handling of racial themes but seem embarrassed, sometimes even angry, at his explicit treatment of gay and bisexual themes. My review of Baldwin's critical reception, in consonance with the objectives of this volume, focuses largely on how the ideology of homophobia, sometimes coupled with racial politics, informs critics' responses and judgments.

Homophobically inspired reactions to Baldwin's fiction assume many forms. First, there is smug condescension from critics whose pretentious, shallow liberalism barely conceals their ignorance and insensitivity. William Barrett, for example, in his review of *Another Country* declares, "Though their [Eric and Yves] love is unnatural by normal standards, it nevertheless has more compassion and humanity than any of the heterosexual affairs" (110). Similarly, Charles Rolo, in his review of *Giovanni's Room*, praises Baldwin for his "exceptional narrative skill, poetic intensity of language," but he proceeds to assert that

this endorsement is made despite the fact Mr. Baldwin's subject is one of which I have had my fill. His story, to sum it up crudely, is about a young American who, when his girl goes off to Spain to decide whether she really wants to marry him, becomes embroiled in a homosexual relationship with a barman in a pansy nightclub. (98)

He then quotes Baldwin's own statement about the novel, which appears as a blurb on the jacket: "David's dilemma is the dilemma of many men of his generation; by which I do not mean sexual ambivalence as much as a crucial lack of sexual authority." Rolo concludes that this is "pretentious nonsense. We know that David's problem is not uncommon; it merits compassion. But surely there is no 'lack of authority' as to whether boys should like girls or other boys" (98). Anthony West, also reviewing *Giovanni's Room*, says that "Baldwin's story is told with solemnity as if it went to the very core of things, although in fact it describes a passade, a ripple on the surface of life, that completely lacks the validity of actual experience." He then concludes by hoping that "Mr. Baldwin, a gifted writer, will return to ... American themes" (22), as if homosexuality is somehow un-American! Moreover, West expends so much of his energy trying to articulate his muddled response to the gay content of the text that he fails to address the text itself in any thoughtful manner.

Sometimes critics, in confused embarrassment, offer grotesque misreadings of Baldwin's text. Donald Gibson's article "James Baldwin: The Political Anatomy of Space" is an excellent case in point. Gibson concedes that "the actual physical relationship between David and Giovanni [in *Giovanni's Room*] is created in such a way as to indicate complete sympathy on the part of the author with [its] legitimacy and beauty" (9). This observation is perceptive enough; but almost immediately, in a bizarre twist of logic, Gibson declares that the resolution of the novel's plot—the abandoning of Giovanni by David and the eventual execution of Giovanni—shows Baldwin's unequivocal condemnation of homosexuality. Baldwin is actually "disdainful of homosexuality," speculates Gibson, who is clearly distressed by the novel and concludes, with an obvious sense of relief, "All in all, the book is about decent behavior and is heavily weighted against homosexuality.... [It] makes clear the author's disgust with fairies" (9–10). In his discussion of *Another Country*, however, Gibson—unable to find any such comforting solutions to his dilemma—reveals his prejudice more candidly: a dismayed and exasperated Gibson complains that Baldwin refuses to create a male character "who might possess the good qualities of an Eric without imposing the necessity of his being in fact bisexual" (13).

A bit more baffling is Colin MacInnes's confused reaction to the gay content of Baldwin's fiction. In his article "Dark Angel: The Writings of James Baldwin," MacInnes prefaces his criticism of *Giovanni's Room* with a blunt statement: "That homosexuality is an aberration cannot be denied ... because it denies one of nature's prime laws, which is the reproduction of our kind" (26). Then, in an abrupt and rather unrelated outburst, he chides the WASP culture for its homophobia but then quickly adds, "the Anglo-Saxon puritan queer—who must surely be one of the most unpleasant and tedious creatures that this globe has ever inflicted on itself—seeks to make out of his deviation a grotesquely vainglorious cult of total boredom and stupidity" (26). A page later he makes an equally curious observation: he speaks of Giovanni's transformation in the novel from a "proud bisexual butch Italian" to a "venal hysterical fairy" (27).

While some critics are merely confused, others cheerfully and confidently articulate their bigotry. Their ideology of homophobia provides a basis to condemn Baldwin as well as his fiction and to arrive at highly questionable aesthetic judgements. James Ivy, commenting on *Giovanni's Room* in the respected and often politically progressive black journal *The Crisis*, begins his review—aptly titled "The Faerie Queenes"—by announcing that in this novel Baldwin "tackles the scabrous subject of homosexual love" and concludes by saying,

It seems a pity that so much brilliant writing should be lavished on a relationship that by its very nature is bound to be sterile and debasing. Frustration, despair, and death are usually tragic, but in *Giovanni's Room* where these elements are served up in a homosexual romance they strike the reader as incongruous and therefore crudely comic rather than tragic. (123)

His prejudice blinds him to the subtlety and poignancy of the text, and his review becomes merely a vehicle to reveal his bias rather than a forum for meaningful assessment of the novel.

Similarly, David Littlejohn is unable to connect with Baldwin's fiction because he finds its gay content too troublesome: in his book *Black on White*, one of the early surveys of African-American literature, he says of *Another Country*, "The over-lyrical poeticizing of homosexual love is one of the real flaws of the book" (129). His bigotry thus becomes the basis for a condemnation of Baldwin's art. Robert Bone's *Negro Novel in America*, which is noted in black academic circles for its racist overtones, is also explicitly heterosexist in its analysis of Baldwin's fiction. Bone's irrational prejudice prompts him to make rather queer observations such as: "To most, homosexuality will seem rather an evasion than an affirmation of human truth" (234). Also, Baldwin's insistent casting of some gay characters in a redemptive role alarms Bone. Angrily he condemns Baldwin for allegedly bringing to his treatment of homosexuality a "proselytizing zeal" and for offering "stubborn heterosexuals" what Bone calls, with alliterative flair, "the prospect of salvation through sodomy" (238).

There are numerous other instances of homophobically inspired distaste for Baldwin's fiction. Richard Gilman states that having to review Baldwin's final novel, *Just above My Head*, was a "disagreeable task"; and soon it becomes clear that one of the reasons that the task is so disagreeable is that the book has an "apologia for homosexuality that seems quite unrelated to the rest of the novel" (30). Evidently, it does not occur to Gilman that he might be unable to discern the relationship. Philip Toynbee, in his review of *Tell Me How Long the Train's Been Gone* in the *Atlantic Monthly*, characterizes the novel as "remarkably bad" because the plot does not have "the faintest penetration from real life and real feeling" (91). He then provides a brief summary of the plot in which, interestingly enough, he focuses primarily on the novel's interracial and homosexual relationships. One has to wonder, then, if it is Toynbee's obvious concern and probable discomfort with the book's treatment of interracial sex and homosexuality that make the novel seem so unreal and remarkably bad to him. Whitney Balliet's reaction to *Another Country* is quite similar. He calls the book a "turbid melodrama" and asserts that the "lovemaking, graphically and frequently presented, seems far larger than life because it is generally between males or between Negroes and whites" (69). But why should sexual acts seem larger than life simply because they are interracial or homosexual or both? Likewise, William Hogan finds the novel "irritating and disappointing" because of what he considers to be the novel's "preoccupation with totally destructive sex" (35). Perhaps Hogan's concept of constructive sex would be the culturally sanctioned and therefore to him less threatening forms of sexual expression.

Sometimes the critics' homophobia is so intense that it reaches hysterical proportions. In the writings of Patrick Cruttwell, Roderick Nordell, and Robert Root, in particular, a potent combination of homophobia, racism, and a general right-wing mentality helps generate some startling observations. Writing about *Another Country* in the *Hudson Review*, Cruttwell begins by assaulting the novel for what he calls its "total obsession with sex," which he claims "has the effect of a disastrous narrowing of interest" (596). A few paragraphs later it becomes evident that what bothers Cruttwell the most is Baldwin's exploration of that complex province of human consciousness where racism and sexuality collide. Cruttwell finds the novel's "picture of a perpetual state of race-sex tension . . . so extreme" that he concludes that the book is merely an extension of Baldwin's own personal "hysteria" (597). He then asks why there is so much denunciation of the United States, and he himself provides an answer to the question—an answer that he declares would surprise the "Communists of Moscow": "The answer is . . . people [in America] are unhappy in bed" (597). *Another Country*, he concludes, "is just one long ugly hysterical chronicle of sex-miseries which are blamed on American society" (597).

Roderick Nordell and Robert Root respond along similar lines. To Nordell *Another Country* is an "obscene book" because it tells a "sordid story of whites and Negroes, bohemians, homosexuality and miscegenation" (11). His racism and homophobia become more obvious when he asserts that Baldwin belabors the racial and sexual themes "to the point of nausea and absurdity" (11). Root, also responding to *Another Country*, says in his review published, not surprisingly, in *Christian Century*, "Here is pottage which surely will nauseate many who are neither effete nor puritan" (1354). He then summarizes the plot in an antagonistic tone; his emphasis, predictably, is on homosexual and interracial sex. He calls the book "crude" and "obscene" and feels that "Baldwin is bent on heading up an Overflowing Garbage Can School of Writing" (1354). Indignantly he concludes his review by saying, "It appears to be Baldwin's view that homosexuality offers as good a chance for love as heterosexuality" (1355).

Even more hysterical is Eldridge Cleaver's infamous essay titled "Notes on a Native Son." He opens the essay by talking about his initial admiration for Baldwin's work, which began to change when he became "aware of an aversion in [his] heart to part of the song [Baldwin] sang" (98). This aversion, we quickly learn, is Cleaver's violent homophobia: "Homosexuality," he declares, "is a sickness, just as are baby-rape and wanting to become the head of General Motors" (110). Cleaver contrasts Richard Wright with James Baldwin; he praises Wright for creating many aggressively heterosexual and thoroughly masculine black male characters and attacks Baldwin for presenting black gay men in his fiction. He accuses black homosexuals in general of a racial death wish, which, he argues, is very strong in Baldwin himself. He adds that black homosexuals "are outraged and frustrated because in their sickness they are unable to have a baby by a white man . . . though they redouble their efforts and intake of the white man's sperm" (102). He talks of Rufus Scott, a character in *Another Country*, letting a "white bisexual homosexual fuck him in the ass" (107). This is a particularly curious assertion because in the novel, though the homosexual nature of Rufus' relationship with Eric is obvious, there is no indication of the occurrence of the sexual act to which Cleaver alludes. It appears that Cleaver, in his racist and homophobic paranoia, coupled with his unimaginative assumptions about homosexual behavior, is picturing events that do not even take place.

Perhaps on some levels the most insidious form of homophobia that distorts critical responses to Baldwin's fiction is silence. The initial reviews of Baldwin's first novel, *Go Tell It on the Mountain*, provide interesting examples. A complex text, *Go Tell* offers one of the most poignant portrayals of developing adolescent homosexual consciousness in American fiction. However, almost no reviewer refers to the novel's homosexual content, focusing instead on other issues. A charitable explanation would be that perhaps Baldwin's subtlety eluded the reviewers, their lack of sensitivity and perceptiveness having blinded them.

More probable, however, is that the silence—at least in some of the critics—is a deliberate ploy. Their silence is not merely a result of blindness but a carefully defined political posture. It is a strategy of enforcing invisibility; it is a way of denying the significance of Baldwin's sexual identity and the gay content of his work. Katherine Gauss Jackson, for example, in her review of *Another Country* does not even hint at the novel's homosexual content. But *Another Country* not only treats homosexuality explicitly—at least explicitly enough to cause hysteria and nausea in some of the other reviewers—it is also integral to the moral vision that Baldwin projects in the novel. James Finn's reaction is similar to Katherine Jackson's: in his 3,000-word review of the book he carefully avoids confronting its homosexual content. Likewise, Richard Gilman, in his 2,000-word review of *Tell Me*, ignores the crucial homosexual theme, other than to make a fleeting reference to the protagonist's bisexuality.

Sometimes critics employ curious rationalizations to maintain their stance of silence. Trudier Harris, in her book titled *Black Women in the Fiction of James Baldwin*, refuses to examine or even to speculate how Baldwin's sexuality might have influenced his creation of black women characters. This is a legitimate area of inquiry that can help us understand Baldwin's texts and his characters more deeply. But Harris quickly dismisses the subject as if Baldwin's homosexuality, which she refers to rather coyly as his "life-style" (205), is irrelevant to her study of black women in his fiction.

This conspiracy of silence exists even after Baldwin's death. The eloquent eulogies by Toni Morrison and Amiri Baraka published in the *New York Times Book Review* reveal the authors' heartfelt sense of loss and their deep love for Baldwin. They speak of Baldwin's fight against racism and his towering position as a black writer. But both Morrison and Baraka conveniently forget to mention Baldwin's struggle against sexual fascism and his central place in gay literature. It took Robert Ferro,* at that time near death because of AIDS, to point out their forgetfulness in his letter to the editor printed in a subsequent issue of the *Times Book Review*.

Such silences continue. A symposium was held at the University of Massachusetts campus at Amherst in 1988 as a tribute to the life and work of James Baldwin. A distinguished panel of speakers—Chinua Achebe, Michael Thelwell, Ira McClaurin-Allen, and John Wideman, among others—gave presentations that were edited into book form by Jules Chametzky and published in 1989 by the Institute for Advanced Studies in the Humanities. The book makes no reference to homosexuality; except for a passing allusion by Thelwell to the fact that Baldwin spoke about sex "openly and honestly" (70), there is determined silence throughout. So Baldwin remains embattled, even in death.

Various covert and open manifestations of homophobia have thus marred the reception of Baldwin's fiction since the 1950s. The ambivalence of many of his critics is, of course, largely a reflection of the extent to which he challenged their conventional cultural assumptions, sexual values, and political beliefs. Baldwin was fully aware of the hostility he provoked. The harsh attacks by some black readers—attacks that gained greater ferocity as his role in the civil rights movement became increasingly more visible—hurt him deeply. That he continued to bear defiant witness to his truth in the face of such antagonism is a poignant testimony to his personal integrity and fearlessness. A look at the homophobically motivated critical violence and textual abuse that Baldwin endured also signals the continuous effort needed to salvage gay artists from such mistreatment—a task that is vital to the construction of a gay tradition in literature.

WORKS BY JAMES BALDWIN

Fiction

Go Tell It on the Mountain. New York: Dell, 1953.
Giovanni's Room. New York: Dell, 1956.
Another Country. New York: Dell, 1962.
Going to Meet the Man. New York: Dial Press, 1965.
Tell Me How Long the Train's Been Gone. New York: Dial Press, 1968.
If Beale Street Could Talk. New York: Dial Press, 1974.
Just above My Head. New York: Dell, 1979.

Nonfiction Prose

"Preservation of Innocence." *Zero* (Summer 1949). Rpt. in *Out/Look: National Lesbian and Gay Quarterly* (Fall 1990): 40–45.
Notes of a Native Son. Boston: Beacon Press, 1955.
Nobody Knows My Name. New York: Dial Press, 1961.
The Fire Next Time. New York: Dial Press, 1963.
A Rap on Race: Margaret Mead and James Baldwin. Philadelphia: J. B. Lippincott, 1971.
No Name in the Street. New York: Dial Press, 1972.
A Dialogue: James Baldwin and Nikki Giovanni. Philadelphia: J. B. Lippincott, 1973.
The Devil Finds Work. New York: Dial Press, 1976.
Evidence of Things Not Seen. New York: St. Martin's Press/Marek, 1985.
The Price of the Ticket: Collected Non-Fiction, 1948–1985. New York: St. Martin's Press/Marek, 1985.

Drama

Blues for Mister Charlie. New York: Dial Press, 1964.
The Amen Corner. New York: Dial Press, 1968.

Poetry

Jimmy's Blues. New York: St. Martin's Press/Marek, 1985.

SELECTED STUDIES OF JAMES BALDWIN

Adams, Stephen. *The Homosexual as Hero in Contemporary Fiction.* London: Vision Press, 1980.
Balliet, Whitney. Rev. of *Another Country* by James Baldwin. *New Yorker* 38 (August 1962): 69–70.
Barrett, William. Rev. of *Another Country* by James Baldwin. *Atlantic Monthly* 210 (July 1962): 10.

Bell, George. "The Dilemma of Love in *Go Tell It on the Mountain* and *Giovanni's Room*." *College Language Association Journal* 17 (March 1974): 397–406.

Bergman, David. *Gaiety Transfigured: Gay Self-Representation in American Literature*. Madison: University of Wisconsin Press, 1991.

Bigsby, C.W.E. "The Divided Mind of James Baldwin." *Journal of American Studies* 14 (1980): 325–42.

Bloom, Harold, ed. *James Baldwin*. New York: Chelsea House, 1986.

Bone, Robert. "The Novels of James Baldwin." *Triquarterly* 2 (Winter 1965): 3–20. Rep. in *The Negro Novel in America*. New Haven: Yale University Press, 1958; 1965.

Campbell, James. *Talking at the Gates: A Life of James Baldwin*. New York: Viking, 1991.

Cederstrom, Lorelei. "Love, Race and Sex in the Novels of James Baldwin." *Mosaic* 17, no. 2 (1984): 175–88.

Chametzky, Jules, ed. *Black Writers Redefine Struggle: A Tribute to James Baldwin*. Amherst: Institute for Advanced Study in the Humanities, 1989.

Clark, John Henrik. "The Alienation of James Baldwin." *Journal of Human Relations* 12 (First Quarter 1964): 65–75.

Cleaver, Eldridge. "Notes on a Native Son." In *Soul on Ice*, 97–111. New York: Dell, 1968.

Cruttwell, Patrick. "Fiction Chronicle." *Hudson Review* 15 (1963): 589–98.

Davis, Arthur. *From the Dark Tower: Afro-American Writers, 1900–1960*. Washington, D.C.: Howard University Press, 1974.

Eckman, Fern. *The Furious Passage of James Baldwin*. New York: Evans & Co., 1966.

Emanuel, James. "James Baldwin." In *Contemporary Novelists*, 82–86. Ed. James Vinson. New York: St. Martin's Press, 1976.

Finn, James. "The Identity of James Baldwin." *Commonweal* 77 (October, 1962): 113.

Foster, David. " 'Cause My House Fell Down: The Theme of the Fall in Baldwin's Novels." *Critique: Studies in Modern Fiction* 13 (1971): 50–62.

Fryer, Sarah. "Retreat from Experience: Despair and Suicide in James Baldwin's Novels." *The Journal of the Midwest Modern Language Association* 19 (Spring 1986): 21–28.

Gayle, Addison, Jr. "A Defense of James Baldwin." *College Language Association Journal* 10 (March 1967): 201–8.

Gibson, Donald, ed. *Five Black Writers: Essays on Wright, Ellison, Baldwin, Hughes, and Leroi Jones*. New York: New York University Press, 1970.

———. "James Baldwin: The Political Anatomy of Space." In *James Baldwin: A Critical Evaluation*. Ed. Therman B. O'Daniel, 3–18. Washington, D.C.: Howard University Press, 1977.

Giles, James R. "Religious Alienation and 'Homosexual Consciousness' in *City of Night* and *Go Tell It on the Mountain*." *College English* 36 (November 1974): 369–80.

Gilman, Richard. Rev. of *Just Above My Head* by James Baldwin. *New Republic* 181 (November 1979): 30.

———. Rev. of *Tell Me How Long the Train's Been Gone*. *New Republic* 159 (August 1968): 27.

Harris, Trudier. *Black Women in the Fiction of James Baldwin.* Knoxville: University of Tennessee Press, 1985.

Hoffman, Stanton. "The Cities of the Night: John Rechy's *City of Night* and the American Literature of Homosexuality." *Chicago Review* 17 (1964): 195–202.

Hogan, William. "Baldwin's Comment on a Sub-culture." *San Francisco Chronicle* 28 June 1962: 35.

Ivy, James. "The Faerie Queenes." *The Crisis* 64 (February 1957): 123.

Kinnamon, Keneth, ed. *James Baldwin: A Collection of Critical Essays.* Englewood Cliffs, N.J.: Prentice-Hall, 1974.

Littlejohn, David. *Black on White.* New York: Grossman, 1966.

Lowenstein, Andrea. "James Baldwin and His Critics." *Gay Community News* 9 February 1980: 11–12, 17.

Macebuh, Stanley. *James Baldwin: A Critical Study.* New York: The Third Press, 1973.

MacInnes, Colin. "Dark Angel: The Writings of James Baldwin." *Encounter* 21 (August 1963): 22–23.

Mayfield, Julian. "And Then Came Baldwin." *Freedomways* 3 (Spring 1963): 143–45.

Nelson, Emmanuel. "Critical Deviance: Homophobia and the Reception of James Baldwin's Fiction." *Journal of American Culture* 14, no. 3 (Fall 1991): 91–96.

———. "James Baldwin's Vision of Otherness and Community." MELUS 10, no. 2 (1983): 27–31.

Nordell, Roderick. "Old and New Novels on Racial Themes." *Christian Science Monitor* 19 July 1962: 11.

O'Daniel, Therman, ed. *James Baldwin: A Critical Evaluation.* Washington, D.C.: Howard University Press, 1977.

Porter, Horace. *Stealing the Fire: The Art and Protest of James Baldwin.* Middletown, Conn.: Wesleyan University Press, 1989.

Pratt, Lewis. *James Baldwin.* Boston: Twayne Publishers, 1978.

Rolo, Charles. Rev. of *Giovanni's Room* by James Baldwin. *Atlantic Monthly* 198 (December 1956): 98.

Root, Robert. Rev. of *Another Country* by James Baldwin. *Christian Century* 79 (1962): 1354–55.

Sarotte, Georges-Michel. *Like a Brother, Like a Lover: Male Homosexuality in the American Novel and Theatre from Herman Melville to James Baldwin.* Garden City, N.Y.: Anchor Press/Doubleday, 1978.

Standley, Fred, and Nancy Burt. *Critical Essays on James Baldwin.* Boston: G. K. Hall & Co. 1988.

Standley, Fred, and Louis Pratt. *Conversations with James Baldwin.* Jackson: University Press of Mississippi, 1989.

Summers, Claude. *Gay Fictions: Wilde to Stonewall.* New York: Continuum, 1990.

Toynbee, Philip. Rev. of *Tell Me How Long the Train's Been Gone* by James Baldwin. *Atlantic Monthly* 222 (July 1968): 91.

Trope, Quincy, ed. *James Baldwin: The Legacy.* New York: Simon & Schuster, 1989.

Wasserstrom, William. "James Baldwin: Stepping Out on the Promise." In *Black Fiction*. Ed. Robert Lee, 74–96. London: Vision Press, 1980.

Weatherby, W. J. *James Baldwin: Artist on Fire*. New York: Donald I. Fine, Inc., 1989.

West, Anthony. Rev. of *Giovanni's Room* by James Baldwin. *New Yorker* 32 (November 1956): 219–24.

BRUCE BOONE (1940–   )

Earl Jackson, Jr.

BIOGRAPHY

Bruce Boone was born on March 16, 1940, in Portland Oregon. He was raised Roman Catholic, and his spirituality was an all-permeating part of his personality and worldview from the time of his childhood and through-out his young adulthood. From 1958 to 1962, he attended St. Mary's College, where he graduated with a double major in English and philosophy. In 1962, in order to focus his religious beliefs and to integrate his emerging sense of self with what he perceived to be his calling, Boone entered a novitiate of Christian Brothers, a lay order of religious men who took the vows of chastity, poverty, and obedience. He stayed there until 1964, when further doubts and other intellectual needs brought him to graduate school at Berkeley. He continued his studies of religion at the theological faculty of the University of Munich, where he studied under Karl Reiner. In 1966, he returned to Berkeley; after completing his master's degree, he spent the next ten years withdrawing and reentering graduate education until he completed his Ph.D. in English in 1976. At one point, in 1969, Boone felt the need to "experience New York City," which he felt was imperative if he were to become a writer. When he first arrived in New York, he got a job at the Marlboro Book Company, where he worked until he became a social worker for the New York City welfare system and the St. Nicholas Center in Harlem. He lived in a converted carriage house with five drag-queen junkies who supported their habits by turning tricks in the bathroom in the afternoons.

After returning to San Francisco in 1970, Boone began to meet other aspiring writers in the Bay Area. In 1971 Boone placed an ad on the San Francisco State University housing bulletin board, seeking gay couples who might want to look for an apartment to share. Robert Glück* and his lover,

Ed, responded. They did not room together, but Glück and Boone began a long friendship that would prove very important to both of them, both personally and in terms of their respective literary careers. In 1975 Boone met Jonathan, whom he describes as "the love of my life." They lived together until 1980, and Boone's coming to terms with both the memories of the relationship and his grief (and incomprehension) over its end informs much of his writing. Socialist politics became increasingly important to Boone, who organized many socialist writers' groups, both gay and mixed, and became central in the leftist writers' community in San Francisco. In 1979, Boone participated in a National Endowment of the Arts sponsored summer seminar for socialist writers on the campus of St. Cloud State College, which he describes in *Century of Clouds*.

Boone's most lasting and pervasive impact on the modern literary scene is the appellation he gave to a group of writers that has in part radiated directly from Glück and Boone or become aligned with them later. Once, while discussing the Language poets with Glück, two fellow writers expressed a need to distinguish their work from them in some way that would crystalize the differences, while acknowledging the stimulus the Language poets at times provided their narrative projects. They needed a name. Boone said, "How about New Narrative? What a stupid name." The name has stuck.

Boone became interested in Buddhism initially when he read an article by Steve Abbott* on the Hartford Zen Center in 1986. Boone visited the center and instantly became an active and fervent member of the group until 1990. In recent years, Boone's fiction writing has been somewhat eclipsed by his translations of French philosophers and French literature, notably Georges Bataille and Jean-François Lyotard, but his presence in the writers' community is still very much felt, and his place in the history of gay male writing in San Francisco is indisputable.

MAJOR WORKS AND THEMES

Boone's recurrent themes in his work are explicitly discussed in *Century of Clouds*. After a long description of his life at the novitiate (focused on the funeral of one of the priests), Boone muses that he has "meandered" too far from the main narrative of his summer in St. Cloud, Minnesota. He writes that his work's apparent formlessness comes from a concern for "what a 'theme' in writing might be," discovering in the midst of his writing that for this text it is a conviction "that telling stories actually has an effect on the world, and that a relation is achieved between the one telling those stories and her or his audience and history" (42). A typical Boone story has a central temporal point that is interpenetrated by other times, other stories, which both dissolve and revivify the main narrative moment into a conflu-ence of personal and political histories, liberating resonances of associations and experiences among the story's focal characters whose meanings cannot be contained by psychological insights or summarized as plot elements. These intermeshing stories, memories, and re-visions also animate the splits between the narrated and narrating "I" that comprise the narrator, always in the midst of self-discovery during self-revelation.

It is easy to synopsize the "plot" of Boone's second novel, *My Walk with Bob*: Bob and Bruce take a brief tour of Mission Dolores on their way to go shopping on Market Street. While in the Mission, Bruce tells Bob an anecdote about his time in the novitiate. What this synopsis cannot reflect is the intimacy in process between the two friends that is captured in the conversation, the walk, and the silences in that conversation. Even a more detailed summary of Bruce's anecdote wouldn't reflect how "Bruce's" memories of sanctity, its symbolisms, beauty, and terror, convey his sense of awe, gratitude, and loss over his love for Jonathan, who had left him shortly before the time of this walk.

Bruce Boone's narratives are often of small, almost indescribably mundane events. But those events are always replete with memory, desire, and an ongoing critical acceptance of life in a sexually and politically metamorphosizing world.

CRITICAL RECEPTION

To date, no one has done a study of Bruce Boone's narrative works. He and his writing figure prominently in Glück's *Elements of a Coffee Service* and *Jack the Modernist*; and *My Walk with Bob* is mentioned in Aaron Shurin's *Narrativity*. Boone's importance to the contemporary literary scene is most often indicated in the number of writers who regularly include his name in their acknowledgements, among them Steve Abbott, Dodie Bellamy, Dennis Cooper,* Robert Glück,* and Kevin Killian.*

WORKS BY BRUCE BOONE

Books

Fuck Up (a play). Sebastian Quill, 1970.
Veins of Earth (poetry). Hoddypoll, 1970.
Karate Flower (poetry). Hoddypoll, 1973.
My Walk with Bob (novel). San Francisco: Blackstar, 1979.
Century of Clouds (novel). San Francisco: Hoddypoll, 1980.
LaFontaine (with Robert Glück). San Francisco: Blackstar, 1981.
The Truth about Ted (chapbook). Oakland: EG, 1983.

Book-length Translations

Georges Bataille. *Guilty*. Los Angeles: Lapis, 1988.
Jean-François Lyotard. *Pacific Wall*. Los Angeles: Lapis, 1989.

Georges Bataille. *A Dead Man*. Illustrated by Sam Francis. Los Angeles: Lapis, 1990.
Pascal Quignard. *Albucius*. Los Angeles: Lapis, 1991.
Georges Bataille. *On Nietszche*. New York: Paragon, 1992.
Paul Virilio. *Vision Machine*. Forthcoming. Lapis.

Stories and Essays

"Gay Language as Political Praxis: The Poetry of Frank O'Hara." *Social Text* 1, no. 1 (1980): 59–63.
"Robert Duncan and Gay Community." *Ironwood* 22 (1983): 66–82.
"David's Charm." *Men on Men*. Ed. George Stambolian. New York: Plume, 1986.

CHRISTOPHER BRAM (1952–   )
Mark E. Bates

BIOGRAPHY

In his first published novel, *Surprising Myself* (1987), Christopher Bram creates a world that evokes many experiences from his own childhood and adolescence. Like the novel's protagonist Joel Scherzenlieb, the author traveled to Europe, spent his summers at camps, and lived in Virginia. Christopher Bram was born in Buffalo, New York, on February 22, 1952. The following year his family moved to Coronado, California, and then later to Norfolk, Virginia, the place he considers home. He graduated from Kimskill High School in Norfolk in 1970. During those high school years he was fascinated with architecture and design and often dreamed of being the next Frank Lloyd Wright. Because such a goal was immediately unattainable for a fifteen-year-old, he turned his creative energies towards writing, a pursuit that gave him more tangible rewards.

Bram continued to write during his college years at the College of William and Mary (1970–1974), and upon his arrival in New York in 1978 he began to submit his work to the *Atlantic*, the *New Yorker*, and finally the gay publication *Christopher Street*. After years of disappointment, he was about to abandon his writing career. He worked on a full-length novel "Gunny" in the early 1980s that remains unpublished. Finally *Christopher Street* published his short story "Aphrodisiac" in 1985 and later included it in their *Men on Men* collection. Before the publication of his short story, Christopher Bram was concerned about his career: "I wondered if there was a market for my work" (excerpted from a telephone conversation with the author on September 22, 1991). Before the publication of "Aphrodisiac," he had already completed work on *Surprising Myself*. After two years of searching for a publisher, the novel was accepted for publication in 1986 and came out in print in 1987. *Surprising Myself* was followed by two successful novels, *Hold Tight* (1988, written during the time before the publication of his first novel), and the most recent novel, *In Memory of Angel Clare* (1989). Christopher Bram has just finished work on his next novel "Almost History," an expansion on one of the characters in his short story "Meeting Imelda Marcos." His new novel, scheduled for publication in 1992, promises to be a departure from his previous three. In addition to fiction, he occasionally publishes book and film reviews.

Christopher Bram readily admits his love for history and enjoys the historical research for background material for his novels. He considers himself to be "an emotional realist" and "heavily into story telling" (excerpted from telephone conversations with Bram). As he considers the plot of a novel crucial in its development, he concentrates on historical detail to add realism to his work. Christopher Bram lives in New York with his partner. He plans to take a short break from writing to relax and adjust, even though he confesses a certain boredom with such vacations. In 1992 he will begin work on his next novel, whose theme and working title are as yet undetermined.

MAJOR WORKS AND THEMES

Any reader of Christopher Bram's work will detect both commonalities and differences from novel to novel. All share three major components: (1) the location of the action of the novel, which is primarily New York City; (2) the focus on gay life during a particular time period, complete with historical and cultural referents; and (3) the use of suspense as narrative device.

Though some events in the novels do occur in other locations, the narrative world in Christopher Bram's novels revolves around New York City. *In Memory of Angel Clare* (1989) depicts the world of New York's professional gay and lesbian cliques in the 1980s. *Hold Tight* (1988) tells the story of Texan Hank Fayette, who has just arrived in New York for shore leave, as many other sailors, during World War II. *Surprising Myself* (1987) portrays the struggles of a young gay couple who come to a post-Stonewall New York in search of themselves and a sense of community. In each novel, characters often seem in awe of the city. Hank Fayette marvels over the oddity of New York City: "It was his first time in New York City and he [Hank] wanted everything to be new. He had spent all morning and the better part of the afternoon riding the trolleys up and down this human beehive, getting a crick in his neck. There was something *wonderfully unnatural* [emphasis mine] about a place where buildings dwarfed the tallest elm tree. The city looked straight out of the planet Mongo in the funny papers" (*Hold Tight*, 8). Joel Scherzenlieb, the first-person narrator of *Surprising Myself*, describes his first impressions of New York, in a way typical of the author's depiction of the city throughout his novels:

New York.

Manhattan.

Capital of the twentieth century, Corey mockingly called it.

I drew deep breaths each time I stepped into it.

Everything had been thrown up into the air. It hung above you—windows, stones, billboards—ready to fall, yet staying aloft a moment longer while you hurried beneath it.

Zurich now seemed as small as Williamsburg, and Williamsburg was remembered as an open air living room. I waited for New York to become familiar, but the city was too vast and various. I kept dealing with it in metaphors. (*Surprising Myself*, 129)

All three novels share a common exploration of gay life in New York during a specific decade, complete with relevant cultural icons and attitudes prevalent at the time. Although *Hold Tight* is chronologically Bram's second novel, it deals with the time period most removed from the reader's experience: New York City of the 1940s. This is a world shrouded in secrecy, where even the most minor sexual indiscretion could lead to imprisonment. The war in Europe has also cast a shadow of doubt upon the patriotism of many citizens, especially homosexuals, as it is believed that their "immorality" makes them untrustworthy and potential Nazi spies. When rumors that a house in Brooklyn is the center of a German homosexual spy ring spread throughout the city, paranoia increases and the association between homosexuality and treason is reinforced. When Hank Fayette is arrested by the Navy police during a routine raid on gay brothels, the officer warns Hank, "Don't move... you stinking Nazi fairy!" (*Hold Tight*, 22).

Surprising Myself explores gay sexuality and political activism in New York during the 1970s. When Joel has become bored with his relationship with Corey, he seeks adventure and excitement outside that relationship through a string of one-night stands, a practice associated with the sexual openness and promiscuity of the time. Specific references are made to gay bars, Julius, the Ninth Circle, and the like, to "cruising at the Met," and to the bathhouses at St. Mark's Place. When Corey discovers Joel's infidelity later in the novel, he responds with the accepting attitude common among gay couples in the 1970s, "And we are male.... I think there's something in male biology that needs this sort of thing. It's just the way men are, especially gay men" (*Surprising Myself*, 338). The other attribute of gay life in the post-Stonewall 1970s, political activism, is expressed by Joel's lover Corey through his participation in neosocialist groups in New York. He eventually joins the "West End Marxists," but he continues to question what his role as a gay man is to be in such an organization. This sense of incompleteness leads the reader to focus on an implied criticism of gay life in New York in the 1970s.

In Memory of Angel Clare, which reads like a travel guide to gay New York, takes the criticism of *Surprising Myself* a step further. The novel portrays the AIDS-contaminated world of gay life in the mid to late 1980s. Gone are the bathhouses, the sexual frenzy of the pickup bars, the casual sex of the 1970s. The politics of gayness has become the politics of AIDS, casual sex replaced by distance, self-assurance by fear. The characters live in isolation, as does Jack Arcalli, film critic and longtime friend of Clarence Laird. As the novel begins, the reader learns that Clarence has died of AIDS, leaving his estate to Michael Sousza, his considerably younger lover. Other characters live in denial, like Ben Slover, the political activist who knew Clarence very well during their years at college. Ben occupies himself with minor political concerns so that he can avoid confronting the difficult problems in his own relationship. Isolation, fear, guilt, and denial have all become a vital part of gay life in the 1980s, as the gay community struggles to cope with the devastating effects of AIDS.

Perhaps the most interesting feature common to the three novels is the use of suspense as a narrative technique. The author captures the reader's interest by creating a suspenseful story line that may or may not deal directly with the major themes of the novel. In *Surprising Myself*, the reader follows the tension created when Joel's sister Liza leaves her career army officer husband Bob Kearney in Germany and flees to New York with her infant daughter Joan. When Bob arrives in New York, apparently AWOL, he searches in vain for his wife and daughter. Soon tension and conflict spiral into several areas of Joel's life. Kearney has discovered Joel's infidelity to Corey and plans to use this information to force Joel to reveal Liza's whereabouts. Joel must rely on his irresponsible father for help. Once Joel is forced to tell Corey the truth, Joel doubts Corey's love for him; this doubt is made more painful by the crisis in Joel's family and the imminent death of his grandmother. Thus tension and theme become interwoven and inseparable in *Surprising Myself*, as reader interest and involvement in the text continue until the resolution in the novel's final chapter.

Because its structure is dependent on suspense, *Hold Tight* could be classified as a mystery or intrigue novel. The plot revolves around Hank Fayette, a sailor who finds himself in the brig after visiting one of New York's many gay brothels. His commanding officers offer him a deal: they will suspend all charges of unnatural sexual acts against him in exchange for his cooperation in a sting operation to catch Nazi spies. They intend to set Hank up as a male prostitute at the same brothel where he was arrested, listening to his activities via hidden microphone. Quite by accident, Hank encounters a wealthy Nazi sympathizer who had hoped to receive valuable information from the same brothel to assist Nazi Germany's war effort. When the would-be spy bungles his mission, he decides to kill Hank to guard the secrets of the spy ring. A frantic chase scene ensues, in which Hank and Erich (one of the officers overseeing the sting operation) flee from their intended killer. Tension in the novel grows rapidly until the novel ends with a bloody shoot-out between government agents and Nazi spies, with one gay man caught between them.

In Memory of Angel Clare presents and develops tensions around a more personal conflict—Michael Sousza's decision to commit suicide. The reader becomes aware of Michael's difficulties in accepting his lover's death and his changing relationships with Clarence's friends. The lesbian couple who purchased Clarence's apartment are anxious for Michael to move out on his own. When Michael learns of the couple's wishes he leaves the house furiously, intent on a self-destructive binge that ultimately is to include suicide. Each of Clarence's friends feels responsible: Danny and Ben because of their aborted attempt at group sex with Michael, Jack because of his suggestion that Michael commit suicide, and Carla and Laurie because of their request that Michael vacate the apartment. As in previous novels, tensions build until the moment when a helpless Jack waits as Michael slits his wrists in his bathtub. The reader remains unsure until the middle of the final chapter as to the success or failure of Michael's suicide attempt. The author himself was unsure as to the final outcome of Michael's suicide: "I hadn't decided until I wrote the final chapter whether or not Michael was going to live or die. I decided that he had to live since his failed suicide attempt would create a greater number of complications for the other characters at the end of the novel" (excerpted from a telephone conversation with Christoper Bram November 12, 1991).

Although undeniable similarities exist among Christopher Bram's novels, each one also presents themes and structures unique to each text. Joel Scherzenlieb, the unreliable first-person narrator of *Surprising Myself*, tells his story with frequent observations about himself even though he lacks the ability to integrate them practically into his life. Bram begins the novel with a quote from Oscar Wilde, "Only the shallow know themselves" (*Surprising Myself*, 7), which immediately suggests that the protagonist's characterization will be complex. Throughout the novel Joel wavers between two options for every decision, often choosing neither option out of inaction or taking extreme or inappropriate courses of action. When he is reunited with his friend Corey from his days at Camp Wolf, he vacillates between acceptance and denial of his sexual feelings for Corey: "I knew exactly why I was so happy, but could only nod at the reason, pretend I didn't know it yet, delayed the moment when I finally looked it in the eye. Because it frightened me. And because I wanted to protect it. I was in love with Corey" (*Surprising Myself*, 61). Joel resolves this dilemma through his rash decision to tell the entire world at once about his feelings:

"Mom?" I began. I had to see if I could finish what my sister had started. "Not a joke. It's true. I'm in love with the large absent minded boy."

You could see my words work their way into the corners of her mouth and eyes.

Her face grew longer. "Oh, Joel," she said, but as if I'd only knocked something over.

"I *am* in love. With a guy. I don't want you to be shocked. But it is surprising, isn't it?" (*Surprising Myself*, 94)

When Joel and Corey move to New York, Joel becomes uncertain about his relationship with Corey. He debates with himself the issue of monogamy versus promiscuity, slowly convincing himself that the increasing frequency of his affairs does not affect his love for Corey. Finally Joel demonstrates ambivalence about his feelings for Corey: he wavers between feelings of love and hatred. He wonders if Corey has been simply a sexual convenience or if he had truly loved him. Again Joel responds with rash action. He decides to stay behind at the farm to allow Corey to return to New York with Joel's father, thus ending their relationship. The reader discovers in the final chapter that Corey never left the farm in Virginia. At the end of the novel Joel tries to make some sense of what his life with Corey has become: "Okay, I wasn't any smarter than I had been a year ago. I still lived in a dream of self, only to wake up periodically, wildly look around and grab for something that proved I could control my life. I'd learned only not to grab so quickly" (*Surprising Myself*, 423).

Unlike *Surprising Myself*, *Hold Tight* is told by an omniscient yet distant third-person narrator unconcerned with intervening in the text. The narrator restricts himself to relaying information to the reader. In addition to the "spy thriller" motif already discussed, the major theme of *Hold Tight* is a challenge to the notion of the unnaturalness of homosexuality. Hank Fayette seems perfectly at ease with his sexual attraction to men: "Gangs of sailors charged up and down the sidewalks, hooting and elbowing each other over every girl they saw, not understanding how much fun they could have with each themselves. Hank had understood since he was fourteen. . . . It should be as natural as eating, but some people were funny and Hank did his best to get along with them" (*Hold Tight*, 11). Other characters, presented in contrast to Hank, demonstrate their disgust for homosexuality. These characters range from Sullivan, one of the chiefs of the undercover operation, to Thomas Blair Rice III, the Nazi sympathizer and would-be spy. The most important of these characters is Erich Zeitlin, another of the directors of the operation, who believes homosexuality to be a sickness. He believes that Hank's sexual orientation results from his limited mental faculties. As the narration progresses, Erich's disgust for Hank turns to sympathy and finally to loyalty. Erich accepts Hank's homosexuality and admits its possibility in himself when he has sex with Hank near the end of the novel. Hank's dream about Juke, the young man with whom Hank had fallen in love, reveals implicitly the author's final comment on the nature of homosexuality: "You're smart to be unhappy with the world. . . . Stay unhappy long enough and something will happen. Hold tight, darling. You ain't alone" (*Hold Tight*, 280).

Christopher Bram's latest novel, *In Memory of Angel Clare*, is told by a third-person narrator who shifts the focus of the novel from character to character in order to emphasize different aspects or situations. The theme of the novel is the conflicting array of emotions that the characters express concerning the death of a friend from AIDS, their gayness, and their lives. The author embodies this theme in a central metaphor, the picture that Clarence gave to Jack before his death: "Michael suddenly looked pained, staring at something: the framed collage of Proust and Charlie Chaplin that perched on the shelf over Jack's kitchen table.... The two metaphysical clowns looked like brothers, especially in comparison to the sexy jock in underpants who stood between them" (*In Memory of Angel Clare*, 95). Just as the picture represents a collage of mismatched images, the novel's characters display a collage of opposing emotions: love for Clarence, guilt over their attitudes towards him as he was dying, fear of the unimportance of their lives and terror of AIDS, anger about their helplessness, and the pain of their grief. This melting pot of emotions causes the characters to behave in impulsive and illogical ways. This is especially true for Jack Arcalli and Michael Sousza. Jack seems bound for a life of self-loathing when he realizes that he had all but ignored Clarence during the months preceding his death. Michael is disgusted with the fear and distance he showed Clarence. Both are self-destructive; Jack chooses the slower route of isolation while Michael chooses the quicker, surer route of suicide. None of the conflicting emotions of the characters finds resolution at the end of the novel. Michael survives his suicide attempt. He and Jack have become "platonic" lovers. Failing to come to terms with the emotions, the characters simply live with them. Michael expresses this acceptance by default in his thought at the end of the novel: "And yet, Michael felt he could live with that, just as he lived with Jack, just as he lived among the foolish, well-meaning men and women chattering around him, just as he lived with himself" (*In Memory of Angel Clare*, 288).

CRITICAL RECEPTION

Numerous reviews of Christopher Bram's novels have been published in *Booklist*, *The Advocate*, *Publisher's Weekly*, and *Kirkus Reviews*, to mention a few. Reaction to his novels have been for the most part extremely positive, especially the commentaries on *Surprising Myself*. Many reviewers have admired the realistic quality of its "homosexual coming of age" theme and found the style refreshing and exuberant. John Brosnahan gave *Hold Tight* a rather negative review, condemning its graphic sexuality and its stereotypical characters. I found this particular review quite homophobic. Other reviewers found the novel well structured and the explicit sexual scenes appropriate. Reviewers praised Bram's most recent novel *In Memory of Angel Clare* as keenly sensitive, especially concerning its treatment of AIDS. No major study of Christopher Bram's novels has been published to date.

WORKS BY CHRISTOPHER BRAM

Surprising Myself. New York: Donald I. Fine, Inc., 1987.
Hold Tight. New York: Donald I. Fine, Inc., 1988.
In Memory of Angel Clare. New York: Donald I. Fine, Inc., 1989.

SELECTED STUDIES OF CHRISTOPHER BRAM

Brosnahan, John. Review of *Hold Tight*. *Booklist* 84 (May 15, 1988): 1573.
Hall, Richard. "Gay Fiction Comes Home." *New York Times Book Review* 19 May 1988: 1, 25–26. Article mentions *Surprising Myself*.
Olson, Ray. Review of *Surprising Myself*. *Booklist* 83 (May 1, 1987): 1332.
———. Review of *In Memory of Angel Clare*. *Booklist* 85 (June 15, 1989): 1778.
Schmieder, Rob. Review of *Surprising Myself*. *Library Journal* 112 (April 1, 1987): 160.
Steinberg, Sybil. Review of *Surprising Myself*. *Publisher's Weekly* 231 (April 17, 1987): 67.
———. Review of *Hold Tight*. *Publisher's Weekly* 233 (May 27, 1988): 52.
———. Review of *In Memory of Angel Clare*. *Publisher's Weekly* 235 (May 19, 1989): 67.

WILLIAM SEWARD BURROUGHS II (1914–)
Gregory Woods

BIOGRAPHY

There is a myth that needs laying to rest: William Burroughs was never, as one critic called him, "the world's richest ex-junkie." His grandfather and namesake was, it is true, the celebrated adding-machine inventor, who did, indeed, turn his ingenuity into a small fortune; his partners took the rest. But after his death the family was prevailed upon to sell most of its shares in the company. Mortimer Burroughs, the author's father, kept some shares until just before the stock market crash in 1929. He was well-off, but not the fabled heir to the adding-machine millions. On the death of Laura, Mortimer's wife, in 1970, William Burroughs inherited $10,000.

William Seward Burroughs II was born in St. Louis, Missouri, on February 5, 1914. If we look at his background and childhood for signals of what he was later to become, we find an unspecified sexual trauma at the hands of his Welsh nanny and her male lover, when Burroughs was four. There is authorship of a sort in the fact that his mother, Laura, wrote three books on flower arranging for the Coca-Cola company. Burroughs' own writing career started when, aged eight, he wrote an "Autobiography of a Wolf." He developed early interests in knife-throwing and firearms and nearly blew one of his hands off when experimenting with explosives. He also formed a lifelong hatred of horses.

In 1929 he was sent to the Los Alamos Ranch School near Santa Fe, New Mexico, a "health school" dedicated to the manly virtues of the rugged outdoor life. The school's director took a close interest in the physical development of his tender charges, to the extent of interrogating them about their masturbatory habits and, at times, making them submit to being scrutinised in the nude. Burroughs' memories of himself at this time often appear in his written work, fictionalized around the awkward, unsavory, and lust-fully smouldering youth Audrey Carsons.

Tirelessly unhappy—taunted and sexually rejected—he left school two months before graduation. At home, he came out to his mother, and she sent him to a benevolent but unhelpful shrink. The Los Alamos school was later taken over by J. Robert Oppenheimer's Manhattan Project and has been associated ever since with the development of the Bomb.

Burroughs' education was not over. When he arrived at Harvard in September 1932, he was an odd mix of naivete (still under the impression that children are born through the navel) and fearless independence of mind, not to mention eccentricity of behavior. He kept a ferret and a .32 revolver in his room. With the latter, he only narrowly avoided shooting a friend by accident. As if he were making up for lost time, in the next few years his sexual education developed apace, but the effects were not invariably happy. He lost his virginity in a heterosexual St. Louis brothel; but his first gay sexual activity, other than boyish mutual masturbation, gave him syphilis. He was later recruited by Herbert Huncke to contribute his sexual history to Alfred Kinsey's national survey.

In 1939, while obsessed with a bisexual hustler called Jack Anderson, Burroughs deliberately severed the tip of one of his fingers. He was temporarily committed to Bellevue until his father intervened and took him back down to St. Louis to recuperate.

In 1942 Burroughs took work in Chicago as an exterminator, an occupation that would provide plentiful material for his fiction. It was during the subsequent period, in New York, that he became associated with the writers of the (younger) Beat generation. He met Allen Ginsberg in December 1943, Jack Kerouac in February 1944. When Lucien Carr fag-bashed Dave Kammerer to death in 1944, Kerouac and Burroughs collaborated on a narrative about these two acquaintances of theirs, in the style of Dashiell Hammett; they called it *And the Hippos Were Boiled in Their Tanks*.

In 1937, Burroughs had married an older woman, a German Jew, to enable her to enter the United States; the couple were granted a Mexican divorce in 1946. By way of a contrast, his second (common-law) marriage, with Joan Vollmer, was not so formally constituted, but was at least built around a relationship. This, in its way, lasted for more than five years. They had a son, whom they took to live in Mexico. However, on September 6, 1951, while playing a William Tell game with an unfamiliar pistol which shot low (a Star .380 automatic), Burroughs killed his wife. Joan was twenty-seven. Their son Billy was four.

This was not the first, but was the most serious, of William Burroughs' many encounters with the law. In May 1948, he and Joan had been arrested for fornicating in the open air in the Rio Grande Valley. In April 1949, he was arrested again, this time for drug and gun license offenses; it was to avoid the subsequent court case that he had moved to Mexico. It became the custom for his family to bail him out. This time, charged under the Mexican legal system with *imprudencia criminal* (criminal imprudence), he was bailed out after thirteen days' imprisonment. Burroughs later expressed the opinion that Joan's death had been instrumental in his birth as a writer.

A sequence of alternating heroin addictions and cures threads itself throughout Burroughs' life, much as it appears as a recurrent motif in his fiction. This is presumably the source of his interest in the ways in which human bodies and minds tend to be controlled by outside agencies. It may also be the origin of some of his books' aggression. When on junk, he used to amuse himself by torturing cats; a paragraph to this effect was excised from *Junkie*, his first book, which was published in 1953. He had written a sequel, *Queer*, in 1952, but it was not published until 1985.

Typically, his first publisher's advance was stolen from him by a Peruvian boy on the day it arrived. He was travelling now, partly in search of the hallucinogenic drug *yage*. After Ecuador, Colombia, and Peru, he ended up on the other side of the Atlantic, in Tangier. It was here that, eventually, he wrote his most notorious novel; and it was here that the book was edited and put together by a committee consisting of Alan Ansen, Allen Ginsberg, Peter Orlovsky, and the author himself. It was published in Paris, as *Naked Lunch*, in 1959.

By then, Burroughs had moved to the famous "Beat Hotel" in Paris, and was at the height of his association with the various transient Beats. It was there that his friend Brion Gysin enthused him with the ideas that led to his development of the disruptive "cut-up" method, whereby written texts were literally cut up and randomly rejoined to form new texts and, supposedly, a new literature. This technique was the main shaping force behind a trilogy of novels, *The Soft Machine* (1961), *The Ticket That Exploded* (1962), and *Nova Express* (1964).

Burroughs' name came seriously into prominence after a major writers' conference at the Edinburgh Festival in 1962; and his reputation, both good and bad, was augmented when *The Naked Lunch* was tried for obscenity in Boston, Massachusetts, and found guilty on March 23, 1965. This decision was overturned on July 7, 1966.

Throughout the period in which his own career was developing, Burroughs watched—often from a great distance—as the life of his son fell apart. Like his father a writer and addict (the author of *Speed*), Billy Jr. was in and out of trouble all his life. He shot a friend in the neck with a .22 rifle in 1962. He nearly died of cirrhosis of the liver in 1976 and was subsequently given a liver transplant. He died in 1981 at the age of thirty-three.

William Burroughs' career as a public figure, addressing writers' conferences and giving readings worldwide, became organized and variably profitable after 1974, when he met James Grauerholz, who became his secretary and amanuensis. In November 1975, the author moved into the most famous of his various residences, usually known as "The Bunker," the kind of retreat in which one might have expected him to hole up: a converted YMCA locker room in New York. The place was windowless and, most evocatively, had porcelain urinals in the bathroom.

The dalliance with drugs—or, rather, the long and difficult relationship, a marriage of convenience and attrition, long past the plausibility of a friendly divorce—continued through these years. In 1975 he came off heroin; by 1979 he was back on; off again by late 1980. He moved away from the metropolis to Lawrence, Kansas, late in 1981; and it was during the next few years that his second trilogy of novels appeared: *Cities of the Red Night* in 1981, *The Place of Dead Roads* in 1984, and *Western Lands* in 1987. William S. Burroughs was elected to the American Academy, not uncontroversially, in 1983.

Burroughs has been well served by the biographer Ted Morgan, from whose book the preceding details have been derived.

MAJOR WORKS AND THEMES

Whether one should unhesitatingly describe William S. Burroughs as a "gay novelist" is open to debate. Of his homosexuality there is no doubt. That it is a crucial element in the shaping of his fiction, where it plays a major and explicit role, is also certain. The problem comes with the casual and all-too-easy use of the word "gay," in its post-Stonewall senses, to describe the writer and his work. There are many readers who would argue that Burroughs is not gay at all, but a rather old-fashioned kind of homosexual who has never contributed, or sought to contribute, to the momentum of social change. His few representations of adult gay couples, as of lesbians, tend to combine unsympathetic humor with real contempt.

The two main reasons for this seem to be, first, his almost exclusive concentration on the sexual experiments of adolescent boys, and, second, his distaste for the very idea of love. Love, he says, is "a con put down by the female sex" and should therefore be resisted. Given that women are "a perfect curse," love needs to be mistrusted as a womanly ruse to lure healthily homosexual boys into vaginal castration. Unreconstructed by the women's movement, Burroughs has remained one of the world's most outspoken misogynists.

He must, however, be read as a comic writer. His sense of humor may not be to every reader's taste, but one should never forget that his steely glare is generally enlivened by a sardonic sparkle. He knows whom he is annoying, whether they be left- or right-wing, female or male (though it is hard to believe he would expect to have a female readership at all).

The Naked Lunch is a self-consciously emetic brew of comedy and carnage, in which Burroughs has abandoned the prescriptive "logic" of linear narrative. Instead he uses techniques that, contrary to his shrillest detractors and supporters alike, are not entirely original, but derive organically from important sources in American culture: in film, but also in the "ideogrammic" methods developed by Ezra Pound. There is no reason for practiced readers to find them surprising or obscure.

This first novel introduced readers to themes and characters that have since become distinctive Burroughs trademarks. According to your sensibilities and preoccupations, your readings of the book are likely to provide abiding memories either of sexual torture—necks snapping as genitals ejaculate—or of wild set pieces of comic *grand guignol*. It is here, for instance, that we first meet the richest man in the world, A. J., flamboyant pederast and mandril-fancier, who cuts a self-indulgently destructive swathe through many of the later books. (In *Exterminator!* he attempts to get a mandril elected president of the United States.)

In its extravagant juxtapositions of different worlds and life-forms, *The Soft Machine*, too, presents us with what can now be recognized as classic Burroughs materials and strategies. Its many sexual acts between male teenagers lead as frequently to death or bestial metamorphosis as to the mere "flash-bulb" of orgasm. Boys are spliced together on tape, on film, and in "reality," with startling, often horrifying, consequences. A pornographic movie of soldiers jacking off while hanging their prisoners is sped up until the men are coming like machine guns; Mayan priests reshape lines of boys, conjoined in mechanical orgy, into a giant, ejaculating centipede; and so on.

As in most of Burroughs' work, however, such scenes of violence and radical transformation are liberally interspersed with nostalgic scenes of affectionate sex (mutual masturbation and anal intercourse) between boys. These are often incidents and relationships remembered, in moments of sentimental vulnerability, by adult narrators to whom, since then, no warmer proofs of human intimacy have ever been granted.

In *The Ticket That Exploded*, Burroughs takes his postmodernist obsession with communications to even further extremes, at which tape recorders have dialogues with each other; everyone is spliced in with everyone else; communication is total. On film, sex takes place in a similar manner, obviating the need for actual physical contact. Lovers send tape recorders, in lieu of themselves, on dates. Why should prerecorded wars not be waged likewise? Then, if nobody is listening, why not switch all the tapes off? Switch off and go home. Communication is thus represented as being both all-important and of no significance whatsoever.

One of this novel's many fragmentary endings consists of a sudden viral takeover and the enforced closure of the Shitola baths. Many of Burroughs' morbid visions have been regarded, in retrospect, as predictions—even prophecies—of the AIDS catastrophe. Certainly, his career-long interest in viral sources of life and death has resonant parallels with the current epidemic. However, his use of viruses in his fiction has not been sufficiently focused to constitute much of a coincidence, let alone a prophecy. He has always had something of a scatter-effect in his attributions of such diverse matters as sexuality and language-learning to viral spread.

Throughout the novels, sexual activity functions as the major means of contact between human beings and between human beings and their environment. Speech generally occurs, in atrophied form (and often in Spanish or broken English), in sexual contexts: propositions, acceptances, voiced desires, instructions, endearments, cries of pain or delight. Where a character speaks for more than a few brief sentences, he is usually giving a speech (a diplomat making an official denial, Doctor Benway ranting about junkies and schizophrenia, a professor giving an incoherent lecture) to which no reply is given.

In its representations of the male half of a world irrevocably divided along the fault-lines of gender difference, *The Wild Boys* is both an extraordinary *tour de force* of lyrical homoeroticism and a further step in its author's marginalization of women. The wild boys, marauding gangs of adolescents in jockstraps, have developed a sophisticated method of homosexual reproduction—physical intercourse with mental images that take boyish shape and spring to life—to augment their number after the carnage of battle. Some of these passages show Burroughs at his most seriously and positively sexy, writing with a control that he has not always been able to muster. The book is one of the most subtle and inventive erotic novels to have been written by an American. For the sake of balance, I long for a cut-up edition, in which it is spliced together with Monique Wittig's equally warlike, but woman-loving, novel *Les Guerillères*.

In a 1965 interview Burroughs said he wanted to write a Western. Two decades later, he did so. But *The Place of Dead Roads* is refreshingly opposed to the hetero-heroism of movie cowboys, as well as to the America of Anita Bryant, the CIA, apple pie, and the pious platitudes of NASA astronauts. It reads like a word-processed transcription of Ovid's erotic nightmares, telepathically spliced into the imaginations of a medieval bestiarist and a Western pulp-novelist. It reeks of the locker room and the grave. It is also the most self-consciously literary of the Burroughs novels. As so much of his work plots a trajectory between American pastoral and Boy's Own adventures from the heyday of the British Empire, Burroughs seems very much at home in the Western genre, even if he does expand and distort it to taste.

In the end, the choice is simple. For those who seek political purity in their reading matter, William Burroughs is best avoided. (The same criterion, however, would force us to ignore the likes of Céline and Genet.) He dramatizes a movement towards sterility and inhumanity, thereby managing to depict both the remnants of tender, affectionate sexuality and the hideous growth of the sexuality of power and "orgasm death." His are books of the dead, books that look back to life, books that long for a return to life but acknowledge the fact that time—relativity notwithstanding—moves in only one direction. They are Pastorals.

CRITICAL RECEPTION

Burroughs criticism has never really grown out of the polarized controversy that attended the publication of *The Naked Lunch*. Intemperate attacks on the book were often countered by ridiculously overstated defenses. It seems that one is expected either to denounce Burroughs as a pornographer or to puff him as the greatest American novelist since Henry James. But in the real world, neither of these accounts is accurate.

John Wain (the poet, not Wayne the masculinist icon) described *The Naked Lunch* as "the merest trash, not worth a second glance" and ridiculed Norman Mailer and Jack Kerouac for their endorsements, quoted on the book's back cover. He said he could not imagine the killjoy Burroughs "looking at a landscape and getting anything out of it." Contrasting Burroughs with the Marquis de Sade, he complained that "Burroughs takes himself with a complete, owlish seriousness" (*New Republic*, 21–23).

In March 1963, the novel was defended by Mary McCarthy. She argued that it was an example of a new type of fiction based on statelessness, other examples being Vladimir Nabokov's *Lolita* and Günter Grass's *The Tin Drum*. She called *The Naked Lunch* "the first serious piece of science fiction," adding that "the others are entertainment"; and she compared Burroughs with Jonathan Swift (a frequent but not particularly sustainable policy of his defenders). But, she said, the main value of the book lay in its humor; otherwise, it was mere "coterie literature" for an audience of junkies and, by implication, homosexuals. Clearly, she was not yet ready to value and evaluate it as gay literature (*The Writing on the Wall*, 42–53).

Others were more positive—in my opinion, too positive—about the literary effects of Burroughs' homosexuality. In *Bomb Culture*, Jeff Nuttall wrote: "A homosexual, his consequent approach to human relationships had the psychological insight of a Proust or a Gide" (99). Hyperbole apart, this statement completely overlooks the great distance between the concerns of French modernism and American postmodernism. Burroughs does not have such insights nor, for the most part, does he seek to. In 1973 Allen Ginsberg called Burroughs "one of the few gay lib 'heroes' " (124). At this distance, since so many heroic women and men have emerged in our movement, especially during the AIDS crisis, it is hard to recognize him as being among them at all.

As the years passed, judgements on Burroughs mellowed somewhat. Several important commentators recognized that his work, far from being as outlandish as the novelty of the early books had suggested, belonged centrally to the mainstream mythic currents of the male literature of the United States. Leslie Fiedler's *Waiting for the End* (1964) was a help in this respect,

assessing Burroughs in the context of an American tradition whose parameters Fiedler had fixed in the earlier book, *Love and Death in the American
Novel*. Burroughs had been granted, according to Fiedler, "an authentic
cosmic vision of the end of man" (168).

Tony Tanner, also, valued him highly, calling him "one of the coolest,
most cerebral and analytic of American writers." In a statement with which,
even today, it is difficult to disagree, Tanner argued that Burroughs "too
often seen as a peripheral figure mongering his own obscene nightmares
and eccentric experiments, in a profound way is an important writer, concerning himself precisely with many of those themes and problems which
are central to American fiction." At one point, Tanner compared Burroughs'
intention of renewing American literature with Walt Whitman's (*City of
Words*, 109–40).

However, the more positive their evaluation of his fiction, the less these
commentators dared confront his sexuality. As a result, there are themes of
his—such as addiction and control—that have been far more thoroughly
and competently covered, critically, than has the theme of sexual relations.
Where the question of sex was raised, it was generally read in entirely
negative terms. A typical early account was as follows: "In Burroughs' work,
sex is usually violation. It is sterile, inhuman, malevolent. It is a perversion
of the life instinct, an organic process turned mechanical. Sadism, masoch-
ism, and pederasty prevail; tenderness, love, and knowledge are absent. Sex
is simply the obscene correlative of alienation." Typically, this "analysis"
constituted a brief paragraph in a nineteen-page essay and was its author's
sole attempt to come to terms with the subject (Ihab Hassan, "The Sub-
tracting Machine," 7).

The outbursts have continued, even as rehabilitations of the sort that
proliferated in the late 1960s and early 1970s have virtually petered out.
The negative comments remain vivid and often amusing: *Port of Saints*
(1980) was called "murderous claptrap" by John Updike. On the "positive"
side, however, we have very little apart from a rather dull festschrift in the
Review of Contemporary Fiction (1984). Generally, critics who value their
tenure have steered clear.

From the point of view of the lesbian or gay reader, the overriding impression created by the critical babble surrounding Burroughs' work is one of
acute homophobia in the academic institutions; of critics measuring their
distaste for anal intercourse or mutual masturbation—the characteristic
Burroughs sex scene—alongside their fear of those other pet subjects of his,
the hypodermic needle and the gun.

WORKS BY WILLIAM SEWARD BURROUGHS II

Junkie: Confessions of an Unredeemed Drug Addict [by "William Lee"]. New York:
    Ace, 1953. Complete edition, Harmondsworth: Penguin, 1977.

The Naked Lunch. Paris: Olympia, 1959. New York: Grove, 1962 [as *Naked Lunch*]. London: Calder, 1964.

The Soft Machine. Paris: Olympia, 1961. New York: Grove, 1966. London: Calder and Boyars, 1968.

The Ticket That Exploded. Paris: Olympia, 1962. Revised edition, New York: Grove, 1967. London: Calder and Boyars, 1968.

Dead Fingers Talk. London: Calder, 1963.

Nova Express. New York: Grove, 1964. London: Cape, 1966.

The Wild Boys: A Book of the Dead. New York: Grove, 1971. London: Calder and Boyars, 1972. Revised edition, London: Calder, 1979.

Exterminator! New York: Viking, 1973. London: Calder and Boyars, 1974.

Port of Saints. Berkeley, Calif.: Blue Wind Press, 1980. London: Calder, 1983.

Cities of the Red Night: A Boy's Book. London: Calder, 1981. New York: Holt Rinehart, 1981.

A William Burroughs Reader. Ed. John Calder. London: Pan, 1982.

The Place of Dead Roads. New York: Holt Rinehart, 1983. London: Calder, 1984.

Queer. New York: Viking, 1985. London: Pan, 1986.

The Western Lands. New York: Viking Penguin, 1987.

SELECTED STUDIES OF WILLIAM SEWARD BURROUGHS II

Bockris, Victor, ed. *With William Burroughs: A Report from the Bunker*. New York: Seaver, 1981. London: Vermilion, 1982.

Goodman, Michael B. *William S. Burroughs: An Annotated Bibliography of His Works and Criticism*. New York: Garland, 1976.

———. *Contemporary Literary Censorship: The Case History of Burroughs' Naked Lunch*. Metuchen, N.J.: Scarecrow, 1981.

Maynard, Joe, and Barry Miles. *William S. Burroughs: A Bibliography 1953–73*. Charlottesville: University Press of Virginia, 1978.

Morgan, Ted. *Literary Outlaw: The Life and Times of William S. Burroughs*. New York: Holt, 1988.

Mottram, Eric. *William Burroughs: The Algebra of Need*. Buffalo, Intrepid, 1971.

Odier, Daniel, ed. *The Job: Interviews with William S. Burroughs*. New York: Grove, 1970. London: Cape, 1970.

Skerl, Jennie. *William Burroughs*. Boston: Twayne, 1985.

TRUMAN CAPOTE (1924–1984)
Peter G. Christensen

BIOGRAPHY

The life of Truman Capote has attracted as much attention as his work, and the traditional outline of reference books is more limiting than helpful. First of all, some of his fiction, such as his best and most famous story, "A Christmas Memory," is strongly autobiographical in nature. Second, he was a self-promoting personality and celebrity for virtually all his publishing career. Third, his idea of the so-called nonfiction novel represented by *In Cold Blood* deserves to be studied with reference to his willingness to blur the actual events of his life with fictional details. Fourth, he has been the subject of many memoirs, one of which he claimed to be a complete lie. Finally, it is clear that he himself lied, for whatever motive, about certain events in his life. Consequently, writing even a brief entry on Capote's life requires weighing evidence from many different sources.

Capote's recent reputation has suffered for several reasons. His last three major efforts, *The Dogs Bark*, a volume of collected essays (1973); *Answered Prayers*, an unfinished novel (1975–1976; rpt. as book 1986); and *Music for Chameleons*, a mix of fiction and nonfiction (1980) not only did not add to his reputation but also contributed toward its negative revaluation. Unfortunately for Capote, he was overpraised at the beginning of his career, he did not write a full-length book of consequence for nineteen years before his death, and he made too many embarrassing public and television appearances. Furthermore, he was replaced by greater, younger American novelists (Gaddis, Pynchon, Oates, Morrison) and writers from abroad. More to the point for some gay readers, he did not become a member of the gay liberation movement. To some gay readers he is an embarrassment.

It is unlikely that Capote's work will undergo a major revival, although his most important works are kept in paperback by Random House and are readily available in bookstores. Nevertheless, he will remain a recognizable name in American literature. The *Modern Language Association Bibliography* lists thirty books, dissertations, and articles on him in whole or part for the period 1981–1990, a credible total. Of these discussions, the issue of Capote and the nonfiction novel is the one to capture by far the most attention. Capote is represented by entries in standard reference tools such as *Dictionary of American Biography* (vol. 2, 1978, and the 1980 and 1984 Yearbooks) and *Contemporary Literary Criticism* (vols. 3, 8, 13, 19, 34, 38, and 58). So far there have been four general studies of his career in English, by Craig M. Goad (1967), William Nance (1970; attacked by Capote in Inge 222), Helen S. Garson (1980), and Kenneth T. Reed (1981), as well as the primary and secondary bibliography by Robert J. Stanton (1980). However, since his death, despite a number of memoirs of him, there has been no book-length revaluation of his literary career.

Any attempt to summarize in a few pages Truman Capote's life is doomed to failure. His early years are remembered and transformed in *Other Voices, Other Rooms, The Grass Harp,* "A Christmas Memory," "The Thanksgiving Visitor," "Dazzle," and "One Christmas." In addition, as is well known, Capote is the model for the boy, Dill, in Harper Lee's *To Kill a Mockingbird*, and Lee herself inspired the figure of Idabel, the tomboy, in *Other Voices, Other Rooms*. There are self-launched stories of Capote as a young boy dancing for Louis Armstrong aboard a pleasure boat on the Mississippi, but they are not to be believed.

Truman Capote was born Truman Streckfus Persons in New Orleans on September 30, 1924. He took the name of his stepfather after his mother remarried. He spent much of his youth with his mother's family in Monroeville, Alabama. During his teenage years he went to schools in New York and Connecticut. He set his sights on a literary career, and he began to work for the *New Yorker*. Publishing short stories in the mid–1940s, he was a much talked-about up-and-coming writer, and his success was consolidated with *Other Voices, Other Rooms* in 1948. He became entranced by the lives of the rich, and he made entry into the circles of such notables as the William Paleys. At the same time he was also a member of gay literary circles. He set out to make himself both a worldly and artistic success, but eventually he found his efforts thwarted after several years of draining work on *In Cold Blood*. A combination of writer's block and addictions led to a derailed career in the two decades before his death (a possible suicide) on August 25, 1984.

Events of his later life are all on the borderline between gossip and public knowledge. This phenomenon is initiated by such slight pieces of personal journalism as the travel writing in *Local Color* (1950) and the account of a theater troupe's trip to Russia to perform *Porgy and Bess* recounted in *The Muses Are Heard* (1956). Later publicized events include a dispute with

Kenneth Tynan conducted in *The Observer* over Capote's relationship to the Holcomb murder case (1966), his glamorous black-and-white party at the Plaza Hotel (1966), a lawsuit with Gore Vidal* (1975–1983), social ostracism after the magazine publication of *Unanswered Prayers* (1976), a disastrous drunken appearance at Towson State University (1977), and the end of his friendship with Lee Radziwill (1979). To these incidents could be added his being rushed comatose from his apartment to a hospital (1981), a much publicized summons to court for a fine for driving without a license (1983), and any number of detoxification stays in hospitals. In short, during the last two decades of his life, he confronted many major difficulties, some of them of his own making. As the first twenty years of his writing career had been generally successful, perhaps even "charmed," the turn-around must have been devastating.

Balancing the flamboyant self-revelatory aspect of his personality, Capote could also be private and constrained. He was not interested in speaking in depth about his sexual orientation. In an interview with Gerald Clarke (1972), he said that he did not speak publicly about it "because I don't want to give the critics an extra stick to beat me with. Everybody *knows* what I do anyway. I don't have many secrets" (Inge, 208).

Capote has become perhaps too famous for saying in "Nocturnal Turnings, or How Siamese Twins Have Sex" at the close of *Music for Chameleons* in 1980: "But I'm not a saint yet. I'm an alcoholic. I'm a drug addict. I'm homosexual. I'm a genius. Of course, I could be all four of these dubious things and still be a saint. But I shonuf ain't no saint yet, nawsuh" (Inge, 364). The recent play, *Tru*, by Jay Presson Allen, has its roots in this image of Capote. Despite a fine performance by Robert Morse, the play does not break new ground in evaluating Capote's paradoxical career.

It does not seem likely that Capote would be seen in a good light by lesbians. In a 1968 interview with Eric Norden, Capote refused to comment on whether Holly Golightly is lesbian or not. He claimed, "It's a well-known fact that most prostitutes are Lesbians—at least 80 percent of them in any case. And so are a great many of the models and showgirls in New York; just off the top of my head, I can think of three top professional models who are Lesbians" (Inge, 143). Furthermore, Holly's constant reference to lesbians as "dykes" reinforces old stereotypes.

In the conversation with Eric Norden, Capote said that he wrote *Other Voices, Other Rooms* to "exorcise my own devils, the subterranean anxieties that dominated my feelings and imagination." Indeed, at the age of forty-four, Capote felt that he had used the "fantastic vein" in his early stories as a means of escape from unpleasant reality (Inge, 116). In his later ambitious project he reworked some of his own personality into the hero-on-the-make protagonist of *Answered Prayers*.

Capote did not attend college, and perhaps as a thinker he was the worse off for it. Also, for all his travels, Capote's knowledge of world literature was not great; and he claimed (facetiously, one hopes) to think of himself as a better writer than Albert Camus, for example. When he started to compare *Answered Prayers* to the great work of Proust (whom he greatly admired), his sense of proportion had really failed him.

The memoirs, collections of interviews, and biography about Capote that have appeared between 1983 and 1989 should all be considered in trying to understand Capote's complex personality. Two memoirs concern his childhood. The first, by Marie Rudisill, with James C. Simmons, *Truman Capote: The Story of His Bizarre and Exotic Boyhood by an Aunt Who Helped Raise Him*, presents an unflattering picture of Capote's family and does not try to follow closely the story of his childhood. Capote's ancestors were plantation slaveholders, and this memoir presents Capote's mother's family, the Faulks, as enmeshed in collective denial of the complicity of the South in its own disasters. It also gives a very unflattering picture of Capote's elderly relative, Sook, the gentle woman of "A Christmas Memory," who is seen here as monstrously bigoted against blacks and living in an unhealthy fantasy land. In contrast, Marianne Moates's *A Bridge of Childhood*, published six years later, tries to recall some specific events in Capote's youth. It was written with information provided by Capote's cousin, Jennings Faulk ("Big Boy") Carter, who was approximately three years younger than Capote. Big Boy was the son of Mary Ida, older sister to Edna Marie (Rudisill) and younger sister to Lillie May Faulk, Capote's mother. This book provides a useful family tree for Capote's maternal relations.

Two other memoirs deal with Capote's career after he became a writer and celebrity. His life companion, Jack Dunphy, has written a combination novel and memoir, *Dear Genius—: A Memoir of My Life with Truman Capote* (1987), in which the story of Capote's fight against despair, alcoholism, and drug addiction is interwoven with the story of a New York priest named Father John Synge. Although an interesting attempt to do something original, the book does not provide much additional insight into Capote's problems. Nevertheless, as Gerald Clarke's 1988 biography is rather severe on Dunphy (who nevertheless cooperated with his research), it is worthwhile reading his point of view. John Malcolm Brinnin, the noted biographer of Gertrude Stein, has chronicled his interaction with Capote over the years in *Truman Capote: Dear Heart, Old Buddy*. An earlier account by Brinnin, appearing in *Sextet* (1981), was attacked by Capote (Grodel, 100).

Lawrence Grodel's *Conversations with Capote*, which appeared in 1985, shortly after Capote's death, sometimes shows Capote in the worst light possible. For example, here he calls Joyce Carol Oates "a joke monster who ought to be beheaded in a public auditorium or in Shea or in a field with hundreds of thousands.... To me, she's the most loathsome creature in America" (140). John Updike fares almost as badly as a blob of mercury swishing around in one's hand. It is in this work that Capote calls Marie

Rudisill's book a lie (49), but in the light of these other comments, it is hard to evaluate the statement. It is interesting that Capote, a victim of writer's block, battered at two authors known for their great productivity.

In contrast, M. Thomas Inge's collection of interviews with Capote throughout his career is very informative, and it is a fine addition to the University of Mississippi Press series. Among the longer interviews included are those with George Plimpton (1966), Eric Norden (1968), Gerald Clarke (1972), and Andy Warhol (1973).

Gerald Clarke, a writer for *Time*, had great cooperation from Capote on his biography (1988); and Clarke thanks him for sharing so much of his time through his enormously difficult last years. Clarke has an obvious sympathy for his subject, and he resists the temptation of writing in this case what Joyce Carol Oates has so well described as "pathography." The biography received mixed reviews, for it is a good but not definitive piece of work. Clarke does not offer much in the way of literary analyses of Capote's works, he does not follow closely the writing and publication of Capote's early short stories, and he tends to overrate his work of the last twenty years.

Clarke, as some reviewers pointed out, is at his best in describing the relationship between Capote and his first long-term lover, Newton Arvin, during the late 1940s. Arvin was to go on to receive praise and fame for his work on Melville, and Clarke also tells about his life after his split with Capote. Clarke does not spend much time on Capote's years before he began to publish. He believes Capote's words that the Rudisill memoir is not to be believed (539), and he further indicates that the short story published by her under Capote's name after his death is most likely not by Capote. In trying for a balanced picture, he makes available disturbing information on Capote's last years, including disastrous romantic involvements, from the huge numbers of interviews he conducted with his associates.

Some things about Capote we may just never know, as a result of Capote's storytelling. Clarke repeats Capote's claim that he went to bed with Albert Camus, and he notes that although this is probably not true, perhaps it was. Stranger things have certainly happened (170).

Clarke implicitly sympathizes with Capote's view that his personal problems were rooted in his sense of abandonment by his parents. He also points out the "too much too soon" syndrome. Capote exhibited defensiveness that led to his making ridiculously aggrandized claims about the value of what he was writing. His work does not reflect a grounding in philosophy, religious studies, or history to a great extent. In addition, in a world of gay liberation, we should surely point out that Capote, who apparently never voted, was incapable of finding some meaning in a larger social cause. Although he did make known his feelings about the misery of convicted criminals waiting on death row, he almost entirely avoided reform movements.

No doubt some readers will still wish to know the models for the figures in *Answered Prayers*, and Clarke does oblige. He is also skillful in indicating the datedness of the source events. For example, the woman who presumably shot her husband and got away with it created a scandal among a certain social set when the incident occurred, but this event happened back in 1955. When Capote began thinking of his novel a few years later, it still had a certain topicality. By the time of the 1976 *Esquire* publication and the later 1986 book publication, it no longer seemed to be very relevant on even the level of gossip.

Clarke does not explore in depth Capote's response to the changes in the gay world about him. He does recount a sad episode in Capote's final years in which he went on a television talk show and made a fool of himself and gay people by suggesting the "bitchiness of fags." For many gays and lesbians today such incidents have more weight than any success he had with *Other Voices, Other Rooms*. Indeed, even this novel may seem dated over twenty years after the Stonewall Riots.

Did Capote commit suicide? Clarke tells us that Capote could probably have taken some action to save himself during his last attack, but because life had become so intolerable, he did not do so. He died in his sleep before Joanne Carson could get him revived.

MAJOR WORKS AND THEMES

Capote's forty-year career was divided among fiction, journalism, and drama and filmscript writing. One could tabulate in several ways the number of novels Capote wrote. Everyone would agree that *Other Voices, Other Rooms* (1948) and *The Glass Harp* (1951) are novels. Some would go further and say that after 1951, at age twenty-seven, he failed to develop his early talent as a novelist. At times, Capote thought of the lead story of his collection *Breakfast at Tiffany's* (1958) as a short novel and of "Hand-carved Coffins" in *Music for Chameleons* (1980) as a novel. Between them, chronologically, we have the "nonfiction novel," *In Cold Blood*, his longest sustained work, and, finally, the incomplete and presumably never completed *Unanswered Prayers*, published in installments in *Esquire* in 1976 and then in book form in 1986. Of these works, *Other Voices, Other Rooms* is the one most concerned with homosexuality, and it is the one work on which Capote's reputation as a gay male author will rest. In addition, some readers have seen homosexuality as a subtext of *In Cold Blood*, a suggestion that Capote denied in detail (perhaps because he did not feel it would help gay people) but that requires further investigation. *Unanswered Prayers*, known for its depiction of the sordid side of homo- and heterosexuality,

contains a very unflattering picture of a writer suggestive of Tennessee
Williams. Of the short stories, only "A Diamond Guitar" from *Breakfast
at Tiffany's* has a gay male relationship at its heart, although "The Headless
Hawk" from *A Tree of Night* features as protagonists a man and woman
who have previously experienced same-sex love.

Other Voices, Other Rooms appeared in 1948, the same year as Gore
Vidal's much more explicit novel *The City and the Pillar* and the limited
edition of Tennessee Williams' first short-story collection. *Other Voices,
Other Rooms* is a boy's coming-of-age story in a small Southern town in
the 1930s. Joel Harrison Knox, a thirteen-year-old, comes to Noon City to
live with relations and is introduced into a world of eccentric and grotesque
characters. At the end of the novel he decides to leave the outer world
behind and take up life with his withdrawn gay cousin, Randolph. *Other
Voices, Other Rooms* has been given several pages of discussion in four of
the standard books on male homosexuality in American fiction: Georges-
Michel Sarotte's *Like a Brother, Like a Lover* (French original 1976, English
translation 1978), Roger Austen's *Playing the Game* (1977), Stephen Adams's *The Homosexual as Hero in Contemporary Fiction* (1980), and
Claude J. Summers's *Gay Fictions: Wilde to Stonewall* (1990). The first two
of these critics are more sympathetic to Capote's novel than the last two.
Sarotte finds the novel to be about a boy's recognition of his homosexuality,
and he concludes that the novel endorses the idea that one should be true
to one's "basic nature against the ideals of a hostile society" (48). Austen
notes that "[a]lthough in tone and atmosphere this book may be regarded
as gay, in actual fact Capote avoids having the main character come to grips
with the problem by keeping his thirteen-year-old safely prepubescent"
(114). In other words, he "remains sexless within the terms of the novel,"
even though we assume that he will grow up to be gay. Furthermore, the
adult gay character, Cousin Randolph, speaks of his love for the prizefighter
Pepe in a way that can be considered as a generalized plea for human love
as much as a statement of specifically gay male feelings (115).

In marked contrast, Stephen Adams stresses the nonliberational nature
of *Other Voices, Other Rooms*. He feels that "the world it creates is ani-
mated by characteristics popularly attributed to the homosexual male: freak-
ishness, affectation and effeminacy. The story of a young boy's discovery
of his homosexuality is decked out with all the trappings of gothic melodrama" (57). Through "Joel's identification with Randolph, Capote implies
that homosexuality is a failure of manliness—an 'ugly room', yet one which
fantasy can prettify" (58). Adams compares Capote's treatment of homosexuality unfavorably with that of Carson McCullers and James Purdy, for
whom the failure of love rather than homosexuality itself is the source of
problems.

Again, in Claude J. Summers's evaluation, Capote is a less interesting and
perceptive author than McCullers. He writes, "Truman Capote creates in

Other Voices, Other Rooms a world of Gothic romance reminiscent of *The Ballad of the Sad Cafe*, but one that lacks the philosophical seriousness and sure vision of McCullers's work" (131). Cousin Randolph is less bizarre than several of the other characters in the novel; nevertheless, "[r]ather than engaging life and challenging or at least defying the world's cruelty, Randolph relishes his victimization" (132).

Since the mid–1970s the treatment of homosexuality has become the central issue for critics of *Other Voices, Other Rooms*. We can see this phenomenon from the articles just considered and that of Annette Runge's Lacanian study (1988). An overview of the criticism from the period before the blossoming of gay studies can be found in the 1970 review article by Dianne B. Trimmier, which treats the critical reception up to 1962, including studies by John W. Aldridge, Nona Balakian, Paul Levine, and Marvin E. Mengling. Craig M. Goad's entry on Capote in the *Dictionary of American Biography* (vol. 2, 1978) is also relevant. Goad (83) notes positive views of the novel by Carvel Collins, Frank Baldanza, and Ihab Hassan against the negative view of John W. Aldridge. Objections to the novel on the basis of its intense interiority may mask antigay prejudices in the sense that the experiences of gay youth are often not of interest to society as a whole.

Critical reaction to the slightly later "A Diamond Guitar" has not gone very far, although the story is skillfully written. This is a tale of two men in a Southern prison camp set in a pine forest. An older inmate named Schaeffer, who has been in the camp for some time, is attracted to a young Cuban knifer named Tico Feo, who arrives with a diamond guitar. It is clear that they fall in love, but there is no overt sexual interaction between them. They plan an escape, but only Tico makes it, and Schaeffer is returned to the camp for the rest of his life. He himself starts to play the diamond (actually "paste") guitar.

In her book on Truman Capote, Helen S. Garson notes that Tico Feo never had wanted Schaeffer to escape. The younger man is a liar, a thief, and a betrayer (93). Nevertheless, in her evaluation, Tico Feo does bring Schaeffer back from the ranks of the emotionally dead. In contrast, Kenneth T. Reed (62–64) in his book on Capote does not point out this element of betrayal. Nor does Ramón Garcia Castro in his book on Capote (120–21). One suspects that the mainstream critics are sometimes reluctant to deal with themes of gay betrayal. In contrast, William L. Nance notes that "the story is a rather explicit rejection of the homosexual option that Joel accepted" (74). Although one should not overstress a story that appeared as far back as November 1950, it does seem typical that Capote is unable even at a later date to imagine a story in which the love of two adult men would lead to mutual salvation or even help.

In *In Cold Blood* male bonding produces violent results. The book recounts the brutal murder of four members of the Clutter family by Perry Smith and Richard Eugene ("Dick") Hickock in Holcomb, Kansas, in November 1959. The murders took place at night, and, as they were out-of-towners and not even acquaintances of the Clutters, the two killers almost got away with it.

In 1966 George Plimpton asked Capote if there was a sexual attraction between Perry and Dick. Capote answered that there wasn't any. He considered that Dick was totally heterosexual and that Perry had little sexual interest: "Yes, Perry had been in love with his cellmate Willie-Jay in the State Prison, but there was no consummated physical relationship. He was not in love with Dick" (Inge 60).

Despite Capote's denial of homosexual attraction between the team of murderers, here we have a chilling example of men who exert what is perhaps a fatal influence over each other in the course of their bonding. It is also clear that by the end of their lives they have had a major falling out. The novel could benefit from an analysis that foregrounds a gay studies point of view, particularly one concerned with the break between the homosocial and the homosexual in American society. In a sense, the novel deals with issues related to repression and sublimation, but as they are not the focus of the novel, interpretation of them remains difficult. Indeed, one set of readers have seen it as a story in which violence substitutes for sexual expression.

Perry himself mentions homosexuality. Reflecting on his experiences as a sixteen-year-old on a boat, he states, "I never minded the work, and I liked being a sailor—seaports, and all that. But the queens on ship wouldn't leave me alone.... A lot of queens aren't effeminate, you know" (156). Before the main part of the story opens, Perry, a bodybuilder, has a homoerotic attraction for his cellmate, a person to whom he reveals the anticipated murder. We are told: "Dick's literalness, his pragmatic approach to every subject, was the primary reason Perry had been attracted to him, for it made Dick seem, compared to himself, so authentically tough, invulnerable, 'totally masculine' " (27). Perry had "no respect for people who can't control themselves sexually" (230). When Perry and Dick try to escape in Mexico, they become temporary guests of an openly gay man.

At another point in the novel it is hard to figure out where Capote's reflections end and Perry's begin: Capote writes, "[N]or did [Perry] care to chance the loss of a manila envelope fat with photographs—primarily of himself, and ranging in time from a pretty–little–boy portrait made when he was in the Merchant Marine" (169). If we consider the famous "pretty boy" photograph of Capote on the dust jacket of *Other Voices, Other Rooms*, it is possible to find a projection of the author himself here. Indeed, one of the most disturbing episodes of Capote's life was his unsuccessful attempt to keep the two men at an emotional distance from himself, especially when Perry began to realize Capote's interest in him would not keep him from execution. Capote avoids direct commentary in *In Cold Blood*, and his lack of evaluation appeared shallow to some reviewers, such as Diana Trilling (Malin 107–14). In any case, it remains difficult to determine his actual feelings on a case in which he was perhaps debilitatingly involved.

Late in the novel a Dr. Jones makes a report in which he contextualizes the personalities of Perry and Dick against those of four other men convicted of apparently unmotivated murderers. He found that to "all of them, adult women were threatening creatures, and in two cases there was overt sexual perversion" (336). In addition, all had been considered "sissies" in their youth. Despite what seems to be Capote's attempt to point out the violent effects of the unjust and bigoted repression of same-sex attraction in America, it is easy to leave the novel confused about where Capote stands in relation to the Freudian-derived views of sexuality that surface in the novel.

Because Capote's veracity in his novel has been questioned and because this issue intersects with Capote's attitude toward the two men, readers may wish to consult two other essays, one an "as-told-to" article that claims to give Hickock's account and another by Philip K. Tompkins that is a direct refutation of Capote's claims to accuracy. Both of these can be found in the critical casebook (along with several important reviews) on the novel edited by Irving Malin in 1968. In 1990 a second "casebook" appeared in *Contemporary Literary Criticism* (vol. 58: 84–136), including lengthy excerpts from many of the reviews in Malin's book, plus the texts of the Capote-Tynan debate, relevant interview material, and parts of four more recent articles. One of these is a discussion by Jack De Bellis (originally 1979) of the changes in the text from the *New Yorker* articles to the Random House edition and their relationship to the book's claimed truth-value. Other statements on this issue can be found in Clarke's biography and Donald Windham's memoir.

Donald Windham's *Lost Friendships: A Memoir of Truman Capote, Tennessee Williams, and Others* (1987) is the only one of the memoirs to give insight into Capote's work as an author and as a gay man. He discusses both the journalism and the fiction. Windham,* a novelist and playwright, gives a piercing view of Capote as an irresponsible weaver of fictions about himself and others, using several of his writings as examples.

Windham challenges Capote on his memories and treatment of gay men such as André Gide. He notes that in *Observations*, a text/image collaboration with the photographer Richard Avedon, Capote describes a last meeting between Jean Cocteau and André Gide at Taormina in the spring of 1950, an encounter that he supposedly witnessed (48). Windham maintains that Cocteau was not in Sicily in 1950 and that Cocteau had written in 1951 that his last encounter with Gide was at Seine-et-Oise in February 1949 (48).

Considering that so much has been written on *In Cold Blood* as a nonfiction novel, Windham's evaluation bears attention. He claims that Capote got at the facts mostly by discounting the stories of Hickock and Smith when they were different and crediting them when they were the same. So, for Capote the true story "was the unagreed-upon versions they both told him" (79). Since the book could not be published until the execution of the two men, when "the book came out, the only living authority for the factualness of much of the narrative was Truman himself" (79). Windham admires the novel, but he thinks that we should scrap the categorization that Capote impertinently and uselessly created for it.

As Capote's most openly gay short story is "A Diamond Guitar," it is worth noting that Windham claims that he gave Capote a copy of his novel *The Dog Star* in 1950 and that this work influenced Capote's later story. He feels that although the events and characters of "A Diamond Guitar," written shortly after, are not taken from his own book, the "assembled properties of his story come from my novel: the emblematic guitar, passed on as an inheritance, the glass jewels; the blondness of the guitar player; the settings—a prison farm, a creek in the woods; the repeated images of sunlight on a woman's hair" (81). He indicates that Carson McCullers also kept track of Capote's borrowings from her, such as a passage in *The Grass Harp* that she matched up with "A Tree. A Rock. A Cloud" (81).

Windham warns us not to take *Answered Prayers* as either a truthful roman à clef or factual reportage. For example, he tells us that even when Montgomery Clift is depicted under his real name in the story "Kate McCloud," there is "no veracity in the incident depicted" (118). Not only does Capote attribute Clift's erratic behavior to a time before it had commenced, Capote's rendition of his meeting with Tallulah Bankhead in the story makes little sense, as they had acted together in *The Skin of Our Teeth* in 1942. Again, we are left with the complicated issue of judging Capote's work both for its literary quality and for its regard of truth-value.

The absence of full-length literary studies on Capote's work since his death is probably an indication that his work is seen as essentially finished by 1966 and that *Answered Prayers* does not add anything to it.

CRITICAL RECEPTION

Even as late as 1985, evaluations of Capote's life and work may fail to mention Capote's homosexuality, as is the case with the three-page entry by Thomas Bonner, Jr., in Rubin's *History of Southern Literature*. Nevertheless, in the case of Truman Capote we cannot say that homophobia lowered the overall critical reception of Capote's work. In fact, to some extent the opposite is true because of the notoriety he gained. Furthermore, he had champions among nongay critics who promoted Southern literature or fiction about American family life. Post-Stonewall evaluations are likely to see Capote as a relic of the closeted age in which happy futures for gay characters and positive evaluations of deep male bonding are relatively unimaginable.

Although there were some initial hostile reviews of *Other Voices, Other Rooms* because of its subject matter, Capote was able to ride them out and to promote himself to a far greater extent than more talented writers of his time. The hostile reaction to *Answered Prayers* can not be attributed to homophobia either. The vulgarity of the published fragments tends to reinforce stereotypes of gay male bitchery, especially in the treatment of the figure inspired by Tennessee Williams. If *In Cold Blood* continues to be studied in terms of the nonfiction novel rather than through a gay-studies approach, we must remember that Capote himself attempted to set criticism along these lines.

Several directions of research are left open. Considering that *Other Voices, Other Rooms* has been treated by many critics as an example of "Southern Gothic," it is worth de-emphasizing the Southern aspect and asking how Capote relates to a tradition of same-sex-oriented writers who, since Horace Walpole, have been prominent practitioners of "Gothic." On another note, we may examine "A Diamond Guitar" in the context of gay men's prison literature. The Smith/Hickock murders in *In Cold Blood* could be related to treatments of the Leopold/Loeb murders in journalism, fiction, and film.

Truman Capote provokes strong emotions to this day as both author and personality. Like his contemporary Andy Warhol, Capote created a public persona for himself, and the comparative strategies of these two men would be worth evaluating in tandem. An in-depth study of the complex web of literary networking among American gay authors and artists could provide new materials for study of Capote as well.

As it stands now, with the academic establishment caught up in debate over the boundaries and comparative strategies of literature and fiction, Capote will be remembered for some time to come mostly as the author of *In Cold Blood*, not as the author of "gay fictions." For those interested in descriptions of childhood, Capote has a respectable place with *Other Voices, Other Rooms*, *The Grass Harp*, and his autobiographical family stories. Indeed, as we attempt to reach out to the thwarted lives and opportunities of gay youth, *Other Voices, Other Rooms* may prove of interest to gay male teenagers (despite Cynthia Ozick's exaggerated claim that the book is "dead and empty" [80–89]). However, Capote's achievement as a revealer of adult feelings is considerably less; and if we take his desire for comparison to Proust seriously, we can only be disappointed.

MAJOR WORKS BY TRUMAN CAPOTE

Other Voices, Other Rooms. New York: Random House, 1948.
A Tree of Night and Other Stories. New York: Random House, 1949.
Local Color. New York: Random House, 1950.
The Grass Harp. New York: Random House, 1951.
The Muses Are Heard: An Account. New York: Random House, 1956.

Breakfast at Tiffany's: A Short Novel and Three Stories. New York: Random House, 1958.
Observations: Photographs by Richard Avedon, Comments by Truman Capote. New York: Simon and Schuster, 1959.
Selected Writings of Truman Capote. New York: Random House, 1963.
In Cold Blood: A True Account of a Multiple Murder and Its Consequences. New York: Random House, 1966.
The Thanksgiving Visitor. New York: Random House, 1968.
The Dogs Bark: Public People and Private Places. New York: Random House, 1973.
Music for Chameleons. New York: Random House, 1980.
One Christmas. New York: Random House, 1983.
Answered Prayers: The Unfinished Novel. New York: Random House, 1986.

SELECTED STUDIES OF TRUMAN CAPOTE

Biographical

Brinnin, John Malcolm. *Truman Capote: Dear Heart, Old Buddy.* New York: Delacorte, 1986.
Clarke, Gerald. *Truman Capote.* New York: Simon & Schuster, 1988.
Dunphy, Jack. *Dear Genius—: A Memoir of My Life with Truman Capote.* New York: McGraw Hill, 1987.
Grodel, Lawrence. *Conversations with Capote.* New York: New American Library, 1985.
Inge, M. Thomas, ed. *Truman Capote: Conversations.* Jackson: University of Mississippi Press, 1987.
Moates, Marianne. *A Bridge of Childhood: Truman Capote's Southern Years.* New York: Henry Holt, 1989.
Rudisill, Marie, and James C. Simmons. *Truman Capote: The Story of His Bizarre and Exotic Boyhood by an Aunt Who Helped Raise Him.* New York: Morrow, 1983.
Windham, Donald. *Lost Friendships: A Memoir of Truman Capote, Tennessee Williams, and Others.* New York: William Morrow, 1987.

Critical

Adams, Stephen. *The Homosexual As Hero in Contemporary Fiction.* New York: Barnes & Noble, 1980.
Aldridge, John. *After the Lost Generation: A Critical Study of the Writers of Two Wars.* New York: Noonday Press, 1951.
Austen, Roger. *Playing the Game: The Homosexual Novel in America.* Indianapolis: Bobbs-Merrill, 1977.
Balakian, Nona. "The Prophetic Voice of the Anti-heroine." *Southwest Review* 47 (1962): 134–41.
Baldanza, Frank. "Plato in Dixie." *Georgia Review* 12 (1958): 151–67.
Bonner, Thomas, Jr. "Truman Capote." *The History of Southern Literature.* Ed.

Louis D. Rubin, Jr., 483–85. Baton Rouge: Louisiana State University Press, 1985.

Garcia Castro, Ramón. *Truman Capote: De la captura a la libertad.* Santiago de Chile: Centro de Investigaciones de Literatura Comparada, 1963.

Garson, Helen S. *Truman Capote.* New York: Ungar, 1980.

Goad, Craig M. "Daylight and Darkness; Dream and Delusion: The Works of Truman Capote." *Emporia State Research Studies* 16, no. 1 (September 1967): 1–57.

———. "Truman Capote." *Dictionary of American Biography* 2 (1978): 81–88.

Hassan, Ihab H. *Radical Innocence: Studies in the Contemporary American Novel,* 230–58. Princeton: Princeton University Press, 1961.

Levine, Paul. "Truman Capote: The Revelation of the Broken Image." *Virginia Quarterly Review* 34 (Autumn 1958): 600–617. Rpt. in Malin, 141–53.

Malin, Irving, ed. *Truman Capote's "In Cold Blood": A Critical Handbook.* Belmont, Calif.: Wadsworth, 1969.

Mengeling, Marvin. "*Other Voices, Other Rooms*: Oedipus between the Covers." *American Imago* 19 (1962): 361–74.

Nance, William. *The Worlds of Truman Capote.* New York: Stein and Day, 1970.

Nations, Mack. "America's Worst Crime in Twenty Years." *Male* 11 (December 1961): 30–31, 76–83. Rpt. in Malin, 8–24.

Ozick, Cynthia. *Art & Ardor.* New York: Knopf, 1983.

Reed, Kenneth T. *Truman Capote.* Boston: Twayne, 1981.

Runte, Annette. " 'Im Kreis des Begehrens': Zur semantischen and narrativen Funktion des Gesichtssymbolik in Carson McCullers Roman *The Heart Is a Lonely Hunter* (1940) und Truman Capotes Roman *Other Voices, Other Rooms* (1948)." *Forum: Homosexualität und Literatur* 3 (1988): 51–77.

Sarotte, Georges-Michel. *Like A Brother, Like a Lover: Male Homosexuality in the American Novel and Theater from Herman Melville to James Baldwin.* Trans. Richard Miller. Garden City: Doubleday, 1978.

Stanton, Robert J. *Truman Capote: A Reference Guide.* Boston: G. K. Hall, 1980.

Summers, Claude J. *Gay Fictions, Wilde to Stonewall: Studies in a Male Homosexual Literary Tradition.* New York: Ungar, 1990.

Tompkins, Philip K. "In Cold Fact." *Esquire* 65 (June 1966): 125, 127, 166–71. Rpt. in Malin, 44–59.

"Truman Capote." *Contemporary Literary Criticism* 58 (1990): 84–136.

MARSH CASSADY (1936–   )

James D. Kitchen

BIOGRAPHY

Reviewers and readers often have remarked how closely Marsh Cassady's *Love Theme with Variations* parallels their own lives. Perhaps it is because the work is highly autobiographical. Like many men of his generation, Cassady's central character, Pete Williamson, married, had children, and lived a straight life-style for many years. After the death of his wife, Williamson no longer could contain his feelings and began his search for a man he could love.

Born Marshall G. Cassady in Johnstown, Pennsylvania (he later legally changed his given name to Marsh), he grew up in Cairnbrook, a bituminous coal mining town in Somerset County, sharing a four-room house with his parents, his maternal grandparents, and at times an aunt. Many of Cassady's short stories are set in the town or on his grandfather's farm nearby.

As a child, Cassady was told repeatedly that he could never be as good at anything as his father. At times he was abused. One such incident is described in REALITIES, as yet unpublished, in which the central character's father slams him down so hard on his bicycle that he breaks the seat.

Early on, the young boy escaped into fantasies. One of the high points of his life was meeting children's book author LeClair Alger when he was eight. She later told him that if he kept at it, someday he would become a writer.

Cassady graduated from Shade High School in Cairnbrook in 1954 and then enrolled in Otterbein College with the idea of majoring in music. He had studied trumpet for nine years. But he became more interested in theater and English.

While at Otterbein, he met Pat Mizer of New Philadelphia, Ohio, whom he married shortly after graduation in 1958. They both enrolled in graduate school at Ohio University but soon dropped out.

For a time Cassady wrote and did amateur theatrics, teaching two years in junior high school and working for three years as a staff writer for the *Daily Reporter* (now the *Times Reporter*) in Dover, Ohio. During this time he wrote short stories that he tried unsuccessfully to publish. He did have a play presented at a high school one-act play festival. In 1960 and 1961 his daughters Kathi and Kim were born.

In 1966 Cassady enrolled in the graduate program in theater at Kent State University. Receiving his M.A. a year later, he took a position as instructor at the Columbiana County Branch of Kent State, where he directed and designed theatrical productions and entered the first Ph.D. class at Kent State in 1969. During this time Cassady and his wife adopted three more children, two girls and a boy. Except for a two-year period after he enrolled at Kent State, he continued to write, occasionally having some of his poetry accepted in regional publications.

In 1972 he received his Ph.D. degree and took a position as assistant professor of speech and theater at Montclair State College in New Jersey. His first success as a writer was with theater textbooks for all levels from junior high to college. The first, written with his wife who entered the graduate program at Montclair State, was published in 1975.

Cassady was to receive tenure during the 1975–1976 academic year, but his wife became terminally ill. The family returned to Ohio, where Cassady again taught part-time for Kent State while he and his wife continued to write together. He also joined Actors Equity Association and performed in summer stock. At the same time he became editorial advisor and later poetry editor of a regional publication, *Buckeye Country*.

In 1978, Cassady's wife died, leaving him to finish rearing the children, the oldest of whom was seventeen, the youngest six. Feeling suicidal and seeing no reason to continue living, he sought psychiatric help for the second time in his life. The first time had been at the age of twenty-six, when his feelings for men and his difficulty in finding a profession he truly liked drove him to seek therapy. For a time Cassady remained in the New Philadelphia area where he continued to act. A year after his wife's death, feeling he no longer could contain his gayness, he met and became the lover of a man from the Dayton area. With the three younger children he moved to Troy to be near his new lover, who then fled because he could not handle his guilt at being gay.

For Cassady this was a double blow, one which sent him into a state of deep depression. However, he continued to write, now placing more and more of his poetry. At the same time a novel he began before his wife's death was rejected again and again. Titled LIGHT, it finally was accepted by a small press, which went bankrupt before the book could be published.

In July of 1980 Cassady met James Kitchen through a correspondence club and decided to move to San Diego. Again bad luck pursued him. An auction sale produced only a fraction of what had been predicted; and Cassady's two positions, one as a half-time instructor in theater at San Diego State and the other as an Equity guest actor at a local theater, fell through at the last moment.

Despite the poor beginning, Cassady credits the relocation as the most important career move of his life. Within a year he began selling short stories in the United States, Britain, and Canada. At the same time he began writing *Love Theme with Variations*, which would take eight years to complete to his satisfaction.

Love Theme became his first published novel (1989). It was followed in 1990 by *Triple Fiction*, a collection of short stories written with two other men, Richard L. Stone and Stephen Richard Smith. During this same year his *Alternate Casts* was published by Banned Books. The novel is a science-fiction murder mystery dealing with time travel back to the nineteenth century and involving a traveling theater company. Other works include *The Music of Tree Limbs*, which won first prize in Cicada Press's annual haiku contest (1990); *Perverted Proverbs*, a collection of humorous short stories (1991); and *To Ride a Wild Pony*, produced in New York in 1985 as a full-length play and later adapted as a novel (1992). Forthcoming is *The Times of the Double Star*, the second in a series after *Alternate Casts*. Cassady also is fiction and drama editor of *Crazy Quilt Quarterly*.

MAJOR WORKS AND THEMES

The most important theme of Cassady's fiction is the need finally to confront what we are and make peace with ourselves. To this effect, in all his published novels and in the forthcoming *The Times of the Double Star*, a central figure confronts great change and transcends it.

This theme is first seen in *Love Theme*, in which the protagonist, Pete, has been married for nearly two decades before the death of his wife. As the novel opens, Pete is in the throes of depression, half-heartedly attempting suicide. He is stopped by his daughter returning from a date. From this beginning Pete acknowledges his homosexuality and begins searching for another man with whom to make a lifelong commitment.

The theme of death and resurrection is central to many of Cassady's works. It is a character's reaction to losing a significant other, often by death, that provides the redemptive change. In "When Benny Came to Town," which takes place in the 1950s, the title character, a black musician, comes to a small, all-white community in Western Pennsylvania to find the nephew of his lover, who had provided Benny with drums and hired him as part of his dance band. Only after the band leader dies does Benny decide not to hide the sexual nature of their relationship. A similar theme is seen in the short story "The Vow," in which a young man is turned down by the girl he loves and vows never to be close to anyone again. Implied is the idea that Bruce is gay but, for whatever reason, will not admit it.

In *Alternate Casts* Lou, who is straight, comes home from his theater to find his wife and two children murdered. This forces him to put together a new life, while remaining true to the old one. The other central character, Willie, has been running for years. Finishing a master's degree in theater and engaged to be married, Willie discovers his fiancée is pregnant with a professor's child. Willie cannot face the fact that it is the professor he loves and not the fiancée. For the next two decades he continues to run from himself. It is only after meeting a gay man who is a member of a traveling theater company that Willie finally is forced to take a long look at himself and admit what he is.

To Ride a Wild Pony is a departure from the others in that it is a tale of dependence, a theme first touched on in the short story "Idiot Savant." In the short story the need for dominance is harsh and cruel, while in the novel it is wrapped in a blanket of love, but no less smothering.

A versatile writer, Cassady seems interested in two different types of fiction, the serious and the playful. For instance, his short story "Fantasy" simply takes a "what if" situation of seeing an attractive man in a dentist's office and letting the imagination go into a realm of the fantastic where fairy tales come true. *Perverted Proverbs* contains twenty-two tales in which good usually triumphs and love conquers all.

Yet, whether writing serious or playful fiction, Cassady has stated that he tries to write about things that matter. In *The Times of the Double Star*, he deals with the horrors perpetrated by the atmospheric testing of the atom bomb in the early 1950s. In both his longer works and his short stories he deals most often with the need to be true to others as well as to self.

One of the strong points of Cassady's writing is his clarity and conciseness. Yet at times the work has a poetic quality. Using carefully chosen words he builds a convincing character, offers insightful dialogue, and evokes the background. His writing often is poignant, as in the short story "Whose Woods These Are," in which an incident at Roy's grandfather's farm has strongly influenced the direction of that character's life, so that he later goes back to confront the memory of a son seeing his father, whom he believed to be omnipotent, tossed by a nephew onto the muddy banks of a stream.

Cassady has the ability to portray human relationships through everyday words and to create characters, such as Pete Williamson or Lou Graham, alone and nearly destroyed by the death of his family, who are three-dimensional and convincing. In REALITIES he concocts a story told from different viewpoints and then steps back to remark upon what really happened. The reader thus discovers that Martin O'Jenkins, the protagonist, has edited his early life to remove the hurt and pain.

CRITICAL RECEPTION

Only in the last few years has Cassady begun to have success with his gay writing, with four novels and two short-story anthologies accepted by gay presses. His shorter work has appeared in a number of gay magazines. As a consequence, mainstream reviewers have not commented on his work.

Neither has he captured the attention of those who comment on books and stories with lengthy scenes of detailed sex. His work, instead, has found approval with reviewers who are interested in writing that features strong characters reacting to real-life situations and relationships, presented with realism and warmth. These critics have noted that his works contain a truthfulness, a universality, that causes people to relate them to their own lives.

WORKS BY MARSH CASSADY

Love Theme with Variations. San Diego: Los Hombres Press, 1989.
Alternate Casts. Austin, Tex.: Banned Books, 1990.
Triple Fiction. With Richard L. Stone and Stephen Richard Smith. San Diego: Los Hombres Press, 1990.
The Music of Tree Limbs. Bakersfield, Calif.: Cicada Press, 1992.
Perverted Proverbs. San Diego: Los Hombres Press, 1991.
The Times of the Double Star. Austin, Tex.: Banned Books, 1992.
To Ride a Wild Pony. San Diego: Los Hombres Press, 1992.

SELECTED STUDIES OF MARSH CASSADY

Barr, Larry. "Time-Traveling & Murder in Ravenna." *Gaybeat* (August 1990): 31.
Cee, Michael. "Love Theme with Variations." *Centaur* (January 1990): 12.
Colley, P. H. "Love Theme with Variations." *Chiron Rising* (November–December 1989): 15.

JOHN CHAMPAGNE (1960–   )
Thomas Piontek

BIOGRAPHY

John Champagne is not only an award-winning novelist and poet but also an accomplished pianist and the author of numerous academic and non-fiction articles. He was born November 27, 1960, in Milwaukee, Wisconsin, the first of six children. A few years later, his family moved to the nearby suburb of Greenfield, where he began studying the piano at the age of eight.

After graduating from Greenfield High School, Champagne attended the University of Wisconsin-Milwaukee for one semester in which he studied English and Art History. At this time his parents learned that John was gay. After a very brief initial period of strife, they became accepting and extremely supportive.

Champagne transferred to Goddard College in Plainfield, Vermont, in the fall of 1980, where he studied acting for one year. Transferring to New York University to study musical theater, he soon ran out of money. From 1982 to 1983, he worked at a variety of jobs: he planned seminars for dentists, taught music and acting at a day-care center, and worked as a wholesale salesman and as an accompanist for cabaret singers and ballet classes.

In the fall of 1983 Champagne was accepted into the honors program at Hunter College, where he also wrote his first novel, *The Blue Lady's Hands*. After his graduation in 1986, he enrolled in the master's degree program in film studies at New York University. He wrote his second novel, *When the Parrot Boy Sings*, in the summer of 1987 and graduated in the spring of 1988.

Since the fall of 1988, Champagne has been a doctoral student in Critical and Cultural Studies at the University of Pittsburgh, where he has also been teaching film, composition, literature, and creative writing. Champagne is currently working on his third novel, tentatively entitled *Not to Say Love*.

MAJOR WORKS AND THEMES

Champagne's major publications focus on the question of what it means to live homosexual desire in the age of AIDS. To some extent, his work reflects the recreational-sex-versus-monogamy debate fuelled by the epidemic. The protagonists of his two published novels seek to create a new way for themselves, somewhere between the values of fidelity and monogamy traditionally associated with the institution of heterosexual marriage and the supposed excesses of the "sexual revolution" and gay liberation.

Champagne's first novel, *The Blue Lady's Hands*, focuses on the twenty-six-year-old, nameless narrator/protagonist's budding relationship with Daniel, a slightly older man. Intertwined with this narrative are recollections of his childhood and his first adolescent love affair with a young man named Michael, dialogues with his therapist Andrea, conversations with his friends Randy and Brian, poetry (which he writes as a therapeutic release), and his personal mythology of the "Blue Lady." The intensity of this rather short novel is due primarily to the youthfulness of its narrator, whose brooding introspection adds further severity and emotion to the narrative voice.

Inspired by a statue of the Virgin Mary in his boyhood home, the protagonist invents the "Blue Lady" of the title when he first falls in love. The terrible pains in his chest, he tells himself, are due to her hands exploring his capacity for love, how much room there is in his heart. The "Blue Lady" becomes a supernatural guide whom he consults in various stages of his relationships with Michael and Daniel and a gauge of his desire to find out what it means to love someone.

Idolizing his mother, whom he resembles in many ways, the protagonist in the beginning tries to emulate his parents' marriage based on the principles of fidelity and monogamy. When, at the age of seventeen, he meets Michael he is convinced he has found the "one and only" love of his life. Michael, however, already has a lover at school and is only looking for a part-time affair for the summer months he spends at home. What evolves between them is a relationship based on the protagonist's emotional dependency: hoping for acceptance and desperately seeking to realize his youthful, romantic dreams, he allows Michael to shape him and to take advantage of him. His hopes, however, are utterly destroyed when Michael finally leaves him for good.

Scared and confused, the narrator starts therapy and does not permit himself to fall in love for years after this traumatic experience—until he meets Daniel. This time he proceeds with utmost caution, not making any demands on Daniel or becoming prematurely attached to him. Like a mantra, he keeps repeating to himself Andrea's words of encouragement, "You're not desperate," and her warning reminder that Daniel and he have no agreement concerning the rules of their relationship. Thus their love affair develops until the protagonist learns that Daniel has a rich secret admirer who showers him with fan mail and gifts. Being possessive to begin with, the protagonist has a hard time controlling his jealousy when he finds out that Daniel also belongs to a jack-off-club. What is he to do when the man he has fallen in love with goes off to a group masturbation party on a Saturday night?

At the heart of the novel, then, is the protagonist's struggle for sexual independence. He comes to realize that his relationship with Daniel can be nothing like his parents' marriage. Yet, by the same token, he refuses the definition of sex as a purely recreational "sport" to which Randy and Brian subscribe. While these issues are not resolved by the end of the novel, we witness the protagonist striving for his own definition of love and sex. In his own idiosyncratic way—and with the help of the "Blue Lady"—he learns to love and to trust, to make room in his heart.

Will, the protagonist of Champagne's second novel, *When the Parrot Boy Sings*, is a young, gay, vegetarian, Marxist collage artist who earns a living cleaning apartments. The first-person narrative voice in this novel is more mature and critically self-reflexive. Will frequently interrupts his narrative with tirades on the impossibility of love and the deplorable state of the world. Crucially, however, he has a sense of humor that effectively balances more serious passages and allows him to develop an ironic distance that keeps him from becoming excessively morbid or too self-righteous.

Like his counterpart in the *The Blue Lady's Hands*, Will is looking for a lover with whom he can share a monogamous relationship. His constant companions are the beautiful Fish Baby and the Parrot Boy, both private mythical creatures who express Will's loneliness and frustration. Will shares with the reader his observations about the city he lives in, his poignant and funny evaluations of his tricks, and descriptions of collages he plans to construct. These collages are his way of commenting on a number of social issues ranging from consumer capitalism to the Catholic Church's attitude toward homosexuality.

In his pursuit of Mr. Right, Will meets a variety of men on different modes of public transportation—Walter, the furniture salesman, on the subway; Gary, a sound engineer, on the Staten Island ferry; and Harry, a stage director, on a bus. In an East Village gay bar, Will finally meets Dennis and Scott, an older gay couple, who try to pick him up for a threesome. Will declines, but eventually befriends Dennis and Scott who like him in spite of—or perhaps because of—his political positions. Dennis and Scott represent everything that Will purports to despise: They are rich, upwardly mobile, politically conservative, sexually promiscuous—and they eat meat.

Yet opposites obviously attract, and Will ends up having sex with them after all. He first sleeps with Dennis, then with Scott, and finally with both of them.

The ménage-à-trois, however, does not develop into the "perfect family" that Will conjures up in his imagination. Dennis and Scott are secure in each other and satisfied with their "open relationship." They continue their individual sexual pursuits and do not seem interested in fully sharing their relationship with Will or making him a permanent partner. Though Dennis and Scott are honest and open about their plans from the start and warn Will not to get hurt, he still gets caught up in his own fantasies and convinces himself that this will be a socialist experiment in monogamous polygamy. In spite of his Marxist rhetoric, Will's values ultimately are utterly bourgeois. He is still looking for a monogamous relationship and his "experiment" turns out to be a mere game of numbers: He wants the three of them to be a couple.

When Dennis and Scott refuse to change their ways, Will breaks off his sexual relations with them. The three men maintain a strained friendship for a short time, but in the end Will is left behind, lonely and frustrated as he was at the beginning of the summer. Importantly, however, he has had occasion to rethink his philosophy of love and sex. By the end of the novel he realizes how diverse gay experience is. Dennis and Scott came out in pre-AIDS New York, and for them learning to incorporate the use of a condom into their sexual practice is a big change—a change they are reluctantly learning to make. They are, however, unwilling to alter their sexual behavior according to someone else's moral standards, standards that remain as foreign to them as their sexual practice remains to Will.

CRITICAL RECEPTION

The AIDS epidemic has led to an enormous reactionary backlash, ranging from the construction of HIV infection as a "gay plague" to calls for mandatory testing and even more extreme legislation against homosexuality. The result has been a systematic infringement on privacy and individual rights that constitutes a serious challenge to the gains of post-Stonewall gay liberation. In this ideological context, the publication of two gay novels with protagonists looking for a monogamous relationship is bound to create all kinds of critical and emotional havoc. Not surprisingly, then, reviews of *The Blue Lady's Hands* in mainstream publications focus their attention on the issue of monogamy, commending the protagonist (and, in some cases, the author) for what they perceive as his laudable stance against gay promiscuity. What these reviews (as well as a number of attacks on Champagne in the gay press) conveniently ignore is the fact that the protagonist undergoes a learning process, a development from the unreflective aping of heterosexual structures to his acceptance of his sexually active partner within the framework of safer sex. *The Blue Lady's Hands* is the story of a young man who comes out in the age of AIDS. Unlike his older lover Daniel, he does not have to unlearn sexual behaviors that can put him at risk. Rather, his is a tale of unlearning the acquired dread of sex that is the result of both his upbringing and his construction as a gay man coming to terms with his sexuality in the time of AIDS.

Admittedly, the protagonist of *When the Parrot Boy Sings* is more outspoken in his rejection of dominant attitudes that represent AIDS as a "punishment" for gay promiscuity. Commenting on his sexual relationships with Dennis, Scott, and others with the hindsight of what we know today, he declares:

If I have anything to feel guilty about, it has nothing to do with AIDS or "promiscuity" or anything like that. To regret what we couldn't have known would be to suggest that we should have led our lives differently, and that is too simple a solution. Sometimes guilt is just too easy. It makes all the difficult questions disappear. (160)

The protagonists of Champagne's novels thus can by no means be construed as a mouthpiece for the agenda of bigots and homophobes; on the contrary, they are advocates for sexual independence. They insist on living homosexual desire according to what feels right to them—with all the uncertainties this entails—rather than the dogmas others seek to impose on them. Champagne's work is an important contribution not only to contemporary gay literature but also to the process of interpreting the meaning of gay male sexuality and the impact AIDS has had on this process.

WORKS BY JOHN CHAMPAGNE

The Blue Lady's Hands. Secaucus, N.J.: Lyle Stuart, 1988.
When the Parrot Boy Sings. Secaucus, N.J.: Meadowlands, 1990.
"Puerto Rico, I Remember." *Pittsburgh's Out* 174 (September 1991): 27 + 29.
"Three Poems of Married Men." *Chiron Review* 10, no. 3 (Autumn 1991): 46.
"At Thirty." *Kenyon Review.* Forthcoming.

SELECTED STUDIES OF JOHN CHAMPAGNE

Geno. "Milwaukee Resident Boughner and Milwaukee Native Champagne Publish New Books *Out of All Time* and *The Blue Lady's Hands. Wisconsin Light* 1 December 1988–14 December 1988: 7 + 10.
———. "*When the Parrot Boy Sings* Is Second Champagne Novel." *Wisconsin Light* 5 April 1990–18 April 1900: 7.
Gould, Christopher. "Laugh While You Can, Parrot Boy." *Washington Blade* 27 April 1990: 21.
Nelson, Bill. "Authors Explore Wisconsin Landscapes, Heartscapes." Rev. of *The Blue Lady's Hands. Milwaukee Journal* 26 February 1989: 9E.

Nelson, Emmanuel. "AIDS and the American Novel." *Journal of American Culture* 13, no. 1 (Spring 1990): 47–53.

Rice, Doug. "Author Exposes Important, Confusing Ideas about Love." Rev. of *The Blue Lady's Hands*. *Pittsburgh Press* 16 September 1989: 9C.

CHRISTOPHER COE (1954–)
William Lane Clark

BIOGRAPHY

Christopher Coe was born in Fountain Hill, Pennsylvania, in 1954 but moved as an infant with his family to Portland, Oregon. Intentionally vague regarding his personal history, he has claimed that, until his parents died in his teen years, "his father was the owner and administrator of a sanitorium for disturbed Eskimoes; his mother ran a charm school" ("Talking to Christopher Coe," 456). Although he declined to verify the accuracy of this personal statement when I talked with him recently (telephone interview with William Lane Clark, February 17, 1992), such charming evasion seems suitable to a writer whose characters are drawn with detailed attention to appearance rather than to subjective depth. "Inner beauty is what counts, but outer beauty is what *shows*," Coe has written; and the high valuation of appearance and surface given his characters is reflected in the author's style as well. Perhaps, the reader might learn as much about Coe by examining his writing; he effortlessly manages the first-person voice, the narrative mode for nearly all his work, with a credibility that suggests origins of deep personal experience. Although Coe spent his early years on the West Coast, he currently divides his residence between New York City and Paris.

MAJOR WORKS AND THEMES

Although he entertains many themes, the subjugation of the dependent son by a powerful father constitutes a common one to nearly all of Christopher Coe's published work. Removal of the father, by parricide, divorce, or unexplained death, occurs in several of the short stories. In the stories "Easy" and "Anything You Want" and in the novel *I Look Divine*, the father or both parents die. Although in "Easy" the son is not portrayed as identifiably gay, both central characters of the latter story and the novel are gay sons. Family dynamics, however, are not explored in any of the works in depth, and the situation of the dependency of the gay male in the context of family serves rather as an emblem for the powerlessness of the deviant in a heterosexual order. Empowerment of the gay individual accrues not simply from the removal of the patriarch but rather by usurpation of his wealth, which grants leverage in the larger (patriarchal) society that may be hostile to homosexuals, but respectful of money. In both of the short stories, the gay character reflects the concerns and needs of the mother, not only in dependency on the wealth of the father but also in dependency on cosmetics in exaggerated concern for personal attractiveness and dependency on drugs and alcohol to endure the powerless state. In "Anything You Want" the mother fails to retain proxy control of the family wealth and attempts suicide the day of the father's remarriage. The mother figure in "Easy," on the other hand, contests the father's dominance much as the sons do in the works. She is revealed as predacious, surviving several husbands by the age of forty, and surprises the son years later by claiming joint responsibility for his killing of the father. Apparently ageless and beautiful when the son sees her years after the father's death, she ironically, in the son's eyes, lives up to the father's sexist maxim, that "a woman, when she is forty, gets the face she deserves" ("Easy," 34). He also recognizes the similarity between the two of them. Deserving respect and the right to exercise autonomy, the problematics of living as a homosexual in a heterosexual social order, underlie Coe's disturbing portrait of two gay sons, principal characters in his only novel.

Christopher Coe's first novel, *I Look Divine*, is a slim, elegant work that burns with the hard gemlike flame of Pater's pre-Raphaelite aesthetics. The laconic, spare style and first-person narrative elevate the contextual importance of description and character over the subjective portrayal of character in the tiny vignettes that comprise the plot. In keeping with an emphasis on surface and appearance, the novel refracts its themes, like light from cut gems, through the mental reflections of a forty-four-year-old man, sitting in the mirrored bedroom of his recently deceased younger brother Nicholas, where he has come to sort through the possessions; the novel is a reminiscence on the homosexual brothers' emancipated lives following the deaths of their parents. Partly fable, partly parable, *I Look Divine* engages the subject of identity, as identity is determined by sexuality in a world of gay sensibility. The nameless narrator is a zygotic half of the author's portrait of the gay psyche, the other half represented by the dominating personality of Nicholas, self-created *exquisite*.

If the Aesthetes and the Decadents lurk in the origins of Coe's conception of Nicholas and his brother, it is Oscar Wilde's field the author works, and Nicholas seems much like a twentieth-century Dorian Gray. Just as youth, beauty, idleness, and appearance dominate the seductive allure of Wilde's character, Nicholas's careful cultivation and manipulation of the same qualities makes him irresistible to others, empowers him in measure equal to his acquired wealth. Wilde's novel amounted to a critique of subjective depth wherein he reversed art and nature, making beauty static artifice in the man and giving physical degeneration to his hidden portrait. Nicholas collects photographs of himself in contrived and flattering poses, images that decorate the room in which the narrator sits at the novel's outset. Nicholas, however, is his own self-portrait, a picture of desire unattached to love. "He would have been happier to have had no body," the narrator muses at one point, "to have been no more than his face" (29). The inevitable corruption of Nicholas's desirable appearance by age and time assures his destruction; he loses his youthful glamour by the age of thirty and is dead at thirty-seven, probably at the hands of a hustler. The older brother, no more impervious to the charms of Nicholas than any other and often compromised by his thrall to filial beauty, nonetheless provides the reader with a normative base from which to judge the glorious and brief impossibility of Nicholas's artificial existence.

A sense of alienation overrides the events of the novel. Both boys seem alienated from their parents as children, Nicholas by his self-absorption and his brother by Nicholas's displacement of him as favorite son. The events recalled by the narrator of their adult years frequently occur in moneyed hotel bars in Rome, Madrid, and Mexico City, where they are foreigners and temporary visitors. Even as adults the boys are alienated from each other by Nicholas's inability to love and his compulsive control of every aspect of their relationship and every situation they encounter together. As homosexuals, the brothers were *both* aliens in the scheme of the traditional family, considering themselves as a fraternity outside the familial order. Both boys rejected the sentimental demands of their grandmother, for example, to say "Cheese" for a holiday photograph: "We could not, even in those years, either of us, believe that we had that kind of grandmother. Nicholas said that she came from a bad family" (2). Even at seven, Nicholas controls the record of his appearance, refusing to smile joyfully as expected, despite his grandmother's pleas for a conventional picture of happy grandsons standing before a holiday tree loaded at the base with their gifts. This moment is important in the narrator's reconstruction of Nicholas's life, however, for it is the single recollection of their sibling relationship when Nicholas temporarily abandons his self-consciousness. The picture taking is preceded by sexual horseplay between the boys at Nicholas's instigation, prefiguring their mutual preoccupation with sex but remembered as a moment when the two managed a temporary communion, not just interdependency. Clutching each other in an awkward embrace, Nicholas "held on to me," the narrator recalls, "his feet planted on mine, and he tipped his weight forward, leaning with it, not to make us fall, but as though he wanted to take flight without leaving me behind" (2). Pinning his brother in place behind him by standing on his feet, Nicholas fondles the other boy's genitals and squeezes his buttocks, all the while evidencing the boyish joy he refuses the camera, laughing with his brother. The spontaneity of the moment preceding the photograph is the only moment witnessed by a carefully observant narrator of any real joy in Nicholas's life. His calculated existence becomes a pose in carefully arranged settings, which are effortlessly designed to foster the greatest adoration. In a bar scene at the height of his sexual attractiveness, he taunts and seduces an older, slightly overweight man smitten by his vivacious charm, claiming the man has élan but no panache. With dramatic irony the man admiringly responds that Nicholas has *suave de vivre*, a misstatement tellingly correct both about the boy's lack of joie de vivre and his control of appearance.

The problematics of (homo)sexual identity presented by the double portrait in the novel are driven by the role of eroticism in framing any definition. The theoretical arguments in gay studies between constructed homosexuality and essential homosexuality vaguely underlie the characters of Nicholas and his brother, respectively. The differences between the two conceptions of the homosexual are reduced, however, because Coe portrays the brothers as interdependent rather than as antagonists. Indeed, the older brother becomes de facto guardian of Nicholas when their parents die, assuming the role of the "father." The brothers lose their parents, appropriately, at times of their own greater autonomy, sexual and social: Nicholas achieving puberty at fourteen, and the narrator his legal majority at twenty-one. The narrator's new sociolegal viability is matched by Nicholas's sexual empowerment. The guardian role has no authoritative value for the narrator in his relationship with Nicholas, however, for the younger brother is superior to his sibling in every way: intelligence, beauty, social sophistication, and sexual awareness. Nicholas never develops these attributes, they are given to him from the moment of his Caesarian-section birth (the birth itself, he claims, made him even "more perfect" than other babies who undergo the *natural* deformations of birthing trauma) and allow him even as a child to control adults and to exercise his erotic appeal. For if the double portrait is an anatomy of homosexual being and homosexual desire, it is dominated by the latter. Eros possesses Nicholas. He is no less subject to the power of this generous but cruel god than he was subject to the father, and even more dependent. He demands adoration and perfects desirability to continue to manipulate older men, who give him lavish gifts that he disdains. Nicholas's obsession with appearance perpetuates a narcissism that, though powerful in its manipulation of others' desire, insures that he will never love and will likely never be loved but only desired. The narrator's admiration for his brother's beauty and its power over others is undercut throughout his revery on the life by an increasing awareness of its eventual attenuation and the inevitable consequences for Nicholas, as well as for himself.

The failure to balance homoerotic desire and homosexual being and the subjection of the latter to the former, as drawn in the relationship of these gay siblings, reflect the discourse on sexual identity in the gay community at the time of its publication in 1987. The epidemic of AIDS and its attendant crisis in the gay community forced revaluation of some of the basic tenets of the gay liberation movement concerning restraints on sexual behaviors, and Coe's novel echoes these concerns without reference to the health crisis and without drawing conclusions. Rather, the crisis for all of Coe's "boy" characters is one of establishing identity and autonomy, of *individual* integration of sexual desire and sexual being in the face of social and familial repression. Although none of his characters manages to do so, the haunting quality of *I Look Divine* comes from the narrator's recognition of its possibility. With all the images of Nicholas left as record of a life, all are as artificial as the subject who created them, and none reflects the Nicholas only the narrator is presumed to have known. The Christmas photograph *not* taken in the opening chapter of the novel, a picture of two boys laughing in precarious balance, the narrator asserts, "would have been a picture worth taking, worth having. It would be worth having now. Now it would be proof" (3).

CRITICAL RECEPTION

As Christopher Coe has published only one novel, the critical response to his writing is limited and confined to reviews of *I Look Divine*. Reviewers as a whole responded to Coe's writing style. Most reviews praised the beauty of the writing, generally conceding its elegance. Richard Burgin, although qualifying his approval by noting "maddeningly elusive" qualities to Coe's style, assessed it as "laconic, subtle and full of lyrical effects" and considered the author "an icy and acute observer." Other reviewers found the book "cleanly written" (*Booklist*), as well as "sleek and troubling" (*Publisher's Weekly*, August 21, 1987). Only one review faulted the style, considering the novel overall as "thin and one-dimensional," derivative of the Aesthetes ("neo-Wildean"), and flawed by shallow characterization, especially Nicholas's "cloying preciosity" and the narrator's "absurdly overdramatic and hushed reverence of his brother" (*Kirkus Reviews*). The disapprobative tone of this reviewer suggests a discomfort with the subject matter of homosexuality not evident in the other reviews. Indeed, one review attempted to place the character of Nicholas in a tradition of characterization midway between characters in Tennessee Williams's short stories and the "just-later 'doomed queens' of Andrew Holleran's* *Dancer from the Dance*." This reviewer also established a historical gay social context for the novel. He perceived Nicholas as representative of the homosexual culture just prior to gay liberation and suggested that his eclipse and death during the period of the "gay macho image" that followed Stonewall make "the novel a glittering memento mori for an era as well as an individual" (*Booklist*).

WORKS BY CHRISTOPHER COE

"Easy." *Harper's Magazine* 273 (August 1986): 32–34.
I Look Divine. New York: Ticknor & Fields, 1987.
"Anything You Want." In *Men on Men 2: Best New Gay Fiction.* Ed. George
    Stambolian, 155–168. New York: New American Library (1988).

SELECTED STUDIES OF CHRISTOPHER COE

Burgin, Richard. Review of *I Look Divine. New York Times Book Review* 92
    (August 30, 1987): 11.
Hempel, Amy. "Talking to Christopher Coe." *Vogue* 438 (September 1987): 455–
    56.
Review of *I Look Divine, Booklist* 84 (September 15, 1987): 107–8.
Review of *I Look Divine, Kirkus Reviews* 55 (August 1, 1987): 1089.
Review of *I Look Divine, New York Times Book Review* 93 (December 25, 1988):
    24.
Review of *I Look Divine, Publisher's Weekly* 232 (August 21, 1987): 54.
Review of *I Look Divine, Publisher's Weekly* 234 (November 18, 1988): 75.

DENNIS COOPER (1953–   )

Earl Jackson, Jr.

BIOGRAPHY

Dennis Cooper was born on January 10, 1953, into an affluent family in West Covina, California. The family fortune came in part from the Cooper Development Company, which designed parts for spacecraft. Cooper's father also worked as a consultant, advising Herbert Hoover and Harry Truman on agricultural policy. Richard Nixon was at one time the best friend of Cooper's father, and Cooper's brother was named after Nixon. Despite the idyllic settings of first West Covina and then the ranch home in Arcadia, Cooper's early intellectual development was informed by an interest in the darker sides of human sexuality and the extremes of aesthetic expression found in de Sade, Baudelaire, and Rimbaud. In his early teens he wrote sex-filled parodies of "Batman" and "The Flintstones," and at sixteen he wrote an imitation of de Sade's *120 Days of Sodom*, which he destroyed, fearing his mother would find it.

A tall, "wimpy" adolescent, Cooper was the object of repeated bullying at public school. In eighth grade, he transferred to a private school, quickly became the leader of a group of outcasts: budding poets, druggies, and punks, who eventually would provide the models for the wayward youths who populate his fiction. By the eleventh grade, his activities led to expulsion, and he returned to public education. After graduating he studied two years at Pasadena City College and spent one year at Pitzer College, but withdrew on the advice of his poetry teacher. In 1976 Cooper went to England where he became involved with the burgeoning punk-rock scene, another major aesthetic strain in his later writings. Also in 1976 he began *Little Caesar Magazine*, featuring interviews with punk musicians and poetry, an interest that led him to founding Little Caesar Press in 1978, which featured the work of upcoming poets Amy Gerstler, Brad Gooch, Elaine Equi, Tim Dlugos, and Eileen Myles, among others.

In 1979, Cooper became the director of programming at the alternative art/poetry space Beyond Baroque, in Venice, California. Under his directorship, performance artists such as Tim Miller and Eric Bogosian made their Los Angeles debuts. In 1984, frustrated with the politics of the L.A. art scene, Cooper moved to New York, living with his Dutch boyfriend, whom he then followed back to Amsterdam. In the Netherlands Cooper suffered from a sense of profound isolation, eventually compounded by a severe case of measles. Sick and depressed in Europe, Cooper wrote *Closer*, taking as initial inspiration a photograph of a boy's back in which someone had lightly carved a Mickey Mouse face (now the cover of the forthcoming Dutch translation).

Returning to New York, he wrote for *Artforum* and began work on *Frisk*. In January 1988, Cooper cocurated an exhibit with Richard Hawkins at LACE, entitled, "AGAINST NATURE: A Group Show of Work by Homosexual Men," which galvanized the divisions between the AIDS activists and the gay avant-garde. Cooper and Hawkins were denounced by both the straight press and political activist-critics such as Douglas Crimp, who views the present crisis as one that leaves no time for pure speculation on gay sexuality. Cooper and Hawkins were subsequently vindicated by Jesse Helms's attack on the NEA over Mapplethorpe, but the rifts have never fully healed and the suspicion with which Cooper is viewed in some gay circles remains strong. Nevertheless, Cooper was the first recipient of the Ferro-Grumley Award for gay literature (for *Closer*), which reflects that fact that Cooper's artistry as a writer is recognized even by those who express reservations about his "message."

Cooper now lives in Los Angeles. Recently he has been experimenting with performance, often collaborating with the choreographer Ishmael Houston-Jones. His most recent performance piece, "The Undead," premiered at LACE in September 1990 and was staged at The Kitchen in New York City in December 1991. Cooper also edited a collection of lesbian and gay short fiction, *Discontents: New Queer Writing*, for Amethyst Press (1992); he is at work on a new novel, and in collaboration with Mark Ewert he is writing a rock opera.

MAJOR WORKS AND THEMES

The reveries within Cooper's prose, from "A Herd" through *Safe* to *Frisk* are haunted by the question of desire and even love: how are they possible and what do they mean in a world without interiority? The sexual obsessions of Cooper's early work are little more than publicist-created images that generate longings that cannot be fulfilled, desires that cannot be reciprocated. The beauty of the desired object, such as Mark Lewis in Cooper's first novel, *Safe*, becomes an enigma with no answer: an ultimate refusal reducible to the photograph of Mark on which the "Dennis" narrator of the center section meditates.

Given the preoccupation with the "blank generation," sexual torture, and murder that characterizes much of Dennis Cooper's recent fiction, it is easy to forget that Cooper began his literary career as a poet. To do so, however, would seriously impair a full appreciation of the difficulty of Cooper's oeuvre. Cooper still commands a lyric "I" that remains operative even within his most horrific prose. In fact, Cooper's "I" is arguably one of the most poignant and plaintive voices in contemporary literature. This "I" can speak only by breaking its own aesthetic laws; it lingers within an environment hostile to it and despite the logic of the world that has apparently vanquished its material validity, like the consciousness of a murdered boy at the scene of the crime in "Dear Todd" (*He Cried*, 29) or the imagined ghost in the windmill in the penultimate chapter of *Frisk* (114–16).

That posthumous remainder of the victim constitutes the traces of the "soul" that beckons through the physical shell but remains elusive. The boys loved or longed for in Cooper's prose texts are as removed from an integrated experience of the corporeal and psychic aspects of "self" as are the teen stars that populate his lyric fantasies in *Tiger Beat* and *Idols*, in a world in which the supersaturation of surfaces precludes depth, meaning has gone out of style, and emotions are a nostalgic embarrassment. Yet the desiring subject continues to pose riddles about the nature of his desire and its source, even in a postmodern environment that seems to obviate such questions. As I have formulated elsewhere:

The plots and themes in Dennis Cooper's texts often involve the same operative paradox: the continuance of obsessive metaphysical gestures within a radically de-mystified world expressing a longing for that X which seems to inhere within the human object of desire that is nevertheless not coextensive with the physical body in which that desire is given shape and through which the desire is brought into control. A desire to know that X—that essence of the person—is overliteralized in acts of mutilation and murder ("Death Drives" 5).

The boys in Cooper's universe are radically bifurcated into a body and a self, the latter being often mistaken for the former, but ultimately beyond apprehension. Cooper's first-person narrator in "Square One" illuminates the problem in his musings over his childhood friend and sometime lover "George M.": "It was [George] I imagined my cock entering each night, not just his flimsy ass, though that's the first thing I opened when I got the chance. . . . If I'd sliced into George I'd have been covered with blood at least. There'd be evidence, if no answer" (*Wrong*, 85).

In a world of pure surface, the "inner self" is displaced onto the internal workings of the body, and the discovery of the "essence" of the person is a grotesque and often fatal intrusion into that body. The doomed heroes of *Closer* often intuit the grisly dichotomies that comprise them. John marvels that "George's skin felt so great . . . at the same time realizing the kid was just skin wrapped around some grotesque-looking stuff" (7). David admits to himself that his obsession with his own beauty "helps me believe in myself and not worry that I'm just a bunch of blue tubes inside a skin wrapper" (22). The boys are also driven by antithetical motivations: a constant search for more stimuli and a need to numb the self. Sex becomes a ritual whose original point is lost in its repetition. This is most grimly illustrated in the sex that takes place between Cliff and Alex after the car accident that leaves Alex parapalegic. Alex holds Cliff to an earlier promise to "fuck him," and the affectless execution of the act is doubly eerie in that it differs only slightly from other sexual encounters in the novel:

Cliff carries Alex, half-lifting, half-dragging his heels on the carpet, toward the bed. "Thanks," Alex says, as Cliff straightens him out then rolls him onto his stomach. . . .
Sometimes Cliff's hand strokes his back very rapidly, as though attempting to rub out a stain. . . . Cliff sighs, "I just can't get it hard." Alex . . . reaches over and takes a porn magazine off the small stack on his night table, hurling onto his back. He hears the pages turn. They feel like wings. "Hey great. I'm in." Alex can't tell the difference. (85)

This scene is a perfect mirror of an earlier scene in which Alex "gets through" sex with a stranger by reading the stranger's porn during the sex act and plotting the film he would shoot, which resulted in his accident (72–75).

The need for ever increasing extremes of physical experience and the profound disinterest in their consequences makes these boys prey to adults who have *ghastly* means of exploring the nature of the boys' beauty. George becomes involved with Phillippe, an older man obsessed with death and murder and a member of a coterie of men with similar interests, one of whom shared a snuff film with the group. The screening of this film is a ceremony that is archaic in the convergence of death and orgasm as two absolute boundaries of human consciousness, that are celebrated as awful mysteries. Dennis Cooper is an archeologist of desire: his fiction is highly reminiscent of Georges Bataille's interrogation of erotic prehistories through cave paintings, particularly one of a man with a bird head and erect penis supine before a dying bison:

Being the first enigma posed by humans, it asks us to descend to the bottom of the abyss opened in us by eroticism and death. . . . Nothing in this whole image justifies the paradoxical fact that the man's sex is erect. . . . This essential and paradoxical accord is between death and eroticism. . . . [the accord] remains veiled by reason of the very structure of human beings. It remains veiled to the extent that the human mind hides from itself. (*The Tears of Eros*, 51–53)

The connection between awe and horror of the body and its ends is most deliberately explored in *Frisk*. Like the word "evidence" in the preceding quote from "Square One," "frisk" belongs to the vocabulary of crime. Cooper's delving into the more obsidian depths of sexuality traverses (and blurs the boundaries between) religion and crime, worship and sacrifice. Cooper takes new risks in *Frisk*, metalinguistic risks, exposing the artifice and mechanics of fantasy and its pornographic representation that he had heretofore manipulated to denude the body of its mystique and desire of its sanctity. More disturbing than *Closer*, *Frisk* implicates the reader directly, creating expectations of murder that it deliberately disappoints. It frisks the reader until it finds evidence against him or her.

From the first sentence the shimmering necromancy of the prose transfixes the reader with a basilisk's gaze; the siren voice of the narrative draws the reader ineluctably into the nether reaches of sexuality. One turns the pages with the fatalistic trepidation of a hero or heroine in a horror film descending into the darkest recesses of a basement where some unknown yet obscenely familiar terror lurks, "too out-of focus to actually explore with one's eyes, but too mysterious not to want to try" (*Frisk*, 4).

In the tradition of Bataille, yet in a thoroughly American idiom and through a bizarrely engaging psychotic lyricism, Cooper obsessively and eloquently articulates the quizzical contingency of being human; reduced to its noisome elements and its unannotated appetites, the human transmits its S.O.S. precariously between its biological grotesqueries and its capacity for cataclysmic ecstacy. If beyond wet dreams there are wet nightmares, Dennis Cooper has already scripted them.

CRITICAL RECEPTION

Dennis Cooper's first major endorsement from the gay literary establishment came from Edmund White,* who wrote an engaging endorsement of Cooper's work as the introduction to *Tenderness of the Wolves*. Here he lucidly distinguishes Cooper's aesthetic strategies from the nihilism of Cooper's subjects: "Cooper is not a naive member of the blank generation. He is its poet, its critic and its mimic. He has mastered its dialect. . . . (x)." White makes precise the locus of the horror in Cooper's murder fiction when he observes that it is so "upsetting precisely because both the murderer and the murdered subscribe to the same code of refinement—a sullen aphasia that conceals a gnawing hunger for sensation" (ibid.).

Other reviews of Cooper's work that distinguish themselves in their insight include Robert Glück's,* Bo Huston's,* and Peter Schjeldahl's (see Selected Studies). The most sustained analysis of Cooper's work to date remains Dodie Bellamy's brilliant reading of *Safe* and *He Cried*, "Digression as Power: Dennis Cooper and the Aesthetics of Distance," in which she pinpoints the central dynamic of Cooper's texts:

Physical Beauty and deep feeling are a deadly combination in two ways: those who possess them die and those who don't become obssessed with those who do, the eventual death increasing desirability. Those who survive do so by elaborate methods of distancing, transforming sex into an image to be manipulated; they in turn are manipulated by images contained within the community. When these abstract constructions collapse and characters confront unadulterated physicality they are stricken with horror. (79–80)

As Dennis Cooper continues to prove his consistency as an important and innovative writer, it is to be hoped that scholars will approach his texts with a courage equal to Cooper's and a critical rigor equal to Bellamy's.

WORKS BY DENNIS COOPER

Tiger Beat. Los Angeles: Little Caesar, 1978.
Idols. New York: Sea Horse, 1979. Rev. ed. New York: Amethyst Press, 1989.
The Tenderness of the Wolves. Trumansburg, N.Y.: Crossing, 1981.
The Missing Men. New York: Am Here Books/Immediate Editions, 1982.
He Cried. San Francisco: Black Star, 1984.
Safe. New York: Sea Horse, 1984.
Closer. New York: Grove Weidenfeld, 1989.
Frisk. New York: Grove Weidenfeld, 1991.
Wrong. New York: Grove Weidenfeld, 1992.

SELECTED STUDIES OF DENNIS COOPER

Abbott, Steve. "Notes on Boundaries: New Narrative." *View/Askew: Postmodern Investigations*, 39–55. San Francisco: Androgyne, 1989.
Aletti, Vince. "Naked Lunchroom: Dennis Cooper's Teenage Wasteland." *Village Literary Supplement* (May 1989): 28–29.
Bellamy, Dodie. "Digression as Power: Dennis Cooper and the Aesthetics of Distance." *Mirage* 1 (1985): 78–87.
Cooper, Dennis. "Sex Writing and the New Narrative." Paper given at the Out/Write Conference, San Francisco, 1990.
Glück, Robert. "Running on Emptiness." *San Francisco Chronicle* 4 June 1989: 9.
Huston, Bo. "The Brink of Darkness." *The Advocate* 1 October 1989: 57.
Jackson, Earl, Jr. "Death Drives across Pornotopia: Dennis Cooper on the Extremities of Being." *GLQ: A Journal of Lesbian and Gay Studies* 1, no.1 (Summer 1993) forthcoming.
Latsky, Eric. "Dennis Cooper Hits Home." *L.A. Weekly* 13–19 July 1990: 20–27.
Meyer, Richard. "Interview." *Cuz*. Ed. Richard Meyer, 52–69. New York: The Poetry Project, 1988.
Schjeldahl, Peter. "Dennis Cooper's Molten Miracle." *Voice Literary Supplement* (June 84): 7.
White, Edmund. "The Lost Boys." *Times Literary Supplement* 5 April 1989: 92.

MICHAEL CUNNINGHAM
(1952–)
Reed Woodhouse

BIOGRAPHY

Michael Cunningham was born on November 6, 1952, in Cincinnati, Ohio, a city even more conservative and banal than the "Cleveland" of his most successful novel (*A Home at the End of the World*). From there his family moved to Chicago, then to Germany for four years, and finally to Los Angeles, where he spent his adolescence. He attended Stanford University, from which he graduated in 1975 with a degree in English, a subject he says he chose because he didn't know what else to study. Stanford he calls a "privileged school" that "didn't feel like good news about the world" (all quotes in this section are from a personal interview with the author, December 21, 1991).

After graduation he moved to San Francisco. As he amusingly put it: "I just wanted to amount to nothing"—an experience apparently forbidden in Palo Alto. For the next two years he drifted about waiting for life to happen: driving to Colorado, then to Nebraska with a woman he was in love with, then ending up back in Los Angeles where he bartended in Laguna Beach. In 1978 he enrolled in the University of Iowa Writers' Workshop, from which he "emerged a writer" (and an M.F.A.) two years later. The following year, he accepted a year's residency at the Provincetown Fine Arts Work Center, then moved to New York City, where he has lived ever since.

Cunningham has not been a prolific writer, and his works seem to have come in two intense bursts: in 1981–1984 and in 1990–1991. In the first period were published three of his five short stories as well as his first novel, *Golden States*. In the second appeared a fourth story, "Clean Dreams," and his principal novel, *A Home at the End of the World*. (A fifth story, "White Angel," which appeared in the *New Yorker* in 1988, is really an excerpt from *Home*.) The six years between the first novel and the second were thus comparatively barren: he himself has called it a period of "hard times."

If the times were hard, they were abundantly compensated by the critical and popular acclaim given the novel that crowned them, *A Home at the End of the World*. It is without doubt his major work so far. Certainly it is the one that most concerns gay readers, and consequently the one I shall discuss here. For while only ambiguously "gay," it nonetheless marks the end of one chapter in gay literature, that of post-Stonewall "community," and initiates another: one of assimilation and, perhaps, of Freud's "ordinary unhappiness."

MAJOR WORKS AND THEMES

Michael Cunningham is one of a new generation of writers who are hardly imaginable earlier than the mid–1980s: writers who, while treating the subject of homosexuality, are both determined and able to make it one subject among others, their gay characters subsumed within a larger social group. That this has become a more available option can hardly be doubted: witness the success of David Leavitt,* with whom Cunningham has been compared. But that success would have been as inconceivable to the fearful closet of the 1960s as (for different reasons) to the defiant ghetto of the 1970s. It is true, of course, that the 1970s saw the publication of such anomalous work as Andrew Holleran's* *Dancer from the Dance* and James Purdy's* triumphantly "self-oppressive" *Narrow Rooms* (both 1978). But they mostly brought forth an aggressively "gay" fiction that mixed pornography, political polemic, and that peculiarly gay *bildungsroman*, the coming-out story.

Cunningham is remarkable for doing without any of these fictional tropes, and even without the two figures Ethan Mordden* calls our central icons: the Stud and the Queen (or, less allegorically, Sex and Camp). Cunningham's characters, who so reluctantly have sex, seem (if anything) scared of it. And although Jonathan and Clare are ironic, it is with the cool postmodern irony of the punk rather than the baroque untruth of the drag queen. Their wit, in other words, does not serve to label them sexually at all, but is rather the lingua franca of disillusioned youth and semi-youth in New York. Neither is Jonathan's a "coming-out" story, for he never denies being gay or encounters any obstacles to it. It is in fact the absence of fear on the one hand (imposed by the closet) and of arrogance on the other (demanded by the ghetto) that gives Cunningham not only his peculiar subject but also his characteristic voice. For if Jonathan never denies his homosexuality, he never glories in it either. (To do so would be to convict oneself of too much certainty.) It is his wary sobriety that characterizes *A Home at the End of the World*.

To bring this tone into focus, consider what New York means to Jonathan and Clare in that novel and what it meant to Holleran's Malone in *Dancer from the Dance*. Could one be sure, for example, which book the following passage came from?

For three years we'd lived together in a sixth-floor walk-up on East Third Street between Avenues A and B, where Puerto Rican women argued in Spanish and drug dealers moved perpetually in and out of basement apartments. Drugged, heartbreakingly beautiful boys danced to enormous radios on the corner. (21)

Pure Holleran! And yet what follows is not: "We lived there because it was cheap, and because—we'd admitted this one drunken night—it struck us as more interesting than the safer parts of town" (21). This defensive, truthful "admission" tells us at once that it is spoken by anyone but Anthony Malone, that rueful, nonironic believer in the magic of the city and the possibility of love. Where Malone saw a beauty composed equally of mystery and squalor (and symbolized supremely in precisely such "drugged, heartbreakingly beautiful boys"), Jonathan sees only self-delusion. Becoming gay has plainly become undramatic, perhaps because there is no longer an audience to play to. There is only oneself: bored, fitful, vaguely despairing. Jonathan is not sure what it would mean to be gay. All he comes up with is occasional, nonecstatic promiscuity and a joyless relationship with his "boyfriend" Erich. Liberation, it would seem, has been gained, but at the price of a loss: "Gay" is no longer enough of an answer to the question, "Who am I?"

In fact, all three main characters—straight, gay, and in-between—share the same sexual bemusement. Afflicted by only minimal desires, they respond to the squalid beauty of the streets by retreating into the private world of "the Hendersons," the family they mock and long to become. Ultimately they will try to embody "the Hendersons" (complete with baby) in upstate New York. But Cunningham does not permit us any sarcastic snicker at their expense: "family" is not a dirty word to him, though it may be an ambiguous one. In this, too, he is different from his immediate predecessors, who tend to view the family either as an absurdity (Malone can tell only the family dog, "I'm gay") or (like Robert Ferro*) as the strong source of their being, the body they seek honorably to join. Cunningham's characters, by contrast, are stronger than their families. For example, the adolescent hero of *Golden States*, David Stark, is touchingly eager to *save* his family, in particular his unhappily engaged sister Janet. And what are Bobby, Jonathan, and Clare doing in their outrageous parody of family life but trying to reinvent it, to salvage something from the wrecks they were born into—and have become castaways from?

How different (despite superficial resemblance) this "solution" is from earlier models. Take, for example, the "We Are Family" contention of someone like Ethan Mordden. No less than Cunningham, Mordden writes about a postmodern New York "family." But this family is composed of gay men; that is, it is *not* a family in any "straight" sense. Their raison d'être is to be gay—that is, not straight—and without that shared identity they would not be together. How different, again, is Jonathan's and Clare's relationship from the classic dyad of fag and fag-hag in Tennessee Williams' "Two on a Party." Oddly enough, despite their palpable self-pity and self-destructiveness, what one remembers about these "two" is their determination and élan. Knowing perfectly well they are not going to survive as "a couple," they nevertheless play the game with intense seriousness, daring each other to new heights of imprudence.

Neither daring nor elitism has a place in Jonathan's relationships, either with Clare or with Bobby. These troubling characters, loving each other without being "in love," come across as confused and sad, indeed as *lost* (hence the attraction for all of them of "home"). Their lostness ontologically precedes their sexuality or any other form of group-identity. In fact, the closest of all the bonds turns out to be that between Jonathan and Bobby, who says of it: "Jonathan and I are members of a team so old nobody else could join even if we wanted them to. We adore Clare but she's not quite on the team." Cunningham's "family" is thus as ineluctable as any biological one, and yet strangely independent of women. And if this male couple is "family," they are so not because they have defied the straight world and set up their own government in exile but because they have fused with each other and denied the necessity of further definition.

Why are they so reluctant to label themselves? What has caused their strange anomie? I would say, their general sense of *belatedness*. (Here Cunningham seems a writer of a younger generation than his own.) What is Cleveland but a city left behind in the 1950s? More poignantly: What is gay New York but a city left behind in the 1970s? What does Bobby listen to but the music his adored, dead brother liked? Where—to their own dishevelled amusement—do Bobby, Clare, and Jonathan end up but at Woodstock, that mocking symbol of 1960s community and passion? Time in this novel is the enemy, not (as in tragedy) because it snatches away youth and beauty, but because it reproaches these latecomers with a glorious past they can neither recover nor abandon.

This, I think, accounts for Cunningham's particular style, which is one of patient, unhysterical truthfulness. To claim to know too much about these characters would seem a kind of lying, and Cunningham's highest value, I would guess, is honesty. The best he can do is to shed on them a mild, perfect, melancholy light. Jonathan's epiphany as he stands in the ice-cold lake with the dying Erich on the last page symbolizes the particular success of the whole book. No hope is falsely held out for long-lasting happiness, no cause for eternal regret. At the same time, "living in the moment," that cliché of spirituality, is not mystically glorified; the moment passes without leaving a trace. If Jonathan's can be called a growing-up (rather than a coming-out) story, it has been a success of attrition rather than expansion, of illusions left behind. Though Jonathan is arguably "reborn" at the end, he is also prosaically cold, pale, and shivering. This is not Blake's radiant figure "Glad Day," naked and rejoicing in the sunlight. The climate is not hospitable, and the month is April.

It is perhaps a mark of the new world (for and about which Cunningham wrote) that few reviewers saw the book as primarily "gay." The "belatedness" that afflicts his characters afflicts us all in the late–1980s. If they are "depressed," so are we; and the depression may be as much an economic as an intrapsychic one. Nor, on the other side, did the gay press see anything odd in Jonathan's desire to be a "father" or a "husband." Indeed, *Home* was quickly taken up by gay reviewers and bookstores as a triumph of "gay fiction." How strange a literary-minded ghetto clone would have found a book whose one gay character is saved only when he is taken into a "family" of two straight people and their baby! And yet, how deeply, troublingly *queer* that family is: much queerer, in fact, than even gay activists might recognize. How utterly it shuts out women (as Clare finally realizes), yet how maternal are its men!

CRITICAL RECEPTION

The critical reception of *Home* was enthusiastic. Nearly every reviewer noticed its seriousness and the subtlety of its prose, though several thought its beauty bordered on preciousness. Cunningham reminded reviewers of other authors, including such predictable ones as David Leavitt, such plausible ones as John Cheever, and such whimsical ones as Sybille Bedford. A number of reviewers compared the novel to *Jules and Jim* without noticing the central and profoundly perverse relationship between Bobby and Jonathan, unnormalized by Gallic joie de vivre. Two long, ambitious reviews, comparing Cunningham with other gay authors, appeared in *The Nation* and *The Advocate*. The latter (by George Stambolian) is particularly fine. A pedestrian but favorable review by Joyce Reiser Kornblatt appeared in the *New York Times Book Review*, and a thoughtful, painstaking one by Chris Nealon in *Gay Community News*.

The fact that the book tells a homosexual story didn't seem to faze anyone—with two exceptions. One was the *Los Angeles Times* reviewer Richard Eder, who wrote that "once she is a mother, [Clare] can no longer avail herself of the refuge, the escape from fundamental choices provided by this comically warm and funky ménage à trois in upstate New York. Lovable and user-friendly to the ultimate degree, it is producer-hostile and as stifling as any unduly prolonged childhood must be" (12). This is the pitying but contemptuous voice of 1950s Freudianism: homosexuals just won't grow up. The other mildly hostile review (in the Chicago *Tribune*) was that of Joseph Olshan. Amid his faint praise for the novel came a bizarre squawk of outrage sounded by no other reviewer. "Why," he asks, "must Cunningham insist on taking the reader through one unsavory sexual act after another?" (8). As Cunningham's characters are bashful to the point of maidenliness, I cannot imagine what book Olshan had in mind when he asked this huffy rhetorical question.

WORKS BY MICHAEL CUNNINGHAM

Novels

Golden States. New York: Crown Publishers, Inc., 1984.
A Home at the End of the World. New York: Farrar Straus Giroux, 1991.

Short Stories

"Bedrock." *Redbook*. April 1981.
"Cleaving." *Atlantic*. January 1981.
"Pearls." *Paris Review*. Fall 1982.
"White Angel." *New Yorker*. July 25, 1988.
"Clean Dreams." *Wigwag*. August 1990.

Selected Reviews of Michael Cunningham

Eder, Richard. "Squaring a Triangle." *Los Angeles Times Book Review* 11 November 1990: 3.
Kaufman, David. "All in the Family." *The Nation* 1 July 1991: 21.
Kornblatt, Joyce Reiser. "Such Good Friends." *New York Times Book Review* 11 November 1990: 12.
Nealon, Chris. "Get a Life." *Gay Community News* 4–10 August 1991: 8.
Olshan, Joseph. "Two trips through the minefields of emotions." *Chicago Tribune Book Review* 4 November 1990: 8.
Stambolian, George. "Searching for Sensibilities." *The Advocate* 23 October 1990: 74.

DANIEL CURZON (1938–   )
John Gettys

BIOGRAPHY

Daniel Curzon (christened Daniel Russel Brown) was born on March 19, 1938, at a hospital in Litchfield, Illinois, a few miles from Farmersville, the small farming town in the Midwest where his parents (Ida and Russell) lived. His father was a farm laborer, then a tavern owner; his mother, born in Tennessee, was a functional illiterate who was a cook and then owner of a small restaurant. Ida already had three other children by her first husband, who had been killed in a car accident.

Having lost their businesses in the Depression, the family moved to Detroit about 1940–1941, Russell taking employment with U.S. Rubber, a tire factory.

Raised Roman Catholic, Daniel attended kindergarten at Lillibridge Public School and St. Rose of Lima Catholic School from the first grade through the twelfth, graduating third in his class of forty-six in 1956. From early childhood, he wrote plays and performed them with neighborhood children, despite the bullies who sometimes interfered with such "sissy" doings.

From 1956 to 1960 the author attended the University of Detroit, majoring in English, overcoming his shyness to become active at the end of his sophomore year in the Players, the university's theater group, acting in several regular productions and directing some student one-acts. It was in the theater that Curzon began to have a full-fledged social life.

In 1960, the author received a fellowship to work on a master's degree at Kent State University in Ohio. He completed this degree in one calendar year, from the summer of 1960 to the summer of 1961. It was at Kent State that the author realized, through a crush on a fellow male student, that he was unequivocally homosexual, though he was not to act on this knowledge for four more years.

From 1961 to 1964 Curzon (as Brown) taught at the University of Detroit, a Jesuit school, though he no longer considered himself a Catholic and hadn't since the age of twenty-one. From 1964 to 1969, with a year off to complete his doctoral course work, he taught at Wayne State University and completed his degree in English there, graduating in May of 1969. His dissertation was titled "The War Within: Existentialism and Naturalism in the Fiction of Nathanael West."

By then he had written poetry, short stories, several plays, and a first novel (*A Crooked Eye*) but had published only scholarly articles. He still regrets turning down an offer on this first novel in 1968 from New American Library because the editor wanted him to add a happy ending and because it was to be "only" a paperback original. "I was so naively idealistic then," Curzon says about his unwillingness to compromise on the book. (All statements attributed to Curzon in this paper are based on personal interviews with him in July of 1991.)

In 1969 he left Detroit to teach for the University of Maryland on U.S. military bases in the Far East and taught college English to American personnel in Thailand, Vietnam, Okinawa, and Japan. In Thailand he began what was to become his first published book, *Something You Do in the Dark*, which was completed in May of 1970 and published by G. P. Putnam in May of 1971.

He lived in London from September 1970, until June 1972. In 1972 he reluctantly returned to the Far East to teach for the University of Maryland extension program because the college-teaching market was impossible to penetrate in other places. In 1974 Curzon was threatened with being fired and was banned from teaching on certain military bases in Asia because he asked the Education Office to make copies of gay material for use in one of his classes. Fortunately, despite the efforts of the chancellor to remove him and the cowardice of certain closeted gays, Curzon managed to escape by winning a one-year appointment at California State University, Fresno. One of the classes he taught was gay literature. He also founded (1975) and edited the six issues of *Gay Literature*, a publication devoted to serious literature on gay themes.

After two years at Fresno, the job over, Curzon moved to San Francisco in 1976, where gay liberation was in full swing but where he lived marginally from 1976 to 1988, on part-time teaching and running IGNA (the International Gay News Agency), which he ran until 1984, supplying news stories and other copy to gay publications around the United States.

In 1988, the local branch of the AFT union found a loophole in the arrangement with part-time teachers at City College of San Francisco, where Curzon had taught part-time since 1980. With full-time status and tenure at last, Curzon became less bitter about the exploitation and financial deprivation he had suffered during the previous twelve years.

He has been lovers with John Gettys, a library technical assistant, since

1980 and sired a child, Zachary, with a lesbian couple in 1983. He now has contact with his son and is pleased both to be gay and to have a child.

MAJOR WORKS AND THEMES

Something You Do in the Dark (1971) is considered by many to be the first gay-liberation novel. "I had never heard of Stonewall," Curzon says, "but apparently my own rage about being considered sub-human for being homosexual coincided with the same feeling in others." The story concerns a young man released from prison after serving time for having sex in a park, having been entrapped by a plainclothes police officer. The young man, Cole Ruffner, then tries to kill the officer, but he does not succeed. It is a dark, angry book written to show the injustice of such a harsh penalty for such a minor "crime" as well as the difficulty of dealing with a homophobic father. In terms of gay sensibility, even though the novel has a tragic ending, it shows a transition in thought from gays as deserving recipients of whatever happens to them to gays as victims of cruel prejudice. The author was at pains not to portray the gay hero as too good or to write mere propaganda.

Some early gay activists such as Lige and Jack of *Gay* magazine and the reviewer for the fledgling *The Advocate* (Jim Kepner) found the book to have a spirit of freshness, while some members of Gay Activists Alliance faulted it for its unhappy ending. *Something You Do in the Dark* is in the tradition of stark realism and was perhaps influenced not only by the author's personal sensibility but also by a graduate course in the naturalistic novel that he had taken at Wayne State University.

The Misadventures of Tim McPick was written in England between 1970 and 1971; first called *Queer Comedy*, it was not published until 1975. It is a picaresque novel, with a gay hero who weaves his way through contemporary society (college, the military, a gang, a sex show, Death Valley, and so on) searching for the meaning of life—only to discover that there is no big "meaning" to life, only little meanings. The dog Zipper, Aunt Nelly (a transvestite), and the selfish twin sister of the hero are major characters.

Curzon here attempts to show that he is versatile, capable of writing comedy as well as the heavy naturalism of his first book. *McPick* is not everybody's cup of tea in its attempt to show the closeness of comedy to tragedy, and some people have found its comedy too strange, although it had (and has) its fans.

In 1972 Curzon wrote a novel called *The Y*, set in a New York YMCA, showing interconnected lives of three gay men (a closeted macho military sergeant, an effeminate older man, and a militant activist) as they encounter a slasher. The book was accepted by several literary agents and even a publisher but for one reason or another has not yet been published.

Endangered Species (1976–1977) uses a basketball-shaped creature from another planet as the main character who witnesses the follies of the species, Homo sapiens. This book has not been published and has been abandoned by the author.

In the spring of 1977 Curzon's first theatrical work was produced in San Francisco. *Sex Show* consists of fifteen skits on sexual behavior, some of them gay. The author produced and directed the show, with five male actors playing multiple parts. It opened at the Gay Community Center, then moved to the Leavenworth YMCA, then was transferred to the Mubuhay Gardens (producer Dirk Dirksen). Its run was six months long, in three locations with two different casts.

In 1978 Curzon published a collection of nineteen short stories called *The Revolt of the Perverts*, stories that varied in style from outlandish comedy ("The Child Molester," about a child who molests old men), to a seriocomic trip to the baths with a young man with cerebral palsy ("Pity"), to an ironic indictment of "Christians" who work against gays and those gays who remain in the closet and help perpetuate hatred through ignorance about them ("The Ulcer"), to several stories set in a military environment, to a thinly veiled scathing portrait of a now-famous woman writer called "Joan Cheryl Holmes" ("Hatred").

Curzon wrote a preface to this book indicating that he thought the greatest gay liberation would come from letting gays be seen as they are in all their variety, good and bad, rather than in "positive" or simplistic agit-prop portraits.

In 1979 Ashley Books reprinted *Something You Do in the Dark*, the author having slightly revised the text to make stylistic improvements and to remove some of the more abrasive moments of the hero. In the same year Ashley Books published *Among the Carnivores*, a novel about a young, idealistic, openly gay teacher at Fresno State University who encounters problems with administrators, conservatives, closeted homosexuals, and his own secretiveness with his mother. Here the author used a realistic style that combines both humor and sadness.

Human Warmth and Other Stories (1981) contains twelve short stories that the author felt displayed his "more touching, more compassionate" side, including "Two Bartenders, a Butcher, and Me" and "Beer and Rhubarb Pie," the former anthologized in *Aphrodisiac: Stories from Christopher Street* and the latter made into a play.

In 1982 Curzon published a mock etiquette book called *The Joyful Blue Book of Gracious Gay Etiquette*, satirizing Victorian books on proper manners as well as Emily Post and Amy Vanderbilt, which has been one of the author's best sellers.

The year 1983 saw the publication of *From Violent Men*, a novel about a conniving gay supervisor and a liberal gay news reporter who become embroiled in a plot to assassinate a Dan White–like killer (Brad Short) while he is still in prison. The book is written in lean, full-throttle prose, the author's second book with revenge as the motive, again with an ironic outcome.

The World Can Break Your Heart (1984) is a novel based on a combination of real-life memories of Curzon's childhood and projections of how his life might have gone had he lived out the heterosexual scenario that seemed most likely. Part I (Benjy) portrays the painful childhood experiences of a sensitive small boy who is raised Catholic and encounters a vicious next-door bully (Jimmy Moznik). Part II (Ben) portrays the adolescence, dating, and eventual marriage of the main character, who fights his homosexual impulses as society and his church tell him he must. Part III (Benjamin) portrays the character breaking away from his marriage and children to establish a life as a gay man in Hollywood as an actor. But instead of finding happiness, he finds minimal work as an actor and eventually contracts AIDS. He writes a book about his life (the very book that the reader is reading) and hopes that his pain has been transmuted into something valuable (art), thus justifying all the hurts he has experienced.

The AIDS Show in 1984 contained a Curzon skit called "Rev. What's His Name," about a "loving" minister talking to Sunday school children about AIDS. The entire evening (produced by Theater Rhinoceros of San Francisco) was well reviewed and toured the United States, and the scripts of all twenty-one skits were published in *West Coast Plays*.

Curzon in Love (1988) is the author's depiction of his three lovers, made up of a separate section devoted to each and yet telling a continuous story via the reappearance of the earlier lovers in later parts of the book, especially the villainous first lover (Jer). Curzon here tries to demonstrate a range of styles from the basically realistic first part ("When Sleazehood Was in Flower") to the high-comedy-down-for-the-weekend flavor of the second part ("When Bertha Was a Pretty Name") to the Arabian Nights feel of the third part ("When Life Was a Wonder").

New novels include *Superfag*, a short satirical book about a semidivine being who is sent to earth by his heavenly father to rid the world of homophobia. It takes a satiric look of two decades of gay liberation. *Superfag* is scheduled for publication in 1992.

Curzon is currently at work on *Only the Good Parts*, a long novel in letters about a gay man's attempt to have contact with the child he has sired with a lesbian couple, one of whom is a female separatist. The major characters are the Jewish professor who is the donor father, his Machiavellian lover, the midwife who arranges the insemination, the lesbian mother of the child, and her lover. Major themes are the conflicts between gay men and lesbians and gay parenting.

CRITICAL RECEPTION

In general the reviews of Daniel Curzon's work have fallen into two categories: praise for his powerful, courageous, or honest story-telling ability, as the following reaction to *Something You Do* reveals: "a stunning masterpiece of believable characters in a world most people never get the opportunity to observe" (John Standring, *Camden Courier-Post*, May 26, 1971), and condemnation: "The author ... loads every confrontation in favor of the hero and his fellow misfits...." " (Peter Thomas, *The Detroit News*, August 22, 1971). Homophobic reviewers have felt no constraints about expressing their displeasure with the subject matter and/or its treatment: "From the evidence presented by Mr. Curzon (a pseudonym), the gay world is a very sick place.... " (John F. Morrison, *Philadelphia Bulletin*, August 8, 1971), while gay or potentially sympathethic reviewers have sometimes found fault with the author's depiction of a bleak world full of disappointments and failure: "unflinchingly defeatist and wantonly anguished, so that any possible instructive catharsis is crushed by Curzon's determination to demonstrate how rotten the world is ... " (Richard Labonte, *In Touch*, 1985). But there is no uniformity of gay approval and heterosexual disapproval. Most often the reviews are absolute contradictions of one another, whether written by gay or nongay reviewers: "This [*Curzon in Love*] is a wonderful book and wonderful on so many levels" (Quentin Crisp, *Insider Magazine*, July 1989). "The wit is paper-thin (literally); you can see right through to the tremendous reservoir of hostility and contempt beneath" ("A.T." [Steven Saylor], *Inches*, 1988).

The failure of mainstream publications such as the *New York Times* to review gay work in general for many years and Curzon's work in particular (ever) has been a major factor in marginalizing his work, whereas these publications have covered women's and other minorities' work much more extensively. Curzon is one of the principal gay writers to walk the minefields of literary and social criticism to make it easier for those who have followed.

SELECTED WORKS OF DANIEL CURZON

Something You Do in the Dark. New York: G. P. Putnam, 1971; New York: Lancer Books, 1972.

Something You Do in the Dark (French translation by Andre Gilliard: De L'autre Cote de la Nuit). Paris: Edition Speciale, Edition et Publications Premieres, 1972.

Something You Do in the Dark. (Dutch translation: *Iets Dat Je Alleen in het Donker Doet*). Uithoorn: Nieuwe Wieken, N.V., 1972.

The Misadventures of Tim McPick. Los Angeles: John Parke Custis Press, 1975.

The Revolt of the Perverts. San Francisco: Leland Mellott Books, 1978.

Among the Carnivores. Port Washington, N.Y.: Ashley Books, 1979.

Something You Do in the Dark (revised version). Port Washington, N.Y.: Ashley Books, 1979.

Human Warmth and Other Stories. San Francisco: Grey Fox Press, 1981.

The Joyful Blue Book of Gracious Gay Etiquette. San Francisco: IGNA Books, 1982.

From Violent Men. San Francisco: IGNA Books, 1983.
The World Can Break Your Heart. Stamford, Conn.: Knights Press, 1985.
Curzon in Love. Stamford, Conn.: Knights Press, 1988.
Superfag. Stamford, Conn.: Knights Press, 1992.

Short Stories

"Two Bartenders, a Butcher, and Me." In *Aphrodisiac: Fiction from Christopher Street.* New York: Coward, McCann & Geoghegan, 1980. New York: A Perigree Book (Putnam), 1982; London: Chado & Windus, 1984.
"Virility." In *On the Line: New Gay Fiction.* Ed. Ian Young. Trumansburg, N.Y.: Crossing Press, 1981.
"Victor" and "Two Bartenders, a Butcher, and Me." In *Mae West Is Dead: Recent Lesbian and Gay Fiction.* Ed. Adam Mars-Jones. London: Faber and Faber, 1983.
"Zwei Barmanner, ein Metzger und ich." In *Aphrodisiac* (German translation). Munich: Knaur, 1986.

SELECTED STUDIES OF DANIEL CURZON

Sarotte, Georges-Michel. *Like a Brother, Like a Lover: Male Homosexuality in the American Novel and Theatre from Herman Melville to James Baldwin*, x, 171, 172, 174, 177–78, 301. Garden City: Anchor Press/Doubleday. 1978.
Curzon, Daniel. "Gay Literature after 'City of Night.' " *Los Angeles Times Book Review* 2 October 1988: 15.

CHRISTOPHER DAVIS
(1951(?)–   )
John H. Pearson

BIOGRAPHY

Christopher Davis is undoubtedly one of the most powerful voices in the literature about gay men. In his fiction, Davis repeatedly confronts the fundamental concerns of gay men, concerns with love, identity, self-esteem, community, and mortality. Davis is as much a literary artist as he is a remarkable storyteller. He seeks implicitly to discover a gay literary tradition and to further that tradition in his own work.

Jealous of his privacy, Davis has never revealed even the most basic of biographical information. One may assume from his fiction that Davis is familiar with New York City and the various enclaves along Fire Island. Yet even these assumptions are risky: Christopher Davis is anything but an autobiographical novelist. He writes from a wealth of experience that is common to gay men, though his lyricism bespeaks a talent rare among even the best of contemporary poets.

MAJOR WORKS AND THEMES

Davis's first book, *Joseph and the Old Man* (1986), is a story of love, sadness, and death. *Joseph and the Old Man* is from beginning to end a novel, like those written by the old man of its title, unerringly about life. Christopher Davis's characters range from the beautiful, sculpted men who come to Fire Island each summer in search of nothing more and nothing less than hedonistic pleasure, to an aging lesbian couple, Elizabeth and Mildred, who must face Mildred's imminent death to cancer and her final days of sickness and fatigue. At the heart of the novel, however, are Joseph and Oswald, who love each other passionately but comfortably, aggressively and intellectually, perhaps even aesthetically.

Joseph is a young, vital historian deeply absorbed in his research on Alexander the Great. He is in awe of the conqueror's phenomenal success, achieved at such a young age; his lover, Oswald (who is referred to throughout the novel as the old man, a nickname he acquires early in his relationship with Joseph), thinks that Joseph is blinded by Alexander's achievements to the Macedonian's brutal means of asserting his authority. In one academic argument while sunning on the beach, for example, Joseph and the old man argue whether Alexander's crucifixion of 2000 enemy men disqualifies Joseph's idol from the ranks of the heroic. The old man is an artist—a writer—who, like Christopher Davis, is far more concerned with morality and beauty and human suffering than with adventure and triumph. In this disagreement we see the essential difference that marks this relationship, a decade-long relationship between two men with thirty years separating them.

The novel begins as Joseph and the old man work side by side in their ocean front study. As time progresses slowly through the course of their tenth summer together, vast stretches of the past are recaptured and brought into the present as the old man reminisces. Joseph met the old man in college, where Joseph enrolled in a creative writing course taught by the old man. In spite of the age difference, the electricity between them was undeniable. At the start, Joseph was the aggressor. Like Alexander, he was the young adventurer and his teacher, the old man, was the exotic object of Joseph's desire. Davis makes the relationship especially poignant by having the old man relate their history to friends shortly after he receives news of Joseph's death.

The rituals of friendship that Joseph and the old man share with their neighbors depict the closely knit summer community of Cherry Grove. The same friends care so gently for the old man after Joseph's death that one cannot help but admire the emotional depth and breadth of the gay community that Christopher Davis has brought to life in this novel.

Davis owes much of his narrative technique to Gertrude Stein, to whom he refers intermittently in this novel and who the old man claims was a great influence on him. Davis's style in *Joseph and the Old Man* is intensely lyrical, often conveying meaning through the rhythm of the language as well as through the meaning of the words. Narrating a sad moment when the old man falls into a memory of his lover, Davis writes: "A small circle of clear memory opened and grew and the old man remembered Joe's face as it had looked in the candlelight at the restaurant and he heard Joe's voice as clearly as though Joe were in the room and had just stopped speaking and the sound of his voice was fading in the old man's ears. The old man remembered with a warmth and a sadness, but then he realized how clearly he was remembering and the circle closed and faded and his mind watched itself separate again" (106). The rhythm opens and closes as the narrative breathes a moment of life into the old man's reverie. And as the language itself becomes self-conscious, so too does the old man, who separates himself from his memory just as the narrative returns to the present moment.

Joseph and the Old Man is a novel of death and survival in the age of AIDS, but AIDS is never implicated here. Joseph dies in a car accident. The old man is left to bury the young and to grieve over a loss for which he could never be prepared. In this sense, Davis's novel transcends the temporal bounds of many recent gay novels of love and loss. It not only offers an emotionally rich landscape on which two men love deeply, but it reaches toward the goal of describing, if not creating, a gay aesthetic of fiction that is reflective, passionate, and painfully beautiful.

Christopher Davis's second novel is *Valley of the Shadow* (1988). The narrator, Andrew Ellis, is a young man dying of AIDS. The story is about his coming of age, but this gay *bildungsroman* ends with the narrator's obituary. The novel opens as a reminiscence of the narrator's youth and his first sexual encounter. As Andrew's sexual history unravels, we come to know him as a kind, fairly conventional young man who seems always in search of someone to lead him into the life for which he longs. Eventually, he finds his guide in Ted Erikson, the man who would become his lifelong, if intermittent, lover.

One of Davis's greatest talents is the ability to write exquisitely wrought prose through which he conveys the most subtle emotion. Early in the novel, he explores the dynamics of three generations of the Ellis family as they spend Christmas together. Harkening back to *Guess Who's Coming to Dinner*, Andrew, the youngest member of the family, brings his lover, Ted, home for the holiday. Davis draws this family portrait with both humor and sadness. Andrew's parents are warm and accepting; Andrew's grandfather is first confrontational and then morose. In this scene Davis establishes the pattern of partial acceptance coupled with partial rejection that characterizes Andrew and Ted's relationship with each other as well as with their families.

As in *Joseph and the Old Man*, *Valley of the Shadow* makes an explicit statement about the strength of the gay community as it struggles to maintain dignity and compassion in the face of death. After a long separation, Andrew passes Ted on the street. The two talk over lunch, and Andrew realizes both that he still loves Ted and that Ted is dying of AIDS. In response, Andrew brings Ted home and cares for him until his death. Davis shows clearly, however, that Andrew is motivated by love and loyalty, not by pity. When Andrew must face his own death from the disease, he sits down to write his memoirs, to leave a record of his love for Ted and of his experience as a gifted, sensual, gay human being.

Both of Davis's novels seek to overcome mortality by making death and grief highly aesthetic experiences. The old man has dream visions of Joseph that forever alter the way he will see the world. Andrew transforms Ted's life and death into his own narrative of growing to love himself and another man as completely as his humanity will allow. Davis seems driven to make enduring through art what has become far too fragile and fleeting—the passionate youth of gay men. Yet to emphasize the profound loss to the gay collective consciousness that AIDS has wrought, Davis allows his second narrator, Andrew Ellis, to lose much of his story in the well of forgetfulness. Personal histories and aesthetic reifications can save only so much of our lives, Davis suggests.

Boys in the Bar (1989) is Davis's most recent work. This collection of short stories begins with tales set in the days after Stonewall and before AIDS. Sexual encounters are not marked with thoughts of death in these first stories; they are moments of intense connection between two men. The final story in the collection, "Histories," is told by an older man in the future, reflecting back on the days before the cure for AIDS was discovered. With this narrative, Davis articulates his belief that AIDS is the cataclysm that brought the gay community out of its adolescence and into its middle age.

Like all of Davis's work, these stories are mostly about upper-middle-class professional men, many of whom have affairs, and sometimes fall in love, with young, not-so-innocent men. In this sense, Davis evokes the tradition of E. M. Forster and Christopher Isherwood.* Age is equated with economic and social status. Frequently, lovers are made Other in classist terms.

CRITICAL RECEPTION

Joseph and the Old Man went largely unnoticed by the critics. It was given a brief, lukewarm review in the *Boston Globe*. *Valley of the Shadow* brought Davis considerable public exposure. As a book about AIDS in the mid–1980s, *Valley* startled at least one reviewer because of its unswerving course toward the narrator's death. Noting that "this novel stirs up those ugly emotions about AIDS that we have all come to know only too well: regret, sadness, anger, loss, and ceaseless fear," Paul Reed* admits that he is "torn between the belief that a novel of despair is an utterly unconscionable creation and the understanding that the story of this novel is completely faithful to every reality about AIDS we have known until now" (61). Emmanuel S. Nelson, on the other hand, finds *Valley of the Shadow* a "poetic novel of remembrance"; Andrew Ellis's narration, "the articulation of his memory of Ted and remembrance of his own life, is a tender act of love, made all the more poignant by its defiant rendering in the face of death" (51–52). *The Boys in the Bars* was praised by Penny Kaganoff as an unforgettable, "compelling collection" of stories that bridges the chasm that AIDS has created in the history of gay culture (96).

WORKS BY CHRISTOPHER DAVIS

Joseph and the Old Man. New York: St. Martin's Press, 1986.
Valley of the Shadow. New York: St. Martin's Press, 1988.
Boys in the Bars. New York: Knights, 1989.

SELECTED STUDIES OF CHRISTOPHER DAVIS

"*Joseph and the Old Man*." *Boston Globe* 20 July 1986: 45.
Kaganof, Penny. "*The Boys in the Bars*." *Publishers Weekly* 30 June 1989, 96–97.
Nelson, Emmanuel S. "AIDS and the American Novel." *Journal of American Culture* 13 (Spring 1990): 47–53.
Reed, Paul. "*Valley of the Shadow*: Shell-Shocked by the Horror in Our Midst." *The Advocate* 21 June 1988: 61.

SAMUEL R. DELANY (1942–   )

Michael J. Emery

BIOGRAPHY

Samuel Ray ("Chip") Delany, Jr., was born April 1, 1942, in New York City. He grew up next to the family's mortuary in Harlem in middle-class circumstances. His mother's influence kept him in contact with the arts—music, theater, books—and he attended good schools at his father's insistence, including the renowned Bronx High School of Science. His high school experience gave him an accelerated education and introduced him to a generation of gifted peers that included Marilyn Hacker, whom he married in 1961 when she became pregnant by him (although she miscarried this child). Hacker, a brilliant poet who later won a National Book Award for her first book of poems, *Presentation Piece* (1974), had an incalculable effect on Delany's life and work. Although he told her he was gay before they were married, they struggled to maintain a relationship that produced a daughter they raised separately, parallel careers as writers, and ultimately a divorce in 1980.

Delany's early adult life emerges fully in his 1988 autobiography, *The Motion of Light in Water: Sex and Science Fiction Writing in the East Village, 1957–1965*, a book that shows him undergoing the beginnings of a gay consciousness well before the Stonewall Riots led to an organized movement. In this brilliant personal narrative, Delany's life is shown to be a series of contradictions: he was a young black gay dyslexic intellectual married to a white Jewish woman, attempting a low-paying writing career instead of a college degree (which he never seriously pursued), and living a subterranean sexual life on the streets of New York. Full of anecdotes about celebrities and unknowns (including a memorable dinner with W. H. Auden and his partner Chester Kallman), the book relates Delany's private sexual encounters with men (given in great detail) to his public life as a writer and husband. It concludes with a heartbreaking account of Hacker and Delany's relationship with Bob Folsom, who was hustling on the streets of New York when they took him in and who subsequently ended up in prison in Florida.

In 1961, Delany began writing science fiction/fantasy novels for Ace Books, where Hacker was then working as an editorial assistant. Well-versed in both pulp sf and "mainstream" literature, especially modern poetry, Delany brought a rich language and sophisticated perspective to traditional sf plots and themes. Delany's quick success in the field led to three Nebula Awards (given by the Science Fiction Writers of America) for the novels *Babel–17* and *The Einstein Intersection* and for the story "Aye, and Gomorrah"—all before the age of twenty-six. At the same time Delany's life was at odds with his success as a writer. He had had little financial reward for his books and had a fitful time reconciling his gayness with his marriage. So he began travelling and considering other directions in life.

For a time in 1967, Delany considered giving up his writing altogether to become a pop musician. Late in the year, he moved into a commune in the Lower East Village with band members of the short-lived group Heavenly Breakfast. His 1979 book of that name documents his life in a casually bisexual atmosphere of mutual tolerance and creativity at the height of 1960s counterculture. Concerned with "life lived humanely, day by day" (91), *Heavenly Breakfast* is a memoir of an experience that lasted only months but affected him profoundly, for all his later fiction proposes communal ways of life that permit varied expressions of sexual behavior outside tightly defined social roles.

Delany returned to the sf field and by 1970 had become one of the best-known and influential sf writers in the world. But the dislocations of his life led him into a massive reconsideration of his career as a writer. Influenced by the French intellectuals Barthes, Derrida, and Foucault and by the emerging liberation movements (black, feminist, and gay), Delany began producing a highly personal and demanding set of books that lost him many of his earlier fans. His best-known book of this period, *Dhalgren*, a long and sexually explicit experimental novel of decaying city life set in the near future, was a bestseller but also unpopular with many sf readers. After *Triton*, a utopia influenced by poststructuralist ideas, he embarked on a ten-year cycle of heroic fantasies set in a deliberately improbable prehistoric Mediterranean culture he called Neveryon. This cycle integrated all of his concerns into an extended meditation on variant sexuality, identity, and language as historical and contemporary phenomena. In 1984 he returned to sf with *Stars in My Pocket Like Grains of Sand*, the first half of a promised "diptych" of novels in a far-future setting. After the last Neveryon book in 1987, he published his autobiography, the first of his books marketed to a gay readership.

In middle age, Delany has settled into fatherhood and several stints as guest lecturer at American universities, including Cornell. He is presently completing the sequel to his 1984 sf novel, and in the fall of 1991 he addressed the conference on lesbian and gay studies held at Rutgers University.

MAJOR WORKS AND THEMES

Delany concerns himself with the importance of the marginal individual in any whole portrayal of life. When society marginalizes a person sexually or racially, it does so through the mechanism of oppression. Delany's oppressed characters embark on a quest for self through an attempt to understand their position in the larger scheme of things. This quest most often takes the form of a confrontation with language as a cultural tool that both oppresses and liberates, depending on one's awareness of the power relations inherent in it. Collectively, Delany's fiction serves to raise consciousness in the receptive reader. Nonrealistic fiction is for him the most congenial means to accomplish his literary task.

Delany's early work merely implies a gay perspective. His first novel, *The Jewels of Aptor* (1962), follows the story of a sea voyage similar to Jason's in Greek myth to restore the jewels of the title to their rightful owners and to prevent their use by evil powers. In the novel's post-holocaust Earth, the jewels are the last remnants of scientific know-how from an earlier culture that destroyed itself. One character on the quest is the thief Snake, a mutated victim of nuclear fallout who seems to be a masked gay figure at times. He is a telepath who sees more than the others but also feels acutely limited by prejudice against mutants. One homoerotic subplot involves Jordde and Ursus, a sadistic enslaver and slave who die fighting one another, locked in a contest of wills that Snake calls both hate and love. Delany later reconsiders this homoerotic situation in his Neveryon cycle.

Delany's first well-known book is *Babel–17* (1966), which won him his first major award. In it, a female poet named Rydra Wong deciphers a highly compressed alien language spoken by an enemy attempting to invade a future earth. *Babel–17* is Delany's first extended meditation on language as a shaper of experience. From a gay perspective, it shows the author searching for an alternative to the conventional heterosexual male protagonist typical of the sf novel. Of interest to gay readers is the three-way bisexual relationship basic to Wong's culture, a speculative variant of marriage based on Delany and Hacker's time with Bob Folsom.

Of Delany's pre-Stonewall work, the short story "Aye, and Gomorrah" has the strongest gay themes. It is one of the best stories written by a gay man in the 1960s. Delany creates in it a new "perversion" based on eroticizing the extinct sexual function of astronauts who have lived outside earth's atmosphere too long. The story's action follows the furlough joyride of several *frelks* (astronauts) to exotic spots, where they attract the attention of the frelk-fixated wherever they go, rendezvousing with them in public bathrooms and backstreet alleys. Indebted to the sexual activity described in his autobiography, the story captures the debasing aspects of the experience as well as its kicky fun. Since the perversion involves an inability to perform, it acts as an ironic metaphor for anonymous sex. That Delany replaces the word "Sodom" with a word of affirmation in his title also suggests the ambivalent feelings he has about the experiences described. Widely anthologized, the story can be found in both of Delany's collections of stories, *Driftglass* and *Distant Stars*.

Delany's post-Stonewall work is more consistently gay in its themes. A little-known work from 1973 that deserves to be better known is *The Tides of Lust*, an experiment in literary pornography that depicts various sexual couplings, mainly S/M and often gay, in a fantastic context. The book was published by Lancer Books shortly before that company collapsed, and only a few thousand copies were distributed. A later British edition was impounded by the government. This book, as well as another unpublished manuscript called *Hogg*—a radical work that follows the work of "rape artists" hired to violate others sexually, a phenomenon Delany says is based in fact—ought to be issued in a new edition by the gay press.

Dhalgren, Delany's sf novel published in 1975, follows the fate of a dyslexic drifter named "The Kid" in Bellona, an American city caught in an oddly timeless limbo that seems more psychological than actual. The Kid has many sexual encounters with people of both sexes, becomes the leader of a street gang of leather toughs, and moves into the city's highest circles. A gay bar provides the watering hole for characters in many of the novel's scenes. Delany's first major response to poststructuralist thought in his fiction, *Dhalgren* features an elaborately tooled language and an eddying plot that maddened many of his earlier fans, but the book found a wide audience outside the standard sf readership. Critics have given it a great deal of attention, primarily focusing on the collapsing social and literary structures in the book. Although its gay elements are diffused by the book's sheer length, they do remain distinct.

Following *Dhalgren*, Delany published *Triton* (1976), a more restrained depiction of a utopian future in which sexual difference is the norm. Sex changes and "refixations" (altered sexual orientations) are routine in this sexual utopia. Interestingly, Delany chose to locate the story's center of consciousness in Bron, a heterosexual male who resists the attitudes of his age and remains a sexual bigot. An ironic protagonist, Bron at one point changes his sex to female in order to pursue an ill-fated relationship (much as the Volker Spengler character does in R. W. Fassbinder's 1978 gay film, *In a Year of Thirteen Moons*). *Triton* critiques intolerance of sexual difference by reversing the terms of power common in the sexual attitudes of its time. It is one of Delany's most interesting books.

The one sf novel Delany has published since *Triton* is *Stars in My Pocket Like Grains of Sand* (1984), a striking work set in a far-future universe with six thousand populated planets. Like *Star Trek*, this future has a multicultural emphasis. The plot involves the relationship between two men—one enslaved by a sexual treatment that terminates his anxiety but makes him emotionally inert, the other an industrial diplomat attempting to bridge the cultural differences between planets. Their love works to change the potential fate of the known universe, but its outcome will not be clear until publication of a sequel, reportedly to be titled *The Splendor and Misery of Bodies, of Cities*. Oddly, the book was not published as a gay novel despite its gay characters and themes, and it deserves a wider readership as gay fiction.

Much of Delany's fiction works to critique conventional heterosexual thought. Nowhere is this trait better displayed than in his Neveryon cycle, a series of four books published between 1979 and 1987. Their titles are *Tales of Neveryon, Neveryona, Flight from Neveryon*, and *The Bridge of Lost Desire*. Only the second is a full novel; the others are linked stories, all concerning a primitive Old World civilization that mirrors important aspects of contemporary America. Taken as a whole, the Neveryon cycle constitutes Delany's most sustained achievement as a gay writer. The cycle portrays homosocial partnerings, both male and female, in a heroic fantasy (or sword and sorcery) narrative complete with dragons, swordswomen, and gay heroes. Most of the described sex involves male prostitutes, for the tales are located at an imagined historical point at which a barter economy is shifting to a money economy in which individuals must market themselves to survive. (One of the telling images of the books is that of slave collars being melted down to make iron coins for the day laborers newly "freed" from slavery; one enslavement simply replaces another.) Except for Pryn, only men who have sex with other men by inclination or for profit get strongly characterized. These books offer a fresh gay-liberation perspective, for the social criticism they contain fully integrates sexual difference into their narrative.

With such a wide canvas on which to create his world—always rendered as a literary construct the reader is aware does not exist—Delany has ample space to bring a varied set of characters to metafictional life. Chief (but not central) is Gorgik the Liberator, a huge and muscular warrior who escapes slavery and sets himself the task of ending slavery in his land. He is not central in that the decentered nature of these postmodern narratives refuses to accommodate him as such. A few of the tales primarily concern him, but mostly he is felt as an absent presence and hope for the future by other downtrodden characters, who hear of him only by rumor or see him only in passing. The story of Gorgik impinges on everyone in Neveryon, however, and his self-empowerment as a gay liberator is one of the most interesting aspects of the books. In opposition to the heterosexual power structures of matriarchy and patriarchy, Gorgik creates a kind of "homarchy" (or rule by gay man, for want of any equivalent term our language has refused us) that balances the heterosexual alliances of power in Neveryon. To do so, he must join the very forces on which he has waged a terrorist war for much of his adult life. The government finally accepts him into its power structure in order to counter a social panic created by the outbreak of an AIDS-like disease in Neveryon. Thus these stories work to reflect contemporary gay life, despite their fantasy.

In the first book, *Tales of Neveryon* (1979), the first and third tales are most important to the cycle's gay themes. In "The Tale of Gorgik," the character's pre-liberation days are recounted. Thrown into slavery as a child, Gorgik works in the mines of Neveryon until he charms some influential individuals and becomes part of the High Court of Eagles. However, he offends one corrupt leader through ignorance of the mazelike social protocol required at court and is then sent away to be trained as a swordsman in military service. This talent he harnesses to lead others to the end of slavery in Neveryon. In "The Tale of Small Sarg," Gorgik purchases a young barbarian slave and has sex with him, but only under the condition that one wear a slave collar during the encounter, for Gorgik has eroticized the collar while a slave. The collar as sexual fetish is not a replication of oppression here or elsewhere in the books; it is a therapeutic reenactment that transfers the terms of power to two men who trade off on master/slave roles and thus take command of their sexual selves. Gorgik and Sarg then develop a strategy of liberation in which one allows himself to be caught as a slave while the other breaks into his prison and frees him and other slaves there. Each raid broadens the base of an underground movement subversive to the so-called civilization that fails to extend its power and protection to the majority of people living within it.

The second book, *Neveryona; or, The Tale of Signs and Cities* (1983), has the most winning protagonist in the cycle. Pryn is a young woman on a picaresque quest for selfhood and a clear place in life. She meets Gorgik early on in the novel, while his rebellion is still precarious and at a time when his first lover Sarg is murdered for betraying the cause by the man who becomes his second lover, Noyeed. In her quest for self, Pryn eventually realizes that she has been enslaved to other people's ideas of what she should be and do with her life and finally joins a mummer's troupe to help create the art of her time. In this novel, the terms of liberation shift from gender orientation to gender itself. More than the other books, this one is preoccupied with a poststructuralist debate on language and culture. Although dry at times, the book's debates offer a theoretical foundation for a radical critique of contemporary heterosexual society.

The third book, *Flight from Neveryon*, is the most consistently gay in its themes, particularly in its long third section, "The Tale of Plagues and Carnivals." If the earlier tales show the seams of their fictional origin, this tale has those seams splitting and unravelling. It parallels an autobiographical fiction on the impact of AIDS on contemporary New York with the outbreak of the same disease (though unnamed) in Neveryon. The emotional and social impact of the illness then and now mirrors one another. The New York setting follows the author's relationship with Joey, a junkie street hustler whose already minimal life is further threatened by the disease. Meanwhile in Neveryon, the Child Empress Ynelgo invites Gorgik back to the High Court of Eagles to distract a panicked populace fearful of the new disease. This tale was completed in the spring of 1984, a time when new findings were shifting knowledge of AIDS dramatically by the month. It has the feel of a rushed report from the front and, though premature, offers a sometimes compelling portrait of a time of confusion and urgency about the disease. The book bravely confronts the reality of a sad time.

The fourth book, *The Bridge of Lost Desire*, was the only one originally published in hardcover and is in many ways the best of the four. It contains three tales that move chronologically from the end of the Neveryon cycle back to its beginnings. This movement is artistically satisfying, for it embodies the theme of return that the book's appendix promises it will. The first story, "The Game of Time and Pain," is an extended monologue by Gorgik set six years after slavery has been abolished because of his influence. Recollections of abortive sexual encounters come up in the context of a failed seduction scene. The "lost desire" of the book's title becomes emblematic of sexual loss in an era of gay death. The fullest philosophy of the collar also emerges here, as we realize that the collar is a talisman that spurs Gorgik to create new possibilities of self-expression for himself and others. The collar brings our attention to a larger collar that both enslaves and liberates—language itself. Language deceives and inhibits freedom, but it is also the only hope we have for a greater freedom. As this tale makes clear, it is both our culture's revenge and our own access to power.

The second story, "The Tale of Rumor and Desire," is the single best of the Neveryon cycle. A shrewd reversal of the reader's view of a failed human being, the story gives us the sexual history of Clodon, an unpleasant person who has spent his life committing crimes and hustling on the Bridge of Lost Desire in Kolhari. He refuses to wear a collar to attract those who eroticize it. Instead, he drifts from one bout of trouble to another, until his fate finally catches up with him near one of the last dragon lairs in Neveryon. He has the only sexually fulfilling experience of his life there with a woman who offers herself to him though he has done nothing to deserve her. While the episode does not redeem him, it does show the reader what happens to a marginal individual who has internalized the values of his own corrupt society. That the most epiphanic moment in the cycle is heterosexual is only one of the many ironies that echo throughout the books.

The final tale is an extended version of the first, "The Tale of Gorgik." It makes sense at the end, for its potentialities resonate far more there than at the start. Among those potentialities is Delany's attempt to mythologize homosexuality at the point that heterosexuality was in fact mythologized: in prehistory. Aware that it can only be imagined, Delany remains willing to take the risks involved, knowing this task needs to be done.

CRITICAL RECEPTION

Although widely discussed as an sf writer, Samuel Delany has had a very limited recognition as a gay writer. The shift in his works to a more theoretical bent in the 1970s met a negative reaction that was also homophobically motivated, at least in part. Delany's new direction challenged many readers willing to follow him, but they had little impact on the critics of his work, who have largely ignored his sexual themes. Two articles in the gay press that acknowledged his work appeared in *Gay Community News* in 1980 and *The Advocate* in 1982. Seth McEvoy's 1984 study has a progay perspective but is limited by a simplified format aimed at high school libraries. Most of his recent critics have at least mentioned that he is a gay black man, but they minimize that fact in their consideration of his work. For instance, in an otherwise solid analysis of his novels, John J. Pierce (in "Free Radical") offers a homophobic reading of *Stars in My Pocket*, complaining of the novel's focus "on gay romance" (111). It is only the Hugo Award won by *The Motion of Light in Water* for best nonfiction work about sf in 1988 that indicates any diminution of intolerance for Delany's gay themes among his sf readership. Given his autobiography's success, Delany's gay voice will now be more difficult to ignore in critical treatments of his work. Still, it remains to his gay readers to assess his achievement as an important gay writer now that he is recognized to be one. That recognition is long overdue, for in his intellectually challenging and socially concerned narratives of gay experience, Delany offers a unique voice that deserves to be heard.

WORKS BY SAMUEL R. DELANY

Fiction

The Jewels of Aptor. New York: Ace, 1962.
The Ballad of Beta–2. New York: Ace, 1965.
Empire Star. New York: Ace, 1966.
Babel–17. New York: Ace, 1966.
The Einstein Intersection. New York: Ace, 1967.
Nova. New York: Doubleday, 1968.
The Fall of the Towers. New York: Ace, 1970. (Trilogy originally published 1963–1965.)
Driftglass: Ten Tales of Speculative Fiction. New York: NAL, 1971.
The Tides of Lust. New York: Lancer, 1973.
Dhalgren. New York: Bantam, 1975.

Triton. New York: Bantam, 1976.
Tales of Neveryon. New York: Bantam, 1979.
Distant Stars. New York: Bantam, 1981. (Stories)
Neveryona. New York: Bantam, 1983.
Stars in My Pocket Like Grains of Sand. New York: Bantam, 1984.
Flight from Neveryon. New York: Bantam, 1985.
The Complete Nebula Award-Winning Fiction. New York: Bantam, 1986.
The Bridge of Lost Desire. New York: Arbor House, 1987.

Nonfiction

The Jewel-Hinged Jaw. Elizabethtown, N.Y.: Dragon Press, 1977.
The American Shore. Elizabethtown, N.Y.: Dragon Press, 1978.
Heavenly Breakfast. New York: Bantam, 1979.
Starboard Wine. Elizabethtown, N.Y.: Dragon Press, 1984.
The Motion of Light in Water. New York: Arbor House, 1988.
Wagner/Artaud. New York: Ansatz Press, 1988.
The Straits of Messina. Seattle: Serconia Press, 1989.

SELECTED STUDIES OF SAMUEL R. DELANY

Califia, Pat. "Samuel Delany: Setting Future Limits." *The Advocate* 9 December 1982: 39–41, 65.
Kuras, Pat M., and Rob Schmieder. "When It Changed: Lesbians, Gay Men, and Science Fiction Fandom." *Gay Community News* 27 September 1980: 8–10.
McCaffery, Larry, and Sinda Gregory, eds. *Alive and Writing: Interviews with American Authors of the 1980s*. Urbana: University of Illinois Press, 1987.
McEvoy, Seth. *Samuel R. Delany*. New York: Ungar, 1984.
Pierce, John J. "The Literary Reformation." *When World Views Collide: A Study in Imagination and Evolution*. Westport, Conn.: Greenwood, 1989. 103–12.

MELVIN DIXON (1950–1992)
Wilfrid R. Koponen

BIOGRAPHY

Melvin Dixon was born on May 29, 1950, in Stamford, Connecticut. Dixon says, "Stamford affected my writing a great deal. The large, significant black community I grew up in is one of my reference points." In a neighborhood barbershop, Dixon "listened to the vibrant folklore and stories that the people had brought with them from the South" (Stephania Davis, D6). Dixon's father, Handy, a house painter and contractor, came from Pee Dee, North Carolina, the principal setting in *Trouble the Water* (1989). Pee Dee is also invoked in the opening line (and elsewhere) in Dixon's *Change of Territory*. Dixon's mother, Jessie, a nurse, came from South Carolina. Although both parents maintained close ties with the South, Dixon has said that because of his father's family's reticence Pee Dee was always a place of mystery. Dixon's first poem was published when he was seventeen, before he left Stamford to attend Wesleyan University.

Two of Dixon's plays were produced at Wesleyan. He graduated in 1971 with a joint English/theater major. He aspired to be a novelist by the time he began his graduate work in American civilization at Brown University. In 1973, he completed a novel with themes (a return to the South, etc.) that appear in *Trouble the Water*. He earned his M.A. in 1973 and his Ph.D. in 1975. During graduate school he felt torn between his academic and creative muses (interview, September 26, 1985). Dixon feels that being a published author of poetry and fiction is his greatest accomplishment, despite a list of sterling scholarly achievements, including a Fulbright lectureship in Senegal. In addition to his two published novels and his book of poems, Dixon has translated books of poetry and literary criticism from the French and has published numerous poems, short stories, reviews, and scholarly works. He was professor of English at the

Graduate School and at Queens College, City University of New York (CUNY), a position that allowed him to don the hats of both scholar and writer of fiction and poetry.

On October 26, 1992, Dixon died of complications from AIDS.

MAJOR WORKS AND THEMES

Dixon's skillful use of setting in his novels is anticipated in *Ride Out the Wilderness: Geography and Identity in Afro-American Literature* (1987), which delineates the motifs of wilderness, underground, and mountaintop in African-American literature, settings that figure in Dixon's novels. Dixon evokes and provides ironic twists to the wilderness and mountaintop motifs in *Trouble the Water* (1989), and he explores the underground through the character of Metro in *Vanishing Rooms* (1991).

Escape through the wilderness from the rural South to the urban North has been a staple of black narrative since the Underground Railroad. In *Trouble the Water*, the protagonist Jordan Henry runs away from Pee Dee early in life. He reappears years later, a Harvard graduate and professor whose specialty is New England's colonial history, married to Phyllis Whitehead, the daughter of Boston's most prominent black lawyer. Jordan remembers his childhood upon his return to Pee Dee, secretely orchestrated by Mother Harriet, Jordan's maternal grandmother, the matriarch who raised him. She lingers on her deathbed to exact revenge upon Jordan's shiftless (absent) father Jake for her daughter (Jordan's mother) Chloe's death at the time of Jordan's birth. Harriet's obsession has wounded Jordan deeply, and one wonders at the novel's end if Jordan can be made whole after all the repression and hatred he has endured.

Henry Louis Gates, Jr., praises Dixon for his "manipulation of the unfashionable but still potent form" of the Southern gothic. "He clearly enjoys serving up the devices of the genre" (7). But Dixon critiques the literary archetypes he evokes. He assaults the sentimentalization of black matriarchs in Mother Harriet. The rural South to which Jordan returns is no pastoral panacea. The hilltop of Jordan's childhood home hints of the mountaintop, which suggests revelation, Moses, the Ten Commandments, and the Transfiguration. But the clarity suggested by the mountaintop is lacking at the novel's end. Even when Jordan finally expresses to Phyllis his memory of his sexual experience in the wilderness with his childhood playmate Mason, who died in a car accident shortly thereafter, he is met with incomprehension:

> "And I held him until he came, Phyllis. Like this. But that's all I did. Really.... Harriet said I couldn't love him like that."
>
> "Oh, I see," said Phyllis. (203)

Phyllis doesn't see; and the homoeroticism Jordan recalls, like most of his feelings, remains unarticulated.

Dixon explores gay themes more candidly in *Vanishing Rooms* and tackles gay-bashing, homosexual rape, and an interracial gay relationship, "Dixon is ... trying to nudge gay fiction away from the typical 'coming out' story ... into an exploration of what comes after coming out" (Marks, 27). Whereas *Trouble the Water* plays with images of wilderness and mountaintop, Dixon delves into myths of the sexual underground and the gay urban jungle—Manhattan in 1975, post-Stonewall and pre-AIDS—in his second novel. The pivotal event occurs at the outset: the brutal gay-bashing, rape, and murder of Metro, a white journalist from the rural South, whose black lover, Jesse, a dancer from the urban North, must cope. The narrative consists of first-person chapters from the points of view of Jesse, Ruella, the dance partner he turns to in his grief, and Lonny, whose gang killed Metro. The relationship between Jesse and Metro "is only sketched, not fully painted" (Marks 28). Metro does not appear in the novel in his own narrative voice. Dixon says in *Christopher Street*, "We've heard a lot about white gay experience. . . . [Metro's] absence . . . is deliberate, because we have not heard from Jesse in our literature, we have not heard from Ruella, we have not heard from Lonny" (25).

In one of Dixon's allusions to the mountaintop motif, Jesse ascends seven floors of a gay bathhouse named Paradise, a parody of Dante's *Divine Comedy*, passing sexual fantasy scenes (army barracks, prison, etc.). Ironically, Jesse confronts his Inferno in the highest level of Paradise. Jesse here sees with the clarity of the mountaintop the racism that poisoned his relationship with Metro after they had graduated from Wesman (Wesleyan?) in Connecticut and moved to Manhattan: "I'm Metro, remember. . . . You want it low. You want me to take you there. . . . Well, down under you ain't nothing but a nigger" (114). Surrounded by unrestrained sexual fantasies (an implicit critique of the gay sexual excesses of the 1970s), Jesse realizes that he represented for Metro "the forbidden pleasures of strong black limbs, and the promise of going under the racial barrier" (Grant, 52). Dixon suggests that racism inevitably surfaces in interracial gay relationships. As Dixon insists, a white gay man "can have a black boyfriend and still be racist" (*Christopher Street*, 27).

Dixon defies many taboos in *Vanishing Rooms*. He depicts the occasional heterosexual forays some gay men make via Jesse's liaison with Ruella. Most daringly, perhaps, Dixon fathoms the psyche of a gay basher in the chapters told from Lonny's point of view. Dixon admits, "I've been criticized for even writing Lonny's character" (*Christopher Street*, 25). Randall Kenan* concludes, "Dixon manages to tell us a great deal in his 210 pages, sometimes more than we think we might want to know, but never gratuitously" (48).

CRITICAL RECEPTION

Trouble the Water (1989) won the Nilon Award for Excellence in Minority Fiction. Henry Louis Gates, Jr., says, "Melvin Dixon is best known as a poet, and *Trouble the Water* is...a poet's novel:...it's propelled by the lyricism of its language" (7). *Kirkus Reviews* calls it "an eloquent family saga—at times surreal and expressionistic, at times naturalistic....Dixon adeptly integrates dialect, fairy tale elements, dreams, and old songs into a compelling narrative" (August 15, 1989). A few reviewers berate Dixon: "unfortunately Mr. Dixon's lyrical prose cloys" (Kennedy, 48), but surely Charles and Mitchell are idiosyncratic in saying that "[Dixon's] language rarely rises above the ordinary" (79).

Dixon is at his best in the flashbacks of Jordan and his childhood friend Mason. "Dixon's most luminous writing recalls the death of Jordan's childhood friend and his youthful realization that he loved the boy, body and soul" while "scenes of the northern college town...threaten to derail the book with blandness" (Thulani Davis, 27).

The book's major disappointment is the denouement (*Kirkus Reviews* August 15, 1989), which seems contrived. Gates says, "the moment of catharsis is too easy to be persuasive" (7). Kennedy finds a "false note [in] the unconvincing scene of violence between Jordan and his father" (48), arguably the book's only unconvincing scene. Leonard Feather, however, calls the climax "less than completely predictable" (2).

Critics have praised Dixon's exploration of violent racism and homophobia in his second novel, *Vanishing Rooms*. Although most reviewers have been free from homophobia, Ned Condini is not: "The style purports to reflect life as an intricate dance,...[b]ut the stereotyped dance is ultimately macabre....[The novel is] a lurid manual of homosexual lovemaking that is...tedious and self-indulging" (32). Other reviewers neither criticize nor justify the novel's frank treatment of gay themes, focusing instead upon the novel's literary merits, for instance, the skill with which Dixon uses the Faulknerian device of interweaving different first-person narratives. Kenan calls *Vanishing Rooms* "a poetic rendering of three-part harmony" (46). The *Library Journal* avers, "Each character has a distinct voice" (147), and *Publishers Weekly* claims that "Dixon creates convincing psychological characterizations" (43). Marks states that "Dixon's greatest success is the skill with which he enters into the consciousness of his characters" (27). "Large parts of *Vanishing Rooms* are written with lyricism so perfect that any distinction between poetry and prose is beside the point," John Preston argues (64).

Ironically, much critical reception of *Vanishing Rooms* focuses on Lonny, the white lower-middle-class teenager whose sexual ambivalence and cowardice provoke Metro's murder. Ruella, like Jesse and Metro, has received less attention. "Ruella benefits much from Dixon's graceful prose, but is just a shade too good to be true," one reviewer writes (Grant, 52). Although *Kirkus Reviews* insists: "Neither [Lonny's] language nor his attitudes ring true as those of a white slum kid" (65), like many others, Marks says Lonny "has the most beautiful and powerful language" (28) with plausible psychological intensity.

Comparisons between *Vanishing Rooms* and James Baldwin's *Giovanni's Room* are perhaps inevitable. Though Dixon acknowledges his debt to earlier African-American writers, he is not content to "play it safe" by treading well-worn paths. In exploring interracial gay relationships and gay bashing, from the point of view of victim and basher, and in his fusion of poetic and novelistic elements, Dixon breaks new ground. Jim Marks speaks for many in concluding that "Dixon gives every promise of making substantial contributions to American literature" (28).

WORKS BY MELVIN DIXON

Change of Territory (poems). Callaloo Poetry Series. Lexington: University of Kentucky, 1983. Rpt. Charlottesville: University Press of Virginia.

Translation. *Drumbeats, Masks, and Metaphor: Contemporary Afro-American Theater.* By Genevieve Fabre. Cambridge, Mass.: Harvard University Press, 1983.

Ride Out the Wilderness: Geography and Identity in Afro-American Literature. Urbana, Ill.: University of Illinois Press, 1987.

Trouble the Water (novel). Boulder: University of Colorado and Fiction Collective Two, 1989.

Translation and Introduction. *The Collected Poems of Léopold Sédar Senghor.* Charlottesville: University Press of Virginia, 1991.

Vanishing Rooms (novel). New York: Dutton, 1991.

SELECTED STUDIES OF MELVIN DIXON

Charles, Nick, and Angela Mitchell. "Book Bag: Lifting Every Voice: Books That Speak for Us." Rev. of *Trouble the Water. Emerge* January 1990: 79.

Condini, Ned. "Three Lives Entwined in Macabre Dance." Rev. of *Vanishing Rooms. National Catholic Reporter* 10 May 1991: 32.

Davis, Stephania H. "Stamford Arthor Comes Back Home." *Stamford Advocate* 25 February 1990: D1, 6.

Davis, Thulani. "Black Novelists Head for the Mainstream." Rev. of *Trouble the Water. Voice Literary Supplement* May 1990: 26–28.

Dixon, Melvin. Interview. "Memories of a Long and Angry Night." With Darryl Grant. *Washington Blade* 26 April 1991: 43, 52.

———. Interview. "Other Voices, Other Rooms." With Clarence Bard Cole. *Christopher Street* 14, no. 1 (1991): 24–27.

Feather, Leonard. "The Homecoming of a Black Preppie." Rev. of *Trouble the Water. Los Angeles Times* 1 October 1989: 2.

Flanagan, Margaret. Rev. of *Trouble the Water*. *Booklist* 86 (15 October 1989): 426.

Forbes, Calvin. "Writing from the African Diaspora." Rev. of *Trouble the Water*. *Washington Post* 4 March 1990: 1.

Gates, Henry Louis, Jr. "Eros and Thanatos Both." Rev. of *Trouble the Water*. *American Book Review* July–August 1990: 7.

Grant, Darryl. "With *Vanishing Rooms*, Melvin Dixon Makes Powerful Appearance." *Washington Blade* 26 April 1991: 52.

Kenan, Randall. "Bookbag: Closed Doors Opened: Portrait of a Gay-Bashing." Rev. of *Vanishing Rooms*. *Emerge* April 1991: 46–47.

Kennedy, Constance Decker. Rev. of *Trouble the Water*. *New York Times Book Review* 9, no. 4 (24 September 1989): 48.

Marks, Jim. "Mean Streets and Shades of Baldwin." Rev. of *Vanishing Rooms*. *Lambda Book Report* May/June 1991: 27–28.

Peterson, V. R. "Melvin Dixon: Wrestling with Baldwin." *Essence* 22, no. 4 (August 1991): 42

Preston, John. "Victory Dance." Rev. of *Vanishing Rooms*. *Outweek* 10 April 1991: 64.

Rev. of *Trouble the Water*. *Calaloo* 13 (Fall 1990): 913.

Rev. of *Trouble the Water*. *Kirkus Reviews* 57 (15 August 1989): 1186.

Rev. of *Vanishing Rooms*. *Kirkus Reviews* 59 (15 January 1991): 65.

Rev. of *Vanishing Rooms*. *Library Journal* 116 (January 1991): 147.

Rev. of *Vanishing Rooms*. *Publishers Weekly* 18 January 1991: 43.

Satuloff, Bob. "Improvising Destiny." Rev. of *Vanishing Rooms*. *New York Native* 29 April 1991: 30.

LARRY DUPLECHAN (1956–   )
John H. Pearson

BIOGRAPHY

"My life is an open book," Larry Duplechan is fond of saying. In fact, his work has strong autobiographical overtones. Duplechan admits that Johnnie Ray Rousseau, the protagonist of his first two novels, "is my alter-ego. Just about all Johnnie Ray's likes, dislikes, attitudes, beliefs, political leanings, sexual quirks, and bad jokes coincide strikingly with my own" ("CS Interview with Larry Duplechan," 61). A black man raised in a predominantly white environment, Larry Duplechan came of age as an outsider who, ironically, found himself at the center of things. He was born on December 30, 1956, in Panorama City, California. He grew up in Los Angeles, spending two years in Sacramento. After high school, Duplechan attended the University of California at Los Angeles, where he received a B.A. in English.

Although he has always been both a voracious reader and, according to his teachers, a gifted writer, Duplechan was never fond of writing. His first career, and his first love, was music. Duplechan spent six years after graduating from college singing in clubs in and around Los Angeles. His first novel, *Eight Days a Week* (1985) draws heavily on Duplechan's experiences during this period of his life.

After leaving the music business, Duplechan sought an outlet for his creativity and turned to writing fiction. He writes during the evening and on weekends, when he's not working to support himself at a Los Angeles law firm. Central to his life, however, is his sixteen-year relationship with his lover, Greg, whom Duplechan calls in the acknowledgments of *Blackbird* "the best 'author's wife' a guy could ask for."

MAJOR WORKS AND THEMES

Eight Days a Week is a comic love story about a black nightclub singer who falls in love with gorgeous white men. Duplechan explores the sense of otherness that Rousseau feels when the white men he dates confess that he is the first black man they have made love to or that he is the first black man that they have ever been attracted to. In short, Rousseau is frequently made aware that his blackness is considered his most important attribute. The feeling, of course, is one of anger mixed with some resignation. Duplechan also notes how other gay black men react to Johnnie Ray's preference for white men: "I was once told by a black alto sax player named Zaz (we were in bed at the time, mind you) that my preference for white men (and blonds, the whitest of white, to boot) was the sad but understandable end result of 300 years of white male oppression" (28). Yet as Charles I. Nero explains, Johnnie Ray's "sexual attraction to white men is anything but the result of 300 years of white male oppression.... It allows Duplechan a major moment of signifying in African American literature: the sexual objectification of white men by a black man" (237).

Duplechan is deeply concerned in this novel with both the problems and the pleasures of interracial gay love. To emphasize the difference between Johnnie Ray and his white lover, Keith, Duplechan stereotypes Keith as a blond, blue-eyed body builder who works at a bank, listens to Wagner while he reads the *Wall Street Journal*, and who likes to be in bed, preferably making love to Johnnie Ray, by 10 p.m. Johnnie Ray, on the other hand, is fond of staying up all night at a local diner with his best friend and accompanist, Snookie. Differences of temperament, life-style, ambitions, and careers seem embodied somehow in the racial difference that so strongly attracts Johnnie Ray and Keith to each other. Duplechan suggests in *Eight Days* that what so strongly attracts equally repels: Johnnie Ray and Keith break up because they cannot reconcile their diametrically opposing desires. Yet difference, or otherness, is exactly that which both men seek. Neither wants or seems capable of falling in love with a man like himself. Johnnie Ray is repeatedly attracted to white men; Keith becomes involved with others who look very much like him but for one clear distinction—they are women.

In *Eight Days* Duplechan suggests that for Johnnie Ray Rousseau, being gay has a greater influence on his identity than being black. In an interview with Christopher Davis, Larry Duplechan asserts that this reflects his own experience: "My gay identity is much more important to me [than my black identity]. But more than that, I am very much an assimilationist. By that I mean, I have no desire to set myself apart from the white gay men ... or from black gays or white heterosexuals or Native American bisexual leather dominatrixes, for that matter" ("CS Interview with Larry Duplechan," 62). Johnnie Ray affirms his gay identity repeatedly in *Eight Days* and often in the most heterosexist circumstances, such as his place of employment, a very posh Los Angeles law firm.

Blackbird (1987) is the coming-of-age story of Johnnie Ray Rousseau. We meet the young Johnnie Ray when he is still in high school. His fascination with beautiful white boys and the isolation he feels because he imagines himself to be the only gay person he knows nearly overwhelm him. Yet this is the story of Johnnie Ray's triumph over the small-mindedness of the suburbs, for it ends in what seems like Johnnie Ray's apotheosis as he enters the gay student union at UCLA to discover the community for which he had yearned most of his life.

Duplechan draws this portrait of adolescence with great care. For example, he explores the hopelessness and anguish that are so often part of youth, gay or straight. When one of Johnnie Ray's friends becomes pregnant, she is sent away by her father, a Baptist minister, to have her baby in obscurity. Soon after she leaves, however, she attempts to abort the baby; the attempt ultimately costs her her life. Her boyfriend then disappears, returning only briefly to say good-by to Johnnie Ray before riding his motorcycle off a cliff. Johnnie Ray's struggles are honestly depicted but softened by retrospection: Johnnie Ray is telling his story after surviving his teenage years. His is the voice of reason and compassion in a world that seems insanely focused on propriety, status, and appearance. When Johnnie Ray's best friend, Efrem, is brutally beaten by his father, for instance, Johnnie Ray confesses both his horror at the sight of his friend in the hospital and the sudden joy to discover the reason for the attack: Efrem, like Johnnie Ray, is gay. These interwoven stories of late adolescence reveal the struggle for control over one's life and the equally compelling desire to remain a child that consume most every teenager.

Perhaps the most talked about scene in *Blackbird* is Johnnie Ray's exorcism. After the family minister reveals the secret of the boy's sexuality to Johnnie Ray's parents, the family and the man of God take Johnnie Ray to a local exorcist who will, they believe, deliver Johnnie Ray from the demons of perversion that are fighting for his soul. Duplechan's comic touch is nowhere else so welcome as here. Johnnie Ray screams "Hallelujah" after an hour of keening and praying for deliverance. The scream is one of hysterical annoyance at the goings-on and an attempt to be delivered from the inquisitory horse-and-pony show in which he is being forced to participate. The exorcism parodies the many attempts to "cure" homosexuality, which are attempts really to vilify and subjugate homosexual men and women.

While the politics of race are less pressing in this novel, they are seldom far from Duplechan's mind. Johnnie Ray is inevitably coupled with the only black girl in his crowd. Like Keith in *Eight Days a Week*, Johnnie Ray seeks sexual gratification in otherness: a black *woman*, a *white* man. This theme dominates Duplechan's first two novels, though it takes an unusual turn—

unusual, that is, to all but the readers of James Baldwin's* *Giovanni's Room*—in Duplechan's third novel, *Tangled Up in Blue*.

Tangled Up in Blue (1989) addresses the AIDS epidemic through the lives of Maggie and Daniel Sullivan and their gay friend Crockett. When Crockett is diagnosed as HIV-positive, Daniel decides that he should be tested too, and that is when Maggie first discovers that her husband and her best friend were once lovers. The emotional range of this novel is expansive. Duplechan writes about a woman's sexual desire with sensitivity and deep feeling. He also describes the emotional crisis that binds and separates Maggie, Daniel, and Crockett.

Daniel and Crockett meet while performing in a small production of *A Midsummer Night's Dream*. Daniel is straight; Crockett is gay. Yet Crockett will not rest until he seduces Daniel—the man who looks so much like Christopher Reeve that people repeatedly mistake him for Superman. Their relationship is steamy at first, for Daniel is undeniably attracted to Crockett. When they decide to become platonic and when Daniel decides to marry Maggie, Crockett remains a central figure in Daniel's life and eventually becomes Maggie's best friend. That is what makes *Tangle Up in Blue* so poignant. It is not the story of a triangulated love, nor is it the story of one man's inadvertent outing. In *Tangled Up in Blue* Duplechan rigorously explores the horrible truth that AIDS can and does invade and destroy the lives of its victims. And its victims include many who are not infected with the virus. The polemical occasion of this novel was the first televised announcement that Rock Hudson had AIDS. Only then did AIDS enter the vocabulary of popular culture. Duplechan's response is *Tangled Up in Blue*, the story that foretold how severely our loyalties and our hearts would be tried by the disease.

What is startling about this novel when it is read in the context of Duplechan's other work is that all the main characters are white. Both Daniel and Crockett could be the usual objects of desire in Duplechan's other novels. Daniel is tall, dark, muscular, and devastatingly handsome. Crockett is blond, blue-eyed, and beautiful. Duplechan has absented himself from this story perhaps in an effort to maintain his focus on the issues of AIDS, sexuality, and the nature of love among friends. And because race is not one of the variables in this novel, the other forms of difference are more thoroughly and convincingly depicted.

This novel was a risk for Duplechan. With his first two books, he had developed a following of readers hungry for fiction that universalizes the experience of being young and gay and that particularizes the experience of being young, gay, and black. When *Tangled Up in Blue* first appeared, Duplechan found himself compared to Baldwin when Baldwin was alienated from the black literary community for breaking ranks with Richard Wright and for writing *Giovanni's Room*, another novel with no black characters.

In short, some of his readers felt betrayed. Yet by focusing his energies on material that does not reflect his own experiences, Duplechan has grown as a writer. *Tangled Up in Blue* is not as successful as *Blackbird*, but it is a far more ambitious and a far more serious novel. Moreover, it is his first novel written in the third person. One might conjecture that Duplechan is an observer of the novel's stage, not the performer at its center.

CRITICAL RECEPTION

Eight Days a Week and *Blackbird* were virtually ignored in the straight press. Both novels, however, were noticed by the gay press and were lauded as the novels of gay black experience that had long been awaited. Duplechan is so candid about the politics of race in the gay community and in mainstream American society, and he is so honest about his black characters' desires to be immersed in a culture that describes them as an outsider that he is able to write coherently and effectively to both the black and the white reader.

In "Toward a Black Gay Aesthetic," Charles I. Nero gives Duplechan's first two novels their most extended critical treatment. In the context of his discussion of prevailing heterosexist ideology in the African-American novel, Nero suggests that Duplechan writes against the conspiracy of the black middle class and the mental health professions "to label a black person's sexual attraction to a white as pathology" (237). Nero then cites Duplechan's exposure of "an unholy alliance between the church and the middle classes" who use "prayer, talk, and counsel" to ensure conformity, as evidenced in *Blackbird*'s exorcism scene (241, 240).

Christopher Davis,* author of *Joseph and the Old Man*, *Valley of the Shadow*, and *Boys in the Bars* wrote to Michael Denneny, Duplechan's editor, that "*Blackbird* is wonderful. I found it almost impossible to stop reading it, I loved the writing itself, and it was a book that made me feel good about being gay" ("CS Interview with Larry Duplechan," 60).

Tangled Up in Blue has been Duplechan's most successful book in the marketplace. It received a mixed review from Carolyn See of the *Los Angeles Times*, who cited underdeveloped characters as its greatest weakness. Scott Poulson-Bryant of the *Village Voice* also gave an unfavorable review. Sybil Steinberg, however, found the novel "arresting, heartwrenching." She also notes that "this moving, inspirational story commands attention whatever one's sexual orientation," thus gesturing toward the common belief that gay fiction is suitable and of value to the gay audience alone (91). The most controversial issue was the novel's focus on white men and women to the exclusion of black characters. Most reviewers agree, however, that Duplechan's depiction of the emotional struggles brought on by the AIDS epidemic is moving and very well crafted.

Michael Denneny of St. Martin's Press and Sasha Alyson of Alyson Publications have been extremely supportive of Larry Duplechan's work. They have included his voice among those who speak for the current generation of gay men and women in America, and for very good reason. As the critics who know Duplechan's work agree, Duplechan is warm, funny, poignant, self-assured, and utterly readable.

WORKS BY LARRY DUPLECHAN

"Peanuts and the Old Spice Kid." *Black Men/White Men*. Ed. Michael Smith. San Francisco: Gay Sunshine Press, 1983.
Eight Days a Week. Boston: Alyson Publications, Inc., 1985.
Blackbird. New York: Stonewall Inn Editions of St. Martin's Press, 1986.
Tangled Up in Blue. New York: Stonewall Inn Editions of St. Martin's Press, 1989.

SELECTED STUDIES OF LARRY DUPLECHAN

Davis, Christopher. "CS Interview with Larry Duplechan." *Christopher Street* 10 (1987): 60–62.
Nero, Charles I. "Toward a Black Gay Aesthetic: Signifying in Contemporary Black Gay Literature." *Brother to Brother: New Writings by Black Gay Men*. Ed. Essex Hemphill. Boston: Alyson Publications, Inc., 1991.
Poulson-Bryant, Scott. Review of *Tangled Up in Blue*. *Village Voice* 34 (July 18, 1989): 61.
See, Carolyn. "Story of Love Ends with Blunted Points." *Los Angeles Times* 8 May 1989: 4.
Steinberg, Sybil. Review of *Tangled Up in Blue*. *Publishers Weekly* 235 (January 6, 1989): 91.

DAVID B. FEINBERG (1956–   )
Jane S. Carducci

BIOGRAPHY

David B. Feinberg, born in Lynn, Massachusetts, grew up in Syracuse, New York. He recalls a normal childhood, but as he confesses to Joel Weinberg, "I thought I was weird all the time" (47). In an interview with David Friedman, Feinberg goes on to describe himself during these years as a typical nerd: small, skinny, and a good student in both math and English: "Born to ace the SATs, that's me" (43). Even though he wrote his first story, "Esion"—*noise* spelled backward—for the high school newspaper, Feinberg was not considering a career as a writer at that time; he says, "Writing seemed fun, but frivolous" (43).

After high school, Feinberg attended the Massachusetts Institute of Technology (MIT) in Cambridge, (where he took a fiction-writing course from John Hersey), graduating in 1977 with a degree in math. Feinberg also experienced his first homosexual encounters at MIT: "Tacky, sordid things, anonymous encounters in a park. I felt incredibly guilty" (Friedman 43). He continues by recalling that he first publicly acknowledged his homosexuality after he moved to Los Angeles: "I went to a Gay Pride Parade, then made the mistake of writing my mother a letter where I told her what a kick I got out of the pom-pom boys." Feinberg's sister warned him, "You better call mom. She's worried sick you're gay." "I am gay," Feinberg said.

It was also in Los Angeles that Feinberg wrote his first bad novel (still unpublished), *Calculus: The Novel*. Smitten with Susan Sontag's crystalline style, Feinberg named every chapter after titles from her essays and stories. He describes *Calculus* as a novel that "only a MIT math major could have written. The style changed every third page" (Friedman 43).

Confessing that he always wanted to live in New York, Feinberg returned there in 1979. He attended graduate school at New York University where

he completed his M.A. in linguistics and began his job as computer programmer at the Modern Language Association (MLA). He also studied
writing with Meg Wolitzer, trying to find a distinctive voice, but recalls that
the gay writing group he joined (advertised in the *New York Native*) influenced him more than Wolitzer's class. He says to Friedman, "We got this
great idea to write a collection of short stories set in a bar. One of us wrote
about the bartender, the rest of us, including me, each wrote about a patron"
(43). This was the first time Feinberg wrote openly about a gay main character. He continues, "The collection never got published, but I liked the
voice I was using" (43). That voice would become B. J. Rosenthal, the
protagonist in Feinberg's two novels, *Eighty-Sixed* (1989) and *Spontaneous
Combustion* (1991).

Currently, besides his full-time job with the MLA and the promotion of
his books coast-to-coast, Feinberg finds time to participate as an AIDS
activist in the gay organization ACT UP. He is no longer fascinated with
New York; but, as a self-described cultural parasite, he is still enamored
with its culture and art. He seems perplexed at his own artistic success,
convinced that he has fooled just about everyone. In fact, he sees himself
as a computer programmer who writes because he is guilty. He confesses,
"I should be writing more. . . . Guilt is my main motivation in writing. Guilt.
Jewish guilt. And a little angst" (Reyes 29).

Asked about his personal goals, Feinberg quips, "I'd like to get five books
under my belt. I want to go to Italy. I want to be the PWLTC [Person With
Lousy T-Cells] poster boy" (Keenhan 43). Feinberg adds that he is finished
with B. J. for now. He tells Jim Provenzano that he is "working on a novel
that is a gay version of *Three Men and a Baby*. It's *Two Fags and a Dyke*"
(36).

MAJOR WORKS AND THEMES

One of the important issues in Feinberg's life is his sense of identity as a
writer. He reads, for example, Edmund White,* Andrew Holleran,* Joe
Keenan,* Michael Nava,* Stephen McCauley, and Sarah Schulman. One
of his Jewish heroes is Woody Allen, but he admits that he is different from
Allen in that Allen is "in a long-term relationship" (Keenhan 43). Feinberg's
goal as a writer is to be "the gay Philip Roth" (Weinberg 47). Indeed,
Feinberg writes primarily for a gay audience, aiming "to reflect experiences
of being HIV-positive and gay life so that people can recognize their feelings"
and be less isolated ("Front Line" 76).

In fact, Feinberg's first novel, *Eighty-Sixed* (slang for "ejected" or
"killed") deals with the gay life-style in New York both before and after
the onset of AIDS. Catherine Texier describes part 1, the "before" section,
as a "hilarious account of gay life in the fast lane at its peak" (9). This part
of the book, entitled "1980: Ancient History," opens: "The priest rarely

masturbated during confession. For one thing, it was too cramped, too confining" (3). From this farcical beginning Feinberg chronicles the sexual excursions of B. J. Rosenthal before AIDS—when it was fun to be gay. We find B. J. in and out of bed with any number of anonymous tricks, all the while ironically offering expert advice about relationships. For example, he counsels the reader on how to get rid of a trick who won't leave, or how to tell when a relationship is on the rocks. This comic beginning is short-lived, however, as Feinberg moves into the second section of the book, "1986: Learning How to Cry." Here Feinberg explores the horrors of AIDS and how it destroys B. J.'s world. Many of the protagonist's friends now fall prey to the HIV virus, and in fact, at this point in his journey, B. J. becomes the attendant to a former trick who is dying of AIDS. Only at the end of the novel does B. J. realize fully the destructive power of AIDS: "It begins as a gentle rain. Just a drop, for each illness, each death. And with each passing day it gets worse. Now a downpour. Now a torrent. And there is no likelihood of its ever ending" (326).

Spontaneous Combustion continues the saga of B. J. Rosenthal, who now tests HIV-positive himself. This novel, another first-person account, covers the years 1985–1990. Felice Picano* names this novel a "virtual primer on big-city gay life today," teaching us "how to exist with grace, humor, love and strength while AIDS is eating at you from inside and people around you are dying like flies" (82). B. J. continues as his neurotic, sarcastic, but lovable self, using humor as a survival mechanism to distance himself from his pain: "lean was out in San Francisco because it held that 'sudden unexplained weight loss' aura about it, and that everyone had a good ten pounds to spare, as if ten pounds could protect one from death" (150).

The protagonist himself is a mouthy, sarcastic, twenty-three-year-old college student who has moved to New York City from Rochester. Catherine Texier describes Rosenthal as the "typical Christopher Street homosexual: trimmed mustache, steely pecs, skintight Levi 501 jeans and an endless supply of one-night stands" (9). She notes that he uses his sarcastic humor as both a weapon and a shield in his terrifying world. This is not unlike Feinberg himself, who feels, "If you can laugh at a situation, it's no longer completely in control of you. You have taken some control over it" (Streitfeld 15).

In fact, when asked by Owen Keenhan if these recent works are truly 97 percent autobiographical, Feinberg admits, "I was lying. It's not 97%. Though I incorporated large elements of my life into both" (29); Feinberg tries more for emotional truth rather than literal truth. Yet, he confesses to "plundering" his own past and jokes, "The important thing to do is smile and lie. . . . I'm actually straight. You wouldn't believe that amount of research I had to do" (Streitfeld 15).

When encouraged to specify how he and B. J. Rosenthal differ, Feinberg offers, "B. J. and I aren't the same person exactly. I'd say he's sixty to seventy percent me. We're both gay, of course, and HIV positive. But, for one thing, I write novels and he doesn't. And, while he's more well-endowed, I'm a better lover" (Friedman 43).

CRITICAL RECEPTION

Eighty-Sixed is the first book to receive both the Lambda Literary Award for Gay Men's Fiction and the American Gay/Lesbian Book Award for Fiction and has been named one of the "Books to Remember" by the New York public library. Ten thousand hardcover copies have been sold so far (nearly four times the average for a first novel), and twenty-two thousand have been sold in paperback. *Spontaneous Combustion* was chosen by the Book of the Month Club and the Quality Paperback Book Club, and twelve thousand copies were sold on the first printing.

Even so, both of these works have received mixed reviews. Emmanuel S. Nelson praises *Eighty-Sixed* as "one of the best novels in the entire genre of AIDS literature" (50). Ray Olson supports this notion when he calls *Eighty-Sixed* "the best sustained work of gay male humor ever published" (120). Catherine Texier agrees that this novel "stands out for its frankness, ferocious wit and lack of sentimentality or self-pity" (9). Bob Summer adds that in *Eighty-Sixed*, "Feinberg reaffirms life in the face of the day-to-day terrors of living"; the novel offers "a cathartic perspective, devoid of romanticism" (10). Ben Davis affirms that this is "an engrossing novel on the effect of AIDS on the lives of ordinary New York homosexuals" (4).

More specifically, Michael McGuire notes, "One of the extraordinary things about *Eighty-Sixed* . . . is that Feinberg has offered a character of such modest virtues, and then taken him through a completely believable slow-but-steady growth experience" (24). Summer agrees that B. J. is, indeed, a rounded character: "From '80 to '86, the difference in tone measures the distance our hero has covered. In stark contrast to the novel's Firbankian opening, its ending tolls with a muffled dirge" (10). This is where Daniel Curzon* disagrees: "The book seems to have been written to show that a superficial, snotty man can remain true to himself throughout the AIDS crisis by continuing to be superficial and snotty" (6). Curzon also suggests that this amateur first novel will be an embarrassment to Feinberg when he learns to write better books.

Spontaneous Combustion has also received a broad range of reviews. Scot Bradfield praises the book because Feinberg "manages to make the tragedy of AIDS both humanly urgent and narratively convincing" (11). Joel Weinberg agrees that this novel is "by turns raunchy, hilarious, and heart rending" (44). Michael Bronski finds this novel to be a "raucous, free-wheeling account—both hilariously funny and mordantly terrifying"; he calls Feinberg's style a "dazzling mixture of controlled hysteria, high queen sarcasm, and truth telling" (3). Robert Friedman continues, "Feinberg dazzles with his excoriating wit and flawless sense of irony" (37).

Daniel Mendelsohn, however, sees only "unfulfilled potential" in this novel, arguing that Feinberg "lacks the self-restraint necessary to sustain really devastating ironic comment" (78). *Kirkus Reviews* calls this novel "disjointed and derivative" (15), one that is not for the mainstream nor a ground-breaker in gay fiction. *Forecasts* complains that the "repartee wears thin" (48); and Dennis Cooper,* himself a gay novelist, dismisses *Spontaneous Combustion* as mere doggerel. Bob Satuloff is impatient with Feinberg's "adolescent antics," even though he does credit Feinberg with a well-written chapter, "The Very Last Seymour." Satuloff insists that Feinberg substitutes "shallowness, posturing, and self-aggrandizement for depth of feeling that exists beneath the defense of a brittle gay facade" (7).

Feinberg realizes that his books do not work if the reader does not think they are funny. He goes on to attack Satuloff personally as a "gay Stalinist," someone who will strike "if you disagree with [him] about anything" (Friedman 43). As for Dennis Cooper, Feinberg counters with another personal assault, "This is a guy who writes books about older guys who (bleep) young boys, then rip out their entrails. He's been called the Bad Boy of Gay Lit. What he really is is the Gay Boy of Bad Lit" (Friedman 43).

WORKS BY DAVID FEINBERG

"The Age of Anxiety." *Men on Men 2*. Ed. George Stambolian. New York: NAL, 1988: 32–48.
Eighty-Sixed. New York: Viking, 1989.
Spontaneous Combustion. New York: Viking, 1991.
"Notes from the Front Line." *New York Quarterly* 6 January 1992: 49–50, 76.

SELECTED STUDIES OF DAVID FEINBERG

Interviews

Keenhan, Owen. "The Inspirations of David Feinberg." *Outlines* December 1991: 29, 43.
Provenzano, Jim. *New York Quarterly* 8 December 1991: 36.
Reyes, Nina. "The Guilt behind the Book." *Next* 8 March 1989: 26–29.
Weinberg, Joel. "Epidemic of Laughter." *The Advocate* 14 March 1989: 46–47.

Reviews

Bradfield, Scott. "Young, Single, and HIV-Positive." *New York Times* 17 November 1991: 11.
Bronski, Michael. "Between the Lines." *The Guide*. December 1991: 19.

Curzon, Daniel. "Bounced from the Bar of Life." *Los Angeles Times* 5 March 1989: C21.

Davis, Ben. "First Novel Examines Homosexuality." *The Hartford Courant* 6 March 1989: B4.

Finkle, David. "AIDS: Metaphor for Defeat and Hope." *New York Post* 10 February 1989: 60.

"Forecasts." *Publishers Weekly* 11 October 1991: 48.

Friedman, David. "Positive with Attitude." *New York Newsday* 7 January 1992: 43–44, 60.

Friedman, Robert. "The Further Adventures of B. J. Rosenthal." *Sentinel* 21 November 1991: 37.

Jensen, Michael. "The Risk in Everything." *The Northwest Gay and Lesbian Reader* 3, no. 6 (November/December 1991): 6, 11.

Kirkus Reviews 1 September 1991: 88.

Mendelsohn, Daniel. "Laugh Lines." *Voice* 26 November 1991: 78.

McGuire, Michael. "Coming of Age in Plague Time." *Next* 3 August 1989: 24–25.

Nelson, Emmanuel. "AIDS and the American Novel." *Journal of American Culture* 13, no. 1 (Spring 1990): 47–53.

Olson, Ray. Review of *Spontaneous Combustion*. *Booklist* 15 September 1991: 59.

Satuloff, Bob. "Enervating Rhythm." *Christopher Street* 168 (1991): 4, 6–7.

Streitfeld, David. "Young and Gay." *Book World* 15 January 1989: 15.

Summer, Bob. "AIDS—This Side of the Abyss." *Lambda Rising* February/March 1989: 10.

Texier, Catherine. "When Sex Was All That Mattered." *New York Times* 26 February 1989: 9.

ROBERT FERRO (1941–1988)
Joseph Dewey

BIOGRAPHY

Robert Ferro was born October 21, 1941, in Cranford, New Jersey. Recognized as early as high school for his interest in storytelling and a love of language, Ferro received a B.A. in English from Rutgers in 1963 and, after a period of traveling in Europe, an M.F.A. from the Creative Writing Program at the University of Iowa in 1967. During the mid–1960s, Ferro traveled widely in Europe; there, in the tonic freedom of the Continental lifestyle, he not only defined his sexual identity but began experimenting with pieces of short fiction, many of which would become part of the storytelling episodes in *The Others*. While at Iowa, Ferro met Michael Grumley, an artist and writer who would become Ferro's lover for the next twenty years. The fact of Ferro's homosexuality proved enormously difficult for Ferro's upper-class, conservative Catholic family, particularly his father, despite unconditional support for Ferro during the 1970s while Ferro worked out much of his apprentice writing and continued extensive travels abroad.

Ferro's first published work came from an eccentric idea of searching for Atlantis, suggested to Grumley by a chance purchase in Rome of a book on Edgar Cayce, who predicted signs of Atlantis would reveal themselves sometime around 1969. In late 1968, Ferro and Grumley returned to America and set off on what became a six-month exploration to the Bahamas aboard Ferro's family yacht. As novice sailors and fledgling writers (their preparations included consulting Tarot cards, and their cargo included typewriters and more than fifty books on topics ranging from astrology to archeology), Grumley and Ferro collaborated on a slim journal of the expedition after the crew documented sightings of previously unrecorded evidences of a buried city. The response to *Atlantis* stirred momentary celebrity status, including a book tour and some talk show appearances. After the notoriety passed, however, Ferro returned to New York with Grumley and struggled (despite unstinted financial support from his family) in routine jobs, including waiting tables with a catering business, while completing more than five years of work on *The Others*, a gothic mood piece deeply indebted to a graduate school admiration of Isak Dinesen.

Ferro's identifying works, however, were written amid the heady freedom of the post-Stonewall explosion in gay expression. As part of the generation of gay writers who emerged in the 1970s, Ferro could explore his sexual identity self-consciously, trying to locate its appropriate orientation within a larger heterosexual culture without defensive subterfuge, furtive innuendo, the restrictive gesture of apology, or the exotic sense of marginality. Although Ferro did not directly write about homosexuality until five years before his death, his decision to turn toward frank treatment of the material of his own life marked a critical turn in his fiction. Ferro was central in organizing The Violet Quill, a small group of seven New York–based gay writers who met informally between 1979 and 1981 (the group of emerging writers, most in their twenties, included Edmund White,* Felice Picano,* Andrew Holleran,* George Whitmore,* Christopher Cox, and Grumley). In lengthy sessions to critique works-in-progress, these writers discussed the possibilities, risks, and necessities of the autobiographical impulse as the first generation of gay writers able to command, even to expect, a reading audience. It was in just such a heady atmosphere of a discovered brotherhood that Ferro turned to the difficult implications of testing his own autobiography, his decade-long commitment to Grumley as well as his own strained relationships within a family deeply splintered by the fact of his life-style.

With the publication of his three major works within a five-year span in the early 1980s, Ferro garnered appreciative national attention in the gay press (including citation as *The Sentinel*'s Writer of the Year in 1988) and in national news magazines (including mention in a lengthy article in *Newsweek* on emerging gay writers) as well as initial recognition by the scholarly establishment. Indeed, at 46, Ferro seemed poised to assume a major place in what was quickly emerging as a most important literary movement. In addition to regular speaking and reading engagements, he had begun regular work as a critic in the gay press and had accepted an adjunct teaching post in creative writing at Hofstra University. But it was not to be. Although Ferro had been diagnosed with Kaposi's sarcoma as early as 1984, he had worked on completing *Second Son*, even while nursing Grumley, who was himself stricken with AIDS. Ferro's sister, Dr. Camille Burns, recalls Ferro's buoyant optimism, his emphatic certainty that the disease could be managed through vitamins and a regimen of medication, and his refusal to concede to closure or to the endgame of regrets. When Grumley died shortly after the release of *Second Son*, Ferro, himself emotionally and physically exhausted and unable to coax back the optimism he had so steadfastly maintained, died quite suddenly less than ten weeks later on July 11, 1988, in his father's house in New Jersey. At the time of his death, he was working on editorial revisions to complete the ending of Grumley's autobiographical novel, *Life Drawing* (subsequently published by Grove Press in 1991). Ferro's ashes are buried next to Grumley's on a bluff overlooking the Hudson beneath a white marble stone that bears an epigraph from Shakespeare's Sonnet 115, "Love is a babe."

MAJOR WORKS AND THEMES

Atlantis: The Autobiography of a Search, a nonfiction account of the 1969 excursion to the Bahamas, is an uneven achievement. A split narrative, authorship of its chapters is divided between Grumley and Ferro. Grumley's methodical recording recalls a nautical log with detailed digressions on the wealth of Atlantis lore and the writings of Edgar Cayce; Ferro, who does not share the enthusiasm for Cayce or psychic experiences, develops in his sections more intimate discourses on a variety of subjects, including the purpose of writing, the importance of the imagination, and—most important for his emerging vision—a naive terror over clock time and a vehement hate of the idea of death.

Bored by daily recording of the expedition itself and uninterested in Atlantis as set of coordinates, Ferro concentrates rather on the idea of Atlantis, more specifically on the immense scale of time suggested by Atlantis—how, preserved from the simplifications of archaeologists who would lock Atlantis within the dreary parameters of linear time, it offers not another dreary civilization come and gone but rather an incredible persistence of the idea of a great cultural past in a garden larger and more technologically developed than Eden, which he finds diminished in an age so unconvinced by the idea of a God. Atlantis as an idea suggests to Ferro a defiance of clock time, a fantastic exception, a place apart, a loophole in the otherwise irontight demands of mutability, an event outside the rigidity of history. The radical moment of discovery itself—finding evidence of stone pillars and an ancient roadbed in the fanning sands of the ocean bottom off Bermuda—receives, on the whole, muted celebration by Ferro, who surrenders Atlantis to the white noise of archaeological experts and the media.

The Others (1979), coming nearly a decade later, offers a radically different reading experience. It is a slender fantasy-allegory, the first of what will prove to be Ferro's characteristic genre-testing experiments. It exposes telling ancestry in Kafka and Dinesen (indeed, a casual reference early in the cruise suggests that all the characters on board are in fact elements in one of Dinesen's stories). The plot does not lend itself to summary, as so much of what happens passes in a dream-like suggestivity that renders any plot ironic. Peter Conrad, ill in his parents' country retreat, is invited for a cruise in the Mediterranean. At the moment of his invitation, he has a striking vision of a large white ship, something of a ghost ship, glowing in the distance. He makes a quick series of drawings of the vision and, when he arrives in Italy, is disturbed (and fascinated) to find the yacht a near-copy of his own designs, thus commencing a struggle in the young man's mind for what is real, what is fantasy. He is introduced to a handful of fellow voyagers, each of whom will in turn relate a story centered on questions of the efficacy of art, the struggle of the artist to break through illusions into the real, the mystery lurking just beneath the obvious, the banal. Each tale, related in the heady atmosphere of what becomes a more and more tenuous setting, has an eerie sort of gothicism to it, in touches of violence, radical loneliness, and aberrant behavior patterns, as the isolated Peter begins to wonder if his life, so apparently real, is indeed a fantasy.

Such heavy-handed Chinese boxing that tests so baldly the line between the real and the fantastic threatens the obvious exercise in the self-indulgent imagination. Ferro offers no real plot, no attempts to define character beyond sketches, no developed tension (save batting about the fog for what is real), no reassuring resolution, and no social, political, or sexual agenda. The work is an intellectual exercise, a performance of an imagination interested in defining the springs of its own powers of invention, the prose drunk on its own perfume. Yet, once again, the most striking passages come when Ferro addresses the idea of death. The Others, two androgynous characters, faceless and voiceless, are so hungry for the experience of closure that they throw themselves off the ship in a struggle to confront what, as fictional creations sealed within the eternal present, they never encounter— the termination of experience. *The Others* is a strangely affective reading experience, testing as it does Ferro's conception of the potent power of the imagination, the accessibility through its magic to a silvery world unlimited by the narrower parameters of the quotidian.

Although *The Others* is clearly autobiographical as it defines the problematic role of the artist as creator and created, it was not until *Max Desir* (1983) that Ferro first worked directly with autobiography. The result is a powerful achievement in which Ferro seeks to resolve his terrors over clock time—against the immense, irresistible pull of death he balances the fantastic potency of sexuality, or more specifically the powerful possibilities of the erotic expressed in the special perceptions of those able to mature along the margins of upper-middle-class respectability. Given his naive refusal in *Atlantis* to work within the stark vocabulary of mortality and his decadent curiosity about its nature in *The Others*, a critical achievement in *Max Desir* is surely Ferro's determined exploration of death. Few novels in recent memory so graphically chart the event of death as Max records with unblinking eye the months after his mother is struck with the first symptoms of what proves to be an inoperable brain tumor. Ferro will not negotiate this experience; rather, in step after deliberate step, the reader follows the diagnosis, the lingering summer at the family summer cottage tending the rapidly deteriorating mother, the lurching spasm of death itself, the macabre business of touching up a badly displayed body in a local funeral parlor (including Max hastily readjusting the wig and removing the excessive makeup), and finally the tedious details of interment and landscaping the burial plot, itself taking a Kafkaesque turn as foundations of a never-completed mausoleum are unearthed over his mother's burial plot.

Against the family's pivoting about the dying matriarch, Ferro charts initially in flashback Max Desir's awakening to his sexual identity, beginning with a powerful memory of a wrestling match in the attic with a school friend that ends with a mutual masturbatory act that Ferro offers as a defiant expression of power, release, and freedom. When Max travels to Europe to pursue his writing, Ferro celebrates that sexual identity, its athleticism, the sheer indulgence of erotic extremism. Sexuality and its expression emerges in Max's awareness that the tonic bolt of attachment creates a hunger for violation, for touch, for penetration. In Europe, Max discovers the circuit, the unrestrained nightworld of Eurosexuality, to which he responds hungrily, addicted, he concedes, a "simple animal . . . within a garden of abundance" (58).

Yet Max is not satisfied with the momentary, anonymous connections in bars and public restrooms. He forges a strong relationship with Nick Flynn, a part-time actor. The critical role of the monogamous relationship will emerge as central in Ferro's unapologetically romantic vision of the potent power of the heart. Max finds in Nick the security of the singular attachment, a commitment that is perhaps called into being by the powerful draw of the carnal appetites but is sustained through dignity and mutual support. When Max and Nick return to States, the Desir family, with the stubborn exception of the father, embraces the fact of the relationship. Yet when Nick and Max are included as part of an embroidered family tree that is to hang in a defiantly public part of the Desir summer cottage, the consternation created in the father by such a gesture of inclusion is enough to fracture the family for months despite the ongoing attempts to minister to the dying mother.

As the mother slips into her final coma, the family itself seems terminal. After his wife's death, the father withdraws from the family, even entering a local monastery for a time. And, after the funeral, Max struggles as a waiter in New York City unable to forgive his father, whose half-hearted efforts at salvaging some sort of apology evidences his deep-seated repugnance for his son's lifestyle. This would seem to define Ferro's novel as a realistic exploration of the inevitable tension between a collapsing, dysfunctional family and the striking power of the bond forged between Nick and Max, a caring, supportive commitment that defies the larger family's unconditional surrender to the quiet terrors of time and mortality, to selfishness and distance.

Yet Ferro threads within this starkly realistic family drama elements of defiantly supernatural dimension, inexplicable strokes that intimate planes of experience undetected by the sensual apparatus. There is Clive, Max's bizarre voodoo lover whom he visits in the city, never a threat to his commitment to Nick but rather a walk on a darker, wilder side of unrestrained sexuality, nights of indulgent splendor by candlelight and jazz; there is the voice Max hears while he shaves one morning, a signal identified as a communication from Iala, the third orbiting planet from the star Arcturus, a civilization that watches our planet with the same bemusement we lavish on television. Most defiantly, there is the closing experiment in fiction, Max's own re-creation of the diary of a mid-nineteenth-century gay British explorer who tells of his adventures in the Brazilian interior when natives mistake the beautiful, athletic, blond creature for some unanticipated river god, a sexual deity who ministers prodigiously in nightly rituals. Amid masked natives, swirling bonfires, and pounding drums, the explorer indulges intimacy without ties in a primitive expression of the identical potency of uninhibited sexuality Max first sensed in the trembling explosion in his attic.

Ferro's book closes with an unnerving conjunction of Max and this river god/explorer. In a sudden intimacy of first-person writing, Max defiantly accepts his dazzling position as deity, an embodiment of the river god who participates as much in potent sexuality as in spirituality, a striking metaphor for Ferro's own conception of the homosexual artist: brazen, self-involved, defiantly sampling the richest experiences and, in that very brazenness, standing as a dazzling presence against the flat, ordinary world of the jungle natives (the colder world of New York where Max hustles as waiter) whose uninterrupted plainness finds its static ordinariness suddenly sundered by the presence of a powerful outsider gifted with special perceptions and unlimited power. It is Max Desir finding in his own sexual identity a counterpressure to the melancholic pull of mortality that so draws the book's larger narrative line. It is a fantastic explosion of possibility that sparks, without warning, in the closing pages, much as the defiant explosion of life in the Desir attic. It is Max finally living up to his name—maximum desire.

If *Max Desir* is a powerful examination of a gay artist coming to terms with the potency of his art, *The Blue Star* (1985) is an outright rhapsodic celebration of desire, a lyric coming-of-age novel set in the splendid freedom of Europe. It is surely Ferro's most centrally sexual work, a work within the gay genre of coming-out fiction set in exotic foreign worlds, works where the assertion of sexual identity can only be realized outside the oppressive rigidities of the American culture. Ferro picks up the story of Peter Conrad, now an aspiring writer in Florence, where he feels considerable freedom as he experiences the sexuality long denied him in America. Imprisoned after a police sweep, Peter meets and develops a fast friendship with the perfect Chase Walker, another American, a sort of Jamesian heiress living an opulent lifestyle on a massive trust fund. Through Chase's connections, the two spend an odd weekend in a country home of decadent

Italian nobility, who press a bewildered Chase to accept an arranged marriage with a niece as part of a deal to produce offspring to carry on the family name and wealth. Coerced by a considerable amount of money, Chase acquiesces to the marriage.

Against such a decadent abuse of heterosexuality, Peter defines his own passionate hunger for a young nephew of the woman who runs the boardinghouse in Florence where he stays. Distracted by his unreturned attention and unable to write, he resolves to return to America. The night before he is to leave, however, the youth demurely offers himself for a night of unrestrained "prehistoric sex" (45) that Peter marks as the night he discovered himself. The memory of such bold connection will stay with Peter for fifteen years, despite, by his own confession, experiences with hundreds of men. With a sensitivity that never panders to purient detailing or to the shock tactics of graphic rendering, Ferro suggests again the potent spell of the heart.

Fifteen years pass. Peter returns to Florence unable to forget Lorenzo. He finds Lorenzo married, the father of two sons, but, after a sharing a drink, the two return to bed. Peter decides Lorenzo should return to America with him; the obsession he feels convinces him that in making love he makes himself stronger. But Lorenzo cannot walk away from his family. Meanwhile, Chase's wife, now fifteen years into a soured marriage and desperate to rekindle the sexual attentions of a husband she believes to be an indifferent heterosexual, proposes a cruise down the Nile in a yacht called the Blue Star, all four will journey down the Nile aboard an extravagantly outfitted luxury ship, a sort of microcosmic decadent world coaxed into magic by potent drugs and uninhibited sexuality, another of Ferro's places apart where with fantastic ease each voyager's wish is fulfilled. It is a demanding close, a far cry from the opening realistic narrative, one that requires a suspension of skepticism and a concession to the powerful possibility of fantasy.

Set against this lush fantasy is Ferro's re-creation of a bizarre Masonic plot in mid-nineteenth-century New York to construct a fabulous secret temple underneath Central Park even as the park itself is being laid out. By the novel's close, the interchapters on the temple are revealed to be part of a diary handed down finally to Chase (a distant descendant of the designer of the temple) and read aloud during the drift down the Nile. Such a rich and opulent temple, so within the urban sprawl and so vitally apart from it, emerges as Ferro's rich metaphor for homosexuality itself—a necessarily secretive brotherhood that transports its fortunate membership into a sort of parallel dimension of baroque splendor. It is the vantage point available only to those who stand outside, in the margins. Like Atlantis, like the Amazonian river basin, the Masonic Temple boldly challenges the puny measure of clock time, sorely tests the boundaries of reality and fantasy (indeed, as the novel closes, Chase, now in the employ of the city park department, pokes about an abandoned shed in Central Park hoping to find evidence of the temple secret entranceway).

As with *Max Desir*, Ferro here moves wildly about genre lines. What begins as realistic, if campy, social satire on the decadent machinations of spent heterosexuality set against the tonic impulse of homosexuality turns toward an unironic incantation of the luxury cruise, a stunning leap of the imagination as much romantic as erotic. What figures to be a coming-of-age chronicle of life abroad is suddenly spliced with apparently straight-faced historical narrative that documents the elaborate underworld of the Masonic tribe, while all the while moving away from history to explode finally into a fantastic celebration of the imagination in Ferro's opulent description of the completed temple, passages which recall the rich peroration of *Max Desir*. From such a deliberate fantasy, Ferro would turn in his closing effort to a far more ghastly reality. The radical impact of the fact of AIDS on Ferro's writing is measured by the achievement of his last novel, *Second Son*, published within months of his death. Within the complicated response to the inevitable sense of futility and waste occasioned by death at an early age, Ferro wrestles with the very mortality he had defiantly avoided since *Atlantis*. He confronts the grim fact of closure that had been carefully mediated by the possibility of that fantastic dimension just beyond the strength of the senses to tap. Death emerges not as a family tragedy or some metaphor slayable by dint of the imagination; rather, death becomes a private act, an undeniable reality, although Ferro never names the illness directly (he feared such a potent buzzword would lose itself in the politics of the moment, associations that would in time limit the novel's argument).

Once again, the relationship is central to Ferro's vision. Mark Valerian develops a simple, profound relationship with Bill Mackey. They have both tested positive and begin, even as the relationship develops, to feel the first symptoms. That construction, so apparently defined by AIDS as infected, offers within Ferro's book the possibility of healing. Against yet another family that must struggle with irresolvable divisions and unretractable distances, a family unable to accommodate completely the curious problem of the second son, a family whose estrangement is merely intensified by the diagnosis of the son's condition, we witness the emergence in graceful counterpoint of Mark's relationship with Bill Mackey, a set designer and theatrical lighting specialist whom Mark meets while on a working vacation in Rome.

This relationship defies the grinding inevitability of the virus. When they first make love in Rome under the fabulous sunsets spoked into color by the poisonous radiation cloud from Chernobyl as it passes over southern Europe, Mark and Bill construct a marvelously fragile bond that revives for both of them emotional responses denied in two years since their diagnoses. Their commitment here becomes Ferro's place apart, a tonic invitation to believe in the magic restoration of romance able to suspend death at least for the moment (Mark's hobby, after all, is a loving, ongoing restoration of his family's huge, run-down summer cottage).

Under the tonic of their commitment to one another, Mark and Bill register defiant, inexplicable remission. During the slow, late-summer days when Mark and Bill return from Rome to the Berkshires to disperse the ashes of Bill's longtime companion, Mark rows to the middle of a lake one evening on Bill's instructions. He turns toward the distant haze of the shore and in the fading twilight sees a flickering against the descending dusk on shore, a "fabulous necklace of lights . . . bleeding into the darkness," complemented by a sixty-foot jet stream of water arching in the simplest grace of a rainbow. It is a gift from Bill. Mark is enthralled by the lambent moment of magic that speaks a "language of brightness," all produced by Bill's creative impulse, aided by a noiseless generator and miles of extension cords (44–46). Like the fragile connection made between Bill and Mark, the display is not permanent; rather, it can be maintained only for the gorgeous moment. But Bill's gesture suggests the magic of the artificial that is powerful precisely because it must flicker, because it must certainly give way to the darkness. Their emotional bond is an assertion against a natural world represented by the sunset poisoned by radiation, by the shoreline hushing into night, by the AIDS virus itself.

But AIDS cannot permit magic; the disease demands closure. Against a subplot of an exchange of letters from a friend of Mark's (who is likewise infected, the reader gathers from remarks in the letters) who writes about money invested in a farfetched plan to launch a rocketful of homosexuals to a distant planet there to recover and live in peace (a secret brotherhood that recalls the Masonic temple), Mark and Bill shoulder their way toward what must be with only the simple, steady reassurance they offer each other that neither will go it alone. That commitment offers a healing of sorts, a summer that is in its brevity the very mother of beauty.

There Ferro closed his fiction, tempering the earnest frivolity of his earlier meditations on the imagination, his wild flights on the backs of untamed white horses, his restless search for the geography that dispelled the onerous burden of the real. In this closing book he turns from Atlantis, from the Temple Chamber, from the erotic wonderland of the Amazon, from the cerebral construction of a radiant ghost ship. Yet even as death became irresistible, Ferro fashions a resolution that finds its expression in the earnest closeness of souls in a splendid resistance to the natural pull toward death. Prior to *Second Son*, only richly imagined worlds offered central characters unnervingly immediate experiences with the possibilities of worlds not soured by exposure to the real elements of time and space. Such places became real because they were fantastic. In this closing effort, the solution is fantastic only because it is real. In *Second Son*, that provocative exploration of the realm beyond the senses finds itself hastened to the periphery. Here, Splendora is accessible, a trembling hand reaching out for another.

Only in this final work, confronting his own circumstances, could Ferro find the magic in a place defined not by the fantastic parameters it establishes but rather by the people it encloses. When Mark Valerian imagines the porch of his family's summer cottage as a great prow of a ship headed for the stars, it is a defiant act of the imagination that is moving only because Mark reaches across to the hand of Bill Mackey.

CRITICAL RECEPTION

The critical attention focused on Ferro's later work inevitably begins with Ferro's lush and intoxicating prose, which either commands more attention than the unfolding narrative or seems to usurp it completely. Critical attention seldom found Ferro's prose line equal to the stories he elected to tell. Only in *Max Desir* (defined most persuasively by David Bergman as part of the important new genre of gay family fiction) did Ferro find his style not an issue.

In Ferro's two last works, however, critical response found harsher dissonances between style and argument. Response to *The Blue Star*, for instance, centered largely on the prose itself. William Harding, writing in the *New York Times*, argued that Ferro turned away from the conflicting emotions of gay men created by the opening half of the novel with its exploration of sexual initiation and self-discovery and that Ferro was finally too "content with glittering surfaces," a reference to Ferro's prose style lavished on the inconsequential historical romance of the pleasure palace beneath Central Park. Yet it is just that polished prose style able to retouch the obvious depravity of the European world that redeems the novel, according to Albert Mobilio, who argued that while the Central Park digression proved finally unworkable the high romance in Italy was as intoxicating a tale rendered in lushest prose.

Reaction to *Second Son* was equally divided. Reviewers quickly acknowledged the important confrontation with AIDS, although Ferro drew some criticism, his insistence on distilling hope from the virus's cold logic and his refusal to concede to the frustration occasioned by the endgame of the disease mistaken for escapism or a somehow "light" treatment of the epidemic. Yet more problematic was Ferro's dramatic reliance on the internal realpolitik of his badly splintered family to counterbalance the emerging relationship between Mark and Bill. Laurie Stone, in the *Village Voice*, dismissed as trivia the family drama. While acknowledging the impact of such an eloquent record of the illness (although she rejects Ferro's decision not to name the disease), she finds much of the novel badly miscalculated, specifically the lengthy explorations into the family and the Splendora subplot.

It is a critical response that consistently finds problematic what most defined Ferro's writing—his flagrant flaunting of established genre lines, his willingness to reinvent virtually every genre he invoked until genre itself becomes wondrously irrelevant, each novel a masterstroke of reinvention, an experiment in transforming genres by juxtaposing apparently conflicting types of stories. His books mesh with wondrous alchemy the grim melodramas and domestic frictions of family chronicles, the traditional sexual bildungsroman of gay coming-of-age fiction, the supernatural and touches of science fiction, erotic fantasies, fairy tales, and, above all, the unapologetically romantic love story. Such genre-busting performances argue that any reality is at best a tenuous, temporary moment, a banal geography beyond which is a most fabulous plane of experience, available only to the imaginative, the sensual, the creative, the romantic, those who, finally, revel amid the margins. That potent faith in the primitive strength of those who are both gifted and marginal (a very Whitmanesque celebration of the gay artist) enabled Ferro over the dozen years of his writing career to come full circle and to confront what his imagination at first assured him was most easily avoided—death itself. In his closing work, pressured by absolute absence, Ferro offers a timeless testimony that is unapologetically romantic, thoroughly vibrant, and defiantly hopeful.

WORKS BY ROBERT FERRO

Atlantis: The Autobiography of a Search. With Michael Grumley. Garden City: Doubleday, 1970.
The Others. New York: Scribner's, 1977.
The Family of Max Desir. New York: Dutton, 1984.
The Blue Star. New York: Dutton, 1985.
Second Son. New York: Crown, 1988.

SELECTED STUDIES OF ROBERT FERRO

Bergman, David. "Alternative Service: Families in Recent American Gay Fiction." *Kenyon Review* (1986): 72–90.
Harding, William J. Rev. of *The Blue Star*. *New York Times Book Review* 14 April 1985: 26.
Hoctel, Patrick. "A Talk with Novelist Robert Ferro: *The Sentinel*'s Writer of the Year." *San Francisco Sentinel* 25 March 1988: 17–18, 28.
Holleran, Andrew. "A Place of His Own: How to Remember Robert Ferro." *Christopher Street* 126 (1988): 4–9.
Lynch, James F. "Two Writers Set Sail for Caribbean to Hunt Lore of Lost Continent." *New York Times* 23 January 1969.
Mobilio, Albert. "Passion Plays." Rev. of *The Blue Star*. *Village Voice* 3 September 1985: 46.
Prescott, Peter S. "Out of the Closet onto the Shelves." *Newsweek* 21 March 1988: 72–74.
Shewey, Don. "Robert Ferro to the Max." *Village Voice* 1 November 1983: 43.

Stambolian, George. "Michael's Room." Afterword. *Life Drawing: A Novel.* By
     Michael Grumley, 143–56. New York: Grove Weidenfeld, 1991.
Stone, Laurie. "Sick Transit." Rev. of *Second Son. Village Voice* 15 March 1988:
     55.
White, Edmund. "Out of the Closet, onto the Bookshelf." *New York Times Magazine*
     16 June 1991: 22–24, 35.

JOHN FOX (1952–1990)
Mark E. Bates

BIOGRAPHY

Any informed reader of John Fox's only published novel, *The Boys on the Rock* (1984), must wonder to what extent the novel is autobiographical. Like the author, the novel's protagonist Billy Conners grew up in the Pelham Bay area of the Bronx, New York, and experienced the difficulties of being a gay teenager during the turbulent decade of the 1960s. John Fox was born on May 26, 1952, in the Bronx, New York, the son of middle-class Catholic parents. After his graduation from Lehman College, he moved to Manhattan, where he lived and wrote until his death in 1990 of complications due to AIDS. He was an intensely personal man who was typified as a "loner" by those who knew him best. Michael Denneny, editor of *Christopher Street*, described John Fox as "extremely serious about his work" and as "a writer who didn't travel well in other circles of gay writers since he had roots, a family in New York, unlike many other writers who came to New York from other places in order to write in a supportive gay environment" (excerpted from a phone interview with Michael Denneny, September 20, 1991).

John Fox published his first short stories, "The Superhero" and "Over the Pyrenees," in *Christopher Street*; they were later included in the 1986 compilation *First Love/Last Love: New Fiction from Christopher Street* and the first of the *Men on Men* series respectively. His only novel, *The Boys on the Rock* (1984), was written during his tenure at the Columbia University Creative Writing Program in 1982–1983. The liner notes of the novel mention that he was "working on a second novel," which was never published. His diagnosis with AIDS curtailed his contacts with the outside world and diminished his relationship with his family in the Bronx. Michael Denneny reported that during that time he "would occasionally have lunch with

John [when] he would speak passionately about his writing". John Fox died at home on August 14, 1990, at 4:10 P.M.

John Fox's funeral revealed many of the conflicts between his family and personal life. Apparent tensions arose between the family and those friends who were more supportive of his gay life-style. At the funeral his younger brother and sister were choked with emotion. The priest officiating the funeral offered consolation: "Your tears are as eloquent as words" (from a telephone conversation with Diana Finch of the Ellen Labine Management Agency on October 10, 1991). A group of three women then spoke of his life. Trudy Ditmar, a close personal friend, broke the mood of the occasion by stating, "John would have wanted everyone to know that he was gay" (interview with Diana Finch). In spite of these difficulties several members of his immediate family, especially his mother, have "remained intensely loyal to John's work . . . [and] should be counted among his biggest fans" (interview with Diana Finch, 1991).

MAJOR WORKS AND THEMES

If the statement "intensely personal" best sums up John Fox's life, the same phrase can also be applied to his literary production. Both his 1984 novel *The Boys on the Rock* and his short stories (especially "The Super-hero") portray the moment or early stages of adolescent sexual self-discovery, which demonstrates the author's desire to relate the "coming out" stories of gay teenagers and perhaps to reexamine his own sexual self-awareness. The biographical section of this study suggests that the author may have struggled with his own sexuality during his teenage years and subsequently embodied these conflicts in his novel and short stories. Whatever the relationship between the author and his texts, there exists an undeniable autobiographical undercurrent throughout his work.

Thus *The Boys on the Rock* typifies the *bildungsroman* of the gay teenager of the 1960s in the United States, a time of social upheaval in which the author himself was a teenager. Narrated in a rambling and often disjointed first-person narrative style, the novel tells the story of Billy Conners, a sixteen-year-old who, amid the political and social chaos of the 1968 Presidential elections, slowly comes to terms with his own (homo)sexuality. Having read the first few pages of the novel, the casual reader will identify Billy Conners as a "normal" average teenager; he socializes with his group of friends, has a girlfriend, and participates in school and extracurricular activities. On the surface, Billy seems remarkably similar to the other teenage boys in his peer group at the beginning of the novel.

As the narration unfolds the reader quickly discovers the flaws in Billy's psychological armor of friends, heterosexuality, and school activity. Although Billy does have his circle of close friends (typically he will double date with Tommy and Lorraine, two teenagers whose passions often lead to personal conflict, and/or Joey and Roxanne, whose need to fulfill carnal urges makes all else seem unimportant), he often feels alienated and withdraws from them: "I thought about Tommy and Lorraine and Joey and Roxanne and Sue and I figured I acted like a turd the way I sat in that cab and watched Sue run into her house crying and I wished that Joey had just driven us all home" (12). Billy prefers to live in his masturbatory fantasy world, where the twins from his swim team and his current romantic interest, Al DiCicco, became his imaginary sexual partners.

The narration immediately creates doubts in the reader's mind concerning Billy's assumed heterosexuality. Although Billy does have a "girlfriend", Sue, a girl he met at a dance at St. Kathleen's Academy for Girls, he expresses ambivalent feelings towards her. He feels obligated through peer pressure to have a girlfriend: "The whole thing made me kind of nervous, I guess because I didn't have any desire whatsoever to talk to her or do anything at all with her. The only reason I was considering going over there was because although I had somehow gotten away with not having a girlfriend up till then, I figured it was about time I got one" (17). In fact Billy was more interested in a boy he had seen when he first met her. Billy likes Sue as a friend and tries to experience sexual feelings towards her but fails miserably: "She [Sue] uncrossed her leg and it touched mine so she moved it away but then I brushed my leg up against hers and held it there. She didn't pull away, but I didn't feel anything. I mean I felt her leg but I didn't feel anything, if you know what I mean" (19).

School and extracurricular activities offer no escape from Billy's dilemma. Although Billy is a member of the swim team, a popular sport at his high school, his obsession for technical anatomical terms (especially concerning the male anatomy) throughout the novel reveals his secret sexual desires which, in spite of his frequent erotic fantasies about other males, don't seem to penetrate his waking conscious mind. He becomes fascinated with Kevin and Evan, the identical twins on his swim team who share a rather odd relationship of mutual affection. Billy identifies with the pair without understanding why. It is only after these secret fantasies become reality through his relationship with Al DiCicco that Billy becomes aware of his true sexuality.

Billy's coming out process is slow but sure. He first redirects his sexual fantasies toward Al, whom he had recently met at the local McCarthy for President headquarters. One fantasy begins after a day in the campaign office, "I took a bath and imagined making out with Al in his Kharmann Ghia, feeling up each other's crotches" (37), and another after a rather awkward telephone conversation between the two, "I took my hard-on into my room. . . . I took a shower and laid down in the tub and soaped up my cock and beat off to <<Me and AL in 69 in the Woods by the Fire>>" (53). Soon Billy recognizes his feelings towards Al and defines them as a crush, which leads to their first kiss (66). Billy finally confides in his swim coach, Mr. Bieniwicz, who challenges him for the first time with the word "homosexual":

"I think it's absolutely natural because it feels fine, it's the way my body feels, I like the way it feels—"
"Are you saying you're homosexual?"
"What?"
"Are you homosexual?"
"Uh, well—"
"Do you like other guys—sexually?"
"Yeah."
"Haven't you heard the word homosexual before?"
"Of *course* I've heard the *word*, it just sounds so stupid." (89)

Billy's final acceptance of his homosexuality comes when he declares his love for Al and uses the word "homosexual" in reference to their relationship (129).

Another major theme that appears in *The Boys on the Rock* and his short story "The Superhero" posits homosexuality as a natural phenomenon that the protagonists may not fully understand but eventually accept without shame or guilt. Dennis Grogan, the preadolescent protagonist of "The Superhero," experiences an odd same-sex fantasy with his best friend Gary Peachey. Despondent over his friend's absence on one particular summer day, Dennis pores over copies of his old comic books: "He tried concentrating on Element Lad—blond, handsome, perfectly built, generous and earnest. He reminded Dennis of Gary Peachey, and was therefore his favorite among the Legion of Superheroes" ("The Superhero," 42–43). Dennis fantasizes that Gary has indeed come to visit him, then experiences a moment of surrealistic homoeroticism in which the two boys become one. When Dennis returns to himself, he longs for that which he had just experienced. He returns home and clearly expresses his open acceptance for his experience when he declares to his sister, "I feel like going into the woods" ("Superhero," 53), the site of this most unusual event.

Once the narrator of *The Boys on the Rock* comes to terms with the reality of his gayness, he seems distressed about society's failure to accept his newly discovered sexuality. He has accepted these feelings and resents his lover Al for his lack of self-acceptance,

"Why don't you go to a shrink and get cured?," I said. Looking out at the ocean, he lifted his head an inch off my chest.
"—If you hate it so much."
"Hate what?"
"Being a homosexual."
"I can't stand that word," he said. (129)

At the end of the novel Billy agonizes over the loss of his lover but reaffirms his own self-acceptance. He tells his woman friend Emo about his relationship with Al, quite pleased about her positive and supportive response. He becomes the Boy on the Rock, alone and unsure of the future yet self-assured in himself and his sexuality.

CRITICAL RECEPTION

Critical reaction to John Fox's work has been minimal, limited to liner notes from his novel or the *Christopher Street* anthologies that contain his short stories. Included are comments from Edmund White* and Richard Price. Reviews of *The Boys on the Rock* emphasize the sexual-discovery aspects of the novel and in general are quite positive. Reviews can also be found in nonliterary sources such as *Torso* magazine or *The Advocate*.

WORKS BY JOHN FOX

The Boys on the Rock. New York: Plume Books, 1985 (originally published by St. Martin's Press, 1984).
"Over the Pyrenees." In *Men on Men.* New York: Plume Books, 1986.
"The Superhero." In *First Love/Last Love: New Fiction from Christopher Street.* New York: St. Martin's Press, 1986.

SELECTED STUDIES OF JOHN FOX

Henderson, David W. Review of *The Boys on the Rock. Library Journal* 109 (August 1984): 1466.
McCoy, W. Keith. Review of *The Boys on the Rock. Interracial Books for Children Bulletin* 16 (1985): 25.
Steinberg, Sybil. Review of *The Boys on the Rock. Publisher's Weekly* 225 (April 27, 1984): 73.

SANFORD FRIEDMAN (1928–   )

Joel Shatzky

BIOGRAPHY

Sanford Friedman was born on June 11, 1928, in New York City, the son of Leonard and Madeline (Uris) Friedman. He received a B.F.A. from the Carnegie Institute of Technology (now Carnegie-Mellon University) in 1949 and began his involvement in theater when he was barely out of his teens, as playwright-in-residence at University Playhouse on Cape Cod, Massachusetts. After graduation, he moved to London, where he worked as a clerk for a year.

From 1951 to 1953 Friedman served in the United States army as a Military Policeman. He served in Korea and received the Bronze Star. He returned to theater in 1954 as a producer for the Carnegie Hall Playhouse, then supported himself as a writer from 1958 to 1975. He was a part-time instructor in reading poetry at the Julliard School in New York City from 1975 to 1979. From 1985 until the present (1991), he has been conducting workshops in creative writing at S.A.G.E. in New York City. Since 1985, he has also been a member of the Executive Board of the P.E.N. Center.

In 1965, Friedman received the O. Henry Award from the Society of Arts and Sciences for "Ocean," a segment of his first novel *Totempole*. In 1984 he was honored with an award in literature from the American Academy and Institute of Arts and Letters.

Until *Totempole* was published in 1965, Friedman was primarily a playwright, although many of his works were unproduced. At the age of nineteen, however, his first play, "Dawn from an Unknown Ocean," was presented at University Playhouse in Mashpee, Massachusetts. Sections of *Totempole* first appeared in the *Partisan Review* and *New World Writing*. After *Totempole*, Friedman published three more novels. The first, *A Haunted Woman* (1968), did not center on gay themes, exploring the crisis of a widowed woman whose late husband's play is about to be produced. In 1975 Friedman's best-received work, *Still Life: Two Short Novels*, examined sexuality in a far more symbolic way than in his first work. His most recently published novel, *Rip Van Winkle* (1980), completely departs from his earlier concerns.

MAJOR WORKS AND THEMES

Friedman's first novel, *Totempole* (1965), focuses on Stephen Wolfe, a young man growing up in a New York Jewish family during the Depression. The novel concerns Stephen's developing awareness of his homosexuality.

Stephen's relationship with a counselor at a boys' camp is sensitively portrayed. In his review of the novel, Granville Hicks states: "I do not know of any piece of fiction that deals more perceptively with preadolescent sex" (21). The approach that Friedman uses, however, is analytical, and seems to be a reflection of the earlier forms of gay fiction, in which a plea for understanding as much as an assertion of sexual identity is emphasized.

The novel connects Stephen's sexuality from infancy to his psychological neuroses, including the episodes in which his father parades around in only pajama tops to the distress of his mother and the delight of Stephen. But physical description at times predominates over psychological insight, as if Friedman is trying to provide evidence in order to support his protagonist's feelings about his sexuality.

The pressures on Stephen to conform are evident when he attempts a heterosexual affair in college and fails, but he arrives at reasonable emotional stability through male companionship in Korea. What is clear throughout is that Friedman did not try to disguise the sexuality of the protagonist through subtlety or metaphor at a time in which such a novel was still considered daring. Reflecting the climate of opinion in 1965, one reviewer, J. M. Carroll, asserted that the "perversions and inversions" of Friedman's sexual descriptions "seem excessive" (3309). Where the novel suffers most is a reflection of the time in which it was written. It has the elements of a case study that can be used to advance a cause, a cause that no longer had to be argued by the time Friedman's next novel about gay issues was published a decade later.

Friedman's second novel, however, *The Haunted Woman* (1968), is a depiction of a modern, sensitive woman who is at a crisis in her life concerning her own future and that of her dead husband's work. The author shows his emotional range by not dealing as directly with the subject of his first novel. The interest in psychological analysis that surfaced in *Totempole*, however, remains.

It was in his third book, *Still Life* (1975), two short novels, that Friedman combined his exploration into the deeper elements of the psyche with his sexual concerns. Through the juxtaposition of the two works, the first set in contemporary New York, the second in mythic Greece, Friedman explores the sexual imagination in its physical and symbolic manifestations.

The title work of the book concerns Danny Wahl, the son of a highly cultivated French-Jewish family. He has returned home in order to see if he can adjust to "normal" life after his stay at a mental institution. Danny's inability to accept his sexuality ends with a brutal description of his suicide. The fact that he is only an adolescent points to the pressures toward sexual conformity, even in the 1970s, that could motivate him to such a terrible act.

Friedman delves into myth in the second novella, "Lifeblood," which tells the story of Agdistis, Dionysus' hermaphrodite half-brother, who is castrated by order of a council of the gods. The beautiful youth Attis, however, becomes Agdistis' lover and eventually his self-castrating, sacrificial victim. The linking of the two novellas occurs not only through the act of denying one's sexuality, one through death, the other castration, but also through the use of a "council" that Danny imagines, which mirrors the council of Olympians in "Lifeblood."

Thus the novel's two parts, separated though they are by time and imagination, complement one another in exploring the connection between myth and delusion, madness and its symbolic representation. Friedman is attempting to discover in these two works the archetypal forms for the emotional dislocations that homosexuals go through when they do not have the psychological support system that they need to sustain them against social alienation.

It is perhaps significant that, after a gap of seven years, Friedman's most recently published work, *Rip Van Winkle* (1980), has nothing to do with homosexuality, as if he had laid the subject to rest. Perhaps his desire to explore that theme was more in keeping with the pre-Stonewall era than with the more recent period of sexual liberation. But it is far more likely that Friedman's view transcends any narrow definitions of subject matter. At present, he is at work on a novel about Beethoven.

CRITICAL RECEPTION

Although Friedman's protagonist's sexual experiences are referred to as "perversions" in *Totempole* in J. M. Carroll's review of the book, Granville Hicks praises the novel for its "honest" representation of Stephen Wolfe's sexuality. Hicks specifically admires the way in which "Friedman treats the homosexual theme ... with great candor and no lubricity" (21).

On the other hand, in the *New York Times Book Review*, Webster Schott criticizes the sexual detail as "a guide to technique ... and a plea ... for homosexuality as a form of romantic love" (26). Carroll, in fact, does not recommend the novel for fiction collections, and Schott considers it "talent spent on a Cause" (26).

In contrast, the reviews for *Still Life* may reflect the work of a writer who is more confident of his craft, as well as the critics of a different era. W. R. Evans regards the title story as "a minor masterpiece" (196), and John Hollander in the *New Republic* described the two sections of the novel as "a subtly but powerfully unified work" (30).

The first of the two novellas fares better than the second, however, as Evans regards much of the talk among the gods in "Lifeblood" as "phony conversation." Bruce Allen also takes Friedman to task for "a cloying emphasis on masochistic butchery" in "Still Life" (1153). Yet the sexual nature of the materials is no longer alluded to with any indication of moral censure but merely, in Allen's review, as "ambivalent sexuality" (1153).

Overall, the reception of *Still Life* was very favorable, with far less emphasis on the subject itself as controversial and far more upon its artistic merits than in the critical response to *Totempole*. Friedman's interest, however, seemed to move away from gay themes in *Still Life*, in comparison to the earlier novel, and more toward myth and archetype. As a strategy for examining and attempting to come to grips with his sexuality, Sanford Friedman's work deserves careful examination as an arresting example of homophilic literature at a time when the subject itself was a source of great controversy. Yet perhaps the best summation of his fiction was expressed by R. W. B. Lewis when Friedman received the award for literature from the American Academy and Institute of Arts and Letters: "Sanford Friedman's fiction explores the realm of prose romance in which inner states and outward representation enter into allegorical relation."

WORKS BY SANFORD FRIEDMAN

Totempole. New York: Dutton, 1965. Reissued by North Point Press, 1984.
A Haunted Woman. New York: Dutton, 1968.
Still Life: Two Short Novels. New York: Saturday Review Press, 1975.
Rip Van Winkle. New York: Atheneum, 1980.

SELECTED STUDIES OF SANFORD FRIEDMAN

Allen, Bruce. Review of *Still Life*. *Library Journal* 1 June 1975: 1153.
Carroll, J. M. Review of *Totempole*. *Library Journal* 8 August 1965:3309.
Hicks, Granville. Review of *Totempole*. *Saturday Review* 21 August 1965: 21.
Hollander, John. Review of *Still Life*. *New Republic* 14 June 1975: 30.
Long, Barbara. Review of *Totempole*. *Book Week* 9 September 1965: 24.
Schott, Webster. Review of *Totempole*. *New York Times Book Review* 29 August 1965: 35.

JOHN GILGUN (1935–   )
Jerry Rosco

BIOGRAPHY

John Francis Gilgun is best known as the author of *Music I Never Dreamed Of*, a refreshingly unique short novel of time and place. The time is the repressive era of the 1950s in America, the place is the Irish working-class neighborhood of South Boston, and the protagonist is Stevie Riley, a young man who comes to terms with his homosexuality despite all the odds. That the book took nearly three decades to see print is very much a part of the author's life story.

Born on October 1, 1935, in Malden, Massachusetts, Gilgun received his B.A. from Boston University in 1957, but he is largely a product of the Iowa Writers' Workshop, with an M.A. in 1959, M.F.A. in 1970 and Ph.D. in 1972 from the University of Iowa, Iowa City.

During his college years he began a longtime friendship with another promising young writer, Carl Morse, later well known as playwright, poet, and editor. There exists a manuscript of over one thousand pages of correspondence between Gilgun and Morse; one striking note is the slow, lonely process each friend experienced coming out sexually in pre-Stonewall America.

Gilgun's precocious writing talent flourished at Iowa City. Notably, his M.A. thesis of stories contains the forty-one-page "In a Yellow Wood," which represents the first draft of his popular novel. Stored in the University of Iowa Library, "In a Yellow Wood" concerns Christian, a Boston College student living in a dorm on Kenmore Square and struggling with his sexuality. Some of the main characters and plot of the future novel appear in this early gay fiction. What distinguishes the early draft are the emotional elements, clear characterization, and strikingly good dialogue.

Gilgun began the summer of 1959 sharing an apartment with Carl Morse at First Avenue and First Street in New York. He then returned to Boston to face a two-month battle with the U.S. Army, which processed him out as a homosexual. Afterwards, he returned to the University of Iowa where he received a fellowship and began to write for the *Daily Iowan.*

Influenced by Jack Kerouac, Gilgun hitchhiked to San Francisco in May 1960. He associated with the Beats at the Co-Existence Bagel Shop, while working as a billing clerk for the Red Stack Tugboat Company. Then he took his first teaching job, at a junior college in Kokomo, Indiana. After two semesters, his ambitious writing career took over.

During 1960, Gilgun's nongay story, "A Penny for the Ferryman," appeared in *New World Writing #16*, alongside work by John Knowles, Anne Sexton, and Thomas Pynchon. This and his promise of a novel led to a small cash advance from Macmillan and the more substantial Eugene F. Saxton Memorial Trust Award from Harper and Row.

The Saxton Award required a year away from work, and in 1961 and part of 1962 Gilgun lived in Mexico, first in Mexico City, then in San Miguel del Allende, producing 700 pages of his prospective gay novel. When it was time to return to teaching, he did, surviving what he called a "dreadful" year at Clarkson College in Potsdam, New York. Then in 1963 he used his small savings for a year in Spain, living on the island of Ibiza and completing a full 800-page draft of his novel about a young man coming out in Boston in the 1950s.

Gilgun returned to New York in April 1964, living for a time at the Vanderbilt YMCA. An editor at Lippincott, Ms. Tay Hohoff, offered a contract and a cash advance for the book.

Gilgun taught at Drake University in Des Moines, Iowa, from 1964 to 1968. There the good news of his novel turned worse and worse. Tay Hohoff cut the manuscript from 800 to 300 pages, which destroyed it. Gilgun recalled in a magazine interview: "We had a corpse on our hands. She broke the contract. She also broke me. I didn't write anything after that for four years" (*Torso*, 20). He suffered a serious decline in health in 1967 and then slowly recovered.

After teaching a semester at the University of California, Santa Barbara, he turned back to Iowa City and to writing from 1969 to 1972. "Dr. Stranglehold," a 250-page manuscript about a man facing hard economic times, and "America Can Break Your Heart," alternately humorous and sad stories about men and women surviving in the 1960s, earned him his Ph.D. and M.F.A., respectively. In 1972, he accepted a position at Missouri Western State College, Saint Joseph, Missouri, and has lived there ever since, making frequent visits to both coasts.

Throughout the 1970s, Gilgun experienced a revival, publishing Iowa City material, as well as his unique animal "reincarnation fables," in such journals as *Iowa Review, Mississippi Review, Four Quarters, Pequod, Paragraph*, and others. At the same time that his fiction writing was reborn

through traditional little magazines, his most ambitious lifelong theme—
the pre-Stonewall coming-of-age story—began to appear in post-Stonewall
gay publications. His gay fiction in Dan Curzon's* *Gay Literature #6* and
in issues of *Blueboy* encouraged him to return to his early gay novel and
rewrite it as a small, well-honed narrative work called "Green." (Gilgun
had published his early gay stories under the pseudonym "Jerry Green.")

In 1981, Gilgun's witty, aphoristic fables were published as *Everything
That Has Been Shall Be Again*. But "Green" remained stymied, first by an
agent's interference with a Gray Fox Press acceptance, then by the financial
limitations of Toronto's Stumblejumper Press. Finally, the novel was accepted by Amethyst Press. Editor-in-chief Stan Leventhal suggested a title
change to *Music I Never Dreamed Of*, as well as a few flash-forwards and
other minor revisions. Published in December 1989, it met with universal
praise in the gay press and a second edition was published in 1990.

Gilgun has turned to prose poems in recent years and two collections
appeared in 1991, *The Dooley Poems* and *From the Inside Out*. His work
has been published in many journals, magazines, and anthologies.

MAJOR WORKS AND THEMES

John Gilgun's place in contemporary gay literature is very much that of
the pre-Stonewall writer whose voice finally was heard many years into the
post-Stonewall era. Yet, if success is measured by quality rather than quan-
tity, the long road to publication may have been paved in gold. Although
it might not console a writer whose major work was suppressed for nearly
three decades, perhaps Gilgun's Iowa City writing and the success of his
fables transformed a fine manuscript into its extraordinary final revision,
Music I Never Dreamed Of, a novel that is a strong candidate for crossover
re-publication on a large scale.

Gilgun's narrative gift was strengthened by the clear, unfettered quality
characteristic of the Iowa City school of writing. The vivid first-person
narrative voice of the animal fables in *Everything That Has Been Shall Be
Again* heightened the truth-telling ardor of a writer strongly influenced by
Walt Whitman and Herman Melville. And praise for the fables did much
to heal Gilgun's writer's heartbreak of the 1960s.

During the late 1970s and early 1980s, Gilgun wrote several short pieces
of powerful gay fiction, all pre-Stonewall in nature: "Beauty" (*Four Quarters*, vol. 28, no. 4, 1979), "The Centipede" and "The Subtle Body" (*Blueboy*, September 1979 and March 1980), and "Tragic Event" in Ian Young's
On The Line anthology (1981). "The Subtle Body" and "Tragic Event"
strongly evoke themes of his eventual first novel, *Music I Never Dreamed
Of*; and another story, "Boppin' " (*James White Review*, vol. 1, no. 3,
1984), became its emotional first chapter.

Music I Never Dreamed Of takes place in working-class Irish South

Boston in the 1950s. Every family watches Milton Berle on their black-and-white television sets. In Washington, Senator Joe McCarthy thunders against communists and homosexuals. Nonconformity is out of the question. Yet nineteen-year-old Stevie Riley is determined to find his way to his true sexual identity and happiness. But the road is not easy.

Having "washed out" of seminary school, Stevie returns to his parents' home. Before he can settle his duffle bag on the kitchen floor, his mother greets him with the Help Wanted pages. His sexy, ungettable friend Ralph helps him get a job at a box-cutting factory, where he meets Luanne, who first seduces him, then befriends him when she understands his private struggle. Most striking is the fresh clarity, immediacy and—most important—believability of the narrative. Steve Riley's innocent and endearing voice is strongly reminiscent of Holden Caulfield's, and Gilgun's novel has the same irresistible quality as J. D. Salinger's *Catcher in the Rye*. Indeed, in his *Torso* interview, Gilgun stated, "This book is my attempt to save all the gay kids before they fall off the cliff" (22).

As to the powerful narrative voice, Gilgun explained that he tape-recorded the 1980 version of his novel as he wrote it. "I knew when I got the sound of Stevie's voice—working class Boston Irish—I could complete the novel successfully" (*Torso*, 22).

More than any other aspect, it is the working-class sensibility of *Music I Never Dreamed Of* that distinguishes its place in American gay literature. Here are humble, moral, hard-working people, manipulated and abused by the political and economic system. Steve's quiet, defeated, taxi-driving father asks for nothing more than some quiet and his beer. His sweet rheumatic older brother Brian is forced by their Catholicism into an early marriage, and by marriage into a lifeless job at his Uncle Tim's manufacturing company. Even his hardbitten mother can move Steve to tears. A minimum-wage waitress who works long hours at a hotel, she feels she must be tough with her sons or they will end up like her husband. When Stevie escapes from his own career-talk with Uncle Tim, he sees "my mother standing in the hall. She was wearing the green nylon blouse she wore every Saint Patrick's Day and she had a plastic shamrock in her graying hair" (74).

These are real people, from a background experienced by many gay people but seldom captured in our literature. The working-class theme and the novel's excellent illumination of the McCarthy era in America are reasons why *Music I Never Dreamed Of* will continue to reach a wider audience.

Ultimately, Steve's emerging sexuality leads him to a sophisticated Jewish boy named Hal and an escape from the U.S. Army or the fate of his brother Brian. After their first encounter, Hal asks Steve how he knows if he's really gay or just experimenting. Steve answers, "I know it in my soul" (148).

CRITICAL RECEPTION

Although not part of Gilgun's gay fiction, *Everything That Has Been Shall Be Again* was important to his development and his return to fiction writing.

Printed in both deluxe and paperback editions, it won four awards, including the Chicago Book Clinic Award and the Midwestern Book Award. In July 1982, *Fine Print* (vol. 8, no. 3) praised the beauty of the book itself and of Michael McCurdy's wood engravings and also offered keen perceptions of Gilgun's skills: "These are voices that recall those of Edgar Lee Master's *Spoon River Anthology*, educated by death (by many deaths, in fact, and many lives). . . . Speaking of Masters, the American sound of some of the monologues makes a noteworthy contribution to the genre of the fable and stakes out some ground for the New World in this decidedly Old World field" (98).

Although *Music I Never Dreamed Of* was not reviewed in the mainstream press, this omission may have indicated the fledgling status of the publisher no less than homophobia. Surprisingly, it was praised in the heterosexual alternative magazine *SCREW* (20). Praise for the book in the gay press was especially meaningful because Gilgun was and remains a total outsider, not associated with any group of gay writers. Yet the book was nominated under best male fiction for a Lambda Award and by the American Library Association. Good reviews and word of mouth led to the novel's success. Five hundred copies were distributed in London.

Among the reviews, *The Guide* noted that Steve Riley "never loses the honesty and innocence which gives his story not only its center but its edge as well" (16). Likewise, *Bay Area Reporter* remarked, "We are in Steve's mind, body and feelings consistently" (31). Michael Bronski in *The Advocate* perceptively noted that Gilgun's "cadence and the collision of class, religious, ethnic and sexual identities has created a world we almost never read about in gay fiction" (67). Harold Norse in *Lambda Book Report* wrote that the book, despite the thirty years' delay, "has appeared at the right time and, I suspect, with its shining prose, insight, emotional honesty and clear-sighted passion, it may be around a long time, like *Huckleberry Finn* and *Catcher in the Rye*, to challenge future generations with its truth and beauty" (42).

WORKS BY JOHN GILGUN

Everything That Has Been Shall Be Again: The Reincarnation Fables of John Gilgun. Saint Paul, Minn.: Bieler Press, 1981.
Music I Never Dreamed Of. New York: Amethyst Press, 1989, 1990.
The Dooley Poems. Los Angeles: Robin Price, 1991.
From the Inside Out. Mulvane, Kans.: Three Phase Publishing, 1991.

SELECTED STUDIES OF JOHN GILGUN

Livingston, Mark C. "The Bieler Press." *Fine Print* 7, no. 3 (July 1982): 98.
May, Hal, ed. *Contemporary Authors #117*. Detroit: Gale, 1986: 2608.
Bronski, Michael. "Books in Review." *The Guide*. February 1990: 16.
Rosco, Jerry. "An Interview with John Gilgun." *Torso* April 1990: 18.

Shaw, Marvin. "Coming Out Equals Manhood." *Bay Area Reporter* 12 April 1990: 31.
Norse, Harold. "Sweet Dreams." *Lambda Book Report* May/June 1990: 24.
Bronski, Michael. "Life of Riley." *The Advocate* 5 July 1990: 67.
Perkins, Michael. "Hard Copy." *Screw* 27 August 1990: 20.

GARY GLICKMAN (1959–)
Philip Gambone

BIOGRAPHY

Gary Glickman was born on March 20, 1959, in Morristown, New Jersey, into, in his words, a "very significant matriarchy." (All quotations in this biography are from an interview with Philip Gambone, October 14, 1991.) His maternal grandmother's family had been among the first Jews to settle in Morristown, where they helped to found both synagogues. Much like Rose Keppler in Glickman's novel *Years from Now*, Glickman's grandmother, Esse Yawitz Schlosser, had eight sisters. It was amidst this large constellation of great-aunts, aunts, and cousins that Glickman was raised.

Glickman's parents were divorced when he was young, another bit of his biography that is echoed in the novel, where the parents of David Rosen, the protagonist, are similarly divorced. "I hated my childhood," Glickman reports. "My mother married a man [full of] self-contempt and unexamined rage. Which translated into virulent homophobia. I grew up in the middle of enormous hatred."

During high school, Glickman pursued musical and literary interests, what he calls "proto-faggot stuff." He played saxophone in the school band, bassoon in the orchestra, and piano. Throughout his school years, he was also writing: poetry, essays, a long fragment of an early novel, and, in his senior year, the class play.

In the fall of 1977, Glickman entered Brown University, where he double-majored in English and music. During his junior year, he met classmate Meg Wolitzer, who was shortly to publish her first novel. "Meg was the one who taught me you can say to the world and to yourself, 'I am a writer,' " Glickman states. The two became close friends.

After college, Glickman worked as assistant director and general factotum at Pine Orchard Artists Festival in Palenville, New York. The following year, 1982, he enrolled in the Writers' Workshop at the University of Iowa. Though he was not particularly happy with the program, Glickman acknowledges that one of his teachers at Iowa, the writer Lynne Sharon Schwartz, "had a big effect" on him.

In 1984, Glickman moved to New York, where, for a time, he shared an apartment with Meg Wolitzer. Later that year, he met David Leavitt,* who had just published his first collection of stories, *Family Dancing.* "For the next five years," Glickman reports, "David and I spent every minute together." During that first year in New York, Glickman completed a novel, based in part on his experiences in Palenville. "It was about a big Catholic family, except they were Jews." When the novel was rejected for publication, Leavitt suggested that Glickman write about his own family and his own Jewish heritage. From Leavitt's suggestion emerged Glickman's story, "The Four Questions," which eventually became a chapter in *Years from Now.*

A year after they met, in the fall of 1985, Glickman and Leavitt moved to East Hampton. "We were a very public couple," Glickman notes. "Our living together and making appearances together was a very strong statement. To us it was just being, but I know to many people it was very challenging and upsetting."

In 1988, Glickman visited Tunisia, a trip that had a significant effect on his life and fiction. "I loved being on my own and in a weird place. I loved being a stranger in the world. I finally had met what I had felt like my entire life, a total stranger: gay, Jewish and an artist." From that trip, Glickman began to formulate ideas for a new book, a nonfiction work, which he eventually titled *To the Place of Trumpeting: Travels in a Diaspora.* Now complete but as yet unpublished, it is a book of stories about various places that at one time were important in Jewish history. "I went there as a Jew," Glickman notes, "to write about what it was like to be there now. I found that going out into the world as a Jew, I was going out into the world more as a gay person. Each time I went to look for Jews I found gay people; and each time I went to find gay people I found Jews."

The trip to Tunisia also helped Glickman identify dissatisfactions in his life with Leavitt. By the summer of 1990, the two had permanently separated and Glickman had moved to Boston to teach in the freshman writing program at Tufts University. The following winter, Glickman was awarded a grant from the National Endowment for the Arts. The award allowed him to leave his teaching position at the end of the academic year and move, that summer, to Provincetown, Massachusetts, where he lived and wrote for the next two years.

In addition to the travel book, Glickman has completed a second novel, *Sylvia Threefoot,* and is at work on a new novel set in Provincetown. Glickman continues to compose as well. In August, 1991, his comic opera, *Orlando, or Love of a Leg,* based on Virginia's Woolf's novel, received its first full-length performance at the Euro Cafe in Provincetown.

MAJOR WORKS AND THEMES

Glickman's one published novel to date, *Years from Now*, opens with a beautifully evoked picture of Lewistown, New Jersey, the hometown of his central character, David Rosen. "It was there," Glickman writes, "that Thomas Paine came for refuge, that Alexander Hamilton found his bride, and that Samuel Morse first tapped out his amazing code" (3). Refuge, love, communication—these become the broad themes that Glickman weaves into his story, one that spans four generations and encompasses a large cast of characters.

Years from Now is both an episodic chronicle of the Keppler family, David's maternal grandmother's clan, whom we see at all the ritual gatherings of middle-class American Jewish life—weddings, funerals, seders—and a specifically gay novel, which follows David from his adolescence through his early adult years. In addition to the family, the novel focuses on two "outsiders" who enter David's world, his college girlfriend Beth Bauer, a sometime lesbian, and Andrew Chase, a blond gentile who eventually becomes David's lover.

Each member of David's family, but especially his mother Zellie, is individually and carefully drawn. Collectively, warts and all, Glickman presents them as a source of strength and love. For Zellie, Glickman writes, love "was no abstract idea." It was "large as loneliness, but whole and palpable and close" (5). At age seven, Zellie experiences her first romantic crush, for the fiancé of her cousin Gloria. Years later, divorced and the mother of three, she remarries. Although this episode in the novel suggests that romantic love is a healing and redemptive power, another, perhaps stronger, implication is that the appeal of the traditional family nucleus, a husband and wife, is what ultimately has prompted Zellie's remarriage. "I always felt married," she explains. "Even when I wasn't. I just had to find someone to be married with again" (71). For Zellie, love's locus is the family, and family is "all . . . that finally mattered" (216).

Family love and the heritage of Judaism also make their appealing claims on David, the perfect representative of the next generation; but, as a gay man, he finds that he cannot always fulfill the familial and tribal expectations. At times, he feels left out and disenfranchised. The clan, as nurturing as it is, doesn't always feel like enough. The dramatic tension arises from these conflicting demands of family loyalty and personal integrity which David tries, with appealing honesty, candor, and humor, to reconcile. The long central chapter, "The Four Questions," in which David brings Andrew home for the family seder, masterfully evokes this complexity of issues, organizing them around the image of the "stranger" in the midst.

In the second half of the novel, the central issue becomes Beth's desire to have a baby with David. David, too, feels that it's a kind of destiny for him to have a child. "For the Jews," (197) he tells a jealous and uncomprehending

Andrew. The child, both figuratively and literally, is to become, as Beth at one point imagines, "all of these loves... coming together as one" (225). Nevertheless, David feels some anxiety about this unorthodox way of raising a child. Would it lead them "too far" ever to return to the path—and the refuge—of the family? (236).

Glickman avoids easy answers. He suggests that "for better or worse," we are all "stuck firmly among" family and what comes with it (246). And yet, the richness and scope of the novel do not allow for simplistic notions about sticking with one's own kind, especially if one is a gay man. By the final chapter, narrated in first person by David, he and Beth have had a son, who is being raised, alternately, by David and by Beth's mother, Barbara. "If life was slapping us in the face," David says, "it was also waking us up to our brief, meager power to slap it back, and shape it a little bit to our own designs" (258). And though he does not know what the future will hold, David comes to affirm what he is, "surely," both a father and a homosexual (262). (This complex awareness of roots and loyalties and the many options for organizing one's life is evident in Glickman's published short stories as well, especially in "Magic," which appeared in *Men on Men 2*.)

As Glickman has noted elsewhere, "I wanted to say [in the novel], 'Look, my life isn't special; I'm as ordinary as can be, but it contains both this mainstream or traditional world and the homosexual man, the bar mitzvah boy who sucks cocks' " (interview with Philip Gambone in *Bay Windows*, April 13, 1989).

Years from Now is a complex, dramatically satisfying novel about the power of love, in all its many incarnations, to transform us into real people.

CRITICAL RECEPTION

Years from Now met with mixed reviews. Even the harshest critics, such as Daniel Harris in the *New York Native*, acknowledged that it was "extraordinarily competent" and that, as a first novelist, Glickman exhibited "the skill others seldom attain after five" (September 7, 1987; 28). Indeed, a theme in many of the reviews was Glickman's promising talent. At least three reviewers praised the writing as "rich"; others noted the novel's sensitive vision, its ambitiousness, and Glickman's considerable gift for characterization. *Books* called it "the most moving gay novel of the spring" (April 1988, 16). "[S]entence by sentence, paragraph by paragraph," wrote Richard Dyer in the *Boston Globe*, "Glickman's novel reveals that he is a writer of wide range and deep sympathy" (March 14, 1989; 26).

Several reviewers noted with particular pleasure the scenes of family celebrations and religious rituals. "It is in capturing these ceremonies and the older family members who hold fast to them that Mr. Glickman is at his best," wrote Robert Houston in the *New York Times Book Review*. "His ear...is wonderfully accurate. His ability to quickly sketch memorable characters is impressive. And his sense of the rhythms, the beauty, the absurdity, the poignancy of the family as it participates in its rituals is delightful" (October 18, 1987; 20).

At the same time, many of these same reviewers found the novel ultimately flawed. Three major criticisms emerge: the novel's structural problems, including too many characters and lack of a central focus ("in effect two novels," wrote Houston); Glickman's tendency toward sentimentality and overwriting; and, most scathing of all, the political incorrectness of the novel's vision.

James Wolcott, in a piece about Leavitt and Glickman in *Vanity Fair*, criticized the "timidity" in both authors' works. "So it isn't the gay element of being a guppie that holds Leavitt and Glickman back," he wrote; "it's the yuppie element, the protective coloration of being contented consumers" (March 1989, 46). Even more disparaging was Harris' *Native* review, which excoriated the novel's premise of "two soul-searching Jewish New Yorkers rummaging greedily among asphyxiatingly fetid emotional rubbish for their religious and familial roots." Harris castigated Glickman for indulging in "his squalid ideology, his sopping-wet immersion in the black lagoon of the gay status quo." Harris not only scorned the novel's "peanut-butter-and-jellyization of gay life" but also the mainstream publishers who "prefer subjects that represent the very assimilative process I have been describing." In Harris' opinion, to be a gay man, like Glickman's David Rosen, "who reenters society, settles down, forms families, often even having children, often even getting religion," is to be a "pasteurized, expurgated homosexual." Another version of this inability to accept the novel's reality is found in Karen Heller's review for the *Philadelphia Inquirer*, where she faulted David's mother and grandmother for accepting his homosexuality "in record time" (September 27, 1987; 7).

A more moderate view, one that accepts the world of the novel as Glickman depicts it, is that taken by gay author and critic Richard Hall,* who, in his review for the *San Francisco Chronicle*, placed *Years from Now* within the tradition of the novel of identity formation. "Will David, we wonder, be able to invent himself—construct an identity, forge a freedom, that will permit him to encompass all these conflicts?...Will he, in short, come to resemble the heroes of countless other novels who slam the front doors of their dollhouses and head for a golden gay ghetto in order to find—not freedom, but at least a set of chains they can bear?" (August 23, 1987; 8).

WORKS BY GARY GLICKMAN

"The Triumph of Dora Barensky at the End of the World." *Mississippi Review* (Spring 1986): 112–21.
Years from Now. New York: Alfred A. Knopf, 1987.

"Magic." In *Men on Men 2*. Ed. George Stambolian. (New York: Dutton, 1988): 229–321.

"Question and Answer." *Bomb* (Spring 1989): 64–65.

"Whispers in the Dark." *Frontiers* 10, no. 21(1992):42–43.

"Buried Treasures." *Penguin Anthology of Gay Literature*. Forthcoming, 1993.

SELECTED STUDIES OF GARY GLICKMAN

Bittmann, Joe. "An Imperfect Portrait of Gays." *Cleveland Plain-Dealer* 6 September 1987: B4.

Dyer, Richard. Review of *Years from Now*. *Boston Globe* 14 March 1987: 26.

Hall, Richard. Review of *Years from Now*. *Vanity Fair*. *San Francisco Chronicle* 23 August 1987: 8.

Harris, Daniel. Review of *Years from Now*. *New York Native* 7 September 1987: 28.

Heller, Karen. Review of *Years from Now*. *Philadelphia Inquirer* 27 September 1987: 7.

Houston, Robert. Review of *Years from Now*. *New York Times Book Review* 18 October 1987: 20.

Kashner, Rita. "Guess Whose [*sic*] Coming to Seder?" *Washington Post Book World* 27 September 1987: 9.

Kendall, Elaine. "Gay Son Enlivens Ethnic Family Saga." *Los Angeles Times* 11 September 1987: V18.

Korelitz, Jean Hanff. "Doctor's Dilemmas." *Times Literary Supplement* 19 February 1988: 186.

Review of *Years from Now*. *Books* (April 1987): 16.

Wolcott, James. Review of *Years from Now*. *Vanity Fair* (March 1987): 46.

Zabusky, Charlotte Fox. Untitled review. *Wilson Library Journal* December 1987: 84.

ROBERT GLÜCK (1947–   )
Earl Jackson, Jr.

BIOGRAPHY

Robert Glück was born into a Hungarian Jewish family in Cleveland, Ohio, on February 2, 1947, and was raised in the neighborhoods of Cleveland Heights and of Woodland Hills, a suburb of Los Angeles. An undiagnosed dyslexia gave him severe problems in school; in fact, he did not learn how to read until fourth grade. Eventually an IQ test uncovered his intelligence; he worked with a tutor, and in six months he moved from children's books to Dickens. Intellectual pursuits were encouraged by his mother, who was proud of the literary figures in their heritage, including both writers and rabbis. The importance of poetry was particularly emphasized; his mother used to recite Poe and Dryden.

His father was a salesman and owned several businesses, including a bedding company. He worked for the magazine *Highlights for Children* and was transferred to Los Angeles in 1958. Reading had already become Glück's refuge, but became even more so as his isolation intensified in a tumultuous family life and the arid tract-house environment of Woodland Hills. Glück waited out his childhood; he painted and hoped to become a visual artist. Unable to connect with other students, he made friends with misfits and usually made a "pal" of an older woman teacher. In his sophomore year of high school, his English teacher Margery Bruce discerned how promising Glück was and encouraged him toward a literary career. The day she showed his class what a sonnet was, Glück went home and wrote one, his first poem. He had a painterly interest in making objects with words.

In 1964 he began an English major at UCLA, his general alienation now informed by an anxiety due to his wanting to be a gay man but not knowing how. In 1966 he went to Edinburgh for his junior year abroad. He decided to become a Shakespeare scholar; his interests shifted to Chaucer, then to twentieth-century literature. He hitchiked around Europe and, by the time he returned to the states, came to feel institutional academia was no longer an option for him. His discovery of the poetry of Frank O'Hara heartened him with the possibility it offered of both sexual and artistic freedom. In 1967 Glück transferred to Berkeley, where he became a peace activist. In a poetry class taught by Peter Dale Scott and Robert Grenier, he began a period of intense writing—two or three poems a day. After graduation he moved to a commune on a farm outside Grass Valley.

At the commune Glück lived in idyllic poverty, his experience of nature amplified by drugs, but he did not find any real support for his literary pursuits among the other residents. In the fall of 1970, Glück moved to New York City, where he worked the night shift unloading trucks at the Grand Central Station post office; he participated in Ted Berrigan's poetry workshops at the St. Mark's Poetry Project (which he initially enrolled in because of Berrigan's ties to Frank O'Hara). Berrigan liked Glück's work, and Anne Waldman published some of his poems in *The World*.

Glück fell in love with a young man. While they hitchiked around the United States and Canada, Glück wrote the long poem that became his first published chapbook, *Andy*.

In 1971 Glück moved to San Francisco. One night, waiting for a bus after seeing Warhol's *Trash*, he struck up a conversation with a Japanese-German American man named Ed Aulerich-Sugai (later to become a noted painter), who had just hitchhiked to San Francisco from Tacoma. They became lovers almost immediately and lived together until 1977. It was during these years that Glück constructed his literary life.

In 1972 he enrolled in a master's degree writing program at San Francisco State. For his M.A. orals Glück read Proust, which was a key moment in his life. He became part of a group of writers who saw themselves as "surrealists." Another important event in this period was meeting writer Bruce Boone.* Glück has always considered Boone his real teacher. Boone was supportive and constructively critical of Glück's work and introduced him to the work of Georges Bataille, structuralism, Marxist philosophy, and much else. (The poet Kathleen Fraser would become Glück's next invaluable reader.)

In 1973, *Andy* was published by Panjandrum Press. In 1976 Glück began working as a volunteer at Small Press Traffic. He eventually became codirector of that organization, in charge of workshops and readings. Three workshops emerged under Glück's direction: an open group, a gay group, and an older writer's group. Each workshop had its own nexus of creative stimulation and intimacy, and each became a group romance. Writers who emerged from one or more of these workshops include Steve Abbott,* Michael Amnasan, Dodie Bellamy, Sam D'Allesandro, Edith Jenkins, Kevin Killian,* John Norton, and Camille Roy, as well as the literary journals

Mirage and *No Apologies*. His experience with these groups and running a literary organization qualified Glück for the assistant directorship of the Poetry Center at San Francisco State University (1984–1987) and eventually the directorship (1987–1990).

There was as much sexual experimentation as literary in the late 1970s in Glück's circles. In 1981, Glück contracted hepatitis B, which he now credits with saving his life, as it put him out of commission sexually in the most dangerous year of the AIDS pandemic.

In 1982 Glück and Boone launched the Black Star Series with Glück's *Family Poems* and Boone's *My Walk with Bob*. The two writers began to receive attention from the larger San Francisco literary community. They went on to publish books by Steve Abbott, Dennis Cooper,* and others. In the same year, Robert Duncan showed Donald Allen one of Glück's stories. Allen asked Glück to write a book for Four Seasons Press. Glück considers this one of the major honors of his life: Allen is both a legendary poetry editor and Frank O'Hara's literary executor. The collection of short stories, *Elements of a Coffee Service*, appeared in 1983.

From 1982 until 1986 Glück was a member of a gay direct-action affinity group, Enola Gay. They were involved in guerrilla theater, benefit readings, rallies and protest marches—anti-U.S. interventionism, antinuclear, and the like. Glück was frequently arrested, and in 1983 he spent two weeks in the Santa Rita prison for an action against Livermore Labs.

In the early 1980s Felice Picano,* impressed with *Elements*, asked Glück for a book for his Seahorse Press. The result was *Jack the Modernist*, which Glück considers his "valentine to the gay community."

In 1986, George Stambolian included "Sex Story" from *Elements* in his first volume of *Men on Men*, which expanded Glück's readership and established his national and international reputation.

Glück has developed many friendships with writers (Kathy Acker, Dodie Bellamy, Dennis Cooper,* Lydia Davis, Robert Duncan, Kathleen Fraser, Judy Grahn, Thom Gunn, Christopher Isherwood,* Kevin Killian, Lynne Tillman, Edmund White*) that greatly enrich his own work and vision and, in his words, "enlarged the scale of what is possible in writing."

At present Glück teaches writing part time at San Francisco State and has been a visiting assistant professor for the spring quarters of 1991–1992 at the University of California, San Diego. He is currently completing a collection of stories entitled *Everyman*, which includes a novella about Margery Kemp, the fifteenth-century would-be mystic and author of the first autobiography in English.

MAJOR WORKS AND THEMES

If both Dennis Cooper and Robert Glück represent "literary postmodernism" the concept itself must be nuanced to remain meaningful. Perhaps

Cooper's work can be typified as a dystopian, Los Angeles–centered post-modernity, and Glück's a warmer, San Francisco postmodernity of identity politics and, in his words, "autonomous movements and rainbow coalitions" ("Truth's Mirror," 40). Language takes on dual purposes—one of communal affirmation ("I'm interested in the way we exist for each other in language" ["Truth's Mirror," 40]) and one of defiance, in that Glück's texts are written against the erasure of gay life from the "general public," counter to the "tenet that homosexuality does not exist verbally" (*Elements*, 15).

Glück's philosophy of language and its literary deployment comes in part from his intellectual confrontation with the language poets, who became a force in the late 1970s and early 1980s. He states that "Bruce [Boone] and I met them with resistance and admiration. The language poets insisted on a theoretical underpinning to writing. We wanted to develop a writing that allowed for the politics of community to enter—for us that meant narration. We were exploring narration from opposite ends: the language poets dismantled it and displayed its parts and operations, we continually recontextuated it." (Note: Direct quotes without source cited are personal communications from Glück to the author.) In their discussions of the language poets and their relevance, Glück and Boone established the "New Narrative," a loose group of writers each of whom came to writing with a relation to either the poetry world or the art world.

Glück has proposed two regions whose interactions and dynamics inform and condition his artistic negotiations with the world, the local and the sublime, in a recasting of Bataille:

By local I mean: intimacy, the circumstance of knowing others and being known, being the subject of one's story, sharing gestures over a period of time, sharing ideology. By sublime I mean: transgression of ego boundaries, merging, transcendence, horror/awe, discontinuities of birth, sex and death. ("Allegory," 112)

The local situates the narratives and focalizes the faith ("the willing suspension of disbelief") in the value of experience and "self." The local can range from helping Bruce shop for a leather jacket ("Night Flight," *Elements*) to a visit to an orchid farm with Ed ("Violence," *Elements*) to descriptions of his dog, Lily, waiting for muffin pieces to be tossed to her (*Jack the Modern* 15:16), to an account of his elderly neighbor's death from cancer ("Everyman"). The sublime inheres in the local but also transgresses it, particularly in sexual ecstasy in "Sex Story" and the bathhouse scene in *Jack* (54–59).

Jack the Modernist (1985) is one of the most important accomplishments in contemporary gay literature. In writing it Glück felt like "an explorer" and something of a colonizer, bringing gay male desire "into the realm of articulation." Innovative in its thematic concerns as well as in its narrative design, it remains an influential novel of the 1980s.

CRITICAL RESPONSE

Many critics comment on Glück's revolutionizing language to accommodate both gay sexual and emotional experience. Edmund White has called Robert Glück one of his favorite gay novelists and cites *Jack the Modernist* as an exploration of "nuances of love never annotated before" (24). Glück himself observes that his work is "boyfriend oriented," that "the boyfriend becomes a disjunction to project into, a longing for unity, and the medium through which form itself is contemplated as a mystery."

Aaron Shurin notes Glück's direct address of the reader as a transgressive form of engagement:

By confronting the reader, Glück not only breaks the window of his narrative but creates and engages an audience, creates a social registration for his writing by direct address. . . . The foregrounding of devices and codes does not neutralize them, they are too full of historical determination, but it can ritualize them, or expose their ritualization; reveal them not as necessities but constructions—open to change. (*Narrativity*, 4–5)

In my own work on Glück, I point out his debt to feminism for some of his models for engagement, commitment, belief in the significance of experience, and the specificity of subject positions. His work seems the most vital and dazzling example we have of reimagining the gay male body as one of wondrous play and plenitude.

WORKS BY ROBERT GLÜCK

Andy. Los Angeles and San Francisco: Panjandrum Press, 1973.
Marsha Poems. San Francisco: Hoddypoll Press, 1973.
Metaphysics. San Francisco. Hoddypoll Press, 1978.
Family Poems. San Francisco: Hoddypoll Press, 1979.
Elements of a Coffee Service. San Francisco: Four Seasons Foundation, 1982.
La Fontaine. With Bruce Boone. San Francisco: Black Star, 1982.
"Allegory." *Ironwood* 23 (1984): 112–18.
"Who Speaks for Us?" *Writing/Talks.* Ed. Bob Perleman, 1–6. Carbondale: Southern Illinois University Press, 1984.
Jack the Modernist. New York: Sea Horse, 1985.
"Sex Story." *Men on Men.* Ed. George Stambolian. New York: New American Library, 1987.
"Truth's Mirror Is No Mirror." *Poetics Journal* (1987): 40–45.
"The Purple Men." *Everyday Life.* Ed. George Tysh. Detroit: In Camera, 1989.
Reader. Los Angeles: Lapis, 1990.

"Workload." *High Risk*. Ed. Ira Silverberg and Amy Scholder. New York: New American Library, 1990.
"Denny Smith." *Gay Short Fiction*. Ed. Edmund White. London: Faber and Faber, 1991.
"Marker." *Dear World*. Ed. Camille Roy and Nayland Blake, 19–20. San Francisco: privately published, 1991.

SELECTED STUDIES OF ROBERT GLÜCK

Abbott, Steve. *View/Askew: Postmodern Investigations*. San Francisco: Androgyne, 1989.
Benson, Steve. "Aesthetics of a Relationship." *San Francisco Chronicle*. June 29, 1986: B11.
Dahlen, Beverley. "The Invention of Childhood." *Poetry Flash*, no. 128 (November 83): 8.
Hasbany, Rick. "In Quest of a New Language." *The Advocate*. 7 August 1985: 102.
Jackson, Earl, Jr. "Scandalous Subjects: Robert Glück's Embodied Narratives." *differences* 3, no. 2 (Summer 1991) *Queer Theory*. Ed. Teresa de Lauretis. 112–34.
MacClean, David. "Moderns in Love." *Body Politic* (July 1986): 27.
Person, Glenn. "Organized Neurosis." *New York Native*. No. 145 (Jan 27–Feb 2): 37.
Shafarzek, Susan. "On *Elements of a Coffee Service*." *Library Journal* 15 December 1983: 4.
Shurin, Aaron. *Narrativity*. Los Angeles: Sun and Moon Press, 1990.
———. "If the Trap Fits, Bear It." *Bay Area Reporter* 30 June 1983: 33.
Stambolian, George. "Thrills and Spills of Perception." *The Advocate* 12 November 1985: 88.
White, Edmund. "Out of the Closet, Onto the Bookshelf." *New York Times Magazine* 16 June 1991: 22–24, 35.

CLAYTON R. GRAHAM (LARRY PAUL EBMEIER) (1950–   )
Donald Callen Freed

BIOGRAPHY

Clayton R. Graham is the nom de plume of Larry Paul Ebmeier, whose first three novels were published by Knights Press under the "Graham" name. Ebmeier's fourth novel, *Engineman* (1993), was published under his real name. "Clayton" comes from his mother's maiden name, Shirley Clayton, and "Graham" is selected from the character Henry Graham in Elaine May's film, *A New Leaf*. In addition to the four novels, Ebmeier also has a short story in press.

Larry Ebmeier was born June 15, 1950, at Good Samaritan Hospital in Kearney, Nebraska, somewhat distant from his parents' Bertrand, Nebraska, farm. But it was a Catholic hospital, and it was fitting that the firstborn son of devout Catholics be born in the area's largest Catholic hospital.

Larry has always regretted not being named Lawrence or Laurence, a formality of name overlooked by his parents in the less formal "baby-boom" era. He has always considered himself "*A Man of Taste*," like Reginald Marne in his first novel by the same name—definitely more a Laurence than a Larry.

The family farm, located in Gosper County, Nebraska, is not unlike many in the area. It is in the "transition" part of the prairie, where the land begins to rise between the Great Plains and the High Plains, westward toward the Rocky Mountains. It was on the farm that Larry spent his childhood, among cornfields and cattle and under the open sky, in wide-open spaces that might encourage larger-than-life daydreams and fantasies, although Larry claims to have drawn no inspiration from the prairie. Despite this, an acquaintance with aspects of prairie life is evident in his books.

One of the author's earliest recollections is that of entertaining brother, sisters, and children from neighboring farms with his imitation of Alfred

Hitchcock (he was a "husky" child). Larry would hold a flashlight under his chin in the dark to create a silhouette, introducing his stories with Hitchcock's familiar "Good Evening." Thus began the Ebmeier penchant for telling stories.

This penchant was encouraged and developed by Mrs. Maxine Carlson, the Bertrand High School English teacher who demanded that all her students, freshman through senior, complete weekly a 300-word theme that was due every Friday. This was quite a rigorous standard, even for the time. Ebmeier credits Mrs. Carlson with honing his skills as a writer, as well as challenging his imagination.

Following high school, Larry enrolled at the University of Nebraska. His parents, survivors of the Depression, encouraged him to pursue a career that would always earn him a good living, even when times were bad. "Get a job that will support you and give you a good salary," was their message, although it was often contradicted by, "You'll be a creative person," indicating their ambivalence toward Larry's writing ability. The first career considerations were medicine and veterinary science, but a career in pharmacy was settled upon instead. To this day Larry is a pharmacist, and he has done much of his writing while "moonlighting" behind counters, in front of countless shelves of pills, and on hospital work-breaks. He also does a good deal of writing on trains, train travel being Larry's favorite escape from pharmacy, as seen in *Engineman*, his latest work, to be published in 1993.

From 1974 to the present, Larry has been a pharmacist in Lincoln, Nebraska, and is currently on staff at a large hospital. Larry now cites the encouragement of friends as being important to his writing. He currently lives in Lincoln with his lover, Donald Callen Freed.

MAJOR WORKS AND THEMES

"For the most part, almost always, there is, in one way or another, a struggle of the characters finding some kind of threshold of life—energy, ability, whatever it takes—for them to listen to and obey inner voices or overcome inner demons. In the gay sense, this almost always requires more than average courage, as anyone who grew up when I did can tell you." This is the author's commentary upon his own works, works that nearly always engage and employ humor in the pursuit of this quintessential struggle. This bittersweet element of self-discovery and self-disclosure—"coming to grips with oneself"—surrounded by humorous situations is a hallmark of the Graham/Ebmeier style.

The two or three main characters in each novel—*A Man of Taste*, *Walkin' Matilda*, *Tweeds*, and *Engineman*—are seeking or discovering a love relationship, around which the humor and self-disclosure occur. The characters' flaws are earthy, humorous, and profound—an important aspect, says the author, in his characters' trueness to life. Often, the main character is older than the younger man whose affection he seeks. Ebmeier/Graham novels are set in the Midwest—the first three in cities and *Engineman* in rural Kansas.

To date, *Tweeds* is the most significant and best-selling work. Set in Chicago, the central characters in *Tweeds*—Corey Reese, a librarian, and Scott Summerfeld, auto mechanic and community theater actor, former schoolmates in their native Grinnell, Iowa—rediscover each other and themselves in the early days of AIDS. But this is more than just an AIDS novel. It is about gay men coming to terms with themselves, both in and out of crisis. It is written in the first person, Corey telling his own story of learning to trust others to the point of life. *Tweeds* is bittersweet, tracing the development of friendship into relationship, and coming out, in a most humorous yet painfully serious manner.

Corey is not quite ready to admit to the world he is gay, and barely does so to himself. Scott says to Corey, "Corey, you're gay, too! You're a faggot, just like me!" Corey's response: "Scott, I am a homosexual; *you* are a faggot" (129–30). Graham illustrates Scott's outrageous "out-of-the-closetness" and Corey's clinical, detached approach to life in general and coming out in particular—humor cloaked in seriousness, or is it the other way around?

Of the lighter works, *A Man of Taste*, the first Graham/Ebmeier novel, is quite humorous, light, and tongue-in-cheek. It is about a wealthy Denver socialite, Reginald Marne, and a young man, Willie Vanis, a fundamentalist nephew, of whom he becomes guardian. Reginald is fond of having poetry readings and concerts at his mansion; his aspiration is to become the poet laureate of Colorado, but until he finds love, his poetry is pure pabulum. Marne's dry humor in speaking with people is at once both subtle and sophisticated, as constructed by Graham/Ebmeier: "William, long ago I resigned myself to the fact that I affect people adversely. It's because I'm basically selfish, absurdly meticulous, and of course, carelessly insouciant ... oh, *especially* insouciant, William" (219).

Set in Lincoln, Ebmeier's current city of residence, *Walkin' Matilda* involves Carson Giles, "Friends of Man Petuary" pet cemetery owner, and Paul, an exchange student from Australia with an artificial leg (which Paul calls "Matilda"). Almost slapstick, the characters in this novel sometimes illustrate the fine line between humor and reality in life.

Engineman, set in rural Kansas, is the story of Russell Rossheimer and Sherman Truckee, 25 and 16 years old, respectively. It is a period piece, set in 1961 in the fictitious town of Fawntella, Kansas, which seems very real through Ebmeier's description and is much like his home town of Bertrand. Young men find the courage to come out, even in this unseemly time and place. But this is no gay melodrama; it is salt-of-the-earth with believable characters.

"Requiem Evita," to be published in an anthology edited by Judith Pastore, *Literary AIDS: The Responsibilities of Representation* (1992), is an account of persons the author has known with AIDS and how AIDS affects both straight and gay communities.

CRITICAL RECEPTION

The first three novels have received positive reviews since their publication; these reviews have appeared mostly in gay periodicals and newspapers, as might be expected. Those available have been summarized in this section; there may be others (the indexing of even major gay periodicals remains a problem). In general, commentators have praised the Graham/Ebmeier sense of humor and, in *Tweeds* in particular, the combination of its seeming nonreality with lifelike seriousness.

Referring to *A Man of Taste*, David K. Krohne stated: "Combine some outrageously zany and heart-warming characters with an equally outrageous plot and, if you are Clayton R. Graham, you come up with a delightful Gay romance" (23).

Walkin' Matilda has been lauded for its descriptive, colorful, humorous qualities: "It's a grand story. If a producer can find a broadshouldered young Australian with one leg to play Paul and a yellow cat who can attack fingers, crotches and thighs on cue, *Walkin' Matilda* could become a hilarious and invigorating movie" ("From Zero to Jackpot," 9).

Tweeds has received the most critical acclaim. Richard LaBonte identified it as one of the best AIDS novels of the year in 1987, "an affecting blend of romantic comedy and AIDS tragedy" (60). It is the "conglomeration of heightened events" ("Automatic Pilot," 17) and sometimes complex intertwining of emotional elements that have fascinated critics of *Tweeds*. Jack Garman, in particular, best summarized these characteristics of *Tweeds*:

The pain, the humor, the fear, the love, the anger, the joy, all the complex emotions Corey has held back within and around him comes rushing out in a torrent. The book is necessarily messy (not sloppy) in its rendering of sentiment, a quality that causes the general tone to ring more true. There are moments of low comedy, slapstick, and piercing sadness that are so very much like daily life that one is truly moved.

The combination of elements—bittersweet—so skillfully summarized by Garman is an increasing hallmark of Larry Ebmeier's work, refreshingly real. This style continues in the soon-to-be-released *Engineman*.

WORKS BY CLAYTON R GRAHAM (LARRY P. EBMEIER)

A Man of Taste. Stamford, Conn.: Knights Press, 1984.
Walkin' Matilda. Stamford, Conn.: Knights Press, 1984.

Tweeds. Stamford, Conn.: Knights Press, 1986.
Engineman. San Diego: Los Hombres Press, 1993.
"Requiem Evita," in *Literary AIDS: The Responsibilities of Representation*. Ed.
Judith Pastore. Urbana: University of Illinois Press, 1993.

SELECTED STUDIES OF CLAYTON R. GRAHAM (LARRY P. EBMEIER)

Garman, Jack. "Living with AIDS: Fact & Fiction." *Lambda Rising Book Report* 1, no. 1 (1987): 8.
Kay, Burf. "The Automatic Pilot." *GO Info* (Montreal), December 1987–January 1988: 17.
Kay, Burf. "From Zero to Jackpot: His Second Novel Is a Bloody Miracle!" *GO Info* (Montreal), April 1985: 9.
Krohne, David K. Review of *A Man of Taste*. *The Washington Blade* 9 November 1984: 23.
LaBonte, Richard. "AIDS Books Prevail in a Strong Year for Gay Literature." *The Advocate* (5 January 1988): 46, 60ff.
Nelson, Emmanuel S. "AIDS and the American Novel." *Journal of American Culture* 13, no. 1 (Spring 1990): 47–53.

HARLAN GREENE (1953–   )
Thomas Dukes

BIOGRAPHY

Harlan Greene was born on June 19, 1953, in Charleston, South Carolina, and has spent most of his life to date there, something that has affected his writing greatly. His parents, however, had neither the old blood nor the old money so prized by the powers that be; rather, his parents were immigrants, and Greene reports "it was odd and rewarding being an outsider in such a settled city." Graduating from the College of Charleston with a B.A. in English, Greene started graduate school in various places but never completed a program. From approximately 1976 to 1989, he worked in a variety of positions with the South Carolina Historical Society, a rare-book and manuscript library in Charleston. His positions ranged from research consultant, to bookkeeper, to archivist, to assistant and then acting director. Other employment included work in a rare-book store.

In the summer of 1989, he moved to Chapel Hill, North Carolina, with his lover Olin Jolley, a medical school student then beginning a psychiatric residency in Chapel Hill. Greene wrote a federal grant proposal for a group of librarians and archivists and has been administering that grant for the group, which subsequently organized as the North Carolina Preservation Consortium. Working as a preservation educator and advocate, in charge of encouraging various constituencies in North Carolina to work together to address preservation issues in their collections, Greene at this writing is seeking to keep the grant and his work as an archivist thriving in North Carolina.

Greene has published two novels, *Why We Never Danced the Charleston* (1984) and *What the Dead Remember* (1991).

MAJOR WORKS AND THEMES

In a written interview with this writer, Greene says that his gayness, Jewishness, and his life as an "outsider" in Charleston are integral to his art.

These elements of Greene's background, which concern him so much, are movingly and profoundly seen in his first novel *Why We Never Danced the Charleston*. Set in Charleston in 1923, the novel recounts the love affair between the handsome Jew Hirsch Hess and the indefinable, passive artist Ned Grimke as witnessed by an unnamed narrator, himself a lover of Hess. The title gets its meaning from the dance of the same name, originated by black children on the streets before finding its scandalous way into the parties of upper-crust whites, only to be banned. The narrator is part of an underground, self-acknowledged gay group, the Sons of Wisteria. The men of the group spend much of their time in a gay bar called Peacock Alley. Greene's southern gothic setting includes hot Charleston nights, cruising along the Battery, and a dwarf at the entrance to the bar. Although the narrator and Hess have a love affair, the narrator loses Hess to Ned; Hess's infatuation with Ned Grimke borders on the obsessive. In one important section of the novel, the narrator, who drives up only after the fact, tells how Hess, Grimke, and Miss Wragg, who runs the museum where they work, go scavenging in an abandoned, rural house and find a dead black man hanging in the attic and a dead white woman and baby on the floor below.

Now enraptured with each other, Hess and Grimke think nothing of doing the Charleston on the dance floor of Peacock Alley, the dance given a "modern" quality by Grimke's club foot. The night of a costume party, the bar is raided, the violence an echo of the pogrom's violence Hess's parents had fled from in Europe. Hess, Grimke, and the narrator escape. Hess, however, realizing that because he, a "queer," will always be chased, runs from Grimke, whom he loves, because Grimke made him believe in the possibility of love. Hess flees Charleston to unknown places (though the narrator speculates what may have happened); Grimke, accepting the guilt Hess has thrust upon him, descends into madness and casual sex, and his body is found floating off the Battery. The narrator survives and is called to the Battery for cruising where there are men who blame, such as Hess, and those like Grimke who believe.

Greene says that "[i]t is the internalization of outside thoughts and views into the individual—his reaction to what he has been taught to believe— that interests me." Greene also says he is not a political or didactic writer; rather, his themes appear in his writing "intuitively or emotionally." He "fear[s] the idea of politicizing my writing—probably because I was taught that propaganda and literature repel each other." In fact, *Why We Never Danced the Charleston* is a perfect example of political themes arising naturally out of a story. Although the novel shows undeniably the damage done by oppression (and not just gay oppression; consider the dead black man and white woman in that house), the story is a perfect evocation of its time and place and what it may or may not have meant to be gay in that setting. Greene's artfulness comes from the particularizations of his characters; Hess, Grimke, and the narrator are by no means Everygayman. The integration of theme—the relationship between the outsider and the larger culture, and the damage the outsider does to others and himself—and story are exquisitely realized in the novel.

Greene says he loved the work of Carson McCullers "as a kid" and has "devoured" James and Faulkner. He also found Proust "liberating" and is currently "intrigued" with Elizabeth Bowen. He notes the impact of "B" writers: "I love the feeling I get in reading them. . . . I can . . . sort of enjoy it ["B" writing] emotionally as I am intellectually diagramming it." Local-color writing, particularly that of George Washington Cable, has also been important.

These influences are easily identified in *Why We Never Danced the Charleston*. The "grotesques" (if that is what they are) of the novel are spiritual cousins of those in McCullers and O'Connor. The powerful sense of place marks Greene as a southern writer in the tradition of Faulkner, O'Connor, and Welty; in this novel and his next, Greene stakes out Charleston as Faulkner does his fictional county, O'Connor her rural Georgia, and Welty her delta. Greene acknowledges that

place is very important in my writing. I think I imprinted on Charleston: I was a loner and spent so much of my time wandering the streets and had some of those Wordsworthian "transcendent" experiences with nature and setting of the city when I was young. Its visual impact, the sensuousness of the landscape, the primal lushness and drugging heat have infected my psyche. Charleston has also held a metaphor for me—the presence of the past, the overpowering tug of history. The setting not only exerts a pull on me but is very exotic compared to a rather homogenized America—so why not use it?

Greene elaborates the tragic theme and consideration of Charleston in his next novel, *What the Dead Remember*. The unnamed narrator is deposited in Charleston with an aunt and uncle when he is thirteen and most of his family is in Europe. He becomes acquainted with old Charleston and its history; he steals magazine pictures of men in BVDs at a local pharmacy. At his aunt and uncle's home on Sullivan's Island, he tries to make friends with boys his age on the beach, but is able to get only the friendship of a retarded boy, Stevie. He tries to be mean, but is eventually won over. The narrator's first act of betrayal of Stevie is to destroy a dam built painstakingly, but the narrator is able to blame it on a storm to Stevie and his sister, Dulcie, whom the narrator likes. He spends more time with Stevie, telling him the story of Atlantis under the sea. Although the narrator returns to his family, his uncle's death causes him to return to Charleston and the beach with his mother, although he has been accused of stealing by his aunt. The boys show up, and despite his sense of impending disaster, the narrator goes with them, only to be forced into group sex, though the nature of this coercion is ambiguous.

Back home, the narrator continues his sexual activity with high school boys. As he becomes a man, he looks for love while engaging in a series of one-night stands, then returns to Charleston where he is reunited with Dulcie and Stevie. At the bars, beautiful men reject him, he feels, but he becomes more and more a part of Dulcie's and Stevie's lives. Eventually, the narrator makes a friend, Ricky, who pulls him into the elite—and closeted—of gay Charleston. He comes to realize that the little group that he is now in is, in fact, made up of the boys on the beach from his childhood trips; they are beginning to hear and suffer the effects of AIDS. The narrator takes up with Jim; one night when they are together, the narrator has left Stevie alone at home during a storm. The next morning, the narrator learns that the man he has been with is, in fact, the worst of the boys on the beach who teased him as a child and that the man now has AIDS. After racing back to the island, the narrator discovers that Stevie has disappeared, no doubt gone into the ocean to get to Atlantis. At the novel ends, the narrator discovers he has AIDS. Knowing he is dying, the narrator nonetheless feels as happy as he was as a child, first seeing the ocean.

As is true of the first novel, the influence of McCullers can be seen in the narrator's racing toward tragedy even as he witnesses it in the making. In the metaphoric use of Charleston, Greene shows what can lie behind the facade of southern beauty and gentility of places and people, including his narrator. This quality of Greene's novels echoes such works as McCullers' *The Heart Is a Lonely Hunter, The Ballad of the Sad Cafe*, and Faulkner's stories and novels, particularly "A Rose for Emily," "Barn Burning," and *Sanctuary*. Furthermore, the use of the retarded man Stevie in *What the Dead Remember* reminds one of O'Connor's *The Violent Bear It Away* and Faulkner's *The Sound and the Fury*. As in O'Connor and Faulkner, the use of the retarded is ironic commentary on the supposed intelligence of the "normal" people. Greene's development of these metaphors of setting and character can be found in his use of gay characters; he is merciless in dissecting gay and straight culture, reminding one of Brecht's admonition that art is not pretty. The characters in Greene's fiction search for love and contentment and fail to find it. They are oppressed: their failures are those caused by being closeted and by their own personal deficiencies. This dramatization of failure is what makes Greene's novels tragedies.

What the Dead Remember marks a considerable development in Greene as a novelist. The canvas is wider than in *Why We Never Danced the Charleston*. Especially in his characterizations of Stevie and Dulcie, Greene develops a greater sensitivity for those outside gay culture. Their interactions with the narrator are more complicated than, say, those interactions between the gay characters and Miss Wragg in *Why We Never Danced the Charleston*; and Greene's kindness is as much on display here as is his recognition of the tragic condition of people. Additionally, the use of AIDS as a metaphor for the destructively closeted Charleston gay community adds another layer of meaning to the tragedy that Greene shows. Greene despises dishonesty, sees the ruinous consequences of hypocrisy, yet he also sympathizes with the people in a repressed culture even as he exposes the cruelty visited upon and by them.

Greene's novels dramatize the disastrous effects of closeting and the tragic results that stem from the injustice of it. If he is very much a southern writer in the Faulkner-McCullers-O'Connor tradition, he is also an openly gay writer illuminating yet another element in the paradox of the South, particularly Charleston: a place where superficial beauty is held to be more valuable than honesty. In his two novels to date of the destructive nature of southern closets, Greene shows immense empathy for his characters even as he is appalled by their actions. He and his narrators are Jamesian witnesses to the destruction, exposing the beast in the jungle as well as the beasts in Charleston and in ourselves.

CRITICAL RECEPTION

Why We Never Danced the Charleston received generally positive if mixed reviews. As *What the Dead Remember* had just been published at this writing, reviews of the novel were unavailable for comment here. However, given the novel's quality, they should be favorable; and as gay studies grows in importance, Greene will no doubt come to the attention of scholars who recognize his place in the tradition of the southern gothic and the contemporary gay novel.

WORKS BY HARLAN GREENE

Fiction

Why We Never Danced the Charleston. New York: St. Martin's, 1984.
What the Dead Remember. New York: Dutton, 1991.

Nonfiction

Charleston: City of Memory. Greensboro, N.C.: Legacy, 1987.
"Charleston, South Carolina." *Hometowns: Gay Men Write about Where They Belong*. Ed. John Preston. New York: Dutton, 1991.

SELECTED STUDIES OF HARLAN GREENE

Milton, Edith. Review of *Why We Never Danced the Charleston*. *New York Times Book Review* 24 June 1984: 29.

Nelson, Emmanuel S. Review of *Why We Never Danced the Charleston*. *Choice* (November 1984): 424.

Review of *Why We Never Danced the Charleston*. *Kirkus Reviews* 1 April 1986: 312.

Review of *Why We Never Danced the Charleston*. *Publisher's Weekly* 13 April 1984: 51.

Review of *Why We Never Danced the Charleston*. *West Coast Review of Books* March 1985: 30.

ALLAN GURGANUS (1947–   )
B. Austin Wallace

BIOGRAPHY

Allan Gurganus was born on June 11, 1947, in Rocky Mount, North Carolina, a hometown he fondly remembers as "a good place to start out, a good place to get out of" ("Mouth of the South,"114). He was the eldest of four sons of Ethel Gurganus, a school teacher, and M. F. Gurganus, a supermarket manager and born-again fundamentalist Baptist preacher. Gurganus was brought up in a religious household where, he says, "being forced to go to church three times a Sunday...cured me of any conventional religious beliefs I've ever had" (telephone interview with Austin Wallace, July 7, 1991).

From an early age Gurganus began to show an interest and talent in art. At the age of twelve he was given a one-man show of his oil paintings, modeled after Matisse and Cezanne, at the local art center. His creativity continued through high school where he ran school assemblies and put on talent shows. After graduating from Rocky Mount Senior High in 1965 he embarked on his art career and attended the Philadelphia Academy of Fine Arts ("Mouth of the South," 116–17). In 1966, in order to avoid being convicted as a Vietnam draft dodger and spending six years in prison, he decided to join the Navy; after all, he thought, that's what Melville and Conrad did (ibid., 117).

After a year of horrendous training in Chicago he was stationed on the *U.S.S. Yorktown* and traveled to Denmark, Italy, France, and the Philippines, but he never quite made it to Vietnam. It was while on the ship that he changed his focus from artist to writer. He picked up a copy of Henry James' *Portrait of a Lady* and "read[ing] this profoundly dignified and compassionate description of a girl," he says, "seemed to coincide with so much that I wanted for myself, ... maybe [I could] do something as a writer" (*Poets & Writers*, 36). He eventually read every book on board.

In 1970 after being discharged from the Navy he enrolled at Sarah Lawrence College where he was given two years of credit for the more than 1200 books he had read at sea. It was at this time that Gurganus officially "came out" at the age of 21. He had known for some time he was attracted to men, but his religious upbringing and Navy career had made it difficult to be open about his sexuality. Graduating in 1972, he won a scholarship to the prestigious Iowa Writers' Workshop, where he met his friend and mentor, John Cheever. In 1974 Cheever secretly sent one of Gurganus's stories, "Minor Heroism," to the *New Yorker*. It broke a long-standing taboo and became the magazine's first published story about homosexuality. He continued to be a regular contributor to the *New Yorker*, the *Atlantic*, *Harper's*, *Paris Review*, and various other magazines.

His stories garnered him national attention. He received two PEN Syndicated Fiction Prizes, two National Endowment for the Arts grants, an Ingram Merrill Award, and the Wallace Stegner Fellowship. He had a brief stint as a Jones lecturer at Stanford and followed this with a position at Duke University. In 1978, he moved to Manhattan and got a part-time teaching job at Sarah Lawrence College and supplemented his income by becoming a sperm bank donor. In 1981, while at an artists' retreat, he saw a *New York Times* article about living Confederate widows still receiving Civil War pensions which sparked his imagination and he immediately wrote thirty pages of what was to become his first major novel. In 1983, on the basis of 210 pages, Knopf bought the manuscript ("Mouth of the South," 119–22). It took another six years of writing, condensing, rewriting, and working with novelist friend Mona Simpson, but he eventually finished the 718-page tome that would become known as *Oldest Living Confederate Widow Tells All* (1989).

The novel hit bookstores in the spring of 1989 and became an immediate smash. It spent months on national best-seller lists, and Gurganus was featured in articles and interviews from the *New Yorker* to *People Magazine*, where he made no attempts to hide his homosexuality. In the fall of 1991 he followed up his success with a collection of previous published works entitled *White People*, which included his gay-themed stories. Gurganus currently divides his time between his Manhattan flat and his cottage in Chapel Hill, North Carolina, where he is at work on his second novel, titled *The Erotic History of a Southern Baptist Church* and on the miniseries version of *Oldest Living Confederate Widow Tells All*.

MAJOR WORKS AND THEMES

Allan Gurganus says he remembers seeing the events surrounding Stonewall on the news, but that it never really had a major impact on either his life or his writing (telephone interview with Austin Wallace, July 7, 1991). This can be seen in the fact that, though the majority of his writing was done after 1969, his work has a decidedly pre-Stonewall slant. While some of the stories included in *White People* (1991) are gay oriented, for the most part, Gurganus seems to regale in the intrigue involved in homoerotic excitement between seemingly heterosexual men, a style reminiscent of D. H. Lawrence, and nowhere is this more evident than in his first work, *Oldest Living Confederate Widow Tells All* (1989).

A good deal of the male interplay occurs near the beginning of the novel when we meet thirteen-year-old Willie Marsden and thirteen-year-old Ned Smythe, as they traipse off to join the Civil War "holding hands like girls that age would" (chapter 1, p. 4). The author characterizes the boys as more than bosom buddies and closer than blood brothers. Ned, an angelic-looking boy with golden ringlets of hair, is looked after by Willie, who never leaves his side. The boys even sleep together, holding each other tighter as the bombs burst over their encampment. When Ned is killed, Willie is unable to let go. He even digs the body up several times after it is buried. Willie's wife, the narrator and title character of the novel, says he loved Ned more than anything, possibly even her. When Willie goes to visit Ned's mother, Winona, to tell her of his death, upon sight of her "he'd experienced a certain manly stiffening below the waist . . . part of it was how much Winona looked just like her dead boy [Ned]" (47).

We also experience the nude swimming escapades of the boys' division, enjoying each others' company in what Gurganus calls an erotic yet "non-genital atmosphere" (telephone interview with Austin Wallace, July 7, 1989). It is a scene akin to the two nude men wrestling in Lawrence's *Women in Love*. The only other gay subreferences he alludes to are seen in minor characters like the bachelor choir director who "was not exactly a major menace to unchaperoned womankind" (35) and Jerome the nursing home orderly, who loves disco dancing, studying acting, and stitching quilts. Here Gurganus is letting us know they are gay without actually saying so.

In *White People* (1991), even though Gurganus opens up about gay sexuality with more overt references, for the most part homosexuality still serves as an undercurrent; we know the people are gay even though they do not profess their sexuality openly to the reader. For instance, in the first story, "Minor Heroism: Something about My Father," which is semi-autobiographical, we meet the eldest son Bryan, who is a mystery to his father. As a child he was very artistic, never liked sports, and did not make many friends. Now, he is a writer living in New York, supporting himself by writing articles on modern dance for *Dance World*. He even has an actor/ model roommate who wears black nail polish and loves talking about big band music. For those in the know, their life-style appears obviously gay.

"Art History," a story told from differing viewpoints, concerns an art professor who sacrifices his career when he feels up a sculpture of a young male beauty, then tries the same thing on the cop who is watching him. In "Adult Art," which originally appeared in *Men on Men 2*, a school superintendent who loves his wife and kids has "this added tenderness...that sneaks up on [him] every two or three years" (109). He meets a young man named Barker and goes home with him to see porno movies. There he experiences a bizarre afternoon tryst. He even fantasizes that Barker will turn up at his kid's Little League games sensing his gratitude but knowing they could not speak openly. "Adult Art" is Gurganus's most blatantly gay story. It sets the stage for his one foray into the post-Stonewall generation, with a story titled "Reassurance." It is a letter from a dying young Pennsylvania soldier in a Washington, D.C., Civil War hospital to his mother as dictated to Walt Whitman. The story deals with AIDS metaphorically; it is an elegy for all those who have died from the disease. Gurganus says that as a gay man living in New York City during the AIDS epidemic, he and his writing could not help but be affected by it in some way (telephone interview with Austin Wallace, July 7, 1991).

The lack of overt homosexuality in Gurganus's work can be attributed partly to his religious upbringing where sexuality is known about and implied at times, but is not discussed openly. This, however, does not make his writing any less relevant and powerful. Being gay and being a writer have, for him, an amplifying fit. He says, "Being gay gives you the passport to go anywhere" (*Poets & Writers*, 36); such imaginative freedom is most evident in the variety of voices he embodies in his writing. Gurganus maintains his grip on his own integrity as a writer and as a gay male. He makes gay literature more accessible to the mainstream not by forcing it down people's throats, but by subtly introducing it into their psyche.

CRITICAL RECEPTION

Since the beginning of his career Allan Gurganus has received raves from gays and straights alike. Grace Paley, his first professor at Sarah Lawrence College, says "Allan didn't need to be taught, he was always fine and fluid and imaginative. There was no question he was going to be a great writer" (*People Magazine*, September 19, 1989, p. 70). John Cheever even sent Gurganus a note saying he considered him "the most morally responsive and technically brilliant writer of his generation ("Mouth of the South," 110).

With the debut of his first novel *Oldest Living Confederate Widow Tells All* (1989), every major review from New York to Los Angeles lauded him and his book, making it one of the most acclaimed first novels of our time as well as one of the few literary works to have a lengthy run on the bestseller lists. The *New York Times Book Review* said, "he takes and shares pleasure in imagining, then bringing forth a rich variety of voices" (6). *The*

Nation called the book "a performance of the historical imagination that never grassed over into mere 'historical fiction' " (April 15, 1991, p. 492).

The appearance of his collection of short stories, *White People* (1991), further enhanced his position as a contemporary gay novelist with its inclusion of Gurganus's gay-themed stories. In a recent article about the state of gay writing, Edmund White* called him one of the best new novelists to emerge in recent years, straight or gay (27). *Lambda Book Report*, a contemporary review of gay and lesbian literature, said he has the "freedom to range across the human spectrum with an astonishing accuracy of voices" (vol. 2, no. 9 [March/April 1991]: 27).

It seems fitting that after years of working to be called a writer, Gurganus has now received the acclaim and attention he deserves. As he himself says, "I've spent six days a week for 20 years learning how to write. Now, finally I'm going to be allowed to be a writer" (*People Magazine*, September 19, 1989, 70).

WORKS BY ALLAN GURGANUS

Oldest Living Confederate Widow Tells All. New York: Alfred A. Knopf, 1989.
Blessed Assurance: A Moral Tale. North Carolina: North Carolina Wesleyan Press,
    1990 (an illustrated chapbook whose story appears in *White People*).
White People. New York: Alfred A. Knopf, 1991.

SELECTED STUDIES OF ALLAN GURGANUS

Garrett, George. Review of *White People*. *New York Times Book Review* 3 February
    1991: 6.
Gates, Henry Louis, Jr. "Art and Ardor." *The Nation* 15 April 1991: 492–93.
Prince, Tom. "Mouth of the South." *New York* 21 August 1989: 110–23.
Review of *The Oldest Living Confederate Widow Tells All*. *Lambda Book Report*
    2, no. 9 (March/April 1991): 27.
Scheuer, Jeffrey. "Black & Blue & Gray: An Interview with Allan Gurganus." *Poets
    & Writers* November/December 1990: 24–38.
Tolson, Jay. Review of *Oldest Living Confederate Widow Tells All*. "Wounds of
    War." The *New Republic* 30 October 1989: 37–41.

RICHARD HALL (1926–   )
Claude J. Summers

BIOGRAPHY

In his recent novel *Family Fictions* (1991), Richard Hall offers a riveting—artistically shaped but largely accurate—account of his family and its secrets; other facets of his life—including his fascination with Puerto Rico, his skepticism about psychoanalysis, and his love of music—are reflected in his other works. He was born Richard Hirshfeld in New York City on November 26, 1926, into an extended family of transplanted Southern Jews. In 1934, his immediate family moved to the New York suburb of White Plains, where his mother became active in the Episcopal Church and he and his sister were baptized. In 1938, after an anti-Semitic incident involving his sister's admission to a church-affiliated camp, Hall's mother changed their name and moved the family to another Westchester county suburb, New Rochelle. Hall graduated from New Rochelle High School in 1943 and immediately entered an accelerated wartime program at Harvard, where he majored in English literature and graduated cum laude in January 1948.

After graduation, Hall spent several months attempting (without success) to write stories for the *New Yorker*, while holding down various clerical jobs. He worked as a junior copywriter for the J. Walter Thompson advertising agency from 1949 until 1952, when he established his own publishing company, Alumni Publications, which created materials for large corporations to distribute to their employees and which he managed until 1964. In the 1950s, Hall underwent deep Freudian analysis in an attempt to change his sexual orientation. In 1960, he abandoned psychiatric treatment and fell in love with a transplanted Texan named Dan Allen (portrayed as Gerald in "The Boy Who Would Be Real" and as Patrick in *Family Fictions*). The couple lived together in New York from 1960 to 1965, when Allen, whom Hall describes as the major influence in his life, moved to

Boston to pursue his Ph.D. After Allen's death from AIDS in 1985, Hall was able to establish, through a successful lawsuit with Allen's family, a Dan Allen Memorial Scholarship for gay and lesbian students at City College of San Francisco.

Hall worked for various corporations in public relations activities from 1964 through 1969. In 1970, weary of corporate culture, he entered New York University to earn an M.A. in English education. Upon graduation, he accepted a job at Inter American University in San Juan, Puerto Rico, to teach literature and language courses and then to serve as acting director of the University Press, a job he held until 1974. During the 1970s, he published *The Butterscotch Prince* (1975), wrote a novel that has yet to appear, taught part-time at New York area universities, established a long-lasting relationship with Arthur Marceau (to whom he dedicated *Couplings* [1981] and who died of AIDS in 1989), and began publishing both fiction and nonfiction in the newly vital gay and lesbian media, as well as writing regularly for such publications as *Opera News* and the *Village Voice*. In 1976, he became contributing editor for books of the gay newsmagazine *The Advocate*, a position that he held until 1982. As contributing editor, Hall published numerous interviews with writers, including Merle Miller, Marguerite Yourcenar, and Leon Edel. Hall's theory, outlined in articles he wrote for the *New Republic*, that Henry James was in love with his brother William was endorsed by Edel in his revised, one-volume edition of his biography of Henry James. In 1978, Hall was elected the first openly gay member of the National Book Critics Circle.

Hall concentrated on writing plays and short fiction in the early 1980s. He served on the board of directors of The Glines, New York City's principal producer of gay drama; and his plays *Love Match, The Prisoner of Love*, and *Happy Birthday, Daddy* were produced in New York and around the country and collected in *Three Plays for a Gay Theater* (1983). Two short-story collections also appeared: *Couplings: A Book of Stories* (1981) and *Letter from a Great-Uncle & Other Stories* (1985). Hall's semi-autobiographical novel *Family Fictions* was begun in 1988, after a year's residence in the San Francisco Bay area during a period of personal crisis. It was published in 1991 by Viking, which will also issue a third collection of Hall's short fiction, *Fidelities: A Book of Stories*, in 1992.

MAJOR WORKS AND THEMES

Although old enough to have begun writing before the advent of the Stonewall insurrection, Richard Hall is a peculiarly post-Stonewall writer, confronting in his work the dilemmas of gay men in a period of exhilarating and sometimes confusing change. While Hall's themes are universal, his subject matter is unabashedly and almost exclusively gay. His fiction, most frequently set in urban gay areas or resorts, focuses on issues of gay identity and community, on the problems of intimacy and commitment between men, and on the intersection of the public and the private in the process of self-fashioning. His work features a wide variety of gay men who are captured at moments of crisis, grappling with the legacies of hurtful pasts as they struggle to achieve coherence and authenticity. Hall's fiction mirrors the pain and joy, the doubts and fears, the tenderness and strength, the self-questioning and affirmations of gay people as they seek to define themselves and to link with others in the brave new world created by gay liberation.

Hall's first major publication is *The Butterscotch Prince*. Although it originated in Hall's attempt to write a pornographic novel, the work is sexy without being salacious. A mystery novel, its plot revolves around Cord McGreevy's search for the murderer of his colleague and sometime lover Ellison Greer, a handsome young high school teacher who is the "butterscotch prince" of the title. Since Ellison is both black and gay, the police seem less than interested in pursuing the identity of his killer. Cord is the only one who cares enough to undertake the task of detection. His odyssey, which is a search for his own authentic self as well as for the murderer of his friend, leads him through the byways of New York's gay underworld of the mid–1970s (updated in the 1983 revision, which also provides a fuller and more convincing account of the villain's motivation).

The Butterscotch Prince rises above the general run of formula fiction by virtue of Hall's exceptionally evocative and sometimes arrestingly beautiful prose and his full characterizations of Cord and Ellison. The brooding introspection of Cord allows insight into his self-doubts and fears, while the revelations concerning Ellison highlight his contradictions and pain. Hall presents their hurt and vulnerability as a paradigm of the gay experience in a homophobic world. At the heart of the novel are two related issues: the difficulty of combining love and sex and the internalized homophobia that besets the protagonist and the victim, who both attempt to flee their homosexual impulses, one through a futile psychiatric treatment, the other through a doomed marriage. By the end of the novel, these issues are tentatively resolved, at least for Cord. In the final scene—tellingly set at a gay rights demonstration—Cord is in a relationship with a young filmmaker with whom he seems able to combine love and sexual passion at least for the present; in his final action, he boldly affirms his homosexuality, his new relationship, and himself by joining hands with his friend in a "double power salute to the world" into the eye of the television news camera covering the demonstration.

Hall's first collection of short stories, *Couplings*, reveals extraordinary skill and suggests that his talent is preeminently suited to the compressed form of the short story. Like *The Butterscotch Prince*, the eleven stories of *Couplings* are also concerned with self-affirmation, though only one—the semi-autobiographical, but archetypal "The Boy Who Would Be Real"—is explicitly a coming-out story. The stories involve pairs who test their relationships or individuals who seek intimacy with others or former lovers who are haunted by lost relationships, hence the name of the collection. The stories are varied in their settings, their characters, and their modes, demonstrating Hall's ability to encompass a wide range of character types and situations within a vision that can span the comic and the satiric as well as the tragic and the mythic. Indeed, Hall's mastery of tone is such that his stories frequently elicit contradictory emotions, as in "A Touch of Fat," which manages at once to be heartbreaking and reassuring, hugely sad yet irresistibly comic, or "The Household God," which is ironic not only by virtue of its comic plot device but also, and more complexly, because of its haunting awareness of possibilities missed, in which it recalls Forster's "The Road to Colonus." Three of the stories are self-conscious literary experiments, retelling James's *The Aspern Papers* ("The Taste of Spring"), Conrad's *Heart of Darkness* ("Colors"), and Mann's *Death in Venice* ("Death in San Juan") from different perspectives. The success of these stories is that they work naturally on their own terms; only occasionally do the parallels with the classic stories seem intrusive or forced. Hall writes in the preface to *Couplings* that he is "concerned with the suffering that arrives on our doorstep in the shape of a friend, a lover, an ex-lover," and these stories—even when comic or satiric, as "The Prisoner of Love"—are in fact about suffering. It is characteristic of Hall's breadth of vision that he sees the suffering beneath the skin of even his least likable characters. His compassion extends even to the homophobic sister of "The Bad Penny."

This same compassion informs the eight stories of *Letters from a Great-Uncle & Other Stories*, a collection that is even stronger and more assured than *Couplings*. Again, Hall places characters in situations that culminate in epiphanies of self-revelation. Obsessed with the past and with the inexorable yet mysterious progress by which the past evolves into the present, these characters desperately, sometimes reluctantly, always painfully, seek to discover the truth of their lives, undertaking the difficult task of distinguishing it from rival truths and from illusions of all kinds, including especially self-deception. The title story imagines the life of Hall's great-uncle, born to Polish immigrant parents in Texas just after the Civil War, who was homosexual and had to flee to New York because of a sex scandal. By framing the letter in which the uncle attempts to tell the truth of his life to his family with the struggle of the nephew to understand the connection he feels with his uncle, Hall shows the relevance of the past to the present and the future. This same point is also made in the collection's two strongest pieces, "The Lost Chord" and "The Lesson of the Master." In the former, an elderly black doctor is forced to reexamine his own version of the truth of the interracial relationship that most profoundly shaped his life in the face of a competing version of that truth; in the latter, a scholar forges a document in an attempt to rewrite the past in order to correct the present only to discover that both his career and his personal life were based on evasion and self-deception.

Issues of deception are also at the heart of Hall's fine autobiographical novel, *Family Fictions*, which pivots on Margaret Schanberg's decision to change the name of her family from the Jewish patronym to the more ordinary Shay. With remarkable economy, Hall traces the fate of this family through the voices of four characters, who narrate carefully selected episodes that cumulatively sketch a saga that spans four decades. By means of a narrative technique that articulates multiple perspectives and concentrates on representative but heightened moments of crisis, Hall is able to bring to bear on the expansive form of the novel the techniques of his short stories, which are typified by epiphanic moments, an empathetic approach to character, and an awareness of the complexities of truth. The consequences of Margaret's denial of her family's past are neither simple nor felt uniformly by the other members of the family. For Margaret and her daughter Mag, the fiction of ordinariness offers compensations, while for her husband Judd and son Harris, the lie constitutes a betrayal. Especially interesting are the effects of the fiction on Harris, who is led to question his own identity in multiple ways. "Who was Harris Shay?" he muses, "It had a cut-off sound, like a piece of him was missing." He sees the denial of his name as judgment on himself, "there must be something wrong with [his name], and by extension with him" (62). The shame and denial that attach to his Jewish heritage also attach to his emergent homosexual desires. Only later when he is able to claim his dual identity as a gay man and as a Jew is he able to accept his doubleness and to reconcile with his past.

CRITICAL RECEPTION

Not only does the American urban gay experience provide the subject matter of most of Hall's fiction, but his writing career itself also exemplifies the way explicitly gay literature has only grudgingly been accepted into the mainstream of American publishing. In his afterword to the 1983 revision of *The Butterscotch Prince*, Hall describes how Pyramid Books regarded the work with acute embarrassment, refused to promote it properly, and quietly dumped it, despite its selling almost 25,000 copies on the basis of reviews in the gay press and a single advertisement in *The Advocate*. As he observes, "It is only since 1978 . . . that the trade has changed its policy toward gay books. In this, as in so many areas of gay life, profit rather than justice was the chief motive of change." After *The Butterscotch Prince*, Hall published his creative work almost exclusively in the gay media, until Viking, somewhat to his surprise, accepted both *Family Fictions* and *Fidelities*. Hall's confinement to the gay media had positive consequences insofar as it permitted his participation in the remarkable "mini-Renaissance" of the gay short story—the genre in which he most excels—that the emergent gay magazines of the 1970s encouraged, as he explains in the preface to *Couplings*. But Hall's segregation in the gay media also accounts for the fact that he has not received the critical attention he merits from the mainstream literary community.

Richard Hall deserves wide recognition as an important chronicler of the post-Stonewall gay male experience and as an accomplished artist, a master especially of the short story. In carefully shaped fictions, distinguished by exceptionally resonant prose, fully credible situations, and deeply imagined characters, Hall has explored crucial issues of American gay life in the aftermath of liberation with empathy, clarity, and genuine insight. As Michael Lynch observed in 1985, "the straight literary world has resisted recognizing Hall's fictional and critical achievements because of his material—our lives" (36). Nevertheless, he remains "one of our prime cultural resources" (36).

WORKS BY RICHARD HALL

The Butterscotch Prince. New York: Pyramid Books, 1975. Rev. ed. Boston: Alyson, 1983.
Couplings: A Book of Stories. San Francisco: Grey Fox, 1981.
Three Plays for a Gay Theater. San Francisco: Grey Fox, 1983.
Letter from a Great-Uncle & Other Stories. San Francisco: Grey Fox, 1985.
Family Fictions. New York: Viking, 1991.
Fidelities: A Book of Stories. New York: Viking, 1992.

SELECTED STUDIES OF RICHARD HALL

Clark, J. Michael. *Liberation and Disillusionment: The Development of Gay Male Criticism and Popular Fiction a Decade After Stonewall.* Los Colinas, TX: Liberal Press, 1987:69–74.
Lynch, Michael. "Reflections at Middle Age." *Body Politic* August 1985: 36.
Stadler, Matthew. "Why the Schanbergs Became the Shays." *New York Times Book Review* 28 July 1991: 6.
Upchurch, Michael. "A Family Denies Itself." *San Francisco Chronicle Book Review* 7 July 1991: 8.

JOSEPH HANSEN (1923–   )

James W. Jones

BIOGRAPHY

Born July 19, 1923, in Aberdeen, South Dakota, Joseph Hansen remembers his first ten years as marked by solitude and poverty. When he was seven, a strep infection forced him to move out of the bedroom he shared with his teenage brother, Bob (to whom *Obedience* is dedicated) and into the bedroom which his sister had left upon moving to California. This enforced solitude, which lasted eight months, led him to begin to develop a writer's most important tool: his imagination.

His father owned a shoe store, but the Depression struck the Hansen family particularly hard. In 1933, they sold almost everything and moved to Minneapolis. Over the next three years, his father and older brother worked at a variety of jobs, but finally, in 1936, the family decided to follow the lead of Hansen's sister and move to southern California.

During his high school years, Hansen remained attracted to good writing. He remembers the stories in the *Saturday Evening Post* as excellent instructors in the construction of fiction. His teachers at school were generally less helpful, except for one, whose denunciation of Gertrude Stein influenced Hansen to read her work. Hansen recalls Stein teaching him "in one astonishing morning the most important lesson in writing I ever learned— that every word contains a small explosive charge" (Winks, 115).

In 1943, Hansen married Jane Bancroft, and they have one daughter. Hansen stated in a 1987 interview "I am homosexual," but he has never identified himself as a "gay author" (Burton, 41). His work has consistently delineated the lives of gay men in conflict with a homophobic world. In his private life, he has remained married to Jane, to whom he dedicated both of his "mainstream" novels, *A Smile in His Lifetime* and *Job's Year*, as well as his second novel, *Strange Marriage*.

Most of what little biographical information is available on Hansen's life has been provided by the author himself in essays where he also discusses why he writes about a gay detective. He has had very little to say about his adult life outside of his writing. Whether he served in World War II, for example, or his relationships with other members of his family are not discussed. Hansen published poetry under his own name in such magazines as *Harper's*, the *New Yorker*, or the *Atlantic*. Until 1970, anything with a gay theme, which included short stories, novels, and some poems, he published under the pseudonym "James Colton."

Hansen played a leading role in the cultural aspect of the gay liberation movement in Southern California from 1962 to 1970. Using both his real and his pen names, Hansen wrote fiction and poetry and provided line drawings and cover art as well as interviews, book reviews, and articles for *One*, the monthly publication of the Mattichine Society. In 1965, several members of *One* decided to form a new journal devoted strictly to literature and to cultural themes. Hansen cofounded this publication, *Tangents*, and served as an associate editor for its first year.

As "James Colton," Hansen became a successful author of "homosexual literature," which is to say literature for and about "the homosexual minority," as it was conceived prior to Stonewall. His eight novels were generally well received in the gay press and were distributed through the "Guild Book Service" whose book reviews and advertising inserts appeared in the proliferating abundance of "male physique magazines." Hansen published these novels with, as he calls them, "small West Coast publishers of doubtful virtue" (Winks, 115), that is, publishers who usually published pornography, because they were the only outlet he could find for a more positive portrayal of homosexual characters.

Hansen finally discovered a way to achieve his goal of breaking down prejudice and destroying stereotypes about gays with his creation of the matter-of-factly gay, middle-aged insurance claims investigator David Brandstetter. The first Brandstetter novel, *Fadeout*, appeared in 1970. It received favorable reviews in the *New York Times* and other influential publications. That book began a series of twelve novels which Hansen concluded in 1991 with *A Country of Old Men*.

The success of that first novel was not, however, immediate. Hansen wrote two more novels as James Colton and even took another pseudonym, "Rose Brock," to write two gothic novels in 1971 and 1974. His works also include a volume of poetry and four collections of short stories or novellas.

In 1974, Hansen was awarded a grant from the National Endowment for the Arts to work on the novel *A Smile in His Lifetime*. He spent much of 1975 continuing his work on that manuscript while in Great Britain on a British Arts Council Grant. Until his retirement in 1988, he taught mystery writing at the UCLA Extension. At present, he is working on a new series of novels that seem aimed at telling more of his own life's story than his fiction previously has.

MAJOR WORKS AND THEMES

Throughout the early 1960s, Hansen continually expressed a desire to find among the increasing numbers of gay characters in fiction "a decent, ordinary homosexual . . . [t]o help the straight reader keep things in perspective." (James Colton [pseud.], rev. of *Swing Low, Sweet Harriet* by George Baxt, *Tangents* 2/3 [December 1966], 29) Hansen wanted the character's "homosexuality" per se to be unexceptional because in literature, as in American society of his time, the revelation of an "other" sexual orientation became the single defining characteristic of a person, severed his bond to the rest of humanity, and imprisoned him within the category of sexual orientation.

Hansen himself decided to take up the task of using fiction to make tolerance and acceptance a reality. Other major themes—among them, the creation and sustenance of gay identity and community, the fear of homophobia, the experience of love between two men—all derive from this. At first, Hansen was able to develop these themes only in short stories published in the gay press or in novels brought forth by publishers of largely pornographic works. While in some ways limiting (length, the necessary focus on the sexual element), the genre of the "porn novel" also liberated him to present the theme of homosexuality with at least much, if not all, of the honesty he believed it deserved.

Two of his "Colton" novels demonstrate these themes. In *Strange Marriage* (1965), twenty-four-year-old Randy Hale, the central character, is abandoned by Corky, his lover of three years. With a tomboyish, dominant (at times domineering) woman, Ruth Landers, he experiences heterosexual passion and marries her. Eventually, he does find sexual and emotional love with a young man. But even the suicide of another closeted married man, George, does not deter Randy from wanting to remain in this marriage. George's suicide note reveals Randy's secret, and Ruth leaves him. The town's liberal-minded country doctor enlightens Ruth (and the reader) as to the "facts" about homosexuality. The novel concludes with the doctor urging Randy to accept his homosexuality and with Ruth expressing her willingness to accept a redefinition of their marriage.

For all its attempts to defuse prejudice, this novel remains largely trapped within the limits of the "homosexual problem novel." The main character's sexual orientation serves as the center of the novel; a homosexual character commits suicide; a physician provides the "truth" about homosexuality; yet, homosexuality remains an aberrant phenomenon, serving more as the object of prurient heterosexual interest than as a tool for understanding.

This pre-Stonewall novel differs significantly from a later work, *The Outward Side* (1971), which treats a similar theme. A married pastor in his early thirties, Marc Lingard, finds himself in an emotional crisis: he can no longer control his sexual fantasies about males. To this inner turmoil is added not only the revelation that the town's librarian, Jerome Howard, has been having sex with teenage boys but also that the teenage son of one of Lingard's parishioners is homosexual. Howard's home is burned by arsonists, and Lingard futilely preaches tolerance. The boy, Skip, expresses the love he has long felt for Marc. After their night spent making love, Marc is able to accept his homosexuality and decides to come out publicly.

This novel shows important differences from *Strange Marriage* because of its post-Stonewall context. Here the teenager, Skip, provides the arguments for the naturalness of homosexuality that the doctor previously stated, and now all trace of psychological theory has been erased. Here no self-inflicted violence occurs; instead, groups from the majority lash out at individuals in the minority. Most importantly, *Strange Marriage* ends in heterosexual tolerance of homosexual feelings, but *The Outward Side* ends in the hope of liberation and of full achievement of gay identity.

Not until the character David Brandstetter did Hansen find a way to create his ideal character. In the first Brandstetter novel, *Fadeout*, Hansen sets the tone and the outline for the eleven to follow. A murder has been committed and Brandstetter arrives to investigate it on behalf of the company that insured the victim's life. Here a man, Fox Olson, has been killed by his son-in-law, who hoped to gain the insurance money. But homosexuality or, more precisely, homophobia also plays a role. Fox rediscovers his first love—for Doug Sawyer, his boyhood friend—and leaves family and career for him. Fox is killed only when he returns to his family and town for help.

Hansen presents a spectrum of homosexual characters who contrast sharply with the heterosexuals: Brandstetter's twenty-year relationship with Rod Fleming has ended only because of his lover's death from cancer, while Dave's father has been divorced eight times. Brandstetter presents a typically "masculine" temperament but other gays, including his lover, are effeminate and make no apologies for it. Hansen introduces many in the recurring cast of characters, including Madge Dunstan, a lesbian friend, and Doug Sawyer, who will become Dave's lover for a few years.

Having shown that homosexuality is not an illness or psychological aberrance in the first novel, Hansen can make a gay character the murderer in his next two novels without seeming to portray homosexuals per se as depraved. In *Death Claims*, a gay owner of a bookstore kills his partner for the insurance money, murders a closeted film star, and frames the son of his partner. The homophobic reaction to homosexuality forms a central theme of the first several works in the series. Parents in particular despise their homosexual offspring, for example, the fundamentalist Christian mother of the movie star or even the murder victim who cast out his gay son.

In *Troublemaker*, a psychotic man kills the wrong person, having intended to kill the man who had spurned his love when they were both teenagers. But Hansen provides other gay relationships in contrast: the victim and his lover; the budding love between Kovaks and Ray Lollard, another of the community of friends who provide Dave with information to help solve these murders; and the relationship between Dave and Doug.

The fanatic hatred by rightwing zealots recurs again and again in these works and supplies the central theme of the next three novels (*The Man Everybody Was Afraid Of, Skinflick, Gravedigger*). More and more Hansen demonstrates how social outsiders (because of their sexual preference, gender, or skin color) are made victims. But, in the process, he also shows how these outsiders create a community and identity that sustain them and indeed often make them the more humane characters.

As the series proceeds, Hansen chooses other topical themes in which to set the murders that Dave (along with Cecil Harris, a much younger African-American who increasingly becomes his partner in and out of bed) solves: illegal disposal of toxic waste (*Nightwork*), drug-pushing (*Obedience*), and the white supremacist movement (*The Boy Who Was Buried This Morning*). One of the best of these, *Early Graves*, describes a tangled set of murders of gay men who have AIDS or are infected with HIV. A gay man driven mad by the desire to seek revenge on the man who "infected" him sets out to murder every one of his previous sex partners. When he himself is killed while trying to commit another murder, the case would seem solved. However, another of the victims—closeted, married, father of a young child—was not murdered by him. He was killed by someone who found his homosexuality abhorrent: his son by a much earlier marriage. That son had become a religious zealot and believed he was performing God's will in killing his estranged father.

This novel, with its plot twisting around the shreds of the heterosexual family, continues another theme which runs through Hansen's works: the disintegration of the "traditional family." That family of (tainted) blood is replaced, however, by the family of choice. Indeed, Brandstetter's wide circle of friends and lovers enables him not only to solve these murders but also to solve the increasingly difficult questions of living his own life, which Dave faces as he ages over the more than two decades spanned by this series. It is with that family of choice that Hansen's gay characters continually create and renew their sense of identity and community. The return to this family forms the theme of the last Brandstetter novel, *A Country of Old Men*. Madge, Dave's closest lesbian friend, who has had a variety of lovers throughout the novels, adopts a little boy whose parents do not want him. Ray Lollard cares for Kovaks, his lover who is dying of AIDS. Dave Brandstetter is settled into his relationship with Cecil and leaves retirement only to help unravel the murder that the boy had witnessed. The novel concludes with Brandstetter collapsing, but not dying, from a heart attack.

Hansen has written three other mystery novels: *Known Homosexual, Backtrack*, and *Steps Going Down*. In addition, he has written two non-mystery novels: *A Smile in His Lifetime* and *Job's Year*. Similar themes and concerns motivate these works: the fear of having one's homosexuality revealed, the stifling confines of the closet that often lead a gay man into heterosexual marriage, the lethal limits imposed by small-town mentality and Christian fundamentalism. Although Hansen generally voices a certain pessimism about human nature, that pessimism is balanced in the Brandstetter series by Dave's pursuit of justice and his adherence to a gay community, whereas in the other novels that pessimism often overwhelms the reader.

CRITICAL RECEPTION

Hansen faced enormous resistance in his attempt to write novels that would portray "a man who has made a healthy, secure and stable life while not compromising his homosexuality" (Hansen, rev. of *The Tortured Sex* by John S. Yankowski and Hermann K. Wolff, *Tangents* 1/4 [January 1966]: 25). *Fadeout*, written in 1967, found a publisher only after three years. He worked on *Backtrack* and searched for a publisher for twelve years. Despite that initial reluctance, Hansen's works, especially the Brandstetter series, have been widely and positively reviewed in both gay and "mainstream" publications. James Levin describes the significance of *Death Claims*: "It indicated to publishers that a reading audience sufficient for financial success would accept a gay detective who operated in a milieu that was often filled with other homosexual men. Furthermore, the homosexuals could be free of neurosis and villainy and still not offend readers" (Levin, 302).

Reviewers most often praise Hansen's plotting ability, realism, and terse, evocative sentences. They also see the influence of Southern California in more than just his settings or characters. His style itself reminds critics of a cinematic style, with jump-cuts weaving together extensive sections of dialogue. Irony is a hallmark characteristic of this author, with the very name of his detective ("Brand's daughter") as a perfect example. Ernest Fontana sees the Brandstetter novels as "anti-pastorals" which "affirm the cosmopolitan values of voluntary rather than inherited relationships, of civilized pleasure, and of racial and sexual diversity and tolerance" (Fontana, 92).

For an author who has written over two dozen novels, it is surprising that so little critical reception of him exists. Perhaps this lies in his choice of genre: The detective novel has become a subject of academic criticism only within the past decade. Indeed, Hansen himself has written more essays about his novels than critics have. The gay press has always reviewed his work, whether as "James Colton" or under his own name. Reviews in nongay publications have been generally favorable, but have sometimes been offended by Hansen's insistence on integrating gay themes and characters.

The source of this critical silence and of gay/nongay difference in response can perhaps be found in Hansen's often-stated aim to portray a variety of homosexual characters so as to chip away at the destructive power of thinking in stereotypes. Those who find too much homosexuality in Hansen's novels object to his insistence on reminding his readers of the simple existence of gays and lesbians. Others, like James Levin, object to Hansen's not always flattering portrayals of his gay characters, in particular his insistence that even gays can be murderers.

What is striking about the novels Hansen has published under his own name and in the mystery genre is that his gay characters have remarkably little sex. Indeed, a reviewer for the *New York Times Book Review* praised Hansen for not making "a big thing of Dave's sexual habits" (Walters, 47). That paucity of sex scenes (perhaps a reaction to those he had to include in the "Colton" novels) is, however, what makes these books acceptable as products for review in nongay publications and by major publishing houses.

Hansen opened the path to the mystery genre for gay detectives. That was an enormous step forward for gay characters: from the status of victim to the role of hero. Hansen helped define the genre and led the way for its development into one of the most popular kinds of writing read by gay and lesbian audiences today.

NOVELS BY JOSEPH HANSEN

As James Colton

Lost on Twilight Road. Fresno: National Library, 1964.
Strange Marriage. Los Angeles: Argyle Books, 1965.
Known Homosexual. Los Angeles: Brandon House, 1968. Rev. ed. (under his own name) *Stranger to Himself*, Los Angeles: Major Books, 1978; and reissued as *Pretty Boy Dead*, San Francisco: Gay Sunshine Press, 1984.
Cocksure. San Diego: Greenleaf, 1969.
Gard. New York: Award, 1969.
Hang-Up. Los Angeles: Brandon House, 1969.
The Outward Side. New York: The Other Traveller, 1971.
Todd. New York: The Other Traveller, 1971.

As Rose Brock

Tarn House. New York: Avon, 1971.
Longleaf. New York: Harper and Row, 1974.

As Joseph Hansen

Fadeout. New York: Harper and Row, 1970.
Death Claims. New York: Harper, 1973.
Troublemaker. New York: Harper, 1975.
The Man Everybody Was Afraid Of. New York: Holt, Rinehart and Winston, 1978.
Skinflick. New York: Holt, 1979.
A Smile in his Lifetime. New York: Holt, 1981.
Backtrack. Woodstock, Vt.: The Countrymen Press, 1982.
Gravedigger. New York: Holt, 1982.
Job's Year. New York: Holt, 1983.
Nightwork. New York: Holt, 1984.
Steps Going Down. Woodstock: The Countrymen Press, 1985.
The Little Dog Laughed. New York: Henry Holt, 1986.
Early Graves. New York: The Mysterious Press, 1987.
Obedience. New York: The Mysterious Press, 1988.
The Boy Who Was Buried This Morning. New York: Viking Penguin, 1990.
A Country of Old Men. New York: Viking Penguin, 1991.

INTERVIEWS WITH AND ESSAYS BY JOSEPH HANSEN

Burton, Peter. "Joseph Hansen." In *Talking To . . .*, 34–41. London: Third House (Publishers), 1991.

Hansen, Joseph. "Matters Grave and Gay." In *Colloquium on Crime: Eleven Renowned Mystery Writers Discuss Their Work*. Ed. Robin W. Winks, 111–26. New York: Scribner's, 1986.

———. "The Mystery Novel as Serious Business." *Armchair Detective: A Quarterly Journal Devoted to the Appreciation of Mystery, Detective, and Suspense Fiction* 17, no. 3 (Summer 1984): 250–54.

———. "Rev. of *The Tortured Sex* by John S. Yankowsky and Herman K. Wolff." *Tangents* 1, no. 4 (January 1966): 25.

STUDIES OF JOSEPH HANSEN

Baird, Newton. "Joseph Hansen." In *Twentieth-Century Crime and Mystery Writers*. Ed. John Reilly, 725–28. New York: St. Martin's Press, 1980.

Fontana, Ernest. "Joseph Hansen's Anti-Pastoral Crime Fiction." *Clues* 7, no. 1 (Spring/Summer 1986): 89–97.

Levin, James. *The Gay Novel*. New York: Irvington, 1983.

Milton, John R. "Literary or Not." *South Dakota Review* 26, no. 2 (Summer 1988): 3–5.

Pike, B. A. "Joseph Hansen," *Detective Fiction*. Ed. John Cooper and B. A. Pike, 90–92. Somerset, England: Barn Owl Books, 1988.

Walters, Ray. Reviews of *Fadeout*, *Death Claims*, and *Skinflick*. *New York Times Book Review* 12 October 1980: 47.

ANDREW HOLLERAN
(1943(?)–   )
Gregory W. Bredbeck

BIOGRAPHY

Andrew Holleran may or may not have been born around 1943; he more than likely is white, American, and middle class; he probably lives in New York. Determining more than these mere possibilities is an impossible task, for "Andrew Holleran" is a pseudonym and the author who has adopted it guards his anonymity tenaciously. Yet one primary factor affecting Holleran as a writer is also the primary fact signalled by this obfuscatory biography: Holleran has chosen to remain at least partially in the closet, a choice that is reflected everywhere in his two major novels.

Some details of Holleran's life can be gleaned from a rare and important interview he granted to *Publisher's Weekly* in 1983. Focusing primarily on a discussion of his then just-released novel *Nights in Aruba*, Holleran admitted a personal tension resulting from being a devoted son to upper-middle-class parents and, at the same time, living a homosexually promiscuous life in New York similar to that portrayed in his earlier novel, *Dancer from the Dance*. Holleran, at the time of the interview nearly forty, described *Aruba* as being loosely based on the general facts of his own life: he was schooled at an exclusive prep school, later attended Harvard, served in West Germany with the Army, and afterward began studying law but abandoned it in favor of advanced training in writing at the University of Iowa. In 1971 he moved to New York City and has continued to be a productive name in the small but influential group of gay Manhattan writers who regularly contribute to *Christopher Street* and the *Village Voice*. He has published two critically acclaimed novels, and twenty-three of his short essays about AIDS have been recently gathered into one book, *Ground Zero*.

WORKS AND THEMES

Holleran's two novels, *Dancer from the Dance* and *Nights in Aruba*, in many ways form a single text. *Dancer from the Dance* chronicles the life of "that tiny subspecies of homosexual, the doomed queen, who puts the car in gear and drives *right* off the cliff!" (18). The characters in it are all what might be termed "circuit queens"—young homosexual men fixated on the social round-robin of Village discos and house parties on Fire Island. Central to the novel is the enigmatic figure of Malone, a solitary and beautiful gay man who captures the imagination of the entire circuit but who also curiously remains distant. *Nights in Aruba* initially seems to change course, for it focuses almost entirely on the bittersweet relationship between one gay man and his family. Yet the link between the two novels is strong, as Holleran himself witnessed: "[I] drew on the material that is now in the first person in *Aruba* for Malone's life in *Dancer*, even though they are certainly not the same person at all" (*Publisher's Weekly*, 72). Although Holleran would not say certainly that these details are drawn from his own life, the affinity between Malone, the narrator of *Aruba*, and Holleran himself seems certain: Malone is, after all, "a partygoer manqué" (137); the unidentified speaker of *Aruba* remains, for all practical purposes, a narrator manqué; Holleran, as the use of a pseudonym suggests, is an author manqué.

Dancer from the Dance is frequently grouped with Larry Kramer's* *Faggots* as one of the first novels to attempt to form a literature of the modern gay urban male. Although this classification dismisses a great deal of important earlier literature, it is indeed true that Holleran's novel broke into the central arena of publishing in a way that was quite unprecedented. The novel begins and ends with a series of letters between two unidentified gay men, one who is living in New York and is contemplating writing a novel about his past life in the city, the other who formerly lived in the city but now resides someplace in the Deep South. The novel per se becomes one of the letters between the two men—a device that interestingly redirects our assumptions of literary address. This novel is, both literally and figuratively, a homosexual missive. And the message it sends is in many ways an intentional cliché. An anonymous narrator tells the tale of Malone, a white upper-middle-class man raised with traditional values, who moves to New York, becomes the perfect New York homosexual, and in the process loses himself. Malone becomes "the central beautiful symbol" (133) of his community, and hence his career and decline become synoptic of the world in which he moved. If the story sounds familiar, it is, and is meant to be so. This is a gay *Great Gatsby*, with East and West Egg replaced by Fire Island and the Pines.

There is within both of Holleran's novels, but especially within *Dancer*, an overpowering sense of the burden of history. The reader in the Deep

South provides a summary that we might easily accept as the dominant motif of the novel: "Your novel might serve a historical purpose—if only because the young queens nowadays are utterly indistinguishable from straight boys. The twenty-year-olds are completely calm about being gay, *they* do not consider themselves doomed. Someone should record the madness, the despair, of the old-time queens, the Great Queens whose stories, unlike Elizabeth of Austria (!), have never been told" (15). The impulse to bear witness here betrays a larger tension within the novel. On the one hand, the novel glamorizes an organic and atemporal image of urban gay male culture. Malone, for example, clings to one central rule, "Over a long enough period of time, everyone goes to bed with everyone else" (33), as if this community is as "natural" and "inevitable" as the food chain. When both Malone and Sutherland, a bitchy queen who orchestrates the social circles of the novel, die at the same Party on Fire Island, the novel rewrites this end as a part of a larger continuance: "A professor from Rutgers pointed out that John Quincy Adams and Thomas Jefferson had died on the same day, not four hours apart, on the Fourth of July; and the departure of Malone and Sutherland on the same night was just as curious, and even more symmetrical to some queens" (234). The community trudges onward with the same inevitability as history. Yet this almost mystical sense of continuance is sharply counterpointed by an anxious fear of its opposite. The bonds that join the members of this community are figured as tenuous and transient, and the community itself frequently seems to be mounting a last defense against inconsequentiality. As Sullivan succinctly phrases it, "We live, after all, in perilous times . . . of complete philosophic sterility, we live in a rude and dangerous time in which there are no values to speak to and one must cling to only concrete things—such as cock" (95). Yet most striking of all is the strong sense that this communal identity somehow occludes the possibility of any identity: "our central struggle, always, [is] to isolate from the mob the single individual" (30).

If *Dancer from the Dance* is generated by an irreconcilable tension between gain and loss, *Nights in Aruba* rewrites this tension in terms of one man's personal life. The novel tells the life of one man: his early childhood on Aruba, where his father was an executive at a refinery; his service in West Germany in the military and the bonding with other gay men he met there; his subsequent move to New York and his visits to Jasper, Florida, where his parents have retired. Whereas *Dancer* begins with a need to bear witness to a lost community, *Aruba* begins with a need to bear witness to a lost past: "And I wondered if it was not time now to look out for myself—to go south farther next winter, as if there I would find a self which had disappeared in false fears and the desire to please others during the intervening years" (14).

The sense of history and loss that permeates *Dancer* becomes additionally stressed in *Nights in Aruba* by the emergent fear of AIDS. Explaining his dwindling fervor for the promiscuity that marked his early New York life, the narrator tells us, "By this time I was wary of disease, aware keenly of the limitations of these brief encounters, and considered homosexual love affairs as likely to survive as a kamikaze pilot" (182). *Nights in Aruba*, published in 1983, appeared only two years after the *New York Times* ran its first brief story about the "rare cancer" found in forty-one homosexuals, yet the impact of the disease on the urban community Holleran anatomizes is poignantly obvious in the novel: "Celebrities of our sexual demimonde were dying of bizarre cancers, and an epidemic of intestinal parasites had subverted the pleasures of promiscuous sex as abruptly as OPEC ended the era of cheap energy" (231). The historical change brought about by AIDS is overtly explored in Holleran's collection of essays, *Ground Zero*, wherein the long catalogue of "Notes on Promiscuity" ends with "92. Not anymore" (120), and the similar catalogue, "Notes on Celibacy," ends with "67. Celibacy is the future"(129). This change in free pleasure is strongly linked with a sense of historical loss in *Nights in Aruba*, for the novel ends with a striking rumination on the historicity of the gay community itself: "The style which was so masculine in my youthful eyes . . . was now discredited"; "Moustaches and beards were now as unpopular among young homosexuals as the Gang of Four was with the current regime in Peking" (231). If history, be it personal or cultural, is purportedly a source of knowledge, *Nights in Aruba* accepts a much darker view, for it ends with the hypothesis that just as Neptune is covered with nitrogen, or Venus with hydrochloric acid, "were one to look at Earth from afar one would say it is covered completely in Ignorance" (240).

The split between gain and loss, between melancholy and optimism, that motivates both of these novels is undoubtedly linked to the central topic that joins them: the split inherent in a closeted identity. In *Dancer from the Dance*, the entry into gay urban community is inextricably tied to a denial of personal history; the emphasis is on anonymity. While the locale of *Nights in Aruba* vacillates between the narrator's gay life in New York and his domestic life in Jasper, the narrative as a whole is generated precisely by an inability to recognize either of these places as a stable site. As the narrator says of Jasper, "the decision to explain nothing about my life . . . left an odd void . . . where a life should have been" (161). Vittorio, a friend of the narrator who has similarly split his life between New York and Jasper, recognizes a similar rupture: "I was an Eagle Scout. Valedictorian! Basketball captain. . . . And that has nothing—absolutely nothing— to do with my life anymore. Nothing" (164). Fixating on the possible visit of gay friends from New York, the narrator, while in Jasper, summarizes both the problem and its effect: "The tension of this approaching collision of two selves angered me so, I found myself talking out loud to the flowers I cut to put in the spare bedroom" (165). Nor is life in New York a secure career: "I slept with countless people during those years but always kept the same apartment and telephone number in order to appear reliable and fixed" (156). In the most telling comment of his interview with *Publisher's Weekly*, Holleran labels this split self "absolutely and completely" reflective of his own life and further calls it a problem "with no resolution, finally. It seems to me they are simply two worlds, and one has to participate in both, one has duties in both—to yourself and your family" (72). If this prompts us to ask, where does this leave a gay man? it is a question that has not been lost on Holleran; it is, rather, the question that creates both of his novels.

Holleran's work has sometimes been criticized by the gay community for presenting a myopic viewpoint catering to circuit queens, but there is also an element of his writing that seems to delimit the sometimes narrow and tragic world he so well re-creates. In the final letter of *Dancer from the Dance*, the transplanted New Yorker writes of "that day we marched to Central Park and found ourselves in a sea of humanity, how stunned I was to recognize no more than four or five faces" (249). He goes on to criticize and limit the group who has been the focus of the novel, suggesting that "our friends were all at the beach . . . they couldn't be bothered to come in and make a political statement" (249), and recognizes that "there were tons of men in that city who weren't on the circuit" (249). In *Nights in Aruba*, the narrator recalls how, when seeing the "feminist revolution" on television, his mother sensed "that she had missed, for purely historical reasons, an opportunity" (162). This same sense of simply being born at the wrong time is recapitulated near the novel's end when Mr. Friel, a gay friend of the narrator's, awaits a phone call from a "young man who is going to teach me to unite love and sex"—a newer generation, in other words, will complete the central challenge of *Dancer from the Dance*. These moments tend to limit the authority of the frenetic post-Stonewall urban world Holleran sketches. Yet the novels are not without optimism. Near the end of *Aruba*, the narrator's mother introduces his name for the first and only time: "Be careful going out, Paul" (234); the final letter in *Dancer from the Dance*, the letter that subtly critiques the apolitical circuit, also ends with the writer finally signing his real name: Paul. There is a characteristic ambivalence within these revelations, a sense that if the urban gay circuit somehow results in loss, in the process one can also gain a name. Perhaps the point is that both loss and gain are inevitable conditions of identity— an idea which the final lines of *Dancer from the Dance* poetically reshape: "Go out dancing tonight, my dear, and go home with someone, and if that love doesn't last beyond the morning, then know I love you" (250).

CRITICAL RECEPTION

In 1978, when *Dancer from the Dance* was released, gay New York was in the ninth year of its post-Stonewall high. Yet while the gay community had had literally a lifetime of oppression to prepare them for the idea of liberation, straight New York had a harder time coming to terms with what it meant to have an openly homosexual community flourishing in its midst. As much as telling about the novel, reception of *Dancer from the Dance* documents this tension. Four important reviews center Holleran's text within a heated debate on what it means to be "gay" "political" and "out"—and two of them, not surprisingly, link the novel with Larry Kramer's *Faggots*, which was released the same year.

In the most laudatory review, John Lahr, writing in the *New York Times Book Review*, claimed that the novel demonstrates "a style of laughter" in which can be found "a seriousness that much of the straight world is afraid to hear, that registers a lack of faith in both the peace it seeks and the pleasure it finds" (39). Paul Robinson hailed the novel as "beautifully written, singleminded and at once evocative and hilarious" (33). Robinson recognized a political danger, in that the novel "acknowledges a politically damaging fact about homosexual life, namely that it is narcissistic" (33), but at the same time recognized what this "danger" represents: "the novel isn't the slightest bit apologetic; there is no sense among the characters of answering to anyone beyond themselves" (33). For Robinson, the novel is a gay coming of age, a point where "political shrewdness" has given way to "truth" (33). In a more literary vein, Valentine Cunningham claimed, "what's important about *Dancer from the Dance* is that it's neither overwhelmed by Huxley's horror over homosexuals . . . nor wholly given up to Genet's excitements over outlawry and blasphemy" (171).

Yet these three reviews considered together paint a falsely optimistic view of the novel's reception. Jeffrey Burke, writing for *Harper's Magazine*, took on the task of reviewing "six books by, about, or for homosexuals" that had appeared "in as many months," and the focal point of the review is a double massacre of *Dancer from the Dance* and *Faggots*. Both novels are, according to Burke, "strong arguments that fiction . . . can do without subtlety, eloquence, characters, general appeal" (122). He derides the novels as being written from a perspective that "is always 3-D—discos, dancing, and drugs" (122). Yet perhaps the most telling comment of the review is a snide aside that opens it, in which Burke concedes that "reality requires an occasional facing, including the recently uncovered feature that not all men and women are heterosexual" (122) and suggests that this "recent" uncovering follows too closely the revelation that "not all women want to be housewives" (122).

Ironically, Holleran's career seems to be plagued by the same burden of history that permeates his novels. If *Nights in Aruba* is in some ways a more mature, personalized rewriting of *Dancer from the Dance*, critics, while praising the novel, singled out this change as a flaw. Caroline Seebohm recognized in the *New York Times Book Review* that there are "brilliant passages and observations" but also complained that it "lacks both the intensity and the flashing wit of the earlier book." She suggested that "Mr.

Holleran seems to have become sobered by the difficulties of his own past, and 'Aruba' reflects this burden" (30). Holleran himself has admitted the possibility of such an interpretation, and it is indeed true that *Aruba* unravels at a pace considerably less invigorating than that of *Dancer*.

Yet if there is a burden at work in Holleran's canon, it is the burden of producing texts in a world that changes as fast as one can write about it. This, at least, is the verdict borne by more recent criticism of *Dancer from the Dance*. In a vitriolic diatribe published in *Boston Review* in 1986, Daniel Harris, under the camp banner "La Cage au Dull," condemns Holleran for "capitaliz[ing] on the perceived exoticism of the subculture, exaggerating its wickedness, its decadence, creating storms of dissipation out of nothing more profligate than a puff of poppers and a Donna Summer song" (13). Ignoring that creating storms out of poppers is in itself a considerable feat, he further complains that "maybe all of this...is Oz...to Holleran..., but to many, Toto, it is just plain Kansas" (13). One does not question the applicability of this statement to the world of 1986; one does question, however, whether it is valid criticism of a novel written in 1978. In a similar vein, a lengthy 1988 article in *Newsweek* about gay writers and AIDS tosses off *Dancer from the Dance* as "a pre-AIDS period piece" (73)—a label that, we should remember, might just as well describe every play written by Shakespeare. What is present in all of these condemnations is a lack of historical sense, a desire to hold Holleran's novels accountable at all times for all facets of a gay world that is as historically mutable as its straight counterpart.

WORKS BY ANDREW HOLLERAN

Nights in Aruba. New York: William Morrow and Co., 1983; New York: New American Library, 1984.
Dancer from the Dance. New York: William Morrow and Co., 1978; New York: New American Library, 1986.
Ground Zero. New York: William Morrow and Co., 1988; New York: New American Library, 1989.

SELECTED STUDIES OF ANDREW HOLLERAN

Burke, Jeffrey. "Of a Certain Persuasion." *Harper's Magazine* 258 (March 1979): 122–23.
Cunningham, Valentine. "In the Wry." *New Statesman* 98 (August 3, 1979): 171.
Harris, Daniel. "La Cage au Dull." *Boston Review* (December 1986): 13–14.
Lahr, John. "Camp Tales." *New York Times Book Review* 14 January 1979: 15, 39–40.
"Out of the Closet, Onto the Shelves." *Newsweek* 21 March 1988: 72–74.
"PW Interviews Andrew Holleran." *Publisher's Weekly* 224 (July 29, 1983): 72–73.

Robinson, Paul. "Dancer from the Dance by Andrew Holleran." *The New Republic* 179 (September 30, 1978): 33–34.

Seebohm, Caroline. "Husbands, Lovers and Parents." *New York Times Book Review* 88 (September 25, 1983): 14, 30.

BO HUSTON (1959–   )
Earl Jackson, Jr.

BIOGRAPHY

Bo Huston was born Paul Huston on June 10, 1959, in Chagrin Falls, Ohio, to a Jewish mother and protestant father, both attorneys. The family moved to Cleveland Heights when he was seven. Although Huston was made aware of his Jewish heritage, he was raised in a secular fashion, and the family attended the Unitarian Church, stressing reason and intellect. Both his parents were Kennedy-style liberals, who felt somewhat embattled during the cold war era. As an adolescent he witnessed what this kind of outward-directed social conscience did to the children of his parents' friends. The concentration on world issues left no time for interpersonal dynamics within the family, and the children experienced a subtle form of neglect. Huston himself found later as a writer it was difficult to adopt the necessary concern for self-awareness, as the kind of liberal interest in humanity in which he was raised had nothing to do with self-awareness, and in fact viewed it with suspicion as a form of selfishness.

Huston had a very hard time adjusting to junior high school and became rebellious, sneaking into gay bars at night and shoplifting during the day. At sixteen he ran away from home briefly, hitchhiking across the country. After he placed himself in an alternative high school program, he became a more serious student. In 1977 he enrolled in Hampshire College in Amherst, Massachusetts. In three and half years he graduated with a degree in writing with a concentration on cinema studies. During his years at Hampshire his drug use increased dramatically, and he also discovered the importance of writing. He spent much of his time writing journals, stories, while experimenting heavily sexually with both men and women. This was where he first became concerned with developing a personal aesthetic and understanding formal concerns about writing. Studying film also helped him map the distinctions between scene and character. He adopted cinema as his model for aesthetic structures and the act of writing as the force of expression within those structures.

Huston took the first gay course taught in college in the United States, a course on gay film taught by Tom Joslin. Vito Russo, who at that time was writing *The Celluloid Closet*, did several guest lectures in that class based on his notes for the book. In this class Huston realized that being gay was a politically and culturally valid identity and something more than the desire for other male bodies.

In 1980, Huston moved to New Haven, Connecticut, which geographically expressed his psychic ambivalence in that it was halfway between Boston and New York, halfway between an academic community and the drug community, the latter of which was gaining increasing importance in his life. His cocaine habit eventually gave way to a heroin habit: he moved to New York and entered New York University in a master's program in film studies, but his drug addiction and his sexual adventures eventually led him to withdraw from the program. He then took courses briefly at the New School, but this also became impossible to continue.

Huston worked as a typesetter and became very involved in the New York club scenes. He would wake at 2 P.M., go to work, and afterward party at the clubs until 8:30 the next morning. He would frequent first the straight or mixed dance clubs—particularly the Mud Club, Cee Bee Jee Bee's, the Rock Lounge, and Studio 54—and then move on to the more notorious gay bars: the Anvil, Mineshaft, and the Hellfire Club. In 1981 Huston met the poet Tim Dlugos in the backroom of the International Stud. They became lovers at first, but remained close friends until Dlugos' death in 1990. Dlugos introduced Huston to Dennis Cooper* and the other Little Caesar poets. When Cooper returned to New York from Amsterdam, he read Huston's stories and gave him his first real encouragement for his writing.

In 1983, tormented by his drug addiction, Huston moved to Rheinbeck, a small town on the Hudson, to dry out and to concentrate on writing. He wrote a novel, which he later abandoned, and the story "The Heart Itself," based on his experience there, which is one of the key stories in *Horse*. In the town he was completely alone and very sick from withdrawal. The town with its white picket fences and apparently happy families both repulsed and attracted him: It is the town that symbolizes home and comes up in many of his stories and is the model for the town in his novel *Remember Me*. During his stay in Rheinbeck he received the news about the first of his friends to die of AIDS ("Robby," whom he puts in his story "After the War") and also became intensely determined to kick drugs. When he returned to New York, however, his resolution failed; and it was not until 1985, when he checked himself into a hospital, that he successfully ended his use of narcotics and alcohol.

Huston returned to typesetting and was able to typeset many of his own stories (for example, "Flies" and "Seven Kinds of Pity") while working on brochures for an upscale travel agency that specialized in yacht cruises. He fell in love with a French man, but when that relationship failed Huston decided to visit San Francisco. Huston was so impressed by San Francisco that he decided to move there, in early 1987, and got a job as a typesetter for the art department of a San Francisco ad agency. At a Christmas party the same year, Huston met Dan Carmell, a young man of extraordinary grace and charisma, who could even tame cats on the street by talking to them. They became lovers almost immediately.

Dennis Cooper showed Huston's stories to Ira Silverberg, and the two men in turn brought them to Stan Leventhal, who published them as *Horse and Other Stories*. In the spring of 1988, Huston was diagnosed with ARC; he decided to quit his job to concentrate on writing. The reviews of *Horse* were extremely positive, and he became a regular columnist for the *San Francisco Bay Times*. As a cofounder of the first Out/Write Conference in 1989, he met Kevin Killian,* Dodie Bellamy, and Dorothy Allison and began to be a part of a writer's community, while working on his novel *Remember Me*.

The process of writing *Remember Me* was a painful one, as were the reviews it received. Partially as a reaction against the heavily meditative tone of that novel, Huston began a new novel almost immediately, entitled *The Dream Life*, which was deliberately "unreflective" and in which the phenomena are presented with no attempt at explication or analysis.

At present Bo Huston and Dan Carmell share a beautiful home in San Francisco with their four cats, and Huston is continuing his work as a journalist for the *San Francisco Bay Times* and other publications, occasionally teaching writing, and has begun a collection of thematically related short stories.

MAJOR THEMES AND WORKS

Bo Huston's stories are somewhere between extended haiku (without the faith in the inherent sanctity of experience that informs that aesthetic) and the writings of J. D. Salinger—slices of unannotated life. The themes and principal preoccupations of Huston's novels are found in earlier but more condensed forms in the stories in *Horse*: false homes (the boardinghouses of "Flies" and "The Heart Itself," the vacation bungalows of "A Phony Laugh"); temporary stations on an ill-defined journey (the motels of "Horse," "Seven Kinds of Pity"); random encounters ("Sex in Public Places," "Dark Springtime," "My Monster"), and the sense of being an outsider ("Man without a Country," "The Heart Itself"). In fact, Huston's first novel, *Remember Me*, is essentially an expansion of the story "Little World."

Remember Me is a portrait of the relationship between a gay man (an unnamed first-person narrator) and Charlotte, a young agoraphobic woman, his lifelong friend, with whom he shares a house in a small town near New York City. The man, an aspiring writer, has AIDS, although he is not yet critically ill. The plot consists of the rhythm of their daily lives, quiet, at times desperately so, but with a richness of nuanced intimacy between the two that sustains the narrative. When the prospective publisher discusses the narrator's manuscript, his criticism serves as a metacommentary on the novel at hand: "What's problematical . . . is the pacing. . . . Not much really happens, does it? . . . The plot does not move. . . . You seem to let your characters wander" (96–97).

Actually quite a bit happens, but it is generally in the interior lives of the two main characters, as if the epiphanic moments of the short stories resurface in the novel; but here the sense of their inherent significance, both psychological and spiritual, is allowed to emerge, albeit retrospectively.

Huston's real masterpiece to date is *The Dream Life*. The novel is told by two first-person narrators: Holly and Jed. Holly met Jed when Jed was thirteen, hired by Jed's wealthy but cold mother to tutor the boy. Eventually the two fall in love, and Holly "kidnaps" Jed. They flee across the United States, eventually setting up house in Los Angeles, where Holly sends Jed out as a prostitute, as Holly had been when he was young. Almost every event in the story is relayed twice, from each perspective, and filtered through the tragic childhoods of each narrator. In beautifully restrained prose, Huston maps the fluid contours of intimacy, sex, memory, grief, loss, love, and retribution in one of the most moving experiments in contemporary fiction.

CRITICAL RESPONSE

The critical response to *Horse and Other Stories* was generally very good, many writers noting Huston's gift for character and scene, which seem somewhat anachronistic in the avant-garde. Dorothy Allison's description of the collection is among the best:

Huston's characters are matter-of-factly queer; their homosexuality is subtext, not subject. Silence, recovery, and self-acceptance are the focus of his delicately rendered tales—not sexuality. . . . Huston sketches in what it means to be queer, desperate, and still vulnerable in the last decade of this millenium. His characters remind us that breathing is sometimes the outlaw's best accomplishment. ("Margin Chronicles")

Reviewers of *Remember Me* seemed to allow AIDS to eclipse the real subject-matter of the novel (Dennis Cooper's review being a notable exception). Sarah Schulman's review was particularly unfortunate, in that it also confused the novel with Huston's own diagnosis (something which he himself had not made public at the time of her review):

people with AIDS are living longer and, in Bo Huston's case, creating thoughtful and honest investigations of this devil in our midst.... As in much fiction by people with AIDS, the reader can sense Huston's desire to stretch, to race against the clock. ("Death Kit")

In the only sustained critical treatment of Huston's work to date, David Jansen-Mendoza situates AIDS within the novel in a far more useful way. After drawing a comparison between Huston's novel and the gothic, in their shared motifs of expulsion from a formerly perfected "home," Jansen-Mendoza observes:

The home that the narrator in *Remember Me* finds himself "fallen" from, or outside of, is not only the idealized family hearth but the body which illness has abducted. This disassociation of the body from the self is, however, ultimately configured positively and illuminates the intrusion of a social system into the stratification of identity. Like the gothic, such disassociation opens horizons beyond social patterns, rational decisions, and socially sanctioned emotions.... The disassociation between body and self... that AIDS evokes is entangled with the illness's proximity to the narrator's sexual behavior and history. The illness forever foregrounds the narrator as a specifically sexualized and transgressive body. At the same time, it is this gap that offers the narrator an opportunity to sort through the "identities" projected onto his body. It is the unveiling of these mis-identities that eventually sets him en route to a "home." ("Foreign Body[ies]," 1–2)

WORKS BY BO HUSTON

Horse and Other Stories. New York: Amethyst, 1989.
Remember Me. New York: Amethyst, 1991.
The Dream Life. New York: St. Martin's, 1992.
"I Am Waiting." *Mother Jones* 17, no. 1 (January/February 1992): 56–59, 72.

SELECTED STUDIES OF BO HUSTON

Allison, Dorothy. "Margin Chronicles." *Village Voice* 24 April 1990: 59.
Benderson, Bruce. "Bo-He-Me-Ah!: Remembering with Bo Huston." *Outweek* 1
     May 1991: 59–60.
Bennett, Adam. "Review of *Horse and Other Stories*." *Torso* (March 1990): 67.
Cooper, Dennis. "Worldly Vision." *The Advocate* 18 June 1991: 84.
Jackson, Earl, Jr. "A Conversation with Bo Huston." *Lavender Reader* (Summer
     1992: 38–40, 31.
Jansen-Mendoza, David. "Foreign Body(ies): The Exposition of Identity via Illness
     in *Remember Me*." Senior thesis, University of California, Santa Cruz, 1991.
Karr, John F. "Review of *Horse and Other Stories*." *Manifest* (June 1990): 43.

Killian, Kevin. "Review of *Horse and Other Stories*." *James White Review* 7, no. 4 (Summer 1990): 21.
Satuloff, Bob. "Tales from the Darkside." *New York Native* 3 June 1991: 39.
Schulman, Sarah. "Death Kit." *Village Voice* 29 October 1991: 54.
Silverberg, Ira. "Goodbye, Guppies." *Outweek* 3 January 1990: 62–64.

CHRISTOPHER ISHERWOOD
(1904–1986)
Claude J. Summers

BIOGRAPHY

Few writers have so exclusively distilled their art from personal experience and so self-consciously blurred the boundaries separating autobiography and fiction as has Christopher Isherwood. His life is the fundamental source of his work. He was born Christopher William Bradshaw Isherwood on August 26, 1904 in High Lane, Cheshire, the son of Kathleen Machell-Smith and Frank Bradshaw-Isherwood. An old and distinguished family of landed gentry, the Bradshaw-Isherwoods were among the principal landowners in Cheshire. In 1915, while a student at St. Edmund's preparatory school in Surrey, Isherwood learned that his father, a professional soldier, had been killed in action in France. In early 1919, he entered Repton, a prestigious public school, where he formed a close friendship with future novelist Edward Upward, whom he joined at Corpus Christi College, Cambridge, in 1923.

Sent down from Cambridge for answering examination questions facetiously in 1925, Isherwood took a job in London as secretary to a string quartet and began to write novels. At this time, he frankly acknowledged his homosexuality to himself and to his mother. In 1925, he also renewed his friendship with W. H. Auden, whom he had met during his last year at St. Edmund's. For over ten years, the two shared an unromantic relationship in which sex gave their friendship an added dimension. Two and one-half years his junior, Auden cast Isherwood in the role of literary mentor and soon introduced him to a fellow Oxford undergraduate, Stephen Spender. The trio formed the nucleus of what would later be called "The Auden Gang," the angry young writers who dominated the English literary scene of the 1930s.

Isherwood's first novel, *All the Conspirators*, was published in 1928. Its poor sales did not encourage the pursuit of a literary career. After an unsuccessful attempt to study medicine at King's College, London, Isherwood departed on March 14, 1929, for a brief visit to Berlin. In Berlin he felt liberated from the sexual and social inhibitions that stifled his development in England, and he determined to move there. Immersing himself in the bohemian world of male prostitutes, he lived almost anonymously in shabbily genteel and working-class areas of the city, where he revised his second novel *The Memorial* and translated his experience of the demimonde into what would eventually become the unsurpassed portrait of pre-Hitler Germany, the Berlin Stories. In 1932, he fell in love with a German working-class youth, Heinz. After Hitler's appointment as chancellor in 1933, Isherwood and Heinz determined to leave Germany, a decision made urgent by Heinz's eligibility for conscription into the German military. For the next four years, the two wandered restlessly from one European country to another, searching for a place where they could settle together. The odyssey ended when Heinz had to return to Germany, where he was arrested and sentenced first to prison for homosexual activities with Isherwood and then to service in the German army.

During the 1930s, Isherwood rapidly gained a reputation as the most promising novelist of his generation. The publication of the Berlin Stories, comprised of *The Last of Mr. Norris* (1935) and *Goodbye to Berlin* (1938), sections of which, including "Sally Bowles," had been published earlier, established him as a penetrating observer of the disturbing events in Germany. He became friends with his hero E. M. Forster, the only living writer whom he regarded as his master, and was hailed by Somerset Maugham. By collaborating with Auden on three avant-garde plays and by supporting various left-wing causes, Isherwood gained a reputation for ideological commitment. But partly because of his growing awareness of himself as a homosexual, he deeply distrusted communism; and he became more and more dissatisfied with the emptiness of left-wing rhetoric. In 1938, he and Auden traveled to China to report on the Sino-Japanese war. On their return, they stopped briefly in New York. The results of this trip were *Journey to a War* (1939) and the fascination of both writers with America.

In January 1939, Isherwood and Auden emigrated to the United States, a decision that reflected both their disenchantment with England and their loss of political faith. On board the ship bringing them to America, Isherwood realized that he was a pacifist, a conviction prompted by his fear that Heinz might be serving in the German army. When Auden and Isherwood arrived in New York, Auden almost immediately found the city stimulating and enjoyable, while Isherwood was overcome with despair. At the invitation of the philosopher Gerald Heard, he traveled to California, where he was to settle for the rest of his life, working largely in the motion-picture industry but occasionally accepting teaching appointments at area universities. He became a U.S. citizen in 1946.

Soon after his arrival in Los Angeles, Isherwood was introduced to Swami Prabhavananda, a Hindu monk of the Ramakrishna order who was head of the Vedanta Society of Southern California. Isherwood embraced Vedantism and seriously considered becoming a monk. His conversion after a long history of opposition to religion acknowledged a spiritual need that the narrowly moralistic Christianity of his youth could not satisfy. The importance of Isherwood's conversion can hardly be overestimated, for all his later work is informed by Vedantism, most obviously *The World in the Evening* (1954) and *A Meeting by the River* (1967) but also *Prater Violet* (1945), *Down There on a Visit* (1962), and *A Single Man* (1964). In addition, he collaborated with Swami Prabhavananda on translations of several Hindu religious works, edited the journal *Vedanta and the West,* and wrote a biography of Ramakrishna (1965), as well as personal accounts of his religious experience, *An Approach to Vedanta* (1963) and *My Guru and His Disciple* (1980).

In the winter of 1953, Isherwood fell in love with an eighteen-year-old college student, Don Bachardy. The discrepancy in their ages scandalized many of their friends, but the relationship proved to be the most enduring union of Isherwood's life. Bachardy subsequently achieved independent success as an artist, and he and Isherwood collaborated on a number of motion picture and television scripts, as well as on a dramatization of *A Meeting by the River.* At the conclusion of Isherwood's 1976 biography, *Christopher and His Kind,* he describes Bachardy as "the ideal companion to whom you can reveal yourself totally and yet be loved for what you are, not what you pretend to be" (339).

In 1971, Isherwood published a biography of his parents constructed from their diaries and letters. Pointing the direction of his increasing interest in autobiography, *Kathleen and Frank* proved to be "chiefly about Christopher." It contained the casual but explicit revelation of Isherwood's homosexuality, a fact that he had never hidden but had also never before confirmed in print. As part of the promotional effort for the book, the author appeared on several television interview programs and openly discussed his sexual orientation, explaining its centrality in his life. From that point onward, he became an active participant in the burgeoning American gay liberation movement, frequently appearing on behalf of the equal-rights struggle at political rallies and fund-raising events. By the time of his death on January 4, 1986, he had become a deeply revered icon of contemporary Anglo-American gay culture, a courage-teacher who vigorously protested the heterosexual dictatorship and who unashamedly expressed solidarity with his "kind."

MAJOR WORKS AND THEMES

Isherwood's homosexuality undoubtedly had a major influence on his art, all the more obviously so because his is primarily an art grounded in autobiography. He sometimes appears to be a face looking over his own shoulder, monitoring with a curious objectivity his fascinating journey from angry young man to ironic moralist and gay-liberation activist. His interest in certain psychological predicaments and in recurring character types and themes, especially such mythopoeic types as the Truly Weak Man, the Truly Strong Man, and the Evil Mother and such obsessions as war, The Test, the struggle toward maturity, and the search for a father, may all be directly or indirectly related to his homosexuality. Certainly, Isherwood's fascination with the antiheroic hero, his rebellion against bourgeois respectability, his empathy with the alienated and the excluded, and his ironic perspective are probably all intertwined with his awareness of himself as a homosexual.

Homosexuality is a crucial element of Isherwood's work. Even when it is suppressed or disguised for legal or artistic reasons, it makes its presence felt in the novels, for it is an indispensable aspect of the personal and literary myth of the outsider that Isherwood cultivated so assiduously. But Isherwood goes beyond simply portraying the homosexual as alienated outsider. He also sees the homosexual as a faithful mirror of the human condition, a symbol of individuality and uniqueness and also of the variousness of human possibilities. Isherwood's work anticipates the gay-liberation perspective that would flower in the aftermath of the 1969 Stonewall riots.

Homosexuals in Isherwood's early fiction are an important constituency of "The Lost," a group that he describes in the preface to *Goodbye to Berlin* as including "those individuals respectable society shuns in horror" (v). Homosexuality features in the early novels in many guises, from the repressed passions of *All the Conspirators* (1928) to the fuller depictions of homosexual characters and situations in *The Memorial* (1932), where Edward Blake is never able to escape the impact of the loss in World War I of his best friend; and from the coyly comic portrait of Baron Kuno von Pregnitz, whose secret fantasies revolve around English schoolboy adventure stories in *The Last of Mr. Norris* (1935) to the spoiled homosexual idyll of Peter Wilkinson and Otto Nowak in *Goodbye to Berlin* (1929). In these early works, Isherwood presents homosexuality unapologetically and without the self-consciousness and melodrama that mark contemporaneous treatments of the issue. He refrains from sensationalizing the gay subculture; he deftly defuses and domesticates aspects of gay life that lesser writers might have rendered as decadence or depravity; and he reveals considerable insight into the dynamics of gay relationships. Moreover, what is faulted in the early fiction is the repression rather than the expression of homosexuality, a repression that underlies the isolation of the narrator of *Goodbye to Berlin*, who clearly is attracted to Otto Nowak's "naked brown body so sleek with health," but whose inability to connect meaningfully even with the characters with whom he is in most intimate contact mirrors the essential loneliness of Berlin itself.

In the early fiction, Isherwood depicts his gay characters as infected (along with many others) with the soul sickness that denies life and distorts reality. They manifest symptoms of the obscure dread that pervades post–World War I England and pre-Hitler Germany. For example, Edward Blake of *The Memorial* is a version of a recurrent character type in Isherwood's early work, the Truly Weak Man; he constantly needs to test himself and is unable to combine love and sex. But Blake's unhappiness (which leads to a suicide attempt) is due not to his homosexuality but to his predicament as a casualty of World War I; adrift in a world without purpose, he fails his self-imposed tests, as do all the other characters in a novel shadowed by the all-encompassing failure represented by the war. Similarly, the unhappiness that characterizes the gay characters in *The Last of Mr. Norris* and *Goodbye to Berlin*—Baron von Pregnitz, Otto Nowak, and Peter Wilkinson—is attributed not to their homosexuality but to their failure of commitment to life, a failure that they share with all the other characters in the novels. In the early works the gay characters are juxtaposed with the heterosexual characters to reveal beneath their apparent polarities a shared reality of the deadened spirit. As one character in *Goodbye to Berlin* remarks, "Eventually we're all queer" (193).

Isherwood's later novels, beginning with *The World in the Evening* (1954), probe more deeply and focus more intently on the plight of the homosexual in a homophobic society. In these works, gay characters are both more numerous and their homosexuality defined more sharply in terms of their social roles and the obstacles they face than is the case in the earlier fiction. The dilemma faced by the gay characters of the later novels is epitomized by their apparently incompatible needs to assert their individuality and to feel a sense of community. This conundrum is felt by Bob Wood, the Quaker artist of *The World in the Evening*, one of the earliest sympathetic portraits of a gay activist in Anglo-American literature. The angriest of Isherwood's gay characters, Wood describes himself as "a professional criminal" and bitterly attacks the heterosexual majority for its failure to accept the gay minority. Sick of the futile discussions of the etiology of homosexuality, he would like to "march down the street with a banner saying, 'We're queer because we're queer because we're queer' " (112); but even this protest, wildly unlikely in the early 1940s, when the action of the novel takes place, is impossible: his lover, Charles, a Jew who has changed his name, "is sick of belonging to these whining militant minorities" (112). Charles's prescription for Bob's dilemma is the improbable creation of "Quaker Camp," but, tellingly, the solution Bob finds for himself is political at base. At the end of the novel, he joins the Navy. His motives are not conventionally patriotic: "Compared with this business of being queer, and the laws against us, and the way we're pushed around even in peacetime—this war hardly seems to concern me at all." But he refuses to accept exemption from military service on the basis of his sexual orientation, "because what they're claiming is that us queers are unfit for their beautiful pure Army and Navy—when they ought to be glad to have us" (281). The solidarity that Wood feels with his fellow homosexuals is extremely rare in the literature of the period. Isherwood's conception of homosexuals as a legitimate minority with real grievances anticipates the emerging gay liberation movement of the late 1960s and his own fuller treatment of the issue in *A Single Man.*

In the "Ambrose" section of *Down There on a Visit* (1962), Isherwood creates a haunting portrait of the homosexual as persecuted victim. The title character is an expatriate Englishman who has created a self-sufficient anarchic community on the Greek island of St. Gregory. Described in terms suggesting saintliness and otherworldly absorption, Ambrose retreats to his island, where he reigns over a disorderly menagerie like "one of Shakespeare's exiled kings" (92). Like Prospero's in *The Tempest,* his retreat is not voluntary. Permanently scarred by the trashing of his rooms at Cambridge by a group of undergraduate hearties, he has been frequently harassed. On St. Gregory, he attempts to create a brave new world of his own imagining. His fantasy of a homosexual kingdom is revealing as a parody of the unjust reality that provokes his alienation. In this fantasy, it is heterosexuality that is illegal: "Meanwhile it'll be winked at, of course, as long as it's practiced in decent privacy. I think we shall even allow a few bars to be opened for people with those unfortunate tendencies, in certain quarters of the larger cities" (92–93). This comic riff embodies the homosexual's bitterness at being excluded from the larger society. Moreover, it also betrays Ambrose's hidden desire for involvement in the world, albeit at a level beyond the reality that he finds unacceptable. Ambrose, no less than Bob Wood, suffers from the absence of community—an absence that will eventually be addressed by the gay-liberation movement.

The need for community is also an issue in *A Single Man* (1964), which is both Isherwood's finest novel and a masterpiece of gay fiction. The protagonist of the novel, George, a late-middle-aged and lonely expatriate Briton grieving at the death in an automobile accident of his lover of many years, is the most fully human of all Isherwood's gay characters. He shares the alienation and anger of characters like Bob Wood and Ambrose, but he is a more central and a more rounded character than they. Indeed, George emerges in the novel as an Everyman figure, with whom anyone can identify. In addition, *A Single Man* more fully develops the context of gay oppression than do the earlier novels and places it within a still-larger context of spiritual transcendence. Dealing with universal themes of commitment and grief, alienation and isolation, the book concretely explores the minority sensibility and masterfully balances worldly and religious points of view. It regards the assertions of individual uniqueness and of minority consciousness as indispensable worldly and political goals, but it finally subsumes them in the Vedantic idea of the oneness of life. In making concrete this resolution, the novel presents a sustained and moving portrait of male homosexual love and explores insightfully the homosexual plight, presenting homosexuality as both a metaphor for alienation and a faithful mirror of the human condition.

The minority consciousness of *A Single Man* helps make possible the balance the novel strikes between assertions of tribal identity and a wider view in which differences are merely circumstantial and insignificant. But another reason for Isherwood's minority consciousness is clearly political. To portray homosexuals as simply another tribe in a nation composed of many different tribes is both to soften the stigma linked to homosexuality and to encourage solidarity among gay people. And by associating the mistreatment of homosexuals with the discrimination suffered by other minorities in America, such as the blacks, the Jews, and the Japanese, Isherwood legitimizes the grievances of gay people at a time when homosexuals were not recognized as either a legitimate minority or as valuable members of the human community. *A Single Man* presents homosexuality as simply a human variation that should be accorded value and respect and depicts homosexuals as a group whose grievances should be redressed politically. Isherwood's dual insistence on the common humanity of gay people and on the need for a tribal identity among homosexuals are vital contributions to gay fiction before the Stonewall insurrection. Presaging the gay liberation movement, *A Single Man* recognizes the need for gay community even as it articulates a transcendent vision in which a universal consciousness subsumes individuality itself.

Isherwood's last novel, *A Meeting by the River* (1967), is set in a Hindu monastery on the banks of the Ganges and incorporates most directly the religious values that more obliquely inform *A Single Man* and the other late novels. The slight plot pivots on the unsuccessful attempt of a bisexual movie producer to dissuade his younger brother from taking final vows as a swami. The producer, Patrick, is among the most unpleasant characters in all of Isherwood's fiction; he is attracted toward a vision of homosexual union "in which two men learn to trust each other so completely that there's no fear left and they experience and share everything together in the flesh and in the spirit" (109), but he retreats to a cowardly and hypocritical conformity. Still, there is hope for Patrick. The union of the brothers at the end of the book is the consummation of their long searches for symbolic brotherhood. These quests lead one to the glimpse of a Whitmanesque ideal of gay love and the other to the achievement of spiritual brotherhood in a monastery. Finally revealing the commonality within the two very different siblings, the novel offers the concept of brotherhood as a means of escaping the imprisoning ego.

More forthrightly than any other major writer of his generation, Christopher Isherwood embraced the contemporary gay-liberation movement. That allegiance was altogether appropriate, for his novels—all written before the Stonewall riots that traditionally date the beginning of the gay-liberation movement—incorporate gay-liberation perspectives, especially the need for solidarity among homosexuals and the recognition of homosexuals as an aggrieved minority. Isherwood's greatest achievement, however, is in creating gay characters—preeminently George in *A Single Man*—whose homosexuality is a simple given, an integral part of the wholeness of personality, and in placing those characters in situations and contexts where their homosexuality functions as an emblem of their common humanity.

CRITICAL RECEPTION

Although he was among the best writers of his generation, Isherwood—for a variety of reasons, homophobia not least among them—was denied the full popular and critical recognition he deserved. After being extravagantly praised in the 1930s, his reputation precipitously declined in the 1950s and 1960s, and not simply because of the relative failure of *The World in the Evening*. He was widely regarded as having betrayed the promise of his earlier work by having adopted—in W. W. Robson's condescending words—"Californian eccentricity and religiosity," a phrase in which "eccentricity" no doubt means homosexuality. Among British critics there may have been resentment over his expatriation, and his larger audience may have been unprepared for the new spiritual dimension of his later work and for the increasing frankness with which he treated homosexuality. As Robert Funk has observed, "the irrationality of homophobia has surely had a significant effect on Isherwood's critical reputation" (xiii).

Perhaps equally significant in denying him a central place in the literature of the 1950s and 1960s was the persistent pigeonholing of him as a 1930s writer, the creator of Sally Bowles. Protesting the lack of recognition extended the later novels, Carolyn Heilbrun declared in 1970 that "in failing to appreciate Isherwood we have failed to understand ourselves" (46). His portrait of Berlin in the 1930s continues to haunt the imagination, and it has been extended in altered—somewhat distorted—form through the adaptations of John van Druten's play and film *I Am a Camera* and John Kander and Fred Ebb's musical play and film *Cabaret*. But the most significant element in the recent rehabilitation of his reputation was the rediscovery of the novels written during the 1960s, especially *A Single Man*. Moreover, the publication of *Christopher and His Kind*, a sexual and political autobiography, may have garnered Isherwood a new audience of younger gay readers and activists. In any case, in the 1970s and 1980s Isherwood's reputation was solidified. Described by Gore Vidal* as "the best prose writer in English," he is now widely recognized as a masterful stylist, a subtle ironist, a witty and compassionate moralist, and an extraordinarily insightful observer of the human condition.

MAJOR WORKS BY CHRISTOPHER ISHERWOOD

All the Conspirators. London: Jonathan Cape, 1928.
The Memorial: Portrait of a Family. London: Hogarth, 1932.

The Last of Mr. Norris. New York: Morrow, 1935. British title: *Mr. Norris Changes Trains.* London: Hogarth, 1935.

With W. H. Auden. *The Dog Beneath the Skin, or Where Is Francis? A Play in Three Acts.* London: Faber, 1935.

With W. H. Auden. *The Ascent of F 6, a Tragedy in Two Acts.* London: Faber, 1936.

Sally Bowles. London: Hogarth, 1937.

Lions and Shadows: An Education in the Twenties. London: Hogarth, 1938.

With W. H. Auden. *On the Frontier: A Melodrama in Three Acts.* London: Faber, 1938.

Goodbye to Berlin. New York: Random House, 1939.

With W. H. Auden. *Journey to a War.* London: Faber, 1939.

Prater Violet. New York: Random House, 1945.

The Condor and the Cows: A South American Travel Diary. New York: Random House, 1949.

The World in the Evening. New York: Random House, 1954.

Down There on a Visit. New York: Simon & Schuster, 1962.

A Single Man. New York: Simon & Schuster, 1964.

A Meeting by the River. New York: Simon & Schuster, 1967.

Kathleen and Frank: The Autobiography of a Family. New York: Simon & Schuster, 1971.

Christopher and His Kind, 1929–39. New York: Farrar, Straus & Giroux, 1976.

My Guru and His Disciple. New York: Farrar, Straus & Giroux, 1980.

Where Joy Resides: An Isherwood Reader. Ed. Don Bachardy and James P. White. New York: Farrar, Straus & Giroux, 1989.

SELECTED STUDIES OF CHRISTOPHER ISHERWOOD

Finney, Brian. *Christopher Isherwood: A Critical Biography.* New York: Oxford University Press, 1979.

Fryer, Jonathan. *Isherwood: A Biography of Christopher Isherwood.* London: New English Library, 1977.

Funk, Robert W. *Christopher Isherwood: A Reference Guide.* Boston: G. K. Hall, 1979.

Heilbrun, Carolyn C. *Christopher Isherwood.* Columbia Essays on Modern Literature 53. New York: Columbia University Press, 1970.

Hynes, Samuel L. *The Auden Generation: Literature and Politics in England in the 1930s.* London: Bodley Head, 1976.

King, Francis. *Christopher Isherwood.* Writers and Their Work 240. Harlow, Essex: Longman, 1979.

Lehmann, John. *Isherwood: A Personal Memoir.* New York: Holt, 1987.

Piazza, Paul. *Christopher Isherwood: Myth and Anti-Myth.* New York: Columbia University Press, 1978.

Schwerdt, Lisa M. *Isherwood's Fiction: The Self and Technique.* London: Macmillan, 1989.

Summers, Claude J. *Christopher Isherwood.* New York: Ungar, 1980.

———. *Gay Fictions: Wilde to Stonewall.* New York: Continuum, 1990.

Wilde, Alan. *Christopher Isherwood.* Twayne's United States Authors Series 173. New York: Twayne, 1971.

ARTURO ISLAS (1938–1991)
David Román

BIOGRAPHY

Arturo Islas was born in 1938 in El Paso, Texas, and died in 1991 in Stanford, California. Nine months before he died of complications due to AIDS, at a conference in New York sponsored by the Dia Center for the Arts on "The Politics of Imaginative Writing," Islas began his presentation by situating himself on the borders of the Americas: "My grandparents were from Mexico, and my parents are first generation North American citizens" (*Critical Fictions*, 72). Islas continued his presentation by explaining the various contradictions and challenges of living between and within two very disparate traditions. His first language was Spanish, but he was brought up and educated in English. Throughout his early years, Islas would struggle, negotiating what he describes as his double life "between cultures, between languages, between sexes, and between nations" (ibid.). Rather than assimilating into an identity prescribed by a dominant culture, Islas aligned himself early on with the Chicano movement. His Chicano identity emerged with, and was fostered by, the grass-roots activism of the political movements of the 1960s.

At Stanford University, where he received his undergraduate, master's, and doctoral degrees in literature, he was able to formulate and refine his ideas of the literatures and cultures of the Americas. For Islas, the fundamental significance of an American literary tradition was to be found in the relationship among the writings of all of the Americas. Among his early influences and loves were William Faulkner, Wallace Stevens, Juan Rulfo, and Gabriel García Marquez. As a professor of English at Stanford, he received various honors, including the prestigious Dinkelspeil Award for outstanding service to undergraduate teaching. He spent ten years in the 1970s writing his first novel, *The Rain God*, finally published in 1984. In

1990, he published his second novel, *Migrant Souls*. Up until his death on February 15, 1991, he was working on the final novel of his planned trilogy.

MAJOR WORKS AND THEMES

The two novels of Arturo Islas's planned trilogy describe the trials and tribulations of three generations of the Angel family living in the Southwest. One of the central protagonists, Miguel "Chico" Angel, is a gay university professor struggling with his (homo)sexuality in a family and culture heavily invested in patriarchal ideologies and norms. Miguel Chico, the presumed narrator of the novels, recounts the history of his family from the era of the 1911 Mexican Revolution up to the present day. Both of the novels, while focusing on various members of the expansive Angel family unit, can be read in the tradition of the bildungsroman. The reader follows Miguel Chico's coming of age in a social milieu laden with homophobia, class oppression, racism, and the internalized aspects of each. Islas, however, eloquently details in these short novels the various contradictions men of color face when up against dominant prescriptions of sexuality, especially in relation to culturally determined definitions of a "gay identity." One of the major concerns of Islas's novels is to explore the often vexed relationships between various borders imagined and real: Mexico/United States, gay/straight, nature/culture, memory/history, and even fiction/autobiography. For many readers of contemporary gay literature, Islas's depiction of same-sex desire may seem understated, if not down right dismal. The gay characters in these novels are victims of abuse, both self-inflicted and socially constituted. Yet rather than presenting these characters as embodiments of pathos and self-loathing, Islas demonstrates how the dominant culture establishes a network of oppressions for these "gay" men. Islas's fiction exposes various ideological systems that oppress these characters and illustrates the price these characters have had to pay to negotiate their sexual desire.

The Rain God, Islas's first novel (1984), begins with a memory. Thirty, single, educated and successful, Miguel Chico sits in a hospital after a near fatal operation. He recalls a photo of himself with his grandmother, the family's matriarch, that captured the moment of their "flight from this world to the next" (p. 4). The photo—of the eldest and the youngest of the clan together in flight—introduces the major impulse of the novel. Islas will relate the ramifications of this moment of border crossing for the entire family, he will demonstrate how despite seemingly unreconcilable differences among family members, it is precisely this liminal moment of being at the border of something that joins them. For Miguel Chico, the combined impact of his operation and this memory initiates a series of thoughts regarding the events and characters in his life. Quickly, as if we were intimates of the family ourselves, Islas throws his reader into the family dynamics and politics that have led Miguel Chico to his current self-exile in San Francisco.

The novel charts the early years of Miguel's life in short, loosely related chapters. Yet rather than focusing on solely the personal experiences of Miguel Chico, these sections offer snapshots of various members of his extended family. These stories are told in third-person narratives that move backward and forward in time and that provide multiple perspectives on various intratextual events. Thus, Islas provides the architectural frame for the shifting ideologies of Mexican and Chicano identities, demonstrating how various family members perceive the events around them and how these incidents have then contributed to Miguel Chico's own personal identity. We hear of a grandmother who refuses to identify with an "indian" past, of aunts who disdain the "illiterate riff-raff from across the river" (p. 15), of a mother who endures the humiliation of a cheating husband's affair with her best friend, of a father who attempts to assimilate in a white hegemonic power structure, of a cousin's surrender to drugs and addiction, and finally of an uncle's hideous death at the hands of a gay-basher. All of these characters and the incidents they recall reveal the historical and political contexts for the formation of Miguel Chico's sense of self. The wonderfully complicated and multiple-perspective family saga demonstrates the effects of competing dominant ideological discourses—of the family, religion, and nation, for example—on each of these "migrant souls." Though Islas generously describes these other characters with ample detail and insight, it is their effects on Miguel Chico's identity that concern him most. Like William Faulkner and the new narratives of Latin American writers, Islas combines elements of magical realism with aspects of psychological modernism to engage the reader in a complex poetic network of associative images and events.

The murder of Uncle Felix, for example, demonstrates all too clearly the limited options available for men desiring men within Mexican American culture and within the larger and equally stifling U.S. culture where they now live. Married with children, Felix holds a job as a factory foreman. On the one hand, this job provides him the means to exploit the Mexican workers he hires who must undergo various humiliations simply to work in the United States. Felix, however, sees himself as a well-meaning friend who is able to find work for men who without his assistance would be wageless. He sees his ritual fondling of these men (under the pretext of a medical examination) as a harmless and even complicit exchange between employer and employee. Still, these occasional examinations prove unsatisfactory in the long run as Felix begins to seduce young men from the nearby military base: "Most of all, he loved their youth and lack of guile. Even the most experienced among them had a certain purity and gravity, not worldliness, pulled down with the passing of time. They were in their prime, and when he was in their company and they permitted him to touch them, he tasted his own youth once again" (135). Islas, like many gay novelists of his generation, romanticizes masculine ideals and the erotics of rough trade.

Felix dies brutally when one such encounter slips out of his control. Islas writes of the murder in chilling detail and, moreover, goes on to describe the responses of the rest of the family as murderous as well. His death, as Rosaura Sánchez notes, "is portrayed as a case of civil rights discrimination against Mexicans when it is covered up by the military personnel at the base where the young man was stationed" (121). The family, except for one of Felix's daughters, participates in yet a second cover-up concerning the issue of his sexuality. Islas poignantly demonstrates how oppression based on homosexuality and ethnicity are, in fact, interrelated. Felix's double death—as Mexican American and as homosexual—reminds us that his desire had no place in either culture. Its eradication seems inevitable. For Miguel Chico, his uncle's murder and his family's response tellingly reveal to him what he may one day have to face if he chooses to come out to them.

Migrant Souls, which continues the family story, finds Miguel Chico, now older and alcoholic, attempting to resolve many of the issues raised in the first novel. The first half of the novel focuses on his cousin Josie, a divorced mother of two who struggles with the limited roles available for women in either culture. Josie, like Miguel Chico, attempts to arrive at an identity that at once recognizes the importance of family and remains true to her own self. Josie and Miguel Chico form a mutual support system, a refuge from the troubled dynamics of the conservative Angel clan. The second half of the novel, which focuses on Miguel Chico, also introduces other cousins who have been able to fashion American identities that accommodate their ethnicity. That these cousins are heterosexual men only calls attention to the complexity of problems that face Josie and Miguel Chico. American culture has room, it seems, for Chicano men to articulate their positions but Chicano gay men and Chicana single mothers must remain on the fringes of both cultures. Islas demonstrates how Miguel Chico attempts to negotiate an identity for himself given these conditions. By the end of the novel, various members of his family begin to voice their concern while expressing their love. The final novel of the planned trilogy supposedly was to focus on the repercussions of Miguel Chico's coming out to his family.

CRITICAL RECEPTION

Unfortunately, the novels of Arturo Islas have been virtually ignored by both mainstream and gay critics. If it weren't for the efforts of a select group of Chicano scholars, Arturo Islas's novels would be unavailable to any reading public. In fact, José David Saldívar has demonstrated the insidious racist response *The Rain God* received when it was first circulating among New York publishing houses in the 1970s. The novel was rejected by more than twenty publishers before it was finally published by a small press in Northern California in 1984. While many of the publishers claimed that the novel lacked believable ethnic characters, Saldívar argues that, in essence, these readers did not see the novel conforming to marketable stereotypical "ethnic themes." Once published, Islas's novel received some reviews but essentially relied on word of mouth recommendations to account for its over 10,000 sales.

With the publication of *Migrant Souls* in 1990, Jeff Gillenkirk writing in *The Nation* heralded Islas's fiction as a "profound and long-overdue literary journey into the heart of Latino America." In the fall of 1991, Avon Books reissued *The Rain God* and published *Migrant Souls* in their commercial tradebook series. While Chicano critics and leftist publications have championed Islas's works, reviewers in the gay media have contributed to the "invisibility" of his work within the gay community. Furthermore, scholars in Chicano studies have failed to discuss adequately the implications of homosexuality in his writings. The result, of course, is that the works of Arturo Islas have yet to be critically engaged on their own terms, that is, as the writings of someone who was both Chicano and gay.

Arturo Islas's work deserves a wide readership as well as critical discussions that can situate his significance in American literature and culture without obscuring his sexuality. Arturo Islas wrote, after all, about the intersections of ethnicity and (homo)sexuality. His writings describe the ramifications of a Latino "gay" subjectivity in cultures that refuse to acknowledge the possibility of such a stance. His writings should be read as an invaluable contribution to the contemporary literatures of the Americas. Gay readers of all colors should especially welcome Islas's fiction for its depiction of the often-unheard experiences of Latino gays. For as Islas himself claimed about his work: "It was not intended solely for a Chicano audience" (*The Dialectics of Our America*, 108).

WORKS BY ARTURO ISLAS

The Rain God: A Desert Tale. Palo Alto: Alexandrian Press, 1984; New York: Avon Books, 1991.

Migrant Souls. New York: William Morrow, 1990; New York: Avon Books, 1991.

"The Politics of Imaginative Writing." *Critical Fictions*. Ed. Philomena Mariani, 72–74. Seattle: Bay Press, 1991.

SELECTED STUDIES OF ARTURO ISLAS

Bruce-Novoa, Juan. "Homosexuality and the Chicano Novel." In *European Perspectives in Hispanic Literature of the U.S.*, 98–105. Houston: Arte Publico Press, 1988.

Gillenkirk, Jeff. "Crossing Over." *The Nation* 5 March 1991: 313–14.

Saldívar, José David. "The Hybridity of Culture in Arturo Islas's *The Rain God*."

In *The Dialectics of Our America: Genealogy, Cultural Critique, and Literary History*, 105–20. Durham: Duke University Press, 1991.

Sánchez, Marta E. "Arturo Islas' *The Rain God*: An Alternative Tradition." *American Literature* 62, no. 2 (1990): 284–304.

Sánchez, Rosaura. "Ideological Discourses in Arturo Islas's *The Rain God*. In *Criticism in the Borderlands: Studies in Chicano Literature, Culture, and Ideology*. Ed. Héctor Calderón and José David Saldívar, 114–26. Durham: Duke University Press, 1991.

JOE KEENAN (1958–   )
Michael Schwartz

BIOGRAPHY

Joe Keenan, born on July 14, 1958, grew up in Cambridgeport, a working-class neighborhood of Cambridge, Massachusetts. From early childhood, Keenan's gay identity found expression in a passion for theater. As early as during grammar school, Keenan was writing comedy with a distinctly gay bent. When he was nine, he wrote a soap-opera parody and cast himself as a matriarchal villainess modelled on Gale Sondergaard. He later attended a Jesuit high school, where the Jesuits themselves, many of them gay, provided an education in camp sensibility. At sixteen, he wrote a skit for a high school production, about a women's theatrical club that stages *Oedipus Rex*. They hire a professional director, played by Keenan and inspired by the flamingly gay director from Mel Brooks's *The Producers*. The director insists that his younger male "protégé" play Oedipus. In the skit, *Oedipus* devolves into a musical à la *Gypsy*, and Mama Jocasta and Oedipus live happily ever after.

Wanting to write for Broadway, Keenan attended Columbia University, with disappointing results. The theater department was overrun with pretentiousness, he felt (the great sin in Keenan's later farces), and Keenan left in the middle of his junior year. After a brief stay in Cambridge, he returned to New York in 1980, working as a copywriter, but also writing plays and lyrics for Off-Off Broadway and workshop productions whenever possible. In June 1983, he met Gerry Bernardi; they became lovers, and Bernardi provided support (both emotional and practical) during the difficult years. To focus his theatrical ambitions, in 1984 Keenan enrolled in a two-year master's program in musical theater at New York University.

Halfway through this program, Keenan began to write his comic stories. Being between apartments in New York, he was spending the summer with his parents and writing a daily four-page letter to Bernardi. The volume of output convinced him that he could be writing fiction. Taking P. G. Wodehouse as a model, Keenan began his first Philip and Gilbert story. This eventually became his first novel, *Blue Heaven*, published in 1988 by Penguin Books as a paperback original. A second novel, *Putting on the Ritz*, was published in hardcover by Viking Penguin in 1991. Keenan's short story, "Great Lengths," appeared in 1990 in *Men on Men 3*.

Keenan continues to live in New York with Bernardi. He is working on screenplays and television comedy series. He also writes books and lyrics for the musical theater, and his musical *The Times* received the 1990 Richard Rogers Development Grant from the American Academy and Institute for Arts and Letters. He promises that there will be more Philip and Gilbert books.

MAJOR WORKS AND THEMES

One of the most striking aspects of Keenan's works is how densely plotted they are. In this, Keenan owes an obvious (and acknowledged) debt to P. G. Wodehouse. Yet Keenan's stories are even more deliriously intricate than Wodehouse's, in large part because each of Keenan's plots is about plots. His specialty is the traditional farce situation of plotters and counterplotters, all of whom launch elaborate schemes only to fall victim to their own devices. Thus, in *Blue Heaven*, Gilbert Selwyn, a young gay man, plots to marry Moira Finch in order to rake in the gifts from his rich stepfather and her mother, a duchess. Gilbert enlists the help of his friend and former lover, Philip Cavanaugh (who narrates all three works). Moira, however, has her own ruthless schemes, and Gilbert's stepfather belongs to the Mafia, ruthless plotters in their own right. In "Great Lengths," Philip will do anything to get an avant-garde director into bed but is bested in the end by a counterplot from Gilbert. In *Putting on the Ritz*, Philip is asked to write songs for Elsa Champion, wife of Peter Champion, a Donald Trump–like real estate developer. The songwriting is actually a cover for espionage, carried out for Champion's rival, Boyd Larkin, a closeted magazine publisher reminiscent of Malcolm Forbes. Philip agrees because he lusts after Tommy Parker, assistant to Larkin—a lust that has him plotting against Gilbert, who also wants Tommy.

The comic effect of all this plotting is expressed by the title "Great Lengths." In farce, the energy invested in the means is insanely out of proportion to the desired end. Keenan's characters resemble that archetypal farce figure, Wiley Coyote, who expends great resources of intelligence and technology in a futile attempt to satisfy a lowly animal appetite: hunger for a scrawny bird. Similarly, Keenan's characters enslave their intelligence to serve the basest desires: revenge, greed, lust. For these ends, all loyalties are jettisoned, as is all morality and all taste. In "Great Lengths," Philip not only pretends to have a retarded sister in order to bed the beauteous Humphrey; he then tricks his friend, Claire Simmons, into unknowingly acting the part of the sister. This violation of all taste measures precisely the great lengths and lower depths that our appetites will drive us to.

But these slaves of appetite at least have something vital about them. Keenan saves his sharpest barbs for characters whose god is not their id but their ego—especially the artistic ego. Bad artists make great farce characters. Their pretensions so outstrip their talent that they are in a constant state of self-delusion and ego inflation—perfect targets for the prick of farce. In *Blue Heaven*, Keenan gives us Soho "found object" artists and a musical based on *The Bell Jar* (called *Bong!*). In "Great Lengths," Humphrey assaults his audiences with an antiwar theater piece called *Hors d'Oeuvres in the Abattoir*. In *Putting on the Ritz*, Peter Champion erects colossal buildings in a style described as "Albert Speer Goes to Las Vegas" (17). The only artists not savaged are Philip and Claire, who write musical comedy, a commercial medium that must please an audience and therefore does not encourage the excesses common to the avant-garde.

In keeping with the demands of farce, Keenan restricts most of his characters to a single dimension, ruled by a single passion, although he allows his main characters a little more complexity. Claire, who frequently rescues Philip and Gilbert from their messes, has a basic common sense that allows her to hold both low appetite and high pretentiousness at bay. Gilbert, on the other hand, is devoid of common sense. He is pure appetite, with no reality principle: he cannot imagine any obstacles to his desire or any consequences to his actions. He has a radical innocence, in that he has no scruples and is surprised when others do. He behaves as if morality had not yet been invented.

Philip, unlike Gilbert, has some scruples and a minimal grasp on reality. The comedy comes from watching how quickly he loses both. As narrator, Philip's voice owes a lot to Wodehouse's Bertie Wooster, but the differences are worth noting. Bertie often seems to be telling the story in spite of himself. He isn't fully aware of the actions in which he is involved, and he certainly isn't aware of his own foolishness. Philip, however, can narrate, with full self-knowledge, his own descent into folly. The self-awareness, with its concomitant self-mockery, strikes a tone that sounds particularly gay. Gay men in love often behave like schoolgirls—with the difference that gay men also have the verbal skills to describe their own foolishness in painful, glorious detail.

Perhaps the most important of Philip's verbal skills is another acknowledged borrowing from Wodehouse, what Keenan calls the "larky comic metaphor" ("Smiling Through," 16). These metaphors charge Keenan's language with comic intelligence: They are funny because they are so smart. Keenan combines improbable images to achieve a vividly precise description: for example, to describe a nervous man, he says, "Even in his calmer moments he reminded me of a hummingbird awaiting biopsy results" (*Blue Heaven*, 177). Cultural allusions are frequent, often in equally improbable combinations: "Mrs. Pilchard grimaced like a chicken doing Chekhov" (*Putting on the Ritz*, 108). The cultural allusion may be high or low: Peter Champion's building, so ornate it doesn't seem real, looks like "some stunning but two-dimensional set built for the finale of Radio City Music Hall's *Salute to Mammon*" (*Putting on the Ritz*, 39). Though Bertie may mangle Shakespeare or Browning, he seldom descends to popular culture. In contrast, Philip's easy mix of high and low culture seems the product of a specifically camp sensibility. The same is true of this passage about the "employees of Marvelous Parties, the season's hottest caterer": "They were all possessed of those attributes which were MP's trademark: thick wavy hair, jaws you could cut yourself on and a certain icy hauteur that made them seem less like waiters than unusually polite storm troopers" (*Blue Heaven*, 104). The throw-away allusion to Noel Coward, the keen (and double-edged) appraisal of male beauty, and the familiarity with the attitude of waiters—these all create a voice that we recognize as gay.

Plot, character, language—these are the comic elements that Keenan deploys. What do they add up to? Some reviewers assume that Keenan is writing satire, but this seems wrong. *Blue Heaven* is not a satire of heterosexual marriage, or "Great Lengths" a satire of avant-garde theater, or *Putting on the Ritz* a satire of Donald Trump, any more than the Jeeves books are a satire of the British class system. Keenan's comic ancestor is Plautus, not Aristophanes. The righteous anger of satire has no place in his comedy. If he draws his characters from current reality—the Soho art scene or the New York moneyed set—it is only because art and money expand the ego to the elephantine proportions favored by farce. Peter Champion may be inspired by Donald Trump, but his real source is the *miles gloriosus* and other puffed-up braggarts of the farce tradition. Besides, Champion is attacked not for his shady financial dealings, but for his esthetic excesses and his kinky sexual desires—subjects for farce, not satire. Satire must take its targets at least a little seriously, as a threat worthy of attack. In Keenan's world, about the worst thing that can happen to you is bad art—and the comedy he derives from it almost justifies its existence.

CRITICAL RECEPTION

The straight press has received Keenan's books with praise, although often the faint praise reserved for fiction that is merely comic. While the *New York Times* liked both novels, it felt compelled to remind us that *Blue Heaven* "may not be ethereal literature" (30) and that *Putting on the Ritz* "won't be mistaken for weighty literature" (18). In contrast, Henry Louis Gates, Jr., discusses Keenan's comedy in the context of Wilde, Shaw, Wodehouse, and Kazuo Ishiguro and says of *Putting on the Ritz* that it "is not high-minded satire but—something much rarer—pure-hearted camp" (5). In general, the straight press has not been hostile to the gay content, although one review does sound a vaguely homophobic note: "While the motor that drives [*Putting on the Ritz*] is Philip's crush on another man, the shenanigans should have equal appeal to everyone—that is, everyone who appreciates bitchy, campy fun" ("An amateur sleuth finds misadventure," 9H).

Reviewers for the gay press take Keenan's work more seriously—seriously enough to make demands on it, to ask it to do more than just entertain. Felice Picano* contrasts Keenan with older gay writers, whose work arose from "the underlying belief that we're part of a community still oppressed, still under attack, still not free." ("Lost Horizons," 82). Picano says that *Putting on the Ritz* "has as much of a sense of gay community as does an aging drag queen on drugs roller-skating on spring ice. But the novel also displays that figure's inherent sense of style, an absurd flair for complications, and a fireworks of wise-cracking one-liners to boot" (84).

Other gay critics assume that Keenan is writing satire, which is more serious than comedy. Jim Marks deems *Blue Heaven* a success because "Keenan showed himself a steely purposed satirist, his target that rallying cry of the Jesse Helms set, the traditional family" ("Frolicking," 29). But Marks complains that the rich are not punished in *Putting on the Ritz*: "In a climate of financial dread and loathing, we want revenge on those who created this mess, not guffaws."

In contrast, Michael Bronski says that *Putting on the Ritz* "exposes the economic injustice and sheer stupidity of our social system, especially the immoral excesses of the Reagan years" (16). Bronski locates Keenan in a tradition of gay satire: "*Putting on the Ritz* is reminiscent of the '30s musicals of Cole Porter, the satiric vision of Saki, and the comic timing of Thorne Smith.... There is a long tradition of gay male writing... which posits its barbed social criticism in the guise of sophisticated, seemingly frivolous comedy" (17). Interestingly, Walta Borawski puts Keenan in the same tradition and condemns him for it: "Perhaps Keenan's shortcomings lie at root in his attraction to a genre that has... long been the stronghold of apolitical-to-conservative white men: Saki, E. F. Benson, P. G. Wodehouse" (12). In reviewing *Blue Heaven*, Borawski faults the book for its white male heroes, its "virulent hatred of woman," its stereotypes about Italians, and its failure to mention safe sex.

This last charge—that Keenan ignores AIDS—is one that Keenan himself has addressed in several interviews, saying that his fiction is in fact escapist. Bob Satuloff goes further in Keenan's defense, again by placing him in a gay tradition: "Keenan's novels... speak to what I construe to be our gay heritage, a tradition of wit, energy, and well-crafted artifice that is passed on from one generation to the next" (13). By creating a world without AIDS, "Keenan's work becomes, at least by default, political" (13), because gay culture cannot be reduced to AIDS; and Keenan's comedy can "pass on a cultural tradition that, with any luck, will outlive us all" (14).

WORKS BY JOE KEENAN

Blue Heaven. New York: Penguin Books, 1988.
"Great Lengths." In *Men on Men 3: Best New Gay Fiction*. Ed. George Stambolian. New York: Plume, 1990.
Putting on the Ritz. New York: Viking Penguin, 1991.

SELECTED STUDIES OF JOE KEENAN

Borawski, Walta. "Escapist Fiction of the Cheapest Sort." *Gay Community News* 4 September 1988: 12.
Bronski, Michael. Review of *Putting on the Ritz*. *The Guide* March 1992: 16–17.
Bruni, Frank. "An Amateur Sleuth Finds Misadventure." *Detroit Free Press* 17 November 1991: 9H.
Hornaday, Ann. Review of *Blue Heaven*. *New York Times Book Review* 29 January 1989: 30.
Gates, Henry Louis, Jr. Review of *Putting on the Ritz*. *Voice Literary Supplement* 100 (November 1991): 5.
Leonard, Sandy. "Smiling Through." *Bay Windows* 28 November 1991: 15–16, 23.
Marks, Jim. "Frolicking with Manhattan's Naughty Hoity-Toity." *Lambda Book Report* January/February 1992: 28–29.
Picano, Felice. "Lost Horizons." *The Advocate* 588 (October 21, 1991): 82–84.
Satuloff, Bob. "Joe Keenan: The Triumph of Arch." *Christopher Street* 167: 12–13.
Sonenberg, Nina. Review of *Putting on the Ritz*. *New York Times Book Review* 15 December 1991: 18.

RANDALL KENAN (1963–   )

Robert McRuer

BIOGRAPHY

Randall Kenan's novel *A Visitation of Spirits* (1989) and his collection of
short stories *Let the Dead Bury Their Dead* (1992) both focus primarily
on a small African-American community in the fictional town of Tims Creek,
North Carolina. Tims Creek is modelled on the southeastern North Carolina
town of Chinquapin, where Kenan spent most of his childhood and youth.
Although he was born in Brooklyn on March 12, 1963, Kenan lived with
his mother in Brooklyn for only a short time. When his maternal grandfather
heard that he had a grandson, he sent for the child; and at the age of six
weeks, Kenan came to live in Wallace, North Carolina. A large portion of
his extended family was living in North Carolina, and eventually Kenan
was placed in the home of his great-aunt in Chinquapin, a rural community
with a population of about 1,000.

Kenan began his elementary education at the time that integration was
first occurring in Duplin County, North Carolina; he attended an all-black
kindergarten, but entered an integrated first grade a year later. At the time,
Kenan was not wholly aware of the meaning of what was happening, but
when he reached high school, he better understood the ramifications of
integration. In *A Visitation of Spirits*, Kenan draws on these early experiences, placing Horace, the young, black, and gay protagonist, in an integrated high school in Tims Creek. In 1981, Kenan himself graduated from
East Duplin High School in Beulahville, North Carolina, and went on to
the University of North Carolina (UNC) at Chapel Hill, where he planned
to study physics. Writing had been an activity he had engaged in during his
youth, but he had never thought of writing as a viable concern for someone
in southeastern North Carolina.

In college, however, Kenan's plans changed. He began to take writing and literature courses, and he came under the influence of instructors such as H. Maxwell Steele, head of the writing department at UNC. Steele encouraged Kenan to broaden his exposure to literature. Up until this point, Kenan had primarily centered his attention on science-fiction writers, and he had not given black literature much thought. During the winter break of his sophomore year, however, Kenan shifted his focus and began reading black literature, particularly everything that Toni Morrison had written. When he returned to school, Kenan proceeded to take fewer physics courses and more literature courses. Kenan spent a summer as an undergraduate at Oxford University studying the criticism of drama as literature and the literary history of Oxford; during this summer, he decided to devote himself to writing. He worked his way through the honors writing program at UNC and graduated with a B.A. in English in December 1984.

Doris Betts, a writer and instructor at UNC, was particularly instrumental in helping Kenan to acquire a position at Random House. Betts wrote to Toni Morrison, who wrote to Kenan and eventually spoke to some people at Random House, who offered him a job. Kenan moved to New York in February 1985. Although he began at Random House as what he describes as an "office-boy-in-waiting," Kenan advanced quickly; within a year, he was working as an assistant to one of the senior editors at Knopf, a subsidiary of Random House. Kenan's work in publishing provided him with a unique opportunity that few writers have: the opportunity to understand the publishing industry from the inside.

During this period, Morrison's work continued to influence him, but Kenan also credits William Faulkner, Katherine Anne Porter, and Gabriel García Márquez as literary mentors. The content of Kenan's own work shifted particularly as he began to read writers such as Yukio Mishima and James Baldwin.* Kenan realized that his best writing would grow from the experiences he knew best; he could use the specificity of growing up black and gay in a fundamentalist Christian community in the South as a literary advantage, just as Mishima and Baldwin had used intensely personal (and often homosexual) experiences as a basis for their work. In 1989, Kenan's first novel was published by Grove Press, and the content did indeed reflect the experiences of growing up black and gay in the South.

In 1989, Kenan accepted a position as a guest lecturer at Sarah Lawrence, where he was able to write as well as teach. In 1991, Knopf approved a proposal from Kenan for a travel narrative focusing on black experiences in North America, tentatively titled *Walk on Water*. In preparation for this book, Kenan interrupted his appointment at Sarah Lawrence and began a journey through the United States and Canada, visiting major cities, gathering information, and conducting interviews. In 1992, his collection of short stories, *Let the Dead Bury Their Dead*, was published.

MAJOR WORKS AND THEMES

Kenan does not want to disavow the debt he owes to the gay political movement, but he nonetheless sees himself in an ambivalent relationship with the current generation of post-Stonewall, contemporary gay novelists. Kenan is often uncomfortable with the rhetoric of the political movement when it does not turn its attention to diversity within communities. Kenan's own work reflects an attempt to understand difference in a postmodern, postindustrial American society. His work explores complex intersections of identity, and hence gay identity is not always the primary organizing principle in his characters' lives. Regional, racial, and religious identities also crucially shape the experiences of Kenan's characters and the themes of his writings.

Kenan's work often reflects the influence of Morrison, García Márquez, and others who have written what has been called "magic realism." The distinction between reality and fantasy in Kenan's writing is always a tenuous one; spirits and demons actively cavort with and influence characters in the "real" world. Kenan himself, however, insists that categories such as "magic realism" are inadequate and peculiarly Northern attempts to categorize what some Southern writers are doing. He himself sees his work rather as "another way of looking at the truth," and indeed the "unreal" elements in his fiction do serve to critique and expose the inadequacies and injustices inherent in "reality." Kenan's consistent exploration of the varieties of religious experience connects to this search for "truth." His writing often turns on the distinction between "faith" and "religiosity." Although Kenan ironically portrays his characters' pompous and homophobic "religiosity," he nonetheless validates "faith" as a genuine force that can bring about connections between human beings.

Kenan's first novel, *A Visitation of Spirits*, concerns itself with several members of the Cross family, an African-American family living in Tims Creek, North Carolina, in the mid 1980s. The novel focuses particularly on Horace, the youngest member of the Cross family, and on Jimmy Greene, Horace's older cousin, the young minister at the First Baptist Church of Tims Creek and principal at the Tims Creek Elementary School. Horace is intelligent and successful, but he is attempting to come to terms with his homosexuality, which is out place in the religious community of Tims Creek. Horace's story is told in five sections that are set in the late night and early morning of April 29–30, 1984. Horace has become dissatisfied with his life and has decided to transform himself via a magic spell into a bird. The magic spell of course fails, but Horace's flirtation with magic inaugurates a night of fanciful visions and experiences. During this night, a demon gives Horace a tour of his past and present life, much like Scrooge's ghosts in Charles Dickens's *A Christmas Carol*, but without the happy ending. Horace watches himself and his family at the First Baptist Church of Tims Creek, where the Reverend Hezekiah Barden, the minister from Horace's childhood, delivers a scathing, homophobic sermon. Horace watches himself with the other boys as they tease an effeminate boy named Gideon, and Horace also observes his growing attraction and eventual affair with Gideon. Horace abandons Gideon and engages in a series of sexual encounters with the actors from a touring company that is visiting Tims Creek. The visions ultimately become apocalyptic, and Horace emerges from the woods on the morning of the 30th and shoots himself in the head before the horrified Jimmy.

Narrative time in Kenan's novel is fragmented, and the events of April 1984 are intertwined with the events of December 8, 1985. Although the various sections are headed by exact locations in time—"December 8, 1985; 8:45 A.M.," "April 30, 1984; 2:40 A.M.," and so on—the fragmented narrative provides the reader with a persistent sense of dislocation; the certainty of time is abandoned, along with the reassuring sense of what constitutes "reality." In the end, the omniscient narrator teases the reader with questions of whether or not the spirits Horace encountered "really" existed. As Horace's suicide is detailed in uncompromisingly "factual" scientific language, however, the distinction between "reality" and "fantasy" becomes irrelevant. For the black and gay main character of *A Visitation of Spirits*, the "reality" of the homophobic world he escapes is as inadequate as the "fantasy" he has experienced.

Kenan's collection of stories *Let the Dead Bury Their Dead* continues a deconstruction of the opposition between "fact" and "fantasy." The title story for this collection is "Let the Dead Bury Their Dead: Being an Oral Annotated History of the Former Maroon Society First Called Snatchit Then Called Tearshirt and Later Tims Creek," and it consists entirely of a conversation between Zeke and Ruth, two of the elderly characters from *A Visitation of Spirits*. Again Kenan provides traditional, recognizable "facts" that come in the form of footnotes and ledgers, but again Kenan blurs the lines between these "facts" and "fantasy": Zeke and Ruth tell a story that deals with the dead rising and with African sorcerers. *Let the Dead Bury Their Dead* is an exploration of origins and of identity, but gay identity is not necessarily primary. Many of the characters from *A Visitation of Spirits* return in this collection, but Horace is not among them. Kenan's collection suggests that other facets of identity, such as regional or racial identity, are as important as sexual identity.

CRITICAL RECEPTION

A Visitation of Spirits sold 7,000 copies while still in hardcover, which is quite good for a first novel. Undoubtedly Kenan's own experiences in the publishing world as well as the fact that *A Visitation of Spirits* was published by a large publishing house contributed to this success. The few reviews that came out about *A Visitation of Spirits* were positive, stressing the experimental style and the richness of Kenan's prose. *Kirkus Reviews* praised the novel's originality, but did so in homophobic and racist terms: "This stylistically daring novel steers wide of the literature of oppression and uplift, and shares even less with tales of coming out." In short, as far as *Kirkus Reviews* was concerned, *A Visitation of Spirits* was good precisely because of its difference from both gay and African-American literature. Nonetheless, Randall Kenan and *A Visitation of Spirits* have received some attention outside of the gay press. African-American writers and publishers particularly have begun to pay attention to Kenan's work, and his current project on black experiences in North America should ensure that this trend will continue. There have been at this point few published responses to Kenan's work, but his fiction has been included in collections focusing on contemporary African-American literature. Terry McMillan included an excerpt from *A Visitation of Spirits* in *Breaking Ice*, her 1990 collection of contemporary African-American stories; and McGraw-Hill has approached Kenan about including his story "Foundations of the Earth" from *Let the Dead Bury Their Dead* in another forthcoming anthology of African-American writing. Kenan's work deserves more attention within gay communities as these communities begin to focus more seriously on diversity. Recent attention to black gay cultures has tended to stress Northern, urban, and secular experiences. Kenan's work consistently explores new ground, challenging any such homogenizing understandings of black gay experiences. His work is a significant addition not only to the growing body of contemporary gay fiction but to African-American, Southern, and postmodern fiction as well.

WORKS BY RANDALL KENAN

A Visitation of Spirits. New York: Grove Press, 1989.
Let the Dead Bury Their Dead. San Diego: Harcourt, 1992.

SELECTED STUDIES OF RANDALL KENAN

Review of *A Visitation of Spirits*. *Kirkus Reviews* 57 (May 1, 1989): 650.
Review of *A Visitation of Spirits*. *Publisher's Weekly* 235 (May 12, 1989): 283.
Review of *Let the Dead Bury Their Dead*. *Lambda Book Report* 3.5 (July/August 1992): 20–21.

KEVIN KILLIAN (1952–   )

D. S. Lawson

BIOGRAPHY

Kevin Killian was born on December 24, 1952, on Long Island, New York, to Raymond Killian (a research engineer) and Catherine Doyle Killian (a schoolteacher). He is the oldest of five children, having two younger brothers and two younger sisters. At the very beginning of *Bedrooms Have Windows* Killian evokes the Long Island of his childhood: "I grew up in Smithtown, a suburb of New York, a town so invidious that still I speak of it in Proustian terms—or Miltonic terms, a kind of paradise I feel evicted from. Smithtown, Long Island, kind of an MGM Norman Rockwell hometown, a place so boring they gave it a boring name" (1). He attended Fordham University and graduated with a B.A. in English in 1974. His education continued in the graduate English program at the State University of New York at Stony Brook. He received the M.A. degree in 1977. After completing coursework for the Ph.D. and passing his oral examinations, he never finished his dissertation on child pornography. In 1986 he married the author Dodie Bellamy (*Feminine Hijinx*), a fact which might surprise readers of Killian's novels, which are often filled with graphic accounts of presumably autobiographical gay sex. Concerning this matter, Killian has said, "Sexual difference and gender studies have often intrigued me in life as well as art. I would hardly consider myself a straight or even bisexual writer. Sexual difference . . . confuses me too much. Like the characters in my books, I don't know where my sex impulses come from or where they lead. I have no theory that my own experience doesn't contradict." (This and all subsequent quotes in this section are derived from correspondence with the author.) Together he and Bellamy run the reading series at the bookstore Small Press Traffic in San Francisco and write a review column, "Signals," for its in-house newsletter, *Traffic*.

His memoir *Bedrooms Have Windows* was originally written for Felice Picano* at SeaHorse Press, who was himself working on a parallel kind of memoir, eventually published as *Ambidextrous*. By the time Killian's book was finished, however, SeaHorse was not actively publishing and thus the book went to Amethyst Press. *Desiree*, a short prose fiction work written in a style mocking eighteenth-century novels, was originally a section of *Bedrooms Have Windows*, but Picano advised him that the piece threw out the balance of the book, so *Desiree* was published separately. The "Kevin Killian" of the novel *Shy* is much more fictional, even a different age than the author was in 1974, the year in which the book is set. Many of the characters are, however, modeled on actual people, but the names were changed. The short story "September," published in the initial volume of the *Men on Men* series, became part of *Shy*. Killian sporadically publishes the little magazine *Mirage* and has said of it, "I regard it as a kind of diary of my own enthusiasms which tend towards the avant-garde and the indescribable."

His work in progress as of late 1991 includes a new novel, *Arctic Summer*; a sex book for children entitled *The Secret Garden*, in collaboration with Dennis Cooper's friend Mark Ewert (born Atlanta, 1971); and a biography of the American poet Jack Spicer (1925–1965), in collaboration with Lew Ellingham. *Arctic Summer* takes its title from an unfinished novel by E. M. Forster (who appears briefly as a character in Killian's novel). The novel is set in 1952, the year of Killian's birth, and concludes with the birth of a baby on Christmas Eve, Killian's birthday. *The Secret Garden* is a transformation of the classic children's book by Mrs. Hodgson Burnett into a book about AIDS and AIDS activism. A chapter from *The Secret Garden* was published independently in the Toronto magazine *Bimbox* under the title, "Sex on the Beach."

The influences on Killian's work range from Christopher Isherwood's* memoirs and documentary novels to practitioners of the "new narrative" such as Dennis Cooper,* Robert Glück,* and Bruce Boone.* His friendships with several avant-garde poets have also influenced his work. Indeed, Killian is an actively publishing poet ("I am a sex writer and a poet, I don't know which one to call myself first"), and his poem "Pasolini" appeared in the inaugural volume of *The Best American Poetry*.

In addition to his novels, Killian has had two plays produced. His play *That*, produced in 1966 at Intersection for the Arts in San Francisco, is set in present-day San Francisco; *That* conflates the stories of Paul and Jane Bowles and Paul McCartney and Jane Asher. His play *The House of Forks* was produced in 1991 at The Lab in San Francisco and at Beyond Baroque in Venice, California.

Killian was one of the organizers of Out/Write, the first national gay and lesbian writers' conference in 1990, and of its sequel, Out/Write 91, held the following year. Killian has acted in theater (appearing in the original production of his play *The House of Forks*) and in experimental video, notably *Swamp* (1991) by Abigail Child and *Coal Miner's Granddaughter* (1991) by Cecilia Dougherty.

Killian currently lives in San Francisco where he writes and works as the secretary to the president of a janitorial company.

MAJOR WORKS AND THEMES

Kevin Killian's writings celebrate the power of the word to reinvent the world, to shape reality. His characters are always telling and retelling their stories, often with subtle or major shifts of details, inventing themselves anew for each listener (or, by extension, reader). Indeed the line between his fictional works (e.g., the novel *Shy*) and his nonfictional works (e.g., the memoirs of *Bedrooms Have Windows*) is often a thin one. *Shy*'s narrative practice is a development of Christopher Isherwood's documentary novels; it features an overtly autobiographical character who is called "Kevin Killian" and a couple of the subsidiary characters in *Shy* appear by name in *Bedrooms* as well. In his essay entitled "Sex Writing and the New Narrative" Killian says,

Words have a separate system, an integrity of their own, and they can't be used to formulate a representation of Life.... All narrative is corrupt insofar as it attempts to ape the realities of our lives. These include the disjunctions, strangenesses and confusions of sexual gender.... Narrative is a faulty analogue for our experiences. (13)

A reader is left wondering to what extent a story or part of a plot line is accurate in the journalistic sense and to what extent the prose is created as a fictional literary artifact. Perhaps this is the point of Killian's narrative aesthetic: gay men's lives both parallel and diverge from the limits delineated by mainstream heterosexual lives just as Killian's writings both use and subvert dominant narrative practices.

One passage from *Shy*, purportedly about "Kevin's" mysterious downstairs neighbor Gunther Fielder, appears almost word for word in *Bedrooms* as about Killian himself. In *Shy* the narrator Kevin is busy writing a novel, which one quickly comes to understand is *Shy* itself. Killian engages in metafictional tricks like discussing "the character Harry" of his novel with Harry as we read him in *Shy*. After they have read together an earlier part of *Shy*, "Harry" and "Kevin" have the following discussion:

"I forgot I told you that dumb lie...," Harry said. "Can't you leave that part out, it was a lie."

"I think it helps the story," I objected. "It shows how the character Harry lives in a dream world."

"It makes me sound so punk."

"You are punk.... If you want, I'll take it out," Kevin said....

"Will you, I mean, thanks ... Like all that sex business I don't mind, not really, I mean wow," Harry giggled, "you and me really got off.... You could put in more," Harry said drowsily, "about how good Harry is in bed."

"The character Harry."

"The character Harry," Harry agreed. (*Shy*, 227–228)

The shift between a first-person narrator who represents himself as "I" and a third-person narrator who is denoted as "Kevin" runs throughout the novel, as though *Shy* were some kind of interface between a subjective account of one summer on Long Island and a speciously objective report on those same events. Harry is a character in *Shy* as well as a character in the novel Kevin writes during *Shy*. His desire to help shape his presentation as a "character" serves to foreground the notion that "Kevin" himself is shaping all these events, even the ones that pretend to be more objective. Harry's admission that part of what he *told* "Kevin" was in fact a lie underscores the idea that the whole novel negotiates among "real life," mistaken or misinformed accounts of "real life," and a life that historically speaking exists only in Killian's imagination. Just as Harry's narrative of himself to "Kevin" was partially untrue, Killian's narrative to his readers is made up in places as well. When Killian writes *Shy* or when readers read it, the "dream world" he sees the character Harry as living in becomes the locus for all attention. Thus the novel as a whole, with its recurring elisions from "Kevin" to "I," through its narrative fluctuations, subtly modulates reader response and foregrounds the metafictional nature of the text.

On occasion, "Kevin" reports accounts of events he cannot possibly know because he was not present at them and has not heard reports of them. In *Bedrooms* Kevin reports on the current life of his childhood friend George, who married a woman named Karoll and moved to Hawaii. Killian describes them as running a tourist service specializing in finding island sex spots for adventurous visitors and tells of them watching *The Golden Girls* and meeting the stars of that television show. After recounting how he has searched unsuccessfully to find George after all these years, Killian writes:

If he reads this book, he may reach for me.

I may hear from him via my publisher, a call may come late at night, his voice on the wire. Wondering. "How did you know I'm still in Hawaii?"

"I didn't—I just guessed."

"You were right about that, but wrong about Karoll. She hates *The Golden Girls*." Or, "Karoll's dead!"

Oh, gee, I'm really sorry to hear that! I'll say. (*Bedrooms*, 132)

Killian's writings create a world of guessing and, based upon those guesses, dictating what reality might be. Everyone probably wonders what old friends, gone for years, might be up to; and Killian takes this commonly practiced narrative of imagination to a higher level in the service of his art. All writing is an expression of creativity, but Killian's is creative in a special, narrowly defined way. He is overtly aware that, even in "real life," we imagine and invent those with whom we interact, so he proceeds quite openly to invent the characters, including himself, whom he represents as being otherwise quite real. After all, what is the "real me" but simply an invention, a mask we show to ourselves? By taking liberties with the mundane real-life events he could conceivably report more flatly and by boldly adding events he can only imagine and create out of whole cloth, Killian finds a narrative voice in the gay literary world that is distinctly his own but has learned from its elders (especially Isherwood). Furthermore, this delicate dance between truth and fiction might be understood best as a formal literary parallel to the kinds of lives gay men lead, balancing themselves between modes of behavior and expression sanctioned by the heterocentric world and behaviors and expressions that would be more natural to homosexual men. Every gay man at some time or other in his life has lived a lie or pretended to be something he is not—has, in fact, reinvented himself for public consumption.

The narrator of the short story "Spreadeagle" follows in this trend, though he is not presented as a "Kevin Killian." He manufactures phony Audrey Hepburn autograph letters for a living, inventing feelings and events in her life, so that these ersatz letters "will sell for $$$ to a besotted queen in San Antonio" (198). Like the autobiographical narrators of Killian's full-length works, this character also devotes his time to the creation of stories that pass for reality.

Of course the subject of Killian's prose is often sex: who is having sex with whom; how the obsessive search for sex turns out; what having sex with someone or with scads of people does to one's integrity of personality. Killian usually avoids romanticizing sex in favor of describing it merely as one of many activities—pleasurable and meaningful, perhaps, but also mechanical and hydraulic, as akin to eating or moving through a room as it is to a fundamentally life-altering or life-enriching experience. The world of his characters is often violent as well: murder, S&M, bruises and bleeding, heavy drinking all are features of the stories he tells. Taking on violence as a subject allows Killian to limn the ordinariness of violence. It is not horrible or frightening, but it too is mechanical and hydraulic. Rather than warping his characters' lives forever, the violence in Killian's work is more just another thing they must put up with before the novel ends and they can get out from under the scrutiny of various anonymous readers (and of the writer himself for that matter).

Here form and content merge: Killian's narrative voice and the stories it chooses to tell are both often mundane—stories centered around daily events told by a voice as familiar and unremarkable as an old friend retelling a story the listener has heard for years. Indeed love and violence are daily events and, in that respect, not remarkable at all. Only when a reader is consciously aware of the craft and ideas behind the narrative thread does Killian's true worth become apparent. Killian is an important voice in contemporary gay literature; when he begins telling his story, he is like Harry, inventing himself before the reader's very eyes, using the power of the logos to make a world.

CRITICAL RECEPTION

As might be expected, most of the critical attention paid to Kevin Killian's work has come from gay literary magazines; this is less a comment on the merits of Killian's prose than on the ghettoization of work by writers who deal openly with homosexual themes, situations, and characters. Given that context, the reviews of Killian's works have been mostly quite positive.

In the pages of *Lambda Book Report*, a leading gay literary review, Philip Gambone writes of *Shy*,

Novels used to be called "romances," and *Shy* is a lyric romance, though one written "through the haze of sexual pleasure." It's a sensual, careening ride Killian takes us on, full of the old novelistic pleasures of plot and character. (14)

Gambone's insistence on the connection between Killian's work—on the surface quite different from anything that has come before in the literary mainstream—and earlier notions of what constitutes fiction is important; although Killian's fictional situations are different from those explored in the great tradition of the novel, his tools are recognizable to any reader familiar with that tradition.

Echoing these comments, Robert Friedman writes of *Bedrooms Have Windows*,

Killian blurs the distinction between novel . . . and memoir. . . . Is this a memoir in the manner of *I Was a White Slave in Harlem*—that is, pure whimsy? Or is this a gay *One Writer's Beginnings*, an introspection like Christopher Isherwood's autobiographical works? *Bedrooms* is probably a little of both. (15)

Friedman goes on to call the volume of memoirs "more poetic than *Shy*" (15). Thus Killian's memoirs are put on a par with those of two of the undeniably great writers of the twentieth century. Just as Eudora Welty does in her memoirs, Killian is exploring for himself and in a gay context the source from which a writer springs, the touchstones of the literary art, the youth and maturation that lead to creativity.

Sarah Schulman calls Killian, "the gentleman sleaze novelist" (60) and sees him as part of an evolving literary movement...which includes people like Eileen Myles ...in New York and Gail Scott in Montreal. This trend consists of gay and lesbian writers who are informed by the last 30 years of the avant-garde but [who] show feelings, don't think they're better than other people and put words together in a way that everyone can understand, even while using unusual rhythms and word orders. It's like a kinder, gentler avant-garde. (60)

Killian's prose is resonant with allusions ranging from trash popular culture stars to literary works. His work exists simultaneously in the realm of the popular and transitory and of the literary and the universal.

WORKS BY KEVIN KILLIAN

Desiree. Berkeley, Calif.: Exempli Gratia, 1986.

"September." *Men on Men: Best New Gay Fiction*. Ed. George Stambolian, 316–30. New York: Plume/NAL, 1986.

"Pasolini." *The Best American Poetry 1988*. Ed. John Ashbery, 82. New York: Collier Books, 1988.

Bedrooms Have Windows. New York: Amethyst Press, 1989.

Shy. Freedom, Calif.: Crossing Press, 1989.

"The Dennis Cooper–Kevin Killian Letters." *400 Rubs* (1990): 82–93.

"Sex Writing and the New Narrative." *The Sodomite Invasion Review* (August 1990): 13.

"The Real and the Unreal: Hayley Mills vs. Annette." *Dear World* (1991): 8–9.

With Mark Ewert. "Sex on the Beach" (chapter 7 of *The Secret Garden*). *Bimbox* 4 (Spring 1991): 10–28.

"Spreadeagle." *Discontents*. Ed. Dennis Cooper, 194–98. New York: Amethyst Press, 1991.

SELECTED STUDIES OF KEVIN KILLIAN

Friedman, Robert. Rev. of *Bedrooms Have Windows* by Kevin Killian. *Lambda Rising Book Report* 2, no. 1 (October/November 1989): 15.

Gambone, Philip. "Nuclear Novels at the Danger Level." Rev. of *Shy* by Kevin Killian. *Lambda Book Report* 1, no. 11 (June/July 1989): 14.

Karr, John F. "Three of San Francisco's Most Popular Gay Authors Talk about Their New Books." *Bay Area Reporter* 14 December 1989: 1+.

Schulman, Sarah. "Lust on Long Island." Rev. of *Bedrooms Have Windows* by Kevin Killian. *Outweek* 29 October 1989: 60.

LARRY KRAMER (1935–   )
Joel Shatzky

BIOGRAPHY

Larry Kramer was born on June 25, 1935, in Bridgeport, Connecticut, the son of George L. Kramer, an attorney, and Rea W. (neé Wishengrad), a social worker. Kramer graduated from Yale University with a B.A. in 1957, the year in which he served in the U.S. Army. He began his career in a training program with the William Morris Agency in 1958 and went to work for Columbia Pictures in 1958–1959.

He had a number of positions at Columbia, including assistant story editor in New York, 1960–1961, and production executive in London, 1961–1965. In 1965 he became assistant to the president of United Artists and associate producer of the film "Here We Go Round the Mulberry Bush" in 1967. In 1969 Kramer wrote the screenplay for "Women in Love," which he also produced.

Kramer is best known for his activist work since the start of the AIDS epidemic. In 1981 he became cofounder of the Gay Men's Health Crisis Center in New York City, and in 1988 he founded ACT UP (AIDS Coalition to Unleash Power).

Kramer has received considerable recognition for his three best-known works. In 1970 his screenplay for "Women in Love" was nominated for an Academy Award by the Academy of Motion Picture Arts and Sciences as well as by the British Film Academy. In 1986, his play *The Normal Heart* received the Dramatists Guild Marton Award, the City Lights Award and the Sarah Siddons Award for the best play of the year, and a nomination for the Olivier Award for best play of the year. In 1987 the Human Rights Campaign Fund awarded Kramer the Arts and Communication Award. His novel, *Faggots* (1978), although it received a decidedly mixed reception when it first appeared, eventually became a best-seller. It was reissued in 1987.

Kramer is a regular contributor on political issues to periodicals, including the *New York Times* and the *Village Voice*.

MAJOR WORKS AND THEMES

When *Faggots* was published in 1978, the reactions to the novel ranged from "sensational trash" (Barbara G. Harrison) to "a satire written, like all good ones, from the inside" (Samuel McCracken). The book is a record of Fred Lemish's search for ideal love during the 1970s in the gay community on Fire Island in New York. The scenes shift from bathhouses to discotheques peopled by such characters as Randy Dildough and Jack Hump-stone, but the book is less satire and more criticism of gay life-style in the sexually liberated 1970s.

Kramer's own view of his book reveals his conviction that it is, indeed, a work badly needed as a corrective to the celebratory nature of the image that was being projected by gays at the time. "I purposely made the chief characters in my book intelligent, educated, and affluent men who should be role-models for the rest of us. Instead, they're cowardly and self-pitying persons who retreat into their own ghetto because they feel the world doesn't want them. . . . It just seems that we should be angry at our own cowardice instead of the world's cruelty" (interview by Richard Christiansen in the *Chicago Tribune* in Janice E. Drame, *Contemporary Authors*, vol. 126, Detroit: 1989, 240).

Indeed, the book is filled with a sense of self-loathing by Lemish, and Kramer makes no apologies for what he feels was a need for being honest and candid about the seamier side of gay life. The negative reaction of the gay community, including some gay critics, however, is a reflection of the extreme position that Kramer takes in his depiction of a life-style of which he vehemently disapproves. The picture he portrays of the excessive use of drugs, sadomasochism, and desperate, temporary relationships was certainly a side of gay scene at the time. But it is also a valid criticism to question some of the implications of this portrait of a particular circle of gay men at a particular place and time, presented as if it embodied the whole of a sexual group as varied within its relations and practices as that of any other.

A decade after its publication, Kramer asserted that "the lesson I learned from *Faggots* was so important to me; the original anger turned into acceptance" (Drame, 241). But it was subsequent events as much as the tenor of the novel itself that gave Kramer's critique immediate relevance when the AIDS epidemic began.

It was for *The Normal Heart* in 1985 that Larry Kramer received what became international recognition. His projection of himself in the person of Ned Weeks, the activist who defied not only the straight but the gay establishment, embodied the crusading figure who argued that extreme measures were necessary in order to control the epidemic, even if it meant sexual abstinence. Praised and honored when it first appeared in New York, the play is a fascinating combination of drama as history, polemic, and scenes of moving tenderness. But, as with *Faggots*, Kramer seems most comfortable by presenting an extreme and controversial position. As he said of his most recent work, "Just Say No": "The play is by far the most controversial thing I have ever written; I have no idea if the play will or will not be a success, but it is going to attract attention" (ibid.).

CRITICAL RECEPTION

Faggots received a decidedly mixed reception when it first appeared in 1978. Barbara G. Harrison, in her "Book World" review in the *Washington Post* (December 17, 1978, E4), finds the book objectionable because of its lack of sympathy with characters who are both "taunting the straight world" and yet looking for "someone to *blame*" for their lives. She regards the work as doing an "enormous disservice" to the homosexual world Kramer depicts and concludes: "I [can't] think that anybody but Anita Bryant and her crowd will be made happy by this book; it will serve to confirm all their wicked propagandistic nonsense."

Martin Duberman regarded *Faggots* as "a foolish, even stupid book" (*New Republic*). His objections to the novel, however, were as much aesthetic as political. "The book's wooden dialogue, strained humor and smug disdain are no match for the inventive flamboyance of Fire Island hedonism when viewed from an angle wider than primitive moralizing."

Significantly enough, Duberman himself disavows the Fire Island scene as one "who can't stand the place, who thinks it magnifies the worst aspects of gay male life. . . . " But he goes on to argue that "a serious dissection of the self-absorbed frivolity of this subculture within a subculture would be well worth having," and concludes that this life-style may have "contained the seeds of a far-reaching social transformation." He regards *Faggots* as "a plastic, trashy artifact of the worst aspects of a scene to which it high-mindedly condescends" (30–31).

Samuel McCracken, in *Commentary* (19–29), however, regards *Faggots* as a successful satire. He described it as "an extraordinary new novel," and recognized that "it holds some positions critical of homosexuality that would be unusual even among the most critical anti-homosexuals." He anticipated the storm of protest over the novel, noting that "Kramer is of course already beginning to be denounced by the activists" (23).

John Lahr's own assessment of *Faggots* in the *New York Times Book Review* (39–40) compares it to another novel about the gay scene in New York, *Dancer from the Dance*, by Andrew Holleran. "Where Mr. Holleran honors the sadness as well as the sensations of homosexual life, Mr. Kramer merely exploits them." Lahr concludes by regarding *Faggots* as "an embarrassing fiasco" (40).

Yet despite the generally hostile view of the novel, both in terms of its treatment of subject matter and its artistic quality, *Faggots* has remained in print for over a decade and has continued to receive attention and even praise when it was reissued in 1987.

The question must remain, however: Is Larry Kramer's controversial approach to such subjects as the Fire Island scene in the 1970s and the AIDS epidemic a matter of style or substance? Certainly, there is no question of his political courage in confronting the "Establishment" when the epidemic was responded to with bureaucratic indifference in the early 1980s. Since it was established in the late 1980s, ACT UP has been receiving headlines for its controversial and confrontational approaches to keeping the seriousness of the epidemic in the public mind. It is also true, however, that Kramer relishes the notoriety of his position; and, as the AIDS crisis has become more and more a mainstream issue in the straight community, one wonders if his confrontational approach will become counterproductive.

The fact remains that Larry Kramer has proven in relatively few works his ability to stir the interests and passions of a great many people who might be more moved or more uplifted aesthetically by other works about gays or AIDS but might not be provoked to think or act as a result of reading them. He has shown himself to be a very angry man, but he has also shown his capacity to turn that anger into effective writing.

WORKS BY LARRY KRAMER

"Women in Love" (screenplay; adapted from the novel by D. H. Lawrence), United Artists, 1969.
Faggots (novel). New York: Random House, 1978. Reissued in 1987.
The Normal Heart (play). New York: New American Library, 1985.
Reports from the Holocaust: The Making of an AIDS Activist (nonfiction). New York: St. Martin's Press, 1989.

SELECTED STUDIES OF LARRY KRAMER

Duberman, Martin. Review of *Faggots*. *The New Republic* 180, no. 1 (January 6, 1979): 30–32.
Harrison, Barbara G. "Love on the Seedy Side." Review of *Faggots*. *The Washington Post Book World* 17 December 1978: 4.
Lahr, John. "Camp Tales." Review of *Faggots*. *The New York Times Book Review* 14 January 1979: 39–40.
McCracken, Samuel. Review of *Faggots*. *Commentary* 67, no. 1 (January 1979): 19–29.

DAVID LEAVITT (1961–   )
D. S. Lawson

BIOGRAPHY

David Leavitt was born on June 23, 1961 in Pittsburgh, Pennsylvania, but grew up in Palo Alto, California, where his father, Harold Jack Leavitt, is a professor of organizational behavior at Stanford and his mother, the late Gloria Rosenthal Leavitt, was a housewife and occasional political activist. He is the youngest of three children, having an older brother and sister. Leavitt was a Phi Beta Kappa graduate of Yale University in 1983 with a B.A. in English. For a time he worked as a slush reader for Viking Press.

In 1983 at the age of 21, while still a student at Yale, his short story "Territory" was published in the *New Yorker*, bringing him instant acclaim and attention. His first collection of stories, *Family Dancing* (1984), included that story and his subsequent *New Yorker* story, "Out Here," together with seven other short pieces of fiction. *Family Dancing* was nominated for the National Book Critics Award and for the PEN-Faulkner award. Leavitt has since published two novels, another collection of stories, and numerous essays, including a series of travel essays for *Vogue*. His stories have appeared in such magazines as *Harper's*, *Mother Jones*, and *Prism*. His writing is among the most successful gay male writing in the literary mainstream.

In 1989, Leavitt received a John Simon Guggenheim Foundation fellowship and became foreign writer in residence at the Institute of Catalan Letters in Barcelona. He now lives in East Hampton, New York, and his current project is a screenplay about AIDS for director John Schlesinger. To this point in his career, AIDS has not played any significant role in his work. Concerning this subject, Leavitt has written:

It used to be that when people asked me why I hadn't written about AIDS, I'd get angry. Because I had published a book of short stories and a novel that dealt with themes of homosexuality and illness, I suppose they assume the subject would come naturally to me. So what? I'd shout back. I'm not obligated to write about *anything*. Only if and when I was inspired to write about AIDS would I write about it. But the truth was that AIDS scared me so much I wanted to block it out of my mind. ("The Way I Live Now," 30)

Leavitt says an awareness of those writers who, because of illness, could not afford to wait for inspiration provided the impetus for his taking on the subject of AIDS in his current project.

MAJOR WORKS AND THEMES

David Leavitt's novels and stories chronicle the lives of young urban gay males; he is the John Cheever of the "guppies" of the 1980s and 1990s. He predominantly centers his works around educated, middle-class, articulate young men, depicting their families, their loves, and their lives with attention to his characters' psychology and also to the passing fads and trends and products that make up so much of modern life.

His work is often associated with the present tense, absolutely current-with-products-and-fads style stereotypically seen as endemic to the *New Yorker*. Perhaps one of his great strengths as a writer is that he chronicles a life and a place not being written about by any other gay male writer in America.

His collection of short stories, *Family Dancing*, tackles the subjects of sexuality, finding a direction in life, and getting along with parents as roles and behaviors change with the increasing age of both the parent and the child. "Territory" is often cited as the most notable story in the collection and it was through this story's appearance in the *New Yorker* that Leavitt became known in literary circles.

The Lost Language of Cranes seems familiar territory to anyone who has read *Family Dancing*. The story of Rose and Owen Benjamin and their gay son Philip is at once realistic and symbolic. Philip's travails with his lover Eliot seem the stuff of many gay novels, but the twist comes in the subplot of Owen's homosexuality, which increasingly has forced its way into his life and consciousness. When Philip finally announces his sexuality to his parents, the time has come for Owen to face himself. A man leaving his wife for a male lover is also the central focus of "Houses," one of the short stories in *A Place I've Never Been*.

In one of the most perfectly realized scenes of the novel, Owen (the admissions officer at a tony private boys' school) invites home for dinner a handsome, athletic young teacher, ostensibly for Philip, but at least partially for himself. Rose recognizes this fact and the scene—from preparing the spaghetti through washing the dishes afterwards—centers around Rose's conflicting but increasingly accurate perception of the events of the meal.

When the young man offers Philip a ride after the meal and then takes him quite the long way around, the scene is neatly concluded with a symbol for the misdirection and waste of time this heterosexual man has caused.

Rose is the copy editor for a small publishing house. She is expert at correcting infelicities of language, catching typographical errors, finding synonyms for words. Indeed, playing human thesaurus with whatever word comes to mind is one of her favorite games. Perhaps part of her problem in dealing with first her son's and then her husband's sexuality is that she cannot make the leap from words to life, that she cannot see their sexual urges as in any way related to or synonymous with her own experience of desire.

The other family in the novel is that of Philip's first real lover, Eliot, who was raised by Derek Moulthorp, a famous children's author, and his gay lover after the deaths of Eliot's parents. Whereas in the Benjamin house books are corrected or studied (Owen started out as an academic, a scholar of Renaissance poetry), in the Moulthorp home books are written and created. As a product of his childhood, Philip grows up to be a man consumed with need for attention and love, but Eliot seems supremely self-confident, able to leave love when it draws too much from him or requires too much of him.

The novel's title, drawn from the unfinished dissertation of Jerene, Eliot's black lesbian roommate, is important: the languages we learn as tiny children—what is said to us, what we hear said—tend to influence the way we think about life for the rest of our lives. When we lose those languages (like the crane baby in the study), we lose something which is irrecoverable but which also continues to haunt us.

Equal Affections likewise centers around a family coping with homosexuality, only this time both the son and daughter are gay. Curiously, both of the homosexual family members here tend to model their lives and behaviors around heterosexual models: Danny, the son (a lawyer), speaks of his long-term relationship with Walter (another lawyer with whom he lives a comfortable suburban life) in terms of marriage; April, the daughter (a folksinger in the Joni Mitchell mode), goes so far as to get pregnant through artificial insemination to have a family of her own.

With characters like the mother, Louise, who has waged a twenty-year battle with cancer (as did Leavitt's own mother), and Nat, the father, a professor at a California university (like Leavitt's own father), *Equal Affections* has been seen as an autobiographical novel. Leavitt himself dislikes this idea, saying, "I suppose it's a natural impulse . . . but it doesn't lead very far. If a particular character resembles my mother or my sister, so what? It's just gossip, and not even very interesting gossip" (Staggs, 48).

It is tempting to see the stories of *A Place I've Never Been* as a departure from Leavitt's previous work (as the title, significantly, might indicate). If the first three books are a kind of very polished and able apprentice work, the fourth book finds an author well in command of his considerable skills. Staggs comments upon this new direction in Leavitt's work:

Phrases such as "The Early Work" and "The Middle Years" of course recall Henry James, and the allusion is apt. Leavitt, like James, has discovered Europe, or more specifically, Americans in Europe, as a prodigious theme which he exploits in several excellent stories in *A Place I've Never Been*. (47)

Though he is still young, Leavitt's published work has shown a great depth and range. He presents the inner lives of his characters through very skillfully detailing their actions, their speech, and their surroundings. Rather than slipping often into the modernist trap of internal monologue, Leavitt chooses mostly to show what his characters are thinking and feeling by showing his readers what they do and say; by giving these unmistakable signposts, Leavitt reveals a very sophisticated fictional technique and a highly intelligent mind at work in the prose.

CRITICAL RECEPTION

Success came to Leavitt at a relatively young age. One of the dangers of publishing well (stories in the *New Yorker*, books by Knopf) while still young is that reviewers and critics cannot resist the temptation to see later work as not living up to the promise of the early stories. This seems to have happened to Leavitt who, though still young, has now assembled an impressive body of work. Generally speaking, he has been accorded more respect and attention in Europe than in the United States.

Writing of a recurring motif in Leavitt's work in general, Carole Iannone says,

A central figure in the Leavitt landscape is the rejected or superfluous female, sometimes unmarried, more typically divorced, abandoned, or neglected, a victim, in a sense of changing cultural patterns. She has often been left for another woman, or for another man, or for more casually miscellaneous reasons like business or travel. ... Leavitt's intricate portrayals of these females' unhappy bewilderment are what his admirers partly have in mind when they wonder how anyone his age could demonstrate so much empathy, understanding, and insight. The truth may be that he rather enjoys detailing—if, again, to no particular literary purpose—the humiliations of women. (58)

So much of Leavitt's work centers around women and their problems and insights that this last sentence would seem to be unfair. It might be more accurate to say that Leavitt sees the world as a place where there are great possibilities for fulfillment as well as for unhappiness and that women, as a result of how differently from men they are socialized, are more keenly aware of the different gradations of both happiness and misery, of both accomplishment and waste.

Leavitt's American critics have often been quite harsh in reviewing his work. In *Hudson Review*, Michael Gorra writes of *The Lost Language of Cranes*:

Leavitt himself is too fully assimilated to the conventions of contemporary magazine fiction, in which brand names replace history, to try to extend his fascination with his characters' private lives to a fascination with the society from which they come. He fails to give his characters the now unfashionable historical significance, as representative figures of their time, that the traditional realism with which he works nevertheless demands, and which even his title suggests. (145)

Perhaps the world of brand names and currently fashionable gay bars (several real-life Manhattan nightspots of the mid–1980s are easily recognizable in *The Lost Language of Cranes*) is one with historical significance. As the historian of that world, Leavitt is recording an era that, in the time of AIDS, no longer exists in the same way it once did.

Phillip Lopate gives *The Lost Language of Cranes* a mixed review in the *New York Times Book Review*, saying it "reads like a real novel: Mr. Leavitt's sense of pacing, his graceful sentences and his storytelling abilities dovetail nicely. On the other hand, the book *feels* young—experientially thin, intellectually timid, contrived, erratic, and, understandably, not yet wise" (3). Lopate goes on to make an interesting observation about the novel, calling it "a strange Oedipal tale . . . with Oedipus and Laius going off to do their male bonding while Jocasta is left out in the cold" (3). Echoing Gorra's comments about the cultural world of Leavitt's fiction, Lopate writes, "Mr. Leavitt's generation was the first to be saturated with children's culture" (3).

Beverly Lowry's treatment of *Equal Affections* in the *New York Times Book Review* is quite positive; she says the novel "does not compromise itself with easy answers. It is a gritty, passionate novel that should settle the question of David Leavitt's abilities" (7). Perhaps even the book reviewers of the mainstream press are beginning to concede that Leavitt's early promise is indeed being fulfilled, that his later fictions are worthy successors to his stories.

Edmund White* sees David Leavitt as one of the few gay writers who has crossed over to mainstream success. Because Leavitt's novels "show gay men living in the larger context of straight friends and relatives" (35), White sees how a more separatist band of gay writers can reject him, but the universality of Leavitt's concerns would indicate one reason for his capacity to cross over.

WORKS BY DAVID LEAVITT

Family Dancing. New York: Knopf, 1984.
"The New Lost Generation." *Esquire* May 1985: 85–88+.
"New Voices and Old Values." *New York Times Book Review* 12 May 1985: 1+.
"Introduction" [to a special issue entitled, *These Young People Today: Writers under 35*]. *Mississippi Review* 14, no. 3 (Spring/Summer 1986): 5–6.
The Lost Language of Cranes. New York: Knopf, 1986.
"Italy's Secret Gardens." *Vogue* June 1988: 178+.
Equal Affections. New York: Weidenfeld and Nicholson: 1989.
"The Way I Live Now." *New York Times Magazine* 9 July 1989: 28+.
"Almodovar on the Verge." *New York Times Magazine* 22 April 1990: 36+.
"Mad about Milan." *Vogue* March 1990: 180+.
A Place I've Never Been. New York: Viking, 1990.

SELECTED STUDIES OF DAVID LEAVITT

"David Leavitt." *Contemporary Authors*, vol. 122, 285–89. Detroit: Gale, 1988.
Gorra, Michael. "Fiction Chronicle." Rev. of *The Lost Language of Cranes* by David Leavitt. *Hudson Review* 40, no. 1 (Spring 1987): 136–48.
Iannone, Carol. "Post-Counterculture Tristesse." *Commentary* 85, no. 5 (February 1987): 57–61.
Kakutani, Michiko, "Ordinary Lives Filled with Love and Loss." Rev. of *Equal Affections. New York Times* 31 January 1985:16.
Lopate, Phillip. "Sexual Politics, Family Secrets." Rev. of *The Lost Language of Cranes* by David Leavitt. *New York Times Book Review* 5 October 1986: 3.
Lowry, Beverly. "Everyone Is Someone's Child." Rev. of *Equal Affections* by David Leavitt. *New York Times Book Review* 12 February 1989: 7.
Martin, Wendy. "Everybody Loves Somebody Sometime." Rev. of *A Place I've Never Been* by David Leavitt. *New York Times Book Review* 26 August 1990: 11.
Staggs, Sam. "PW Interviews: David Leavitt." *Publisher's Weekly* 24 August 1990: 47–48.
White, Edmund. "Out of the Closet, Onto the Bookshelf." *New York Times Magazine* 16 June 1991: 22+.

ARMISTEAD MAUPIN (1944–   )
Barbara Kaplan Bass

BIOGRAPHY

Armistead Jones Maupin, Jr., was born in Washington, D.C., on May 13, 1944, the eldest of three children of a prominent lawyer and his wife. A descendant of a North Carolina Confederate general, he grew up in Raleigh, North Carolina, "a tight-assed little Republican kid, an Eagle Scout" (Dyer, 32). Although an English teacher at Broughton High School in Raleigh encouraged his talent, Maupin didn't immediately follow a career in writing, although as an English major at the University of North Carolina (UNC), he did write a column for the *Daily Tarheel*, "a jaunty mixture of Art Buchwald and William F. Buckley, Jr." (Maupin, "Growing Up Gay," 13).

After he graduated, Maupin enrolled in the UNC law school, but at the end of his first year, unhappy and bored, he applied for naval officers' candidate school. A lieutenant in the Navy from 1967 to 1970, Maupin served in Viet Nam with the River Patrol Force, returning after his discharge as a volunteer to build housing for disabled Vietnamese veterans. For this effort, he was presented with the Freedom Leadership Award by the Freedoms Foundation at Valley Forge, an award Anita Bryant had won two years before, and President Nixon invited him to the White House, honoring him as the very model of patriotic young Republicanism (Fitzgerald, 30). Maupin recalls, "I was an utterly different person twenty years ago. I couldn't sit in the same room with me then now" (Maupin, telephone interview).

In 1971, when he left his reporting position at the *Charleston News and*

I would like to thank Donald Craver, Chair of the Department of English, World Literature and Linguistics at Towson State University, for his insight, advice, and criticism, and Terry Anderson and Armistead Maupin for their cooperation.

Courier to accept a position with the Associated Press in San Francisco, Maupin's life began to change. Once in California, he found a climate of tolerance that he had never experienced in the South. He was working as a reporter for the San Francisco edition of *Pacific Sun* in 1974 when he decided to come out of the closet. "A magazine wanted to include me in their list of the ten sexiest men in San Francisco. . . . I said they could include me as long as they said I was gay" (Clifton, 77). By doing so, *San Francisco* magazine hurtled Maupin into the public realm, and his career as a gay-rights advocate was born.

In 1976, the *San Francisco Chronicle* began serializing Maupin's "Tales of the City," stories set amid the sexual and social diversity of San Francisco. The success of the series furthered Maupin's position as a public figure, a role he welcomes, and he has emerged as a national spokesperson on gay matters. He serves on the board of advisors of numerous gay and lesbian organizations and gives freely of his time in both fund-raising and advocating for gay rights.

MAJOR WORKS AND THEMES

When Armistead Maupin first introduced "Tales of the City" in the *San Francisco Chronicle*, he had no thought of turning the daily columns into a book. His original plan was to produce a series of vignettes depicting famous San Francisco settings, institutions, and characteristic local lifestyles (Dyer, 32). In fact, he wrote none of his daily 800-word installments very far in advance because he liked responding to his readers' feedback about the characters and plot. At the time, Maupin said of his writing, "I have a rough idea of the journey ahead with a little idea of the side trips. I map out the overall theme, some sort of emotional resolution that I want for all the characters. But there's enough room to surprise myself in the process" (Spain, 53).

The central themes in Maupin's fiction focus on two major issues: the search for domestic contentment and the conflict between appearance and reality. Introduced in *Tales of the City*, these themes develop throughout the six novels around Maupin's main characters, at the center of whom is Anna Madrigal, the eccentric, maternal, transsexual proprietor of the tiny apartment house located at 28 Barbary Lane. Here Maupin depicts a new social arrangement in an extended urban family and sets the stage for a loving, supportive, and connected group.

The spiritual core of the novels, Anna Madrigal is the character against which all the others must be measured. Even in the novels where her role in the plot is minimal, her presence is always thematically and structurally significant. Like the mythical Teresias, Anna is a seer and a central consciousness in the stories, and her mystical ability to know all seems to increase throughout the novels. "Be careful," Mary Ann warns herself in

Babycakes. "A nice old woman who used to be a man could very well know what's on everybody's mind" (164). However, Anna, "the true mother of them all" (*More Tales*, 3), doesn't attempt to change people. Instead, she accepts her "children" for what they are and offers them unconditional love.

Mrs. Madrigal serves as an ironic earth mother in these stories, ironic not only because she is a transsexual, but also because none of her "children" is really her own. However, because of her selflessness and concern for her charges, she is able to create this family and remain at its center, maintaining connections with all of the other characters throughout the series. She plays the role of both mother and father and is most content when she is surrounded by her family. "I'm a cranky old hen," she says in *Further Tales*. "I like all my eggs in one basket" (190). In these stories, the boundaries blur between sons and daughters, husbands and wives, mothers and fathers, male and female. When she finally is told of her connection to Anna, Mona comes to think of her as "[my] father, mother, best friend, and landlady, all rolled into one joyful and loving human being!" (*Further Tales*, 101).

In the first novel, Mrs. Madrigal instructs Mona, "There are all kinds of marriages, dear . . . lots of things are more binding than sex. They last longer, too" (115). Alienated in one way or another from their own families, the characters spend much of their time searching for someone or something to belong to, even if on a purely physical level. All but Anna seem bewildered, careening through the stories searching for love and security in an uncertain world, yet ultimately realizing that they must find peace through emotional, internal commitments. As he matured over the fifteen years he spent with these characters, Maupin "learned more about the power of love, friendship, and compassion" (Dyer, 32). And as the series develops, Maupin stresses the conflicts between the misguided easy answers to human relationships that lie in sex and the more difficult but true answers found through family connectedness and love.

Maupin's fiction also focuses clearly on the conflict between appearance and reality. He recognizes that the humanity of others goes beyond their external differences. As Jon Fielding asks in *Further Tales*, "What the hell does gay have to do with anything?" (65). But it isn't simply the distinction between gay and straight that Maupin proves superficial. In these novels, he also dissolves the artificial categories that separate genders, social classes, age groups, professions, and geographical areas. Underneath the surface, Maupin seems to be saying, we all have the same universal needs. "The human heart," he has said, "is pretty much the same organ in every individual" (Anderson, telephone interview).

In Maupin's writing, the conflict between appearance and reality becomes political as he attacks hypocrisy, an attack that permeates his work and grows stronger with each successive novel. His main target is those gays who hide behind a heterosexual facade. Maupin believes that more could be done to stem the AIDS epidemic if gays in high places spoke out rather than denied their sexuality. "The world won't change until gay people become visible and proud. We have our own dead to honor, and their blood is on the hands of the indifferent" ("Growing Up Gay," 13). His characters demonstrate not only how difficult it is to be different, but also how sincerity and genuineness are preferable to conformity and lies. "The best way to take charge of your life," says Maupin, "is to abandon your secrets" ("Growing Up Gay," 13).

Maupin sees himself as a fiction writer with journalistic roots and demonstrates his gifts as both a reporter and social ironist in his work. He gives credit to E. F. Benson and the *Lucia* novels: "The contained cast that has adventures over a period of years and the sort of assurance that you are given by having a sort of homey center to it" and to Jan Struther, who serialized *Mrs. Miniver* in the *Times* of London as World War II was breaking out (Hayes, radio interview). He credits his early love for Alfred Hitchcock movies "with their wry mix of sex and death" for spawning his preposterous plot lines. Maupin was also influenced by Christopher Isherwood.* "He was one of the few literary figures that gave me support early in my career, who recognized what I was doing and applauded me for doing it, and encouraged me to continue to do it" (Allen, 20).

Although Maupin claims to have read little of Charles Dickens before beginning *Tales of the City*, his work seems to follow the tradition of the nineteenth-century serialist. Even the series' title is a variation on the Dickens title *A Tale of Two Cities*. Certainly Maupin's plot twists and surprise connections are Dickensian in nature. Also like Dickens's work, Maupin's fiction brings social issues to life for the masses (Spain, 53), each book representing a sociological portrait of the era in which it was written.

Although *Tales* is not directly autobiographical, many of the episodes are based on Maupin's real-life experiences, and the characters do reflect aspects of Maupin's life. He recognizes that all but one of the principal characters reflect parts of his own personality: the cynic, the romantic, the sexual lothario who becomes domestic, the lesbian with a society past. Although Mrs. Madrigal and Maupin share the same initials, and she does have the strongest voice in the series, Maupin claims that she "isn't me at all, but the person I aspire to be . . . her spirit is that of my grandmother, who was the biggest influence on me in my childhood. She was a suffragette, a vegetarian, theosophist, palm reader . . . she was a generous, loving spirit . . . her spirit is what rescued me in the long run; she was the explainer and the forgiver" (Dyer, 32).

As a gay author, Maupin treats the gay experience truthfully and frankly, but fewer than half of the significant characters are gay or lesbian and certainly his themes are universal. "From the very beginning," says Maupin, "my goal has been to create a framework which is large enough to include most of humanity" (Warren, 24). One can safely assert that Maupin has followed the dictates William Faulkner laid down for young writers in his

1950 Nobel Prize Address, instructing them to write only of "the old verities and truths of the heart, the old universal truths lacking which any story is ephemeral and doomed—love and honor and pity and pride and compassion and sacrifice."

Although Maupin has decided to end the Tales series "to explore new territory and avoid growing stale" (*Back to Barbary Lane*, introduction), he is now involved in writing a new novel, *Maybe the Moon*, published in 1992 by HarperCollins. Set in Los Angeles, it is written as the first-person diary of a young woman, a character based on a friend of Maupin's who recently died. It is not surprising that Maupin has chosen to write this new novel from a woman's perspective. He has already demonstrated his ability to write with ease about what it means to be a human being.

CRITICAL RECEPTION

Armistead Maupin has been reviewed in publications as varied as Britain's *Punch* and the *New York Times Book Review*. His writing has been praised in publications such as *People*, *Publisher's Weekly*, the *Village Voice*, and *Mother Jones*; and he is highlighted in "The Castro" section of Frances Fitzgerald's best-selling examination of communities, *Cities on a Hill*. Critics especially single out his flowing conversational style and his skill for crafting dialogue. Reviewers refer to Maupin as "glib," "cheeky," and "a master of compression" and to his writing as from "cozy and charmingly innocent" to "urbane." He has been favorably compared to such diverse writers as Charles Dickens, P. G. Wodehouse, Wilkie Collins, George Eliot, Anthony Powell, and Jonathan Swift. Most reviewers also allude to Maupin's accessibility: "Maupin writes for everyone: gay, straight, single, married, hip or square," says David Feinberg. "Acceptance is a given" (26).

However, for Maupin official literary recognition has been slow in coming. His philosophy that nothing is sacred, coupled with his early reputation as a San Francisco journalist may have contributed to this reception. Maupin, however, is much more than just another West Coast humorist. As his series' title implies, the books are indeed tales of San Francisco, but through the struggles of his characters, Barbary Lane has become a microcosm for San Francisco, and the city itself has become a microcosm for modern America, perhaps even for the modern world, pulled apart by a variety of forces yet drawn together by love, truth, and commitment.

Still, some critics insist upon labeling Maupin as merely a translator of pop culture rather than a serious mainstream satirist, emphasizing the local-color aspect of his writing and noting his popular success. He draws readers from a variety of backgrounds, both gay and straight; and popularity often detracts from even well-deserved literary respectability. Adam Block notes that Maupin's fiction does have the quality of escapist literature, "yet it counsels the readers to confront their dilemmas, not to flee or conceal them"

(45). Maupin seems finally to have received the literary recognition he deserves. He has recently been included in *The Faber Book of Gay Short Fiction* with such literary heavyweights as Henry James, E. M. Forster, Tennessee Williams, and James Baldwin.*

WORKS BY ARMISTEAD MAUPIN

Tales of the City. New York: Harper and Row, 1978.
More Tales of the City. New York: Harper and Row, 1980.
Further Tales of the City. New York: Harper and Row, 1982.
Babycakes. New York: Harper and Row, 1984.
Significant Others. New York: Harper and Row, 1987.
"Growing Up Gay in Old Raleigh." *The Independent* 16–29 June 1988: 11–13.
Sure of You. New York: Harper and Row, 1989.
28 Barbary Lane/Back to Barbary Lane: The Final Tales of the City Omnibus. New York: Harper Collins, 1991.

SELECTED STUDIES OF ARMISTEAD MAUPIN

Allen, Chuck. "Armistead Maupin." *Frontiers* 3 November 1989: 18–21.
Anderson, Terry. Telephone interview. 24 September 1991.
Block, Adam. "Teller of Tales." *Outweek* 29 October 1989: 42–45.
Clifton, Tony. "Mainstreaming a Cult Classic." *Newsweek* 30 October 1989: 77.
Dyer, Richard. "For Fifteen Years, He's Told Tales of San Francisco." *Boston Globe* 20 November 1989: 32.
Feinberg, David. Review of *Sure of You. New York Times Book Review* 22 October 1989: 25–26.
Fitzgerald, Frances. *Cities on a Hill.* New York: Simon and Schuster, 1981: 25–119.
Maupin, Armistead, radio interview by Suzanne Hayes. Adelaide College of Tafe, Australia, 1990.
Spain, Tom. "A Talk With Armistead Maupin." *Publishers Weekly* 20 March 1987: 53–54.
Warren, Steve. "Travails of the City." *San Francisco Bay Guardian* 11 October 1989: 24.

JAMES MERRILL (1926–   )

D. S. Lawson

BIOGRAPHY

The details of James Merrill's life are as well known as those of any openly gay writer alive today. Largely as a result of his highly respected, widely reviewed, and prize-winning poetry, Merrill seems likely to remain a fixture of American literature of the second half of the twentieth century. One imagines literature students of the future reading *The Changing Light at Sandover* in the same kinds of classes in which today's students read Yeats's or Blake's or Milton's or Dante's or Langland's visionary poetry. Certainly a handful of his shorter lyrics—for example, "Lost in Translation" and "The Power Station"—have likewise found for themselves a permanent place in the literary canon. Although Merrill's fictional output has been small, it must be accounted a place of importance in his overall oeuvre.

Merrill was born on March 3, 1926, in New York City, the son of Charles Edward Merrill (stockbroker, financier, and founding partner of Merrill/Lynch) and his second wife Hellen Ingram Merrill. His was a privileged childhood, filled with culture, a nanny who taught him foreign languages, and general material prosperity. Both of his parents wrote: his mother was a journalist before her marriage and his father was known for his long, lucid letters. His mother was both proud and critical of Merrill's early attempts at writing. The divorce of his parents when he was twelve has had an undeniable impact on his later life and work (see, for example, his poem "The Broken Home").

He attended the Lawrenceville School, where he began writing poetry because his close friend Frederick Buechner did. He has said of his urge to write, "I needed to feel that I was fulfilling myself in the face of heartless indifference" ("Condemned to Write about Real Things," 33). During his senior year at Lawrenceville, his father had a volume of Merrill's short stories and poems privately published under the title, *Jim's Book*. His collegiate years at Amherst College (his father's alma mater) were interrupted by service in the army in 1944–1945, but he graduated in 1947, writing an honors senior thesis on metaphor in the works of Marcel Proust.

Beginning in 1959, for twenty years he spent six months of each year in Greece. Since then, he has shuttled between his home in Stonington, Connecticut (the locale from which his book of poems *Water Street* takes its title) and David Jackson's summer home on Key West (see the poem "Clearing the Title"). He is still an actively publishing poet, apparently at the height of his powers over words.

Through his poetry, many coveted literary prizes have come his way: National Book Awards for Poetry in 1967 (for *Nights and Days*) and again in 1979 (for *Mirabell: Books of Number*), the Bollingen Prize from Yale University in 1973 (for *Braving the Elements*), and the Pulitzer Prize for Poetry in 1976 (for *Divine Comedies*). In addition to the two novels—*The Seraglio* (1957) and *The (Diblos) Notebook*, (1965)—and the poetry, he is also the author of two plays, *The Immortal Husband* (1955) and *The Bait* (produced 1953, published 1960).

Merrill certainly runs the risk of being forever known as the "Ouija" poet for his long, mystical poem based upon thousands of sittings at the board with his lover of many years, David Jackson. As such, he is the target of attacks that state that his poetry is frivolous or too utterly personal (as in fact the *New York Times* did attack him upon his receipt of the Bollingen prize). In his introduction to a volume of essays of literary criticism of Merrill's poetry, however, David Lehman points out Merrill's important historicity:

It is an amusing historical irony that it should be Merrill, of all American poets, who might succeed in identifying history with himself. Having felt like a candidate for abduction in the wake of the Lindbergh case, he could publish a depression kidnapping fantasy that was a prophetic step ahead of events: "Days of 1935," whose protagonist feels grateful to his kidnappers, seems eerily aware of the future history of Patty Hearst. And having grown up in "18 West 11th Street," the house blown up by Weathermen in 1970, gave Merrill a special impetus, and perhaps a special authority, to examine that incident and its implications—and to see his own life pass before him during the slow-motion replay of the blast. (16–17)

It seems germane to note that the impetus for the Ouija poems was a warning from the other world about the potential for a nuclear disaster. The material from the Ouija board, though Merrill's most famous (or notorious) work, is by no means all that he writes about. Significantly, the Ouija board plays a small but important role in *The Seraglio*, and scholars generally have failed to investigate the important connections between Merrill's fiction and his poetry. Though it is doubtful that his place in American letters would be secured by his fiction alone (as it most assuredly would be by his poetry), in his two novels Merrill does have things to say which he does not say in the poetry and any picture of him or his work that ignores his fiction would necessarily be incomplete. Furthermore, there are often interesting and illuminating parallels or areas of overlap between the poetry and the prose.

MAJOR WORKS AND THEMES

In some important ways, James Merrill's two novels seem as though they were written by different authors. *The Seraglio* is a relatively conventional novel of manners, slightly reminiscent of Henry James's style, with an omniscient narrator and wealthy characters based upon Merrill's own family. *The (Diblos) Notebook*, on the other hand, is a tour de force of formal technique: a novel that attempts to duplicate in the reading the manner in which it was written: a novel blending a contemporary social story with significant psychological and mythic elements.

The Seraglio tells the story of Francis Tanning, the aesthete son of businessman Benjamin Tanning, a man surrounded by riches and women—his ex-wives, ex-mistresses, potential new wives and mistresses, a daughter, a granddaughter, and a woman sculptor commissioned to do a bust. Curiously, his son seems quite the opposite of the father, interested neither in women nor in business. Although Francis' sexuality is never addressed directly, he is at one point questioned as to whether he likes girls or boys. At the very center of the novel Francis nearly kills himself when, psychologically overcome by the tremendous sexually charged atmosphere that envelops his father's life and household, he attempts to castrate himself in the bathtub. Certainly this scene could be read as Francis' frightened reaction to an awareness of the true direction of his sexuality.

The very first image of the novel is a portrait of a family member being accidentally defaced; this is a telling symbol of the book as a whole. The image the family has of Francis is not real. If Francis Tanning is meant to be seen as a portrait of the youthful James Merrill, then in the course of this novel he becomes aware of his homosexuality, even though the subject is never overtly raised. Just as the picture gets damaged, so as well must Francis' image—both within the family and within his own consciousness.

Francis is surrounded by artists of one kind or another—the aforementioned sculptor and a young composer who writes an opera entitled *Orpheus*. In his poetry from the Ouija board, Merrill specifically deals with the relationship between homosexuality and art, arguing that homosexuality was created so that music and poetry could thrive. In *The Changing Light at Sandover*, Merrill comes to realize that he was chosen as a medium because, like the spirits, he is childless; a parallel theme is also the subject of the well-known poem "Childlessness."

Midway through the novel, Francis becomes fascinated with the Ouija board and discusses with his friends some of the spirits with which he has communicated via the board. Along with the poem "Voices from the Other World" (written in 1955 and published in *The Country of a Thousand Years of Peace*), this is the earliest treatment of material from the Ouija board in Merrill's writing.

The (Diblos) Notebook is altogether another type of fiction, heavily experimental and intellectually demanding. Ostensibly, the plot of this novel follows a writer (John/Sandy) who goes to Greece to trace the events of his brother Orson's life there in hopes of writing a book. The form taken by the novel is that of a notebook kept by the writer/brother, who sometimes merely observes, who sometimes recites past history (both real and imagined), and who occasionally overtly introduces mythic parallels to his brother's story by comparing him to Orestes. The novel is full of false starts, crossed-out words, plot threads that lead nowhere, and radical shifts in subject and point of view from first-person narration to third-person.

The form could arguably be seen as emblematic of sexuality: oscillating between culturally predetermined poles (first-person/third-person, homosexual/heterosexual); always in a constant state of change and revision, even of reaction to the events which transpire; and ultimately never capable of enclosing the "truth" about the characters, just as sexuality is never the whole of any human being. The fascination with a brother is a staple of gay fiction, of course.

It is important to note that the story from the Ouija board that became *The Changing Light at Sandover* was originally intended to be a third novel, the manuscript of which was lost in a taxi and never recovered (compare the poem "The Will").

CRITICAL RECEPTION

Merrill's writing is reviewed in the most respected magazines and journals; furthermore, he receives critical and scholarly attention in conference papers, journal articles, and books written by some of the finest minds in academia today. Largely, of course, all this writing focuses on his poetry and the fiction gets the short end of the stick. Nevertheless, what has been written on the fiction has generally been quite positive.

In his review of *The Seraglio* in *The Nation*, David L. Stevenson sees the novel as "a Freudian diagram enlarged to the shape of a novel" (329). Indeed the sexuality of the father's household and the son's reaction to it (which ultimately encompasses an attempt at sexual self-defacement) takes up a good deal of the novel's space. In the *New York Times Book Review*. Richard Sullivan praises the novel: "The writing in this first novel is admirably controlled. There is a genuine intimation of ennui, sophistication, decadence—all brightened by wry humor" (19).

Charles J. Rollo in *The Atlantic* was more negative, however, writing, "Francis' attempt to come to terms with life is the central theme of the

story, and the author's handling of it seemed to me faltering and unsatisfactory" (85). After comparing *The Seraglio* to novels by Henry James,
Whitney Balliet in the *New Yorker* argued, "Yet, while he perfected all of
James's outward pirouettes, he has taken on none of the always surprising,
naive positiveness that keeps James's work alive" (134).

The (Diblos) Notebook received its share of attention as well. F. D. Reeve,
writing in *Hudson Review*, sees the strength of the novel as being its me-
diation between fiction and reality and argues that this is a parallel to the
way most people interpret the world and their own lives in it: "Our lives
are the stories we have made ourselves believe about ourselves, the stories
in which we are prominent" (290). In an essay, Merrill himself subscribes
to this view of his work: "The unities of home and world, and world and
page, will be observed through the very act of transition from one to the
other" ("Condemned to Write about Real Things," 33).

Wilfrid Sheed in the *New York Times Book Review* compares the novel
to books set in the Mediterranean by E. M. Forster and Cyril Connolly. He
goes on to say, "The experiment is self-liquidating and can hardly be used
again.... This is the kind of novel it is a pleasure to take seriously, a disciplined, adventurous performance in the best tradition of fictional experiment" (4).

In the only academic article yet published that is solely devoted to Merrill's
fiction, Morris Eaves says,

On the one hand the book seems to be the work of Penelope as she knits in the
sunshine and unravels in the moonlight. On the other, it is the great model of all
Unfinished Business, a work of construction that is all angles—an edifice of irregular
stones notched and fitted until it stands, a wonderful feat of balance without sym-
metry. (156)

Merrill's attempt to write fiction in which the seams still show, to re-create
in the reading some aspects of the formulation of the writing of the novel,
must be judged only a partial success according to Eaves, who sees the
narrator as a kind of Prufrockian character who never actually gets around
to asking his overwhelming question; Eaves calls both Sandy and Prufrock
"revisers" (164).

Jefferson Humphries says,

The (Diblos) Notebook is not really a novel at all.... It is a fiction about the writing
of a novel—uncompleted phrases, scenes, crossed out and rebegun beginnings, failed
attempts to conclude. If it were a novel, it would be a novel about the uncompleted
writing of a novel, so about its own failure to be a novel. A fiction whose subject
is itself and its failure to become what it means to. (39)

He sees the novel as evidence of Merrill's fascination with form (indeed,
most of his poetry is highly form-centered). Humphries defends Merrill's

unique fictive voice: "The language of the novels resembles Merrill's poetry more than anyone's prose" (37). Merrill's work in prose narrative would thus seem to have important and as yet underexamined links to his more noted poetry.

WORKS BY JAMES MERRILL

First Poems. New York: Knopf, 1951.

The Immortal Husband. Playbook: Plays for a New Theatre. New York: New Directions, 1956.

The Seraglio. New York: Knopf, 1957; reissued with new preface, New York: Atheneum, 1987.

The Country of a Thousand Years of Peace. New York: Knopf, 1959; rev. ed., New York: Atheneum, 1970.

The Bait. Artist's Theatre. Ed. Herbert Machiz. New York: Grove Press, 1960.

Water Street. New York: Atheneum, 1962.

The (Diblos) Notebook. New York: Atheneum, 1965.

The Fire Screen. New York: Atheneum, 1969.

Braving the Elements. New York: Atheneum, 1972.

The Yellow Pages. Cambridge, Mass.: Temple Bar Bookshop, 1974.

Divine Comedies. New York: Atheneum, 1976.

Mirabell: Books of Number. New York: Atheneum, 1978.

Scripts for the Pageant. New York: Atheneum, 1980.

The Changing Light at Sandover. New York: Atheneum, 1982.

"Condemned to Write about Real Things." *New York Times Book Review* 21 February 1982: 11+.

From the First Nine: Poems 1946–1976. New York: Atheneum, 1982.

Late Settings. New York: Atheneum, 1985.

Recitative. San Francisco: North Point, 1986. Includes the short stories "Rose," "Driver," and "Peru: The Landscape Game."

The Inner Room. New York: Knopf, 1988.

Selected Poems 1946–1985. New York: Knopf, 1992.

SELECTED STUDIES OF JAMES MERRILL

Balliett, Whitney. "Books: Content and Form." Rev. of *The Seraglio* by James Merrill. *The New Yorker* 30 March 1957: 130+.

Eaves, Morris. "Decision and Revision in James Merrill's *(Diblos) Notebook.*" *Contemporary Literature* 12, no. 2 (Spring 1971): 156–65.

Humphries, Jefferson. "James Merrill's Voice within the Mirror." In *Losing the Text: Readings in Literary Desire*, 21–54. Athens, Ga.: University of Georgia Press, 1986.

"James Merrill." *Contemporary Authors: New Revision Series*, vol. 10, 322–29. Detroit: Gale, 1983.

Kalstone, David. *Five Temperaments.* New York: Oxford University Press, 1977.

Leavitt, David. "Stockbroker Father, Poet Son." Rev. of the reissue of *The Seraglio* by James Merrill. *Los Angeles Times Book Review* 25 October 1987: 1+.

Lehman, David, and Charles Berger, eds. *James Merrill: Essays in Criticism*. Ithaca: Cornell University Press, 1983.

Moffett, Judith. *James Merrill: An Introduction to the Poetry*. New York: Columbia University Press, 1984.

Reeve, F. D. "An Island of Form." Rev. of *The (Diblos) Notebook* by James Merrill. *Hudson Review* 18 no. 2 (Summer 1965): 290–92.

Rollo, Charles J. "Reader's Choice." Rev. of *The Seraglio* by James Merrill. *The Atlantic* May 1957: 80 + .

Sheed, Wilfrid. "We Know Everything, We Know Nothing." Rev. of *The (Diblos) Notebook* by James Merrill. *New York Times Book Review* 21 March 1965: 4.

Spiegelman, William. "James Merrill." *Dictionary of Literary Biography, vol. 5: American Poets Since World War II, Part 2, L–Z*, 53–65. Detroit: Gale, 1980.

Stevenson, David L. "Four Views of Love: New Fiction." Rev. of *The Seraglio* by James Merrill. *Nation* 13 April 1957: 329.

Sullivan, Richard. "Tycoon's Harem." Rev. of *The Seraglio* by James Merrill. *New York Times Book Review* 21 April 1957: 18–19.

White, Edmund. "The Inverted Type: Homosexuality as a Theme in James Merrill's Prophetic Books." *Literary Visions of Homosexuality*. Ed. Stuart Kellogg, 47–52. New York: Haworth, 1983.

Yenser, Stephen. *The Consuming Myth: The Work of James Merrill*. Cambridge: Harvard University Press, 1987.

LARRY MITCHELL (1938–   )
Craig Allen Seymour II

BIOGRAPHY

After graduating from high school in his hometown of Muncie, Indiana, Mitchell left for Colby College in Maine. In 1960, Mitchell graduated cum laude with a degree in philosophy.

Mitchell moved to New York City shortly thereafter to study sociology at Columbia University. He writes: "One reason why I began to study sociology was my need to understand homosexual existence" (*Great Gay*, 31). He wanted to write his dissertation on this topic, but he feared people would then know he was gay. Despite these obstacles Mitchell received his Ph.D. from Columbia in 1968.

In addition to being a period of intellectual growth for Mitchell, the late 1960s were also a period of political growth. He was active in many antiwar demonstrations of the time, including the 1968 takeover of Columbia University's administration building. He states that he was politically ready for the Stonewall Rebellion when it occurred in June of 1969. Although he did not participate in the events at Stonewall, he became involved in the Gay Liberation Front following the rebellion.

Around this time Mitchell was also a member of the Gay Liberation Front Study Group. The group read the works of various political theorists in order to construct political analyses of gay oppression.

In 1970, 1971, and 1972, Mitchell taught a course in Gay Oppression and Liberation at the City University of New York's College of Staten Island. The class consisted mostly of lesbians, gay men, and those whom Mitchell calls "fuzzies," people who were not yet sure of their sexual identity. Again, the goal of the class was to develop political analyses of gay oppression.

Mitchell's political interests of the time also fostered an interest in communal living. Mitchell lived communally off and on from 1969 to the late

1970s. Initially he lived with both heterosexual and homosexual people. Later, however, he lived only with homosexuals, viewing this in itself as a political act.

Mitchell's writing career began as the result of these communal living experiences. In 1972, a representative from Times Change Press asked him and the other members of the commune to write a book on communal living. This work eventually became *Great Gay in the Morning*.

Mitchell began his next book in 1975 following a short trip to San Francisco. In San Francisco, Mitchell was struck by the "new gay energy" of the city, a phenomenon that would not have been evident just a few short years earlier. Mitchell wanted to write a book to celebrate this newfound energy. *The Faggots and Their Friends between Revolutions* became this book.

Because *The Faggots and Their Friends between Revolutions* was originally conceived as a children's book, Mitchell wanted it to have the look of a children's book. He asked Ned Asta, a woman living in the commune with him, to illustrate the book in the manner of a Victorian children's book. Both the illustrations and the thematic content of the book made it very hard for Mitchell to find a publisher. After being turned down by several publishers, Mitchell decided to publish the book himself. Thus Calamus Books was born.

Once Mitchell published his own book, he used Calamus Books to publish gay male writers whose books, in his opinion, helped to "aid progressive forces within the Gay male/Lesbian movement" (*Faggots*, 113). Ron Schreiber, Gary Indiana, and Robert Patrick were among the writers he published.

The second book Mitchell published on his own was *The Terminal Bar*. This and all of Mitchell's subsequent books began as an experiment. For *The Terminal Bar* Mitchell wanted to write a novel, because he had never written one before. He also had just moved to Manhattan's Lower East Side and was inspired by the many gay artists living there.

In Heat, Mitchell's second novel, was his attempt to write a heavily plotted novel. Unlike his other books, *In Heat* was published not by Calamus Books, but rather through Gay Presses of New York, a coalition formed by Mitchell, Felice Picano* of Seahorse Press, and Terry Helbing of JH Press. *My Life as a Mole and Five Other Stories* began when the editor of an anthology of new gay male fiction asked Mitchell to write a few short stories. The editor subsequently rejected all of them. Mitchell then expanded one (which became the novella "My Life as a Mole") and wrote a few more. Once completed, he published the collection himself; and the collection went on to receive a Lambda Literary Award.

His most recent (as yet unpublished) novel, *Acid Snow*, consists mostly of dialogue. It also addresses the mothers of gay men, because of the strength he witnessed watching mothers care for their sons with AIDS.

MAJOR WORKS AND THEMES

The writings of Larry Mitchell have a particularly post-Stonewall character. They reflect the inclusive, anti-assimilationist politics espoused by gay-liberation movements, like the Gay Liberation Front, immediately following the Stonewall Rebellion. Unlike the earlier homophile movements, many gay liberation groups, coming from a predominately white male center, viewed gay liberation as a part of a larger movement to liberate all oppressed peoples, including women and people of color.

In his first book, *The Faggots and Their Friends between Revolutions*, Mitchell takes this vision of liberation and transforms it into a fairy tale. He creates a place called Ramrod, populated by many different groups of people. The "faggots" are the main characters of this fairy tale. The term "faggot," however, does not apply to all of the gay men of Ramrod. "The queens" are another group of gay men in the book. They differ from the faggots in that they "often make fun of the faggots for their drab uniformity and their addiction to the men's fashions . . . "(63). There are also "the queer men," who move among the "men (read as straight)" during the day and the "faggots" at night. Despite the differences between the groups, Mitchell includes all of them in the revolution. He writes: "EVEN WEAK LINKS IN THE CHAIN ARE LINKS IN THE CHAIN" (27).

Other groups populating Ramrod include "the men," and "the women who love women." "The men" rule Ramrod. They came to power after the first revolution, which "destroyed the great cultures of the women," and the second revolution, which made "a small group of men without color very rich" (1). "The women who love women" are friends of the faggots and integral parts of the revolution. They even wrote a song for "the faggots" called, "Anything you do that the men don't like is o.k. by us" (47).

Using these various characters in short vignettes, rarely longer than a page, Mitchell not only promotes an inclusive revolution, he also engages stereotypes of gay male sexuality, encoding these stereotypes with new meanings. On sexual promiscuity, Mitchell writes: "The faggots consider it their sacred pleasure to engage in indiscrimimate promiscuous sexuality. No faggot, regardless of age, race or physical appearance, should ever be horny" (12).

In his second book, *The Terminal Bar*, Mitchell leaves the fantasy world of Ramrod for the reality of Manhattan's Lower East Side. His view of Manhattan, however, does not differ significantly from his view of Ramrod. They are both empires on the verge of collapse.

The characters in *The Terminal Bar*, like the groups in *The Faggots and Their Friends between Revolutions*, are fiercely political. The politics of the characters in *The Terminal Bar*, however, manifest themselves in intensely personal and often amusing ways. Mitchell writes of Barnaby, a gay male character: "He has begun to realize that his politics are pushing him into a completely untenable position. He hates men. They are violent, competitive and destructive. . . . Yet he is a faggot and so loves men. Hating maleness makes being a faggot absurd" (49).

In *The Terminal Bar*, Mitchell also tackles environmental issues. These concerns often mediate talks of revolution as in the following exchange:

"There must be something to believe in—the revolution."
"Except by the time we'd win there would be nothing left to enjoy. Victorious on a dead planet" (25).

The emphasis on the interplay between social revolution and the environment shifts in Mitchell's second novel, *In Heat*. Here Mitchell focuses on the relationships between a small group of friends and lovers. The novel takes place as AIDS begins to slowly and subtly affect the lives of the characters. It examines mortality, not specifically with respect to AIDS, but through aging. Mitchell uses aging as an opportunity to present elements of a decidedly gay male history. In doing this he implicitly asserts a gay male future, despite the ravages of both age and AIDS.

The action of the novel revolves around a bookstore in Manhattan owned by Gregory, a gay octogenarian. A gay man in his sixties, Samuel Cranshaw, now runs the bookstore. Throughout the novel the bookstore and its owner, Gregory, are linked with a variety of gay male writers and artists, most importantly, Jean Cocteau. This link to Cocteau makes Samuel, or more specifically Samuel's cock, especially appealing to Jonathan, a male nurse in his forties. Jonathan explains this to a friend:

"It's a historic dick."
"You mean old, don't you?"
"No, historic. He (Samuel) sucked off Gregory and Gregory sucked off Cocteau. So if I suck off Samuel's I have a direct link to Cocteau. . . . "(42)

For *My Life as a Mole*, Mitchell returns to the political terrain of *The Terminal Bar*. In the six years separating the books, however, this terrain has changed for the worse. Economic conditions for many Lower East Side residents have significantly worsened; and the full-scale assault of new moneyed urban developers has made it increasingly hard for many residents to keep their homes. Compounding these economic problems is the intensified presence of AIDS and the general phobic reactions to PWAs by the society at large. In this 106-page tour de force Mitchell records not just the presence of this phenomenon, but the way in which it pervades every thought and colors every action.

In comparison to his other novels, Mitchell's latest novel, *Acid Snow* is most like *In Heat*. The emphasis is far more personal than political. In short cinematic sequences, Mitchell tells the story of Jake, a middle-aged Jewish gay man and his dealings with his communist parents; his sister, who has "sold out to Wall Street" (7); her girlfriend, who can't decide "whether to open an art gallery or have a baby" (17); and the increasing number of his friends dying with AIDS: "Three funerals in a week makes you wish one of them were yours" (3).

Similar to *In Heat* too is the role of history in the novel. In *Acid Snow*, however, the focus is not on collective history, but the loss of personal history due to AIDS. As Jake observes: "I'm losing my past. Soon everyone who remembers me will be dead (63)." The novel asks: how does one live with the past disappearing behind one, and no vision of the future yet in sight?

CRITICAL RECEPTION

To date, the works of Larry Mitchell have received little critical attention beyond brief book reviews in the lesbian and gay press. Of all his books, *In Heat* and *My Life as a Mole* are the most favored by critics. In *The Alyson Almanac*, Richard Labonte includes *In Heat* as one of the ten best gay books to date. He writes: "Mitchell's 1985 novel quietly captures the post-Stonewall, pre-AIDS world of pretty common gay guys . . . and does so with gracious, gorgeous writing" (34).

On *My Life as a Mole*, John Preston* in the *Lambda Rising Book Report* wrote that it "breaks away from all the middle-class gay male fiction and instead demands that the reader look at the world through eyes which see the hypocrisy, violence, and intolerance that rule America today (1).

WORKS BY LARRY MITCHELL

Great Gay in the Morning [by "The 25 to 6 Baking and Trucking Society"]. Washington, N.J.: Times Change Press, 1972.
The Faggots and Their Friends between Revolutions. New York: Calamus Books, 1977.
The Terminal Bar. New York: Calamus Books, 1982.
In Heat. New York: Gay Presses of New York, 1985.
My Life as a Mole and Five Other Stories. New York: Calamus Books, 1988.
Acid Snow. Unpublished, 1991.

SELECTED STUDIES OF LARRY MITCHELL

Labonte, Richard. *The Alyson Almanac*. Boston: Alyson Press, 1989.
Preston, John. "A Cry of Rage in a Troubled Time." *Lambda Rising Book Report* 2, no. 2 (December 1989–January 1990): 1.
Saslow, James M. "Taking Note at the End of the Empire." *The Advocate* 11 November 1982:65.

PAUL MONETTE (1945–   )
David Román

BIOGRAPHY

In his autobiography, *Becoming a Man: Half a Life Story*, Paul Monette explains, in his by now typical sardonic style, that "until I was twenty-five, I was the only man I knew who had no story at all." Monette is writing of his years in the closet, a time familiar to countless gays and lesbians, where personal identity, more often than not, is determined by an insidious homophobia that permeates all aspects of everyday life. "The story where nothing happens," as Monette describes his closet years in the autobiography, can be told only now, over twenty years later, in the aftermath of Stonewall and in the midst of the time of AIDS. Fueled by Monette's own relentless commitment to leave a testimony of how gay men have lived and loved, the complete works from the publication of his first novel, *Taking Care of Mrs. Carroll*, in 1978 to the current *Becoming a Man* chart the often-troubled history of contemporary gay male fiction and its critical reception by both mainstream and gay audiences. These works also begin to suggest the emerging politicized role of the writer, one which Monette consistently advocates and champions, to thoroughly engage gay and lesbian readers in the critical social issues facing all gay and lesbian people in contemporary society.

Paul Monette was born in Lawrence, Massachusetts, in 1945. He was educated at the prestigious schools of New England: Phillips Academy Andover and then Yale University, where he received his B.A. in 1967. He began his prolific writing career soon after graduating from college, writing poetry exclusively for eight years. During this time he taught at Milton Academy and Pine Manor College. The turning point in Monette's life was his coming out in his late twenties. When he was twenty-eight he met Roger Horwitz, his lover for over ten years. It was also during his late twenties that he grew disillusioned with poetry and shifted his interest to the novel. In 1977, Paul Monette and Roger Horwitz moved to Los Angeles, where they were successfully able to live productive and happy years. During the late 1970s and early 1980s, both men contributed to the growing gay community of Los Angeles on many levels. In particular, they were dedicated in their commitment to the Los Angeles Gay and Lesbian Center and various other gay organizations and agencies. Throughout these years, Monette also wrote a number of screenplays that, while never produced, provided him the income to write. Along with the early novels, *The Gold Diggers*, *Lightfall*, and *The Long Shot*, he wrote various novelizations of films including *Scarface* and, most recently, *Havana*.

Paul Monette's life changed dramatically when Roger Horwitz was diagnosed with AIDS in the early 1980s. Since Roger Horwitz's death in 1986, Paul Monette has written extensively about the years of their battles with AIDS (*Borrowed Time: An AIDS Memoir*, 1988) and how he himself has coped with losing a lover to AIDS (*Love Alone: 18 Elegies for Rog*, 1988). Readers unfamiliar with these works are missing two of the most powerful accounts written about AIDS thus far. The publication of *Borrowed Time* and *Love Alone* catapulted Monette into a national arena as a spokesperson for AIDS. Himself a person with AIDS, he has continued to address AIDS issues in various capacities and to diverse audiences. Paul Monette, along with fellow writer and activist Larry Kramer,* has emerged as one of the most familiar and outspoken AIDS activists of our time. Given the fact that very few gay men have had the opportunity to address national issues in mainstream venues at any previous time in U.S. history, the high visibility profile of Paul Monette since 1988 should be considered one of his most lasting and accomplished achievements.

In recent years, Paul Monette has been an active supporter of ACT UP (AIDS Coalition to Unleash Power) and has continued to work tirelessly as an advocate for all people with HIV or AIDS, AIDS activism, gay and lesbian rights, and anticensorship campaigns, appearing regularly in print and television media to address these issues. In 1988, he fell in love with Stephen Kolzak, a member of ACT UP/Los Angeles and a talented television executive. (Among his many successes, Stephen Kolzak cast the original talent for the TV hit *Cheers*.) They were able to spend over two years together before Stephen Kolzak died of complications from AIDS in September 1990. Currently, Paul Monette lives in Los Angeles and is once again in love. "I have never been more alive," he offers (*The Advocate*, April 9, 1991, 40).

MAJOR WORKS AND THEMES

In each of his six novels, Paul Monette has unabashedly depicted gay men who strive to fashion personal identities that lead them to love, friendships, and self-fulfillment. These novels generally begin where most coming-out stories end; his protagonists have already come to terms with their sexuality long before the novel's projected time frame. Paul Monette shows gay characters negotiating family relations, societal expectations, and personal desires in light of their decision to lead lives as openly gay men. Refreshingly for gay fiction, a secure gay male identity is the norm in his novels. Two major themes emerge: the spark of gay male relations and the dynamic alternative family structures that gay men create for themselves in contemporary society. These themes are placed in a literary form that relies on the structures of romance, melodrama, and fantasy. Monette does not attempt to portray realistically the inner struggles and social realities of gay people in such a way to merit his work in the "serious" mode of sociorealism. Instead, these are love stories, ironic in form but sincere in their conviction that gay men can, and do, find love and happiness. Moreover, Monette is highly aware of popular genres; he manipulates the conventions of romance by punctuating his narratives with an acerbic wit and an ironic grin.

Paul Monette's first novel, *Taking Care of Mrs. Carroll*, for example, involves a madcap scam to save a wealthy old woman's pastoral estate from the hands of greedy developers. The story takes place the summer of Mrs. Carroll's death; with humorous detail, Monette introduces a cast of mainly gay characters who cleverly join forces to dupe the enemy by the end. This escapist romp is told by Rick, the gay narrator/protagonist, who by the end of the novel is transformed by the events of the summer. *Taking Care of Mrs. Carroll* is, like all Monette's fiction, a multilayered text. On the one hand, it tells the amusing story of a group of gay men who leisurely indulge in the pleasures available to their class in the tradition of Hollywood's best screwball comedies. Yet, on the other hand, these same men also embark on journeys of self-discovery that result in deep-felt realizations about their identity as gay men. Characters engage in various symposia on love, sex, and commitment that by the novel's conclusion subtly demonstrate the fluidity of expression and desire available to gay men in the late 1970s. Furthermore, these characters form a support system—a community—that allows them the possibility to grow and learn about themselves.

The summer at Mrs. Carroll's estate, like the best of all pastoral worlds, is only a temporary retreat from the darker realities awaiting them in the city. It functions mainly as the transformative location where these gay men are able to cast aside static old scripts for newer and more dynamic identities. Rick, whose story of coming to terms with the past and celebrating the present is at the heart of the novel, invokes this sentiment when he describes at the novel's end his main epiphany, "I gave up the past I wanted to invent all along with the one I spent my life burying" (271).

These same motifs emerge in his next two novels, *The Gold Diggers* and *The Long Shot*. Both novels continue to exploit popular genres; *The Gold Diggers* can be best described as a postmodern Western and *The Long Shot* as a murder mystery/Hollywood exposé. In both novels, the gay characters establish alternative family systems that sustain them through the unexpected twists and turns of the fast-paced plots. Like the earlier *Taking Care of Mrs. Carroll,* these two novels focus on characters determined to come to terms with the past in order to engage the present without remorse or regret. Similarly, the novels are exceptionally witty and even more sexy. Monette writes erotic scenes between men that extend beyond cliché and celebrate the many pleasures of the flesh. His characters enjoy sex, never succumbing to the fear and trembling associated with guilty, self-loathing pathos. (Nor do they go to the other extreme by hyperromanticizing all gay male sexuality as some sacred exchange of the initiated.)

Unlike *Taking Care of Mrs. Carroll,* which is set in a mythic pastoral landscape in New England, *The Gold Diggers* and *The Long Shot* are unequivocally novels of and about the gritty, seductive, and always enigmatic city of Los Angeles. *The Long Shot,* in particular, demonstrates gay men's seduction by Hollywood. The novel begins with the main character, the down-and-out unemployed screenwriter with a heart of gold, Greg, forcing himself *not* to watch the television broadcast of the Academy Awards. Disenchanted with the current state of Hollywood film, Greg boycotts the Oscars only to be launched into the star-making machinery by the mysterious death of an industry legend. The apparent double suicide—could it be murder?—of a fading major screen idol, Jasper Cokes, and Greg's next-door neighbor heartthrob Harry sets the plot in motion and initiates the critique of Hollywood that becomes one of the novel's finest features. *The Long Shot* presents an uncanny depiction of gays in Hollywood that exposes the homophobia normalized by the entertainment business. Jasper Cokes, the murdered star, happens to be gay, but in the hands of Hollywood publicists he is forced to marry and live his gay life in secrecy at his wealthy estate:

It was past time, meanwhile, for Jasper Cokes to take a wife. At twenty-eight, he ought to have had a first marriage over and done with. Not that the public suspected any irregularities. The public believed what it wanted to—that a man with everything ate up life like candy, girls included. Concern over Jasper's waking hours in bed came down direct from the executive suite, where the Gelusil accountants toted up the grosses. (18)

The press is to blame as well for their complicit perpetuation of Jasper's constructed heterosexuality. Greg, our hero, finds this stance incredible: "How was it, he wondered, that no one had ever said this in the press? There had always been an unwritten rule that barred a reporter from letting it out that Jasper Cokes was queer" (187).

Although these early novels tackle some social issues relevant to gay men, it would be misleading to identify them as overtly political novels. The major contribution to gay literature found in these earlier works remains the positive depiction of gay men affirming their gayness in relationships, through sex, and the friendships, including those with women, that are formed around each. It's not until Monette's brilliant novel about three AIDS widowers, *Afterlife*, that personal relationships and activist politics merge in a method previously unseen in modern gay male fiction.

It's tempting to divide Monette's fiction into two camps: before AIDS and since AIDS. Yet though AIDS is undoubtedly the major issue of his later work, Monette continues to write about relationships, friendships, alternative family structures, and most of all, love. *Afterlife* and *Halfway Home*, while certainly his best novels, share with the earlier works their penchant for romance, melodrama, and even humor. In fact, it is this precise merging of the themes and modes inaugurated in the early novels with the current reality of AIDS that makes these later works so interesting and successful. Still, while he continues to write novels about gay male relationships, the context of AIDS cannot be denied. These later works are about AIDS and should be read as such.

Afterlife tells the story of three AIDS widowers who, having met in the most dire of circumstances, continue a friendship way past the long, round-the-clock hospital vigils of their first encounters:

None of the three had ever met before the waiting room on the ninth floor, where each had come to watch the world end. Victor was in 904, Marcus in 916, Ellsworth in 921. The death-watch lovers quickly became a kind of combat unit, reeling in and out of their separate chambers of horrors, outdoing one another with unspeakable details. By the time it was all over—Marcus on Tuesday, Victor Thursday, Ellsworth midnight Friday—the widowers knew one another better than anyone. Or at least how they cried and took their coffee. (6).

The widowers—Steven, Sonny, and Dell—represent three very different ways of reacting to grief, terror, and anger. Monette begins the novel a year after their initial meeting and depicts how each widower copes with his loss and his own HIV-positive status. Steven, the novel's central character, who "ballooned in a year from 160 to 185" (1), hosts their frequent Saturday gatherings; Sonny, on the other hand, lives at his West Hollywood gym flexing muscle and attitude with a vengeance that can only be countered by a heavy dose of California New Age mysticism; and Dell, the novel's most enigmatic character, rages against an antigay televangelist when he's not on the 900-number phone lines. Each man undergoes a powerful journey that results in a complete restructuring of his life. Together, they teach each other about the challenges and possibilities of living in the afterlife, "this extra piece of time after a lover dies" (6).

Perhaps the most important aspect of *Afterlife* is the idea that, once again breaking new ground for gay fiction, gay men can live meaningful, productive lives in the plague years. Some, if they are lucky and interested, may even find love once more. *Afterlife* is, however, by no means a novel of denial. Monette's characters know only too well what it means to be gay in the age of AIDS. Instead, Monette offers his readers characters who decide to take this time in the afterlife to put their lives in order. As usual in his work, the main plot device Monette employs to articulate this position is the love story. Early in the novel, Steven meets up with the terribly sexy Mark (who to Steven's dismay had had a brief affair with his lover, Victor, before Steven and Victor met); and although their subsequent courtship begins with a round of bad sex and awkward affections, by the end theirs is a love story in the grandest tradition of the nineteenth-century English novel. *Afterlife* reads like Jane Austen in West Hollywood—courtship, social critique, irony, and, of course, AIDS. Add to this love story a dash of the best revolutionary resistance narratives, and you have the first gay novel written about AIDS that fuses personal love interests with political activism. *Afterlife* is a major achievement in gay fiction. It is a novel about finding love in the age of AIDS; of living sex-positive lives; of fighting the enemy by whatever means possible; and finally of establishing unflinching bonds in the face of a raging epidemic: all told with wit, anger, and an urgency that cannot be denied. It is Paul Monette's finest achievement so far.

Halfway Home, Monette's next novel, moves from the broad landscape of the Los Angeles gay scene found in *Afterlife* to concentrate on one man's battle with AIDS. Tom Shaheen, a notorious radical queer performance artist with AIDS whose stage persona, Miss Jesus, rattles the fundamentalist fringe, narrates his story from a secluded beach house in Malibu. *Halfway Home* is the story of Tom's reconciliation with his straight brother Brian. After a long hiatus from any communication with his gay brother, Brian shows up unexpected at the beach house to seek refuge from his own deteriorating life. Brian's failing marriage and collapsing career are paired against Tom's own troubles with AIDS. At first, neither brother completely understands the other's pain and loss. In order to reach any sense of connection, Brian and Tom must reconfigure their relationship by coming to terms with an abusive past and tortured present. Tom at least has the support of his extended gay family: Gray, Gray's wise Aunt Foo, his lesbian friend Mona, and a group of adoring fans who eagerly await the return of Miss Jesus. As Tom and Brian begin to mend the scars of their childhood, Tom finds a new, nearly forgotten passion for living in his growing relationship with his lover Gray, his friends, his fans, and finally, his blood family. Above all, *Halfway Home* is a novel of reconciliations.

Halfway Home also foregrounds a new theme in Paul Monette's fiction. At the heart of the novel is Tom's relationship with his brother, marking the first time that family bonds determined by blood are the focus of any of his novels. Monette ably depicts many of the complexities affecting gay men, especially gay men with AIDS, that result from the heterosexist family unit. Critiques of the family unit as dysfunctional are plenty in this novel, although Monette offers poignant exceptions as well. Some of the novel's best moments focus on the relationship between Tom and his brother's young son, Danny. Danny lacks the homophobic biases that are so ingrained in his parents' view of gay people and AIDS. For Tom, Danny becomes the hope of the future:

> In any event I only wanted one thing for Daniel—that he learn to cry when he lost something, or how would he ever be sure he truly had it, or know what to look for again.
>
> The oldest wish of the race, that the child should have it easier. So: let him not grow up among people who learned too late how to feel. I knew about this, down to the marrow. I looked across into my lover's eyes, flashes of amber in the firelight, knowing it could be stolen at any second, the next time pitching me all the way down, broken on the sand.
>
> Not that I had any regrets for the life that brought me here, not a minute of it. The slightest turn might have diverted me from the perfect balance of our three hearts. At last, to feel everything down to the marrow. If it only lasted a moment more, it had come to me in time. (180)

The tableau of Tom, his lover, and his nephew caught in a moment when Tom's health begins to falter captures Monette's hope that someone will learn from AIDS and the fears and discriminations that surround it. This scene, while uniting what at first seems like an improbable trio, shifts the novel's tone from the antagonistic tension of the brothers to the fully realized reconcilations that find expression by the novel's end. It is here, in the arms of his lover and filled with hope for his young nephew, that Tom recognizes that he is halfway home.

CRITICAL RECEPTION

Not surprisingly, the critical reception of Paul Monette's work reveals more about the reviewing processes of both mainstream and gay publications than it does about the work. His early novels received favorable reviews in gay publications and yet were virtually ignored by mainstream critics. It was not until *Borrowed Time: An AIDS Memoir* that Paul Monette was even reviewed in the *New York Times*. Since then his work has received wide critical attention, including prepublication publicity arriving in the form of interviews, feature articles, and biographical blurbs. Monette has been successful in turning these forms of advance publicity, in part solicited from the extensive book tours that accompany his publications, as forums to educate the uninformed about gay and lesbian issues and AIDS concerns and as opportunities to galvanize and inspire his devoted readers across the country. His recent novels have been widely reviewed in major publications, gay and straight, throughout the country. The reviews of *Afterlife* and *Halfway Home* suggest the complicated responses that his work engenders.

Although critics were nearly unanimous in praising the merits of *Borrowed Time* (it was nominated for a National Book Award), the subsequent novels have met with mixed response. On the one hand, nongay reviewers and mainstream publications tend to universalize many of the gay contents of the novels and thus ignore the specificity of gay male experience Monette so powerfully describes. Many of these reviewers proclaim, for example, that these novels "transcend the label gay novel" suggesting that there may be something inherently negative in such an identification. Critics in gay publications, on the other hand, while for the most part praising the novels, complain that the novels are not realistic enough, suggesting on their part a bias for gay male representations that can be grounded only in the "real" experiences of gay men in contemporary society. Marv Shaw in his review of *Halfway Home* claims, as do others, that "the departures from probability weaken the book" (30) and neglects to notice that the elements of fantasy and melodrama are ironic and add to the reader's overall experience of the novel. Most critics, regardless of their venue or sexual orientation, generally fail to comment on Monette's gift for manipulating such popular forms as romance, melodrama, and irony. In fact, it is often these very aspects that form the basis of their complaint.

Some critics also have noted the class and race biases of Monette's protagonists, who are almost exclusively affluent gay white men. Yet, as I argue elsewhere, the Latino character in *Afterlife* embodies the revolutionary anarchistic impulse many gay men, including men of color, feel is a necessary and legitimate response to AIDS. Dell Espinoza is never judged by any of the other gay characters as the ethnic stereotype that the novel's dominant institutions construct. Instead, Steven, the novel's main character, understands completely Dell's actions. Still, on the other hand, the novel fails to address why Ray Lee, the only person who dies of AIDS, also happens to be a gay man of color. While much could be said of the discriminatory lack of access to health care many people of color with AIDS must confront, Ray's death is never fully accounted for in *Afterlife*. However, it's important to recognize that *Afterlife* and *Halfway Home* are essentially love stories where secondary characters, including women and gay men of color, play a supporting role to the novel's main protagonists.

Some critics, almost exclusively gay writers, astutely realize that Monette's excursions into melodrama and romance form the strength of his novels and that he doesn't attempt to provide a fictional documentary about AIDS, race relations, or the politics of gay and lesbian interactions. One of the best reviews of *Afterlife*, written by John Weir, the author of the popular novel *The Irreversible Decline of Eddie Socket*, recognizes Monette's deliberate manipulation of popular styles and goes so far as to suggest that "this book has the feel of a '40s 'women's picture' " (3). For Weir, *Afterlife* is a "war novel" that "holds your interest not because the beauty of its language, but the urgency, and the immediacy, of the story" (3). While other gay critics ignore the campy invocations of melodrama, Weir notices Monette's ironic depiction of the traditional narrative form. Walta Borawski, writing in *Gay Community News*, offers one of the best reviews of *Halfway Home*. Borawski anticipates "the sardonic reader putting [the novel] down as romance, *China House* with an AIDS sensibility and better cover art" (9), by spending a considerable chunk of the review explaining how significant it is to have a gay novel where the main character is a person with AIDS who finds love *and* sexual pleasure in the height of the epidemic.

Much could be said, as well, of the bias that East Coast literati, both gay and straight, hold against anything written outside of the confines of Manhattan. Gay West Coast writers have traditionally fought a double battle to be taken seriously, because of their queer identities and regional identifications. Anything about Southern California, especially Hollywood, is already marked as either frivolous or a sell-out. Monette has been accused of both throughout his career. In one review, gay novelist David B. Feinberg,* writing in the now-defunct New York publication *Outweek*, charges Monette with both crimes in his bitter assessment of *Afterlife*. After offering the prefatory disclaimer that "*Afterlife* is a necessary book and I'm glad Monette wrote it," Feinberg continues: "yet there's something altogether too slick about Paul Monette's writing: the sheen is too polished, the artificial veneer too smooth. He tries too hard and it shows" (59). Such a nebulous complaint offers little insight into the novel and yet seems minor compared with Feinberg's final blow, where he exonerates himself by glibly offering the following confession: "I admit I have a bias against an author who lists novelizations of *Nosferatu*, *Predator* and other screenplays beneath novels, poems and nonfiction. Maybe *Afterlife* was too Hollywood slick for me" (66). In this one review, Feinberg demonstrates only too well how Monette has been viewed by gay critics with absolutely no sense, let alone appreciation, for his writing. Perhaps it's best to notice then what some other reviewers have said of the novel. Jesse Monteagudo's comments, written away from either New York or Los Angeles biases, suggest what many of Monette's readers believe, when he claims in Miami's gay publication *TWN* that "*Afterlife* is the greatest novel ever written about AIDS" (6). Monteagudo convincingly sums up the achievement of the novel by concluding: "In the end, Monette and his characters seem to agree with Michael Callen (another survivor) that love is all that matters, if only because love is all we have" (6).

It seems inevitable that Paul Monette will be remembered most for *Borrowed Time: An AIDS Memoir*. Yet gay people who invest in reading his extensive body of fiction will no doubt find much to celebrate in his writing. While the early novels now seem slight compared to the AIDS novels, they too are worth reading if mainly for their lively, likable characters. Throughout his career, Monette has offered his many readers enjoyable and highly provocative novels that add to any understanding of what it means to be gay in the years since Stonewall and what it means to endure in light of AIDS. His continuing career as writer, AIDS activist, and spokesperson for gay and lesbian issues positions him as one of our history's greatest heroes. Let the record show as well that, among his many roles, Paul Monette is always, perhaps above all else, an inspiring romantic. "As for me," he reminds us, "I'd still rather be remembered for loving well than writing well" (48).

WORKS BY PAUL MONETTE

Taking Care of Mrs. Carroll. New York: St. Martin's Press, 1978.
The Gold Diggers. New York: Avon Books, 1979; Boston: Alyson Publications, 1988.
The Long Shot. New York: Avon Books, 1981.
No Witnesses: Poems. New York: Avon Books, 1981.
Lightfall. New York: Avon Books, 1982.
Borrowed Time: An AIDS Memoir. New York: Harcourt, Brace, Jovanovich, 1988.
Love Alone: 18 Elegies for Rog. New York: St. Martin's Press, 1988.
Afterlife. New York: Avon Books, 1990.
Halfway Home. New York: Crown Publishers, 1991.
Becoming a Man: Half a Life Story. New York: Harcourt, Brace, Jovanovich, 1992.

SELECTED STUDIES OF PAUL MONETTE

Borawski, Walta. Review of *Halfway Home*. *Gay Community News* 21 April–4 May 1991: 7.
Clum, John M. " 'The Time Before the War': AIDS, Memory, and Desire." *American Literature* 62, no. 2 (1990): 648–67.
Davis, Christopher. Review of *Afterlife*. *Lambda Book Report* 2 no. 3 (1990): 20–21.
Feinberg, David B. Review of *Afterlife*. *Outweek* 4 April 1990: 59.
Kaufman, David. "All in the Family." *The Nation* 1 July 1991: 21–25.
Labonte, Richard. "Fire and Ice." *The Advocate* 13 September 1988: 65–66.
Maggenti, Maria. "No Half Measures." *Outweek* 8 May 1991: 56–58.
Monteagudo, Jesse. Review of *Afterlife*. *TWN* 25 April 1990: 6.
Román, David. "Tropical Fruit?: Latino "Gay" Men in Three Resistance Novels of the Americas." Forthcoming in *Tropicalizations*. Ed. Francis Aparicio and Susana Chávez Silverman. Philadelphia: Temple University Press, 1993.
Shaw, Marv. Review of *Halfway Home*. *Bay Area Reporter* 23 May 1991: 30.
Simpson, Janice C. Review of *Halfway Home*. *Time* 6 May 1991: 72.
Viorst, Judith. Review of *Afterlife*. *New York Times Book Review* 29 April 1990: 7.
Weir, John. Review of *Afterlife*. *Washington Post* 26 April 1990: 3.
Williams, K. Orton. Review of *Halfway Home*. *San Francisco Sentinel* 9 May 1991: 21.

ETHAN MORDDEN (1949–   )

Michael Schwartz

BIOGRAPHY

In "Interview with the Drag Queen," the first story in Ethan Mordden's first collection, the narrator listens to a drag queen's tale of Miss Titania, who ruled over a pre-Stonewall bar. Afterwards, he discovers that the drag queen *was* Miss Titania, who lied in order to tell the truth about herself— something every writer does. The story ends, "God make me as honest a storyteller as the drag queen was." Such "honesty" describes Mordden's own writing, which is autobiographical fiction or fictionalized autobiography. He there tells the important truths about his family and his life as a gay man. The facts in this essay therefore focus on his career as a writer.

Born on January 27, 1949, Mordden grew up in Heavensville, Pennsylvania, a small town near Wilkes-Barre. His father was a building contractor. Mordden was the middle of five boys: brothers figure prominently in his fiction. He attended Friends Academy, in Locust Valley, New York, and then the University in Pennsylvania, where he received a B.A. in history. After college, he went to New York City, to develop as a writer and (less consciously) as a gay man. This move, in 1969, put him in New York right as the Stonewall revolution was beginning and positioned him to become the historian of Stonewall.

In New York, Mordden's first jobs reflected his encyclopedic knowledge of culture, both high and low. He first worked at *TV Guide*, writing plot descriptions for syndicated series, and later was editor of the Romance division at D. C. Comics. From 1974 to 1976, Mordden was an assistant editor at *Opera News*. This was his last "day job." In 1975, his friend and eventual agent Dorothy Pittman introduced him to an editor at Viking Press who was eager to do a book on the Broadway musical. Mordden's extensive knowledge led to an immediate book contract. This was the first of (at last count) fifteen nonfiction books on such topics as opera, theater, film, and jazz—books that are ruthlessly learned and fearlessly opinionated.

Two of these books were published by St. Martin's Press. Pittman had introduced Mordden to Michael Denneny, an editor at St. Martin's who specialized in gay titles. In 1983, Denneny took Mordden to the men behind *Christopher Street*—publisher Charles Ortleb and editor Thomas Steele— thinking that Mordden could write reviews for the magazine. At the initial meeting, Mordden started telling stories about his grandmother, and the other men convinced him that his true subject was autobiographical. The resulting column, "Is There a Book in This?" was a regular *Christopher Street* feature for several years. These first-person pieces were occasionally about his family but more frequently described his friends and acquaintances in gay Manhattan.

A first collection of these pieces, *I've a Feeling We're Not in Kansas Anymore*, appeared in 1985. Two more collections followed: *Buddies* (1986) and *Everybody Loves You* (1988). During this period, Mordden also wrote a novel, *One Last Waltz* (1986). Denneny was the editor on all of these books.

The editor on one of the nonfiction books was Bob Gottlieb of Alfred A. Knopf. When Gottlieb became editor of the *New Yorker*, Mordden's association with him continued, and he has written long, detailed "Critic-at-Large" pieces on *Show Boat*, Judy Garland, and Cole Porter. He has also published fiction in the *New Yorker*, once under the name M. J. Verlaine. In 1991, a collection of stories by "Verlaine," *A Bad Man Is Easy to Find*, was published.

Mordden still lives in New York and is currently at work on *Stonewall*, an epic novel about the evolution of gay culture in America.

MAJOR WORKS AND THEMES

Some gay writers assert their desire to go "beyond the ghetto," to show gay life as one thread in a complete tapestry, and to write books that would not threaten a straight reader. In contrast, Mordden's focus is unapologetically on the ghetto: "A people as chosen as gays are must erect a ghetto not so much for segregation as for concentration: to learn what gay is" (*Buddies*, 41). Mordden means to threaten, and he does it well. Just the word "chosen" leaps beyond gay pride into gay arrogance. With this one sentence, Mordden claims gay life as a valid literary subject, on its own terms, isolated from any straight context.

Mordden has one subject: "what gay is." His characters don't "just happen to be gay." Their gayness is their reason for being. Mordden even uses "gay" as an abstract noun: in the phrase "what gay is," or his assertion that on Fire Island "we find gay stripped to its essentials" (*Kansas*, 105). "Gay" is not an adjective describing one aspect of a noun. Gay is its own state of being, to be lived and analyzed. Specifically, gay is to be found in Manhattan, and most specifically in post-Stonewall Manhattan, because Stonewall is the process of gay coming to know itself. As the historian of Stonewall, Mordden is also the theorist of gay.

The stories center on four gay men. As the historian of Stonewall (not its fiction writer), Mordden presents the stories as autobiographical, and Bud Mordden is the aggressively intrusive narrator of virtually all the tales. (In this essay, "Bud" refers to the narrator, and "Mordden" to the author.) Bud is the writer who observes and analyzes but seldom participates. Bud's best friend is Dennis Savage. (Bud always uses his full name.) Their interaction consists largely of comic insults, but the bickering conveys a shared history and intimate knowledge, as well as an affection so strong it can be expressed only in this indirect, peculiarly masculine, way. In Mordden's Stonewall, friendship—not love, not sex—is the primary bond; and the friendship between Bud and Dennis is always present in the background of these stories, an implicit point of reference for the other Stonewall relationships.

The other two main characters complement Bud and Dennis. Dennis's lover, Little Kiwi, although in his twenties, has a childlike, almost presexual, innocence that justifies his nickname. Little Kiwi is the next generation of gay, the wave of settlers after the Stonewall pioneers. Opposite to Little Kiwi is Carlo, "pure hunk and our set's contact with Stonewall as absolute sex" (*Buddies*, 54). (Mordden has based both Dennis and Carlo on actual friends. Little Kiwi is more purely fictional.)

Obviously, these four characters were chosen for their symbolic value. As the theorist of gay, Mordden makes each character, major or minor, both a sharply observed individual and a representative of a gay type. For example, a story about a hustler ("Three Infatuations," in *Kansas*) also asks, What is a hustler? Mordden's passion for definitions and categories is evident throughout his nonfiction books, which sort their subject—opera sopranos or movie studios—into revealing categories, to see what new definitions emerge. For Mordden, the individual is always emblematic of its type, and identifying the type tells you something essential about the individual. This isn't simpleminded pigeonholing or reductionistic stereotyping. The categories are frequently of Mordden's own devising, and his definitions always arise from original observation: in defining a hustler, Bud offers the unique proposition that "a hustler has no opinions" (67).

Mordden's stories are adventures in taxonomy. The point is often to define a Stonewall type or experience: what is S&M? what is love? and always, what is gay? Sometimes Bud explicitly plays detective, trying to fit a stranger into one of his categories. Yet the drama of these stories—and their honesty—lies in the fact that Bud's categories, though provocative, are finally not definitive. Mordden always includes other voices to answer Bud's dialectics: Dennis's own cranky intellectualizing or Carlo's mellow, street-based feelings. Conversation is central to Mordden's stories, because in it we hear the gay community in the process of understanding itself. In this conversation, no single definition, not even the narrator's, stands as final.

Moreover, in each story, the narrative itself asserts a complexity beyond Bud's categories. Even the two basic categories—straight and gay—lose their sharp boundaries. With his passion for categories, Bud believes that the underlying category, gay itself, must be absolute. Yet Mordden always includes stories about men who are not clearly straight or gay, or who discover they are gay only late in life, or who are completely straight except in their choice of sexual partners. These crossovers, as Mordden calls them, are the most glaring affront to Bud's faith in taxonomy. The crossover keeps Bud humble, by proving that there is more to gay than his own experience can tell him.

An example of Mordden's narrative strategy is "The Straight; or, Field Expedients," in which Bud's friend Alex is having sex with his "straight" neighbor, Joe. The plot is slender, just enough to fuel the debate that is the real point of the story: Is Joe straight or gay? and, more basically, What is gay? When Bud first meets Joe, he thinks, "He didn't *seem* gay, lacking both self-willing sensuality and self-spoofing satire" (*Kansas*, 15). This breathtakingly arrogant generalization is pure Mordden. It offers no diluting qualifier, no concession that this may be true of "some gays" or "some East Coast urban gays." Yet Bud's definition of "gay" does capture a hitherto undefined aspect of gay self-presentation, the way it is at once assertive and ironic. It is brilliant taxonomy.

But it doesn't explain everything. In the end, after everyone has discussed Alex's orientation, the narrative comes to its own conclusion. In the final scene, Joe and Alex are arguing about Joe's refusal to call himself gay; in counterpoint, Bud and Dennis Savage are bickering comically, in what Alex calls "fag vaudeville." The argument is real, but the "fag vaudeville" wins out. Bud instructs Joe to tell Alex to "go fluff his puff." Joe, while crying, does so. Everyone laughs, and Joe is accepted: Bud's final words to him are "Welcome to gay." By mouthing the campy words, Joe symbolically adapts himself to gay style; but his nongay style also forces a redefinition of what gay is. What finally matters is that room is found for the crossover in the accommodating untidiness of Stonewall.

In Mordden's first collection, *I've a Feeling We're Not in Kansas Anymore,* "Interview with the Drag Queen" serves as prologue, describing the writer's mix of truths and lies. It also shows a pre-Stonewall New York, where the gay world is "just queens, johns, trade, and cops" (4). The rest of the stories show how Stonewall has multiplied the categories of gay. Almost every story defines a type. In addition to the Drag Queen and the Straight, there is "The Homogay" (a term Mordden invents for an uneasy blend of sexuality and camp), and "The Case of the Dangerous Man" (a detective story that explores the archetypes of Chatty Cock and Murder Cock). Other stories define the Hustler ("Three Infatuations"), the Rich ("A Christmas Carol"), and the Love Affair (described as "The Shredding of Peter Hawkins"). The book ends with "The Disappearance of Roger Ryder," a gay actor who sells his soul for the power to change his appearance at will. This fable is about the gay freedom to choose among types, and about the reality (or lack of it) conveyed by these types.

Two other stories present gay life under ideal laboratory conditions: on Fire Island. In "The Precarious Ontology of the Buddy System," Bud and Dennis take Little Kiwi on his first trip to the Island, "the place where all men are forms of lovers because they hunger so, the gayest place on earth, all ours" (63). Complementing this erotic vision, "And Eric Said He'd Come" is about non-erotic bonds. Bud strolls about, encountering friends, acquaintances, and men he has seen for years but never spoken to. The stroll adds up to a revivifying of that cliché, "the gay community" (116).

The introduction to Mordden's second collection, *Buddies*, describes an archetypal gay novel, with "its desperate flight from the family, its attempt to reconstruct an existence without any relations but those we choose our-selves" (xi). *Buddies* is about Bud's two families: his biological one and his chosen one. Unlike some gay writers, Mordden is not torn between the two. His biological family inspires neither horror nor nostalgia, only an affec-tionate bemusement. He left this family to find his gay one. Going back would be failure, insanity, or even betrayal.

The first four stories define the biological family that he leaves. "On the Care and Feeding of Parents and Siblings," a humorous childhood recol-lection, is not specifically gay until the end, when Bud visits New York and discovers gay possibilities. His response is unambivalent: "I came home ready to leave it" (15). In contrast, "Hardhats" is about sexual ambivalence and the cost of not leaving the straight world. The hardhats are Bud's ironworker brother Jim and Jim's friend Gene, whose feelings for his "buddy" are painfully erotic. "Confessions of a Theatregoer," about Bud's childhood immersion in Broadway, is also about how the theater nurtures a budding gay self in ways a biological family cannot. In "A Weekend with Straights," Bud shares a Fire Island house with his brother Jim. He ac-knowledges the powerful bond, violent and loving, between the brothers; but in the end the family is merely a subject for his stories and has no further claim on him.

Other stories in *Buddies* also involve family matters. "Kid Stuff" is about a gay man's adolescent sexual relationship with his older straight brother. In "Rope," a man who ties up his sexual partners evokes family memories, of Bud's brother and Carlo's father. In these stories, the familial relationships still haunt the present, charging it with erotic power. Among the nonfamily stories, "I Am the Sleuth" features Bud as the taxonomist/detective, trying to solve another crossover mystery, this one involving a straight actor in gay porn and a street pickup who may be straight and/or a Hawthorne specialist.

As the first stories were about the biological family, the final four affirm the gay family. "Raw Recruits" recalls how Bud, Carlo, and Little Kiwi first arrived in New York and how friendship shaped their lives there. It is also about departures, as Carlo, despondent over the growing AIDS crisis, returns to his biological family, which is the subject of the next story, Carlo's "Three Letters from South Dakota." In Carlo's absence, "The Hottest Man Alive" is about an anti-Carlo, a hunk who, without friends, becomes a hustler and sinks to the bottom of gay Manhattan. Mordden here acknowledges the dark side of gay life, but he thereby affirms the supreme importance of friends. The final story, "Sliding into Home," celebrates two homecomings. The literal homecoming is Carlo's return from South Dakota. The other is that of a crossover—a fraternity "paddle buddy" of Little Kiwi's father—who, after twenty years of marriage, discovers he is gay. The collection ends as this newest "raw recruit" is accepted into the Stonewall family.

The biological family is also the subject of Mordden's novel, *One Last Waltz*, which appeared about six months before *Buddies*. The novel starts with Johnny Keogh, who moves from Dublin to New York, and continues with his three sons: Johnny, a small-time hoodlum; Mike, a builder (who recalls Bud's ironworker brother Jim); and Dennis, the gay son who becomes a successful songwriter. The novel is the complete opposite of the stories. Where the stories are about categorizing and explaining, *One Last Waltz* is, as the prologue says, "a novel without many explanations," more Celtic saga than realistic narrative. The narrator, although intrusive, tends to be lyrical rather than analytical. Causality seems determined by plot parallels to an "ancient" tale of the King of Tara and the Scornful Witch of Fooley. Even the central mystery—how one family can produce such different children—is referred to myth, not psychology.

The novel is about family: its violence—emotional and physical—and its fierce loves and hatreds. But the gay family, so central to Mordden's stories, is missing; and the gay son, Dennis, can choose only between his family and isolation. Even though the novel takes place in contemporary New York, it is as if Stonewall never happened. When Dennis leaves the family, he enters a show business world of flash and shallowness, a world without friends. To be redeemed from this enchantment, he must reconcile with Mike, the builder brother whose values offer the only solidity in the novel. The final scene finds Dennis in the garage of his brother's Long Island home, thinking about his mother. It is the inverse of the "homecomings" that end *Buddies*. It is as if Mordden excludes the Stonewall option to compel himself to focus exclusively on the biological family, and to confront the forces that, in his stories, are part of a safely distant past.

Toward the end of his third collection, *Everybody Loves You*, Mordden announces that this is "I am very nearly positive, [the] final volume of tales on my New York adventures" (302–3). Two of the stories first appeared in the *New Yorker* and, though not explicitly gay in content, become so in context. "I Read My Nephew Stories," about Bud's vacation with his brother's family, is an outsider's look into the tense dynamics of the nuclear family. "The Complete Death of the Clown Dog," about growing up in a small West Virginia town, is about being different and therefore about being gay. The other stories are specifically gay. In "The Boffer," Dennis goes to his college reunion with Bud and Little Kiwi—best friend and lover, the gay nuclear family—and confronts the lies of his "straight" past. "The Ghost of Champ McQuest" is about ghosts that must be exorcised: most literally the ghost of a dead gay man, but also the dark side of the gay past that killed him.

The collection ends with five stories that provide a sense of valediction to the world Mordden has created in these three volumes. Four connected stories concern Cosgrove, a "Littler Kiwi" whom Little Kiwi adopts. These stories, as one title puts it, are about finding "The Right Boy for Cosgrove"—symbolically, finding a place for Cosgrove in the Stonewall family. Since there is a Littler Kiwi, then time has passed and things are changing in Stonewall. Bud and Dennis reflect on their passing youth. Dennis in particular fears losing Little Kiwi. AIDS is making its presence felt. Some adjustments must be made. Little Kiwi grows up into his real name, Virgil, and he even gets the chance to be on top: such details matter. On the final page, Bud asserts the continuity of the gay family: "I am determined that my family find a place for the elf child, because I have not forgotten how lonely it felt to be one myself, when I was very young and didn't know the way to Stonewall City" (308).

The sequence of Cosgrove stories is interrupted by "The Dinner Party," which is Mordden's AIDS story. It takes place, of course, on Fire Island, among four men whose interrelationships—sex, love, and especially friendship—become emblematic of the Stonewall achievement that has been Mordden's one subject: "I've been trying to tell you something else in story after story; is it taking? I've been trying to tell you that a man-to-man system that doesn't fear sex creates the ultimate in man-to-man friendships" (220). Of the four men, Cliff in particular embodies everything that Mordden has admired: he is unapologetically sexual, relentlessly intellectual, chauvinistically progay, and a genius at friendship. Through Cliff, Mordden re-creates in microcosm the world that his stories have chronicled over the years. In describing this world one more time, Mordden editorializes, eloquently and vehemently, on how much it means to him and to all gay men. And then he shatters the world, with one more diagnosis. Other stories about AIDS lament the loss of an individual—a lover or a friend. Mordden, because he has always found the universal in the particular, can make us see the loss of an individual as the loss of an entire dream. "It was," the story concludes, "like the end of the world."

CRITICAL RECEPTION

The critical response to Mordden's fiction often seems based on who feels included in Mordden's Stonewall and who feels left out. One gay reviewer, who defines a good gay book as one you could give to a straight reader (a definition that is anathema to Mordden), singles out "the unspeakable *I've a Feeling We're Not in Kansas Anymore*" because of its emphasis on Fire Island: "What are the rest of us supposed to read?" ("Zeitgeist or Poltergeist?," 8). Similarly, a reviewer for the West Coast *Advocate* can find things to praise in *Everybody Loves You*, yet only after saying, "Sometimes, Ethan Mordden is just too New York for words, but he goes on writing anyway" (70).

In contrast, unqualified praise comes from Michael Bronski—like Mordden, a cultured East Coast, ghetto-dwelling Stonewall veteran. Bronski's praise is precise and literate: Mordden is "a witty social commentator: like a miniaturist Dickens or Trollope, a Sheridan rather than a Wilde, he can capture, pin down and dissect gay male conventions and mores, exposing not only their foolishness but their emotional necessity." Bronski calls Mordden's brand of storytelling "not only important but absolutely vital" ("Buddy Stories," B1, B8).

The straight press will obviously feel left out, because Mordden insists on the validity of strictly gay themes, a subject the *Boston Globe* finds distasteful: "Mordden has the capacity to write affectingly, a capacity he perversely suppresses. His characters have no identity beyond their sexual identity, no interest beyond their sex lives and those of their friends. . . . By accentuating the lurid, Mordden ensures second class citizenship for his work" (B11). Significantly, the same reviewer later calls *One Last Waltz* a "small and rather fine coup" (A13), probably because the novel isn't as gay as the stories. In fact, many straight press reviews of *One Last Waltz* manage to describe the plot without mentioning the gay element at all.

The straight press can also diminish Mordden's comic achievement by insisting on the sadness of his stories: gay life is an acceptable subject if it is tragic, or at least unpleasant. The *New York Times* reviewer of *Buddies* professes "considerable admiration" for the collection, but seems to have read the wrong book. He says "the most powerful piece . . . draws a striking parallel between the sheerly human needs of two lonely men—one a straight hard hat, the other a homosexual" (18). This apparently refers to "Hardhats," in which a straight ironworker suffers intense homoerotic feelings. But there is no lonely homosexual in it, unless the *New York Times* believes that all homosexuals are inherently lonely.

Mordden has written his own scathing review of reviewers, first denouncing straight critics who ignore or savage gay books: "A bad review of a good gay book is a political act, an oppression" ("Gay Writers and Their Critics," 38). But he also attacks gay reviewers for the sins of jealousy, illiteracy, and politics. More recently, in an interview with his protégé Joey Manley, Mordden responds to Manley's concern that he might not be writing what gay critics want: "They have no business wanting anything. It's the authors of the fiction who decide what that fiction shall be. We are the lit" (13).

WORKS BY ETHAN MORDDEN

I've a Feeling We're Not in Kansas Anymore: Tales from Gay Manhattan. New York: St. Martin's Press, 1985.
Buddies. New York: St. Martin's Press, 1986.
"Gay Writers and Their Critics: Do Bad Reviews Hurt Our Culture?" *The Advocate* 447 (May 27, 1986): 38–39, 127–29.
One Last Waltz. New York: St. Martin's Press, 1986.
Everybody Loves You. New York: St. Martin's Press, 1988.
"Southern Boy Makes Good: Ethan Mordden/Joey Manley Interview." *Lambda Book Report* November/December 1991:12–13.

SELECTED STUDIES OF ETHAN MORDDEN

Bronski, Michael. "Buddy Stories Your Buddy Never Told You." *Gay Community News* 21 December 1986: B1, B8.
Heller, Amanda. Review of *I've a Feeling We're Not in Kansas Anymore*. *Boston Globe* 29 September 1985: B11.
———. Review of *One Last Waltz*. *Boston Globe* 27 July 1986: A13.
Maves, Carl. "Third Time Out." *The Advocate* 514 (December 20, 1988): 70–72.
Olshan, Joseph. Review of *Buddies*. *New York Times Book Review* 11 January 1987: 18.
Witomski, T. R. "Zeitgeist or Poltergeist? Why Gay Books Are So Bad." *Gay Community News* 2 February 1987: 8–9.

MICHAEL NAVA (1954–   )
George Klawitter

BIOGRAPHY

Michael Nava was born in 1954 in Stockton, California, a third-generation Mexican American and the second oldest of six children. His great-grandparents had fled the Mexican Revolution, become migrant workers, and settled in the Sacramento valley. Nava grew up in Sacramento, attended Norte del Rio High School, where he was captain of the debate team, school president, and valedictorian. He has described himself as a compulsive overachiever. After taking a degree in history at Colorado College in Colorado Springs, he was awarded a fellowship to study the Latin American poetry of Ruben Dario. For this project he spent a year in Buenes Aires. His translations of several Dario poems were published by the University of California at Irvine. Back in the United States, Nava applied to law schools at both Harvard and Stanford. He took a law degree from Stanford, where he wrote his first novel while studying for the bar exams and working the night shift in a jail. First employed in the office of the City Attorney of Los Angeles, Nava left public service after three years to work for a private law firm. Presently he is employed by an appellate-court judge in Los Angeles as a research attorney.

Although Nava has been writing since the age of fourteen, the age at which he was first aware of being gay, he did not publish until 1980, the year *Blueboy* printed one of his short stories. It was his first and final publication in the gay glossies. He attributes much of his interest in writing mystery fiction to Joseph Hansen,*a gay mystery writer Nava began reading in the 1970s. The other writer he admires is Ross MacDonald. Although Nava has published verse, his last poems appeared in *LA Poetry* (1983); his critical energies have since been spent on writing gay mystery novels.

In the early 1990s his popularity as a public reader of his fiction accelerated. Nava was awarded two literary awards by *Lambda Rising* for the novel *Goldenboy*, one for best gay mystery of the year. His novel *How Town* also won a Lambda award for best gay mystery of 1990. He has edited a collection of mystery short stories for Alyson Press, a collection that includes one of his own pieces of short fiction, "Street People."

MAJOR WORKS AND THEMES

Although *The Little Death*, Nava's first novel, is a mystery, it does not read as a mystery for the first fifty pages. The setting up of characters and scene early in the novel is gentle, lacking the anxious suspense that characterizes whodunits. In this way, Nava interests his readers in characterization, particularly that of his narrator Henry Rios, before they become distracted by suspicious events. When Aaron Gold, the narrator's lawyer friend, indicates that he knows more than he is telling, readers can begin to feel the tone tighten and the momentum move from where and how to why and who. Interestingly, the delayed action does not impede the flow of the early pages: readers are involved with Rios's personal identity crisis with the law and sense only later that the burned-out lawyer theme is essential to get Rios unemployed in order to pursue a murder full-time.

The narrator is, perhaps, an extension of Michael Nava, a lawyer himself: both are Hispanic, both work in California, both are gay. The novel is filled with law jargon, some of it intricately complicated, all of it, however, necessary to support the apparatus of the crimes involved and the final lawsuit designed to bring the evil rich to justice. At one point, the dead man's mother tells Rios, "I cannot follow you when you start quoting the law at me." Nava takes great pains to phrase the law in terms simple enough for the ordinary reader to understand. Although Rios is the main character, he undergoes little change in the novel and is thus not as well fleshed out as other characters, particularly Hugh Paris and Aaron Gold. Because he is the narrator, Rios never describes himself, and readers get only oblique ideas of his looks. Because Rios is the author, readers get few objective evaluations of his personality. We sense, however, he is hard-working, sensitive, intensely committed to justice. The character in the novel who changes most is Aaron Gold: we see both his good and bad sides.

The Little Death is particularly good in short interview scenes. Nava is able to bring minor characters into sharp focus with a few pages of writing. For example, Rios's first interview with Katherine Paris is vivid, her character upstaging the narrator's as he fumbles to get information on her son (his lover).

The gay love theme that permeates this novel is tempered at every turn with a theme of justice. Without the love between Rios and Hugh Paris, there would be no motivation; and without Rios's passion for justice, there would be no denouement. If Hugh were not gay, he would not have met

Rios, and Rios, of course, would not have been brought into the Paris family crisis at all. Once involved, Rios lets his sense of justice take over, and the second half of the novel rides on the justice theme rather than the gay love theme.

Nava's style in his first novel is tight and energetic. At times the poet in him shines through. He remarks on "the hole where my heart had been" and notices "a pot of yellow chrysanthemums blazed on a coffee-table." Such close attention to words makes many of the scenes visually alive. Nava's rhetorical structures are unobtrusive, although occasionally they stand out. In describing the Paris family money, Nava wields parallel structure in three paragraphs, one beginning "Famous money," a second, "Corrupt money," the third, "Endless money." The title of the novel is vaguely poetic, the French term for orgasm (*la petite mort*). Its significance for the novel as a whole is not clear.

Nava's second novel, *Goldenboy*, appeared two years after his first and features the same narrator as *The Little Death*; he is still a lawyer and still gay, but now beyond his burnout and resurrected from two years of alcohol addiction. Henry Rios is still bright and brash (he does not mind stepping on wealthy or homophobic toes), and he still retains a touch of the self-effacement that made him so endearingly vulnerable in *The Little Death*. He finds himself aging, distrusts his appeal, but nonetheless attracts a young lover who does not die on him this time.

The title *Goldenboy* refers to two characters: one a teen who dies before the novel begins and the other an obnoxious chicken-hawk who does not die soon enough. The novel itself splits into two distinct sections because the boy we think is going to be the hero, Jim Pears, vacates the novel by page eighty. Only the drive in Henry Rios to vindicate Jim keeps the latter an enduring force in the novel. With Jim's exit, the story's energy shifts even more to the narrator, who becomes the nemesis for the many villains.

The gay atmosphere that was almost incidental in *The Little Death* becomes paramount in *Goldenboy*. Without the gay theme, there would be no story. It motivates all major activities in the novel and becomes the excuse for standard episodes of coming out to one's parents, dealing with a homophobic psychiatrist, and struggling with age difference in gay relationships. The justice theme is strong in *Goldenboy*, but it shares the élan of the novel with the gay theme; and in this novel we feel immersed in the gay subculture of California with an intensity that Nava's first novel did not need or exploit. It seems as if Nava were first testing his talent as a novelist in his first book and then flexing his talent as a gay novelist in the second. It is, of course, wonderful that the same narrator controls both stories, even though there is little change in him. As Henry Rios is Michael Nava, we expect the kind of consistency that a character identified with a real person would demonstrate.

Nava's successful delineation of a woman character (Katherine Paris) in

The Little Death is matched by that of an equally successful woman character (Irene Gentry) in *Goldenboy*, but the latter convinces even more than the former because she surprises us more frequently. Once we apprehend Katherine, we have her, but Irene changes significantly throughout her novel. Her initial description is also more elaborate than Katherine's: Nava is clearly goddess-struck with the Irene character and thus works harder to move her out of stereotype and into personality.

Nava's second novel, unlike his first, is obviously a mystery from the first pages: We are swept into Rios's tension with the first phone call he receives inviting him to handle the defense of a gay teen. *Goldenboy* uses detective-fiction strategy to unravel the who more than any other aspect of the Brian Fox murder. We are never so much interested in why or how as we are in who, probably because everyone in the novel is convinced Jim Pears is the murderer. Such mass conviction invites any reader to challenge the accepted obvious. The suspicion, of course, pays off.

Goldenboy is a more satisfying gay novel than *The Little Death* because of its more obvious gay milieu and gay love scenes. As sentimental as it may be, Henry Rios's fulfillment in love is a plus for his second novel. Although *The Little Death* narrator is interesting, the psychosexual stability of the maturer narrator in *Goldenboy* affords readers an opportunity to focus on solving the crime without the distraction of wondering when and if Rios is going to get his love act together. An added gay angle comes into this novel with the framing appearances of Rios's friend Larry Ross, who is dying of AIDS. He opens the novel by getting Rios involved in the Pears case, and he exits from the novel by flying to Paris for AIDS treatments.

How Town, Nava's third novel, finds Henry Rios settled down with the young lover he found in the previous novel. The lover is HIV-positive, and his subplot gives to this novel its primary gay theme because the main plot concerns not a gay man but a heterosexual pedophile. Outside of occasional appearances by the gay lover, primarily at the beginning and end of the novel, the only gay-related material in *How Town* is the homophobic comments that Rios has to parry from cops, teenagers, and the accused man himself. For *How Town* the gay issue is secondary but always there, running beneath the thread of the plot. The reader is, of course, always conscious that Rios is gay because his private life not only enters the novel through the character of his lover but also becomes the topic of various conversations with Mark, Henry's best pal back in high school, and with Ben, a cop on the case. Both men are foils to Henry's stable sexuality because the pal has been through a failed marriage and is now on his way to alcoholism (compounded by bankruptcy and jail). The cop was sexually molested as a teenager and now does not know where his sexuality lies: he calls Henry a queer, but he himself gets an erection when he sees Henry with the young lover in a hotel room. Clearly, the best relationships in *How Town* are

Henry's and the straight marriage of his *Little Death* cop partner, Terry Ormes.

A new twist on gay love surfaces in *How Town*: there is a lesbian relationship, but its evolution is anything but pleasant, either to Henry or to the reader. We suspect its presence early in the novel by way of hints that Nava drops, but its revelation is very late; and when it does blossom, one of the lesbians is coldly mechanical, the other downright nasty. Its use in the novel is peripheral, most of its energy used to round out a corner of Henry's background that we did not get in the earlier novels.

As Nava continues to spin his Henry Rios novels, he can draw on a host of minor characters to fade in and out of his writing. Already mentioned, Terry Ormes is a stereotype of the good woman cop who will go behind her bosses to help Henry solve his mysteries. Freeman Vidor, a private investigator who appears first in *Goldenboy*, is a more-rounded minor character. Black, straight, and given to unexpected comments, he adds a comic touch to the novels that is much needed, given Henry's bone sober and sometimes brutal seriousness. Grant Hancock, Henry's rich friend from law school days, has purpose in *The Little Death*, but his brief appearance in *Goldenboy* deadends. He does not resurface in *How Town*.

CRITICAL RECEPTION

Reactions to Michael Nava's fiction have been positive. Clair Peterson has praised him for writing with "a gut-level integrity that may heighten reality but never overlooks it"(61). Such fundamentally strong talent has led members of the American Booksellers to tell Nava how much they liked *Goldenboy* "even if it wasn't appropriate as stock in their stores" (Peterson, 61). The *Booklist* notes that Henry Rios is a complex and vital character, an opinion shared by many critics including Victor Zonana, who sees Rios as "a kinder, gentler Philip Marlowe, the perfect mystery protagonist for the multicultural and multiracial Los Angeles of the 90's" (8). What undoubtedly endears Rios to many readers is his believable human frailty. Julie Reynolds describes him as having "circumnavigated the emotional block often enough" (69). The finest praise comes from Larry Romans, who believes that "Henry Rios has become a better realized character than David Brandstetter" (14). As Nava idolizes Joseph Hansen's Brandstetter, to surpass his master is achievement of the highest order. Nava's minor characters too have earned critical praise. Gillespie comments on Nava's ability to engage readers "in each of the characters, including the unpleasant ones" (10).

Nava's plots have caught readers from the very first novel. Zonana singles plot out as one of the characteristics that initially won Nava a solid following when *The Little Death* was published. By the time his third novel appeared, critics noticed how neatly "puzzle pieces fall into place without too much fuss" (Nolan, A11) and how expertly Nava handles courtroom scenes. John Preston enjoys the culmination of plot in the ending of *How Town*, "one of the best gay-themed detective novels yet written" (63). For Preston, the ending "is not a trick played on the reader but a genuine surprise" (63). In fact, Nava had to do some fancy stylistic dancing to end life for one of the *How Town* villains far removed from the eyes of the "I" narrator Henry Rios, who has to be present, one way or another, for every scene readers experience.

Beyond plot, Nava has impressed critics with his sensitivity to the human condition. Zonana notes that while Nava sticks close to mystery conventions, his novels are "set apart by their insight, compassion and sense of social justice"(E1). Nava admits he chose a theme for *How Town* (pedophilia) before he began writing the novel and deliberately set out to distance gay men from child molesters, a linkage all too often made by homophobic minds. His intention has not escaped critics like Larry Romans who sees it as basic to revealing "a complicated person that we want to know better" (14). As a lawyer, Nava is uniquely knowledgeable among gay fiction writers to tackle the finer points of the law and weave them into mysteries that depend to a large degree on Rios's ability to understand and manipulate legal minutiae.

Although Nava denies he is Rios, readers cannot help but note the similarities: Hispanic origin, law degree, gay life-style, and, as Zonana notes, recovering alcoholic. Nava may protest to interviewers that he is a very private person, but his character is laid before the reader every time Henry Rios opens his mouth or has a thought. Nava concedes that *The Little Death* had much of himself in it, but he contends that *Goldenboy* has less "because Henry Rios has become a real character and has taken on a life of his own" (Hopbell, 8). Nava, however, will have difficulty explaining to his fans that the character is not autobiographical: Any image they conceive of Henry Rios is filtered through the Nava photograph on the book jacket.

WORKS BY MICHAEL NAVA

The Little Death. Boston: Alyson Publications, 1986.
Goldenboy. Boston: Alyson Publications, 1988.
Finale. Boston: Alyson Publications, 1989.
How Town. New York: Harper and Row, 1990.

SELECTED STUDIES OF MICHAEL NAVA

Review of *How Town*. *Booklist* 15 April 1990:1611.
Gillespie, Noel. "*How Town*: The Best Yet from Mystery Writer Michael Nava." *The Washington Blade* 11 January 1991:29.

Hopbell, Ph. "Lawyer's Moonlighting a Mystery," *Lambda Rising* 1, no. 5 (1987): 1, 8.

Nolan, Tom. Review of *How Town. Wall Street Journal* 11 May 1990: A 11.

Peterson, Clair. "Enter Goldenboy." *The Advocate* 10 October 1988: 60, 61.

Preston, John. Review of *How Town, Outweek* 1 August 1990: 63.

Reynolds, Julie E. Review of *How Town. Los Angeles Daily Journal* 30 May 1990: 7.

Romans, Larry. "Whodunit?" *Dare* 19 October 1990: 9, 14.

Smalling, Allen. "The Mysteries of Writer Michael Nava." *Outlines* June 1990: 35.

Zonana, Victor F. "Poetic Justice," *Los Angeles Times* 6 May 1990: E1, E13.

FELICE PICANO (1944–   )
Will Meyerhofer

BIOGRAPHY

Felice Picano's life can be characterized from early on as a profound ques-
tioning, if not an active rejection, of the status quo. "I'd already been a
fornicator and petty criminal at eleven years old, a drug addict and homosexual at twelve, a seducer, a sexual exhibitionist and a successful purv-
eyor of pornography by thirteen" (180), he writes in *Ambidextrous: The
Secret Lives of Children*, the first volume of his memoirs. The setting for
all this alleged childhood depravity was a middle-class neighborhood in
eastern Queens during the sleepy complacency of the "Eisenhower-placid
'Fifties." The realization at a young age that a Big Lie—composed of intolerance, censorship, denial, and exploitation—lay at the core of the quin-
tessentially "normal" suburban world where he grew up leads the author
to a vital conclusion on the book's closing page: "I always tried to keep to
and tell the truth, to point it out, to defend it as I had experienced it, knew
it, even when all around me didn't want to acknowledge it, denied it for
reasons of policy or business."

As a student activist at Queens College (CUNY) in the early 1960s Picano
took part in sit-ins supporting racial integration. He went on to become a
social worker in East Harlem for two years before leaving for Europe, as
he writes in *Men Who Loved Me*, the second volume of his memoirs, "to
break all ties with the past—and to become homosexual" (22). After a year,
and a romance in Italy, he returned to New York in 1967, worked at a
variety of jobs, experimented with psychedelic drugs, and became a gay-
rights activist. His first published novel, the psychological thriller *Smart as
the Devil*, came out in 1975. It sold well, was selected by the Mystery Guild
Book Club, and was a finalist for the Ernest Hemingway Award for best
first novel. Neither *Smart as the Devil* nor the two novels that followed it,

Eyes (1976) and *The Mesmerist* (1977), were gay novels, although *Eyes* did feature minor gay characters. Picano was writing and publishing gay short fiction and poetry, but it was not until 1979 that he published a gay novel: "I was leading a double life—at least in publication" (*Contemporary Authors Autobiography Series (CAAS)*, 226). Despite dire predictions from advisors within the publishing industry, Picano "came out" literarily with *The Lure*, a violent, fast-paced thriller based upon a series of unsolved murders of gay men in New York City during the 1970s. Like the author's previous works, *The Lure* quickly became a best-seller, as well as "my most controversial [novel], and until recently the best known" (ibid., 229).

Picano had founded his own publishing house, the SeaHorse Press, in 1977. In creating one of the first gay houses in New York City, the author had a mission: "I'd begin my own publishing house and publish *nothing* but the work of gays. I'd hire, utilize, and work only with gays—artists, type-setters, printers, binders, distributors. I'd stock my books in lesbian/gay-owned bookstores ... [It] would be called the SeaHorse Press—after the marine species in which the male bears and gives birth ... " (ibid., 228). SeaHorse went on to publish the first-ever volume of gay history, Martin Duberman's *About Time: Exploring the Gay Past*, and the first anthology of lesbian and gay writing, *A True Likeness*, as well as works by Doric Wilson, Alan Bowne, Robert Peters, Gavin Dillard, Dennis Cooper,* and Brad Gooch. Picano also utilized this outlet for two of his works: a collection of poems, *The Deformity Lover* (1978), and a novella, *An Asian Minor* (1981). The author later collaborated with two other small gay presses under a new imprint, Gay Presses of New York (GPNY). By 1985, GPNY's combined catalogue showed seventy-five gay and lesbian titles in print, including Harvey Fierstein's acclaimed *Torch Song Trilogy*, Picano's short-story collection, *Slashed to Ribbons in Defense of Love* (178), and his first volume of memoirs, *Ambidextrous* (1985).

Between 1979 and 1981, Picano met with other influential gay authors with whom he was friendly, including Robert Ferro,* Andrew Holleran,* Edmund White,* and George Whitmore,* to react to and discuss works-in-process. This informal group, the first composed entirely of openly gay writers, came to be called the Violet Quill Club: "Separately and together, we were the first 'gay' authors the world had ever seen. ... we went around the country publicizing our books as gay authors. Nobody had done that before us, not Capote nor Tennessee Williams nor Gore Vidal*" (interview, October 8, 1981). The club's members went on to produce much of the best gay fiction of the period.

The 1980s brought stylistic experimentation from Picano: a novel, *Late in the Season* (1981), a novella, *An Asian Minor: The True Story of Ganymede* (1981), a short-story collection, *Slashed to Ribbons in Defense of Love* (1982), and two volumes of memoirs, *Ambidextrous* (1985) and *Men Who Loved Me* (1989). In addition to these gay works, he wrote two straight, more "commercial" novels, *House of Cards* (1984) and *To the Seventh Power* (1989), which hailed back to his best-sellers. Returning to an earlier style seemed only to further spur the author's eagerness to branch out into new forms and genres. In 1986 he tried playwrighting for the first time, adapting *An Asian Minor* for the off-Broadway stage under the title *Immortal!* That summer his one-act play, *One O'Clock Jump*, was also produced off-Broadway, and he adapted his novel *Eyes* for film with director Frank Perry.

AIDS has taken a terrible toll of Felice Picano's friends, colleagues, and acquaintances. The author remains committed to his craft despite the loss of so many peers: "As those few friends left to me continue to sicken and suffer and die, I often wonder if that's the reason I lived through those times, knew those people, suffered those losses, became a writer . . . so that eventually I might bear witness to that era, those people, this great loss, and make it literature." He continues to explore, experiment, and challenge readers, and to produce new work. He is coauthoring a complete revision of the classic *Joy of Gay Sex* with Dr. Charles Silverstein, has completed a marvelous, as-yet-unpublished gay science-fiction epic, *Dryland's End*, and begun a new volume of memoirs (interview, October 7, 1991). Still very much an activist, Picano recently helped found and develop the Publishing Triangle, a national organization of gay writers, publishers, and booksellers.

MAJOR WORKS AND THEMES

With nine published novels to his credit, as well as volumes of poetry, plays, short stories, a screenplay, and many essays and reviews, Felice Picano is a prolific and diverse author. He is also an avid experimenter, creating at one time or another works of historical fiction, mystery, horror, comedy, and science fiction. There is, too, a sort of schizophrenia to his career, as he has been the author of both best-selling "commercial" thrillers—with the important exception of *The Lure*, all straight—as well as openly gay, often experimental, "literary" efforts directed at a more specific audience.

The constants amid this experimentation are twofold: Picano gravitates toward controversial topics, presenting characters with unconventional lifestyles, living arrangements, and manners of dress and style, and examining the reaction of the surrounding society to their nonconformity; he is also fascinated by mind control, direct or as the effect of unconscious outside influences upon one's ideas, beliefs, and perceptions. These common themes appear throughout his work, including his first three novels. In *Smart as the Devil* (1975), a brilliant, possibly deranged boy, Nicolas De Luca, controls the lives of those around him, including his psychologist, Dr. Peter Mazur, by convincing them that he is either schizophrenic or possessed by a malicious spirit. An unconventional living situation appears as a plot element when Mazur, hired to treat Nicolas, finds himself falling in love with the boy's unhappily married mother. In Picano's second novel, *Eyes* (1976), a woman voyeur, Johanna Poole, controls the relationship with the man she loves by observing him in his apartment via binoculars and making disguised telephone calls to him under a false identity. Ultimately, Johanna is attempting to control her troubled relationship to all men through these unconventional means. In *The Mesmerist*, Picano deals with mind control directly, fictionalizing a true event in which a dentist arrived in a Midwestern town at the turn of the century and through hypnosis took control of its prominent citizens' lives. An unconventional life-style is presented in the widow, Carrie Lane. The great lady of the town, she is reduced to a social outcast when forced to admit in open court that she is addicted to morphine and has committed adultery under hypnosis.

In terms of style and content, Picano's first gay novel, *The Lure* (1979), serves as a linchpin in his career, linking his first three commercial novels and the openly gay stylistic experimentation that emerged through SeaHorse Press and the Violet Quill Club. Like Picano's earlier work, the novel is a tightly plotted thriller, involves criminal behavior and occasionally very violent scenes, and asks the reader to suspend disbelief, for example, to accept that a corrupt psychiatrist and police investigator would use psychiatric methods to control the mind of the protagonist, predicting his behavior and "programming" him into a murder weapon. Unlike the earlier novels, *The Lure* is set entirely in a realistically portrayed gay milieu, through the point of view of a character who is slowly transformed to a gay sensibility; and it carries the resounding political message that gays must organize and work together against opposing forces, both legitimate and criminal.

The Lure is a novel of revelation. The ostensibly heterosexual central character, Noel Cummings, is cycling past a warehouse on the abandoned West Side Highway when he hears a scream and realizes he has interrupted a murder in progress. Hurrying for help, he encounters "Whisper," a secret investigative branch of the New York Police Department, whose chief agent, Loomis, eventually recruits Noel to work undercover in the gay bar scene. His mission is to identify and capture "Mr. X," the gay man believed responsible for this and other murders. Noel is to use his position as a professor of sociology as a cover, simultaneously conducting research for a book on the gay life-style. By the novel's conclusion, Noel realizes the whole situation was a set-up: "Whisper" and Loomis are corrupt, in league with the Mafia to destroy Eric Redfern, an educated, openly gay businessman who is attempting to organize a gay political group. Moreover, Noel ultimately comes to terms with his own long-repressed desires and falls in love with Eric, the very man Loomis enlisted him to destroy.

Once again in *The Lure*, Picano explores favorite themes. The controversial life-style is the explosively liberated 1970s world of New York City's gay bars, clubs, and promiscuous sex. The author's honest depiction of this "seamier" side of gay life brought much criticism: "A lot of people put it [*The Lure*] down because of the area of gay life I chose to illustrate. Hell, I wrote a thriller; I purposely didn't show the happy gay couple at home because of the nature of my novel. I gave the reader a world that was realistic" (interview, *Gay Life*, vol. 5, no. 33, February 1, 1980, 12). Notable in Picano's depiction of the bar and disco scene in *The Lure* is his refusal to be judgmental. Rather than laden his presentation with disapproval, pity, or undue exaggeration, he fairly and evenly describes what he has seen, presenting a realistic, if heightened, version of a gay reality and allowing the reader, like Noel, to decide whether he likes it or not.

Picano's second major theme is presented as a plot element in *The Lure* as Loomis uses psychiatric methods to control Noel's mind and emotions, counting on the young man's disgust, fear, and homophobia. But the issue takes on greater resonance when these methods are recognized as a metaphor for the pervasive mind control by which contemporary Western society attempts to convince the homosexual he is an isolated freak, diseased, unwell, doomed to unhappiness unless he conforms. Noel's realization that he is being controlled by Loomis parallels the realization that he has been societally programmed to reject the sexual attraction toward other men he has felt all his life: "Eric hugged Noel closer, and Noel reached an arm around Eric's waist as they descended the short flight of steps onto the street. Noel felt as though after a journey of almost twenty years' duration— destination unknown—he was finally finding his way. Still uncertain as he was of that destination, he was at least certain it coincided with Eric's" (438).

The Lure is a culmination, Picano's thriller masterpiece, one with a twist that pushes the genre to new limits by opening it for the first time to a gay reality and a gay sensibility realistically portrayed. It remains the finest existing example of the gay thriller, a classic.

With his next, fifth novel, Picano chose an entirely different tack: "*Late in the Season* was published by Delacorte, although with a tenth of the attention given *The Lure*—because it was a 'smaller' book. It was in fact something new: an 'idyll,' a love story . . . a series of prose poems: aquarelles even" (CAAS-ibid., 232). From the opening chapter, it's clear that the author of best-selling thrillers was experimenting with prose style: "the morning felt so clear and sunny, so absolutely cloudless he felt he might strike it with the little glass pestle in the dining room bowl, and the day would ring back echoing crystal like a gamelan orchestra" (3–4). Picano explains: "I was tired of writing the tightly plotted 'perfect' novel. I wanted to reach out, experiment with my style, try a new form" (interview, October 7, 1991).

In addition to a new, more richly descriptive style, *Late in the Season* is different from Picano's previous books in that its plot is a model of simplicity. Centering on a brief, two-week affair between a gay man, Jonathan, and a college-age girl, Stevie, while Jonathan's lover Daniel is away on business, the book contains no violence beyond a splinter lodging in someone's foot—in fact, at the book's conclusion Jonathan and Daniel end up reunited. The novel is written through the alternating points of view of Jonathan and Stevie, further adding a sense of intimacy; and Picano takes his time, savoring each word, often pausing to dwell pensively on a particular detail in the landscape or to present a stream of consciousness as a character muses in silence.

Late in the Season, as its title suggests, is about periods of change in life. For Stevie, it's the coming of maturity, and her first taste of adult love; for Jonathan, it's the arrival of middle age and the realization that his relationship with Daniel may be evolving into a lifelong commitment. As one season in each of their lives fades into another, Jonathan's and Stevie's short-lived affair proves to be only a shared rite of passage. Picano once again depicts a controversial relationship, that of a gay man who finds himself sexually attracted to a woman, which was bound to stir up controversy in a hypersensitive gay community. Picano admits he could easily have drawn the character of Stevie as a young man, a fact he telegraphs through her name. He chose the more complicated relationship to stretch the definition of what a gay novel could be: "I did it to cause trouble, I admit it, but I also thought that it introduced the possibility for a much larger conflict because it would be a social conflict, a real alteration in his [Jonathan's] life, as well as a personal alteration." (interview, October 7, 1991). *Late in the Season* remains a stylistically rich, emotionally accurate account of two lives meeting in crisis.

Picano published another book that year, an unusual short novella, beautifully illustrated with erotic drawings by David Martin. *An Asian Minor: The True Story of Ganymede* retells, as its campy title suggests, the classic Greek myth of Ganymede, much expanded from Ovid's few lines and with a very modern, post–gay-liberation twist. At times the book gets quite silly. In the last scene, Zeus comes to seduce Ganymede as a bolt of lightening, and the young Trojan isn't buying any: " 'What happens when I come to you?' I asked, and answered myself. 'I become barbecued boy, right? Well, forget it' " (113)! In other places, the prose becomes reminiscent of older translations of the myth, only to revert to a jarring modernism, with humorous results: "So I was shunted off to a lesser man, a corporal named Leonides. But even though he had a reputation for being the cruelest of taskmasters in the great allied army of Trojans, Phrygians and Sardinians getting ready to invade the northern states on the Pontus Sea, Leonides became a babbling pussy cat whenever I stepped into his tent" (47). With its campy humor and lighthearted treatment of the myth upon which it is based, *An Asian Minor* is a uniquely imaginative and offbeat entertainment. It also represents, to my knowledge, the first modern attempt to update a Greek myth to include not merely homoeroticism but a genuine, proudly gay sensibility.

Picano wrote two volumes of memoirs during the 1980s, *Ambidextrous: The Secret Lives of Children* (1985), covering his grade-school years from about age ten to fourteen, and *Men Who Loved Me: A Memoir in the Form of a Novel* (1989), which begins with the author about twenty, working as social worker, and leaves him making his first attempts to become a writer. Picano makes no bones about how he feels about them: "They . . . are the books I'm most proud of: they contain all I've learned so far of style, form, and technique in rendering the funny, tragic, sad, frustrating, incomprehensible, and ambiguous quotidian of our lives" (CAAS-ibid., p. 234). Both in content and in style, they represent the author's boldest, most successful experimentation.

Picano claims the organization of the books grew out of music—sonata form, variations, and fugues (interview, October 7, 1991), and it is not hard to see these influences. *Ambidextrous*, for example, is in three chapters, like movements in a symphony, each split into two parallel themes, one concerning a sexual went and the other a social event that led him toward self-discovery. Each chapter culminates in a new set of realizations, propelling the reader ahead. In the middle chapter, "A Valentine," for example, Picano describes his first same-sex experimentation with Ricky Hersch, a sixth-grade coeval, then parallels it with an equally passionate recounting of his discovery of literature via his first reading of *The Iliad*. The chapter ends with a climatic scene in which an ugly, overweight boy in Picano's class is publicly spurned by a beautiful, popular girl through a returned Valentine's Day gift. The young Picano realizes that this boy's adoration, grotesque as it is, symbolizes his own love for Ricky and presages its ultimate failure, and he experiences his first dose of heartbreak. Hurt and bitter, he seeks solace in books, launching a lifelong intellectual pursuit.

Men Who Loved Me, by comparison, is two long chapters, with multiple recurring, interwoven stories. In the second section, "The Jane Street Girls," the stories of the author's trials as a magazine editor, his rocky affair with the playwright Bob Herron, his unusual friendship with actor George Sampson, and other romances are interplayed like related themes in a canon to a gradually accelerating tempo. The two long sections of the book are broken by a short, humorous narrative, "Interlude," which, as in classical drama, both links the two parts and comments on their major themes. The effect of Picano's elegant experimentation with form is that these two volumes never devolve into episodic narrative but rather hold together as a carefully woven fabric of related anecdote, guiding the reader to profound insights into the development of the artist and the man.

As for the books' style, it's understandable the author selects them as representing a new plateau of effectiveness in his writing. Where the rich, lush descriptiveness of *Late in the Season* may occasionally seem mannered, in the memoirs Picano has combined the tight, carefully planned storytelling of his earlier novels with a more subtly sophisticated subject matter, a deceptively casual presentation, and a voice that is flexible and supple, encompassing sudden shifts of scene, mood, time, and place with ease.

The subject matter of *Ambidextrous*, especially its unabashed recounting of childhood sexuality, proved controversial. As ever, Picano defended his artistic choices and remains adamant he's done nothing but present the truth: "Some British critics called the books flat-out lies, assuring their readers and me that children never have sex. But I'll continue to experiment with and develop this new style" (CAAS-ibid., 234). Of the two volumes of memoirs, *Ambidextrous* evokes a more universal feeling of identification, perhaps because of the very nature of childhood. It is not so much the memories Picano recounts that evoke this feeling as the eternal condition of childhood itself, which he masterfully recreates, including, as Stephen Greco has put it: "that constant sense of untrustworthiness instilled in a young mind not just by people and their often unwelcome attentions, but by the things and places that are comprised in a seemingly innocuous American hometown" (58). When the ten-year-old Picano rebels against Mr. Hargrave, the tyrannical fifth-grade teacher who insists he write with his right hand instead of his left, we not only see the beginnings of the author's lifelong commitment to activism and his hatred of mind control, we also see our own first realization that the world brings us enemies who must be battled.

Men Who Loved Me, by contrast, is a passage through memories of a world just passed. The book resounds with the theme of a time forever lost. The author dedicates it to an old friend and fellow gay writer with the words: "For George Stambolian, who remembers Rome in the 'Sixties." The great age of the Roman *Cinecittà* is just one of the entirely vanished worlds that Picano describes in *Men Who Loved Me*. At times the events Picano recalls merge with gay history. Andrew Holleran has called the book, "A funny and sad remembrance of a New York that has entirely vanished: gay Greenwich Village in the 'Sixties." In one episode, Picano describes meeting and becoming friendly with the celebrated gay poet W. H. Auden. In another he has a crucial confrontation with a closeted lover, Bob Herron, over his decision to live openly as a gay man. Their words, as they argue, define the chasm between two generations of American gay men: " 'What would happen,' Bob argued, 'if every faggot in America did what you're doing?' 'For one thing, America would see how many faggots there actually are,' I said" (307). At a pivotal point Picano describes leaving a party in Greenwich Village late one night in June of 1969 with a handsome Texan named Buzz, the two stumbling drunk on tequila. Rounding a corner onto Sheridan Square, they encounter a tumultuous scene: "a batch of police cars was filling the streets, and scores of cops appeared to be massed in front of one of the storefronts. . . . People surrounded them, throwing flaming bottles, flaming wooden boxes, flaming purses, flaming anything.... One police car appeared to have been pushed into a fire hydrant that had split up from the sidewalk.... [it] suddenly shot up in flames" (315).

These events are of course now gay history, recorded from the vivid perspective of a participant in its shaping. Just as at Stonewall the separate voices of hundreds of gay lives seemed to come together in a single cry of rebellion, so in the pages of Picano's memoirs his life merges at a historic crossroad with the lives of his readers, gay and straight, who have felt their worlds altered by modern gay liberation. As Allen Smalling put it: "The more he [Picano] talks about his life the more we come to realize he's talking about us all" (26). In these, only the first two volumes of a memoir still being written, Picano has provided his reader with a vibrant account not only of one celebrated gay life but also of seminal events in the forming of a new gay consciousness.

CRITICAL RECEPTION

As *The Lure* was published at almost exactly the same time that the controversial film *Cruising*, starring Al Pacino, was released, the two were often compared in the press. This is ironic, as although they share some basic plot elements, the film presents a hateful message diametrically opposed to that of Picano's novel. While many critics chose to lump the novel and film into one review, in almost every case the comparison concluded with praise for Picano at the film's expense. An anonymous reviewer in *Malebox* wrote: "*The Lure* ... is in a different league than *Cruising* when it comes to attitude and viewpoint" (review of *The Lure*, December 1979, 5). John Mitzel, in *Gay News*, compared the novel and the film at length, concluding: "*The Lure* is a fanciful concept, stylishly executed (as you'd expect from a craftsman like Picano).... Friedkin's script for "Cruising" is a different kettle of fish" (Review of *The Lure*, December 28, 1979, 9). Critics who dealt with the novel independently of the film usually had positive things to say. Mary A. Pradt, writing in *Library Journal*, termed the novel "a real shocker, action-packed and cinematic, yet thought-provoking and psychologically probing" (Review of *The Lure*, October 1, 1979, 12). Despite the controversy surrounding it, *The Lure* went on to become a best-seller, the first gay novel ever chosen as a featured selection by the conservative Literary Guild. Something of a classic, it has been translated into six languages, became best-seller in Germany and Brazil, and has only recently gone out of print in this country.

Late in the Season, a less-commercial title, received less attention, but the reviews were usually favorable. *Publisher's Weekly* gave it a respectable short review: "The ending is bittersweet and credible, and this engaging tale is a fresh and different kind of love story" (48). Joseph Arsenault, in *Mandate*, termed it "An excellent, well written novel, treating adult relationships with sensitivity and deeply appreciated nuance. A book to be embraced by gay and straight readers alike for its uncompromising honesty and wonderful sophistication" (Review of *Late in the Season*, October 1981, 20).

An Asian Minor received slight critical notice, but Rick Archbold reviewed it in *The Body Politic*, closing thus: "Maybe if he [Picano] hadn't tried so hard to be cute, this brief entertainment would have more substance than it does. Whatever his motives, Picano and (more often than not) the reader both have a good time" (Review of *An Asian Minor*, March 1983, 18).

Both volumes of memoirs, *Ambidextrous* and *Men Who Loved Me*, brought Picano widespread attention from the gay and straight press. The *San Francisco Sentinel*'s Robert Burke gushed: "Picano has, in *Ambidextrous*, gone beyond his basic obligations as a writer to entertain and instruct. In *Ambidextrous*, Picano has bestowed a gift upon us" (Review of *Ambidextrous*, January 1986, B9). Stephen Greco, in *The Advocate*, similarly heaps praise: "Deftly, Picano evokes those placid Eisenhower years of bicycles, boners and book reports. It is, in fact, in making us remember what it feels like to be a child . . . that *Ambidextrous* really glows" (58). *Men Who Loved Me* received more mixed notices. David W. Henderson, writing for *Library Journal*, stated that the book's "often pretentious, self-indulgent, and gossipy tone . . . suggests a put-on. . . . It is further marred by loose editing . . . and a weak ending" (Review of *Men Who Loved Me*, November 1, 1989). The gay press was more enthusiastic, on the whole. Jere Real, in *The Advocate*, wrote that "Picano manages to capture the free-wheeling spirit of the era and explores the nature of gay life" (Review of *Men Who Loved Me*, November 1989, 20).

An irony of Felice Picano's career is that, as one of the first openly gay writers and an alumnus of the Violet Quill Club as well as a working author, he finds himself in the strange position of being simultaneously lionized and resented by the gay literary community. On the one hand, gay and straight critics are apt to include him in lists of familiar names—White, Holleran, Ferro, Whitmore . . . Picano and treat them with enormous collective respect, as befits their position as literary trailblazers. On the other hand, resentment of their success and the attention afforded them has existed among younger authors. Back in 1980, Dennis Altman wrote about Picano and his contemporaries under the title, "A Movable Brunch: The Fag Lit Mafia," poking fun at them for their dominance of the gay literary scene (10). Revered groundbreaker or literary godfather, Picano remains a significant presence in gay fiction, and his work provides ample pleasures to fascinate and intrigue readers, both gay and straight, for a long time to come.

WORKS BY FELICE PICANO

Fiction

Smart as the Devil. New York: Arbor House, 1975.
Eyes. New York: Arbor House, 1976.

The Mesmerist. New York: Delacorte, 1977.

The Lure. New York: Delacorte, 1979.

(Editor) *A True Likeness: An Anthology of Lesbian and Gay Writing Today*. New York: SeaHorse Press, 1980.

An Asian Minor: The True Story of Ganymede (novella). New York: SeaHorse Press, 1981.

Late in the Season. New York: Delacorte, 1981.

Slashed to Ribbons in Defense of Love and Other Stories. New York: Gay Presses of New York, 1983.

House of Cards. New York: Delacorte, 1984.

Ambidextrous: The Secret Lives of Children (memoir), vol. 1. New York: Gay Presses of New York, 1985.

Men Who Loved Me: A Memoir in the Form of a Novel. New York: New American Library, 1989.

To the Seventh Power. New York: Morrow, 1989.

Poetry

The Deformity Lover and Other Poems. New York: SeaHorse Press, 1978.
Window Elegies. Tuscaloosa, AL: Close Grip Press, 1986.

SELECTED STUDIES OF FELICE PICANO

Altman, Dennis. "A Movable Brunch: The Fag Lit Mafia." *The Soho News* 19 November 1980: 10.

Collins, Jack. "A Dazzling Lure." *The San Francisco Sentinel* 16 November 1979: 12.

Greco, Stephen. "Sweet Mysteries of Youth." *The Advocate* January 1986: 58.

Smalling, Allen. "Destiny's Darling." *Bay Window* 14 June 1990: 26.

Smith, Wendy. "The Un-Authorized Life of Novelist Felice Picano." *Publishers Weekly* 30 January 1981: 48.

DAVID PLANTE (1940–   )
Thomas Dukes

BIOGRAPHY

Born in Providence, Rhode Island, on March 4, 1940, David Robert Plante, the sixth in a family of seven sons, is of French-Canadian and Indian descent (Kaiser, 298), a fact that has had considerable bearing on his work. After schooling in Catholic schools in Providence, he received his degree in French from Boston College; his undergraduate work included a year spent at the University of Louvain in Belgium (Kaiser, 299). Following a brief teaching stint in Rome, Plante worked as a researcher for *Hart's Guide to New York* while writing "on the side" (Baker, 12). After failing to get a novel published in New York, Plante went to London; although expecting his visit to be a brief one, Plante became an expatriate and continues to reside in London. Following the first publication of a short story, "The Buried City," in *Transatlantic Review*, Plante published several other stories before the publication of his first novel, *The Ghost of Henry James*, in 1970 (Kaiser, 299). He has since written eleven other novels—*Slides* (1971), *Relatives* (1974), *The Darkness of the Body* (1974), *Figures in Bright Air* (1976), *The Family* (1978), *The Country* (1981), *The Woods* (1982), *The Foreigner* (1984), *The Catholic* (1986), *The Native* (1988), and *The Accident* (1991). Plante has also produced a number of short stories, nonfiction pieces, and a nonfiction account, *Difficult Women* (1983), of his relationships with Jean Rhys, Sonia Orwell, and Germaine Greer. His work has appeared in such periodicals as the *New Yorker*, *Esquire*, the *New York Times*, the *Paris Review*, *Tri-Quarterly*, and *Grand Street*.

Plante has been writer-in-residence at the University of East Anglia (1977–1978), University of Tulsa (1980–1983), King's College (1985–1986), Adelphi University (1980–1989), and the Université du Québec à Montréal (1990). He has received awards from the British Arts Council Bursary and the American Academy and Institute of Arts and Letters as well as a Guggenheim Fellowship.

MAJOR WORKS AND THEMES

In a letter to this writer, Plante offers a forthright aesthetic and political view of himself as a writer: he asserts his many identities—American, Québecois, New Englander, Catholic, part–Native American, homo/heterosexual—and insists that all of these dimensions of his inheritance are inseparable from one another and vital to his sense of self. Similarly, he argues that no one in contemporary societies can completely disconnect himself or herself from the influences of other social classes or cultural groups. In other words, we cannot speak of an independent gay culture, just as we cannot speak of a separate Catholic culture or a Native American civilization that is completely "unpolluted" by European influences.

This belief in the inextricability of the parts of the self from each other and the inextricability of the self from the larger culture is central to Plante's novels. Indeed, if any one quality can be said to link Plante's twelve (to date) novels, it is that struggle of individuals to reconcile themselves to themselves, to each other, and to society. This struggle takes place in an effort to understand what may be called "the other," and the other can be many things: another person, a place, a feeling; and these others may or may not be bound up in homosexuality.

Plante's first novel, *The Ghost of Henry James*, at once sets a kind of pattern that Plante will follow in some of his subsequent novels and also deviate sharply from in others. In *The Ghost of Henry James*, the gay character, Charles, pursues and is pursued by a crafty male lover; yet Charles is no different from his brothers and his sister, equally important in the novel, in that he is unable to sustain contact with the outside world. Like them, he withdraws from the world after the death of one brother and retreats to the family. In Plante's second novel, *Slides*, reconciliation to the world by the gay character (Jim) and the straight characters is ultimately achieved at the end of the novel where these young people wandering through Europe have a group epiphany under the apse of San Clemente. Jim is no more and no less lost and searching than his straight friends and, like them, is in a room that "might have been filled with the ghosts of initiates sitting about, shoulder to shoulder on a stone bench, all silent, sweating, their pulses beating audibly, waiting in the darkness for whatever would shock them into some other awareness" (185–86).

In both of these novels, the characters, gay and straight, are essentially drifting, waiting for something to happen; those in *The Ghost of Henry James* are essentially trapped, while those of *Slides* appear to see something larger than their own drifting experiences at the end of the novel. Although both novels illustrate the impossibility for their characters of remaining completely alone or becoming completely one with the other, the gay characters are neither better nor worse off than the straight ones. Plante's orthodoxy of integration can be seen in sharp relief in these novels; he uses the integration of his gay characters as simply one more way to show how his different people struggle to understand their relationships with the world.

Plante restricts his scope to three characters in his next novel, *Relatives*; in so doing, his examination of love and the idea of the body becomes even more focused than before. The relationship between the brother, Val, and the sister, Ann, borders on the incestuous, a closeness heightened by the unexplained disappearance of Val's wife. Ann creates a triangle when she takes Russel, a stranger, as her lover. Both Val and Ann have sexual feelings for Russel, yet only Ann consummates the relationship physically. They seem to interchange roles and identities: at one point, Russel puts on Ann's blouse, she puts on his socks, Val wears Russel's sweater. By the end, Russel has left with Ann, but she returns alone, reuniting with Val; they admit that Russel could not choose between them, and Ann could no longer sleep with Russel because it would have felt " 'incestuous' " (221). Russel appears again at the very end, but the nature of the reunion with Val and Ann is ambiguous, to say the least. That sexual and emotional ambiguity is again found in Plante's next novel, *The Darkness of the Body*. On a cruise from one country to another, Valerian meets a married couple, Jonathan and Marion. If at first Valerian seems drawn to Jonathan, he soon loves Marion. Their passion is deep, its source mysterious and inexplicable, like all passion in Plante's novels. This novel was followed by Plante's first overtly gay novel, *Figures in Bright Air*; it is also Plante's most obvious effort to "revitalize or somehow completely change the course of the traditional twentieth-century novel" (Kaiser, 201). The romance between the unnamed narrator and Ewan is troubled by the problematical relationships both have with their parents; the love affair ends, and Ewan drowns. This novel represents Plante's most experimental attempt to bring together his concerns with the desires of the body, communication among people, and their reconciliation with the world. In spite of its overt gay subject, however, it is little different in theme from the previous four novels; if anything, this novel relies even more than the others on the interior monologues and extensive narration of characters' thoughts that mark much of Plante's writing and his integration of love, relationships, and the body as ideas in the novel. Its experimental form and the lack of significant characters other than Ewan and the narrator makes this book the most experimental of the novels in the first half of Plante's novelistic canon.

Plante's next three novels mark a radical departure from the experimental nature of his first five novels, which concentrate almost entirely on characters' emotional lives and very little on traditional plot action. *The Family*, *The Country*, and *The Woods* constitute a trilogy, with obvious autobiographical overtones, of the French-Canadian Francoeur family of Rhode

Island. *The Family* is by far the most traditional and accessible novel by Plante; if one misses the daring experimentation of his first novels, the coming-of-age story in *The Family* offers its own rewards in recounting the awakening of twelve-year-old Daniel Francoeur to the complications of family life. In some ways, the traditional action of *The Family* lets us inside Daniel's thoughts as well as if not better than Plante's heretofore typical use of interior monologues and explorations of consciousness. In the second novel, *The Country*, Plante jumps ahead to Daniel's adulthood, when he must come to terms with the aging of his parents, his changing relationships with his brothers, and his father's death. Finally, in *The Woods*, Plante returns to Daniel's youth when he finishes his first year at college, has a brief affair with a woman at his parents' summer cottage, and then returns to college. While these novels have no overt gay themes, they represent major achievements in Plante's work in their concentration on the individual coming to understand his family and his role in it as best he can.

Following the atypical memoir *Difficult Women*, *The Foreigner* tells the story of an unnamed nineteen-year-old narrator (who has the same-named college roommate and brother as Daniel of the Francoeur trilogy) and his encounters in France and Spain with several people, most notably Angela and Vincent, a crazy man with whom the narrator is in love. He feels a sexual response to Vincent and Angela together, finally being told by Vincent to watch Angela and him make love. Vincent kills himself, and the narrator finally goes to another city in Spain. The triangle here is reminiscent of those in *Relatives* and *The Darkness of the Body* in its exploration of the varieties of love and its treatment of the pair of lovers and the outsider emotionally drawn to that couple. Once more, gay sexuality is presented simply as one part of the narrator's experience, no more or less important than any other.

Plante's most directly gay novel to date is his next, *The Catholic*. Now in college, Daniel Francoeur of the Francoeur trilogy seeks to reconcile the haunting of his libido by his religious upbringing. After sexual encounters with his male roommate and a girl, Daniel becomes involved in an obsessive affair with Henry. Although the affair ends, it allows Daniel to escape the constraints of his Catholic upbringing, enter the world of the erotic, and explore the relationship of the body to the soul, of society's teaching to one's own desires. Although Plante's previous novels have been frank about sex, this work is by far his most directly gay and homosexually explicit. Yet, its concerns harken back to his first, pre-Francoeur trilogy novels in its explorations of the varieties of love and sexual experience. *The Catholic* cannot really be said to be Plante's "gay novel" because, like his other works that feature gay characters among straight, this novel uses homosexuality—among other things—to examine the protagonist's relationships to the larger culture.

With *The Native*, Plante returns to the history of the Francoeur family, concentrating on the stories of Antoinette, Reena, and Jenny. While the novel fleshes out the story told in the Francoeur family, it has understandably little to do with Plante as a a gay writer, although the book does much to confirm Plante's reputation as a first-rate novelist.

Plante's most recent novel, *The Accident*, again features an unnamed narrator, aged nineteen, who is in Belgium to study after a summer in Spain; the time seems to be roughly after that of *The Native*, but any connection between the two novels is not entirely clear. Believing that God "wouldn't ever possess me and make me His" (3), the narrator longs to return to Spain. Eventually, he starts the trip with the naive but friendly and well-meaning Tom and two other companions, Karen and Vincent. Shortly after their car crosses the border into France, the car, with Vincent driving, crashes in the passing lane into an oncoming truck; Tom is killed. The narrator breaks down in a memorial mass said for Tom in Belgium; the novel's powerful final pages, and especially its last line, emphasize the ironic blessing of the narrator's survival and his relationship with God.

Thus, Plante's collection of novels is as varied in subject and treatment as is his awareness of the many elements that form his own background; his canon of novels integrates homosexuality as thoroughly as other themes.

CRITICAL RECEPTION

David Plante's novels have been reviewed in the popular press, with most of the attention going to the Francoeur trilogy and that attention being largely, if not entirely, favorable. That Plante's trilogy should be so praised is hardly surprising: those novels are his most accessible and least threatening stylistically and thematically, with overt homosexuality simply not presented as a major concern. His more challenging novels, especially his gay-themed work, have gotten less attention in the popular press, but *The Catholic* did receive some friendly reviews in newspapers around the country. Although Plante is too young to have attracted the attention of many scholars, this negligence will no doubt change as Plante's novels continue to add up. It will be especially interesting to see whether Plante's integration of homosexual characters in some of his novels will put him in the shadow of novelists who are more consistently militant in their presentation of gay sexuality (although it is hard to imagine a more specifically gay novel than *The Catholic*). Given Plante's talent and the volume and quality of his novels, with no doubt more to come, it is highly unlikely that his view of gay sexuality as "just" one more element in character and society will prevent him from getting the critical attention he deserves.

WORKS BY DAVID PLANTE

Novels

The Ghost of Henry James. Boston: Gambit, 1970.
Slides. Boston: Gambit, 1971.
Relatives. New York: London: Cape, 1972.
The Darkness of the Body. London: Cape, 1974.
Figures in Bright Air. London: Gollancz, 1976.
The Family. New York: Farrar, Straus & Giroux, 1978.
The Country. New York: Atheneum, 1981.
The Woods. New York: Atheneum, 1982.
The Foreigner. London: Chatto, 1984.
The Catholic. New York: Atheneum, 1986.
The Native. New York: Atheneum, 1988.
The Accident. New York: Ticknor and Fields, 1991.

Selected Short Stories

"The Buried City." *Transatlantic Reivew* 24 (Spring 1967): 78–85.
"The Fountain Tree" and "The Crack." In *Penguin Modern Stories I.* Ed. Judith
    Burley. Harmondsworth: Penguin, 1969.
"The Tangled Centre." *Modern Occasions* 1 (Spring 1971): 356–60.
"Mr. Bonito." *The New Yorker* 7 July 1980: 30–34.
"This Strange Country." *The New Yorker* 7 January 1980: 32–40.
"Work." *The New Yorker* 21 September 1981: 41–48.
"The Accident." *The New Yorker* 9 August 1982: 28–38.
"Paris 1959." *The New Yorker* 4 June 1984: 44–54+.
"A House of Women." *The New Yorker* 28 April 1986: 32–33+.
"The Secret of the Gentiles." *The Faber Book of Gay Short Fiction.* Ed. Edmund
    White, 291–308. London: Faber and Faber, 1991.

Selected Nonfiction

"Preface." *Beyond the Words: Eleven Writers in Search of a New Fiction.* Ed. Giles
    Gordon. London: Hutchinson, 1975.
"The State of Fiction: A Symposium." *New Review* 5 (Summer 1978): 59–60.
"Jean Rhys: A Remembrance." *Paris Review* 21 (1979): 238–84.
Difficult Women. New York: Atheneum: 1983.
"Profiles" [Steven Runciman]. *The New Yorker* 3 November 1986: 53–56+.
"In the Heart of Literary London." *New York Times Magazine* 11 September 1988:
    42–43+.

SELECTED STUDIES OF DAVID PLANTE

The Author's and Writer's Who's Who. Sixth ed., 638. Darien, Conn.: Hafner,
    1972.

Baker, John F. "David Plante." *Publishers Weekly* 24 December 1982: 12–13.

Contemporary Authors. A Bio-Bibliographical Guide to Current Authors and Their Works, vols. 37–40. Ed. Ann Envoy. First Revision, 437–38. Detroit: Gale, 1979.

Contemporary Literary Criticism, vol. 7. Ed. Phyllis Carmel Mendelson and Dedria Bryfonski, 307–8. Detroit: Gale, 1977.

Contemporary Literary Criticism, vol. 23. Ed. Sharon R. Gunton and Jean C. Stine, 342–47. Detroit: Gale, 1983.

Contemporary Literary Criticism, vol. 38. Ed. David Marowski, 364–73. Detroit: Gale, 1986.

The International Authors and Writers Who's Who, 7th ed. Ed. Ernest Kay, 472. Cambridge: Melrose, 1976.

The International Authors and Writers Who's Who, 8th ed. Ed. Adrian Gaster, 814. Cambridge: International Biographical Centre, 1977.

The International Authors and Writers Who's Who/International Who's Who in Poetry. Ed. Adrian Gaster, 513. Detroit: Melrose/Gale, 1982.

Kaiser, John R. "David Plante." *Dictionary of Literary Biography Yearbook 1983*, 298–304. Detroit: Gale, 1983.

Nye, Robert. "David Plante." *Contemporary Novelists*. Ed. James Vinson, 1088–89. London: St. James; New York, St. Martin's, 1976.

———. "David Plante." *Contemporary Novelists*. Ed. James Vinson, 523–24. New York: St. Martin's, 1983.

JOE ASHBY PORTER (1942–   )
John M. Clum

BIOGRAPHY

Joe Ashby Porter's novels and stories offer an unusual combination of place and rootlessness. His *Kentucky Stories* (1983) are clearly located in his home state and reflect a temporary identity as a regional writer, but the sense of being an exile "somewhere else" dominates much of his other fiction, from his brilliant novel *Eelgrass* (1977) to his collection of short stories, *Lithuania* (1990). This paradox expresses the movement of Porter's own life.

Born into a Kentucky coal mining family, Porter moved on to the most elite of academic institutions: Harvard (B.A., 1964), Pembroke College, Oxford (1964–1965), and Berkeley (Ph.D., 1973). His years in Berkeley spanned the turbulent period known as "the sixties," which are chronicled so imaginatively in *Eelgrass*, which was begun in 1970. Then came the itinerant life of a young scholar-teacher in the rocky academic marketplace of the mid–1970s: positions in Baltimore, Seattle, Virginia, and Kentucky, before settling down in his present position in the Duke University English department in 1980. There have also been residencies in England, North Africa, and France. Porter speaks French and has noted that French literature is one of the major influences on his work. His imaginative relationship to these varied environments is the starting point for *Lithuania*.

Joe Ashby Porter is also Shakespearean scholar Joseph A. Porter, who has two major books to his credit: *The Drama of Speech Acts: Shakespeare's Lancastrian Trilogy* (1979) and *Shakespeare's Mercutio: His History and Drama* (1988). While Joe Ashby Porter heads the creative writing division of Duke's English Department, Joseph A. Porter teaches Shakespeare and English Renaissance literature and has coedited the annual volume *Renaissance Papers*. The two names reflect an interest in maintaining and controlling separate identities.

MAJOR WORKS AND THEMES

Porter has not been discussed as a writer of gay literature though he strongly wishes his work to be seen as that of a gay author. Yet one has to begin by saying that Joe Ashby Porter is not a gay writer in the sense of demonstrating a commitment to writing about what can very loosely be called "the gay experience" in America. One story in *Lithuania*, "Aerial View," recounts a trip to Tunisia Porter took with his companion of many years, but Yves is referred to as Porter's "friend" and no further details are given of their relationship. Like many of the stories in *Lithuania*, "Aerial View" raises the artistic questions that are clearly Porter's primary interest in this collection—questions about what a story is and about the differences, or lack of same, between personal anecdote and fiction. "Aerial View" begins a section entitled "*Contes*," which has as its epigraph the paradoxical definition of *contes* offered by a French dictionary: "Short account in prose or verse, of marvels or events drawn from reality.... Untrue discourse or narrative." The latter definition summarizes "Aerial View," an account more than a tale, in which the sense of being a stranger in an alien culture is more important than the relationship to his companion, though the story recounts a visit to Yves's birthplace. The stories in *Lithuania* are chaste narratives in which the relationship to place is everything. As the epigraph tells us that Lithuania is "a country and no country," so all of the places in the collection are and are not sources of meaning for their inhabitants and visitors.

The one work in Porter's oeuvre that could be considered gay-related is the delightful novel *Eelgrass*, in which homosexual acts are placed in the larger context of an idyllic 1960s pansexuality, but, as is typical of gay literature, the scopular object in *Eelgrass* is male.

Eelgrass takes place on an island off the coast of South Carolina, a kind of Prospero's island but one in which women own the property and magic comes from a variety of drugs. One cannot help but be reminded, as one reads Porter's tale, of Shakespeare's great comedies: the gender confusion and romantic entanglements of *Twelfth Night*, *As You Like It*, and *A Midsummer Night's Dream* and the magic of the latter and *The Tempest*. There is a Caliban, a savage called Babe who roams the island, but he is nobody's slave. The most ethereal character, our Ariel, is Carter, who is the center of the attention and desire of a group of stoned young people who live in a large farmhouse on the island. Porter's physical descriptions tend to be general and suggestive rather than specific, yet Carter's "beautiful gold hair, beautiful face, beautiful body" (3), suggest an ideal of adolescent male beauty. While the wild Babe's focus is on his nocturnal feeding, Carter is all sexual appetite. His semicivilized state, more libido than superego, is reflected in his constant state of semidress: "He has a white tee shirt and faded dungarees, nothing else—no footwear, no jewelry, no underwear" (3–4). Carter's natural state is "hardly thinking at all" (12). Sexual desire motivates everything. Carter has sex with most of the women in the book, including the villainess, whom he rapes. However, the most idyllic sexual encounter, occurring at midpoint in the novel, is that between Carter and another young man, Jimbo. Their encounter has a sweet sense of discovery about it that separates it from the other conjoinings in the novel: "Now there is a quite different silence as each from moment to moment thinks, 'Far out' and 'What's going to happen next?' "(101). Carter and Jimbo seem to have, for a moment, entered Miranda's "brave new world." The Edenic landscape for their tryst is like that of a children's story. To return to their friends, they must travel, "a narrow path which always seems about to end but does not," along which "flowers open and close"(101). Their homosexual activity takes place in a setting that is more Oz than nature and is metaphoric in that it suggests the future companionship and travels Carter proposes to Jimbo.

It is hinted that the two young women who are the drug pushers for the young people probably have a sexual relationship though, as with all their peers, their desires cannot be neatly categorized.

The activities of the young people are in conflict with the strivings of their elders, who are all scheming and ambitious. Shakespearean Porter has created a Forest of Arden in which the young people's spirit triumphs over malevolent concerns about power and possession and in which gender and sexuality are, happily, unstable. It is only in this environment that homosexual acts are celebrated. Like many pre-Stonewall gay writers, Porter does not find space in his work for homosexuality as a life-style or the basis for a sexual politics. One finds Joseph A. Porter's recent critical work more "gay," in a political sense, than his fiction.

CRITICAL RECEPTION

In the description of the format of this volume sent by editor Emmanuel S. Nelson to contributors, he noted that one key purpose of this section would be "to establish the extent to which homophobia shapes the critical reception of the gay novelist." In Porter's case, like that of many other gay writers, homophobia and heterosexism may have caused the author's reticence about his homosexuality. Porter's fiction has been received favorably by critics on its own terms. In a *Baltimore Sun* review of *Lithuania* (May 12, 1991), Jaimy Gordon noted: "Ever since his luminous and sly island romance "Eelgrass" appeared in 1977, Joe Ashby Porter has been a writer's writer—that is, a writer admired by other writers and almost unknown to the general reader" (B9). *Eelgrass*, a delightful book, has been unduly neglected beyond initial favorable reviews in trade publications like *Publisher's Weekly* and *Best Sellers*. Yet Porter's volumes of stories are indeed the work of a "writer's writer" self-consciously absorbed with questions of form. It is not surprising that they have been published by a university rather than a commercial press. Yet they have garnered favorable reviews from major newspapers. *Kentucky Stories* won Porter the National Endowment for the Arts/P.E.N. Syndicated Fiction Award in 1983, and his work has been printed in *The Best American Short Stories*.

WORKS BY JOE ASHBY PORTER

Eelgrass. New York: New Directions, 1977.
Kentucky Stories. Baltimore: Johns Hopkins University Press, 1983.
Lithuania. Baltimore: Johns Hopkins University Press, 1990.

WORKS BY JOSEPH A. PORTER

The Drama of Speech Acts: Shakespeare's Lancastrian Trilogy. Berkeley: University of California Press, 1979.
Shakespeare's Mercutio: His History and Drama. Chapel Hill: University of North Carolina Press, 1988.
"Marlowe, Shakespeare, and the Canonization of Heterosexuality." In *Displacing Homophobia: Gay Male Perspectives in Literature and Culture*. Ed. Ronald R. Butters, John M. Clum, and Michael Moon, 127–48. Durham, N.C.: Duke University Press, 1989.
Untitled short essay on fiction. In *Writers and Their Craft: Short Stories and Essays on the Narrative*. Ed. Nicholas Delbanco and Laurence Goldstein, 197–99. Detroit: Wayne State University Press, 1991.

SELECTED STUDIES OF JOE ASHBY PORTER

Campbell, Don B. Review of *Lithuania*. *Los Angeles Times* 30 December 1990: D21.
Gordon, Jaimy. "Porter's Stories Strip Away the Conventions of Fiction." *The (Baltimore) Sun* 12 May 1991: B9.
Ward, William S. *A Literary History of Kentucky*, 428–29. Knoxville: University of Tennessee Press, 1988.

JOHN PRESTON (1945–   )

Jane L. Troxell

BIOGRAPHY

Editor and author John Preston, in 1991's *Hometowns: Gay Men Write about Where They Belong*, tells of the sense of entitlement that his New England boyhood gave him. Even though in high school Preston felt compelled to discover new gay worlds away from his native Medfield, Massachusetts, his early sense of being entitled to the American Dream and belonging to a community underscores what is undeniably the most productive career in contemporary gay literature. Preston was not content simply to write gay fiction; he inspired a generation of gay readers with positive (and almost superhuman) role models like characters Alex Kane and Mr. Benson and with the credo that all gay men are entitled to a home in the world and in literature.

Born December 11, 1945, John Preston grew up the oldest child of old-line working-class parents. An affinity for books and a dislike for sports failed to make Preston feel like an outsider, although it did make the young "class brain" feel different. Today, it is hard to imagine Preston, physically imposing at six-foot-one and an ardent baseball fan, being the stereotypical high school nerd.

It was as a teenager in the 1960s that Preston acted on his feelings of difference. Living a double life, he attended proms in Medfield while pursuing homosexual sex in Boston's Park Square. Having heard rumors of a "different world," Preston would go into the city more and more frequently, supposedly to visit urban cousins; he would stay, instead, in the Greyhound terminal, where seasoned gay men would offer the rites of initiation. He also snuck off to New York City and Provinceton, Massachusetts, meccas where the young man could uncover the secrets of an exciting gay life.

The emphatic desire to travel even further away from home informed

Preston's choice of colleges. Lake Forest College in Chicago provided that distance. There, he started to come out, albeit tentatively, as openly gay. He also attempted his first relationship with a man. When that man committed suicide because of his homosexuality, Preston decided to come out with a vengeance. Obtaining his undergraduate degree, he moved to Minneapolis to complete his coming out.

Preston's activism flowered during this time. Around 1970, he established the country's first gay community center in Minneapolis and ran it for two years. Because counseling played such a big part in the center, Preston enrolled in the sexual health program at the University of Minnesota Medical School. That graduate degree eventually gave him the opportunity to move to New York City to edit a newsletter produced by the Sex Education Council of the United States.

Preston had lived as an out and active gay man in New York for a couple of years when *The Advocate*, then a fledgling magazine, offered him its editorship. It was 1975, and the West Coast-based *Advocate* sought a high-profile "New York" editor. Preston naturally took the position, the best "gay job" in America at the time, and stayed with the magazine for over a year during frequent moves between San Francisco and Los Angeles as the new magazine tried to plant roots. The position proved unsatisfying, and Preston fled the West Coast to return to New York.

A period of unemployment and a subsequent stint in "temp" typing (serious letdowns for Preston after having been at the helm of the nation's premier gay magazine at age twenty-nine) actually instigated Preston's writing career. He had never considered himself a writer, merely an editor of other writers' words, but a nine-to-five job gave him a lot of time on his hands. His imagination and evenings free, the activist/editor started writing.

His favorite of the new gay male periodicals was a magazine called *Drummer*. For the now world-weary Preston, *Drummer* presented a rougher editorial stance than the other, more polished gay rags. With *Drummer* in mind, he wrote a short story that "rambled on for 20 or so pages," composing it on a portable typewriter in his basement apartment in the East Village. If the humble short story he had written was indeed accepted by *Drummer*, Preston rationalized, at least his friends wouldn't see it. On the contrary, two days after Preston mailed the story to *Drummer*, editor John Embry called Preston and asked him to expand the short story into a novel. *Drummer* serialized the S/M classic *Mr. Benson* in 1978, and Preston became a cult hero.

As his first attempt was so well received, Preston took his writing more seriously. He followed up *Mr. Benson* by cranking out erotic stories, developing essays, and taking on review assignments for *Drummer*, *Mandate*, *Inches*, and other publications. As his career quickly grew, so did the distractions of New York. The pace, the noise, and the expense of the city became too much for a man who was having to monitor his mail slot for checks from porn magazines in order to make rent. In December 1979, Preston moved to Portland, Maine, to become a full-time writer. He could save some money, return to the familiar territory of New England, and still reach New York in an hour by plane.

Back in his geographical element, Preston was immediately productive, writing a novel within the first year. *Franny, the Queen of Provincetown*, a series of monologues by the drag queen hero and his young charges, adapted easily to the stage and was first performed in Ogunquit, Maine, on June 5, 1982. The relatively new gay press Alyson Publications published *Franny* the next year—the same year that San Francisco's Alternate Publishing published *Mr. Benson* in book form.

To pay his bills, Preston wrote in quick succession a surprising number of successful and pseudonymous pulp adventure novels. In the five years after his publishing breakthrough in 1983, mass market publishers Dell, Avon, and Worldwide Library published over twenty of Preston's paramilitary, Rambo-esque tales. Some of Preston's bread and butter ran off into his gay writing as well, as he wrote the popular gay adventure series featuring superhero Alex Kane. Alyson published the six Kane books between 1984 and 1987.

Nor did Preston ever leave his pornographic writing. The S/M "Master" series, published between 1984 and 1989, proved ample successors for *Mr. Benson* fans. *The Heir*, a tale of gay S/M among the privileged class, followed in 1988; but its small-press publisher let it go out of print before the book could find its audience.

The AIDS epidemic had started shortly after Preston's move to Portland. Having been trained in sex education and health, Preston felt particularly suited to meet some of the challenges the gay health crisis brought about. He lectured from coast to coast, kept tabs on AIDS research, and wrote (with Glenn Swann) the 1987 mainstream release for gay men, *Safe Sex: The Ultimate Erotic Guide*. As the pornographer's antidote to AIDS' devastating effect on gay men's sex lives, he also prepared *Hot Living: Erotic Stories about Safer Sex* (Alyson, 1985). Through much of the 1980s, Preston was, as he puts it, "Mr. Safe Sex."

In Maine, he also heard the old activist's call to arms. He eagerly became the Portland gay community's representative to the local media and helped to found the Maine Health Foundation and later became the president of the AIDS Project of Portland, for which he is still writer-in-residence. Supported by grants from the state, Preston began two ongoing projects: to record the oral histories of gay men in Maine and to establish a process whereby those Maine residents with HIV and AIDS could work with him on their own writing.

Because he had been an early safe sex practitioner, Preston was not prepared for his own HIV diagnosis in 1987, which was discovered during a routine checkup with his ear, nose and throat specialist. At the peak of his literary success, Preston froze as a writer for almost two years. Busying himself with medical consultations and treatments and sinking emotionally as he got daily reports about sick friends around the country, Preston was unable to produce more than the occasional column for gay periodicals. He eventually found relief through his writing, completing an anthology of writing on AIDS he had begun before learning of his HIV status. *Personal Dispatches: Writers Confront AIDS*, a collection of essays by fifteen gay men and a lesbian, was published by St. Martin's Press in 1988.

Since that harrowing time, Preston has regained his ground. While he has not written a novel since 1989's *In Search of a Master*, he has enjoyed great success as an anthologist and nonfiction writer. *Hometowns* and *The Big Gay Book: A Man's Survival Guide for the Nineties* were picked up by the Book-of-the-Month Club. *Flesh and the Word: An Erotic Anthology* will be published by E.P. Dutton in 1992, and contracts for four more books— none novels—are already in-hand. Also in progress are a memoir and two mysteries. Preston's trademark prolificacy only gains momentum.

Through his own activist and literary efforts, John Preston is now one of a handful of prominent gay male writers who are able to make their living from their writing. Still living in the Portland apartment he took ten years ago, Preston has created a writer's life out of his dreams for all gay men.

MAJOR WORKS AND THEMES

Thirteen of John Preston's two dozen published gay-themed books are novels, and these are all early works. Decidedly post-Stonewall, the erotic novels glorify the gay sexual experience, while the adventure novels and *Franny* present gay heroes—a boon to a community then in need of heroes.

Mr. Benson began Preston's literary exploration of the uniqueness of gay sex, sadomasochism, and the power dynamics between sexual partners. Aristotle Benson is the archetypal master. Told from the viewpoint of his slave, *Mr. Benson* captures the explosive aspects of gay lust. This same theme of sex as catharsis runs throughout Preston's "Master" series. Not always a prelude to love and commitment, sex has meant for many gay men an introduction to homosexual life and a pleasurable self-affirmation. S/M codifies these rites of passage, with "masters" establishing the rules and inducting "slaves." The encounters in *Mr. Benson* reflect this constant re-initiation to gay life. Like John Rechy's* earlier *City of Night*, *Mr. Benson* had at its core the ungovernable decadence of the urban sexual underground.

While much of the writing is sexual fantasy, the "Master" series is about much more than sex. The books provide a picture of real gay life, of how gay men were thinking and acting at the time, and of how they established the parameters of their intimate lives. Characters investigate the power and possibilities of sex; they question and uncover their true natures. Of his pornography, Preston has said, "I write [it] because it's a form of gay men's vernacular literature, created in our own language about our own passions and the ways we use our own bodies to express those passions."

Franny, Preston's sole nongenre novel, is a timepiece—a paean to the pre-Stonewall generation of gay men who survived to create the gay community. Through example and through her unconditional love, the avocado-shaped drag queen in muumuu shows younger men that being gay is okay. The book addresses the redefining of the family, as Franny and her young friends—some cut off from their traditional families—build a new clan within the gay community.

The Alex Kane adventure novels also expand the boundaries of family constructions. Alex, his young lover Danny, and Joseph Farmdale, his late lover James's father, unite to exact justice for hate crimes directed toward gay men. A precursor of Queer Nation's activists, superhero Alex Kane does not sit idly by as terrorists and bigots extort and kill factions of the gay male community: he pulls out an Uzi. Preston's theme in these works is literature's most enduring: the conflict of good and evil—this time with homosexuals being the good guys.

The plots of the Kane books vary little beyond the location (all are set in big cities): Gay men are under seige by homophobic fanatics. Alex Kane employs his superior intelligence, finely tuned body, and rich resources to fight the attackers. The books' emphasis on justice for gays was buoyed by the listing of the National Gay Task Force's address at the beginning of *Stolen Moments* and a true story of fatal gay-bashing starting off *Deadly Lies*. The author encouraged action of his readers as well.

Finally, in all of his fiction, Preston is creating and breaking down myths. His protagonists are quasimythical creatures with unwavering integrity, stunning bodies, and/or powerful passions.

CRITICAL RECEPTION

St. Martin's editor Michael Denneny called John Preston "the most accessible" of the "first-generation" gay writers (quoted in Lemley, E1–2). This accessibility stems from much more than the fact that Preston is also the most prolific. Preston's success as a writer also comes from his wide range. Pornography, adventure mysteries, a charming novel, S/M classics, sex manuals, intelligent and significant anthologies, and self-help books all add up to a well-respected body of work for Preston.

Early on, Preston became a stumbling block for critics. Relying on predictability in writers, some reviewers were challenged by the fact that Preston would produce pornography (albeit significant and well-done) and then would write in other genres with decidedly non-erotic themes. Eventually, though, most reviewers came to expect the unexpected, respecting the author's diversified talents and interests. Denneny even hazarded that Preston may be the "best-known gay writer"—not off the mark for those who recognize the existence of the general gay readership in America. For his achievements, *Lambda Book Report* named Preston one of the twenty-five most-influential men in gay publishing and writing in the last decade.

Of course, Preston had auspicious critical beginnings. When *Mr. Benson* came out, it was an immediate hit. At the time, the *Village Voice* hailed it "a cult classic" (review of *Franny*, November 1983, 3). A decade later, *Outweek* put it like this: "[B]oys across the land [were] slapping, ramming, and dressing in time to [Preston's] directives" (42). *Mr. Benson* fan clubs sprang up at which members read the installments and then acted out Preston's scenes among themselves. Meanwhile, the author received fan mail and successfully sold by mail T-shirts that read "Looking for Mr. Benson"— with or without a question mark. Preston was soon to be dubbed "the contemporary overlord of male erotica" by *Lambda Rising's* annual mail order catalog.

Preston considered his second book-length work, *Franny, the Queen of Provincetown*, his "first novel" and a test of his artistry: could he pull off a successful nonpornographic novel? Now that *Franny* has been through a few printings and has been performed on stage many times across the country (as recently as 1991), it is safe to say that he could. Alyson published the book to rave reviews, and the dramatic version won the Jane Chambers Memorial Award as one of the best gay plays of the year.

Gay critics appreciated Preston's effeminate hero, who followed right on the heels of Arnold Beckwith in Harvey Fierstein's more mainstream *Torch Song Trilogy*. "Best gay novel of the year" (Rofes, 1), said North Carolina's gay paper *The Front Page* of *Franny*. *The Weekly News* of Miami, Florida, echoed, "John Preston is Author of the Year" (Monteagudo, 31).

Heterosexuals also appreciated Preston's efforts to bring a part of gay history to life. The author received thank-you letters from straight people who claimed new understanding of gay life. *Franny* received good notices from mainstream vehicles, *Library Journal* included. *Franny's* only scathing review came from Preston's local paper, the same *Maine Sunday Telegram* that in 1991 ran a large, gay-positive profile of Preston but then published an ill-informed, homophobic review of what is really too sweet a story to pan.

While he was receiving his first mainstream reviews with *Franny*, Preston was collecting the stories for *I Once Had a Master*. The "Master" series as a whole was well-received, lauded for the "skilled simplicity" with which it described sadomasochistic acts. One periodical went so far as to call it "the ideal against which all subsequent forays into the genre will be measured" (Terry, 25). As happened with *Franny*, a few critics noted Preston's growing "maturity" as a novelist.

The Alex Kane series was also praised, for its pacing and its outlook. Of the series' first entry, *Sweet Dreams*, the *Washington Blade* stated, "If a book can be judged by how quickly you turn the pages, *Sweet Dreams* is a winner. You may not agree with Kane's methods, but you can't quarrel with his sense of purpose" (Krohne, 23). *The Advocate* also recognized Preston's contribution to gay self-esteem by saying, "Preston's story is a step toward filling a deep need for gay dreams" (Mains, 43).

As Preston's work became better known, the national media granted him more attention. It has only been in the few years since Preston stopped publishing book-length fiction, though, that mainstream review vehicles have routinely given space to gay books (and even then, only to those coming from corporate New York houses). Preston received well-deserved praise for the nonfiction works *Hometowns*, *Personal Dispatches*, and *The Big Gay Book* from *Publishers Weekly*, *Library Journal*, *Booklist*, *Kirkus*, and other outlets. All his works are now featured in the gay and lesbian periodicals that publish book reviews. When Preston publishes his next novel, review channels will be in place and waiting.

SELECTED WORKS BY JOHN PRESTON

Mr. Benson. San Francisco: Alternate Publishing, 1983.
Franny, the Queen of Provincetown. Boston: Alyson Publications, 1983.
I Once Had a Master and Other Tales of Erotic Love. Boston: Alyson, 1984.
"The Mission of Alex Kane" Series:
Sweet Dreams, vol. 1. Boston: Alyson, 1984.
Golden Years, vol. 2. Boston: Alyson, 1984.
Deadly Lies, vol. 3. Boston: Alyson, 1985.
Stolen Moments, vol. 4. Boston, Alyson, 1986.
Secret Dangers, vol. 5. Boston, Alyson, 1986.
Lethal Secrets, vol. 6. Boston, Alyson, 1987.
Entertainment for a Master. Boston: Alyson, 1986.
Love of a Master. Boston: Alyson, 1987.
The Heir. Austin, Tex.: Liberty Books, 1988.
In Search of a Master. Secacas: Lyle Stuart, 1989.

SELECTED STUDIES OF JOHN PRESTON

Krohne, David. "Sweet Dreams." *Washington Blade* 28 September 1984: 23.
Lemley, Brad. "A Gay Writer's Survival Guide." *Maine Sunday Telegram* 27 October 1991: 1E–2E.
Mains, Geoff. "Sweet Dreams." *The Advocate* 5 March 1985: 43.
Monteagudo, Jesse. "Book Nook." *The Weekly News* 21 November 1984: 31.
Palley, Marcia. "Between the Covers with John Preston." *The Advocate* 2 March 1988: 40.
Perry, John. "Writer John Preston's Walk on the Wild Side." *The Washington Blade* 4 October 1991: 41, 51.

Pettit, Sarah. "Bearing Witness." *Outweek* 10 December 1989: 42–44.
Rofes, Eric. "The Revolution of the Clones: Talking with John Preston." *The Front Page* 11–24 October 1983: 1; 25 October–7 November 1983: 1, 11.
Terry, Victor. "I Once Had a Master." *Dungeon Master* Spring 1984: 25.

JAMES PURDY (1927–   )
James Morrison

BIOGRAPHY

The available details of James Purdy's biography are somewhat sketchy. He was born in 1927 in southern Ohio, presumably not far from the rural sections of West Virginia that serve as the setting for many of his novels. He attended the Universities of Chicago, Madrid, and Puebla, Mexico, and taught from 1949 until 1953 at Lawrence College (now Lawrence University) in Wisconsin. Reportedly, he spent time in Mexico during the 1950s and also worked in Europe as a translator. At the same time, his early stories began to appear in magazines ranging from *New Directions* and *Evergreen Review* to *Esquire* and the *New Yorker*. Even in these early days, Purdy's career was marked by a certain resistance on the part of the literary establishment to Purdy's style. Publishing his story "About Jessie Mae," for example, the *New Yorker* purged it of some of the distinctive colloquialisms in which the characters speak, as if to domesticate the story. On a larger scale, his earliest books—*Color of Darkness* and *Children Is All*—were turned down by the major American publishers; according to Purdy, these rejections frequently questioned Purdy's sanity.

Color of Darkness was privately printed abroad in 1956, and the turning point in Purdy's career came when the book was championed by Dame Edith Sitwell, who called Purdy "one of the greatest living writers of fiction in our language." The next year, Purdy received two major awards, one from the National Institute of Arts and Letters and another from the Guggenheim Foundation. Throughout the 1960s, Purdy's reputation as a writer grew steadily as he produced such major works as *Cabot Wright Begins*, *Eustace Chisholm and the Works*, and *Jeremy's Version*. Extending as it does across a range of shifts in literary style and taste, Purdy's oeuvre has remained remarkably consistent in the 1970s and 1980s.

Biographical material on Purdy during that time is limited, for the most part, to the publication of his books. He taught fiction writing for two semesters at New York University in the 1980s, but he has claimed in interviews that he found the experience uninspiring. He lives where he has lived for many years, alone, in a small apartment in Brooklyn with—reportedly—pictures of boxers lining the walls.

MAJOR WORKS AND THEMES

Purdy's first major work, *63:Dream Palace*, sounds most of the common themes that will recur throughout Purdy's fiction. The novel opens with three of its characters reflecting on the fate of a fourth, Fenton Riddleway, a boy from West Virginia who comes with his sickly brother Clair to New York. The bulk of the novel is a complex flashback detailing Fenton's adventures in the grotesque netherworld of Purdy's New York. Like James's "The Turn of the Screw," Purdy's tale never returns to its frame-story, so in spite of the novel's comic portents Fenton's fate remains something of a mystery. Many of the key elements of Purdy's fiction, however, are already in place: the figure of the cynical naif and the gallery of grotesques he encounters in his travels; the intense relationship of Fenton and Clair, a combination of love and hate; the climactic revelation of previously concealed passions through an act of violence. The end of the tale turns on Fenton's repression of his murder of Clair, which is then revealed to his own consciousness when another man attempts to seduce him. The sordid conclusion of the novel places it squarely in a tradition of gay fiction of the 1940s and 1950s practiced by John Horne Burns, Gore Vidal, and others.

For all its power, Purdy's early work seems finally to be a prelude to his mature work. Thus, though his characteristic plot patterns are established immediately, the tone and conduct of his early novels may be seen as faintly derivative. With its gritty grotesqueries and its flamboyant rhetoric of mock-redemption, *63:Dream Palace* suggests the Flannery O'Connor of *Wise Blood*; *Malcolm* with its antic Christian iconography suggests the Nathaneal West of *Miss Lonelyhearts* or *The Dream Life of Balso Snell; The Nephew* with its piercing observation of small-town torpor suggests the Wright Morris of *The Man Who Was There*. With *Cabot Wright Begins*, Purdy's quirks begin to solidify into a distinctive voice and vision, but it is perhaps no accident that it is in the first of his works to treat homosexuality with full openness that Purdy achieves full maturity as a writer.

Eustace Chisholm and the Works remains Purdy's most consolidated work, bringing together as it does the major strains of Purdy's fiction. Like Parkhearst Cratty of *63:Dream Palace*, Eustace Chisholm is a writer, the wayward chronicler of his time and place, with epic aspirations for his work on "a long narrative poem, written in charcoal stick on old pages of the Chicago Tribune"(4). As in *Cabot Wright*, the novel ends with the scribe's renunciation of his offices. With its conflation of homoeroticism and brotherly tenderness, the story of Daniel Haws and Amos Ratcliff follows a line in Purdy's fiction from *63:Dream Palace* to *Mourner's Below*, while the Melvillean sadomasochism of Haws's encounter with Captain Stadger introduces a motif that receives its fullest treatment in the later *Narrow Rooms*. The Gothic picaresque of *Malcolm*, the urban horror-show of *Cabot Wright*, the demonically inverted "family romance" of the later *Sleepers in Moon-Crowned Valleys*—all are present, in admittedly diffused but equally pungent form, in this novel. The title itself refers to the apparently catchall nature of the novel; in the context of Purdy's work, *Eustace Chisholm* does indeed yield "the works."

The catalogue of Purdy's themes we find in *Eustace Chisholm*, moreover, takes shape around two key issues: Purdy's place in the general context of modernist/postmodern literature and the representation of gay sexuality in his work. I will insist finally on a crucial link between these two issues that makes Purdy an unlikely but unavoidable touchstone in the half-formed canon of gay literature. For the present, however, I will consider each issue separately.

In an important sense, *Eustace Chisholm* is a self-conscious novel in the tradition of Barth or Gaddis, two other writers who came to prominence in the late 1950s but who, unlike Purdy, were promptly extolled as representatives of midcentury modernism. In Purdy's novel, Chisholm's "epic" functions as a *mise-en-abime*—a self-conscious reflection in microcosm of the novel as a whole, like Wyatt's forgeries in Gaddis's *The Recognitions* (1955). Moreover, the oddments and refinements of the novel's narrative voice continually draw attention to the artifice of the novel's style much as do the quirks and metafictional hiccups of Barth's narrators to the fictive status of his work. Indeed, the complex structure of *Eustace Chisholm* is redolent of a recognizable tradition in modernist fiction. Like Djuna Barnes's *Nightwood* (1936), Virginia Woolf's *Between the Acts* (1941) or *The Recognitions*, *Eustace Chisholm* is a novel about a disparate, renegade community struggling to unify itself around an artist-figure who in each case proves incapable of providing such unity. Thus in each case the novel's panoply of modernist maneuvers finds its analogue within its own narrative, becoming for all intents a self-contained representation of its own failure, a deadpan joke on the reader.

Purdy's novel obviously fits neatly into this pattern in many ways. The end of the novel, however, presents a problem here. By the time of the novel's conclusion, the seemingly heterosexual Daniel Haws, after acknowledging his love for Amos Ratcliffe, has been beaten to death by Stadger; Amos himself, forced into hustling, has been murdered by a john; and the bisexual Reuben Masterson and Eustace Chisholm have been restored, triumphantly it seems, to heterosexuality. Eustace announces to his wife Carla that he has abandoned his poem, and the novel forthwith ends on the tranquil union of man with woman. Whereas in Barnes, Woolfe, and Gaddis, the artist-figure's renunciation is framed in apocalyptic, almost eschatological terms, in Purdy's novel it is presented as a gently humorous vindication (in a novel whose humor is ordinarily anything but gentle) of Carla's wifely insight into Eustace, opening up the authentic possibility of their renewed love.

What with the high body count of gay men here, the equation of gay sexuality with infernal suffering, and the conclusive note of renewal achieved through restoration of heterosexual order, a gay-conscious reader of the 1990s may well be forgiven for seeing *Eustace Chisholm* as merely an artifact of pre-Stonewall self-hatred. Such a reader could not, however, be forgiven for regarding the artifact as harmlessly quaint along the lines of something like Vidal's *The City and the Pillar*. The hellish ardor of Purdy's novel, its bold refusal to choose between moral gravity and a ferocious objectivity at times suggestive of Georges Bataille—these qualities make the book a profoundly disquieting experience, impossible to laugh off as an antique, from a past sociocultural epoch. For me, more to the point, the force of the novel's tone and its manner of execution, both austere and relentless, render the objection about the novel's "negative images" of gay men quite irrelevant indeed. It's like complaining that Sade lacks propriety.

The problem in gay studies of schematically pitting the "negative" against the "positive," valuing the latter while chastising the former, is a complex one, and this is hardly the place to treat that tendency in detail. The bind in which a critic who rejects such schematism finds himself is this: his rejection itself is likely to be read as participating in the self-hatred of the object under analysis. If I suggest, for example, that the ruthless irony that pervades *Eustace Chisholm* reaches its zenith in the final section of the novel or that, far from legitimizing the heterosexual imperative, Purdy insists that we see how it is bought through the murderous abolition of its presumed antithesis, I open myself to the charge that I am cloaking my own self-hatred in the New-Critical Formalism that decrees irony the most bracing panacea of them all. What I would in fact suggest, however, is that readers who perceive self-hatred in *Eustace Chisholm* share assumptions with critics who have consistently demonized Purdy in the context of modernism/postmodernism.

Consider the last sentence of *Eustace Chisholm*, depicting Eustace and Carla's final coupling:

Staring at her dumbly, he stirred, pulled her head down toward his mouth, covered her neck with silent kisses and then slowly, like all the sleepwalkers in the world, took her down the long hall to their bed, held her to him, accepted her first coldness as she had for so long accepted his, and then warmed her with a kind of ravening love. (215)

On the face of it, this is a sentence that achieves an almost classical modulation, a careful balance that may indeed appear to signify nothing more than the novel's validation of the triumph of heterosexuality. Understood in the context of the novel as a whole, however, that seeming triumph is anything but secure. Carla and Eustace have been so remote from one another throughout the novel, there has been so little preparation for this final embrace, that the classical flourish of the sentence begins to seem excessive. Indeed, prior to this passage, Carla mouths a numbing platitude to Eustace in declaring her love: "All I ever cared about was you." The banality of the lovers, then, is distinctly at odds with the heightened rhetoric of the last sentence. But the rhetoric itself is designed, in effect, to self-destruct. The cumulative effect of the sentence, each of its successive phases layered to drive up, as it were, the rhetorical thermostat, is self-consciously undermined, as so often in Purdy, by a calculated lapse of precision—"*a kind of* ravening love." Finally, the reference to "all the sleepwalkers in the world" is a reference to Daniel's love of Amos, so repressed it could express itself only in Daniel's own sleepwalking. Thus, the image apparently intended to invoke rapturously romantic conventions in the novel's conclusion serves further to undermine them with its reminder of the fates of these other lovers. To be sure, the sentence is one of startling virtuosity, but its virtuosity is anything but simple.

My point here is that Purdy's narration employs a complex, distinctly modernist double-focusing, emphasizing its own artificiality by counterpointing rhetorical effect with structural demand. The reader is asked to see the materials of the fiction under many aspects at once. Purdy's handling of point of view, for example, demands that we see his characters not only as they must appear under the aspect of eternity—as deluded, inane, or doomed—but with equal legitimacy, as they appear to themselves. In other words, the ferocity of Purdy's satire is not won at the expense of his characters, as is that of a writer like Terry Southern (with whom Purdy was compared at the time of *Eustace Chisholm*): In Purdy's work, the infernal vision of a ruthless satirist mingles with the delicate, tender perceptions of a novelist of manners.

The novel's opening chapters are broadly representative of Purdy's approach. With clean strokes, Purdy introduces Eustace, Carla, Daniel, and Amos through a complex interplay of viewpoints. In the first chapter, for example, the reader moves from Eustace's point of view to Amos's to Daniel's to Carla's in almost imperceptible shifts that simultaneously bring about subtle stylistic shifts. The introduction of Eustace encapsulates Purdy's manner of setting the character's own view of himself in opposition to an "objective" view, while refusing to grant either position final privilege:

Eustace Chisholm had been caught up in two tragedies, the national one of his country's economic collapse, and his failed attempt to combine marriage with the calling of narrative poet. He wondered whether it was because of his inability to produce a book or merely the general tenor of the times that his wife, Carla, who had supported him hand and mouth for two years, ran out on him with a baker's apprentice some six months before this story begins.... The original name, like a scar, he reopened each morning while shaving. "I am Eustace," he would mumble into the mirror. (4)

The grandiosity of Eustace's own self-image is registered through the blandly poeticized turns of phrase with which the narrator presents him—the reference to his "calling of narrative poet" here, or elsewhere in the passage to his "coign of vantage." Only as the novel proceeds does the reader see the irony of Eustace's oracular vision of himself, and if Eustace is "caught up" in anything, it is in his own narcissim. The parodic quality of the prose juxtaposes dime-novel pieties against more evenly colloquial idioms, producing an effect of calculated bathos and heightening the novelistic conventionalism of the introduction ("some six months before this story begins ..."). At the same time, the dialogue between these two modes is negotiated by yet another level, that of the piercing poetic images with which Purdy periodically tightens the rein of the narrative. The comparison of the name with a scar is startling in its off-hand brevity and resonant in its paradox: Why a scar and not a wound, as it is reopened every morning? Followed by Eustace's mumbled iteration of his identity, the moment is characteristic of Purdy's prose style in mingling these multiple voices to produce one that is bracingly rangy and utterly unique—by turns mordant, gawky, scorching, playful, simply functional, grandly baroque, a shotgun wedding of Sherwood Anderson, Gertrude Stein, and a third distinctive but unnameable ingredient.

The key to Purdy's handling of point of view, then, is its refraction through these dense layerings of linguistic register. At the same time, Purdy sets into play a mixture of viewpoints suggestive of a nineteenth-century novel in its ability to encompass a range of characters. In the novel's opening, for example, the reader is positioned first with Eustace at his window looking into the street; then shifts to Amos below, calling up unanswered; then briefly to Daniel, who enters the scene and commands Amos to follow him "without waiting to see if his tenant followed"(5). Daniel, in turn, collides with Carla, and the reader follows her as she returns to Eustace. In this instance, point of view does not only define character relations—as in, say, Hardy—by showing us Daniel's indifference, Amos's desperation, Carla's disorientation, and Eustace's position, above it all, as observer who refuses connection to the scene below him (by failing to answer Amos). The gaze defined by point of view here demonstrates, as well, the recalcitrance of its objects and the ineffectuality of mastery, the refusal of desired objects in Purdy's world to answer that desire (again, as in Hardy). Simultaneously, the seemingly random shifts in point of view, in a fiercely visual, almost cinematic way, call attention to the conventions of point of view themselves.

The multiplicity of viewpoints, that is, gives way to the instability of view-point—not so much in the spirit of a comparatively conventional novel like, say, Hardy's *Tess of the D'Urbervilles* but in that of a protomodernist fiction like Melville's *The Confidence-Man.* (Both these examples similarly begin with a scene dependent on multiple points of view.)

I make this point not to assert a stock claim such as that Purdy's characters are all equally validated by the conduct of the narrative—that they are human beings first and gay men or women only afterward. Rather, the manipulation of point of view is intricately connected to the representation of sexual identity in Purdy's work. This connection exists on two levels, that of the construction of gender and that of the construction of gayness.

On the former topic, the character of Maureen O'Dell is the crucial figure to examine. Maureen is one of Purdy's gallery of women characters who observe the intense male-male relationships of the narrative, a figure in whom an intensity of emotional investment is placed within the narrative who yet remains outside the network of sexual bonds that generates the story. Ordinarily, this figure is aging and matronly, placing in her own charge a young man suffering a crisis of sexual identity that, when he finally recognizes this crisis, causes him to betray her. The pattern runs from *63:Dream Palace* to *On Glory's Course* and beyond. Maureen has a definite place in this lineage, but she is unique in recognizing the place to which she has been assigned by the story. She explicitly and bitterly acknowledges her own exclusion from the homosexual bonds of the male characters, and she vents her contempt for them by becoming, as she characteristically puts it, a "serious fucker." Maureen rejects her status as an outsider, and indeed at the beginning of the novel she is pregnant with a child fathered by Daniel Haws and at the end of it she has married Reuben Masterson. Although neither of these events in itself is granted much weight in the novel—and Maureen significantly disappears after her child is aborted—they clearly indicate Maureen's entry into the sphere from which she has been excluded.

Maureen is also unique in Purdy's work for being the only woman character to be associated with the kind of cosmic physical suffering later in the novel to be inflicted, more characteristically, on Haws. The abortion scene is among the most devastating scenes in Purdy's work because of its peculiarly measured tonal registers, weighing a horrific, offhanded whimsy against a titanic recognition of the character's unendurable suffering. In a way, the scene crystallizes the key issues of Purdy's work, providing a point of convergence for questions of sexual representation and modernism/postmodernism.

Generally, Purdy's work refuses binary sexual categories such as homo/heterosexual. The bisexuality of Masterson, Haws, and Chisholm is a case in point; and the ambivalent, shifting sexual identities of, say, the figures encountered by Malcolm in that early novel further suggest the general fluidity of sexual identity in Purdy's work. My point, then, is that whether one conceives of them as modernist or postmodern, Purdy's irony, his complex orchestration of narrative structures, and his play with point of view are an integral part of this subversion of schematic sexual oppositions. However, this fluidity of sexual identity is clearly and disturbingly isolated to male characters in Purdy's world. Purdy's women desire men—tend, in fact, toward unstated "hysterical" longings for men who are unattainable precisely because of the intense but indefinable nature of their sexual personae. In the context of Purdy's work, then, it is significant that Maureen, who does not break out of this pattern but recognizes and takes control of it, should be subject to the intense agony Purdy's female characters are otherwise spared. It is not so much that Purdy's impulse is to punish Maureen (though such an impulse may exist) but that, more generally, Purdy's work suggests an ineffable connection between sadomasochism and self-consciousness. As in Djuna Barnes, whose modernism is similarly distilled through polysexuality, so in Purdy to *think*, to *know*, is to suffer.

With its opulent gore, its operatic Grand-Guignol, the conclusion of *Eustace Chisholm* makes this connection plain. As has been suggested, the scenes of Stadger torturing Haws bring together Conrad and Melville, fully revealing the horror repressed in those more staid authors. Stadger is at once Haws's "secret sharer," who instantly recognizes his deepest sexual impulses, and his darkest nemesis—his name is a variation on Melville's Claggart. His demands that Haws renounce Amos force Haws into the fullest acts of recognition in the novel. In the midst of a climax whose brutality exceeds that of any other American novel, Haws's final lucidity emerges most movingly (in a way, like Billy's last blessing of Captain Vere). Similarly, in the later *Narrow Rooms*, the impulse to sadomasochism becomes a form of identification among characters who, ruled strictly by their passions, yet find it necessary to repress the fiercest of those passions. (The notion of sadomasochism as identification suggests Genet, at least in Sartre's version of his work in *Saint Genet*.) The ending of *Narrow Rooms* holds its own with that of *Eustace Chisholm* both in its torrent of carnage and in the awesome purity left in its wake. In this regard, Purdy's work mines the horror of Jacobean tragedy.

Much of Purdy's later work strives for similarly epic dimensions. *Sleepers in Moon-Crowned Valleys* enlarges Purdy's canvas to Faulknerian proportions, and in complexity of structure and force of character these novels rival *Absalom, Absalom!* Later works in this vein, such as *On Glory's Course* and *In the Hollow of His Hand*, are less ambitious, but continue to reach toward the mythic. Purdy's most recent novel, *Garments the Living Wear*, is an effort, as it were, to rewrite *Malcolm* for the age of AIDS, but its allegorical handling of the subject (the disease is never mentioned but referred to in mock epic/portentous terms as "the pest") undermines some of the novel's depth of feeling.

CRITICAL RECEPTION

At first glance, Purdy's own responses to the critical reception of his work may seem to be nothing more than acute paranoia. In his most recently published interview, Purdy presents himself as something of a martyr to the cause of his own work, mercilessly crucified by ignorant and homophobic reviewers. Describing the reception of *Narrow Rooms*, for example, Purdy claims, "That's the book they crucified me for. On every corner they've lynched me"(68). Yet Purdy blithely agrees with the interviewer when she calmly asserts to the contrary, "Critics said that was your best work" (ibid.), substantially undermining his initial claim. He also claims he will not buy newspapers because "they are trying to destroy me" (ibid.), or that when his books are reviewed badly "what the reviewer is saying is that he wants to kill you"(64–65). Given Purdy's comparatively high standing currently, such remarks are difficult to fathom. A survey of the reviews of Purdy's work reveals them to be, with noteworthy exceptions, overwhelmingly favorable. Yet the consensus appears to be that Purdy's distinction derives from properties uniquely idiosyncratic, integral to his own work instead of drawing upon more general cultural tendencies. In other words, to judge from the reviews, Purdy is very much a pariah—not part of the major currents of twentieth-century literature and not part of the growth industry of gay literature of the 1970s and 1980s. It may, then, be this relegation to no-man's-land that Purdy laments in his remarks about responses to his work.

This is not to deny, of course, that Purdy has received a share of extremely hostile reviews, or that these are frequently motivated by the evident homophobia of the mainstream press. Yet the most hostile vein in criticism of Purdy's work operates at, seemingly, a more basic level, claiming that Purdy is simply an inept writer. Among the most vehement critics making this charge are Stanley Edgar Hyman and Geoffrey Wolfe. Both critics cite presumed abuses of language in Purdy's work to argue for a linguistic insensitivity they see as pervasive. Hyman concludes that Purdy is "a terrible writer and worse than that . . . a boring writer." Wolfe, meanwhile, composes a list of words Purdy allegedly misuses to make a similar case. In neither case does the critic consider the possibility that Purdy's idiosyncratic narrative voice is to be understood in the context of modernist experimentation as a self-conscious reflection of the ingenuously somnolent consciousnesses of Purdy's characters. It is as if, as Purdy himself points out in the previously cited interview, such critics had never read *Huckleberry Finn*.

Two of the three full-length studies of Purdy's work similarly fail to understand the author in context. Bettina Schwarzschild's *The Not-Right House* is an impassioned reading of Purdy's early work, but its conclusion says nothing more impressive than that Purdy chronicles a failed quest for love. Yet Schwarzschild's litany of this failure is notable in its repression of the homosexuality even Purdy's early work insists upon. Love fails, Schwarzschild instructs us, between "mother and child, brother and brother, brother and sister, husband and wife, aunt and nephew, friends, neighbors, strangers . . . "(50). Conspicuously absent from this odd survey are the same-sex relationships that most intensely express Purdy's concern with this theme. The list amounts, then, to a taming of the elements of Purdy's work most disruptive of conventional sensibility in spite of her emphasis on the "unsparing" qualities of Purdy's vision.

In his study *James Purdy*, Henry Chupack simply reads Purdy's work as demonstrating the "hellish and frustrating life that homosexuality involves" (102–3). Just as Schwarzschild's approach depends on a genteel avoidance of homosexuality, so Chupack's depends on a failure to note the social contexts and tonal complexities through which Purdy presents the theme. As late as the mid–1970s, Chupack still finds it possible to read Purdy's work as a critique of homosexuality instead of as an agonized critique of social repressiveness. Chupack's own witless assumptions emerge in the section of his book where he claims to be placing Purdy's work into a larger context, arguing for the current social significance of his work. Again Chupack appeals to the failure-of-love syndrome, constructing a social scenario in which "rape and homosexuality were engaged in by those who, denied love in their own lives, sought it in anti-social actions" (126). Such as it is, Chupack's point is that Purdy's work has obvious relevance to such a scenario, if it only existed. However, the equation of rape with homosexuality, the definition of both as "anti-social actions," and the suggestion that rape can be understood as a search for love illustrate a repulsively normative— though in fact aberrant—perspective from which it is flatly impossible to read Purdy's work with any understanding.

In its own way, each of these books provides a case study of dominant critical approaches to gay literature—both pre- and post-Stonewall. Both are designed to avoid treating critically either Purdy's gayness or its manifestations in his work. Schwarzchild does so by claiming that the experience of love is universal; as homosexual love is part of this universal phenomenon, homosexual love may be ignored in favor of the universal principle itself. The easy and unconvincing equivalence of homosexuality with heterosexuality becomes a way of talking about the latter *as if* one were talking about the former so that, in effect, one never has to talk about the former. Chupack's strategy is more transparent. He ghettoizes homosexuality and addresses it almost obsessively, arguing that it undermines what is for him the ideal state, that of the heterosexual family. One need hardly point out that Purdy's work presents the bourgeois family as itself the source of much of the evil his world depicts.

Stephen Adams's study of Purdy is the best of the three precisely because of its concern with placing Purdy in context. Adams sees Purdy as the culmination of a metaphysical tradition in American literature including

Hawthorne and Melville, and he places Purdy within the grid designed by Leslie Fiedler in *Love and Death in the American Novel*. There, Fiedler argues that the key to American fiction, since "Rip van Winkle," is in its renunciation of "mature" heterosexual union. To be sure, Purdy's fractured families live frequently in the wake of abandonment by the father, and *The House of the Solitary Maggot* makes a very sustained use of the archetypal hold of the Rip van Winkle legend on the American imagination. Yet Adams is on shaky ground with his use of Fiedler's schema, considering its implication that homosexuality is regressive and that the "transcendent" stage of heterosexual union lies somewhere beyond it. It must be noted that Purdy's work, beginning with his earliest stories, routinely attaches imagery of primitivism and infantilism to his portrait of bourgeois couples. Moreover, Adams's treatment of homosexuality in Purdy becomes quite suspect in this regard. Repeatedly, Adams chastises Purdy's characters for failing to accept their own sexuality; yet if gayness has *already been defined* as regressive, why should anyone accept it? The "personal" triumph Adams claims to associate with such acceptance loses its force in the context of his argument as a whole. Once again, the critic reproduces the very ideologies Purdy's work challenges.

In what may still be the best treatment of Purdy's work, Tony Tanner in *City of Words* argues that Purdy's fiction "addresses itself to the process of fiction-making itself" (87). This claim, and the mere fact of Tanner's inclusion of Purdy in his book otherwise devoted to Nabokov, Pynchon, Hawkes, and other writers conventionally regarded as definitive of postmodernism, obviously draws Purdy into the fold of the canon. But Purdy resists being so drawn, and Tanner appears not to know what to do with *Eustace Chisholm*, where Purdy "has abandoned his undermining skepticism towards his own medium sufficiently to write the story of Amos and Daniel." Yet the outcome of the story leaves Tanner reflecting on multiple interpretive possibilities: "Perhaps this [larger failure] is because of the failure of modern society, or that failure of modern feeling which is everywhere evident in Purdy's work..." (117). While Purdy's self-consciousness admits him to Tanner's study, his faith in the possibility to reveal truths (about, say, sexual identity or social formations) makes him, for Tanner, a problematic figure in this context, defying as it does a certain strain of postmodernist orthodoxy.

Thus Purdy remains an outsider. Although two of his novels have been issued in Alyson's "Gay Modern Classics" series (with excellent introductions by Paul Binding), Purdy is not in the mainstream of gay writing. ("They don't like me," he says.) He is himself uncomfortable with such a category. (According to the previously cited interview, he finds it "limiting.") Cited by Charles Newman in *The Post-Modern Aura* as emblematic of the fate of the postmodern storyteller (in a grizzled discussion of *Cabot Wright*), he is yet denied full status in that club as well. Acceptable as neither a "gay writer" because of the breadth of his concerns, nor as a "postmodernist" because of his work's abiding humanism (and, of course, because he is a "gay writer"), Purdy remains where perhaps, after all, he *does* belong: in a sphere of his own.

WORKS BY JAMES PURDY

63:Dream Palace. London: William-Frederick Press, 1956.
Color of Darkness. New York: New Directions, 1957.
Malcolm. New York: Farrar, Straus, and Cudahy, 1959.
The Nephew. New York: Farrar, Straus, and Cudahy, 1960.
Children Is All. New York: New Directions, 1962.
Cabot Wright Begins. New York: Farrar, Straus, and Giroux, 1964.
Eustace Chisholm and the Works. New York: Farrar, Straus, and Giroux, 1967.
Sleepers in Moon-Crowned Valleys: Jeremy's Version. New York: Doubleday, 1970.
I Am Elijah Thrush. New York: Doubleday, 1972.
Sleepers in Moon-Crowned Valleys: House of the Solitary Maggot. New York: Doubleday, 1974.
In a Shallow Grave. New York: Arbor, 1975.
Narrow Rooms. New York: Arbor, 1978.
Proud Flesh: Four Short Plays. Northridge, Calif.: Lord John Press, 1980.
Mourners Below. New York: Viking, 1981.
On Glory's Course. New York: Viking, 1984.
In the Hollow of His Hand. London: Weidenfeld and Nicolson, 1986.
The Candles of Your Eyes. London: Weidenfeld and Nicolson, 1987.
Garments the Living Wear. San Francisco: City Lights, 1989.

SELECTED STUDIES OF JAMES PURDY

Adams, Stephen. *James Purdy.* New York: Barnes and Noble, 1976.
Chupack, Henry. *James Purdy.* Boston: Twayne, 1975.
Hyman, Stanley Edgar. *Standards.* New York: Horizon, 1966.
Lear, Patricia. "Interview with James Purdy." *Story Quarterly* 26 (1989): 55–76.
Newman, Charles. *The Post-Modern Aura.* Evanston, Ill.: Northwestern University Press, 1985.
Schwarzschild, Bettina. *The Not-Right House.* Columbia, Mo.: University of Missouri Press, 1968.
Tanner, Tony. *City of Words.* New York: Harper and Row, 1971.
Wolfe, Geoffrey. Review of *Jeremy's Version. Newsweek* 12 October 1970: 122.

JOHN RECHY (1934–)

Gregory W. Bredbeck

BIOGRAPHY

John Rechy was born in El Paso, Texas. His mother, Guadalupe Flores de Rechy, fled Mexico to escape the purges of Pancho Villa, as did his father, Roberto Sixto Rechy, a Mexican aristocrat of Scottish lineage. These romantic origins form the imagery around which Rechy weaves both his fictions and his life; in a narrative written for Gale's *Contemporary Authors Autobiography Series,* Rechy calls these family stories "inherited ghosts that romanced the memories of others and floated into mine" (Adele Sarkissian, ed. *Contemporary Authors Autobiography Series,* vol. 4, 1986, 253).

The events of Rechy's life are frequently difficult to separate from the stories and anecdotes that have grown around them. He received a B.A. at Texas Western College, where he studied on a journalism scholarship, and then attended the New School for Social Research in New York before serving a tour of duty in Germany with the army. His recollections of his youth, like those of the protagonists in most of his novels, are filled with images of death and desolation. Texas during the depression was decimated by poverty, and drought destroyed nearby Oklahoma. The youngest of five living siblings, Rechy also was influenced by the family's memory of two deceased children: Valeska, the sister who passed away at age twelve before Rechy's birth, and a half-brother also named John. Rechy recalls visiting this half-brother's burial site: "I would stare in fascination at the grave that bore my own name" (ibid., 254).

Of course these recollections must be tempered by Rechy's continual desire to blur the boundary between fiction and fact. Although derisive of critics who read his fictions as factual accounts of his life, he is just as eager to assert the facts of his life as fictions: "My life-as-novel allows me to supply motives that satisfy me, adhering to autobiography by basing them on subsequent evidence, always allowing for mystery" (ibid., 255); he professes plans to someday write a book called *Autobiography: A Novel.*

Rechy's biography supplies "facts" that can account both for the anarchist protagonists of most of his novels and for the distinctly literary mind that creates them. His father gained early fame as a musical prodigy and made his living for a time in a number of music-related jobs: conducting his own orchestra, composing scores for films, owning and directing a touring theater, tutoring children in music. He later entered journalism and operated a Southwestern newspaper until run out of town for exposing municipal corruption. These artistic and rebel impulses surfaced early in Rechy's career. In college one of his first compositions was an essay suggesting that Milton sympathized with the rebel angels, and he subsequently wrote a poem in which Jesus, on the day of judgment, sentences God to hell. By the age of sixteen Rechy had written two other epic poems about the war in heaven, texts undoubtedly derived from the Scottish and Mexican Catholicisms that permeated his youth.

After leaving Texas and relocating to New York City, Rechy began a period of hustling and drifting that has, by and large, dominated criticism's view of him. These wanderings form the basis of Rechy's first novel, *City of Night.* Indeed, that novel began as a personal letter to a friend recounting Rechy's experiences in New Orleans that was then printed in *Evergreen Review* as the short story "Mardi Gras." Since publishing *City of Night* in 1963, Rechy has continued to make his living as a writer, publishing eight novels, one nonfiction "documentary," a play, and a number of columns and essays in major periodicals, including essays about Mexican American oppression and about the torment of resistant American soldiers in Vietnam, which appeared in *The Nation* (189 [October 10, 1959], 210–213; 210 [January 12, 1970], 2–12). Many of his novels deal with homosexuality, but only a few are what might be called overtly gay novels. The majority of his work finesses a rather gray area of concerns roughly marked out by sexuality, ethnicity, and personal history and identity. Rechy currently lives in Los Angeles and teaches at the University of Southern California.

WORKS AND THEMES

Rechy's canon forms a complicated and allusive web stretching between books, and between books and life. In *City of Night,* for example, the nameless narrator recalls the musical career of his father, which leads the informed reader back into the childhood of Rechy himself. Mandy Lang-Jones, the ambitious and brutal newscaster from *Bodies and Souls,* resurfaces in *Marilyn's Daughter,* as too does Sister Woman, an evangelical television preacher. Johnny Rio, the protagonist of *Numbers,* recounts a personal history that imitates the events of *City of Night.* Manuel Gomez, a Hispanic American slaughtered on the freeway in *Bodies and Souls,* reappears in *The Miraculous Day of Amalia Gomez* as the dead son of the title character. *This Day's Death* focuses on an entrapment in Griffith Park, the setting of *Numbers*, and concerns the smothering love between a mother and child—a topic Rechy pinpoints as dominant within his own life and that also becomes the starting point of *Marilyn's Daughter*. *Rushes* explores the politics of S/M, which recalls Johnny Rio's fascination for and repulsion from a nameless man scarred with lash marks. Both *The Fourth Angel* and *Bodies and Souls* focus on vagrant teenagers and the Los Angeles street world in which they wander. Although Rechy's canon manifests this self-referentiality and allusiveness, it is necessary to consider four books in relative isolation in order to ascertain his position as a "gay" novelist. Rechy's first three novels, *City of Night*, *Numbers*, and *This Day's Death*, all written before the Stonewall riots, form a trilogy that anatomizes many of his major themes relating to homosexuality. A later post-Stonewall novel, *Rushes*, then provides a means of assessing some of the novelist's attitudes toward what has come to be known as "gay male identity" in the United States.

City of Night chronicles the wanderings of a nameless male hustler from El Paso, to New York, to Los Angeles and, finally, to New Orleans and intersperses these wanderings with recollections of the narrator's youth in El Paso. As with most of Rechy's novels, the book is motivated by an irreducable tension between a sprawling, colloquial narrative and a self-conscious and highly allusive structure. The novel is drawn in a tight circularity by its opening, which recounts the death of the narrator's dog, and its final plaintive question, *"Why cant dogs go to Heaven?"* (380). The novel also develops a structure that Rechy returns to in many other novels: it alternates between narrative chapters (in this case all titled "City of Night") and chapters that are sketches of various people involved in the narrative and titled after them.

The alternation between narration and character that is marked by these chapters also suggests the tension that generates the novel as a whole. Each "character" chapter builds a knowable person, but then the novel pulls us away from that person and moves us onward. In an ironic way, then, the novel forces us as readers into the position of a hustler: we know someone, and then move on. This transiency between knowing others and not really knowing them obviously derives in part from the actual life of a drifter. But it also signals a larger theme, a standoff between identity and its loss that becomes the central idea of the book as a whole. In the broadest sense, this idea is present in the fact that the novel devotes its entire length to sketching a portrait of the narrator and his life, but then refuses to tell us his name. The novel seems overtly to mock us with this withholding of a name; when toward the end of the novel a trick directly asks the narrator his name, the novel breaks from the dialogue into the third person: "I told him my first name" (345). Later we are also teasingly told, "I told Jeremy Adams my own last name" (345), as if to underscore that the narrator is at once what this novel gives us and what it withholds from us.

City of Night is difficult to label as a "gay" novel precisely because its constant toying with identity affronts post-Stonewall ideas of gay pride and gay identity. And yet in its own time it formed an important step in the development of the gay novel. Gay New York poet Frank O'Hara, in a 1963 review of the novel, praised it for its gay sensibility: "John Rechy... gets marvelously accurately the Exact tone of homosexual bar-talk... Which Is something, since I don't know of any other writer around recently who has managed this feat Unsquarely" (Frank O'Hara, *Standing Still and Walking in New York*. Ed. Donald Allen [San Francisco: Grey Fox Press, 1983, 160). In order to read *City of Night* as a part of gay literary history, it is necessary to recognize that it is produced by a specific historical moment, one that had not yet necessarily formed an idea of gay identity but was, rather, implicated in a set of questions that called the very idea of identity—and especially sexual identity—into question.

Rechy's second novel, *Numbers*, continues with many of the themes of *City of Night* and also introduces several themes and stylistic techniques that dominate Rechy's later works. The novel begins as Johnny Rio, a former hustler, returns to Los Angeles for a visit after a self-imposed exile of three years to his home in Laredo. After wandering through his old haunts, Johnny focuses his activities in Griffith Park and sets himself the goal of tricking with thirty men. The choice of thirty is arbitrary, but it is also a pun. Thirty is the printers term for "the end" or "no more follows." We are faced here with an indeterminacy: will the thirtieth man end Johnny's tricking or, with the tricking ended, will nothing more follow in Johnny's life? On the one hand, there is redemption; on the other, death. The title itself is also a pun, referring at once to the slang name for a hustler's client, the self-imposed test Johnny Rio undertakes, and the book of the Bible. The biblical subtext evoked by the title recalls a similar exegetical motif in *City of Night*, which begins with a near parody of Genesis: "and it begins in the wind..." (9). In *Numbers*, the biblical passage of central concern to Rechy is Numbers 9:16—"during the day the Dwelling was covered by the cloud, which at night had the appearance of fire"—which Rechy associates with the smog and neon of Los Angeles. Both the religious and regional associations conjured by the passage dominate the remainder of Rechy's canon, with the exception of *Rushes* and *The Vampires*.

Numbers initially seems to eschew the ambiguity of identity that marks *City of Night*. Johnny Rio, the protagonist, is introduced by name in the second paragraph and is drawn as a character who contrasts with the almost willful unknowingness of the narrator of *City of Night*: "he's aware of whatever mysterious thing it is that makes him alive" (18). Yet the solidity of Rio quickly decays as the novel traps him in a series of failed narcissistic images: "he looked in the mirror to dazzle himself with his smile; and he saw, instead, a depraved distortion of himself" (33); "predictably, he stands before the Mirror. . . . Suddenly he remembers the time, years ago, when he saw a vision of . . . corruption")120. Rio's personal history and world matches perfectly with that of the narrator of *City of Night*; indeed, one of the first friends he meets upon returning to Los Angeles from Texas reminds him of the "young number" they used to hang around with who has since written "a *book* about *Main* Street and *Hustling* and Pershing *Square* and *queens*" (25)—an obvious allusion to *City of Night*. Yet there is a critical difference in Johnny, for although he once hustled, he now pursues only free sex. The removal of the economic motive creates new possibilities for sexual identity, and these possibilities become the subject of the book.

Johnny's relentless pursuit of "numbers" in Griffith Park becomes a ritual of purgation for him that will allow a new sense of sexual identity. He tells Sebastian, an older, middle-class gay man who has befriended him, that achieving his goal of thirty "numbers" will allow him then to attempt other forms of sex: "It'll be only with people with identity. . . . that's what the Park was all about . . . and the numbers. Losing control and losing identity. But I'm in control again, and that's what I won" (235). Johnny's victory is short-lived, for the novel ends with him back in the park and on his thirty-seventh "number." But unlike *City of Night*, where we are led to believe that continued anonymous sexual wandering is what allows the narrator his "identity," here we are forced to see this accumulation as a "failure" of identity—or at least as a betrayal of Johnny's idealization of it. There is within *Numbers* a sense of homosexuality, an idea of gay identity that hovers throughout the novel even as it constantly eludes the protagonist.

This Day's Death, Rechy's next novel, returns to Griffith Park and the world of free and anonymous sex. Rechy calls *This Day's Death* "a novel that does not understand the situations it attempts to explore, because I did not understand them" (Sarkissian, 262), yet this ambivalence does not diminish the light the novel sheds on the tensions of identity constructed in *Numbers*. *This Day's Death* concerns a young Mexican American paralegal from El Paso, Jim Girard, who, during a trip to Los Angeles, is falsely arrested for having sex in Griffith Park. The novel shifts between El Paso, where Jim cares for his sick elderly mother, and Los Angeles, where he and the man arrested with him face a lengthy legal proceeding. The legal battle parallels the battle Jim faces with his mother, a woman who loves him and is loved by him fiercely but who also, in Jim's mind, uses illness to manipulate him. This interplay between public world and personal biography is another trope characteristic of Rechy's canon and is reminiscent of the similar interplay between past and present in *City of Night*, *Bodies and Souls*, and *Marilyn's Daughter*. *This Day's Death* grows from Rechy's own troubled and deep love for his mother. Jim's taking his mother with him to Los Angeles imitates a similar trip Rechy took with his mother, and the encounter in the park is derived from, as were the encounters in *Numbers*, Rechy's attempt during that trip to "cram my life with sex again—as if to make up for lost years—in an area of a vast park, a sexual paradise..." (ibid., 261).

Although the family narrative of the novel is essential for understanding Rechy's later works (especially *Marilyn's Daughter* and *The Miraculous Day of Amalia Gomez*), its primary importance in this first trilogy is the outrage against institutional homophobia expressed in the legal narrative. Jim, like the protagonist of the other novels, does not identify himself as homosexual. His unconsummated encounter in Griffith Park is the first time he has acted on his homosexual urges, and in El Paso he has an ongoing relationship with a woman. Yet as the trial process drags on and as Jim recognizes the inhumanity and violence of the court, he begins to express what might be called a gay consciousness. After conviction, Jim writes a rebellious summation for the parole officer: "The charges we were found guilty of today didn't occur. The cop lied. But had it occurred, there would still have been no 'crime.' The guilty ones are the cop who lied and the men who chose to believe him despite the evidence—but, more, the men who uphold or ignore the perverted laws that make these charges possible" (219–20). Jim's outrage is bolstered by the inadmissible and unprovable piece of evidence that indicts society in the novel: that earlier in the day Daniels, the arresting officer, had himself tried to pick up Jim in the park. With this symbolic irony, Rechy suggests that society's hatred of the homosexual is a hatred of its own sexuality.

Rechy's first three novels demonstrate a strengthening movement toward an idea of gay identity. In *City of Night*, the narrator shuns any idea of determinate identity; in *Numbers*, Johnny Rio professes an identity troubled by the possibility of gayness; in *This Day's Death*, "the homosexual" is recognized as a specifically oppressed minority, even if Jim Girard remains uncertain about his own sexual identity. Rechy himself has adamantly opposed being labelled a "gay novelist," and to reduce his works to this one idea in many ways betrays them. Yet the pattern of emerging gay identity within the first trilogy is undeniable, and it forms an idea which is the overt topic of critique in Rechy's seventh novel, *Rushes*.

Rushes unfolds a structure that recalls the Biblical allusions of *Numbers* and *City of Night*. Its chapters derive their titles from the liturgy of the Mass, and the bar that serves as its setting is decorated with a series of pornographic paintings that are linked with the medieval Stations of the Cross. But unlike *City of Night*, which supplies a nameless narrator in a variety of well-known locations, *Rushes* flips this perspective and supplies a number of carefully drawn and precise characters in a city that remains nameless. If *City of Night* is structured by places, *Rushes* is structured by people; each chapter begins with the same line (sometimes with minor variations), "As often as he comes to the Rushes...", and then begins with a character's feelings about the S/M and leather bar. The novel constructs a post-Stonewall dark comedy of manners, wherein a group of friends gather in the bar and gradually reveal themselves to the reader—though not always to each other. The primary tension of the novel forms when Lyndy, a female socialite and woman's fashion designer, coerces her way into this all-male bar. Lyndy's presence is a catalyst that allows the novel to ruminate on the meanings of gay-bar culture and identity. Like *This Day's Death*, *Rushes* also manifests an extreme concern with social oppression. Throughout the novel there is a constant fear of the fag-bashers and muggers who roam the piers outside, and one of the central characters, Don, has recently been bashed.

The individual characters of the novel are used to elaborate a series of issues that typify post-Stonewall but pre-AIDS gay America. Chas, a top man, antique dealer, and avid defender of S/M sex, is locked in a battle with Endore, a well-known columnist and former S/M devotee, about the political correctness of S/M and of the "new masculinity" (19) that grew in the communities of the seventies and eighties. Both Chas and Endore advocate "abundant sex—what others but not they call 'promiscuity' " as "an enriching experience not to be denied or surrendered to conventionality posing as liberation; and both agree that sex need not occur with love" (33). Don, aging and aware of it, personifies the preoccupation with youth present in the culture—a culture that routinely posted its gathering places with the warning "No Fats Femmes Over 35s" (203). Bill is haunted by the memory of a lost relationship, and offers a painful tale of the psychic trauma that followed when his lover, a strong "top" man, expressed his desire to be a "bottom." Throughout the novel Rechy implicitly chides the sexual role-playing that the novel suggests typified post-Stonewall metropolitan culture.

If *This Day's Death* critiqued social oppression by demonstrating its attraction to homosexuality, *Rushes* critiques homosexuality by demonstrating its attraction to oppression. One of Chas's earliest recollections in the novel is of his presiding over a "slave auction" that was raided by the police. The narrative stresses the similarity between the sexual play and social repression: "The cop led him next to the naked 'slave' Chas had just 'handcuffed,' the play handcuffs now replaced by real ones. Chas still held the chain in his hand. He dropped it" (28); later the chain is also compared to one used by a basher to assault gay men cruising the piers. Chas proffers the "new masculinity" as a triumph—"we're the *real* men now. *They* imitate *us!*" (117). But Endore, who functions in many ways as the novel's conscience, offers a different interpretation: "Why, after the bursts of 'liberation'—why, now, the courtship of filth, even when sterilized filth? Within the safe, enclosed bars and orgy rooms, why the initiation of the dank tenebrous places into which others had been shoved by oppression—toilets, crumbling buildings, prison cells?" (93). If the law's homophobia masks an attraction to homosexuality, homosexuals' attraction to the images of violence and oppression equally marks a homophobia. Within this novel the line between liberation and oppression is skeptically effaced; as Endore thinks, "the masculine homosexuals had become the new sissy-haters, like the bullies who had taunted them as children" (94).

Rushes demonstrates a strong self-consciousness of both the gains and losses that arose in the wake of the Stonewall Riots. Don, the oldest of the characters, eulogizes the past, when "to be a 'queer'... meant accepting being an outcast" (58). He derides the ugliness of the new "openness" and pinpoints the fall of the gay community: "When did it change? The death of Judy and the Stonewall Inn riot, when the 'queens' fought the cops. For Don, a troubling death, a troubling birth" (58). Yet despite his animosity toward Stonewall, Don cannot entirely turn his back on it. He recalls a night not long ago when he saw a demonstration commemorating the riots: "He ran to avoid it, but the chanting pursued him" (67). The novel as a whole seems to occupy a position similar to Don's, for while it is clearly produced by a post-Stonewall sensibility, it is also clearly derisive of that sensibility. If we read the title with the same religiously punning stress of *Numbers*, we can summarize this tension—rushes, the temporary highs that always fade; rushes, the place where Moses, the deliverer of his people, was found.

We can read these four novels as constitutive of their own gay narrative, a movement from a continued reshaping of sexuality and identity in the pre-Stonewall period to a recognition and critique of a homosexual identity in the post-Stonewall text. By stressing the "sexuality" of this movement, we can see that Rechy's canon indeed constitutes, at least in part, a gay literature. Yet the broader question of identity irrespective of sexuality also structures all of Rechy's novels—texts that, though not overtly "gay," nonetheless comment on and derive from the poetics of Rechy's homosexual novels. Like the gay texts, these other books frequently work in counterpoint to each other. Rechy's fifth novel, *The Fourth Angel*, and his eighth, *Bodies and Souls*, both explore the meandering world of rebellious teenagers in Los Angeles. *Bodies and Souls* perfects the structure introduced in *City of Night*, alternating between chapters entitled "Lost Angels," which recount the wanderings of three teenagers, and chapters titled after and describing individuals tangentially involved in the main plot. The overall structure of the novel recalls Thornton Wilder's *The Bridge at San Luis Rey*, for what unites these characters ultimately is that all are involved at the end of the novel in a highway slaughter perpetrated by Orin, the leader of the "Lost Angels." We also see in this structure a glimpse of Rechy's training in journalism, for everything in the novel leads toward this topic that dominated California news in the early 1980s, and in the process seems to supply "the story behind the story." The novel also examines a topic that is central to Rechy's canon, sublimated homosexuality or, more precisely, a male bonding in which the erotic energy is dispersed through a shared attraction to a woman, a topic that is also overt in *The Fourth Angel*. Both novels also focus on central male characters who have lost their mothers, which probably relates to the death of Rechy's own mother in 1970. The novels return to Rechy's preoccupation with religion, especially in their use of "lost angels." In *The Fourth Angel*, three teenagers randomly search for a fourth teenager or "angel" who will somehow "complete" their purpose, while in *Bodies and Souls* the three "lost angels" are governed by Orin's preoccupation with a television evangelist, Sister Woman, who, Orin has been told, will supply necessary proof to him of an afterlife. The stress on "lost angels" also intersects with Rechy's strong California regionalism, for as early as *City of Night* the novels show a fascination with the image of Los Angeles as the City of Lost Angels. And, of course, all of the imagery implicitly invokes Rechy's early interest in Milton's rebellious angels—a continued influence stressed by the title of *This Day's Death*, a phrase derived from *Paradise Lost*.

Rechy's other three novels, *The Vampires*, *Marilyn's Daughter*, and *The Miraculous Day of Amalia Gomez*, bear similar loose and associative relations with his more overtly gay texts. *The Vampires*, another novel Rechy claims not to understand, is the story of a large cast of characters gathered on an island by a rich and eccentric practitioner of voodoo. Under the guise of voodoo and "entertainment," the group tests and torments each member by staging confrontations that conjure repressed sexual fantasies and anxieties. The Gothic narrative, Rechy claims, derives from Pioe; but obvious associations with Sade's *120 Days of Sodom* are difficult to avoid and again comment on the strange approach/avoidance to sadomasochism that is present in many of Rechy's novels, especially *Rushes*. Rechy's most recent novel, *The Miraculous Day of Amalia Gomez*, taken together with *Marilyn's Daughter*, seems to mark a turning point in his canon. The story concerns a day in the life of a twice-divorced Mexican American woman contending with the stresses of an abusive live-in lover, a past of religious guilt, and an early marriage forced by a pregnancy resulting from rape, a son who has died, another who is a drug addict, and a daughter who, she fears, is heading for trouble. Like *Marilyn's Daughter*, the novel is overtly concerned with documenting and exploring the determinants of female identity in contemporary culture, a theme that seems to be emerging as the primary touchstone of Rechy's more recent canon.

Marilyn's Daughter is a carefully constructed mystery, in which Normalyn Morgan, supposed daughter of Enid Morgan, a once-famous movie star and best friend of Marilyn Monroe, pursued the ramifications of a note left by Enid upon her death telling her that she is Marilyn's daughter. The novel relies on an alternation between past and present similar to that in *This Day's Death*. In many ways Rechy's most accomplished novel, *Marilyn's Daughter* is only tangentially related to the homosexual novels that warrant Rechy a place in gay literature. However, it does culminate the poetics of ambiguous identity present in all of Rechy's work. As Normalyn's quest for truth winds down and she is given the opportunity to prove once and for all that she is Marilyn's daughter, she refuses the chance, preferring to prove herself by living her present life rather than by chasing the traces of the past. *Marilyn's Daughter* also returns us in many ways to *City of Night*, for the novel is structured around Normalyn's friendship with Troja, an African American transvestite prostitute who impersonates Marilyn Monroe and who also recalls the drag queen Miss Destiny, who presides over the central chapters of *City of Night* and also was the subject of Rechy's second published short story.

CRITICAL RECEPTION

By configuring and interpreting Rechy's canon around the topic of homosexuality, we have in many ways replicated the critical reception that has formed Rechy's place in contemporary literature. Reviewers, especially for the early work, consistently demeaned Rechy's novels as sexual gossip or, in some cases, as pornography. As a result, Rechy has come to be known as either a central marginal writer or a marginal central writer, depending on the politics of the reviewer. Although this pattern has begun to erode with the reception of *Bodies and Souls* and *Marilyn's Daughter*, it is still one that clearly demonstrates the homophobia that creates and is created by the literary marketplace in America.

Webster Schott, writing for the *New York Times Book Review*, exemplifies the prejudice that has greeted much of Rechy's work. His review of *Numbers* opens with a full frontal attack on gay culture: "The homosexual assault on United States fiction really began sometime around 1945," and labels *Numbers* as a part of "the great siege" (January 14, 1968, 5). His subsequent review of *This Day's Death* continues the refrain with its opening line—"If you don't know by now what homosexual life is like in the United States, don't blame John Rechy"—and takes the opportunity, in passing, to reduce *City of Night* to "a dark landmark in the literature of sex" (November 22, 1970, 7), again placing Rechy firmly at the center of the margins. Although Schott concedes that *This Day's Death* "isn't wholly a failure," it is clear that Rechy's novels are being held accountable for a great deal more than their own achievements.

Because Rechy's work is uneven, so too have been the reviews. It is true that the movement away from homosexuality in Rechy's writing has corresponded with an increasing control and force that merits praise, but a gay reader is forced to wonder whether this is the only reason that reviewers have been more accepting of the later canon. Alan Cheuse's review of *Bodies and Souls* in the *Times* praised Rechy's "brute lyricism" and, picking up a phrase Rechy uses to describe Los Angeles, calls the book "A 'scarred beauty' " (July 10, 1983, 34). Further evidence for a homophobic bias in reviewers can be seen in the change of tone that greeted the reissue of *City of Night* in 1985. *Books West Magazine*, for example, cites the reissued novel as evidence of "a real talent at work" (vol. 1 [October 1977], 34). It is also worth noting that *City of Night*, in which the narrator doggedly refuses to "be" homosexual, also received the best reviews of the first trilogy.

Finessing the politics of reviews is in most cases a notoriously risky business. But the fact remains that mainstream reviewers have seldom given Rechy's works the breadth of credit they deserve. Rechy himself has noted, though not in overt terms, that homophobia has shaped the reception of his books. As he notes, reviewers have almost universally preferred to critique the content and ignore the form, as if the topic of homosexuality is, in and of itself, enough to remove the need for artistic judgment. It is not surprising then to find a pattern of increased acceptance as the topic of homosexuality becomes less central in the later novels.

Scholarly work on Rechy has yielded a somewhat different picture of the writer. Rechy is both gay and Mexican American, but his place in the popular review market has been determined almost exclusively by his sexual identity. Several interesting studies have addressed the double minority identity of Rechy's texts and in the process have also provided important political insights into gay criticism. Emmanuel S. Nelson, James R. Giles, and Stanton Hoffman have all compared Rechy to James Baldwin*, and the results are instructive. Charles M. Tatum also touches on the subject and provides a worthy summary: "John Rechy holds the same position vis-a-vis contemporary Chicano literature that James Baldwin does in Black literature" (47). Both authors have somehow been ignored by the critical perspectives interested in either ethnicity or sexuality, each view relegating the authors to the other camp. Rechy's place in Chicano literature was reassessed in *Minority Voices* in 1979, an issue in which Tatum's essay and essays by Carlos Zamora and Bruce-Novoa appear. The final factor that has been ignored in Rechy's writings, that he is in many ways a regional writer, has been examined in a general way by Stanton Hoffman's discussion of Rechy and Larry McMurtry in a 1972 edition of *Houston Forum*.

WORKS BY JOHN RECHY

City of Night. New York: Grove Press, 1963; London: MacGibbon and Kee, 1964.
Numbers. New York: Grove Press, 1967.
This Day's Death. New York: Grove Press, 1969.
The Vampires. New York: Grove Press, 1971.
The Fourth Angel. London: W. H. Allen, 1972; New York: Richard Seaver/Viking, 1973.
The Sexual Outlaw: A Documentary. New York: Grove Press, 1977; London: W. H. Allen, 1978.
Rushes. New York: Grove Press, 1979.
Bodies and Souls. New York: Carroll and Graf, 1983; London: W. H. Allen, 1984.

Marilyn's Daughter. New York: Carroll and Graf, 1988.
The Miraculous Day of Amalia Gomez. New York: Little, Brown and Co., 1991.

SELECTED STUDIES OF JOHN RECHY

Bruce-Novoa, Juan. "In Search of the Honest Outlaw: John Rechy." *Minority Voices* 3 (1979): 37–45.
———. "Homosexuality and the Chicano Novel." *Confluencia* 2, no. 1 (Fall 1986): 69–77.
Giles, James R. "Larry McMurtry's *Leaving Cheyenne* and the Novels of John Rechy: From Trips along the 'Mythical Pecos.' " *Houston Forum* 10, no. 2 (1972): 34–40.
———. "Religious Alienation and 'Homosexual Consciousness' in *City of Night* and *Go Tell It on the Mountain.*" *College English* 36 (1974): 369–80.
Giles, James R., and Wanda Giles. "An Interview with John Rechy." *Chicago Review* 25 (1973): 19–31.
Heifetz, Henry. "The Anti-Social Act of Writing." *Studies on the Left* 4 (Spring 1964): 6–9.
Hoffman, Stanton. "The Cities of Night: John Rechy's *City of Night* and the American Literature of Homosexuality." *Chicago Review* 17, nos. 2–3 (1964): 195–206.
Lynch, Honora Moore. "Patterns of Anarchy and Order in the Works of John Rechy." *DAI* 37 (1976): 158A.
Nelson, Emmanuel S. "John Rechy, James Baldwin, and the American Double Minority Literature." *Journal of American Culture* 6 (Summer 1983): 70–74.
Satterfield, Ben. "John Rechy's Tormented World." *Southwest Review* 67, no. 1 (Winter 1982): 78–85.
Southern, Terry. "Rechy and Gover." *Contemporary American Novelists* 28 (1964): 222–27.
Steuernagel, Trudy. "Contemporary Homosexual Fiction and the Gay Rights Movement." *Journal of Popular Culture* 20, no. 3 (Winter 1986): 125–34.
Tatum, Charles M. "The Sexual Underworlds of John Rechy." *Minority Voices* 3 (1979): 47–52.
Zamora, Carlos. "Odysseus in John Rechy's *City of Night*: The Epistemological Journey." *Minority Voices* 3 (1979): 53–62.

PAUL REED (1956–   )
Terrence J. McGovern

BIOGRAPHY

The author of the first novel about AIDS was born Paul Hustoft on May 28, 1956, in San Diego, California, the son of Sigurd William and Melva (Moffat) Hustoft. In 1969, he had his name legally changed to Reed. Although he had studied organ, harpsichord, and piano during his childhood and teenage years and continued to do so in college, Reed chose sociology and anthropology as his major areas of study. He graduated with a B.A. from California State University, Chico, in 1978. In 1981, Reed earned a M.A. in social anthropology from the University of California, Davis, and moved to San Francisco, where he still lives. He has reviewed books for the San Francisco *Bay Area Reporter*, a gay newspaper, and *The Advocate*, a gay newsmagazine. He has also written for the *San Francisco Chronicle*, *University Journal*, *Blueboy*, *Mandate*, and *Drummer*. Since 1981, Reed has worked as an editor at Ten Speed Press/Celestial Arts, Berkeley.

Reed's arrival in San Francisco in July 1981 coincided with the first report of a cancer (Kaposi's sarcoma) and pneumocystis pneumonia among a small group of gay men in New York City and California issued by the Centers for Disease Control (CDC)—the beginnings of the AIDS epidemic. AIDS is the focal point of Reed's writings. When Reed wrote his first novel *Facing It* (1984), he did not know anyone who had AIDS, but he was motivated to write the novel because the epidemic had become the personal tragedy of so many young gay men. During the years following the publication of *Facing It*, Reed met people with AIDS and lost friends to the disease. This firsthand knowledge of AIDS became even more intimate and personal when his lover was diagnosed with AIDS-Related Condition (ARC). His own HIV-positive status completed the personalization of the epidemic. His fears and concerns for his lover, himself, and the gay community in the face of such a devastating disease resulted in *Serenity* (1987, revised edition 1990), a collection of eight essays about overcoming the fear and despair associated with AIDS. In his second novel, *Longing*, Reed puts in fictional context many of the themes discussed in *Serenity*. His most recent work is *The Q Journal* (1991). This journal chronicles his use of an experimental drug called Compound Q as well as his working through grief at the death of his lover from AIDS.

MAJOR WORKS AND THEMES

The major themes of Reed's two novels—death and dying, alienation and loneliness, love and romance—are developed within the context of the gay communities of New York and San Francisco, which are struggling to cope not only with the AIDS epidemic but also with the homophobia of American society, of religion (especially Christianity), and of the United States medical establishment. In both novels Reed juxtaposes the carefree and exhilarating days of post-Stonewall gay liberation of the late 1960s and the 1970s with the concern and the worry of the 1980s about personal health and fear of casual sex as more and more gay men contract AIDS. As in real life, not all of the gay men described in the novels accept the change of life-style required by AIDS. Promiscuity is still prevalent. Bathhouses, bushes in public parks, and back rooms in sex clubs continue to be the favored places for anonymous sex. For some, it is the attitude that it won't happen to them; for others, it is the question of why indeed it happened to them.

Facing It, Reed's first novel, is also the first American novel about AIDS. A brief history of the development of AIDS among gay men in the United States forms part of the story line. The author interrupts the fictional narrative with excerpts from the Center for Disease Control's *Morbidity and Mortality Report*, underscoring the fact that although the characters are fictitious, AIDS is a harsh reality that must be dealt with. A sense of urgency coupled with frustration and anger permeates the novel. The possible causes of the disease and its prevention become one of the principal topics of conversation among the main characters.

The story takes place in New York City in the early 1980s. Andy Stone, a young gay activist, has contracted AIDS. As a result, he and David, his lover of four years, must now face not only death and dying but also the alienation and loneliness that come from both being gay and having AIDS. Andy is no stranger to the alienation caused by homophobia. At the age of fifteen, he came out to his blue-collar suburban Philadelphia family. An initial attempt through therapy to make Andy a man as defined by his father resulted, ironically, in self-acceptance and gay pride, due in no small measure to Andy's knowledge of Stonewall. His newly found gay pride exacerbates the alienation from his family and finally ends in total exclusion. In the final stages of Andy's illness, when confronted by the loneliness of dying, he wants and needs the comforting presence of both his lover and his family. David calls Andy's family to tell them that their son and brother is dying. However, the estrangement from his family is so complete that Andy's virulently homophobic father blames David and Andy's gay life-style for AIDS and wishes them and all gays dead. Further, in one of the most powerfully written scenes of the novel, Andy's father forbids his wife to visit her dying son.

Reed continues to develop the theme of alienation by portraying the medical establishment as a group of individuals who, with few exceptions, are more interested in their careers than in trying to research a disease associated with gays. Reed highlights this alienation by having one of the doctors at the hospital callously make a wager about "how long that crazy fag in room 217 would last" (189) and by creating the character of Dr. Art Maguire, a closeted gay hospital administrator who refuses to give the necessary funds for AIDS research until threatened with exposure.

The straight establishment, however, is not the only source of alienation and loneliness. Members of the gay community also cause pain and loneliness. As soon as it becomes clear that Andy has AIDS, gay friends begin to treat him differently. Andy is especially hurt that a gay friend visiting the couple's apartment refuses to touch or hug him. Fear born of ignorance of the disease on the part of gay friends results in Andy's meal being served on a paper plate at a gay party. Although Andy understands his host's apprehension, the incident heightens his feelings of isolation and loneliness. In counterpoint to the alienation experienced from society is the alienation from self, which results from internalized homophobia. Both Andy and David question the value of their gay identity. They wonder if the homophobes are right in their insistence that AIDS is divine retribution for their gay life-style or that there is a causal relationship between being gay and contracting AIDS. This mode of thinking leads Andy to ask the ultimate question, whether if given the chance he would choose not to be gay. After exorcising the demons of fear, denial, and anger, Andy has faced the fact that he will die and has determined that in spite of the pain, both physical and spiritual, he will die with dignity. In the final moments before his death, Andy quietly and lovingly affirms his gay identity by answering no to his question.

Andy's ability to face death and dying is strongly linked to the presence of love, fidelity, and friendship. Through David's abiding and deep love, Andy found a refuge from alienation and loneliness. True friendship expressed in David's fidelity to his lover echoes the promise made by straight couples to be faithful in good times and bad, including illness, until parted by death. In spite of the obstacles of alienation, loneliness, and death from AIDS, Reed affirms the possibility of a loving monogamous relationship between two gay men. Perhaps the author's subtextual message is that Andy and David's relationship should serve as a paradigm for all gays who seek to affirm and rejoice in their gay identity.

Longing, Reed's second novel, is set in the early 1980s. Through a first-person narrator, Reed tells the story of a young gay man's search to discover life's purpose. It is a story of frustration, obsession, loneliness, alienation, and longing as the young narrator attempts to find love and fulfillment.

At an early age, the narrator realizes that he is alienated from the world of his parents and high school classmates. It is an oppressive world, from which he needs to escape. Leaving home to go to college is the first step on the way to freedom and love. His college experience, however, is a disappointment. As a college student in a small town living in a house with several other people, none of whom are gay, the narrator feels isolated and lonely. He becomes aware that he needs to be in a gay community in order to be free, that is, openly gay, and to find a lover. In the small college town, gay men are invisible except in the bushes of a nearby park. The narrator's sexual encounter with the men he meets in the park are anonymous and unfulfilling, as love is not present. In spite of warnings from friends, the narrator falls in love with Stephen, a straight student, which only adds to the narrator's sense of frustration. Although disappointed in love, the narrator's friendship with Stephen helps to alleviate some but not all of the narrator's loneliness. Stephen's subsequent departure from the college and eventual marriage reinforce the narrator's feelings of alienation and loneliness. He concludes that the only way to fulfill his deeply felt needs is to move to San Francisco, the American gay mecca.

Reed's portrayal of San Francisco is that of a city still caught up in the exuberance of gay liberation. The city is a smorgasbord of gay sex and drugs. Anonymous sex flourishes in bathhouses, sex clubs, parks, and porno theatres. Although mention is made of the role gays played in the gentrification of the Castro area, there is an emphasis on the superficiality of certain segments of the gay community. Singled out are the musclemen of the gym set. These gays are in pursuit of the perfect body in order to obtain the perfect lover. A beautiful face and a well-defined muscled body are the primary criteria for acceptance into this group. For these men, AIDS is not a major concern. The term AIDS is never mentioned. AIDS is marginal to their lives, nothing more than a rumor. This is the gay world that greets the narrator upon his arrival in San Francisco.

Delighted to find himself in a community where he can be himself and feel connected, the narrator initially revels in the hedonism offered by the gay ghetto. As time passes, he becomes bored with anonymous sex and begins to feel isolated and alone. Promiscuity is not the answer. One evening, the narrator meets Keith, a former trick from college days, who introduces the narrator to a select group of the musclemen. Their friendship gives the narrator a sense of belonging, although he is not totally comfortable with their values. As the novel progresses, the narrator becomes disenchanted with the attitudes of his gym buddies. In very strong language, he bluntly rejects their values and behavior, thus beginning his alienation from the gay community. In spite of the negative aspects of his friendship with the gym set, it is through them that the narrator meets Cole, the man who he hopes will become the man of his dreams. Obsessed with Cole, the narrator ignores his friend Keith's warning that Cole already has a lover and remains convinced that Cole is available. The narrator falls in love with Cole, who seemingly reciprocates. For two months the young couple enjoy a romantic interlude. The narrator soon learns the difference between romance and love. He is blind to the faults of Cole, until Cole returns to his former lover Laine, as predicted by the narrator's friend Keith. The narrator is crushed by Cole's lack of fidelity. Not only has the narrator's relationship with Cole cost him the friendship of the gym set, but it has contributed to his alienation from the gay community. Ever hopeful, he makes a final attempt to win back Cole. At this point in the narrative the specter of AIDS reappears. A female friend of the narrator asks him if he is being "careful" (115). The narrator watching the passing scene in the Castro notices the changes that have occurred in his brief time in the gay neighborhood. The carnival of seminaked muscled men, drag queens, and "tap-dancing blonds" (123) has been replaced by a somber procession of "young men shuffling with canes" (123). Not everyone is aware of the seriousness of the disease and his own vulnerability to it. To a group of young gays, AIDS is source of humor:— "Isn't it just too perfect that a *gay* cancer should show up in *violet* spots" (117).

To the tough realities of life in the gay world is now added yet another, the reality of death from AIDS. Keith, who has been for the narrator a kind of mentor in the ways of gay life, reminds the young man that people are changing and so must he. The narrator must change not only his sexual habits but also his attitude towards his life and failed relationship with Cole. In the end, the young narrator passes through the crucible of anger and despair, frustration and loneliness to emerge with a new understanding of the meaning of life.

CRITICAL RECEPTION

Facing It is acknowledged as the first novel about AIDS. The response to Reed's first novel was generally positive. As for the subject matter of the novel, Joseph Interrante sums up the critical reception by stating that *Facing It* "is a welcome addition to our struggle to learn to live with AIDS" (6). Reed's knowledge of the history and development of AIDS is commented on by most of the critics. However, this knowledge can be problematic when Reed tries to weave it into the story. Much of the information on AIDS is conveyed through the conversations of the characters, which according to

Interrante make "the dialogue seem overly didactic and somewhat wooden" (7). This opinion is echoed by John-Manuel Andriote who, although affirming the importance and value of the theme, thinks that "the book's language is often stilted and artificial" (43).

With one notable exception, the critical response to *Longing* is generally positive. The reviewers praise Reed's prose writing skill and his sensitivity to the human condition. Ray Olson and John Malloy comment on the presence of New Age ideas—transcendence, harmony with nature and the universe. The young narrator's negative life experiences, according to Olson, change him "from romantic to nascent New Ager" (542). Several critics note Reed's reprise of the AIDS theme. According to Malloy, Reed has incorporated the epidemic into the plot with "effective subtlety" and "eloquent understatement" (6).

In marked contrast to the other critics is Bob Satuloff's review. At the beginning of the review, he states that, after having read *Longing*, "it's possible to feel as much cultural alienation from the sensibility of a gay novelist as one might feel reading the latest Sidney Sheldon best-seller" (23). Although he acknowledges Reed's skill as a "prose stylist" (23), Satuloff takes umbrage at the portrayal of the gay community as shallow and mean-spirited. The description of gays is so negative that Satuloff thinks that the novel may be a satire. He also takes issue with the novel's conclusion. In an interview with La Padula, Reed acknowledged that he has been criticized in the past for "being overly critical of Gay life in San Francisco" (21). In *The Q Journal*, Reed responds to Satuloff's review. Although Reed finds the review "strange," he "was impressed by the simple fact that he (Satuloff) had evidently read the novel closely and had given it a great deal of thought" (101). In reply to Satuloff's observations, Reed states that he intended the novel to be "an indictment of a subset of gay culture that is unfortunately shallow"; that the novel "is not a satire"; that "the ending is terribly weak, mostly because I simply did not know how the story ended myself. I would have to live a couple more years before I learned" (101).

Ten years have passed since the CDC report announced the beginning of AIDS. Since that time, thousands of gay men have died; many more are infected. In the face of such sorrow and tragedy, Paul Reed's novels give us the opportunity "to rediscover the fighting spirit it takes to go on living and caring about life—and to see how far our community has come" (Bean, 63).

WORKS BY PAUL REED

Facing It: A Novel of AIDS. San Francisco: Gay Sunshine Press, 1984.
Longing. Berkeley: Celestial Arts, 1988.

Serenity: Challenging the Fear of AIDS, from Despair to Hope. Berkeley: Celestial
     Arts, 1987; rev. ed. 1990.
The Q Journal: A Treatment Diary. Berkeley: Celestial Arts, 1991.

SELECTED STUDIES OF PAUL REED

Andriote, John-Manuel. Rev. of *Facing It: A Novel of AIDS. The Advocate* 423
     (25 June 1985): 43–44.
Bean, Joseph W. "Prescriptions for the Here and Now." *The Advocate* 514 (20
     December 1988): 62–63.
Interrante, Joseph. "Learning to Live with AIDS." Rev. of *Facing It: A Novel of
     AIDS. Gay Community News* 12, no. 32 (2 March 1985): 6–7.
Kolata, Gina. Review of *Longing. New York Times* 19 February 1989: 20.
La Padula, Phil. "Longings of a Romantic Idealist." Review of *Longing. Washington
     Blade* 19, no. 47 (18 November 1988): 21.
Malloy, John. "Feet in the Castro, Head in the Stars." Review of *Longing. Lambda
     Book Report* 1, no. 10 (April 1989): 6.
Nelson, Emmanuel S. "AIDS and the American Novel." *Journal of American Culture*
     13, no. 1 (Spring 1991): 47–53.
Olson, Ray. Review of *Longing. Booklist* 85 (15 November 1988): 539.
Ratner, Rochelle. Review of *Facing It: A Novel of AIDS. Library Journal* 1, no. 10
     (1 March 1985): 92–93.
Satuloff, Bob. "No Common Denominator." Review of *Longing. New York Native*
     9 (July 1990); 23.
Umans, Meg. Review of *Facing It: A Novel of AIDS. RFD* 45 (Winter 1985): 6.

PAUL RUSSELL (1956–   )
D. S. Lawson

BIOGRAPHY

Paul Russell was born on July 1, 1956, in Memphis, Tennessee, the son of Jack Russell, a professor of mathematics at Southwestern College at Memphis (now known as Rhodes College) and Margaret Feltner Russell, a musician. He is the oldest of three sons, the others being Mark (born 1958, a computer programmer who lives in California) and Brian (born 1961, a furniture designer who lives in Memphis). He earned a B.A. in English from Oberlin College in Ohio in 1978. He went on to the graduate program in English and creative writing at Cornell University and was awarded the degree of M.A. in English in 1982. He earned an M.F.A. in creative writing in 1982 as well, writing a collection of short stories and a novella called "The Longing in Darkness." He received the Ph.D. in English in 1983 with a dissertation entitled *Vladimir Nabokov: The Habit of Exile*. With Jeffrey Kotzen he cofounded and coedited a literary magazine, *The Poughkeepsie Review*, which published between 1987 and 1990. He currently lives in Poughkeepsie, New York, where he teaches at Vassar College. Among the courses he has taught is a course on gay and lesbian literature called "Queer Alphabets."

His first novel, *The Salt Point*, is set mostly in Poughkeepsie. Russell has said of Poughkeepsie,

While I was writing *The Salt Point*, I used to drive around aimlessly, letting myself get lost in Poughkeepsie's seedy neighborhoods and stricken parks, trying to imagine what it might be like to have grown up here, to have lived a whole life here. I'd moved to Poughkeepsie from Ithaca, NY, a jewel of a town, and had spent much time depressed by Poughkeepsie's rampant ugliness. Writing *The Salt Point* taught me the difference between the beautiful and the merely pretty. After I finished the book, I made a trip up to Ithaca, and that city I'd loved in my younger years now seemed too tidy, too kempt, a roccoco confection, where Poughkeepsie now had a heft, a palpable reality to it that I could feel. Its beauty didn't depend on the merely aesthetic, its beauty was simply whatever IS. I think that was an important turning point for me as a writer, that realization about prettiness and beauty, because my work up till then had been marred by a kind of misplaced aestheticism (as will be painfully obvious to anyone perusing my early published stories). (All quotes in this section are derived from correspondence with the author.)

Russell lists D. H. Lawrence, Joyce Carol Oates, and Patrick White among his influences. Of them Russell writes,

These aren't necessarily my favorite writers, in fact I often can't stand elements of their work. But I learned something from each of them. Lawrence taught me not to be afraid of trying to render the terrific squalor and splendor of human emotions in all their mind-numbing contradictoriness. Characters, like people, should be allowed their internal dissonances. From Oates' work I learned to trust the life around me—whatever my material happened to be, even if it was just a few people living in Poughkeepsie, that was good enough. And from White I learned how to make a scene, to set it in motion, to get characters talking to or at or past one another, and also to undermine even the most ordinary moments with a sense of strangeness and wonder.

Although Russell's hometown of Memphis does not figure in *The Salt Point*, part of *Boys of Life* is set there. Russell says of using Memphis in this novel,

I don't think I really have much to say about Memphis—except that it's taken me a long time to write about it, and one of the surprises of *Boys of Life* was how familiar the territory felt once I'd gotten the characters there. I think the thing that daunted me all those years was the presence of so many powerfully imagined Souths already in the literature—Faulkner's and Welty's and Tennessee Williams' in particular. It was hard for me to see through those visions to my own private, meager version of the place, and it was only by the circuitous route of this novel's plot that I finally arrived there.

He specifically cites Paul Rogers' *Saul's Book* as a major influence on *Boys of Life*.

As of late 1991, Russell's current project is a novel provisionally entitled *Shehzade* which means "prince" in Arabic (compare with the feminine Sheherezade). Of it Russell says, "It's looking like it's going to be fairly long, since it involves a multilayered narrative, some strands of which I haven't even begun to work out yet. It takes place in America and Turkey and on the moon."

MAJOR WORKS AND THEMES

Both of Paul Russell's novels revolve around older gay men who mold and refashion teenaged boys, trying to get these boys to conform to a preconceived aesthetic vision. Anatole, the hairdresser protagonist of *The Salt Point*, sees the exquisitely beautiful Leigh ("our boy of the mall") one day through the window of Reflexion, his salon on Poughkeepsie's main mall; when they later meet, Leigh becomes the center of Anatole's whole existence. Just as Anatole reshapes Leigh's hair to fit his own notion of attractiveness, he attempts to force Leigh to conform to all his notions of the perfect young lover; despite all of Anatole's maneuvers, Leigh and Anatole have sex only once and very perfunctorily at that. One result of Anatole's constant sculpting of Leigh is that Leigh remains mysterious, ultimately unknowable, throughout the course of the novel. Readers do learn some isolated details of Leigh's past—an unhappy crush on a male childhood friend—but not enough to comprehend fully the motivations for all his actions, particularly his leaving Anatole and the circle of friends around him for a stranger met in a bar at the novel's end. One failure of the generally successful and moving novel is that the third-person, omniscient narrator never convincingly details Leigh's personality or history.

Easily the chief attraction of the novel is the character of Anatole's friend Chris, an educated and relatively financially comfortable outsider who has moved to Poughkeepsie to open a record store. Despite the sexual attraction and availability of other characters, both male and female, Chris remains physically aloof, preferring infrequent trips down to New York City where he pays hustlers to have sex in front of him. Chris' voyeurism is perhaps a comment upon the nature of narrative itself—the incessant watching of people who are unaware of the attention. Chris' lack of connection with the other characters borders on being frightening at times and, importantly, it is he who drives off, leaving Leigh at the home of the man they have met in a bar.

By withdrawing, Chris has found one way to survive the conflicting demands of his sexuality and of the normative society. Anatole's way to survive is to fixate upon some object for his romantic fantasies, to numb himself with drugs and alcohol, and to make increasingly frantic and desperate emotional demands upon his friends. The novel ends with an emblem of Anatole's capacity for survival. Bereft of Leigh, sad and alone in his apartment in the middle of the night, Anatole hears his downstairs neighbor complaining about all his noise, insisting that she's just trying to sleep: "And Anatole shouts back, stomping on the floor, jumping up and down, laughing and crying like a maniac, 'I'm just trying to stay *alive* up here,' he cries. 'Don't you understand, I'm just trying to stay alive.' " (210). This is finally the theme of *The Salt Point*: what people do to survive. For Russell's characters, it can mean long alcoholic nights at dreary, depressing bars, or it can involve basing whole chunks of life around fantasies projected onto relative strangers. Finally, however, the characters do survive, do exhibit a kind of strength and dignity in the midst of misery.

The title image is important for the novel as a whole. The salt point is that ever-changing place where the Hudson River changes from salt to fresh water. Like the river, these characters are undergoing fundamental changes, major accommodations in their lives; they try to find a way to make the real world resemble their dreams and fantasies. Strangely enough, as the novel progresses and change becomes more imminent, the characters grow worried and frightened, seemingly afraid both of getting what they want and of not getting it as well.

Boys of Life covers much of the same thematic ground, but through different eyes. It uses Tony Blair, the teenage boy who becomes the subject of the artistic refashioning, as its narrator; thus, unlike with Leigh, the reader is allowed full access to Tony's thoughts, fears, and past. His mentor is avant-garde filmmaker Carlos Reichart, who picks Tony up while on a location shoot in Kentucky and brings him back to the seedy East Village apartment from which he makes his movies. Tony stars in Reichart's next feature, *Next Week in Gomorrah*, which becomes the darling of film scholars. As the films become increasingly bizarre and violent, Tony grows uncomfortable and ultimately runs off to Tennessee with a waitress from a dive where he drinks and plays pinball.

Despite Tony's shaping role as narrator, it is he who ultimately is shaped by the characters surrounding him. He appears to have no fixed sexuality—fantasizing about sex with his younger brother, enjoying sex with Reichart, participating in graphically sexual scenes with other performers in the films, but running away with a young girl whom he ultimately marries and with whom he lives a fairly typical heterosexual life for a time.

In Reichart's films, the dialogue is overdubbed by different actors after shooting has finished; the words that come out of Tony's mouth on the screen are not in fact his at all, not even the words he emits while pretending to be a character. So pervasive is Reichart's influence over Tony Blair that his words in the films are not his own. A reader is left wondering to what extent the words he so voluminously produces in *Boys of Life* are really his and to what extent they are a production of the people and factors influencing Tony's life. At the time the story is narrated, Tony is serving a jail sentence for Reichart's murder, the statue having come to life and destroyed its creator.

Boys of Life suffers from a failure complementary to that of *The Salt Point*. Whereas Leigh remains unknowable in Russell's first novel, Reichart is elusive and opaque in his second. Perhaps it is always difficult to depict a mad genius, but it is particularly hard to do in the voice and with the consciousness of an unsophisticated, relatively uneducated boy who lacks fundamental understanding of the nature of Reichart's artistic medium. The Lower East Side setting of the novel, however, is highly atmospheric and evocative.

With its graphic descriptions of sex and violence, *Boys of Life* must be counted as an example of the "new narrative" whose chief apologist is Dennis Cooper.* Russell's form and technique are much more accessible and mainstream than typical for the new narrative, but in his second novel he clearly ventures into the territory associated with new narrative. Despite the genteel qualities of Russell's fiction, the fascination with pain and horror common to the new narrative remains intact.

Of Russell's short stories, only "Ricky" shares the concerns of these novels in any significant way. Its eponymous narrator, a fifteen-year-old boy who is picked up by an older man at a bus station and then taken on an odyssey across the Far West, exhibits many similarities to Leigh and Tony. When the older man, Robison, finally attempts sex with Ricky, we once again see the sex act divorced from any truly functional sexuality; as Ricky says, "If you play around with me I'm going to get all excited. It doesn't mean anything" (22). Like Russell's other teenage objects, Ricky is bored and has no recourse to those things that have traditionally given meaning and direction to life—religion, family, education, work, and the like. All these young characters see the attentions of older gay men as one means of escape, as one way to fill the time, as something to do.

Russell's exploration of relations between older men and teenage boys is resonant both with hope and despair. Are these men trying to re-live their own adolescent years through the boys they attract? Are they trying to re-create (or at least re-encounter) their own innocence? Artistry and creation play significant roles in Russell's fictive world. Are we meant to see the "artists" Anatole and Reichart as representatives of Russell the artist, weaving the fabric of the characters' lives as he creates them? (One problem in viewing these artists autobiographically is that, at least on the surface, Chris' past life in *The Salt Point* is a closer match to Russell's own life than is Anatole's.) Ultimately a reader is left wondering to what extent these boys are being shaped and to what extent they are being mutilated; especially in the more horrifying scenes of Carlos Reichart's later films, the line becomes blurred, inviting readers to reconsider where the line should be drawn.

With the exception of the story "Opening the Door," whose emotionally distant narrator becomes fascinated with Jared, a man dying of AIDS, the subject of AIDS is not central to Russell's concerns. *Boys of Life* is set before the disease became widespread, and it seems to play only a peripheral role in the lives of the characters of *The Salt Point*. He chooses instead to present his readers with complex psychological renderings of characters within fairly traditional narrative frameworks.

CRITICAL RECEPTION

Perhaps because his novels have appeared from Dutton, a respected press which also handles well-known mainstream writers, Russell has been reviewed in many publications that do not often pay attention to gay literature. He has, generally speaking, received positive press; oddly enough, some of his most savage and negative reviews have come from the gay press. Maybe his conservative narrative idiom seems old-fashioned to reviewers used to more flashy (not to add gory and sensationalistic) prose on homosexual subjects.

On the other hand, Sarah Ferguson in the *New York Times Book Review* sees Russell's "slightly numb prose style . . . [as] perfectly suited to [the characters'] hollow search for affirmation" (23). Madison Smartt Bell, writing in the *Village Voice*, compares *The Salt Point* to "one of the nastier Henry James novels, [which] shows how very possible it is for all of its characters to do unspeakable harm to each other, without allowing themselves to know what they are doing" (77). Bruce Bawer in the *Wall Street Journal* specifically cites the novel as "conspicuous for its genuineness and humanity. . . . [Russell's] accomplishment is to remind us, with surprising poignancy, that the miracle of life is how very much people can mean to each other" (A12).

Despite the positive reviews from the straight press, John Wing in *Out/Week* seems singlemindedly set on assaulting every aspect of *The Salt Point*. He terms it "far from great writing" (68). After quoting a sex scene from the novel, Wing observes, "Russell's sexual descriptions tend to sound like bad take-out Chinese food" (68). He goes on to argue that the novel "shows quite clearly the MTV-ication [*sic*] of American fiction" (72) and ends his review by saying that it is "hard for the reader to keep from shrugging off the characters and from throwing the book away" (72). Many of Wing's criticisms of the book seem gratuitous, more an occasion for publishing waspish, well-crafted barbs than an honest reaction to or assessment of the novel's merits or flaws.

The early reviews of *Boys of Life*, in both the straight and the gay presses, have been more mixed. This certainly is in large part a response to a second novel that bites off more than the first one did, that aims higher and thus appears worse if it even slightly misses the mark.

In *The Washington Post* Andrew Sullivan argues that Reichart's need for vicarious, observed experience is fed by Tony's utter inexperience: "It's clear from the outset that Blair will be for Reichart another experiment in observation and that Reichart will be for Blair a first experiment in actual living. From the beginning, this meeting of temperaments provides the essential theme of the book" (8). Writing in the *San Francisco Chronicle*, David Silva compares *Boys of Life* to a well-known icon of gay culture: "Like a Robert Mapplethorpe photograph, *Boys of Life* explores the unsettling tension between artistry and prurience, aesthetics and morality.... Russell's novel succeeds by presenting a provocative but balanced study of the artist as pioneer in the far reaches of human experience" (9). John Rechy* argues that *Boys of Life*, along with Bret Easton Ellis' *American Psycho* and Dennis Cooper's *Frisk*, "provides further evidence that the novel of sexual violence may be replacing the novel of sexual passion. The object of desire has become the object of mutilation" (1).

Once again, however, Russell received his most negative review from the gay media: writing in *The Advocate*, Felice Picano* chides Russell's fiction for a lack of awareness of a gay and lesbian community, saying, "his characters live in one of those arty, unreal worlds found only in books and movies" (84).

Although one is always happy to see gay literature reviewed at all in the mainstream press (much more so to see it positively and respectfully reviewed), it is discouraging to see gay reviewers in gay publications do to Paul Russell what John Wing and Felice Picano have done. Perhaps the gay literary world has yet to recognize one of its treasures.

WORKS BY PAUL RUSSELL

"The Witch and the Goatboy." *Black Warrior Review* 7, no. 2 (Spring 1981): 72–81.
"Leiza." *Akros Review* 6 (Fall 1982): 83–86.
"After Mariah." *Swallow's Tale* 1, no. 1 (Spring 1983): 96–104.
"Ricky." *Carolina Quarterly* 37, no. 1 (Fall 1984): 12–24.
"Emma." *Souwester* 11, no. 3 (Winter 1984): 41–53.
"Brushes." *Epoch* 34, no. 2 (Summer 1985): 102–11.
"A Hospital Room, a Tesseract, a Box Canyon." *The Crescent Review* 5, no. 2 (Fall 1987): 138–46.
The Salt Point. New York: Dutton, 1990. [In Dutch as *De jonge van de windelpromenade.* Amsterdam: Amber, 1991. In Italian, Italy: Mondadori, 1991. In Swedish, Sweden: Wiken, 1991.]
Boys of Life. New York: Dutton, 1991.
"Opening the Door." *Men on Men 4: An Anthology of Gay Fiction.* Ed. George Stambolian. New York: Plume/NAL, 1992.

SELECTED STUDIES OF PAUL RUSSELL

Bawer, Bruce. "Bookshorts: Thirtysomething and Having a Rough Time." Review of *The Salt Point* by Paul Russell. *The Wall Street Journal* 19 April 1990: A12.
Bell, Madison Smartt. "Three Lives." Review of *The Salt Point* by Paul Russell. *The Village Voice* 24 April 1990: 77.

DeFelice, Jim. "Poughkeepsie after Dark." Review of *The Salt Point* by Paul Russell. *Hudson Valley* June 1990: 37–38.

Ferguson, Sarah. Review of *The Salt Point* by Paul Russell. *New York Times Book Review* 6 May 1990: 22–23.

Picano, Felice. "Lost Horizons: New Gay Novels Display Style and Grace, But What's the Point?" Review of *Boys of Life* by Paul Russell. *The Advocate* 22 October 1991: 82–84.

Rechy, John. "The School of Cruelty." Review of *Boys of Life* by Paul Russell. *Los Angeles Times Book Review* 6 October 1991: 1+.

Review of *Boys of Life*, by Paul Russell. *Publishers' Weekly* 31 May 1991: 60.

Review of *The Salt Point* by Paul Russell. *Publishers' Weekly* 12 January 1990: 47.

Silva, David. "Gritty Surfaces of a Runaway's Career." Review of *Boys of Life* by Paul Russell. *San Francisco Chronicle* 10 November 1991: 1.

Snider, Clifton. "Bitter Truths." Review of *The Salt Point* by Paul Russell. *The Advocate* 31 July 1990: 71.

Sullivan, Andrew. "Walks on the Wild Side." Review of *Boys of Life* by Paul Russell. *Washington Post* 20 October 1991: 8.

Wing, John. "Penny Brown Nipples from Hell." Review of *The Salt Point* by Paul Russell. *Outweek* 18 April 1990: 68+.

JONATHAN STRONG (1944–   )
James Morrison

BIOGRAPHY

Jonathan Strong was born in 1944 in Winnetka, Illinois, and attended Harvard University, dropping out for a time before receiving his degree in 1969. His early work began to appear while he was a senior, and his first two books—*Tike and Five Stories* and *Ourselves*—were published to enthusiastic acclaim in 1969 and 1971, respectively. Throughout the 1970s and 1980s, Strong taught writing at Harvard, the University of Massachusetts at Boston, and Wellesley, as well as at Tufts University, where he continues to teach. Meanwhile, sections of novels or stories continued to appear in such journals as *TriQuarterly*, *Shenandoah*, and *Transatlantic Review*. His next novel, *Elsewhere*, was not published until 1985, to general acclaim but, considering the novel's surpassing brilliance, insufficient notice.

When *Elsewhere* appeared, *Christopher Street* did a spread on the novel, but Strong is not a "gay writer" in the accepted sense of the term; his work places gay sexuality in the context of human sexuality in general. Indeed, his recent response, in defense of Edward Albee, to a piece by Edmund White* in the *New York Times* suggests Strong's understanding of such a category:

The account by David Richards of a writer's dedication to aesthetic values through both the fat and the lean years gave courage to those others of us "writers who are gay" (to adopt Mr. Albee's distinction) who read with some bewilderment Edmund White's canonization of certain "gay writers" in the *Times* magazine of the same Sunday. If literary movements are now defined by sociological subject matter and marketing goals, we need a voice like Mr. Albee's to remind us of our task as explorers of language and imaginers of the range of human experience. (printed June 30, 1991)

MAJOR WORKS AND THEMES

In *Secret Words*, the narrator, Barbara Orsini, amuses herself intermittently by scratching phrases in the steel-and-glass shelter where she waits, mornings, for the bus. The phrases often bear some relation to what is going on in Barbara's life; but the reader is not always sure Barbara herself is aware of that significance, especially because the phrases are, on the face of it, out of keeping with what we know of Barbara's character. She is an overweight woman in her thirties from a working-class family, sometimes narrow-minded but always generous-spirited, unpretentious, matter-of-fact. The phrases, however, seem cryptic, gnomic, antic, remote, oddly poeticized. They express, these "secret words," truths about Barbara's self of which even she may be oblivious, and her triumph in the course of the novel is in her pursuit of these enigmatic inner words, giving herself up to them to see what they tell her of herself, to learn how she might, at last, be able to speak them to others.

Barbara's furtive, half-playful scrawling of these words on the bus shelter plays a relatively minor role in the novel's structure, but in the context of Strong's work as a whole it is a crucially characteristic gesture. For Strong's characters, the deepest words are always secret, and the fiercest impulse is always painfully divided between protecting that secrecy and renouncing it to achieve a degree of intimacy with others. Often such impulses become a key part of the work's structural principles.

Ourselves and *Elsewhere*, for example, are both constructed around private journals kept by the main characters for therapeutic purposes. Xavy, the narrator of *Ourselves*, recounts in a diary the details of his relationship with Jeff Kimberk and Susannah Twombley on the advice of his psychiatrist; Burt Stokes, the narrator of *Elsewhere*, enters his words into the word processor at the office where he works, keeping a journal to try to come to terms with the circumstances surrounding the kidnapping of his wife's child. In both cases, the format of the journal and its interaction with the ongoing events of the story account for the novel's complexity. In *Tike*, *Secret Words*, *Companion Pieces*, and the yet-to-be-published *Offspring*, the narrative style is more immediate and perhaps more conventional, relating usually in the present tense the events as, presumably, they occur; but the tension between the narrators' public responses and their private reflections remains formative of the novels' construction.

An examination of Strong's first-published (and perhaps still best-known) work, "Supperburger," will clarify these issues before we survey the novels in greater detail. In fact, because "Supperburger" has gone through multiple revisions since its first appearance in 1966, it exemplifies the overall evolution of Strong's fiction at the same time that it sounds fully his major theme. Narrated by its eighteen-year-old protagonist Patrick, the story concerns the relationship between the naive, curious, petulantly vulnerable Patrick and an aging, warily disillusioned composer, Arthur Supperburger. During one of Patrick's routine visits to Supperburger's townhouse, amid civilized conversation among Patrick, Supperburger, his wife, and a visiting nephew Louis, Supperburger announces to Patrick in private that their time together is ending. At the end of the story, the four of them marvel at the sky from the roof, and Patrick leaves with Louis, thinking they will become friends. The story's simplicity of surface is deceptive, for a number of basic questions are answered only with insistent ambiguity. The sexual nature of Supperburger's relationship with Patrick, for example, is hinted at in Patrick's memory of their meeting, or in the abruptly physical description of Supperburger's stomach, or in the furtiveness of their embrace: "I hear the door opening and quickly get back all the way on the bed...." (149). Is Patrick a hustler for whom Supperburger has paid, as one of his monologues suggests? Why does Mrs. Supperburger not only tolerate but seem to welcome Patrick, treating him alternately with a sympathy he appreciates and a pity that frightens him? The most explicit reference to homosexuality in the story, in any case, comes in Patrick's description of Supperburger's books: "I have heard of Kipling and there is a big set of his books, and I know about Wilde" (128). Clearly, Wilde, about whom Patrick *knows*, is to be distinguished from Kipling, about whom he has merely *heard*.

In the revision of "Supperburger," Strong simplifies the story's surface and amplifies its ambiguity still further. At the end of the first version, Patrick's father arrives and shouts recriminations up to the roof at Supperburger and Patrick. In the final version, called "Zwillingsbruder," this event is gone; Strong's removal of this climactic incident shows his withdrawal over the course of his career from conventional forms of narrative rhetoric, but it also underlines Patrick's solitude. Moreover, the final version of the story works numerous refinements and modulations of voice, enriching the autumnal melancholy of Zwillingsbruder's twilight soliloquies and increasing Patrick's painfully growing awareness of his own marginal place in Zwillingsbruder's life—and perhaps, by extension, in the world.

Tike and *Ourselves*, also narrated by boys, similarly balance an adolescent viewpoint against a fully wrought subtext. *Tike* is narrated by a college dropout whose first affair with an older girl the story chronicles. Tike is sensitive and withdrawn, but he yearns for connection with others. (A yet-to-be-published revision of *Tike and Five Stories* is called, tellingly, "Among Others.") Where Patrick of "Supperburger" repeatedly expresses his adolescent fear that others will like him more than he likes them, though, Tike is instinctively aware of his own emotional excesses and carefully monitors them, as in this passage of almost Lawrentian content:

I fall on my back and roll around. I lie on my back and pant. The sky is light. I think of Val suddenly. I cannot remember what she looks like...I get up. I am dizzy. I sit down. Now I get up again. I run slowly back to my shoes. I have trouble finding them, but I find them.... (12–13)

The balance *Tike* achieves is that between the amplitude of its emotional content and the starkness of its expression. Tike's name itself, a short form of the more baroque Timon, illustrates the brusque containment of baroque potential that characterizes the novel. At the same time it accurately designates Tike—only a kid, after all—and points to his essential difference from others through the peculiarly foreign quality of the nickname. The novel is, moreover, haunted by figures of High Romanticism. Tike listens to Wagner at top volume and reads Goethe with his lover Val. The distilled simplicity of the sentences repeatedly threatens to burst at the seams in its effort to contain Tike's powerful longings, his potent ardor, so that, for example, a small gesture at the novel's end like the hurling of a stone becomes, in this context, an explosive epiphany.

The wonder of *Tike*—as of much of Strong's fiction—is how Strong is able to express fully *through* Tike's voice an intense authorial tenderness toward the character. That is, Strong gets some distance on the character while entirely retaining an immediacy of narrative pitch, a feat all the more remarkable because Strong cannot draw here upon contrasts between past and present to achieve it. Tike is exclusively a creature of the present, as the impacted present-tense of the prose certifies; and when a voice from Tike's past life does manage to break through, in the form of chatty letters from his mother or a friend, the effect is quite jarring.

Ourselves is a novel that also deals with the rapture and despair of youth, but it depends precisely on counterpointing the past of the story's events with the present of its writing. Thus its narrator, Xavy, emerges as a more calculating figure than Strong's previous narrators, still at the mercy of incalculable longings but more in control of their expression. Reading *Ourselves* in the full context of Strong's work, one senses that Xavy may be the one among his characters most like himself, but he is also the one for whom Strong expresses the least affection.

The tension of *Ourselves* derives from a quality of portentousness that grows out of Xavy's fully modulated voice. One senses throughout the novel that Xavy's journal is a confession of sorts, that Xavy has ultimately done something terrible in the story that he is recounting. (In this atmosphere of anxiety, as well as more generally in its painstaking rendering of young people entering the world of adults, Strong's book is the obvious precursor of a novel like Scott Spencer's *Endless Love*.) Indeed, Xavy casually betrays Jeff and Susannah throughout the novel, and he seems incapable of confronting the intensity of his feelings for Jeff. Indeed, Xavy is so good at deflecting his—and our—attention from the deepest reserves of his own feeling that the novel itself loses some of its potential force.

Strong's work through *Ourselves* concerns characters armoring themselves against emotions, still unrecognized, powerful enough to destabilize the self. What is at stake in these books, then, is less the social consequence than the sheer power of feeling. (Given the ardent and amorphous nature of the feeling, it is noteworthy that neither Tike nor Xavy acknowledges even the faintest possibility of homoerotic desire in himself.) Strong's next two published novels, *Elsewhere* and *Secret Words*, his finest works to date, shift the focus somewhat. Though still much concerned with movements of mind and inflections of voice, both novels present a more detailed social milieu, perhaps simply by focusing on adults whose place in society remains insecure. In both cases, this insecurity is reflected in a sexual involvement that stands in a troubled relationship to society. Burt, the teacher in *Elsewhere*, is sexually involved with his student Liam, while Barbara Orsini of *Secret Words* has, in spite of her deeply conservative upbringing, moved in with a black man. In each case, the narrator's self-discovery hinges on the ability to make a place for these desires in the social world, to bend restrictive convention to individual desire.

In *Elsewhere*, Burt Stokes displaces his fascination with one of his students, Anthony, a gifted writer who has died before the novel begins, onto two others, Liam and Nell. Like Xavy of *Ourselves*, Burt is nearly paralyzed by a sense of moral rectitude, sacrificing his own life as it were by marrying Anthony's lover Nell; at the same time, he is shown to be, by instinct, deeply manipulative (also like Xavy). The novel's first two sections detail Burt's haphazardly formed sexual bonds first with Liam, then with Nell, both of whom were intimate with Anthony. At the end of the second section, Burt reflects as he makes love with Nell:

At moments I felt she was Liam then I knew she was Nell. I was in a dark dream, tumbling, surging. Did she think I was Anthony? I even pretended I was Anthony, at first, to get myself going, even for a moment that I was Anthony with Liam. But I came back to Nell and me. In the midst of it I saw Anthony come running to me, over a hill, barefoot, all in tears, saying Nell's pregnant and she wants an abortion. And here was my Nell beneath me. And I thought that now I'd been inside Liam, and inside Nell, in the two most secret places Anthony had been in his life. (72–73)

What makes this passage both oddly moving and intensely disturbing is the keen rhythm of its prose, alternately poetically stilted and heightened, its supple mixture of expansive solicitousness and crimped rapacity. Amid the inexorable flow of primal images, Burt does not lose sight of "my Nell beneath me." (But is that possessive tender or sadistic—the "my Nell" merely to distinguish her from *Anthony's* Nell?) Although he makes love to her to please her, still the thought of how he uses her presses in on him in the end. Throughout much of the novel, Burt sees himself as a savior: "What can I do to rescue Nell?" he asks of this woman grieving over the death of her lover and the loss of her child. But his efforts at salvation are ineffectual at best; the coiled, terse admission of the first paragraph—"We have an idea where [our baby] is, we know who took her, when and why, but we do not think we will get her back" (3)—suggests the paralysis into which Burt has fallen at the novel's beginning. The "secret places" to which he stumblingly finds admission signal the curious, dreamlike lack of volition in the action of the novel as a whole.

The pastoral, utopian connotations of the novel's title do not prepare the reader for the stark landscape it depicts, a landscape of barren streets and rubble-strewn lots. In fact, the novel is decidedly *not* set in a "world elsewhere": As Burt himself notes, "If I had lived elsewhere I would have letters [from Anthony] too, but I lived here . . . "(3). The novel is about the distance between *here* and *elsewhere*—or between present and past, or self and others—yet what makes it, for all that, unexpectedly luminous *is* its suggestion of a "world elsewhere." Anthony's writing (of which Burt's journal serves as a tortured analogue) first opens up such a world. His own "secret words" transform the grey city into a mythic otherworld. The reader, ironically refused access to this *elsewhere*, remains with Burt and the others in the novel's pressingly immediate *here*—which has, nonetheless, been touched by that other world they, and we, can only glimpse.

At the end of the novel, Burt decides to set off in search of Liam, who is "hiding in this huge country." On the one hand, Burt can be seen here as having fully accepted his desire for Liam and at last set a decisive course of action, having abandoned *here* for *elsewhere*; at the same time, he can be seen as only once again abdicating his real responsibilities, misperceiving Liam as needful and "submissive." The novel's conclusion piercingly portends both the character's first triumph and his final desolation.

Secret Words works at a similar level of complexity, but Barbara's moral courage in forcing her mother to recognize her relationship with Paul confers on the novel an unquestioned purity that shimmers through the utter simplicity of Barbara's own words. Like *Secret Words*, much of Strong's later fiction concerns family dynamics, in contrast to the absent or hopelessly fractured families of his earlier work. The crucial balance of private against public expression still remains in place, however. *Offspring* deals with a father's concern about the place of his three sons in the larger social world outside the protection of the family, while *Doing and Undoing* (one of the two short novels of *Companion Pieces*) is a quasi-Joycean fugue of voices among brothers. Both novels overlay a quality of myth upon family history, and both concern the place of private assumptions in society at large. The boys in *Offspring* sport Biblical names and compulsively mount inexplicable private projects such as digging tunnels in the basement; yet, as their father comments, "Their schoolmates haven't learned the words they know, wouldn't care for the games they play. But no one gives our boys trouble. They're strong from their digging, and good-looking, so they're tolerated"

(2). In Strong's recent work, the family becomes an emblem of private sensibility confronting public demand, as the family is at once an intimate unit—an extension of the self—and a social collective—a group of others. This growing concern for the gestural nuances of social milieu reflects the development in Strong's work—self-consciously signalled by references in *Offspring* to the work of Sinclair Lewis and Edith Wharton—of a post-modern fiction of manners.

CRITICAL RECEPTION

Strong's work has yet to be the subject of full-scale critical analysis, but the reviews of his work have been generally favorable and perceptive. Reviews of the first two books emphasize their immediacy and ability to speak for their own generation. Strong is, according to these reviews, very much a writer of the 1960s. (This claim seems in retrospect shortsighted, failing to note the irony, however gentle, of the work.) Christopher Lehmann-Haupt praises the precise understatement of *Tike*, while Phoebe Pettingell notes that, if Strong's range is limited, he finds a variety of nuances within it. (This comment, too, seems retrospectively inaccurate: Strong's range proves extraordinary in his subsequent career.) For its ability to speak the experience of the 1960s without belying it through overelaboration, *Ourselves* was widely hailed as the *Catcher in the Rye* of its time. Richard Locke describes Strong's work aptly in his review: "*Tike* had power and a tense, expectant sexuality, and the very short, shallow-breathing sentences never missed a step. The echoes of early James Purdy* or Tennesse Williams stories, of Hemingway's sad, deliberate, wounded heroes, of Harold Pinter's menacing minimality, never obscured Strong's own careful, resonant voice" (24).

Reviews of *Elsewhere* are, though fewer, even deeper in their appreciation. Brad Gooch sees it as a family novel that works through principles of substitution. Interestingly, although Gooch is a gay writer of note, he barely mentions the homosexuality in the novel, responding to it as matter-of-factly as, indeed, the novel does itself. In the best review of Strong's work, Marianne DeKoven praises it for its ability to negotiate formal innovation and a humane concern with character.

WORKS BY JONATHAN STRONG

Tike and Five Stories. Boston: Little, Brown, 1969.
Ourselves. Boston: Little, Brown, 1971.
Elsewhere. New York: Ballantine, 1985.
Companion Pieces. Boston: Dancing Bear Productions, 1992.
Secret Words. Boston: Zoland, 1992.
Among Others, revision of *Tike and Five Stories*, forthcoming.
Offspring, forthcoming. (Sections in *Hanging Loose 55*, 1989.)

SELECTED STUDIES OF JONATHAN STRONG

DeKoven, Marianne. "Later and Elsewhere." *Partisan Review* 53 (Fall 1985): 315–18.

Gooch, Brad. "Surrogates." *The Nation* 8 March 1986: 280–81.

Lehmann-Haupt, Christopher. "Short Stories—to Be Taken as Prescribed." *New York Times* 14 April 1969: 43.

Locke, Richard. "Keeping It Short and Subtle." *New York Times* 10 July 1971: 24.

Pettingell, Phoebe. Review of *Ourselves*. *The New Leader* 26 May 1969: 9.

GORE VIDAL (1925–   )
Joel Shatzky

BIOGRAPHY

One of the most prolific, controversial, and inventive authors of the post–
World War I period, Gore Vidal was born Eugene Luther Vidal on October
3, 1925, at the United States Military Academy at West Point. His father,
an aeronautics instructor at the academy, later became Director of Air
Commerce in the Roosevelt administration. Although Vidal was very much
attached to his father, Vidal's greatest influence in his childhood was his
blind grandfather, Senator Thomas Pryor Gore, the first senator from Oklahoma, with whom Vidal and his family lived in Washington, D.C.

In 1935 his mother divorced his father and married Hugh D. Auchincloss,
and the young Vidal moved to the Auchincloss estate, "Merrywood." He
attended the St. Alban's School in Washington, D.C., and the Los Alamos
School in New Mexico and finished his formative education in 1943 at
Phillips Exeter Academy, where he began writing his first novel, which he
never finished.

Instead of enrolling in Harvard after graduation, as his parents expected
him to, Vidal joined the U.S. Army Reserve Corps in 1943 as warrant officer
on a transport ship in the Aleutians. On board the ship he had the opportunity to read, to observe life at sea, and to gather material for his first
novel, *Williwaw* (a williwaw is a sudden and violent storm), which was
completed when he was only nineteen years old. The novel was published
in 1946 by E. P. Dutton and was generally well received, encouraging Vidal
to pursue his vocation as novelist. After being discharged from the Navy
in 1946 and after a brief stint as an editor with Dutton, Vidal moved to
Antigua, Guatemala, for two years to devote himself to writing full time.

A Yellow Wood (1947), about his experiences at Dutton, shortly followed,
as well as a fictionalized treatment of his childhood, *The Season of Comfort*,

published in 1949. Neither novel was well received. It was his third published novel, *The City and the Pillar* (1948), that made Vidal a controversial figure, although it temporarily damaged his literary reputation. Considered by many to be the first American novel about homosexuality, it was negatively reviewed for its "flat" style as well as its controversial subject matter; the *New York Times*, in fact, refused to advertise it. Recounting the story of Jim Willard, a young man from an ordinary family who lived in a small town not far from the Potomac, the novel chronicles his life from his first sexual experience with Bob Ford, a school friend, through his many encounters with men at sea, in Hollywood, and in the underground gay life of New York City. Vidal rewrote the ending in a revised edition in 1965 that was not so pessimistic as the original, in which Jim ends up killing his old friend after a reunion in which Bob rejects him. The negative reception of the novel at the time drove Vidal, after a series of unsuccessful efforts, to begin writing for television, movies, and later the stage. He also wrote three detective novels under the pseudonym Edgar Box.

Writing for television in the middle and late 1950s, Vidal turned out a number of distinguished scripts including *Visit to a Small Planet* (1955) which was made into a successful play, running on Broadway for over a year. *The Best Man*, a play about a presidential candidate that reflected Vidal's own interest in politics (he twice ran for elective office), played for almost two years on Broadway after its opening in 1960 and was later given an award for the best screenplay at the Cannes Film Festival in 1964. Among other notable scripts Vidal produced in the 1950s were television adaptations of *The Turn of the Screw* and *A Farewell to Arms* (1955), an original screenplay, *The Catered Affair* (1956), and the film adaptation of *Suddenly Last Summer* (1959).

Vidal returned to novel writing in the mid-1960s, producing *Julian* (1964) about the Roman emperor Julian, the Apostate, who wanted to reject Christianity and return to Hellenism. In the late 1960s Vidal wrote a series of historical novels beginning with *Washington D.C.* (1967) and continuing with *Burr* (1973), *1876* (1976), *Lincoln* (1984), and *Empire* (1987). Most of these works were well received and added to Vidal's literary reputation; but he also wrote several controversial and highly popular works about sexuality, including *Myra Breckenridge* (1968) (later made into a movie starring Mae West) about a transexual, and a sequel *Myron* (1974).

Vidal is noted not only for his many fictional works but also his acerbic and acute observations on political and social mores in the *New York Review of Books*, several collections of essays on politics and society, and, in the past, his frequent television appearances, the most memorable being his encounter with William F. Buckley during a commentary on the 1968 antiwar protests of the Democratic National Convention in which Vidal accused Buckley of being a "crypto-Nazi" and Buckley called Vidal a "queer."

Vidal has received many awards for his writing. In addition to the one already mentioned, he was given the Edgar Allen Poe Award in 1955, a nomination by the Screen Writers Annual Award for "The Best Man" in 1964, and the National Book Critics Circle Award for criticism for *The Second American Revolution and Other Essays* (1982).

MAJOR WORKS AND THEMES

Although he has written over twenty novels, several successful stage, screen, and television plays, and numerous collections of essays, Vidal's one vital contribution to gay literature is *The City and the Pillar*, the work of a precocious twenty-one-year-old. Certainly, one can consider Vidal's interest in the different modes of sexual identity in such works as *Myra Breckenridge* and *Myron* as part of his concern for understanding and tolerating sexual diversity. It can even be said that in his contribution to the screenplay *Ben Hur* (1959) he introduced a homoerotic element, but in his revised version of *The City and the Pillar* (1965), Vidal appended an afterword that well expresses his attitude toward the issue of sexuality.

Despite current usage, the word [homosexual] is an adjective describing a sexual act, not a noun describing a recognizable type. All human beings are bisexual. Conditioning, opportunity and habit account finally (and mysteriously) for sexual preference, and homosexualists are quite as difficult to generalize about as heterosexualists. (245)

The novel concerns the experiences of a young man who discovers in later adolescence that he is physically attracted to his boyhood friends and, in an idyllic incident, they have sex. Throughout the rest of the novel, although he fails in his attempts to have sexual relations with women, and succeeds with men, Jim Willard is haunted by his desire to return to his first love, Bob Ford. It is this ideal image of adolescence that proves to be his undoing for when, at the end of the novel, he finally has an opportunity to fulfill his dream, he discovers that Bob is not only unwilling to do so but reviles him as a "queer." Vidal's original violent ending, in which Jim murders his friend, is modified so that, although Jim in his rage rapes Bob, he still finds the strength to go on with life and not give in to despair.

Written shortly before the Kinsey Report was released, Vidal said of this third novel, that he wrote it because he was "bored with playing safe" in the first two (245); and as can be seen from his portraits of some of the characters, particularly the movie star Ronald Shaw, even in a serious book Vidal is a born satirist. It is perhaps this satirical bent and his iconoclastic views that have left him an outsider among the literary elite, but much he has written and said has shown his wisdom and insight into the nature of American culture.

If the theme of *The City and the Pillar* is to be set within the corpus of

Vidal's works, it is among the many themes that he has explored in which he attacks the narrow-minded and Puritanical aspects of American life. As a challenge to conventional thinking at the time it was written, the novel is the first of many of his that has fomented controversy. For one to attempt to identify Gore Vidal with any specific label, however, is a perilous undertaking. Since he has shown that his own sexual identity as well as the theme of *The City and the Pillar* are not central to the major corpus of his work, I doubt that he would regard his inclusion in this volume with any great enthusiasm.

CRITICAL RECEPTION

Reaction to *The City and the Pillar* was far from totally negative, although some of the criticism condemned it as "sterile" and "unadorned tabloid writing" (C. V. Terry, *New York Times*, January 11, 1948, 22). R. E. Kingery described the novel as a "serious, discerning and obviously courageous novel having no counterpart in the recent rash of similarly concerned novels." He added, however, that "each library must consider whether this subject in its specific details is locally admissible" (*Library Journal* 76 (December 1, 1947): 1686). R. B. Gehman, in the *New York Herald Tribune Weekly Book Review* described *The City and the Pillar* as "frank, shocking, sensational and often embarrassing, but it is also extremely sympathetic, penetrating and exhortive" (January 18, 1948, 6).

In contrast, the anonymous *New Yorker* reviewer dismissed *The City and the Pillar* as "the kind of dreary information that accumulates on a metropolitan police blotter" (January 10, 1948, vol. 23, p. 81), while C. V. Terry, already quoted, regarded it as "the case history of a standard homosexual," which "adds little that is new to a groaning shelf" (22). In retrospect, one can only wonder to what "groaning shelf" Mr. Terry was referring.

When one reads the novel, however, it is plain that after more than forty years of subsequent fiction on every aspect of homosexuality, *The City and the Pillar* is a significant and pioneering work that considers many of the themes involving sexual identity that have been developed and disputed ever since. Writing about Jim Willard's sexual behavior as a normal part of his emotional development at a time when homosexuality was being treated as a mental illness, Vidal anticipated the "discovery," some thirty years later, by the American Psychiatric Association that there is nothing inherently more neurotic about one form of sexual preference than another.

But Vidal best expresses his own view of his work as well as himself when he says, "I am at heart a propagandist, a tremendous hater, a tiresome nag, complacently positive that there is no human problem which could not be solved if people would simply do as I advise" (Quoted in *Contemporary Authors*, Detroit: Gale, New Revision Series, 1983, Vol. 13, p. 498). A libertarian in the broadest sense of the word and yet a cultural conservative, Gore Vidal is clearly the "correctionist" that he sees himself, whether in matters political, social, cultural, or sexual; as a *Time* writer once said of him, "for [forty] years, he has been a cinder in the public eye."

WORKS BY GORE VIDAL

Novels

Williwaw. New York: Dutton, 1946. Reprinted, New York: New American Library, 1968.
In a Yellow Wood. New York: Dutton, 1947.
The City and the Pillar. New York: Dutton, 1948. Revised edition, 1965.
The Season of Comfort. New York: Dutton, 1949.
Dark Green, Bright Red. New York: Dutton, 1950. Reprinted, New York: New American Library, 1968.
A Search for the King: A Twelfth Century Legend. New York: Dutton, 1950.
The Judgment of Paris. New York: Dutton, 1952. Revised edition, New York: Little, Brown, 1965.
Messiah. New York: Dutton, 1954. Revised edition, New York: Little, Brown, 1965.
Three: Williwaw. A Thirsty Evil: Seven Short Stories. Julian the Apostate. New York: New American Library, 1962.
Julian. New York: Little, Brown, 1964.
Washington, D.C. New York: Little, Brown, 1967.
Myra Breckenridge, New York: Little, Brown, 1968.
Two Sisters: A Novel in the Form of a Memoir. New York: Little, Brown, 1970.
Burr. New York: Random House, 1973.
Myron. New York: Random House, 1974.
1876. New York: Random House, 1976.
Kalki. New York: Random House, 1978.
Creation. New York: Random House, 1981.
Duluth. New York: Random House, 1983.
Lincoln. New York: Random House, 1984.
Empire. New York: Random House, 1987.
Hollywood. New York: Random House, 1990.

Collections of Essays

Rocking the Boat. New York: Little, Brown, 1962.
Sex, Death and Money. New York: Bantam, 1968.
Reflections upon a Sinking Ship. New York: Little, Brown, 1969.
Homage to Daniel Shays: Collected Essays, 1952–72. London: Heinemann, 1974.
Matters of Fact and Fiction: Essays, 1973–76. New York: Random House, 1977.
The Second American Revolution and Other Essays. New York: Random House, 1982.

Selected Plays, Screenplays and Teleplays

Visit to a Small Planet (T.V.). 1955.
The Catered Affair. Metro-Goldwyn-Mayer, 1956.
Visit to a Small Planet and Other Television Plays. New York: Little, Brown, 1956.
Visit to a Small Planet: A Comedy Akin to a Vaudeville. Booth Theatre, February 7, 1957.
Suddenly, Last Summer. Columbia, 1959.
The Best Man: A Play of Politics. Morosco Theatre, March 31, 1960.
The Best Man (screenplay adaptation of the play). United Artists, 1964.
Is Paris Burning? Paramount, 1966.

SELECTED STUDIES OF GORE VIDAL

Dick, Bernard F. *The Apostate Angel: A Critical Study of Gore Vidal*. New York: Random House, 1974.
Kiernan, Robert J. *Gore Vidal*. New York: Ungar, 1982.
Stanton, Robert J. *Gore Vidal: A Primary and Secondary Bibliography*. Boston: G. K. Hall, 1978.
White, Ray Lewis. *Gore Vidal*. Detroit: Twayne, 1968.

PETER WELTNER (1942–   )

James Tushinski

BIOGRAPHY

Born on May 12, 1942, Peter Weltner grew up in a religious Lutheran family in Winston-Salem and Greensboro, North Carolina. He showed an early interest in painting, and when he was a boy his parents sent him to Salem Academy and to St. Leo's Convent in Winston-Salem to study art more seriously. Around the age of fifteen, Weltner says, religion "fell apart" for him; he had a sense that reading and the whole study of art was an attempt to find another source of religious meaning. When he was seventeen, he attended an exhibition of artist Gerald Coble's work in Greensboro and was so excited by what he saw that he got in touch with Coble, who then took him on as a student. For over a year, Weltner went to Coble's cabin every Saturday morning to work on painting and to see more clearly "what making modern art was all about" (all quotes in this section are from a personal interview with Weltner). During the same period, Weltner traveled to New York City, which he had visited often with his family while he was growing up, to see the work of the Abstract Expressionists. These artists had a profound influence upon Weltner, as did the writers he discovered in magazines like *Arts* and *Art News*, which he would buy at a newsstand down Market Street from his family's church after Sunday services.

In 1960, Weltner entered Hamilton College in Clinton, New York. He felt that going to college was in many ways "a digression" from what he had been learning in his friendship and work with Coble. Nevertheless, Weltner received his A.B. from Hamilton and immediately afterward attended graduate school at Indiana University, where he completed his Ph.D. in English Literature in 1969. In August of that year, he moved to San Francisco to teach at San Francisco State University, where he is still employed as a professor.

The years 1969 to 1972 were "three years of the usual coming-out madness," and in the fall of 1973 Weltner met Bob Mohr. They fell in love and lived together for the next eight years. Starting in 1973, Weltner and poets Linda Gregg, Robert Hass, John Logan, and several other writers began to meet regularly at Weltner's apartment on Telegraph Hill to discuss poetry and writing, though at the time Weltner was writing only critical essays and reviews. He sensed that before he could begin writing fiction, he had to free himself from the academic strictures that for the preceding ten years had limited the kind of writing he really wanted to do. More importantly, he had to find "a sense of a world." Until he had that sense of a world and a "sense of comfort in it," he says, "I don't think I could really have started writing." Once he began in 1976, however, he wrote a long story or short novel a year, though he refrained from seeking publication for over ten years.

Weltner met his current lover, medical social worker Atticus Carr, in 1986. In 1989, his collection of stories *Beachside Entries/Specific Ghosts* was published, followed the next year by his novel, *Identity & Difference*. In 1991, more of Weltner's fiction began to appear in print. Five Fingers Press published his collection of three short novels entitled *In a Time of Combat for the Angel*, and his story "At Dawn the Guard Advances in the West" appeared in the special issue of *Five Fingers Review* entitled *Vanishing Point: Spirituality and the Avant-Garde*. In 1992, his long story "The Greek Head" appeared in both the June issue of *American Short Fiction* and George Stambolian's fiction anthology *Men on Men 4*.

MAJOR WORKS AND THEMES

"The responsibility, the challenge of gay writing," Peter Weltner has said, "is to write in an uncoded way without [the writing becoming] sociology or journalism. Coding allowed for an extraordinary development of metaphor, which we can now abandon. We need other kinds of metaphors" (personal interview with James Tushinski). It is this search for other kinds of metaphors to tell the stories of gay men that unites Weltner's published work. In each book, he has found a different narrative and stylistic approach to join with the thematic concerns—redemption, memory and loss, intellect and emotion, the interconnection of geography and sexuality—to create works that both celebrate and examine life without violating the mystery and simplicity of emotions.

Weltner's first book, *Beachside Entries/Specific Ghosts*, is divided into two independent sections separated by a group of Gerald Coble's haunting drawings. The first section, "Beachside Entries," consists of 30 short pieces, each less than a page—prose poems of themes of love and loss. Weltner chooses to ignore linear components of short fiction such as characterization and plot, achieving unity, tension, and climax through his use of recurring imagery. A swirl of Scotts, Dons, Phils, and Joes move through "Beachside Entries," their lives and relationships irrevocably altered by AIDS, while images from fairy tales and mythology and vignettes of natural disaster, war, religious persecution, and pestilence weave in and out. The vague collection of proper names takes on personalities, not from the scattering of information Weltner provides but from one's own memories of dead friends. By the end of "Beachside Entries," the effect of Weltner's skillful image-weaving is profoundly moving. He takes on the emotional enormity of AIDS by creating a patchwork of memory and myth that, when seen as a whole, is formally beautiful and ultimately healing.

Memory also plays a central role in the second part of the book, "Specific Ghosts." Here Weltner uses the classic form of the literary ghost story, borrowing specifically from Mary Wilkins Freeman, to study the effects of the death of a lover or friend on the survivor. "Specific Ghosts" consists of ten brief, but traditionally narrated, short stories, each dealing with the restless dead and the unhappy living. Weltner refrains from ambiguity about the supernatural and makes it quite clear that the spirits depicted are no more or less real than a memory and that memory itself can be quite physical. The strengths of "Specific Ghosts" reside not only in the subtle craft of the ghost stories but also in Weltner's successful transposition of the modern gay male experience onto a classical literary form.

Identity & Difference, Weltner's first novel, alternately tells two unrelated stories. One is about Preston, a self-absorbed gay man in San Francisco who does not need to work and who spends too much time analyzing and agonizing over his relationship with Jim. The other story deals with Darryl, a working-class teenager in San Mateo, California, who is trying to come to terms with the suicide of his older brother, Glenn. Their stories never intersect and are even stylistically different. Preston's is told in a somewhat distant, analytical third person, while Darryl relates his own story in a searching and immediate voice. The novel's two-story structure resembles William Faulkner's *The Wild Palms*, and like that book, *Identity & Difference* succeeds by juxtaposing its stories in ways that are seldom obvious but seem to rhyme with one another.

On the surface, Preston and Darryl are about as different as two young men can be, yet both are deeply involved with trying to understand and accept aspects of their sexuality. Preston, older than Darryl and more experienced sexually, is nevertheless the immature one, groping toward commitment and monogamy in his relationship with Jim. Darryl only begins to accept his homosexuality by the end of the book, but he seems better prepared to face the difficulties of coming out and loving men. Weltner's exploration of the difference between the two men and of analytical and emotional responses to love, instead of pulling the book apart into two distinct narrative and stylistic clumps, weaves together their disparate experiences into a celebration of a shared "gay male experience."

The three "short novels," as Weltner calls them, that make up *In a Time of Combat for the Angel* all take place in the South and center on characters struggling with their sexuality. Yet it would be a grave misreading of these works to call them "coming-out" stories or "Southern" stories. They are, however, all intensely concerned with place and the yearning for a home—both real and imagined. In "Dying," the home is real enough, a familiar place where the narrator, a school teacher, and his younger brother Gerald have come to care for their dying mother. The narrator watches with anger and helplessness as Gerald tries to break away from the sexual and emotional bond the two brothers shared for years. Their home becomes a place of death and waiting, their relationship an uneasy dance of denial and pain. Even so, breaking away from his brother is ultimately as inconceivable for Gerald as leaving the family home is for the narrator. After their mother's death, the brothers draw closer to each other, closing off the outside world for a relationship that seems both comforting and suffocating.

A similar inability to escape from the past haunts Eric, the main character in the second story, "Summers." Now a resident of California, Eric idealizes the summers he spent as a teenager in the South and his love for high school football star David Kittinger. Weltner uses these nostalgic yearnings as an entryway into Eric's past, painting a broader canvas of characters, opening the narrative out and becoming omnipotent, but always returning to Eric in the present. By making these summers so complete and populated, Weltner allows us to participate in and understand Eric's feelings of loss, to examine nostalgia without succumbing to it. "Backswimmers," the final story, again deals with a young boy's yearnings, but this time sexuality is barely understood and home is an emotional vacuum. On their way to a favorite secluded lake, Mark Morehead and his friend Dewey discover Cal, a returning World War II veteran who is squatting on what used to be his family farm. Mark attempts to help Cal rebuild his house and his life, looking for the affection Mark's father, a wealthy businessman who dabbles in poetry and sketching, cannot give him. Mark's relationship with Cal is eventually cut short by the forces of the law, and "Backswimmers" ends with Mark watching business and progress pave over the land he and Cal hoped to restore.

CRITICAL RECEPTION

The paucity of critical attention Weltner's fiction has received points out the difficulty writers have attracting attention when they publish with small presses. The difficulty is inevitably compounded when the writer deals with the gay experience. To date, reviews of Weltner's works have appeared mostly in local gay newspapers, affording little chance of recognition on a wider scale, even within the gay community. Weltner's first book, *Beachside Entries/Specific Ghosts* received only one review. *Identity & Difference* fared much better as far as the number of reviews went (a total of five), but only one of them appeared in a non–gay-oriented periodical, *Publisher's Weekly*. This review was brief and lukewarm. It praised the book's "perceptive and graceful" writing, but found the plot "conventional and lacking in humor" (55).

The four reviews in gay periodicals were mostly excellent and evenly split between national publications and local ones. George Stambolian, in *The Advocate*, cited Weltner's novel as one example of the different gay male sensibilities to be found in recent works of fiction. Calling Weltner an "exceptional talent" (75), Stambolian quotes a passage in which Preston vents his frustration about the ubiquity of heterosexual "stories" and concludes that "one purpose of gay fiction is to end these frustrations and to give us, at last, the stories of our yearnings." Steve Abbott,* writing in the *San Francisco Bay Times*, gives a thorough and sensitive analysis of the work, emphasizing what he sees as the "mythic scripts" in Preston and Darryl's stories and offering an interesting reader/text correspondence. Abbott says that the book is "on one level . . . simply a damn good read" and that "by seeing how others act out *their* mythic scripts, we get clues on how to act out our own" (46).

WORKS BY PETER WELTNER

Beachside Entries/Specific Ghosts. San Francisco: Five Fingers Press, 1989.
Identity & Difference. Freedom, California: The Crossing Press, 1990.
"At Dawn the Guard Advances in the West." *Five Fingers Review* no. 19 (1991): 49–62.
In a Time of Combat for the Angel: Three Short Novels. San Francisco: Five Fingers Press, 1991.

SELECTED STUDIES OF PETER WELTNER

Abbott, Steve. Review of *Identity & Difference*, by Peter Weltner. *San Francisco Bay Times* December 1990: 46.
Review of *Identity & Difference*, by Peter Weltner. *Publisher's Weekly* 20 July 2990: 55–56.
Stambolian, George. "Searching for Sensibilities." *The Advocate* 23 October 1990: 74–76.
Tushinski, James. "Late Bloomer: Peter Weltner Blossoms after Ten-Year 'Apprenticeship.' " *Bay Area Reporter* 13 December 1990: 29, cols. 3–5; 40, cols. 1–5.

EDMUND WHITE (1940–   )
David Bergman

BIOGRAPHY

Now in his fifties, Edmund White retains the dimpled cheeks, the cupid lips bowed in an archaic smile, and most notably, the large, baleful eyes of his youth, features that seem to prove if not the Wordsworthian adage of the child as father of the man, then the more American and gothic proposition that the youth is the spector of the adult and his undying double. White, who has said that all his work is about initiation, remains the eternal ephebe, a Childe Roland who has yet to change his permanent address to the Dark Tower in which he has taken all but residence.

White's fiction reflects the doubleness of its creator. One of the country's most sophisticated writers, White has earned the praise of such demanding and sophisticated critics as Vladmir Nabokov, Susan Sontag, and Cynthia Ozick. A graduate of Cranbook Academy, one of the nation's poshest preparatory schools, and the University of Michigan, where he majored in Chinese and won two Hopwood Awards, White has had a distinguished teaching career, serving on the faculties of Yale, Columbia, and the Johns Hopkins University, as the executive director of The New York Institute for the Humanities from 1981 to 1983, and since 1990 as professor of English at Brown University. Yet something Huck Finnish lingers in his tales of young men making their curious ways through the intricate currents of life, young men who seem either never to have learned or to have forgotten how to read the social signs that would lead them through their journeys. One imagines that at any moment they might exchange their summer shares on Fire Island or their villas on the Riviera for a raft down the Mississippi, that is, if they knew how to. Indeed, one feels that the only reason they haven't is that they have not yet lost the starry-eyed innocence that allows them to stay fascinated with the glittering social world in which they find themselves.

White's odd combination of innocence and worldliness, prolonged naivete and enforced sophistication, is somewhat explained by the vageries of his childhood. Born and raised in Cincinnati, White left the Queen City when his parents divorced. He was seven. But he didn't go far or leave for long. His mother took him and his sister to the Chicago area, where they lived in a number of suburban towns. Yet each summer, he returned to Cincinnati to stay with his father (*States*, 167). Even when he went away to school, he did not leave the Midwest. Thus, White is a product of the American heartland, a child of that austere but endlessly aspiring Protestant ethic against which he intermittently rebels even as it holds him captive.

Of course, White long ago left the Midwest. Upon graduation from the University of Michigan he moved to New York, where he took a job with Time-Life Books from 1962 to 1970. In 1970, he moved to Rome for a year, then briefly served as an editor for *Saturday Review* and *Horizon*. In 1983, he left for France, where he lived until 1990. In fact, today his reputation is greater in Europe than in the United States.

Nevertheless, the importance of Cincinnati, "the Republican Valhalla," cannot be underestimated in White's fiction. Cincinnati not only has played a prominent role in his autobiographical novel *A Boy's Own Story* but also is the model of the rigid, self-enclosed societies White analyzes with almost anthropological detachment in *Forgetting Elena*, his first published novel, and in *Caracole*. "The Cincinnati of my adolescence is indelibly mapped onto my cortex," he writes in *States of Desire*, his remarkable travel book about gay America, "and I could still lead someone through that phantom city. It still exists—shabby, circumspect, as German as knockwurst—in my imagination, but nowhere else" (*States* 168–69).

Cincinnati was a kind of fictional laboratory for White, where, to borrow from his description of his father, White "filled in a grand Balzacian canvas of greed, corruption, competition and disappointment," a canvas that included "everyone's pedigree and pretensions, the scope of their infidelities and the true size of their bank accounts" (*States*, 172). Even if White rejects Balzac's realistic creed, he is always indebted to the sociological and psychological density of his vision. As White told Kay Bonetti in an interview published in *The Missouri Review*, "I believe that we're shaped by our class position. In my own case my father was a small entrepreneur who made a lot of money and then lost most of it during the time when small businessmen were being superseded by big corporations" (100).

Cincinnati also provided White with many of the contradictions in his personality and his work. At the end of *States of Desire* he turns his critical lens on himself and detects his "most maddening fault...a peculiar alternation between socialism and snobbism" (334). By snobbism, White means a desire to curry favor with and to adopt the manners of the wealthy, the socially prominent, and the best educated. By socialism, he means nothing more than a "sympathy" with the victims of racism, sexism, economic exploitation, and social inequality. In a remarkably telling sentence, he explains, "I am by nature more inclined to side with the poor and with the Third World, though paradoxically I'm more at home with rich whites" (335).

Such a split allegiance is a legacy of that Midwest background. White finds that the best part of Cincinnati is evident in "the somber, noble mosaics" that once decorated the train station and have been moved with civic pride to the airport. The mosaic executed in the middle of the Depression depicts a paperworker "in blue coveralls lifting his arms to manipulate a pulley." The man's face and hands are "undifferentiated," but the atmosphere he creates is "one of intense, almost monastic concentration—the patient, humble, religious dignity of work" (*States* 1974). On the one hand such art work celebrates civic snobbism—the economic and cultural superiority of Cincinnati over its neighboring cities—while on the other hand, it promotes democratic populism, the sanctity of the common man, and the dignity of the most humble worker. The tensions between these two contradictory attitudes is both a "maddening" feature of White's work and one of its most compelling strengths.

The lessons of Cincinnati were reinforced when his mother removed him to suburban Chicago, which, though culturally "the chief oasis between the two coasts" (*States*, 175), is nevertheless a place where "doing well on the job is the most important thing" (*States*, 181). His formal education at Cranbook Academy—which houses one of the great collections of twentieth century design, a subject about which White has written extensively—and at the University of Michigan, continued the lessons of his childhood. But the tension between the value of art and that of work does not so much parallel the tension between elitism and egalitarianism as cut across them. White is driven toward both high art and a larger, popular audience, drives that match both his need for respectability through hard work and a desire to shock with an almost aristocratic contempt for labor. In an interview with Jordan Elgrably published in *The Paris Review*, he brings these two contradictory impulses together when he explains that although if he were to write "two or three bad or unpopular books, [he'd] be very, very poor," nevertheless he has "always made it a point of honor to write as though I had a million dollars" (60). Beauty and hard work, respectability and bohemianism continue to be points of conflict in White's life and literature.

MAJOR WORKS AND THEMES

Stylistically White's work can be divided into two groups, the high style of *Forgetting Elena*, *Nocturnes for the King of Naples*, and *Caracole*, and the plainer, colloquial style of *A Boy's Own Story* and *The Beautiful Room*

Is Empty, the first two volumes of a projected tetrology of autobiographical novels. But there is considerable overlap in theme and method. The narrator's imaginary friends in *A Boy's Own Story* bear a striking resemblance to Gabriel's imaginary creatures in *Caracole*. The recurring fantasy in *A Boy's Own Story* that the narrator is "a king or a god" (75) and Jupiter in an "only seemingly powerless incarnation" is paralleled by the narrator's awareness at the end of *Forgetting Elena* that he is the prince of the island. As the last example makes clear, in White's fiction gods can be powerless, and the seemingly powerless can exert an enormous force. The high and the low, the aristocratic and the plebian can change places rapidly or intersect in formally complex and socially anarchic ways. The divisions he so carefully constructs—or that we as readers would like to impose—are constantly collapsing on themselves.

Perhaps the best entry into *Forgetting Elena*, White's first published novel, is through his essay "Fantasia on the Seventies," a short meditation he published in *Christopher Street* on the changing ethos of the gay community. "Fantasia" is useful because *Elena* is in great measure a spoof in allegorical drag of the Fire Island gay scene in the 1960s and early 1970s.

In "Fantasia on the Seventies" White contrasts the staid, respectable, bourgeois world of Rome, in which he lived for the first ten months of the 1970s, with the raunchy, sexually permissive atmosphere of New York, in which fistfucking, "our century's only brand-new contribution to the sexual armamentarium" had become a commonplace (31). For White, the change was highly marked, but for those who lived through this transitional period, the alterations had seemed virtually invisible.

For the longest time everyone kept saying the seventies hadn't started yet. There was no distinctive style for the decade, no flair, no slogans. The mistake...was... looking for something as startling as the Beatles, acid, Pop Art, hippies and radical politics. What actually set in was a painful and unexpected working-out of the terms the sixties had so blithely tossed off. Sexual permissiveness became a form of numbness, as rigidly codified as the old morality....

The end of role-playing that feminism and gay liberation promised had not occurred. Quite the reverse. Gay pride has come to mean the worship of machismo. (31)

From White's perspective the 1970s are both shockingly different from and depressingly the same as the 1960s. The forces of sexual liberation had taken root and created very different and original sexual practices. But the promise of the 1960s has not been realized. The new codes of behavior that the 1960s had hoped to bring about—the end of role-playing, a more expansive consciousness, a greater sensitivity to others, an androgynous ideal—had turned out to be a new numbness, a new narrowness, and a new set of roles. As White recalls, "Fantasy costumes (gauze robes, beaded headache bands, mirrored vests) were replaced by the new brutalism: work boots, denim, beards and mustaches, the only concession to the old androgyny being a discreet gold earbob or ivory figa" (31).

White has described the source of *Forgetting Elena* in this way:

> The idea of writing about a culture that had a surface democracy, but an actual hidden hierarchy, and where morality had been replaced by esthetics, where people no longer troubled about what was good, but only about what was beautiful, fascinated me. It seemed to be true of how a certain group of highly privileged gay men were living in the seventies. (Bonetti, 102)

In *Forgetting Elena*, the unnamed narrator wakes one morning to discover that he has amnesia. Nevertheless, he hopes by remaining calm and attentive he can learn not only who he is, but the mores of the island community—a kind of Fire Island of the mind—in which he lives. (One of the strange and unexplained aspects of the novel, one of the signs that his is indeed a highly privileged circle, is that no one seems to work.) The narrator meets Herbert, an authority figure whose source of authority remains uncertain if not unchallenged; Jimmy, a beautiful young man of ambiguous sexual proclivities; Doris and The Hand, challengers to Herbert's authority; and finally Elena Valentine, who may be the narrator's sister or wife. (Valentine is a name that runs in White's family and is his middle name.) In the course of the very short novel, the narrator switches allegiances several times, in part because he cannot figure out who may have claims upon him. These betrayals cause Elena to commit suicide. In the closing moments of the novel, the narrator both realizes who he is—namely, the former prince of this newly democratized country—and forgets what he has done—caused the death of his beloved Elena. As one memory is awakened, another is buried.

In some way *Forgetting Elena* is the opposite of the Proustian novel despite a similar lushness of language and complexity of syntax, for whereas Proust's epic is predicated on involuntary memory, White's novel is based on spontaneous amnesia. This amnesia provides his narrator with several advantages: First, it allows him to maintain an almost anthropological distance from the events he records, as if he found himself in some foreign but fascinating tribe whose various rites he is trying to understand even as he is subjected to them. Second, it provides him with a convenient starting and ending point for the narrative. Third, it permits him to retain his innocence even while he betrays the people he loves and commits incest with them. For without a real understanding of his relationship to those around him, he cannot possibly be found culpable of immorality. If his innocence is not wholly artificial, then it is not entirely genuine either.

Such moral ambiguities haunt White's second published novel, *Nocturnes for the King of Naples*. (He had composed several novels before and one after *Forgetting Elena*.) Like the narrator of *Forgetting Elena*, the narrator of *Nocturnes* is a nameless man who, in a monologue addressed to his former, much older lover, confesses his undying love and repents his ingratitude. For the flipside of the innocence of youth is its shallowness; and on one level, *Nocturnes* is a defense both of older lovers, who might be accused of exploiting young men, and of the young men who, out of ignorance and uncertainty of who they are, inflict enormous pain on those who love them. Yet *Nocturnes*, while it tries to uncover the complexities of emotion and the intermeshing of power relations to comprehend erotic forces, nevertheless is ultimately concerned with morals; and while it understands why someone would desire the aesthetic suspension of the ethical, it cannot condone it. *Nocturnes* is an elegy, first for the dead older lover whom the youth has so cruelly abandoned, second for the narrator's lost youth whose memory no bout of amnesia can ever erase, and finally for the life not lived because for White the innocent often choose not the truly rich possibilities of experience but the most expedient. For White, our greatest sins against ourselves and others are the products of our shallowness.

Nocturnes for the King of Naples is the work that most intensely plays with the allure of incest. Today the public is so sensitive about incest, blurring the language of primitive taboo with the rhetoric of psychotherapy, that it becomes inflamed by any talk that incest might have an allure, no less, an allure one might play with. But for White, who went through more than the requisite number of years of analysis for a gay man of his class and period and who has spoken rather bitterly about the process, his position is strikingly Freudian. The son desires not the actual experience of incest, but the fantasy, where eros and thanatos can meet in a sublime moment of both stimulation and blissfully numbing joy. Thus, in *A Boy's Own Story*, the narrator confesses, "I feel sorry for a man who never wanted to go to bed with his father; when the father dies how can his ghost get warm except in a posthumous embrace? For that matter, how does the survivor get warm?" (22). In *Nocturnes*, the actual father, whose embrace when it comes is a noxious parody of incest, is rejected for a father figure who is not adequately loved until he is dead. Similarly, in *Caracole*, phantom mothers and alternative fathers appear in rococo profusion, for example, the uncle who is Gabriel's patron becomes the lover of Gabriel's wife, while Gabriel becomes the lover of his uncle's former mistress. So diffuse is the fantasy world of incest, that it hardly takes on meaning in *Caracole*. It is unclear to me whether this diffuseness is White's comment on heterosexuality or a failure of his application of homoerotic poetics to straight psychology.

Civilization, for White, is both a mask to cover the corrupt interplay of power and sexuality and the means of uncovering the hypocrisy of that interplay. As he sees *Caracole*, it is a work divided into three sections: "uncoded, coded, decoded." In the opening chapter Angelica and Gabriel, the central pair of lovers, are living in the ruins of two different civilizations and understand neither the vestigial social organs or the religious rites. They come to the capital of a conquered people and are instructed in their social, religious, and artistic codes. Angelica and Gabriel are willing and able students, but in the end they become aware of the naked powers that these symbolic systems encode and make possible.

We still do not know the overriding structure of White's tetrology because only two of the projected four novels have been written. In an interview with Stewart Kellerman, White suggests that the series will be the "unapologetic portrayal of the development of a gay man" and how the gay culture "oppressed in one generation, liberated in the next [is] wiped out in the next" ("Everything Is Potentially Final," *New York Times Book Review*, March 20, 1988, p. 7). But in many ways the sequence appears to be an extended treatment of the process developed in *Caracole*, but in the tetralogy developed on more clearly autobiographical lines with an overt homosexual subject.

A Boy's Own Story, the first of the series, is widely regarded as White's finest work so far. It narrates the last moments before the erotic, social, and economic codes are firmly traced on the narrator's mind. The opening chapter, originally published as the story "First Love," is really the tale of his last love, his last opportunity to immerse himself in a relationship which is mutual, nonexploitive, and truly loving. The title "First Love" is purposely ambiguous, referring either to the narrator's father or to Kevin, the twelve-year-old, who with his entire family stays for a week with the narrator's family in their summer home. The narrator enjoys a kind of pre-Oedipal *joissance* with his father. Together they bathe themselves "side by side, in those passionate streams [of late Brahms] every night," and the narrator would like "to think that music . . . acted as the source and transcription of a shared rapture" (22). With Kevin he enjoys, at least for a while, an affection uncontaminated by romantic cliches, a love that is "unaware of anything but the pleasure spurting up out of his body and into mine" (19). But this unencoded or barely encoded affection is soon lost, and the narrator, convinced that he had too much power for his own good, comes to desire "someone to betray" (31). In the last chapter, he finds that person, a music teacher at his prep school, whom he seduces even as he arranges to have him fired. Betrayal is the form of love he has learned from the adults, whose love repeatedly takes the form of exploitation and abandonment. It is no surprise that the structure of *A Boy's Own Story* is circular, beginning and ending with his impulse to betray, while the center of the book looks back to expose the narrator's path to betrayal.

The Beautiful Room Is Empty is about the end of the encoding process and the beginning of the decoding process. The encoders for White are school, family, and psychotherapy, but they are not without their benefit as they also give the narrator the means to decode their own constructions. The most obvious example of a process or institution that both provides a disabling code and enabling tools for decoding is psychotherapy. Dr.

O'Reilly, the narrator's psychiatrist, is willing to drive his patients insane in order to make them healthy, but nevertheless gives the narrator the insight to recognize finally that it is O'Reilly who is insane and that the therapist's homophobia is the illness. School is another example of an institution that both disables and enables: It teaches obedience to intellectual forms of authority but, in so doing, promotes disdain for the more brutal forms of social control. Significantly, *The Beautiful Room Is Empty* begins in an exclusive prep school and ends with the Stonewall riots.

If the form of *A Boy's Own Story* is circular, then the form of *The Beautiful Room Is Empty* is a rondo, a recurring theme punctuated by contrasting episodes. The recurring theme is the narrator's love for Maria, a bisexual painter and social activist, whom he loves and has rather feeble sex with. That the Maria/narrator relationship is not strong enough or developed enough to hold the novel together is not entirely a miscalculation on White's part. His narrator admits midway through the novel that his relationship with Maria was not wholly realized. "I knew we hadn't yet quite found the form our love would take, doubtlessly because of the extreme conventionality of my social imagination" (113). The problems with the form of that love is reflected in both the banality of its structure and the emptiness of its expression. The beautiful room of their love is empty because their love was not made for a conventionally beautiful room. Such a love requires new and different accommodations.

CRITICAL RECEPTION

Two aspects of White's work are always examined by his critics, his self-conscious, rich style and his homosexual content. One senses that sexual politics have more to do with the response to White's work than with any of its inherent merits and limitations. Thus when Peter Cowan complains that White is an inadequate guide to gay life because "he never tries to help readers who don't share his sexual preference to understand his assumptions" (13), and when John Yohalem argues that *Forgetting Elena* is a better novel than *Nocturnes for the King of Naples* because in the earlier novel "White disguised his own sexuality, and that incognito seemed to give his art a nervous, mysterious charm, a bewildering but wonderful evasion of certainty" (12), we may read the traces of homophobia dressed up as objective criticism. And when Alan Hollinghurst wonders in print whether White is "intentionally challenging some assumed norm of decorous heterosexual writing by creating a style that is overblowm, self-advertising, narcissistic, the livery of a specifically homosexual literary position" (875), one hears how a gay critic can negotiate between style and subject matter and bring the two, if not into alignment, at least into provocative tension.

In general, White is noticed for his style. Those who have the taste for his often purple, always highly metaphorical prose praise it as one of the advances on the realistic novel that has dominated postwar American fiction. Those who don't have a taste for such things will find it "gooey and fantastic as Italian pastry" (Yohalem, 12).

White is not viewed as a particularly artful storyteller, and the structure of his work is often taken to task even by critics who are otherwise favorable in their opinion.

Among the finest writers on gay themes and gay life, White is compared to Proust, E. M. Forster, and Christopher Isherwood.* The range of subjects, the richness of his material, his insight into social psychology, his highly evolved and unmistakable style have earned him an important place in contemporary American letters.

WORKS BY EDMUND WHITE

Forgetting Elena. New York: Random House, 1973.
With Charles Silverstein. *The Joy of Gay Sex: An Intimate Guide for Gay Men to the Pleasures of a Gay Life Style*. New York: Crown, 1977.
Nocturnes for the King of Naples. New York: St. Martin's, 1978.
States of Desire: Travels in Gay America. New York: Dutton, 1980.
A Boy's Own Story. New York: Dutton, 1982.
Caracole. New York: Dutton, 1985.
The Beautiful Room Is Empty. New York: Knopf, 1988.
With Adam Mars-Jones. *The Darker Proof: Stories from a Crisis*. New York: New American Library, 1988.

SELECTED STUDIES OF EDMUND WHITE

Bonetti, Kay. "An Interview with Edmund White." *The Missouri Review* 13 (1990): 89–110.
Cowan, Paul. "The Pursuit of Happiness," *New York Times Book Review* 3 January 1980: 12–13.
Elgrably, Jordan. "The Art of Fiction CV," *The Paris Review* 108 (1988): 47–80.
Hollinghurst, Alan. "A Prince of Self-Approval." *Times Literary Supplement* 19 August 1983: 875.
Yohalem, John. "Apostrophes to a Dead Lover." *New York Times Book Review* 10 December 1978: 12.

GEORGE WHITMORE
(1946–1989)
Les Wright

BIOGRAPHY

George Whitmore was born in Denver, Colorado, in 1946, where he grew up. After graduating from MacMurray College (Illinois) he did graduate work at Bennington College in Vermont. Whitmore became a conscientious objector during the Vietnam War, serving as coordinator of Planned Parenthood's national abortion referral unit in Manhattan, where he settled. He later worked at the Citizens Housing and Planning Council for affordable and low-income housing. He came first to feminism and after Stonewall to gay activism, working on the media committee for Gay Activist Alliance, then with the Gay Academic Union (publishing a two-volume biography of Thoreau), and in 1974 organized the first major panel on gay journalism.

By the mid-1970s Whitmore was building his reputation as a writer. He joined the Violet Quill Club, a discussion group including Robert Ferro,* Michael Grumley, Felice Picano,* Edmund White,* Christopher Cox, and Andrew Holleran* that addressed problems of writing gay autobiographical fiction. In 1976 Whitmore began writing for the newly founded gay literary journal *Christopher Street*, which showcased gay male writing otherwise ignored in the mainstream press. He contributed to other gay journals, published a poetry chapbook, and saw his first successful play *The Caseworker* produced by Playwright Horizons. By 1981 he had realized two more dramatic productions: two one-acts, "The Flight" and "The Legacy" (1979), and the very popular full-length drama-comedy *The Rights* (1980). *Christopher Street* carried his pseudonymous "Confessions of Danny Slocum" (July 1979), which he subsequently expanded into a novel (1980). His campy "Deep Dish" ran in the first thirty issues of *New York Native*.

In the 1980s Whitmore's interest turned toward journalism. He wrote on art, architecture, design, and travel for a number of nongay journals. He also wrote individual stories for a collection to be called *Out Here: Fire Island Tales*. Although the collection was never published, individual stories appeared in gay journals or anthologies such as *Aphrodisiac*, *On the Line*, and *A True Likeness*. Whitmore became a member of the Gay Men's Health Crisis, the New York–based AIDS organization, and in 1985 he approached the *New York Times* with a proposal to write about AIDS. A year later Whitmore was himself diagnosed with AIDS (Kaposi's sarcoma). The eloquently and eerily moving *Nebraska*, published in late 1987, was overshadowed by *Someone Was Here* (1988), which the *Times* piece had engendered. Whitmore taped interviews and made extensive handwritten notes after his walks around the wards at Lincoln Hospital, talking to staff and patients. "I realized," he commented to Paul Reed, "that the story of AIDS was really about the collapse of the health care system, welfare, poverty, racism, sexism, and politics. . . . I started out writing on the suffering of gay men and ended up writing about how all these things were connected to AIDS. In fact, they were AIDS" (43). At the end he filed suit against a Greenwich Village dental clinic for refusing to treat him because he was a PWA. The clinic was eventually found guilty and fined and went out of business. George Whitmore died on April 19, 1989, survived by his lover Michael Canter.

MAJOR WORKS AND THEMES

Whitmore began his writing career as a playwright and a poet. In 1976 he published *Getting Gay in New York*, a chapbook of confessional poems, and saw his two-act drama *The Caseworker* produced off-Broadway. Over the next five years Whitmore published individual poems and short stories and wrote three more plays: *The Legacy* (1979), *The Flight* (1979), and *The Rights* (1980). These earliest works reveal Whitmore as a poet of great psychological insight and empathy, an astute social observer with a campy sense of humor, and a social worker deeply concerned for other people. *The Caseworker* is a dark, moody drama about "a middle-aged social worker who watches his own mistakes" in the form of a younger roommate. "The Flight" and "The Legacy" were presented under the omnibus title *A Life of Gertrude Stein*. The highly popular comedy-drama *The Rights* offered up a sophisticated examination of the paradoxes of gay manners— Larry, a campy 1950s queen, encounters the butch, subdued post-Stonewall crowd on Fire Island.

Short stories, intended for *Out Here: Fire Island Tales*, began appearing in the gay press. In "The Black Widow," for example, Whitmore observes gay relationships with a rare emotional honesty and integrity. Gerald Manheim, the titular "Black Widow," is a mysterious, aloof summer resident on Fire Island, universally known as the one whose four lovers had died, each in a different manner. From the safety of distance the narrator, a "style queen" clone, becomes infatuated, then intrigued by Gerald, a successful composer. They meet, by chance, on the subway (the narrator takes advantage of the press of people to feel Gerald up). An intense courtship ensues. Gerald rejects "Island faggots" as "disengaged and selfish," leading the smitten narrator to renounce in word, if not in fact, his "style queen" circle. Gerald, he learns all too quickly, is smotheringly possessive and emotionally dependent. The narrator breaks free in a public scene on Fire Island.

In "The Guermantes Way" the narrator has taken in a new housemate for the summer. Booker is "an overgrown Boy Scout" from Louisiana, bookish and fond of Proust, whose older brother used to beat him up. Booker's fastidious habits in the household endear him to the narrator. However, the violent relationship between Booker and his new boyfriend, the big and beautiful Daniel, reveals Booker as a prime candidate for initiation into sadomasochistic practices.

Told through journal entries, notes jotted down, and reported dialogue, *The Confessions of Danny Slocum* (1980) is the story of the homonymous Danny Slocum, a gay New Yorker in late 1970s Manhattan, who seemingly has everything an "out" gay man could want; he is tough, ironic, patient, and popular. But he is unable to ejaculate with a partner present, a problem that appeared after he broke off an abusive relationship. In sex therapy Danny is partnered with a young Italian man from Long Island, just coming out and with the same sexual dysfunction. The first-person narrative links short notes, weaving together reports of sexual practice sessions and regular aspects of gay life in the big city, past and present, journalism and fiction, reality and fantasy. Nominal types, rather than secondary characters, reflect typical urban gay points of view. The Political Friend objects to therapy as brainwashing, the Fire Island Friend celebrates hedonism. Other aspects of Whitmore's person appear as the Novelist, the Dancing Friend, and the like. On one level *Danny Slocum* is about one gay man's fight for individuation from the conformity of the post-Stonewall "clone crowd." On another level it is the story of human intimacy in the face of alienating mechanization, love versus sexual practices. Gay New York stands as a third character, simultaneously attractive and repellent, representing the ironic vision of gay sensibility.

Nebraska (1987) is an unflinching look at the emotional and spiritual wasteland of America from which so many gay men living in urban centers have fled. A kind of American gothic, it captures the working-class idiom and the milieu of repressive, conformist 1950s America. The story of twelve-year-old Craig McMullen is told by an older version of himself through flashbacks and projections, juxtaposing scenes in the style of a film montage of recalled memory and unstated desire. Moody and stylized in a manner reminiscent of Nathaniel West, Craig's poor working-class Nebraska is filled with emotionally crippled people. His father, a handsome Irish redhead, is also a violent drunk. His mother holds the family together, slaving away at the local "Monkey Wards." His Grandpa is an old railroad man and lives with Grandma in a ramshackle house built one room at a time. Then there are his sisters Betty and Dolores, a pal from school who drifts away, and the eagerly anticipated, almost legendary Uncle Wayne, recently discharged from the Navy. In a freakish accident, Craig has been run over by a truck and lost a leg.

Two more major events come to define Craig's childhood. His father, who had abandoned the family, returns a born-again Christian and kidnaps Craig in an ill-advised attempt to redeem his lost family. Failing once again, he shoots himself. The second event concerns the relationship between Craig and Uncle Wayne. Coming home late from a drinking bout, Wayne helps Craig change out of sweat-soaked pyjamas. He touches Craig's scrotum briefly, making a wisecrack about them "dropping." Soon Wayne is picked up by the police at the local tearoom. Craig is pressured into confessing this innocuous "man-to-man" grope to the authorities, thus corroborating the suspicion that his uncle is a homosexual and a child molester. Wayne is ostracized by his family, placed in a mental institution, and forced to undergo electroshock therapy.

Years later, Craig traces his Uncle Wayne to southern California, where Wayne's nebulous plans with his Navy buddy, the Chief, have come to an ironic fulfillment. Irreparably damaged by electroshock, Wayne has become simple and childlike. The Chief, now more brother than lover, takes care of him. In the closing moment, Craig and Wayne come together spiritually as brothers in a gay family, finding a safe haven from a treacherous and homophobic America on the eve of Stonewall.

Typifying Whitmore's renewed dedication to journalism in the late 1980s, *Someone Was Here: Profiles in the AIDS Epidemic* (1988) began as a piece for the *New York Times Magazine* in 1985. "I wanted to document in the straight press what the gay community was doing with AIDS," Whitmore reported. He first profiled Jim Sharp, a thirty-two-year-old advertising executive, and his friend Edward Dunn, who was coming to terms with the recent death of his lover; this became Section One. Section Two follows Nellie Roacha, a Chicana woman caring for her gay son, who has returned home to Greeley, Colorado, to die after living homeless in San Francisco for five years. Section Three is a piece of investigative reporting on the desperately poor, mostly black and Hispanic AIDS ward of Lincoln Hospital in the South Bronx.

Someone Was Here began as an attempt to put a human face on AIDS by studying its impact within the gay community, but it rapidly grew into both an overview of the many faces of AIDS (Whitmore likened it to taking snapshots from a speeding train) and a private view of his own diagnosis. By allowing third parties to tell their experiences, Whitmore is able to represent his own. This distancing effect adds to the power of his message and dramatizes how the personal is political for him. He reports that the urgency of AIDS made him a more disciplined writer and that he engaged in a superstitious hope that as long as he wrote he would be spared. In the prefatory author's note, Whitmore describes a photograph of a monk on a Greek island, holding a box of bones out to view, as if this were his duty. Whitmore identifies with the monk, presenting the book as his own box of bones.

CRITICAL RECEPTION

From his first literary success on, Whitmore showed a gift for engaged reportage, infusing "a life and a warmth that exists independently of the facts" to his works in his "unrelenting adherence to emotional truth and ...passion for validating all human experience" (Bronski, 51). *The Case-worker* was the unadorned portrayal of an average gay man in a typical life, something many gay critics, as Edmund White noted in an interview with Whitmore, had called for in the 1970s, an injunction that they then nonetheless ignored, decrying Larry Kramer's* and Andrew Holleran's self-critical novels for their lack of "positive" gay images.

The Confessions of Danny Slocum addresses the tangled issues of sexual desire and romantic attachment head on, praised by Bronski for bringing "some reality to a world which was becoming increasingly portrayed as nothing but disco, boffing and poppers" (3). Richard Hall remarked on the novel as a "clinical analogue" to our narcissistic and performance-oriented age and traced its literary genealogy to the novels of spiritual dysfunction by the likes of Dostoevsky, Hesse, and Conrad. White hailed "the perfect-pitch integrity of all" (23) as the fulfillment of Whitmore's promise as a writer.

Several critics praised *Nebraska* for being finely crafted and deeply moving. Craig's return to Wayne suggests the creation of a radically new—gay—family, renewing "one of the richest, and least appreciated, myths of contemporary gay fiction—the establishment of a more democratic society of sons opposed to the hierarchical family dominated by the father" (Stambolian, 39). The Oedipal drama Whitmore began to explore in *Danny Slocum* finds resolution here (ibid.). *Nebraska* will likely prove an enduring contribution to American letters.

Written at a time when most AIDS writing was scientific and PWAs were portrayed as faceless victims, *Someone Was Here* broke new ground, "witness[ing] disease with a clear eye," with integrity and honesty, refusing "to indulge in cheap emotions or sanctimonious political rhetoric by comparing one vastly different situation to another" (Bronski, 3). *Someone Was Here* "provides a stark testament to the tolls that AIDS is taking in *human* lives, ...a cross-section of the AIDS epidemic, exposing the many layers and factions of our society affected" (Reed, 49). Over a decade into the epidemic, this remains one of the few such humanizing profiles.

WORKS BY GEORGE WHITMORE

Getting Gay in New York. New York: Free Milk Fund Press, 1976.
Out Here: Fire Island Tales (unpublished manuscript). Ca. 1978–1981.
The Confessions of Danny Slocum, or, Gay Life in the Big City. New York: St. Martin's Press, 1980. Rev. ed. San Francisco: Grey Fox Press, 1985.
"Deep Dish" (serial in 29 episodes). *New York Native* 1–30 (December 29, 1980–February 1, 1982).
Nebraska. New York: Grove Press, 1987. Rev. ed. New York: Washington Square Press, 1989.
Someone Was Here: Profiles in the AIDS Epidemic. New York: Penguin, 1988.

SELECTED STUDIES OF GEORGE WHITMORE

Bronski, Michael. "*Someone Was Here.* Bearing Witness to Pain of AIDS." *The Advocate* 21 June 1988: 51–52.
———. "Writer George Whitmore Dies of AIDS." *Gay Community News* 14 May 1989: 3.
Hall, S.S. "*Someone Was Here.*" *New York Times Book Review* 10 April 1988: 50.
Reed, Paul. "Behind the AIDS Whitewash." *The Advocate* 10 May 1988: 42–44.
Stambolian, George. "Out of *Nebraska* Betrayed Dreams in the Heartland." *The Advocate* 24 November 1987: 39.
White, Edmund. "Edmund White on the Confessions of Novelist George Whitmore." *The Advocate* 12 June 1980: 21–23.

DONALD WINDHAM (1920–   )
Bruce Kellner

BIOGRAPHY

Following a dispiriting youth in Georgia, Donald Windham left when he was nineteen years old and never looked back. Some of his early stories are based on incidents that occurred there, and his finest achievement—a moving memoir of his youth, *Emblems of Conduct* (1963)—derives from his early experiences; but there is neither a Southern gothic nor a Southern eccentric atmosphere in his work. He is a "Southern" author only by birth, whose writing has always shared a sophisticated concinnity with European rather than American writers.

Born in Atlanta on July 2, 1920, the second son of Fred and Louise Donaldson Windham, he was reared by his divorced mother in her family's late-Victorian house. When their fortunes dwindled, they were obliged to move into a tiny apartment, where Windham passed his adolescence, impatient but tolerant of his impractical mother and alienated from his older brother. The emotional climate of those years informs many of his short stories.

Windham graduated from high school with an undistinguished record but with a remarkably rich, self-chosen library behind him: sequentially from William Saroyan to Aldous Huxley to Marcel Proust to James Joyce to Gertrude Stein to Ignazio Silone, only then returning to earlier writers. Given his family's financial straits and the still-depressed economic landscape of 1938, Windham's day-to-day activity was controlled by a job in the local Coca-Cola factory, making barrels and then hauling them around, with nothing ahead of him but the remote possibility of a promotion to an office job. As an escape, he became a second-stringer with Atlanta's avant-garde through a little theater group, and at one of their parties he met Fred Melton, a twenty-one-year-old graphic artist. They left Atlanta together, ostensibly for a holiday in New York, from which they had no intention of ever returning—and didn't.

Windham worked at a number of jobs for the next three years, including one at the World's Fair where he dispensed Coca-Cola, a coincidence he never would have included in the subtle stories he had begun to write at one or another of the variety of addresses he and Melton shared. Windham called Melton "Butch" and Melton called him "Stinky," "to counter my sweet appearance," Windham later wrote.

Tennessee Williams used the nicknames occasionally after he met them in January 1940. A mutual friend had brought him to the furnished room where Melton and Windham were then living in poverty. Williams was impressed by the intensity of their romance. In turn, Williams was the first person Windham knew whose commitment to writing was absolute; not surprisingly, their emotional influence on each other was mutually significant, as it remained through their long and often difficult friendship.

During the three-year period that Windham and Melton lived together—even briefly after Melton married—Windham's circle of friends expanded to include a number of artists and writers: Fritz Bultman, Paul Cadmus, Jared French, Christopher Isherwood,* Anne Ryan, Tony Smith, Glenway Wescott, and a few years later Truman Capote* and also ballet impresario Lincoln Kirstein.

Windham went to work as Kirstein's assistant on *Dance Index* in the fall of 1942; and when Kirstein went into the army five months later, he took over as editor, adding to his acquaintances Pavel Tchelitchew, about whose stage designs he wrote at length in one issue; photographer George Platt Lynes and collagist Joseph Cornell, who contributed illustrations; and George Balanchine, whose "notes" about ballet choreography Windham revised into an essay for another issue. For an aspiring writer, the experience as proofreader, copyeditor, and checker against factual inaccuracies was invaluable; in turn, Windham's issues of *Dance Index* are equally invaluable to aficionados of ballet history in America.

Most of these people with whom Windham came in contact were in one way or another influential on his subsequent life and writings, but no one more so than Sandy Montgomery Campbell, a Princeton freshman, with whom a forty-five-year alliance began in 1943. Their emotional and intellectual symbiosis was mutual and productive, ending only with Campbell's unexpected death in 1988.

With the royalties from the modest success of *You Touched Me*, the play Windham wrote in collaboration with Tennessee Williams, he went to Italy in 1948 to complete his first novel, *The Dog Star*. Published in 1950, it was followed a decade later by a second novel, *The Hero Continues*, and a book of short stories, *The Warm Country*, one of which—"The Starless Air"— Windham dramatized for production in Houston in 1953. In 1960, he was awarded a Guggenheim Fellowship in creative writing, through which he spent another year abroad in Greece, Denmark, England, and Italy, writing his childhood memoir, *Emblems of Conduct*, and amassing material for a third novel, *Two People*.

When publishers proved indifferent to a subsequent novel, *Tanaquil*, Campbell published it in Italy, the first of several private publications through the Stamperia Valdonega in Verona, under the supervision of Martino Mardersteig. This was followed by several other books in limited editions, all sufficiently handsome to eradicate the distinction between a bookmaker's craft and art. Four of these were picked up for trade editions that proved popular enough to result in paperback versions. Windham's editions of letters from E. M. Forster, Tennessee Williams, and Alice B. Toklas, organized in collaboration with Campbell, are models of editorial excellence; and his memoirs of Williams and Truman Capote are luminously informative as literary history as well as art.

Now in his early seventies, Windham continues to add to the journals he has kept for nearly half a century; they should prove of inestimable value in assessing the literary scene in New York and in various European locales.

In reviewing Windham's most recent novel, *Stone in the Hourglass*, Robert Ferro* cogently observed that, although the author had "always lived in the shadow" of Williams and Capote, Windham, "who perhaps came in with a marble or two less, still has all of his and happily many years more to display his prodigious gifts" (13).

MAJOR WORKS AND THEMES

"Gay" is inappropriate as a qualifying adjective for the writings of Donald Windham. More than once he has declared that he has never thought of homosexuality as a subject; instead, his novels have involved people who happened to be homosexual or bisexual. To some degree, the time at which Windham began to write was influential on his work; and like Christopher Isherwood—to whose novels his own bear some resemblance if only in their cool ambience—Windham seems reticent, although revisionist assessment is always questionable. Homosexual activity is lambent in all five of his novels and in many of his stories; its influence is an unspoken motif in his memoirs, but the emotional difference between Windham and almost any contemporary self-described gay novelist is considerable.

The Dog Star (1950), a loose biography of Fred Melton's brother, pits Blackie Pride against an alien world that he ultimately rejects through suicide. Sexually active at fifteen and by turns indifferent and vicious, he is a modern-day Actaeon. In the myth on which Windham embroiders his story, Actaeon is transformed into a vulnerable stag and destroyed by his own hounds when unwittingly he spies the goddess Artemis when she is bathing. As an unrepentant juvenile delinquent, Blackie is no likable protagonist; and Windham's narrative, stripped of both sentimentality and sensationalism, makes the telling all the more shocking. Wounded by the suicide of Whitey Maddox, an equally alienated boy he has loved, Blackie finds the world too hostile, once he leaves the confines of the detention school in which he and Whitey were incarcerated, despite overtures of love from his family, his friends, and a girl his senior with whom he has a passionate affair. His seemingly callous actions against all others, however, are only manifestations of diffidence. Windham asks for no sympathy for his young hero and gets none.

His second novel, *The Hero Continues* (1960) is based on the early career of Tennessee Williams, although it is more concerned with fame as a corrupting influence on both creativity and interpersonal relationships than with Williams himself. In the process of transformation from private man to public icon through his work, Dennis Freeman loses his ability for either love or friendship, paralleled with actual physical losses: an eye, an arm, sexual impotence. Both Freeman and his friend Morgan (a thinly disguised Windham) are explicitly writers and implicitly homosexual; both demonstrate, but in opposite ways, that human and hero cannot be synonymous either professionally or privately. With a decade's firmer control over his material, Windham again challenges his reader's allegiances, but with a new sophistication.

That proves true in his volume of short stories, *The Warm Country* (1960), which appeared at the same time. His characters are feckless or desperate or both, caught in prisons of their own making, but one of the stories, "The Starless Air," transcends its unpromising material to become a worthy American equivalent of James Joyce's early masterpiece "The Dead."

Windham's third novel, *Two People* (1965), is his testament to the significance of love. That it happens to be homosexual love seems almost incidental to the writer's wider vision. Windham has never objected to being called homosexual or to calling himself homosexual, although in his view, like all categories, it is a false one: "This isn't something I thought up for *Two People*," he observed to a friend: "Categories . . . are for me conventions of time and place 'as misleading as they are convenient' that permit us to discuss events too upsetting to examine individually. Homosexuality and heterosexuality are equally artificial categories. As to 'normal,' normal would be bi-sexual, except that 'bi-sexual' is as artificial a category as the other two, necessitated by their artificiality. Love is *not* an artificial category—but at the price that no one agrees on what the word means. I would say the same thing for friendship" (Kellner, xxviii). In *Two People*, a married American businessman in his early thirties and an Italian boy in his teens have a love affair, but the novel's title refers to the cultures they represent as well as to themselves. The novel demonstrates how easily categories— notably those Windham rejected—fail to explain human behavior. That the alliance between Forrest and Marcello is essentially physical, and homosexual, might seem to categorize *Two People* as "gay," even though Windham clearly counters such a limited reading at the conclusion of the novel: "Love's power is that it lets you exist outside your own body.... Its biological end is the creation of a new body, and because of this it has been taught that love between men should remain chaste. But life is not so clearly defined. Forrest had suffered...from a failure to accept what was happening. He accepted it now....And...he sensed that it was at least in part himself that he held in his arms that afternoon" (234–35).

Tanaquil (1977), originally subtitled *The Hardest Thing of All* (1972), offers a broader landscape than Windham's earlier novels anticipate. A twentieth-century American Dickens or Trollope might have written a similar love story about the marriage of Frankie and Tanaquil, ripened with their large supporting cast of eccentrics, many of them thinly disguised portraits of actual artists and writers active in New York at midcentury. At its center, Frankie is another of Windham's seductive, self-centered protagonists, in this case a modern-day version of Samuel Richardson's Lovelace or Jane Austen's Darcy, easily lured into infidelities—both male and female—and fully capable of initiating some of them himself. If his loyal and patient Tanaquil seems too good to be true, Frankie is too true to be good. Windham refuses to persuade his reader to choose sides; instead, Frankie and Tanaquil are merely human.

Windham's most recent novel, *Stone in the Hourglass* (1983), has not been published in America and is available only in its limited edition, printed in Italy. It is a marvelously intricate tale of intrigue and corruption in the arts, an intellectual tour de force pretending to be a thriller, with a preposterous plot, false leads, a little adventitious sex, and murder, all snaked out in wicked humor. But the guilty go unpunished and innocence suffers here, for corruption in the arts, Windham suggests, is as subversive as it is anywhere else.

In his childhood memoir, *Emblems of Conduct* (1963), and his later memoirs of Truman Capote, Tennessee Williams, and others, published collectively as *Lost Friendships* (1987), Windham is never preoccupied with homosexuality as a subject, although it illuminates his material. Even in privately printed, overtly homosexual stories like *The Hitchhiker* (1950) and *The Kelly Boys* (1957), the subject is handled with a casual diffidence. None of Windham's work is essentially "gay" by definition or assessment: homosexuality, like heterosexuality, is merely an emotional articulation of love. It is not the subject of Windham's work, nor, had he begun to write a generation later, would it have been likely to be: "What you need to explain to yourself is what reality is," he wrote in *Emblems of Conduct*. "And although this amounts to explaining your viewpoint to yourself, it is an act that changes your viewpoint in the process. Not until you have finished do you know what you are doing" (168–69).

CRITICAL RECEPTION

From the start of his career, Donald Windham has enjoyed the endorsements of many reputable writers, beginning with Thomas Mann, who called *The Dog Star* "simple, natural, and strong, . . . a good, sincere, and highly gifted piece of work" (Kellner, xxxv, 55). Others have echoed him: J. R. Ackerly, Paul Bowles, Albert Camus, Marianne Moore, Georges Simenon, and Carl Van Vechten. E. M. Forster wrote, in his foreword to *The Warm Country*, "Donald Windham, I understand, has never learnt literature. He merely produces it" (1).

These encomiums have not led to commercial success, however. He is a subtle writer, which has sometimes led to impatience; he writes about sex but never erotically, which has sometimes led to disappointment; he is classified as a homosexual writer, which all too often has led to naked loathing in print. Reactions to his early work was largely favorable, like Jeremy Larner's generous assessment of him as "an uncommon, unfashionable writer [whose] downright power will gain him the eventual audience he deserves" (Kellner 62). *Two People*, however, unleashed the wrath of homophobic critics like Eliot Fremont-Smith, who called it "aenemic," "pretentious," and "so devoid of relevancy that it may, to some, seem art"; Hilton Kramer, who dismissed it as "pederasty without tears"; Stanley Kauffman, who condemned its "queer lives" and "absurd comments" about sexuality and friendship; and Robert J. Kaller, who feared that Windham's delineating "positive virtues in such relationships" marked a "serious social evil" and made his "spiritual skin crawl" (Kellner, 71–74). The hysteria in these hostile reviews written prior to 1965 may be understandable; but it is unforgivable, not only because it has deprived Windham of objective criticism but because it has discouraged readers. More recently, Windham has been given some attention in the gay press through reviews and articles and a reprint of "The Hitchhiker" in *Christopher Street*, a good beginning for the overdue rediscovery that Donald Windham deserves.

SELECTED WORKS BY DONALD WINDHAM

The Dog Star. Garden City: Doubleday, 1950; New York: New American Library, 1951; London: Rupert Hart-Davis, 1951; [as *Canicule*] Paris: Galliard, 1954; [as *Let Me Alone*] New York: Popular Library, 956; [as *Let Me Alone*] London: Harborough, 1956.
The Hero Continues. London: Rupert Hart-Davis, 1960; New York: Crowell, 1960; New York: Four Square Books, 1966.
The Warm Country. London: Rupert Hart-Davis, 1960; New York: Scribners, 1962.
Emblems of Conduct. New York: Scribners, 1963; [as *Emblemes d'une vie*] Paris: Gallimard, 1968.
Two People. New York: Coward-McCann, 1965; London: Michael Joseph, 1966;

[as *Due Vita*] Rome: Arnoldo Mandadori, 1967; London: Penguin, 1971; New York: Popular Library, 1978.

Tanaquil. Verona: Campbell, 1972; New York: Holt, 1977; New York: Popular Library, 1978.

Stone in the Hourglass. Verona: Campbell, 1983.

Lost Friendships. New York: Morrow, 1987; New York: Paragon, 1989.

SELECTED STUDIES OF DONALD WINDHAM

Doepke, Dale K. "Donald Windham." *Contemporary Novelists*, 1526–28. New York: St. Martin's, 1976.

Dlugos, Tim. "His Dailiness: The Works of Donald Windham." *Little Caesar 12: Overlooked and Underrated*, 63–67. Los Angeles: Little Caesar Press, 1981.

Forster, E. M. "Introduction." *The Warm Country*, 1–2. London: Rupert Hart-Davis, 1960.

Holleran, Andrew. "That Generation." *Christopher Street* 118 (December 1987): 3–7.

Kellner, Bruce. *Donald Windham: A Bio-Bibliography.* Westport: Greenwood Press, 1991.

Willingham, Robert M., Jr. "Donald Windham." *Dictionary of Literary Biography* 6, 380–86. Detroit: Gale, 1980.

APPENDIX: SMALL PRESSES AND SELECTED JOURNALS

The following is a selected list of small presses in the United States that regularly publish works of gay fiction. It should be noted, however, that since the mid–1980s a number of major commercial publishing companies such as St. Martin's Press, Plume, Penguin, Harper, and Dutton, among others, have begun to issue gay titles.

Alamo Square Press, P.O. Box 14543, San Francisco, CA 94114

Alyson Publications, 40 Plympton Street, Boston, MA 02118

Amethyst Press, Inc., 6 West 32nd Street, New York, NY 10013

Banned Books, An Imprint of Edward-William Austin Publishing Company, P.O. Box 33280, Austin, TX 78764

Calumus Bks, Box 689, Cooper Square Station, New York, NY 10276

Celestial Arts, P.O. Box 7327, Berkeley, CA 94707

Crossing Press, P.O. Box 1048, Freedom, CA 95019

Gay Presses of America, P.O. Box 294, New York, NY 10014

Knights Press, 190 Henry Street, Stamford, CT 06902

Lavender Press, P.O. Box 998, South Norwalk, CT 06856

Los Hombres, P.O. Box 632729, San Diego, CA 92163

The following is a selected list of journals with sections that are likely to be of interest to students of contemporary gay American fiction.

Advocate, Liberation Publications, Inc., P.O. Box 4371, Los Angeles, CA 90078-4371

Bay Area Reporter, 395 Ninth Street, San Francisco, CA 94103-3831

Bay Windows, 1523 Washington Street, Boston, MA 02118

Cabirion: Gay Books Bulletin, P.O. Box 480, Lenox Hill Station, New York, NY 10021

Christopher Street, P.O. Box 1475, Church Street Station, New York, NY 10008

A Different Light Review, 548 Hudson Street, New York, NY 10014

Evergreen Chronicles: A Journal of Gay and Lesbian Writers, P.O. Box 8939, Minneapolis, MN 55408–8939

Gay Community News, 62 Berkeley Street, Suite #87, Boston, MA 02110-6215

Giovanni's Room, 345 S. 12th Street, Philadelphia, PA 19107

James White Review: A Gay Men's Literary Quarterly, P.O. Box 3356, Traffic Station, Minneapolis, MN 55403

Journal of Homosexuality, Center for Research and Education in Sexuality (CERES), San Francisco State University, San Francisco, CA 94132

Journal of the History of Sexuality, Bard College, Annandale-on-Hudson, NY 12504

Lambda Book Report, 1625 Connecticut Avenue, N.W., Washington, DC 20009

Lesbian and Gay Studies Newsletter, Department of English, Duke University, Durham, NC 27706

Lesbian & Gay Teachers' Association Newsletter, Box 021052, Brooklyn, NY 11202-0023

OurStories, P.O. Box 42126, San Francisco, CA 94142

Out/Look: A National Lesbian & Gay Quarterly, 2946 16th Street, Suite #319, San Francisco, CA 94103-6706

Outlines, 3059 N. Southport, Chicago, IL 60657

R.F.D.: A Country Journal for Gay Men Everywhere, P.O. Box 68, Liberty, TN 37095

San Francisco Bay Times, 288 7th Street, San Francisco, CA 94013-4004

San Francisco Sentinel, 500 Hayes Street, San Francisco, CA 94102

Washington Blade, 724 9th Street, N.W., Washington, DC 20001

INDEX

ABOUT THE CONTRIBUTORS

BARBARA KAPLAN BASS teaches in the English Department at Towson State University. Her research focuses on pedagogical issues as well as on mainstreaming gay and women writers into literature and writing classes.

MARK E. BATES is assistant professor of Spanish at Xavier University in Cincinnati. He is currently researching contemporary Mexican gay writing.

DAVID BERGMAN, professor of English at Towson State University, is the author of *Gaiety Transfigured: Gay Self-Representation in American Literature* and the editor of *Reported Sightings: Art Chronicles, 1957–87*. His volume of poetry, *Cracking the Code*, won the George Elliston Poetry Award in 1985.

GREGORY W. BREDBECK is associate professor of English at the University of California, Riverside, where he teaches English Renaissance literature, contemporary gay and lesbian writing, and queer theory. Most recently he is the author of *Sodomy and Interpretation: Marlowe to Milton*.

JANE S. CARDUCCI is Associate Professor of English at Winona State University, Minnesota.

PETER G. CHRISTENSEN has published widely on contemporary literature. He is now a post-doctoral teaching fellow at the University of Wisconsin at Milwaukee.

WILLIAM LANE CLARK is currently a biomedical writer at Johns Hopkins University.

JOHN M. CLUM is professor of English and drama at Duke University. He is the author of *Acting Gay: Male Homosexuality in Modern Drama*, in addition to numerous essays on gay-related issues in modern art and contemporary drama.

JOSEPH DEWEY is assistant professor in the Department of English at the University of Pittsburgh at Johnstown. He is the author of *In a Dark Time: The Apocalyptic Temper in the American Novel of the Nuclear Age*. His articles on American fiction have appeared in a variety of journals and anthologies.

THOMAS DUKES is associate professor of English at the University of Akron. He has published articles on a number of twentieth-century British and American authors as well as on composition theory and business communication.

MICHAEL J. EMERY is assistant professor of English at Cottey College in Nevada, Missouri. Author of a chapbook of poems titled *Orange Trees Burning Everywhere*, he has published critical essays on American science fiction.

DONALD CALLEN FREED is a singer, composer, teacher, and writer.

PHILIP GAMBONE is the Director of Secondary School Counseling at the Park School in Brookline, Massachusetts, and an adjunct instructor in the Expository Writing Program at Harvard University. A former fellow at the MacDowell Colony, he is the author of *The Language We Use Up Here and Other Stories*.

JOHN GETTYS lives in San Francisco, where he works as a technical librarian.

EARL JACKSON, Jr., teaches in the Literature and History of Consciousness Program at the University of California at Santa Cruz.

JAMES W. JONES is associate professor of German at Central Michigan University. He is the author of *"We of the Third Sex": Literary Representations of Homosexuality in Wilhelmine Germany* as well as articles on AIDS discourses in Germany and in the United States.

BRUCE KELLNER is professor emeritus of English at Millersville University in Pennsylvania. Among the eight books he has published are *The Harlem Renaissance: A Historical Dictionary of the Era* and *The Last Dandy, Ralph Barton*.

JAMES D. KITCHEN, professor emeritus at San Diego State University, is a cofounder and former director of the School of Public Administration and Urban Studies there. Coauthor of a Holocaust biography, *Because of Romek*, he is editor-in-chief of the literary magazine *CrazyQuilt*.

GEORGE KLAWITTER is chair of the English Department at Viterbo College, Wisconsin. In 1990 he edited the complete poetry of Richard Barnfield for Susquehanna University Press.

WILFRID R. KOPONEN teaches literature and the arts in the Cultures, Ideas, and Values Program at Stanford University. He is the author of the forthcoming *Coming Out: Gay Novels as Guides* (1993).

D. S. LAWSON is assistant professor of English at Lander College, South Carolina. He is the author of two forthcoming books—one on intertextuality, another on Joe Orton. In addition to articles on British drama and on AIDS theater, he has published poetry in *The James White Review*, *Bay Windows*, *Amethyst*, and *R.F.D.*

TERRENCE J. McGOVERN is assistant librarian at the SUNY-Cortland Memorial Library.

ROBERT McRUER teaches gay and lesbian literature at the University of Illinois at Urbana-Champagne. He was one of the organizers of the Second National Graduate Student Conference on Lesbian and Gay Studies, held in April 1992.

WILL MEYERHOFER is a free-lance writer in New York City and has written numerous film reviews for the *New York Native*. He has also contributed short fiction to *Christopher Street*. Presently he is at work on his first novel.

JAMES MORRISON is assistant professor of English and Film Studies at North Carolina State University at Raleigh. Currently he is at work on a study of gay filmmakers of Classical Hollywood.

EMMANUEL S. NELSON is editor of *Connections: Essays on Black Literatures*, *AIDS: The Literary Response*, and *Reworlding: The Literature of the Indian Diaspora* (Greenwood, 1992). He has published over two dozen articles on ethnic, postcolonial, and gay literatures.

JOHN H. PEARSON is an assistant professor of English at Stetson University, Florida. He has published on narrative theory, the fiction and criticism of Henry James, autobiography, and the relation of gender and narrative in the work of Zora Neale Hurston.

THOMAS PIONTEK is completing a dissertation on the literature of AIDS at the University of Wisconsin in Milwaukee. He coconvened the First National Graduate Student Conference on Lesbian and Gay Studies held in 1991.

DAVID ROMÁN is assistant professor of English at the University of Washington at Seattle, where he teaches courses in gay and lesbian studies, theater and society, and the literature of U.S. peoples of color. Author of several scholarly articles that have appeared in journals and collections including the *Theatre Journal, Critical Theory and Performance*, and *Gay Theatre and Performance*, he is currently at work on a book-length study of the theater of AIDS.

JERRY ROSCO, formerly a reporter for Gannett Newspapers, has contributed stories and essays to numerous publications, including *Chicago Review, Christopher Street*, and *Amethyst*.

MICHAEL SCHWARTZ works as a technical writer in Boston.

CRAIG ALLEN SEYMOUR II is a staff writer for the *Lambda Book Report*. He currently lives in Washington, D.C.

JOEL SHATZKY is professor of English at SUNY-Cortland. He has published several articles on modern drama and on the theatrical treatment of the Holocaust, in addition to editing *Hitler's Gift to the Jews: Theresienstradt in the Words and Pictures of Norbert Troller*.

SETH SILBERMAN writes short fiction and has taught creative writing.

CLAUDE J. SUMMERS is the William E. Stirton Professor in the Humanities at the University of Michigan at Dearborn. A recipient of the Crompton-Noll Award in gay studies, he is former chair of the MLA Division on Gay Studies and the author of numerous essays and books, including *Christopher Isherwood, E. M. Forster*, and *Gay Fictions: Wilde to Stonewall*.

JANE L. TROXELL is senior editor of *Lambda Book Report*, a national review of gay and lesbian literature. A former columnist for *Feminist Bookstore News*, she serves as director of Lambda Literary Awards Program, which recognizes excellence in gay and lesbian writing and publishing. As a free-lance writer, Troxell reviews books and interviews writers for *The Washington Blade* and *The Advocate*.

JAMES TUSHINSKI has contributed pieces to *The James White Review*, the *Bay Area Reporter*, and *Prism International*. His work has also appeared in the fiction anthology *The Gay Nineties*.

B. AUSTIN WALLACE is currently a book buyer and reviewer for Lambda Rising. In addition, he has worked as a disc jockey and as an information specialist for the National AIDS Hotline.

REED WOODHOUSE, a lecturer in English at the Massachusetts Institute of Technology, is also the music director of the Opera Program at Boston Conservatory. His autobiographical essay "Provincetown, Massachusetts" appears in *Hometowns: Gay Men Write about Where They Belong*.

GREGORY WOODS teaches English and communication studies at the Nottingham Polytechnic in England. Author of *Articulate Flesh: Male Homo-eroticism in Modern Poetry* and an acclaimed collection of poems, *We Have the Melon*, he is currently writing a book on Marcel Proust.

LES WRIGHT completed a dissertation titled "The Chiasmic War: AIDS, Writing, and Gay Community" at the University of California at Berkeley. A founding member of the Gay and Lesbian Historical Society of Northern California, he was the editor-in-chief of *OurStories* until 1992. A contributor to *Hometowns: Gay Men Write about Where They Belong* and *AIDS: The Literary Response*, he has begun work on a book-length oral history titled *Castro Street: Gay Hometown, USA*.